CLOSING THE GAP

SPECIAL LEARNERS IN REGULAR CLASSROOMS

Margret Winzer
University of Lethbridge

Copp Clark Pitman Ltd.
A Longman Company
Toronto

ISBN 0-7730-4620-8

Executive Editor: Brian Henderson
Developmental Editor: Barbara Tessman
Editor: Camilla Jenkins
Design: Lorraine Hulme
Cover illustration: Marcel Durocher
Technical art: Catherine Aikens
Typesetting: Compeer Typographic Services Ltd.
Printing and binding: John Deyell Co.

Canadian Cataloguing in Publication Data

Winzer, Margret, 1940–
Closing the gap

Bibliography: p.
Includes index.
ISBN 0-7730-4620-8

1. Mainstreaming in education. 2. Exceptional children – Education. I. Title.

LC3965.W56 1989 371.9′046 C89-093147-X

Copp Clark Pitman Ltd.
2775 Matheson Blvd. East
Mississauga, Ontario
L4W 4P7

Associated companies:
Longman Group Ltd., London
Longman Inc., New York
Longman Cheshire Pty., Melbourne
Longman Paul Pty., Auckland

Printed and bound in Canada

For Irene

"The world would be so boring
if everyone was the same."

Table of Contents

Preface

In Canada today, educational integration is the prevailing educational ideology. Growing numbers of exceptional students are entering the public school system and classroom populations are being described more broadly.

As exceptional students move into neighbourhood schools and regular classroom settings, new challenges confront the educational profession as a whole. Particularly affected are regular classroom teachers, those crucial professionals who will be most intimately involved in the integrational process. In order to participate successfully in mainstreaming ventures, teachers both in regular classrooms and in special education must develop new skills. Although teaching and curricula will not change dramatically, the addition of an exceptional child to the regular classroom necessarily engenders some changes, specifically in individual planning, instruction, and ways of monitoring student progress.

Generally, books on exceptional students and special education tend to focus on the primary characteristics of the children or of the educational process. Many texts are available that direct their attention to areas such as definitions, prevalence, etiology, characteristics, identification, and developmental consequences of specific conditions. For an introduction to exceptional children in Canada, the interested reader is referred to Day (1985) and Winzer, Rogow, and David (1987).

The present text, however, is not a portrait of the exceptional child. Rather, it is organized around educational considerations: the instructional, physical, and social variables that are important for special learners. The fulcrum on which the discussion turns is the concept of mainstreaming, or educational integration. These terms, which are used interchangeably in the text, imply educating exceptional students in the most appropriate educational milieu, preferably the neighbourhood school. The terms exceptional student and special learner are also used here synonymously.

Once in school, exceptional students may need special instruction in skills that other children master more easily. This text emphasizes the instructional approaches useful for students who require a variety of modifications in teaching goals, methods, techniques, or physical and social environments. Because the discussion deals with those exceptional students who are integrated into regular classrooms, the teaching methods described are primarily intended for mildly handicapped children — rather than children with severe or profound handicapping conditions — and follow a non-categorical approach. At the same time, students with specific sensory and physical impairments are also considered. As well, the text maintains a balance between ideas for elementary levels and secondary levels, and presents suggestions that can be adapted to a wide range of age levels.

Readers will find many of the general suggestions offered to be familiar. Although there are specific competencies directly related to success with special learners, the same teacher behaviours that result in effective programming for students in general are those which are necessary to instruct exceptional learners successfully. Exceptional students must be equipped with the tools for learning; they need to know how to approach subject matter and how to cultivate good learning techniques. They also require daily instruction in basic concepts and language usage. In order to develop these skills in students, teachers need to improve their own skills in individualization, presentation, communication, and classroom management.

The text is divided into four sections. The first provides the framework of the subject by introducing exceptional children and special education. The second section deals with preparing for mainstreaming. It focusses on planning and implementing the educational task and moves from identification and diagnosis to individualized planning and classroom management. The section includes a chapter on the social aspects of mainstreaming and delves into an area of particular importance to teachers, classroom control and discipline with both groups and individuals.

The third section then discusses teaching various academic subjects on a generic basis, from language arts to career education. This text asserts that there exists a core of teaching approaches and techniques appropriate for all exceptional learners, and the section therefore presents a variety of general and specific ideas as well as examples of teaching techniques, lesson plans, and materials.

The final section of the text examines approaches for specific groups of exceptional children. The section opens with a chapter on language problems because deficits in speech and language tend to cut across many areas of exceptionality. In the chapters on sensorily deprived and physically disabled youngsters, the technological aids designed to enhance teaching and learning are especially important; the use of prosthetic and orthotic devices and special technical equipment is too often overlooked in special education. Further teaching ideas are also presented in these chapters, to supplement those presented in the third section.

Although general approaches and particular techniques are specifically categorized in the text, the divisions are only for the purpose of organization and clarity. Many ideas can be adapted to a wide diversity of exceptional learners. If a teacher believes in an approach and if that approach works with a particular student, then it is appropriate. Eclecticism is the key when teaching special learners and teachers should have a variety of strategies at their fingertips.

The range of ideas presented is not inclusive but instead has been selected to illustrate the concepts discussed in each chapter and to provide examples that creative teachers can adopt, adapt, and expand for their own purposes. Some of the suggestions have been drawn from the literature; many come from my own experience with exceptional children and from discussions with practising classroom teachers. A particularly fruitful source has been the E.C. Drury School in Milton, Ontario and the Trillium School on the same campus, where many of the ideas were seen in action. But as many teachers do, I have picked up ideas from others and then adapted them for my own class situations. Although I have tried to acknowledge such material, I apologize for any inadvertent omissions.

Additional material is used throughout to illustrate salient points. In each chapter, readers will find an opening letter from an educator or a parent discussing various points related to the chapter, a list of the main objectives for the chapter, and glossary terms marked for ease of reference. As well, relevant chapters contain special features such as case studies, to illustrate individual mainstreaming experiences, extracts from individual education plans (IEPs), to show how teachers can devise programs for the students described in the case studies, and boxes containing suggestions for dealing with specific situations.

A student workbook complements the text. The workbook contains chapter summaries, key concepts and terminology, lists of relevant standardized tests, and examples of commercial materials. Each workbook chapter also includes a bank of test items related to the material presented in the text.

Many people contributed to this book. I am indebted to all the educators who so kindly contributed letters and information and to the students at Memorial University who were so helpful in delineating the kinds of material that they would like to see in a text. Special thanks to Margaret Baskette, a dear friend and an astute critic, who typed much of the initial draft. I would also like particularly to thank Camilla Jenkins, who patiently edited the manuscript.

Margret Winzer, Ed.D.
Associate Professor
Faculty of Education
University of Lethbridge

PART

1

Laying the groundwork

1 Special education and special learners

Dear Reader,

Although some believe that custodial care developed because of society's fears about the freedom of defective individuals, it is generally held that special education grew out of the social conscience, common morality, and religious beliefs of concerned citizens. No matter what the reason for its beginnings in the mid-nineteenth century, the early practice of segregation was a better alternative than the neglect or exploitation that handicapped people faced outside of institutions. Yet special institutions for the deaf, the blind, the mentally handicapped, and so on were forced to operate within the constraints of very inadequate budgets and, as in many residential settings, their occupants became socially isolated. One was never sure whether the walls were there to keep the inmates in or to keep the community out. The sad results of this system have been well documented; in brief, not only were the occupants deindividualized but society developed an institutional mentality toward exceptional individuals.

Special education itself reinforced this attitude. We started with the belief that important intra-individual differences existed; we proved those differences existed and attempted to explain them; and we organized separate facilities to provide for special needs. This not only resulted in a separate educational system but also strengthened social attitudes, beliefs, and expectations about handicapped people that will prove difficult to eradicate. Indeed, recent studies to determine how regular teachers view exceptional children have not been very encouraging.

In Canada today we do not have to look hard to find students still being removed from regular classrooms because they differ intellectually or behaviourally from their peers. Nor is it difficult to find special education settings that are isolated from regular schools and cope with their students on either a categorical or non-categorical basis. Inevitably the conduct, organization, and validity of special education have been challenged. As a first step to improve the system, efforts were made to resolve the question of institutional versus non-institutional care, and these led to the establishment of special classrooms in regular schools. In turn, the efficacy of the new programs was examined and although the results were somewhat equivocal they bolstered a further movement away from special classes to placement in regular classes, or a form of mainstreaming. This term "mainstreaming," by the way, does not imply that all exceptional students will be returned to regular classrooms. Instead it represents one facet of normalization — namely that handicapped students should be regarded as their normal peers are, as much as possible. The actual mechanism to achieve normalized school experience is placement in the least restrictive environment.

These concepts of mainstreaming, normalization, and the least restrictive environment are even now likely to provoke heated controversy among special educators. This is understandable because at each stage of the special education process — referral, evaluation, placement, and programming — provincial and school board policies and practices historically have encouraged separate education for handicapped students. Of course, regular education teachers also have strong feelings on these issues.

The thesis of this book is that while some students now in special education are properly placed, there certainly are many others who would be better served in a regular education system that gives greater attention to individual needs and applies the established techniques of an adaptive learning environment. This movement will of course involve a greater number of services to support regular school staff and an emphasis on prevention as well as remediation.

I trust that your careful reading of this book and discussions with your colleagues will enable you to examine carefully, and to come to grips with, the current inconsistencies in our educational system. The manner in which you seek solutions to the problems presented in the text will determine the future not only of special education but of general education itself. Above all else I hope that you, the reader, will strive to find what works best for each particular child. We must succeed at this task because it is, in fact, what education is all about.

Bryan R. Clarke, Ph.D.
Professor Emeritus
University of British Columbia

Picture this scene in the teacher's lounge of a large school somewhere in Canada. Over coffee, a teacher bitterly complains about a new arrival in her class. "He can't learn," she says. "He's slower than the rest, can't keep up, and takes too much of my time. Maybe he should be in a special class."

"Well," responds another, "I have the opposite problem. There's a student in my room who works at twice the speed of the others. I can't teach her at one level and everyone else at another, and she's getting bored. She should certainly be in a special class."

A third breaks in, "You all know the difficulties I'm having. I've got a boy who constantly disrupts the class with his talking and poor behaviour. A special placement is certainly right for him."

"Well I have a pupil in a wheelchair. She does her work nicely, but she can't go to gym. Maybe she should be in a special class, too," adds the first.

Finally, the fourth teacher has his say. "The class I take in the mornings is quite difficult. The girls read and spell well and do tidy work but the boys are messy and loud. Maybe we should have a special class for boys" (after MacIntyre, 1984).

Although the scene is obviously exaggerated, it contains at least a kernel of truth. Every year in the public school system there are students of all ages identified as not profiting from regular classroom instruction. Until very recently, special class placement was viewed as the most appropriate educational setting for any student who demonstrated learning and behavioural difficulties. Special education now encompasses a tremendous variety of instructional options and settings, however, and has developed into a very rewarding field. This initial chapter seeks to introduce special learners and Canadian special education; to present the major trends apparent in modern special education; to delineate and explain some of the central themes running through the text; and to lay the groundwork on which the remainder of the text is erected.

Today, we adhere to the notion that all students have the right to learn in the educational environment most suited to their academic and social needs. Within the educational system there is a powerful move to abandon many special classes and replace them with regular class programs supported by special education services. The trend is motivated by increasing awareness of and respect for the different learning characteristics among students, and a belief that educational mainstreaming can accommodate individual differences by developing appropriate programs. Helping exceptional children to fit into the mainstream of school, society, and community life has become a major goal of special education during the past decade.

Contemporary social and educational philosophy rejects the idea of merely caring for or maintaining people with disabilities. In education, specifically, instead of simply helping students to adapt to limitations, educators can attempt the correction and prevention of continued learning disorders. The new approach suggests that exceptional students should be provided with educational experiences as similar as possible to those of other students and dispels the notion that there are two distinct sets of children—handicapped and non-handicapped. Rather, all children are viewed as unique individuals with their own sets of physical, intellectual, emotional, and psychological characteristics.

Scores of exceptional children have therefore moved within the orbit of the public schools. Many of them suffer from mildly handicapping conditions and can be successfully integrated into regular classrooms; others have more severe impairments to learning, but they too are moving into regular school settings. They are riding school buses, attending assembly programs, and participating in art, music, lunchtime, and recess with their non-handicapped peers (Cypher, Hinves, Baine, & Sobsey, 1984).

Approximately 77 percent of Canadian special learners now receive instruction in integrated settings (Council of Ministers, 1982–83). Special education is no longer a retreat for a few children, separate from the mainstream of education; it is now everybody's concern, from the specialist to the regular education teacher. In 1983 there were 251 448 full-time teachers in Canadian schools, of whom 28 884 were providing some special education programming. Approximately one in nine teachers therefore spent some time working with exceptional children or special programs (Council of Ministers, 1982–83). Eventually, as the trend toward integration grows, all regular classroom teachers may be instructing exceptional pupils for at least part of the day. In the meantime, the need for classroom teachers to know more about exceptional youngsters and special education has never been more pronounced. Indeed, surveys of teachers' opinions have revealed that demands for in-service training in these areas head the list of perceived needs (McMurray, 1980).

Integration of exceptional pupils is becoming an imperative rather than a hope, and classroom teachers must develop the professional skill necessary to educate many of these youngsters. Teachers are increasingly being called upon to instruct heterogeneous groups of children, which include individuals who are handicapped or exhibit deviant behaviour, as well as normal and **atypical youngsters** from various ethnic groups, among whom communication often presents special difficulties. Classroom teachers play a crucial role in providing appropriate educational experiences and stimulating environments for exceptional students. In order to create suitable educational programs, teachers are obliged to adopt fresh instructional alternatives and don some new hats.

It is expected that classroom teachers will develop the competencies required to teach classes organized on educational need, rather than on the basis of intellectual functioning or educational achievement. The effective learning environment requires an organized teacher who understands each phase of the instructional process and is able to select the approaches that best meet the individual needs of all students. As well, the effective teacher must assume a range of responsibilities in order to provide comprehensive services to exceptional students (Mandell & Gold, 1984). He or she will have to produce both individual and group programs, and function as part of a school-based educational team.

Many teachers are unaware of, or misunderstand, the philosophy and process of mainstreaming, and are consequently ill-prepared to teach exceptional pupils. Teachers react with anxiety, and even hostility, to the prospect of admitting an exceptional student into their classrooms. Their experience with exceptional children may be limited, and their knowledge of programming for such students virtually non-existent. In a survey of the literature, it was found that teachers worry about dealing with the exceptional child, about their ability to teach the student successfully, and about whether exceptional pupils will dilute educational programs or demand a disproportionate amount of time. (Winzer, 1985b). They especially fear being forced to absorb antagonistic, disturbed youngsters into the regular classroom, because maintaining discipline is often a problem without the added difficulty of coping with extremely disruptive behaviour. Other teachers feel uncomfortable with the idea of mainstreaming because it involves extensive shared responsibility. They may feel that they are losing autonomy, drowning in paperwork, and being held accountable for policies and plans to which they contributed little.

By and large, teachers want answers to some very basic questions about mainstreaming and its impact. They ask, "Why change?" "What are we being asked to do?" "What aspects of current practice will be affected?" and "How will this affect me?" Such questions are entirely reasonable, and the anxieties felt by classroom teachers are realistic. Yet if teachers were asked how schools can best serve all students, their responses would undoubtedly contain statements concerning individual differences. Almost everyone thinks that accommodating a range of differences is a desirable goal of schooling, although articulating the principle is often much easier than achieving it.

Nevertheless, mainstreaming essentially implies painting the populations of regular classrooms with a broader brush. A larger range of students will appear in regular classrooms, and with them a greater variation in ability to learn, to socialize, and to achieve independence. Exceptional students may learn at a different tempo and indeed in different ways than their peers, but they do learn and, if given the chance, they learn most of the same things that non-exceptional students do. There are more similarities than differences between exceptional children and their peers. Once this is recognized, it is clear that mainstreaming, which allows attention to be given to individual rather than categorical differences, is the appropriate response to the educational needs of all children.

The parallels between regular education and special education also outweigh the disparities. The suspicion that the techniques, materials, and approaches of special education are not suitable for the regular classrooom was abandoned long ago, and educators now accept the premise that the same principles and procedures, with some modifications, can be used in the instruction of all children.

Defining the exceptional population

Every teacher daily confronts a room full of faces that mask abundant individual differences. In any given classroom, most students will be capable of handling the regular school curriculum. They may stumble now and then in certain areas and perhaps occasionally rest on plateaus, but eventually, and without much trouble, the majority of schoolchildren learn to read and write, compute and spell, and all the other things that educators are charged with teaching them. A very few will fly through the curriculum and, if provided with guidance and encouragement, thrill teachers with their love of learning and sense of discovery. Another, somewhat larger, group will find learning particularly difficult. These children will stumble more often than is usual and require more support to wend their way through the intricacies of reading, spelling, and mathematics. Many of the students in these latter two groups are exceptional.

Exceptional children or **special learners** may be defined as those who have difficulty in reaching their full human potential. Their intellectual, emotional, physical, or social performance falls below or rises above that of other children. In order to maximize their potential, special children require special education and related services (Winzer, Rogow, & David, 1987). This definition focusses on the very broad characteristics of exceptional children and offers a general prescription for educational intervention. It uses the term exceptional, or special, to encompass those who fall below the norm in some area of functioning, as well as gifted and talented students who require special programming if they are to attain their greatest potential.

Categories of exceptionality

Today, categories of exceptionality based on psychological and medical conditions are considered less significant than groupings based on educational functioning. While the severity of a handicapping condition is a crucial factor in integrational decisions, the type of condition is not as telling. Nevertheless, traditional categories for exceptional children do remain important in Canada.

Categorical orientation has persisted for several reasons. In the certification of teachers most provinces still follow categorical patterns that have limited scope for change (Heller, McCoy, & McIntyre, 1979). Much special education funding is based on categories of exceptionality, and research, too, still adheres to a somewhat categorical orientation. In addition, special education practices often perpetuate a categorical approach. In many school districts, special education exists as a series of separate classrooms organized by categories of exceptional pupils served.

Although there is relatively little standardization in the area of special education, exceptional students tend to be identified by certain general categories. First, there are children with intellectual differences, a category that encompasses both gifted and talented children and those at all levels of mental retardation. Second, children may have communication disorders. This group includes children with speech and language problems, and those who are learning disabled. Third, sensorily deprived children are those with visual impairments or auditory dysfunctions. Many children with multiple handicaps are also included in the category. The fourth category is that of emotional disturbance, which includes children with behavioural disorders, as well as those affected by childhood psychoses. Finally, the category of physical handicaps and health problems comprises a widely divergent range of children, including those with neurological defects, orthopedic conditions, birth defects, developmental delays and disabilities, and conditions resulting from infections and diseases.

Traditional categories are likely to be viewed very differently in the future. Special educators are rapidly moving toward non-categorical instructional approaches that are both desirable and practical. Certainly, special classes continue to serve a purpose, but their programs will increasingly be founded on functional needs rather than clinical diagnostic categories.

Prevalence of exceptionality

In 1982–83 there were 3 610 381 school-age children enrolled in Canada's public schools. Of these, 559 717 or 15.5 percent were receiving some form of special education (Council of Ministers, 1982–83). These figures, however, should only be considered as an estimate and may indeed be a very conservative number in relation to the proportion of school-age children who actually require special services. For many reasons, it is extremely difficult to arrive at an accurate tally of exceptional children, especially those considered to be mildly handicapped. As an example, while more children are being identified as learning disabled, changes in the definition of mental retardation have reduced the number of students eligible for services in that category.

Defining special education

All exceptional children will require special education and related services at some point in their school careers. **Special education** may be viewed as planned intervention designed to reduce, eliminate, or preclude deficits in learning or behaviour. It is especially designed to meet the particular needs of exceptional children: to prevent or ameliorate conditions that hamper the intellectual, communicative, social, emotional, or psychological functioning of pupils.

Special education grew from the proposition that all children can reach their full potential given opportunity, effective teaching, and proper resources. Whenever feasible, therefore, exceptional students should be instructed in regular school settings so that, upon leaving school, they will be better prepared to live and work in normal community settings. Inevitably, there must be alterations in certain aspects of classroom organization, planning, and the knowledge required by teachers. Special education is thus bound to involve changes in learning and life in the classroom.

Successful special education may require special teaching materials, equipment, and facilities. However, while there exists a core of effective instructional approaches and techniques, no one style of education, no single approach, and no one special type of grouping can provide adequate educational services for all the diverse problems that may be encountered in the classroom.

Educators have invented numerous approaches, techniques, and environments, and have even formulated philosophies in an effort to provide the best education in the most appropriate environment. The techniques and materials may alter in response to the type and severity of the conditions, and the student's age. Manual communication for deaf pupils, braille for blind students, and behaviour modification techniques for emotionally disturbed children are examples of specialized provisions that may be needed for exceptional pupils.

Many different kinds of educational setting are also available for exceptional children. Setting constitutes an important consideration of special education and will be dealt with fully in chapter 2. Figure 1–1 briefly illustrates the scope of the field.

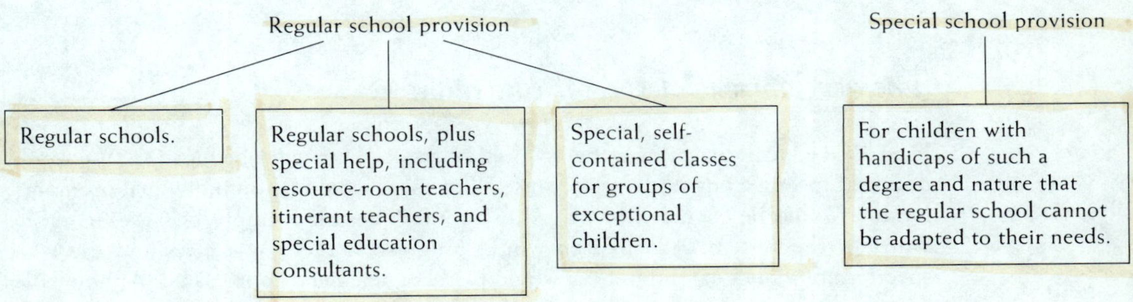

Figure 1–1 Scope of special education

Defining related services

Related or **support services** augment special education. They are the provisions necessary to help exceptional children benefit from special education. Related services keep the academic progress of exceptional pupils up to an appropriate level, or expedite the social and psychological benefits of special education.

Many professional disciplines work together to provide a continuum of services for exceptional learners. Each discipline provides services in its own area, and the involvement of a particular discipline will depend upon its application to the problem. Generally, low-incidence handicaps involve a greater number of professional groups than do high-incidence conditions. For example, a profoundly deaf child may meet a pediatrician, otolaryngologist, audiologist, psychologist, speech therapist, language pathologist, and teacher of the deaf, whereas a mildly mentally retarded student may be assessed by an educational psychologist and taught by regular and special education teachers.

There are many different kinds of support service. Just as physical and occupational therapists, and psychological and counselling personnel provide related services, so do the people who look after transportation and recreation. The contributions of those involved in related services are more fully explored in chapter 2.

Current administrative arrangements

Education for exceptional students may be provided through various administrative arrangements. The least restrictive environment is the setting in which individual exceptional children can best be helped to attain their full human potential. The unique needs of the student largely determine the most appropriate setting; the least restrictive environment for one student may very well be the most restrictive for another.

Mildly disordered children manifest learning and behavioural deficits primarily in the educational environment and they may need only limited instructional support to remain in regular classroom settings. The problems of severely and profoundly handicapped students are more complex; for these youngsters educational intervention may be quite different from traditional forms and may involve people from many disciplines. Generally, children with severe and profound handicapping conditions will not be educated in regular classrooms, although they may certainly be accommodated within the regular school plant.

The development of special education

In an ideal educational system there would be no need for special education. We would not need to single out students, because all of them would be on individual programs. No one would be excluded or placed in an inferior setting simply because he or she didn't fit the system. All children would progress at their own rates and the wide spectrum of individual differences would be recognized and appreciated. Although we are making progress, the gap between the ideal and reality remains wide.

As Bryan Clarke points out in the letter that opens this chapter, the education of special students in Canada has passed through a number of stages. When special education was first initiated in the mid-nineteenth century, children were placed in institutional settings. The large institutions that opened in that period, such as the provincial schools for deaf and blind students, continue today to serve a discrete population, but enrolment is decreasing.

The opening decades of the twentieth century witnessed a proliferation of special classes in Canada's urban areas, to serve mildly handicapped individuals. Physically and health-handicapped children were the first to be taught in special classes, although facilities for children with other conditions developed rapidly (Winzer, Rogow, & David, 1987).

These special classes were established to meet the needs of students who could not make satisfactory progress in regular classrooms. Educators hoped to provide better education through a well-defined curriculum taught by specially trained teachers to homogeneous groupings of exceptional students. It was believed that low student–teacher ratios afforded more individualized instruction and that teachers would be more effective with homogeneous groups. It was also believed that academic failure would be limited and self-esteem simultaneously heightened in children.

The existence of segregated classes, however, implied that educators viewed exceptional individuals as qualitatively different; they tended to focus on the handicaps, disadvantages, and weaknesses of individuals. Children were categorized within traditional boundaries based on medical orientations, and professional groups and programs then emerged around each discrete category. The professionals were responsible for conducting programs tailored to the specific needs in each category of exceptional children.

Segregated classes remained the most important vehicle for service delivery to exceptional children into the post-war period. The 1950s, however, saw the development of a more optimistic view of the potential of handicapped people, particularly in the area of mental retardation. A massive infusion of funding took place in the 1960s, and professional and community interest in the problems of social disadvantage grew rapidly. There was particular concern over the apparently disproportionate number of children from minority groups placed in segregated classes, especially classes for mentally retarded children; it was suspected that these pupils were slotted into such programs more for the convenience of educators than for the good of the children.

During this period the problems of differential programming, along with some possible solutions, were mapped out in detail; these continue today to be the focus of attention in research and service delivery. At the same time, parents began to demand that their exceptional children be provided with educational services within local school districts. Educators, too, started to question the value of special classes, and a series of efficacy studies resulted that delved into the educational justification and effects of instructional segregation.

By the 1970s a more humanistic movement had developed, representing a gradual but positive change in social attitudes toward exceptional people. Awareness of the needs and rights of exceptional individuals became evident in many ways, such as wheelchair ramps, braille signs for blind people, and closed-captioned television shows for deaf individuals.

Society also responded in less tangible ways. Efforts were made to regard exceptional people as individuals and to treat them fairly and humanely. The existence of segregated facilities, which was once taken for granted, was seriously challenged, and many people moved from large institutions into more normal living environments. The first exceptional students were mainstreamed, joining classes in neighbourhood schools.

Several reasons were at the root of the transformation from segregated to integrated educational placement. Empirical data on the effectiveness of special classes and educational litigation and legislation had all accumulated by the 1970s. Concerns had grown about inappropriate identification of children from minorities. As well, knowledge relating to children with learning and behavioural problems became increasingly sophisticated with experience. Research dissuaded educators and related professionals from the idea that homogeneous diagnostic categories existed for exceptional children. Rather, such research argued for individualized educational planning for each student receiving special education (Forness, 1981).

Providing quality services for exceptional learners that were as ample as those given to non-exceptional students created a challenge in the 1970s. In the 1980s, the challenge has been to maintain the initiative in a manner that provides a collaborative, co-ordinated delivery system, to enable all students to receive appropriate education.

Major themes of the text

This text is designed to help teachers overcome their anxiety about exceptional students and mainstreaming. It provides information about exceptional children and presents approaches, techniques, and ideas for effective planning and implementation of educational programs. Concepts and approaches are emphasized that are useful to children who require a variety of modifications, within the regular classroom, in teaching goals, methods, techniques, or physical and social environments. The text presents specific methods by which regular programs can be adapted or modified for exceptional students, and covers a range of strategies applicable to students at both the elementary and secondary levels. Although there is no discussion of specific subject areas for secondary students, many ideas are directed toward remedial programming for older students, and numerous others are flexible enough to be adapted to any age level.

The book also draws together categorical and non-categorical approaches. This is not pedagogical fence-sitting but a pragmatic response to the realities of the school system and teacher-training programs as they exist in Canada today. Although we are certainly moving toward non-categorization of mildly handicapped students, many school districts retain the traditional labels and classifications, and many training programs prepare teachers for only one group of exceptional students.

While most of the discussion focusses on students traditionally labelled as mildly behaviourally or learning handicapped, attention is also given, especially in the final section, to children who need not only program modifications but also specialized technical equipment and alterations in their physical environment. This is not to imply that insurmountable differences exist among groups of exceptional students. Rather, the object is to identify strategies that are suitable for many exceptional pupils and then to provide greater insight into some very specific problems. All of the discussions on language, for example, are directly applicable to hearing-impaired students and these appear in the general section on teaching approaches and techniques. But a hearing-impaired child may require further modifications in the form of amplification equipment, communication systems, or interpreting services, and such specific adaptations are included in the chapter devoted to hearing-impaired students. The text therefore reflects the commonly employed categories of exceptional children as well as the similarities in behaviour among those groups.

There are specific competencies directly related to success with special learners, yet the same teacher behaviours that result in effective programming for students in general are also those that are necessary to instruct exceptional learners successfully. Some of the general suggestions offered throughout the book will therefore sound familiar. In addition, however, exceptional students may need special instruction in skills that other children master more easily. In fact, practically all exceptional learners are given some kind of special skill training to provide them with the tools for learning. They need to know how to approach subject matter and to cultivate good learning techniques, and they also require daily instruction in basic concepts and in language usage. If exceptional students are to develop these skills, teachers will find it necessary to build or improve their own skills in individualization, presentation, communication, and classroom management (Crookall & Land, 1983).

A number of major themes underlie the text:

- All children are unique. Exceptional people should be viewed first as individuals, and only then as exceptional.
- All children can learn. Regardless of the nature and degree of the handicapping conditions, all children are entitled to a free and appropriate public education.
- The principle of normalization, which affirms that exceptional individuals should be integrated as much as possible, both socially and educationally, into the mainstream of society, is the most appropriate and effective precept to follow.
- Expectional students, to the greatest degree that is reasonable and consistent with their needs, should be educated with their non-exceptional peers.
- With support, regular classroom teachers instruct exceptional students efficiently and effectively.
- Teachers are just as distinctive as the children they teach and have developed different management strategies and teaching styles. The use of particular approaches, techniques, and materials is largely determined by the individuality of teachers, and what works in one classroom may not be a comfortable approach for another teacher.
- There exists, however, a core of critical teaching approaches, methods, and techniques that apply to all students demonstrating problems in learning or behaviour. Moreover, the use of such techniques will enhance the learning of all students, regular and exceptional.

The following chapters explore techniques and approaches in special education, and apply them to the classroom.

2 *The philosophy and practice of mainstreaming*

Dear Reader,

In recent years the effort to integrate exceptional children into the mainstream of public education has been renewed. Having first acquired strength in Scandinavian Europe in the late 1960s, integration has swept through the Western world. Recent major documents in Canada (Roberts & Lazure, 1970), in the United States (Public Law 94-142), and in the United Kingdom (Warnock Report, 1978), are formal acknowledgements of the movement. In present educational thought there is a consensus that if exceptional children are placed in regular classrooms, they will perceive themselves as less exceptional and be treated by their peers accordingly. This educational trend reflects recent social efforts, such as the proliferation of community living facilities, stemming from the philosophy of normalization (Bank-Mikkelson, 1969).

Although there is much agreement concerning the merits of normalization, the realities involved in its implementation generate pervasive educational debate. Fervent advocates of integration have described the special education classroom as an anachronism, a home for ne'er-do-well students and teachers; they look with hope to the day when such classrooms cease to exist. Opponents of integration such as Winchel, on the other hand, have decried normalization as a catchword that generates "fake hope for parents, disillusionments for teachers and new possibilities for estrangement and failure for children" (1976, p. 9). Schwartz also denounced normalization, calling it "an idealism based upon philosophic ideas which negate our knowledge of individual and group psychology" (1977, p. 38). Obviously, the integration issue is not clear-cut; nor is it as new as an initial look at recent national documents might suggest. It is interesting to note Johnson's early comment on integration at the twenty-second meeting of the International Council for Exceptional Children in 1944: "Dumping a handicapped child into a pool of normal children where he must sink or swim should not be permitted until all teachers have been trained to be lifesavers" (in Shattuck, 1946).

Integration as it applies to exceptional youngsters is not a constant; its meaning varies with the level of handicap. As defined by the Warnock Report, there are three forms of integration — locational, social, and functional/academic — and each form should be considered when one thinks and plans for exceptional individuals. In the case of moderate, severe, and profound handicaps especially, protracted debates flourish concerning the merits of integration and segregation. Notwithstanding arguments to the contrary, it may be said with certitude that the significant documents of recent years do not advocate the wholesale and immediate movement of all handicapped children, irrespective of the severity of handicapping conditions, into regular classes.

The process of integration parallels the degree of handicap from profound to mild. For the profoundly and severely delayed group of students, for example, locational and possibly some social integration are both desirable and realistic objectives. Clearly, these forms of integration represent a marked improvement over traditional, segregated educational settings. To expect that such children will share in the functional/academic curriculum of the regular classroom, however, is unrealistic.

The moderately handicapped child, the "trainable student" in the somewhat unsavoury traditional nomenclature, can be expected to benefit from both locational and social integration. Teachers can facilitate their participation in dances, library tasks, the student council, teams, school societies, clubs, assemblies, holiday events, and noon-hour activities. With such children, functional/academic integration may be possible individually for a very small percentage of the timetable, in areas that do not hold the likelihood of constant failure. It must be remembered that the moderately handicapped child's rate of intellectual development is about one-third that of non-handicapped chronological age mates. In a very rough equation, the twelve-year-old moderately handicapped child's mental age ranges from approximately four to six years. It is obvious that these children will have problems when confronted with a curriculum based upon an assumed mental age of twelve years. For a large percentage of moderately handicapped children, the special class, where programming is tailored to meet individual needs, is often the least restrictive environment. Nevertheless, this does not rule out social integration in non-academic areas.

It is the mildly handicapped child who has the greatest potential for integration. In almost every class the educable child can be integrated for some aspects of academic programming if the programs are carefully planned and the regular classroom teacher is prepared for a good deal of extra work. In many cases, these students can centre their school day in the regular class, with part-time special help provided in the resource room. Patience, extra help, careful programming, and continuous monitoring of progress are functional requisites.

When deciding who can and should be integrated one must consider a number of crucial questions (Nesbit & Karagianis, 1981). Is integration the most appropriate educational setting for the child? For severely disabled children, integration with non-handicapped children may be more appropriate in social rather than academic settings. Integration becomes a travesty when the child's needs and capabilities are lost.

Are there adequate numbers of support personnel? If the child is to be integrated successfully, the regular classroom teacher must have support. All too often administrators are eager to place exceptional children in regular classes but reluctant to provide further assistance once the classroom door closes. Resource teachers, school counsellors, special education program co-ordinators, and itinerant personnel are among those who provide the many required support services.

Do the teaching staff accept, and are they prepared for, integration in their school? Locational integration, in which a special class is located within a regular school, requires one level of staff support; academic integration involving part- or full-time placement in regular classes requires a much deeper commitment.

Is the class small enough to allow individual programming? In the United States, Public Law 94–142 has made individualized education programs (IEPs) mandatory. There is no similar, prescriptive law in Canada, however, although the policy of individual school boards may require IEPs. The Canadian system therefore has considerable flexibility. Experienced teachers agree that a regular class teacher who instructs twenty or more children does not have the time to develop such programs, and many exceptional children do not benefit from commonly used teaching methods such as heuristic inquiry without extra assistance. Consequently, class size might well be the most critical facet of integration.

What is the child's age and background? Most research on the integration of handicapped learners concludes that integration works best at the primary level. Secondary schools tend to be far more inflexible about program changes, timetables, and individualization of instruction. It is therefore especially important to consider the type of disability, level of intellectual functioning, and social and educational background of exceptional students before placing them at secondary levels.

Have peers been adequately prepared to accept the exceptional student? Various studies indicate that self-derogation and loss of self-esteem frequently characterize the way that exceptional students function in regular classrooms. If this occurs, the student must not be left unattended to watch from the sidelines.

With the influx of exceptional children into regular school settings comes the educational responsibility to help them fit in. Each child's program must be planned carefully and monitored continuously, for without this the most well-intended integration can become educational window dressing. Physical proximity to other children does not ensure learning, and without diligent individual planning and extra effort, the failure of exceptional children is virtually certain. On a brighter note, few would contest the view that integration is a highly desirable and welcome concept. I am a strong advocate for responsible mainstreaming when it is the result of decisions concerning individual children rather than of a universally applied policy. Perhaps I am a grammarian rather than a poet but I feel that sincere aspirations must be tempered by careful judgment.

Wayne C. Nesbit, Ph.D.
Professor and Co-ordinator of Special Education
Memorial University of Newfoundland

If you can, turn your mind back to the mid-1950s. Schools were pretty much the same then as they are today although you would notice much larger classes, much less equipment, and a more restricted range of activities. The careful observer might also be struck by the distinct separation between the special and regular classrooms in the school. Often, rooms labelled "auxiliary class," or "opportunity class," or "special class for the emotionally disturbed" were in the basement or at the end of the corridor, physically separated from the rest of the school.

Children in special classes were often viewed as different, if not deviant, and were given few opportunities for integration or social interaction with their non-handicapped peers. Physical separation also kept regular and special education teachers apart professionally. Regular classroom personnel saw special education as a distinct entity, and believed that special educators were imbued with qualities different from their own, the holders of quite dissimilar philosophies, teaching approaches, and techniques.

Today, the situation has changed dramatically: the separation between special and regular education is crumbling, and the roles of both special educators and regular classroom teachers are changing in order to meet the needs of all pupils most effectively. Special educators have not altered their goals drastically, but they have changed their ideas about the potential and needs of exceptional pupils, and about how to teach them successfully. Because of these changes, special education has become an especially exciting professional area. The social and educational needs of exceptional individuals are now being served in new and sophisticated ways. Mainstreaming has been widely adopted in Canada, and across the country integrated programming is now the most popular educational option for exceptional youngsters. Figure 2–1 shows the percentages of students who have been integrated, across several categories of exceptionality, at both the elementary and secondary levels. Twenty years from now, a history of special education may well report this current period as the time in which special education came of age as a service delivery system, a creditable support system for exceptional students, and a viable component of the public school system (Paul & Warnock, 1980).

A range of philosophical, legal, and educational precepts underlies the current advocacy of integration. The main objectives of this chapter are to

- explain the philosophy and process of educational integration
- discuss the elements necessary for successful integration, and the barriers remaining
- introduce support personnel and detail their contributions to special education
- outline the rationale behind the emergence of non-categorical approaches to educating mildly handicapped students

Mainstreaming exceptional students

Educational and social forces combined in the 1970s to advocate the integration of exceptional students. Pressure from parent associations and interest groups, new educational litigation and legislation (such as the Ontario Education Amendment Act, 1980), and humanistic imperatives in social policy all had a hand in instating mainstreaming as the dominant educational ideology. Educational mainstreaming was thus given impetus by the larger, social goal of normalization, of which it formed a part.

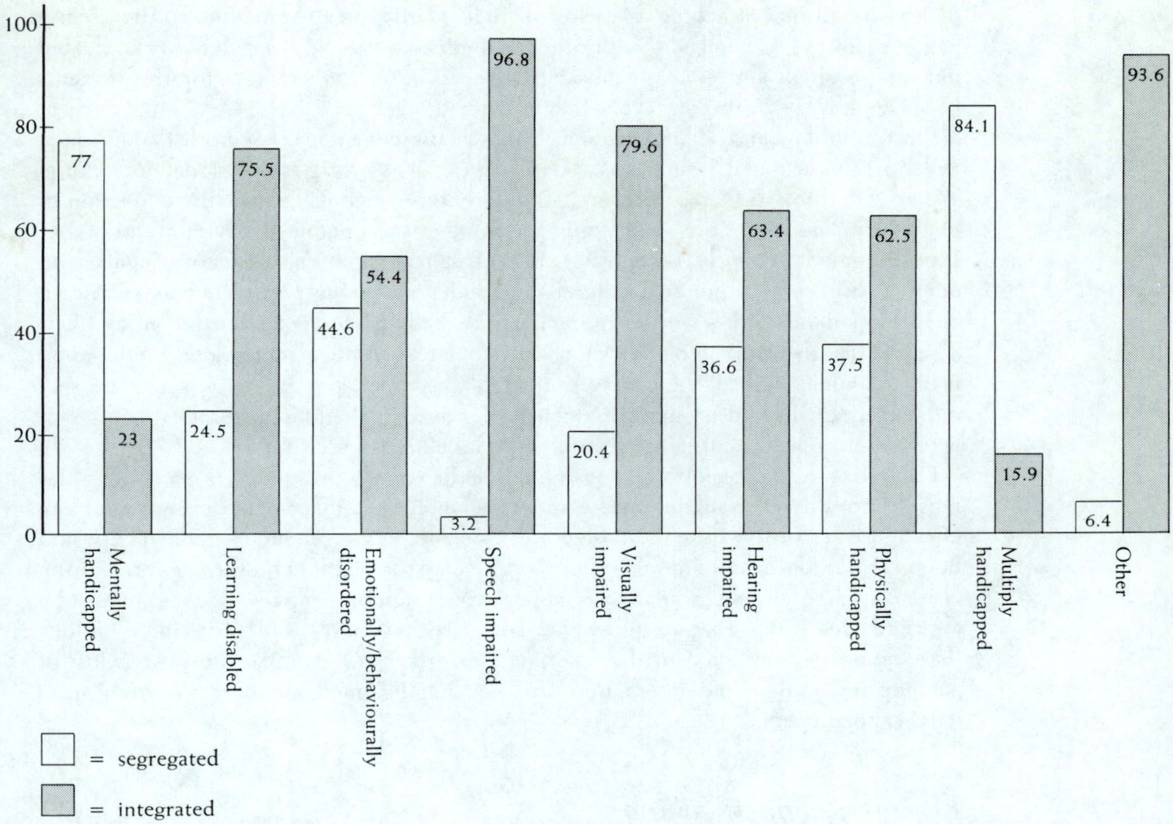

Figure 2–1 Percentages of Canadian students in segregated and integrated settings, 1982–83

Source: Data from *Survey of Special Education in Canada, 1982–83* (p. 17), Council of Ministers of Education, 1982–83, Ottawa: Council of Ministers of Education.

Normalization is the belief that every exceptional person, regardless of the type and degree of handicap, should be provided with a living environment as close as possible to normal. Exceptional people are to have equal access to resources of all kinds (such as recreational and vocational resources, physical access to buildings, and so on), equal opportunities to influence their own situations, productive working roles, and the chance to be a part of the social community.

It would be a mistake to assume, however, that educational integration advanced solely because of positive social forces, generated spontaneously. Equally important was the discovery that between 68 and 75 percent of children in special classes had been unfairly classified and placed (Mortimer & Hammill, 1971; Reynolds & Balow, 1972), and that most of them came from minority groups (Dunn, 1968). As well, numerous studies comparing exceptional students' progress in segregated and regular classes failed to discover superior performance in special class placement. Research demonstrated that attaching a label of mental retardation to students and then segregating them in special classes with other individuals who had been similarly evaluated did not result in any educational, social, or vocational advantages for the students (Goldstein, Moss, & Jordan, 1965; Meyerowitz, 1962).

On the other hand, mainstreaming brings many advantages for both handicapped and non-handicapped youngsters. For exceptional students, educational integration allows wider horizons, greater stimulation in heterogeneous settings, the emulation of better peer models, more group pressure to adopt acceptable behaviour, and higher expectations of progress (Barngrover, 1971). Mainstreaming also expands regular students' awareness of individual differences. Students develop positive attitudes toward handicapped individuals, and an appreciation that all people can learn from one another. There exists, therefore, a beneficial, two-sided nature to the association engendered by mainstreaming. Indeed, educators, anthropologists, and psychologists speculate that non-exceptional children may be unfairly deprived if their opportunities to interact with handicapped children are restricted (Mandell & Fiscus, 1981).

Of course, as Nesbit observes in the letter that opens this chapter, many variables must be considered in integration. A successful integrated placement depends upon the characteristics of the student involved, the specific environmental arrangements, and boundary conditions such as the wishes of the classroom teacher, other children in the class, class size, and the availability of appropriate support services. Educators must be aware of the settings that are most likely to be successful, as well as the interventions that should be employed in these settings, in order to maximize the probability of genuine integration and interaction between handicapped children and their non-handicapped peers.

Defining mainstreaming

Many definitions of mainstreaming exist (Blacher-Dixon & Turnbull, 1979; Kaufman, Gottlieb, Agard, & Kukic 1975; Keogh & Levitt, 1976; Meyen & Lehar, 1980). All of them, however, have the same focus: the best educational placement for the individual exceptional student.

In this text, **mainstreaming** is defined as both a philosophy and a process. It is the physical, intellectual, social, and emotional integration of exceptional students into the regular educational milieu. Mainstreaming demands individual programming, co-operative planning, and a range of educational options and support services.

Mainstreaming is not an end in itself, but rather, an ongoing learning experience, a process through which many exceptional children will be prepared for life and work. Box 2–1 lays out the broad parameters of what mainstreaming does, and does not do.

As a process, mainstreaming offers various forms of integration within the context of the neighbourhood school. Special education services may, for example, be provided in classrooms within the school plant. Students from these classes have access to general school social activities. As well, several types of integration into the regular classroom are possible. Some students benefit from non-academic integration: their core and content subjects are provided in a special class, but they join the regular stream for areas such as art, music, and physical education. Other students are partially integrated:

Box 2–1 Defining mainstreaming

Mainstreaming does . . .	**Mainstreaming does not . . .**
. . . keep exceptional students with their non-handicapped peers as much as possible.	. . . close all special classes and return all exceptional students to regular classrooms.
. . . unite the skills of regular and special educators for the educational benefit of all students.	. . . eliminate the role of special education teachers.
. . . provide every exceptional student with the most appropriate education possible in the most suitable setting.	. . . place exceptional students in regular classrooms without the necessary support services.
. . . focus on the educational needs of exceptional students instead of on clinical or diagnostic labels.	. . . ignore students' needs that cannot be met in the regular classroom.
. . . seek alternatives to help regular educators teach handicapped students.	. . . cost less than self-contained segregated classrooms.

they move between the regular class and the special class as their unique learning needs dictate. Many mildly handicapped children are fully integrated into regular classrooms, but receive additional help in the **resource room**, from itinerant teachers, or from other specialists. For all kinds of integration, support services are essential.

As the definition of mainstreaming suggests, exceptional children in regular classrooms must become members of the class not just physically but also socially, emotionally, and intellectually. Mainstreaming without social integration may actually create a more restrictive environment than segregation does, if exceptional students are debased by their peers, socially isolated, and poorly accepted. Students must be given the opportunity to form peer relationships, earn status and acceptance, and feel comfortable with members of the classroom group. With acceptance, exceptional pupils will gain the corresponding rights and responsibilities of group membership. It is therefore important that scheduling between the various classes that exceptional students must attend be devised to accommodate classroom opportunities for social interaction. Much group work and discussion are involved, for example, in the content areas, such as science and social studies. Moreover, the non-academic areas, such as art and physical education, provide an excellent context for developing social and cooperative skills. They also allow exceptional children to demonstrate talents in areas unrelated to pure academics. The social and emotional integration of exceptional pupils into regular classes is the chief subject addressed in chapter 6.

If mainstreaming exceptional pupils is to be successful academically, individualized program preparation and instructional modification will be necessary. These require the teacher to observe a student's response to instruction continually. Individualized programs are discussed in chapter 4, and instructional modifications are described in the chapters dealing with various subject areas.

Finally, the definition of mainstreaming stresses the need for a co-operative effort between regular and special educators in order to make integration successful. Because the severity of their deficits is often not sufficient to warrant full-time immersion in the special education system, mildly handicapped children are frequently the responsibility of both regular and special educators. Consequently, special education and regular education can no longer exist as separate entities; they must join forces in order to provide the most appropriate education for every child.

Mainstreaming has focussed on elementary levels

It is no secret that handicapped adolescents have received less than their fair share of help. In the past, mainstreaming practices have been more widely implemented at elementary than at secondary levels; special education has not developed much emphasis on a strong, ongoing presence at the secondary level and so opportunities for adolescents have been unsatisfactory. The literature has been, and indeed still is, replete with references to children but much less concerned with youth, partly because so much research regards the primary level as the optimal time for integration to take place (e.g. Nesbit & Karagianis, 1981) Of course, if early recognition automatically implies early intervention and remediation, then the resources of special education can be used much more efficiently at the younger levels.

Another reason for the neglect of secondary special education is that few secondary teachers are offered training in developmental, corrective, or remedial teaching; hence, their ability to provide basic academic skills is hindered. In addition, secondary personnel tend to be more subject-oriented than are their counterparts at the elementary level and to focus more on the transmission of content than on individual needs (Elkins, 1983). Some subject areas lend themselves to mainstreaming more easily than others. Mathematics is particularly difficult to teach successfully in an integrated classroom, for example, which is why chapter 9 of this text focusses on the elementary level. As well, the predominant style of teaching in secondary school is the lecture, which cannot be adapted well to individualization.

The organization of large secondary schools is complex and quite different from that of neighbourhood elementary plants. High schools are organized by department and subject and are much more inflexible about program change, timetables, and individualization of instruction. Moreover, it is more difficult to create individual programs in behavioural and curricular areas at the secondary level; interventions that were satisfactory in elementary school do not provide sufficient support for secondary students. As well, remedial instruction may be viewed very differently by adolescents, who will not generally place a high priority on any component of education that singles them out from their peers.

Where programs have existed at the secondary levels, they have traditionally consisted of teacher-directed procedures. Because techniques and materials needed for modifying course content have not been available at the upper levels, adaptations have used reading, language, and mathematics materials borrowed from general elementary education (D'Alonzo & Miller, 1977).

Generally, the conflict between secondary schools and the needs of exceptional students seems to be dissipating. Several promising trends are emerging that reflect mounting interest in secondary disabled students and a sense of commitment to their needs. Naturally, some aspects of secondary education, such as vocational education, are more amenable to integration than others. Vocational and career education stress the importance of both vocational skills and work experience. Educators also now realize that exceptional adolescents need to work on daily living skills, occupational preparation, and psycho-social problems (Miller, 1975), as well as the remediation of reading and mathematics. Several writers (Alley & Deshler, 1979; Wiederholt & McNutt, 1979) note that a number of different strategies are currently available in secondary special education programs. Exceptional students may be given remedial instruction that focusses on their deficiencies in basic skills, tutorial work to assist in various subject areas, compensatory education that offers alternative methods for performing certain tasks, or training in the functional skills essential in everyday life.

Even as secondary programs are burgeoning, there remains the issue of whether instructional emphasis should be placed on improving academic performance or on developing skills that are needed in adulthood. Moreover, there are serious questions regarding the choice of groups to be served in the various programs available: much consideration is given to the severity of the disability, the level of intellectual functioning, and the student's academic background and needs. The mix of specific educational and social objectives within and between domains will vary considerably according to the degree of functional limitation among individual students.

Making mainstreaming work

Many factors determine the success or failure of any mainstreaming policy. Mainstreaming must be implemented systematically; it demands positive attitudes and new skills from teachers; it necessitates shared responsibilities among educators; it involves adaptive roles for both regular and special education teachers; and it requires sufficient support staff and related services. Each factor is critical and all must be present in order to serve exceptional pupils appropriately and effectively. The following discussion details each of these elements in turn.

Mainstreaming must employ a systematic process

To be successful, mainstreaming takes the form of a systematic, sequential process. Effective implementation involves many tasks, each of which must be completed in turn: the creation of an initial, comprehensive plan, in-service training, acquisition of resources, co-ordination of services and support personnel, and the development of evaluative procedures (Paul, Turnbull, & Cruickshank, 1977). Identification, referral, and diagnosis begin the process.

Early identification is crucial because the so-called low-severity, high-incidence disabilities experienced by school-age children have long-term effects. It is well established that subtle, mild handicapping conditions can seriously interfere with the acquisition of academic skills, adjustment to school life, and the process of socialization. Yet too often a mildly handicapped learner is identified only after he or she has been exposed to enough schooling for teachers to become aware of problems in the student's behaviour or responses to teaching, instead of at the preschool age, through the techniques of early identification. In fact, it is not unusual for a child to be in formal schooling for several years before it becomes apparent that problems in either learning or conduct need to be evaluated formally.

Students who have trouble learning often develop social and emotional problems: their academic inabilities can provoke anxiety, frustration, and anger. If these difficulties are neglected, students may eventually become caught in a spiral of failure and dissatisfaction, losing their self-esteem and motivation in the process (Blackman, Levine, Markowitz, & Aufsaeser, 1983). The later that identification and diagnosis takes place, the harder it is to remediate learning problems and confront accompanying emotional difficulties. Moreover, a delay in recognizing underlying learning dysfunctions can lead to false labelling, parental and professional misunderstanding, and failure to provide appropriate services. As well, academic retardation can cause disappointment to parents and bring ridicule from peers.

Disciplines involved in special education are therefore now pressing for early identification and its corollary, early intervention. Early childhood education, which encompasses infant (from birth to three years) and preschool education (from three to five or six years of age), has originated several methods of identification and intervention. Winzer, Rogow, and David (1987) and Marfo (1988) provide good sources of further information about early childhood education.

At any level of education, planned instruction follows identification, referral, and diagnosis. Objective data are gathered about a student's performance level at the beginning of the planned intervention. Priorities are then established among the skills the student needs to know now and in the future, and the prerequisite behaviours identified that are necessary to develop those skills. During instruction, the student's progress must be carefully assessed and the information used to revise teaching procedures as necessary.

For the exceptional student, some modification is necessary in lesson content, type and complexity of skills to be learned, and learning environment. For mentally handicapped students, for example, the content of a lesson may be modified to make it more concrete and relevant to student's recent experiences. Gifted students, on the other hand, can handle the challenge of expanded lesson content and sophisticated cross-disciplinary references. Also, the pace of the lesson, the rate at which information is presented, may be either accelerated or slowed.

Specific modifications are components of a systematic, planned intervention, based upon identification and diagnosis. Each step in the process of integration is the logical sequel to that which precedes it, informed by a plan for the whole. Particular modifications for mildly handicapped learners are discussed in chapters 7 to 10.

Mainstreaming depends upon teachers' positive attitudes

Regular classroom teachers are particularly affected by the mainstreaming movement, and because they carry the primary responsibility for integrating exceptional pupils into regular classrooms, their attitudes in turn are central to the outcome of any mainstreaming venture. The relationship between teachers' attitudes and successful integration is thus reciprocal: the more favourable teachers are to the concept, the more comfortable they are with exceptional children; the more knowledge they have about special needs, the more they are likely to adopt the principles of mainstreaming. Because they are so vital to the mainstreaming enterprise, teachers' attitudes toward both exceptional children and mainstreaming have been the subject of intense research activity in recent years. (See, for example, Albert, 1980; Goupil & Brunet, 1984; Larrivée & Cook, 1979; Winzer, 1984; and Winzer & Rose, 1987).

Mainstreaming improves teachers' methods and skills

There is no question that mainstreaming requires knowledge and skills greatly expanded from those acquired by many teachers in pre- and in-service training. Teachers must expect to individualize planning and materials, and to use approaches that are both more intense and more extended. The teacher's *methods* — those recurrent patterns of teacher behaviour — have to incorporate enhanced skills in lesson presentation, group work, individual work, and teaching students to solve problems. As well, educators must be thoroughly versed in techniques for direct observation, continuous assessment, interpretation of psycho-educational tests, referral, documentation of behaviour, behavioural management, reinforcement tactics, and methods to pinpoint the specific behaviours that interfere with learning.

The things that make special education special are actually done informally by good teachers every day (see box 2–2), but mainstreaming does involve a wider range of organizational and instructional materials and alternatives than regular teaching does. Teachers need to feel comfortable with a variety of methods and materials in order to choose appropriate instruction for diverse students. Of course, it is also vital to make continual, objective assessments about why particular techniques are succeeding or failing.

While regular classroom teachers are increasing their accomplishments, special educators also need to develop wider perspectives. Many training programs are categorical and a special educator may be trained specifically, for example, in the area of learning disabilities. Additional training not only imparts other skills but also illustrates how already acquired abilities can be modified for use with a range of mildly handicapped students. One of the benefits of mainstreaming lies in the fact that it provides both regular and special education teachers with the opportunity to learn and implement new skills. These enhance the learning of all students while making the job of teaching more organized and systematic.

Mainstreaming involves shared responsibility

In the past, regular education and special education have functioned as parallel rather than integrated enterprises. Successful integration, however, implies alterations in the traditional conception of two separate educational systems. It will not work unless staff, regular students, and exceptional pupils are committed to the idea, and co-operate in finding ways to overcome the obstacles that inevitably and continually arise. Integration must be discussed with the whole school before it is initiated, and classroom teachers given a part in mainstreaming decisions.

Box 2–2 Components of effective teaching

- Have a clear sense of purpose.
- Have a wide knowledge of the subject matter.
- Set clear expectations.
- Give detailed, redundant instructions and explanations.
- Spend an appropriate amount of time actually teaching.
- Structure the instruction.
- Provide many examples.
- Ask many questions.
- Provide continual, active practice.
- Use a variety of concrete materials.
- Stress all aspects of the language hierarchy.
- Assign seatwork, divided into small assignments.
- Monitor and evaluate seatwork frequently.
- Provide feedback, reinforcement, and correction, particularly in the early stages of teaching new material.
- Check homework and mark assignments.
- Conduct review.
- Spiral the learning process and ensure mastery to the point of overlearning.
- Allow each student to experience some success every day.
- Develop a hierarchy of praise for younger students.
- Attend to inappropriate behaviour.
- Command attention from all students.
- Never take anything for granted.

For those who are designing or participating in integrated programs, the following points should be considered:

- All members of the educational system should be involved with and committed to the concept.
- The goals of the program must be clearly delineated in advance.
- All regular classroom teachers should be provided with in-service training in order to build their competence and confidence before the integrated program starts.
- Regular teachers and special education personnel should design the program together. Especially, regular classroom teachers must be helped to plan and carry out individual instruction.
- Communication among staff members must be maintained; time should be scheduled within the school week for staff to consult one another.
- Teachers must be alerted to the value and process of identifying learning and behavioural problems at an early stage. They should be given clues about potential learning and behavioural disorders and provided with systematic referral procedures.
- Regular classroom teachers who teach exceptional learners must be assured of necessary support services.
- Non-handicapped students may also display learning problems and classroom teachers should be helped in their efforts to aid these youngsters.

- Modifications to the physical plant may be necessary to accommodate physically handicapped students.
- Record keeping should be consistent throughout a school but kept as simple as possible.

Staff members work as part of a school-based educational team that considers pupil and parental rights, the least restrictive environment, and the most appropriate program, and then makes educational decisions regarding each exceptional student. School teams are something quite new on the educational scene—they were virtually unknown before 1975 — and they are still not being used as well as they might be. One study, for example, revealed that only 35 percent of teachers surveyed had received either preservice or in-service training to work on a team (Yoshida, 1983). To overcome this lack of preparation for what is rapidly becoming an integral part of school programming, teacher trainers should demonstrate a greater commitment to team approaches (Abelson & Woodman, 1983). The functions of a **school-based team** are addressed in further detail in chapter 4.

Mainstreaming implies changing roles for educators

Many teachers still adhere to strict role boundaries. The idea so central to mainstreaming, that regular and special educators should act in concert, has proven difficult to put into practice for the notion is a new and unfamiliar one. Two intrinsic difficulties beset mainstreaming efforts: special educators are not willing to give their students up and regular educators are not willing to take them. Many regular classroom teachers still feel that remedial instruction for behaviourally and learning-disordered students is not their responsibility (Speece & Mandell, 1980). For mainstreaming to be truly successful, however, these role divisions must be broken down.

Special and regular educators need to acquire a thorough understanding of both segregated and regular programs. Reciprocal understanding might be initiated by the special educator, who may legitimately claim the need for more knowledge of the regular class before recommending a student's placement there. Indeed, in some ways, special teachers may eventually be placed in a perpetual in-service capacity. They will work with classroom teachers, for example, to develop programs and alter instructional strategies for exceptional students. They will assist students to transfer skills learned in the resource room to the regular classroom, and support teachers through in-service training (Bachor, 1983).

Some special educators have feared that mainstreaming might result in a change of roles, loss of responsibility, or even elimination of positions, yet while roles are certainly changing, educators' responsibilities have, if anything, increased. Special educators have already assumed roles that extend beyond the classroom. They participate in conferences, and are required to work with psychologists, language therapists, administrators, and many other people involved in an exceptional student's educational program.

To gain acceptance and respect, however, special educators may find it helpful to become actively involved in school functions not specifically related to special students (Elman & Ginsberg, 1981). They could, for example, socialize with other staff members, attend evening programs, or volunteer for school committees. They should take part in extra-curricular activities and perform yard and bus duty.

With integration, the roles of not only special educators but also of regular educators will change. Classroom teachers may have additional work and anxiety; they might need to devote extra time to assessment and referral, and to meeting with the school-based team in order to develop and evaluate programs.

A number of writers have attempted to catalogue the competencies that will be required of regular educators as they become involved in mainstreaming exceptional students (Anderson, 1979; Goldman & Mosla, 1976; Goodspeed & Celotta, 1982; Haisley & Gilberts, 1978; Rader, 1978). Some of these have been outlined in the discussion of teachers' increasing skills. These, and further competencies may be summed up as follows:

- an understanding of the precursors to mainstreaming, the legislation involved, and the procedures and terminology that mainstreaming employs
- familiarity with resource and support systems
- knowledge about the varied learning styles of exceptional learners
- cognizance of a variety of learning environments and the ability to adapt them appropriately
- knowledge of a variety of assessment measures, and the competence to interpret and explain psycho-educational test results
- ability to set goals and modify or develop curricular materials for exceptional learners
- competence in instruction and management
- ability to implement various behavioural management techniques
- skill in public relations, in order to communicate effectively with other professionals, students, and parents

Extra responsibility and changing roles can mean more pressure for some teachers. As well, the rate at which students learn often does not conform to a bureaucratic timetable, and the conflict between what they learn and what the curriculum says they should be learning may result in elevated rates of stress among educators. Generally, being positive about the profession and the teacher's role in it, keeping in mind the students to be served, setting realistic professional goals and objectives, keeping motivated, and making work as enjoyable as possible all assuage stress. Within the school, teachers should try to develop positive relationships with others, recognize mistakes and learn from them, and pace themselves. They should also use available resources, ask for help when it is needed, and learn to say no. If possible, work should be left at school so that outside time can be enjoyed.

Mainstreaming requires readily available support services

When teachers accept exceptional children into their classrooms, they also accept assistance from a variety of support services. A regular classroom teacher can no longer meet all the needs of all his or her students. Instead, members of several disciplines pool their expertise in order to assist classroom teachers. Although students sometimes leave the classroom for special help, many specialists today work right in the classroom to develop the most effective education for a student, in consultation with the classroom teacher. Obviously, daily schedules must be carefully co-ordinated for students to benefit from all the possible services.

Many mildly handicapped children can be integrated with support help.

Special education draws heavily on knowledge and theory from a number of core disciplines. In consequence, support services provided by those disciplines have grown in concert with special education (see table 2–1) and the roles of the various professionals involved have expanded. School psychologists, for example, today do not simply administer tests; they are important members of school-based educational teams. More and more speech and language therapists are working directly in schools, and social workers, adaptive physical education specialists, and home–school liaison personnel may also have close contact with the school. Probably no exceptional student will need all of these services, or even most of them, but they should be available.

The discussion that follows describes those support services that are directly involved with educational intervention. The responsibilities of personnel in support services are interlocking (see table 2–2), so that a number of people contribute to each aspect of educational organization, planning, practice, and evaluation.

Directors and principals

The director or superintendent of special education ensures that administrative and supportive educational services meet the requirements of school law, regulations, policies, and legislation. Within an individual school, the principal is indispensable to the success of the mainstreaming venture (Payne & Murray, 1974). School p[illegible] organize educational services, hire personnel, establish volunteer programs, [illegible] of school-based teams, and locate appropriate instructional resources.

Educational consultants

Educational consultants provide advice to regular classroom teachers about special teaching methods, equipment, and materials. The consultant's role is vital; in fact, many educators are convinced that exceptional children cannot be educated in the least restrictive environment if consultants' services are not utilized more fully than is currently the case. Although they have few, if any, direct teaching responsibilities, educational consultants help members of the school team to recognize individual differences among students, plan programs, and place students correctly.

Hawisher and Calhoun (1978) describe five main duties for educational consultants:

1. With teachers, consultants deal with classroom management, grading procedures, and instructional adaptations to meet the needs of individual pupils.
2. With students, consultants address problems and concerns related to academic difficulties, social skills, peer relationships, and self-concept development.
3. With parents, consultants discuss educational programs.
4. With volunteers and paraprofessionals, consultants identify roles and responsibilities, discuss classroom management issues, and give encouragement.
5. In the school district, consultants are involved in staff development needs and provide in-service training.

Table 2–1 Support services in special education

Service	Examples of personnel and of services provided
Medical services: services provided by licensed practitioners for children whose physical conditions may result in the need for special education	*Family doctor:* cares for general health *Neurologist:* treats head injuries, traumas *Ophthalmologist:* undertakes identification, treatment, and prognosis of visual problems *Otologist:* undertakes identification, treatment, and prognosis of auditory problems *Pediatrician:* cares for general health in early childhood
Paramedical services: services that supplement medical diagnosis	*Audiologist:* identifies and treats hearing loss; provides amplification equipment *Oculist:* provides equipment for visual problems
Counselling: services provided by psychologists, social workers, counsellors, and many other qualified personnel	*Family counsellor:* helps parents and siblings to cope with the impact of diagnosis of a handicapping condition *Genetic counsellor:* counsels families at high risk from hereditary handicapping conditions *Guidance counsellor:* helps students with social, personal, family, and educational problems

Table 2–1, continued

Service	Examples of personnel and of services provided
	School counsellor: helps students deal with school problems and vocational destinations
Therapy: treatment to improve, develop, or restore some area of functioning; helps to prevent the development of secondary problems	*Occupational therapist:* improves physical functioning through various therapeutic activities and assists students to develop self-help skills such as feeding; provides vocational training in specific settings such as sheltered workshops; helps to develop perceptual skills; and practises methods to enhance learning potential and to employ vestibular, tactile, kinesthetic, gross and fine motor co-ordination *Physical therapist:* works to improve or restore muscular and physical condition to maintain maximum motor functioning *Speech therapist:* helps client to develop speech, or ameliorates and remediates speech problems *Language therapist:* remediates language disorders
Psychological services: services to administer and interpret tests; integrate information about child behaviour; and provide psychological counselling for children and parents	*Clinical psychologist:* works with both adults and children in a variety of settings outside the school, such as hospitals and clinics *Educational psychologist:* tests, observes, and assesses school-age children; acts on school-based teams; serves as a consultant to teachers and parents; counsels children and parents
Social work: a broad range of services that involve the child's functioning at home and in the community	*School social workers, probation officers, child advocates,* and *lawyers:* social workers act as a liaison between school and families, counsel families, and conduct family therapy
Recreational services: services that organize therapeutic and leisure activities	*Adaptive physical education teacher:* modifies programs for handicapped learners (see chapter 10)
Educational services: services that involve teaching and learning	*Directors of special education, school principals, educational consultants, resource-room personnel, itinerant teachers, special education teachers*
Transportational services: services that provide transport to, and between, schools	

Table 2–2 Support services and interlocking responsibilities

Director of special education	School principal	Educational consultant	Resource-room teacher	Special education teacher	Itinerant teacher	Regular classroom teacher
Arranging services	Arranging services					
Hiring personnel	Hiring personnel					
	Acting on school-based teams	Acting on school-based teams	Acting on school-based teams	Acting on school-based teams		
	Locating appropriate resources	Locating appropriate resources	Locating appropriate resources			
	Helping teachers with specific problems	Helping teachers with specific problems	Helping teachers with specific problems	Helping teachers with specific problems	Helping teachers with specific problems	
	Working with students on academic and social problems	Working with students on academic and social problems	Working with students on academic and social problems	Working with students on academic and social problems	Working with students on academic and social problems	Working with students on academic and social problems
	Staff development	Staff development	Staff development	Staff development		
	Communication with parents	Communication with parents	Communication with parents	Communication with parents	Communication with parents	Communication with parents
		Instructional planning	Instructional planning	Instructional planning	Instructional planning	Instructional planning
		Teaching	Teaching	Teaching	Teaching	Teaching
		Evaluation	Evaluation	Evaluation	Evaluation	Evaluation

Resource-room personnel

At present the most common way of educating exceptional students is by a combination of services in the regular classroom and in a resource room. Resource rooms are so classified when students spend less than half their time receiving direct instruction there (Johnson, 1977).

The **resource room** is an instructional innovation originated by special education. The model was developed in the 1960s and evolved for two reasons: exceptional students required more direct instruction and teachers therefore needed support services. In the resource room, behaviour can be assessed precisely, and students are able to accelerate rapidly in areas requiring special attention, while functioning for part of the day in the regular classroom. Resource-room personnel work with individuals or small groups on improving skills, remediating specific deficits, and completing class

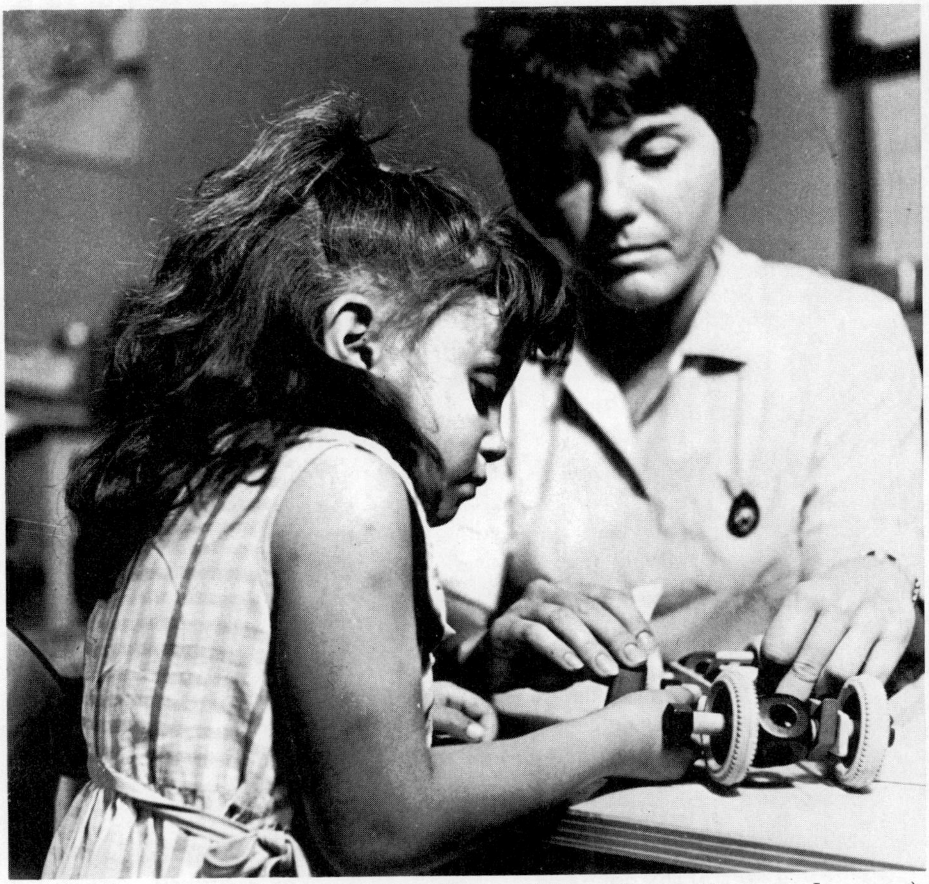

Fine and gross motor training is important for some children. (Sunny View #18, June 1965)

assignments; they design, alter, and present instruction across a number of curricular areas. Placement in the resource room depends only upon a teacher's referral, so no time is lost in waiting for a complete psycho-educational assessment. As well, a pupil's schedule can be altered to suit her or his needs at a particular time so that one hour a day in the resource room may be appropriate in one term, two hours in another.

The resource room is modelled on the principle of normalization; it eliminates the stigma of special class placement while preserving high quality service for exceptional pupils. Resource rooms should never be seen as part-time special classes. Rather, they are best viewed as a placement between the regular classroom and the special, self-contained class, a setting that children enter for specific, regularly scheduled periods of time (Wiederholt, 1974). Resource-room help initiated early in a student's school career may prevent the development of **secondary handicapping conditions**. Intervention, especially before the end of grade three, may alleviate or prevent emotional problems by providing some success in academic ventures.

In Canada, resource rooms have typically consisted of a home base staffed by at least one resource specialist or learning-resource teacher, often with a teacher's aide, and sometimes peer tutors (Wilson & McLaughlin, 1986). Resource-room specialists assess students, plan instruction, teach, evaluate students' work, and act as consultants for regular classroom teachers (Wallace & McLaughlin, 1979). Resource-room personnel are in an ideal position to generate enthusiasm and positive feelings among all staff members about pupils with special needs. Their attitudes can involve other teachers in united support for the students (Klockors, 1982).

Although the intent of all resource rooms — to provide support to students meeting school difficulty—is identical, the model has several variations. Resource rooms usually differ in relation to the population served, and include

- *categorical resource rooms,* which serve one primary type of exceptionality;
- *cross-categorical resource rooms,* in which two or more categories of children are grouped;
- *non-categorical resource rooms,* where students with mild to severe learning and behavioural problems, and possibly non-handicapped children, are given help;
- *specific-skills resource rooms,* in which a particular area of the curriculum, such as mathematics or reading, is pinpointed for work; and
- *itinerant resource rooms,* which travel to various geographic areas as services are required (Hammill & Bartel, 1975; Sabatino & Mauser, 1977; Wiederholt, Hammill, & Brown, 1983).

Adolescents encounter an educational environment considerably different from that found in elementary schools. While it is imperative that students continue to receive support, resource-room models may function slightly differently. Three main models have been identified at the secondary level:

- *the teacher-consulting model,* in which the students involved receive services either directly or indirectly in their regular classes, and do not have to go to another classroom;
- *the pull-out model,* which requires that students leave their regular classes at specific intervals; and
- *the study-period model,* in which students are regularly scheduled for at least one block of resource-room activities per day in the **learning centre** (in either the classroom or another room) in place of an elective course (Wilson & McLaughlin, 1986).

As special education advances, resource-room personnel may be required to expand their duties beyond those in the direct-only service models just described, to provide indirect services such as consultation, in-service education, and co-ordination of individual education plans, schedules, and so on. Increased obligation becomes especially noticeable at the secondary school level, when resource-room personnel may be involved in both direct and indirect tracking of exceptional students. When using direct tracking methods, the resource-room teacher usually has some responsibility for the student, whereas indirect tracking tends to imply that he or she works with the regular teacher, in the manner of an educational consultant. Table 2–3 explains the components of resource-room programs in secondary schools although, of course, many of the responsibilities also concern resource-room teachers in elementary schools.

Because resource personnel and classroom teachers must work so closely with one another, it is essential that they establish some simple rules to govern their working relationships. Klockors (1982) points out that resource teachers should

- present suggestions that are realistic for the regular classroom environment
- show, not tell, how recommendations can be implemented
- be acutely aware of the curriculum and instructional materials at each grade level
- learn all they can about a particular classroom and a particular teacher's style
- adhere to commitments
- establish a schedule and be prompt and dependable
- never arrive unannounced or interrupt a lesson
- treat in-class visits as seriously as they do their direct caseload
- be prepared with a lesson plan before class and a record after of what was achieved

Table 2–3 Resource-room programs in secondary schools

Direct tracking	
Learning strategies	Instructing students in classroom survival skills such as skimming, note taking, outlining, and so on.
Deviant behaviour and peformance contracts	Developing and monitoring contracts for behaviour as well as performance in regular classes.
Charts and graphs	Creating charts and graphs to monitor progress and provide feedback.
Role playing	Creating and enacting situations in the resource room that may be met in regular settings.
Problem solving	Helping students work through problems that they meet in regular classrooms.
Consequences of misbehaviour	Providing consequences when expectations for behaviour in regular classes are not met.
Monitoring and pre-assigning work	Monitoring assignment completion, or giving assignments before they come up in class, thus enabling students to better join in class discussions.
Providing rewards and incentives	When appropriate behaviour is demonstrated, providing rewards and incentives.
Progress reports	Providing these to regular classroom teachers as a means of giving feedback to students and parents.
Budgeting work	Helping students budget their time in order to complete school work.
Crisis intervention	Intervention when students experience crises or conflicts that they cannot resolve.
Behaviour training	Training social and classroom behaviour expected in the regular classroom.
Negotiation training	Teaching negotiation strategies as a method of problem solving with regular classroom teachers.
Compensatory devices	The use of calculators, tape recorders, typewriters, and other compensatory devices and techniques.

Table 2–3, continued

Indirect tracking	
Modifying and substituting assignments	Changing work that students could not otherwise perform so that credit may be earned.
Brainstorming alternatives	Working with teachers to find problem solutions.
Modifying grading criteria	Suggesting that teachers grade students in light of their ability, rather than against class norms.
Problem solving	Helping regular teachers find solutions to difficult problems as situations arise.
Providing low-level materials	Providing commercial materials on secondary subjects at an elementary reading level but without elementary pictures.
Co-facilitating class meetings	Offering to co-facilitate class meetings when they are used for problem solving in the regular class.
Breaking tasks down	Helping the teacher break concepts and skills into smaller steps for exceptional pupils.
Observing and giving feedback	Providing feedback on such areas as proximity to the board, classroom distractions, and classmates.
Sharing ideas	Passing ideas and suggestions both to and from the classroom teacher.
Creating learning packages and modules	Creating learning packages for common units which can be sent to the regular class and used under the teacher's direction.
Developing plans	Working with the teacher to develop a co-operative plan for each student by anticipating problems, rewards, and consequences.
Helping with buddy systems	Arranging for a buddy in difficult classes to sit with a target student and assist in getting assignments, reading from the board, or giving behavioural clues.
Setting up peer tutoring	Arranging for peer or cross-age tutors to provide instruction in the resource room.
Teaching awareness clues and cues	Giving students and teachers a brief language of cues to reinforce good behaviour or provide silent warning before a consequence is invoked.
Crisis intervention	Being available to the regular classroom teacher when a crisis occurs in the classroom.

Source: From "Linking Two Worlds: Serving Resource Students at the Secondary Level" by D.R. Adamson, 1983, *Teaching Exceptional Children, 15*, pp. 70–76. Copyright 1983 by The Council for Exceptional Children. Reprinted with permission.

Itinerant teachers

Itinerant personnel move from school to school to visit exceptional pupils who are enrolled in regular classrooms for most of the day. They provide specialized instruction, either to individual exceptional students, or to small groups, and also serve as a resource for regular classroom teachers. Itinerant teachers may work in or out of the regular classroom, and deal with exceptional students, their non-exceptional peers, and teachers, helping all three groups with the process of integration.

Special education teachers

Among the many responsibilities of a special education teacher is the task of easing the passage between special and regular classrooms from both the exceptional student's standpoint and that of the regular teacher. The designated classroom teacher can be prepared for the transition by having the student's needs, and special needs in general, explained as fully as possible, and being encouraged to focus on strengths as well as weaknesses. Special education personnel also demonstrate teaching approaches, techniques, and materials, and help classroom teachers to prepare or modify individual education plans. In addition, they can ready the regular students for change by giving brief in-class talks and fostering discussions. With the target student, special education teachers must make it a point to reinforce appropriate behaviour.

During and after the integration, special education teachers will maintain close contact with the receiving classroom teacher by evaluating the teacher's performance and the efficacy of the program in a tactful and positive manner, and by remaining available for consultation. In the school as a whole, special education teachers may attempt to involve other staff members positively in the integration procedure, in order to ease the transition for the student. The transition process is more fully discussed in chapter 6.

School and guidance counsellors

Counselling is a process in which a trained counsellor meets with a student, usually one to one, to discuss educational and career choices. Effective counselling is both a process and a relationship; it is designed to explore the student's feelings and to make him or her aware of choices. School counsellors endeavour to discover the needs of students and to assess their potentialities. Guidance counsellors advise students on particular courses of study, and help them to develop their goals, formalize their plans, and begin the process of realizing their ambitions.

Although guidance and counselling are important for exceptional students at all levels, they are particularly beneficial in secondary school. Because counsellors are often the first people to have contact with special students in a new educational environment, they are in a unique position to help students and their parents to cope with the social and emotional difficulties that can arise during the formal educational process.

Counselling is one of the many services designed to individualize education and assist all pupils in developing their full potential. It helps students to adjust to school life, and promotes principles such as self-realization, social skill, and a sense of civic responsibility.

School psychologists

The term "school psychologist" first appeared in print more than sixty years ago (Hutt, 1923), but it took almost three more decades for the American Psychological Association Council to recognize school psychology as a speciality within the field. Today, however, school psychologists are an indispensable component of the school system and of school-based educational teams. Their expertise bridges the gap between the disciplines of education and psychology, allowing the former to draw on the knowledge of the latter. School psychologists are trained to perform a variety of sophisticated functions that range from assessment and instructional planning for students experiencing academic and behavioural problems to individual therapy and behavioural treatment consultation. Like other members of the school-based team, they confer with teachers, students, and families in the course of carrying out their responsibilities.

Teacher aides

Paraprofessionals, and specifically teacher aides, constitute one group of support staff who are of particular value to classroom teachers. Increasingly, teacher aides are receiving training that enables them to provide a valuable helping hand in the educational enterprise. Their active involvment can boost a teacher's efficiency, give students greater opportunities to learn, and improve even a good program. Because they can add so positively to the organization and management of a classroom, chapter 5 contains a more complete discussion of teacher aides.

Mainstreaming benefits mildly handicapped students

No perfect relationship exists between severity of handicap and success in the regular classroom. Few studies, however, demonstrate that integration answers the purpose for trainable mentally retarded students or those with multiple handicaps (Birch, 1976); successful integration is more often reported for mildly disabled students, including those labelled as learning disabled (Ritter, 1978), educable mentally retarded students (Gottlieb, Campbell, & Budoff, 1975), those who are hearing impaired (Reich, Hambleton, & Houldin, 1977), or mildly emotionally disturbed pupils (Macy & Carter, 1978). Even so, studies of the success of integration for mildly handicapped students still present mixed and inconclusive results (Caparulo & Zigler, 1983; Gottlieb, 1981; Polloway, 1984), because so much depends upon the attitudes of classroom teachers. The only consistent finding in recent reports has been that integration works when teachers are able to adapt instruction for all the students in their classrooms, including those with mild handicaps (Madden & Slavin, 1983).

Although many children could be included in the category of mildly handicapped, the term is generally reserved for the three groups traditionally labelled as mildly mentally retarded, learning disabled, and behaviourally disordered. (The last term is currently used almost interchangeably with "mildly emotionally disturbed.") Mentally retarded children have difficulties in all aspects of intellectual functioning: memory, attention, language, and the ability to learn concepts. Their learning difficulties are often accompanied by social and emotional problems, and by reduced motivation to succeed (Harter, 1978). Mildly mentally retarded children have the same range of personality characteristics as other people, but are more likely to experience emotional disturbance, partly because they have limited intellectual tools and fewer skills in social interaction.

By definition, learning-disabled children lag in some or all academic areas: they are unable to acquire skills at a normal rate. Learning-disabled children are likely to have attention problems (Ross, 1976), be less task-oriented and more distractible (Feagans & McKinney, 1981), and face difficulties in social interaction (Bryan, 1978). In addition, learning-disabled students often demonstrate behavioural disorders, which may mask the learning disability.

Compared to the normal distribution of intelligence, a high proportion of mildly emotionally disturbed children fall into the slow-learner or mildly retarded category; most have IQs in the dull–normal range — around ninety — and very few score above the bright–normal range (Hallahan & Kauffman, 1986). Many of these children are underachievers at school, as measured by standardized tests (Kauffman, 1985).

Three case studies are presented below, of children variously labelled mildly mentally retarded, learning disabled, and behaviourally disordered. As you read these, it will become obvious that the children function in similar ways, yet this does not indicate that they will all respond to exactly the same teaching approaches and techniques. Their differences reflect the individuality of all students.

Case study 2–1

Name: Lucia
D.O.B.: 14 March 1981
C.A.: 8–6
Diagnostic category: Mildly mentally retarded

Eight-year-old Lucia attends school in the east end of Vancouver. She is a pleasant, amiable child but often seems slow-moving and apathetic. Lucia is the youngest of nine children of a recently arrived family from southern Europe. Other siblings in school are not demonstrating any learning problems.

Lucia has developed a fair command of conversational English. She has lagged far behind her class, however, in all subject areas since she arrived in school three years ago. This is her second year in grade two but the teacher reports that Lucia's achievement remains far below the norm. Reading is the area of greatest weakness; apart from a few recognition words, Lucia has made no start here at all.

Classroom strengths:

- pleasant, amiable, and friendly
- well-liked by classmates
- developing appropriate oral language, although slowly
- good printing, when copying
- strong in art; shows talent

Classroom weaknesses:

- no start in reading; few sight words and no skills for word attack
- poor comprehension; inability to follow the sequence of stories read aloud to her
- no spelling skills at all
- can count to 100, but has no basic addition and subtraction facts; uses her fingers

Recommendations:

- resource-room placement for reading, arithmetic, and spelling
- integration for all non-academic and content subjects

Instructional approaches:

- sight-word approach to reading to build up a basic word vocabulary
- language experience approach will draw on her strengths in printing while building oral skills, comprehension, and ability to follow a sequence
- concrete materials to teach addition and subtraction facts to 9

Case study 2–2

Name: Nicky C.A.: 8–8
D.O.B.: 2 January 1981 Diagnostic category: Learning disabled

Nicky attends a small school in rural Ontario. His learning patterns have disappointed and worried his teachers since kindergarten. His parents are also becoming increasingly concerned about Nicky's lack of academic progress and his mounting isolation and frustration.

Many deviations are apparent in Nicky's oral language; the syntax is representative of a much younger child. Reading is below grade level with a limited sight-word vocabulary and few word-attack skills. Once he decodes the words, however, Nicky demonstrates adequate comprehension of the message. Printing, written language, and spelling are all well below average. Arithmetic is stronger, although not quite at grade level.

Nicky is becoming increasingly frustrated with his lack of success. He manifests this by withdrawing from the other children and refusing to participate in classroom activities.

Classroom strengths:
- good auditory skills
- usually pleasant and co-operative
- well-liked but often becomes the scapegoat

Classroom weaknesses:
- below-average reading in all areas except comprehension
- poor spelling skills
- poor handwriting
- mathematics needs practice for Nicky to develop automaticity

Recommendations:
- resource-room help for reading, spelling, written language, and arithmetic
- integration for all non-academic and content subjects
- remedial work begun well below entry level in order to ensure success and build motivation

Instructional approaches:
- build basic sight-word vocabulary
- use a basal reading series
- employ concrete materials for mathematics

Case study 2–3

Name: Martin C.A.: 8-5
D.O.B.: 15 April 1981 Diagnostic category: Behaviourally disordered

Martin's parents, both high school teachers, are distressed and perplexed by Martin's learning and behavioural problems. In his grade two classroom, Martin is fidgety, inattentive, overactive, and very poorly behaved. The teacher reports that he has a short attention span, is constantly out of his seat, rarely listens to instructions, is verbally abusive, and throws massive temper tantrums. He is aggressive toward other children and a disruptive element in the class as a whole.

Martin's academic achievement reflects his behavioural problems. He is well behind the class in all areas, especially in reading. His written work is messy, disorganized, and rarely completed; his spelling is poor. On the other hand, Martin is precocious in his use of oral language, demonstrating a wide vocabulary and sophisticated usage. Often, however, language is used as a tool for poor behaviour and as a device to manipulate others.

Classroom strengths:
- above average oral expression
- good auditory skills
- usually co-operative in non-academic, one-to-one situations
- knows addition and subtraction number facts to 19

Classroom weaknesses:
- reading far below the grade average with minimal sight-word vocabulary and non-existent word-attack skills
- extremely poor spelling
- untidy and ill-formed printing, showing many deviations and inconsistencies
- mathematics, although stronger than other areas, reveals difficulties in generalizing concepts and understanding word problems
- disruptive classroom behaviour; aggressive behaviour leading to many fights
- unpopular with the other students

Recommendations:
- placement in a special class for all academic subjects except arithmetic
- integration for arithmetic and non-academic subjects
- a supportive atmosphere in which routines and consistency are given priority
- stress on social and behavioural skills
- instruction that begins below entry levels, to provide success and motivation

Instructional approaches:
- employ phonetic approach to reading, to build on strong auditory skills
- extend sight-word vocabulary through use of a language experience approach
- in printing, stress patterns and letter formations; begin on blackboard and easel
- engage in role play to develop socially appropriate skills
- teach and reinforce the specific behaviour necessary for Martin to function within the rules and routines of the regular classroom

Mainstreaming leads to non-categorical approaches

Although it is likely that some form of categorization will be retained for the purposes of administration and research, educators are tending to decategorize handicaps and to encourage the perception of exceptional pupils as individuals with some special learning problems. Some writers (e.g. Reynolds, 1979) have advocated a generic approach for the so-called mildly handicapped and a categorical approach for the severely disabled. Others (Balow & Balow, 1982) see no reason to perpetuate categorical groupings, such as autism, based on etiology and symptomology. Given that many educators have long been dissatisfied with traditional, medically oriented labels for disability, the current trend toward alternative classification schemes is not surprising. These schemes are simply different models of the non-categorical or generic approach to teaching exceptional children. Although their terminology may differ, alternative classification schemes share a single goal—provision of the best possible education for every person.

The **non-categorical approach** involves methods of placing and educating mildly handicapped youngsters that focus on their learning patterns and behaviours rather than on diagnostic categories. This does not mean that expertise concerned with specific disabilities, such as deafness, will disappear, but rather, that mildly handicapped youngsters are labelled less and taught in closer accordance with their specific and unique needs.

Traditionally, however, it was thought that these children shared neither common etiological factors nor behavioural characteristics, and that their performance levels differed in certain areas. Among the three groups of mildly handicapped children, differences were said to exist in levels of cognitive ability, in academic achievement or underachievement, patterns of cognitive performance, and adaptiveness of social and emotional development. Essentially, the categorical definitions of exceptional children maintained the purity of each population by focussing on discrepant attributes, the unique and elusive characteristics that distinguished one defined population from another in special education. Yet when these students' actual performance in school is examined a considerable overlap emerges, particularly at the level of mild severity (Laycock, 1980a; Wang, 1981), as was suggested by the case studies.

Because of the similarities in learning deficits among these groups, instructional needs, and therefore teaching methods, are remarkably alike. A number of studies further demonstrate similarities in the way that mildly handicapped children function. A recent data-based study of ninety categorically labelled and served junior high school students (Beare, 1985), for example, found that notable differences in all or even most instructionally relevant characteristics did not exist between behaviourally disordered and learning-disabled students. They were virtually the same in IQ, patterns of cognitive ability, and number of behaviours rated as significantly deviant by their teachers. Achievement in reading — lower for the learning-disabled group — was the only conspicuous difference. The mildly retarded group proved to be less proficient than the other two groups in areas directly related to cognitive ability, but not in others. There were very large overlaps in the range of characteristics exhibited by each of the three groups, even in those parts of the study that measured ability, and standardized testing could not identify students as members of separate groups.

Marston (1987) took a somewhat different tack and studied the types of teacher certification in relation to the types of pupils instructed, within the three groups under discussion. He did not find any significant correlation between teachers' certification and students' progress. Over the course of an academic year, learning-disabled students taught by teachers trained in learning disabilities did not improve any more than learning-disabled students taught by teachers trained to instruct educable mentally retarded students.

From these studies, then, it appears that mildly handicapped students share a variety of academic and behavioural characteristics that transcend traditional approaches to classification. Some professionals also maintain that the traditional categories of mental retardation, learning disabilities, and behavioural disorders, do not clearly define or adequately differentiate the *individual* needs of exceptional students in the classroom (Hardman, 1981; Lilly, 1971). Instead of depending upon those divisions therefore, it is practical to focus upon functional impairment, to determine the specific strengths and weaknesses of each pupil. Can the student, for example, use and comprehend written language, follow directions, and interact appropriately with peers? A second alternative is to sort students into groups that correspond roughly to ability in the particular subject matter and skill being taught (Cartwright, Cartwright, & Ward, 1984).

The notion that mildly handicapped students can be best served in a non-categorical framework has been challenged, however, by those who suggest that generic terms are non-functional and that the individual categories are more relevant to educational programming (Becker, 1978; Keogh, Becker, Kukic, & Kukic, 1972). Liebermann (1981), for example, argues that pupils with varying disabilities do not successfully relate to each other in the same special education setting. He also believes that teachers of the handicapped are ineffective when they do not have a comprehensive understanding of the etiology pertinent to a particular student, that non-categorical approaches over-identify students who are not truly handicapped educationally by testing them for the sake of testing, and that new labels will take the place of old ones. These are issues that must be carefully considered when making individual decisions about integration.

Empirical support for either a categorical or a non-categorical approach to the education of any student population is practically non-existent (Brito & Reynolds, 1979), because studies have not achieved any direct comparisons of the two approaches that specifically measure students' progress (Nelson & Greenough Janssen, 1984). Box 2–3 sets out both sides of the issue, to summarize the general considerations that have been discussed above.

Curricular adaptations for mildly handicapped students

In order to achieve the recommended curriculum, all students must develop basic skills and use them to progress in reading, writing, spelling, and language. These fundamental academic goals apply to mildly handicapped as well as regular students. Learning sequences, skill hierarchies, and other aspects of human growth and development are the same for all people. The curriculum for special learners will therefore include academics though it may also stress social and emotional development and career planning. Additionally, mildly handicapped children need special help in dealing with their limitations and overcoming the obstacles in the way of their progress. The curriculum for these pupils therefore differs somewhat from the norm in how the skills taught are differentiated, as well as the actual skills or subjects covered (although the latter is more noticeable at the secondary level). Schooling focusses on those academic areas that will enable the student to proceed to successful life in the community and the home.

Skills are only functional if they serve the student over time. For example, should mentally retarded students have to learn Roman numerals or the parts of speech? Before teaching such units teachers should carefully consider whether these skills, and others

Box 2–3 Considerations in the use of categorical approaches

Benefits of categories	**Objections to categories**
Categorical systems clearly delineate the parameters of each category, which reduces ambiguity and enhances communication among educators, professionals, and parents.	Categories are educationally irrelevant.
Categories provide a basis for determining which students require special education.	Categorical labels imply that the problem is within the student.
Categories provide a system for financial accounting for related services.	Categorical teacher preparation programs result in course redundancy and professional barriers.
Categorical accounting allows school districts to collect funds in proportion to the exceptional students accommodated by the district.	Categories are perpetuated by the administrative organization of funding, rather than by educational usefulness (Blackhurst & Berdine, 1981).
Categories constitute a vehicle for obtaining legislative and public support because lobby and professional groups form around each category (Goldstein, 1975).	Categorical approaches do not take enough account of the strengths and weaknesses of individual pupils, a vital aspect of programming.
The organizational constructs underlying categories facilitate research.	Labels tend to accentuate negative stereotyping.
Categories help the public to understand the specific needs of a population and to make broad distinctions among different areas of exceptionality.	Teachers hold lower expectations for labelled students (Gillung & Rucker, 1977).

of the same type, will be relevant for mildly handicapped students to function independently and successfully in their immediate and general environment. To do so, mildly handicapped people will need skills in many areas, including self-care, mobility, communication, social interaction, academics, health, safety, and vocational and leisure pursuits. Teachers must find useful learning objectives in all of these areas, rather than teaching only the traditional three Rs.

Mildly mentally retarded pupils are the largest group of mildly disabled learners and possess probably the widest variations in skills and needs. There are three major goals in the education of mentally handicapped children: productivity (or performance), independence, and participation. Learning-disabled children may lag developmentally in various areas. They may have problems in sensory motor ability, language, perception, thought processes, memory, attention, emotions, and social behaviour. Their education must focus on acquiring skills in three very broad instructional areas: cognition and performance, language and communication, and independent functioning. Behaviourally disordered students require a precise focus on developmental skills, particularly in reading and mathematics. Special emphasis must be paid to shaping acceptable behaviour (see chapter 6).

Although mildly handicapped youngsters may consistently lag in academic areas such as reading, mathematics, science, and social studies, they do successfully use techniques for remembering and learning. Only the rate and the way in which they acquire the skills may differ. Nevertheless, every class should be divided into groups for individual subject areas, so that the curriculum can accommodate the different rates of learning of all children, exceptional and non-exceptional, within a single classroom.

To carry out a finely tuned instructional program, a teacher must specify the steps within a program, the preparation and procedures, the sequence of learning tasks, and the criteria by which change can be measured, as well as keeping a record of the student's progress. Such a precise focus can only serve to enhance the learning of all members of a given class. Instruction is then geared to each student's level of competence. Before instruction can be individualized in this manner, however, the student's strengths and weaknesses must be carefully assessed. Assessment measures form the subject of the following chapter.

PART

2

Preparing for instruction

3 Assessment

Measures to assess present levels of performance

Formal measures: standardized tests and diagnostic instruments

- Achievement tests
- Diagnostic tests
- Process-oriented tests
- Language tests
- Social measures

Informal measures

- Criterion-referenced tests
- Curriculum-based assessment
- Error analysis

Teacher-made tests

Classroom measures for assessing behaviour

- Direct observation
- Anecdotal reports
- Q-sorts

Dear Reader,

It is interesting that teachers often have contradictory attitudes toward assessment. Sometimes, teachers will treat the results of an assessment by an outside "expert" with scorn because the test results do not seem to show anything that they do not already know from their own observations. On the other hand, teachers will often treat results as if they were delivered from on high, rather as the ten commandments were delivered to Moses. How many times have you heard a teacher say that because a certain child scored ten points higher than another child on an IQ test we should expect better performance from the "smarter" child?

In order to appreciate the value of testing, a teacher needs to understand the strengths and limitations of the assessment process. The first thing to consider is the purpose of assessment. Three important functions of assessment are evaluation, prediction of a child's future performance, and diagnosis of problem areas.

Often tests are not used effectively because a test designed to serve one of these functions is interpreted from the point of view of another. Tests designed for evaluation, for example, are used as measures of general ability; or people speak of achievement tests (such as the Wide Range Achievement Test, or WRAT) and intelligence tests (such as the Wechsler Intelligence Scale for Children, Revised, or WISC-R) in the same breath. Whatever happened to the idea of "capital G" general intelligence, which is supposed to be independent of achievement on particular tasks?

Tests designed for general assessment are sometimes misguidedly used to diagnose specific problems; people try to find patterns of responses on standardized tests that indicate a specific pathology; for example, children with low scores on the Verbal subtests of the WISC-R and normal scores on the Performance subtests are classified as learning disabled. Attempts are made to assess the cognitive development of deaf children by using tests designed for verbal youngsters, or modifications of these measures. Why not develop tests that are specifically designed to measure the behaviour in which we are interested?

Prospective university students are given IQ tests to predict success in university, and while this procedure seems to be relatively successful within certain limits, these predictions are made over a fairly short period of time. Success rates are predicted four years in advance. We know that the longer the time between tests used to predict performance and tests used to evaluate later performance, the lower the quality of the prediction. Also, these tests *only* predict academic success. They should not be used, for example, to predict success in a given career.

The more we stretch tests to do jobs that they were not designed to do, the more problems we are going to encounter. This is especially true in prediction, which is by far the most misunderstood function of testing. Although administering ability measures to future university students has some validity, we should not expect to predict future performance from tests of early behaviour.

We no longer hope to predict, for example, future success in life from scores on the Bayley Scales of Infant Development. This effort was abandoned as a result of Bayley's own research, which showed that there is no relation between infants' test results and intelligence as measured by the Stanford-Binet test at the age of six or seven. Others have found that the correlation between intelligence at one year and at five years of age is only 0.01. Having given up this particular attempt to predict future performance from early correlational variables, however, we cannot resist the temptation to try our hand at prediction in other realms. We give pupils achievement tests at the end of elementary school so that we can predict performance in high school, for example.

Before succumbing to this temptation, we should address the limitations inherent in such an exercise. Three things must be kept in mind. Psychological entities cannot be measured in the same manner as can physical entities. A measuring stick continues to tell height accurately, even though a child grows taller from one year to the next, but if you measure intelligence one year and then measure it the next, a child's score might be different even though the child's intelligence has not changed. This occurs because we have to change the measuring stick as the child matures. A test that is appropriate for a one year old is not appropriate for a five year old. Yet because we have changed the measure it is hard to tell if a change in a child's score is a result of a change in intelligence or whether it simply reflects maturity. The inevitable outcome is that our predictions will be less than perfect.

The second caution concerns the imperfect nature of the tool used to make predictions. We predict future outcomes when there has been a high correlation in the past between the predicting variable and the predicted variable. We may use the results of mathematics tests (the predicting variable) to predict success in the subject area of mathematics (the predicted variable) if it has been found that test results can be used effectively in this way. Just because there is a high correlation between one variable and another, however, does not mean that one predicts the other precisely; this would be true if the correlation were perfect, but that is seldom the case. The point may seem too fastidious, but it has important consequences for our ability to make predictions.

The third consideration may be the most important. If children do not perform at a level that we would expect at a particular age this does not mean that they will not achieve an appropriate level of performance eventually. We have to allow for differing rates of growth at different ages in any individual. Unfortunately, many of the predictions that we make for children are founded on norms based on standardized samples. We expect every child to behave like the normal child at every level of development. It is extraordinary that we should expect this kind of conformity in children when we don't expect it in any other living organism.

Armed with knowledge about the limitations of testing, teachers can become educated consumers of test results, and learn to use them for what they are worth.

Ken Clarke, Ph.D.
Department of Educational Psychology
St. Francis Xavier University

In all aspects of our lives we run into measuring instruments. The principal reason that these exist is to reduce personal and subjective judgments to a minimum. Allison (1982) points out that unless you know your grocer very well, understand his or her biases, and have faith in her or his judgments, you are not very likely to accept that you have really been given a dollar's worth of potatoes or raisins unless you see the bag weighed — personal opinions shouldn't enter into it.

The measures used by your grocer exist because they have been agreed upon, and carefully defined in such a way that anyone can use them. It is not as easy to be objective with people, however, as Clarke observes in the letter that opens this chapter. Unlike raisins or potatoes, human characteristics cannot be quantified, yet being human we keep trying to do so. Assessment is a fact of life for all of us and is especially prominent in the lives of children. In fact, the process usually begins moments after birth, when the newborn is evaluated in the delivery room to provide an Apgar score.

Once started, assessment continues right through school and beyond. The procedures vary, serving several purposes: some are designed to measure physical responses; others measure knowledge, ability to solve problems, or competency in highly specialized areas. The tests are administered by different personnel, and the results used in different ways. Broadly speaking, **assessment** is the process that takes place as we form judgments about people, things, events, or performances. In this chapter, the term refers specifically to psycho-educational diagnosis. Assessment is not an end in itself; tests should never be given simply for the sake of producing a label or filling in the blanks on a student's cumulative record card. A critical assumption of mainstreaming, however, is that the students who can benefit from integration can be identified and properly placed (Zemanek & Lehrer, 1977). Assessment of exceptional youngsters is therefore the process that attempts to discover whether they exhibit developmental problems, what those problems are, the causes, the general prognosis, specific developmental consequences, and the best approaches to intervention and remediation.

We move from assessment to evaluation when we go from asking "How much?" to asking "What does it mean?" When we can answer these two questions we can individualize planning. Assessment and evaluation are inseparable, fundamental tasks in teaching. Indeed, an instructional program that consists only of teaching routine skills is inefficient and may even be detrimental to students. A teacher must always teach, test, and re-teach. Using assessment data to prescribe, implement, evaluate, and revise instructional programs is thus an integral part of contemporary education, both regular and special. Regular classroom teachers play a central role in assessment and evaluation, chiefly by assessing students' progress consistently and evaluating the success of the educational program.

Effective educational programming depends upon proper measurement of students' strengths, weaknesses, acquisition of skills, areas of deficit, interests, and dislikes. We require a detailed picture of their performance across a variety of domains in order to develop appropriate instructional goals. As well, referrals for further, thorough assessment are usually based on information collected and collated by classroom teachers.

Yet many teachers are unsure about the procedures involved: often they have had only one measurement course. The course was probably a component of their education at a time when they were more concerned with learning how to construct classroom tests, or assign grades, or with getting a good grade in the course, than they were with gaining a firm grasp of the finer points of measurement theory. Indeed, teachers generally hold the opinion that courses on measurement and psycho-educational testing are a burdensome requirement that is irrelevant to teaching practice (Deno, 1985). As an example, a recent study has found that teachers of the deaf view assessment as an unimportant factor in instruction (Winzer, Clarke, & Clarke, 1988).

Teachers tend to rely on informal observations of students' performance to evaluate progress; they cede low priority to the concepts of measurement and evaluation. In an Ontario study, both elementary teachers and elementary principals considered observations of children's work by the teacher to be of the utmost importance (Wahlstrom & Donley, 1976). At the secondary level, observation ranked a close second behind standardized testing, but many teachers view standardized tests as being of greater value to people outside the classroom, such as principals, parents, and school boards, than they are to practitioners (Salmon-Cox, 1981). As well, researchers are increasingly critical of some standardized measures. Their scepticism, and that of teachers, has led to a search for additional or alternative evaluative measures.

Nevertheless, effective teachers use a variety of formal and informal data-gathering procedures. With practice, assessment becomes a natural part of each activity in the classroom, whether oral or written, class, group, or individual. It is then possible to create a continuous program for each student; grouping and individualization are made easier, and the lock-step grade system becomes more flexible.

Classroom teachers are not expected to have the same expertise in assessment as do professionals such as psychologists and psychometrists, but they should be acutely aware of the range of tools that can be used systematically in the classroom. Teachers also require more than a nodding acquaintance with the measures employed in in-depth psycho-educational diagnosis. They need to know what is being assessed, why it is being assessed, and roughly how the job is done. In addition, teachers should be able to interpret the results of psycho-educational assessments clearly in order to derive educational objectives from them. This chapter is not intended to teach readers how to administer specific tests. Instead, it familiarizes readers with the purpose and usefulness of a wide assortment of measures.

It is beyond the scope of this text to review the staggering variety of measures available to assess the physical, cognitive, motoric, social, and emotional development of children. The array of procedures numbers in the thousands, and descriptions of tests and other assessment procedures can be found in textbooks on general assessment. An excellent source for critiques of specific tests is the *Mental Measurement Yearbook* (Mitchell, 1985).

This chapter is founded on two premises: that efficient assessment and evaluation underlie efficient programming; and that classroom teachers should assume a central role in the assessment process. The main objectives of the chapter are to

- discuss the purposes, strengths, and limitations of informal and formal assessment measures
- identify and explain the levels of testing, the types of instruments used, and the personnel involved
- detail the steps in the diagnostic-prescriptive teaching cycle

A general overview of assessment

A wide range of conditions and disabilities can interfere with children's learning at home and in school, affect their socialization with peers, and hinder them from attaining their maximum potential. Yet assessment involves looking for not only areas of deficit, but also for a child's strengths. In educational settings, assessment is a multifaceted process that involves far more than administering tests. As Salvia and Ysseldyke point out,

> Assessment is the process of understanding the performance of students in their current ecology. . . . Assessment is always an evaluative, interpretative appraisal of performance. . . . [I]t provides information that can enable teachers and other school personnel to make decisions regarding the children they serve (1978, p. 4).

Assessment and evaluation can be used to

- determine an effective instructional program for all students, allowing programming at a general level and also promoting individualization
- help teachers to collect data on students' achievement that will serve as the systematic basis for grading
- assess the effectiveness of instruction and identify areas that require greater concentration
- provide guidelines for planning
- determine which students are eligible for special education services
- begin the development of **individual education plans** for exceptional students

It can be seen that assessment and evaluation apply to all students, not just to those who are exceptional in some area of their functioning. For exceptional students, however, it is particularly important to use data from assessment to create individual educational plans. The assessment process is useless if it is not followed by educational prescription and then remediation.

Assessment follows some generally accepted guidelines. At the outset, teachers and diagnosticians must determine what is to be assessed. (A developmentally disabled two year old and a mildly mentally retarded sixteen year old should both be assessed for adaptive behaviour, for example; but the two year old may be assessed for skills in communication as well, whereas the sixteen year old would be assessed for vocational skills.) They then select the tests and other procedures designed for the specific purpose. The same measures are not appropriate for every student. As well, whether a single functional area is being measured in any pupil, or an exceptional youngster is being identified, several kinds of assessment will be necessary to answer all the questions posed about the individual. If you have ever seen the folder of an identified learning-disabled student, for example, you were probably amazed at the number and variety of tests that had been administered.

Exceptional students most often share disabilities in both learning and development across a number of behavioural domains: physical, intellectual, linguistic, perceptual, social, and emotional. The domains are not mutually exclusive; each spills over to affect other areas of functioning. Measures therefore assess functioning across a spectrum of learning and behavioural areas. As an example, common procedures with children suspected of having learning disabilities include achievement tests, behavioural assessment, informal reading inventories, **criterion-referenced tests**, and **process-oriented tests** (Hallahan & Kauffman, 1986). With a physically handicapped student, some of these tests may be used, but other considerations demand precedence: assessment looks at how the student performs self-help skills such as dressing and feeding, how much mobility the student has, and the level, clarity, and speed of her or his communication.

The strategies selected depend upon the age and nature of the student, and the purpose of the diagnosis. Older pupils are usually evaluated in order to provide effective remedial help for existing problems; school beginners are frequently assessed in order to prevent or minimize potential problems.

Procedures should also be chosen to achieve a match between the specific characteristics of the measure and the behaviour about which information is needed. If we want to evaluate the mistakes that a child is making in long-division problems, we may use an **error analysis**; if we need summary information about academic achievement we could use a standardized achievement test or a teacher-made, criterion-referenced test.

Assessment data may have to meet the needs of different audiences, most usually administrators, teachers, and parents. Each person employs the data in a different way: administrators require information to determine placements, while teachers want data that will offer guidance for classroom management. Both groups use data to objectify judgments.

Finally, the assessment of exceptional children and youth is not a single, unrepeated procedure; it is ongoing and requires the contributions of many professionals. Figure 3–1 presents an overview of the identification of exceptional students. The crucial role of classroom teachers is obvious, as is the continuous nature of the evaluative process.

Types of assessment procedures

The procedures that make up the assessment process can be broadly categorized as informal and formal. Both types are used with exceptional youngsters. The term **informal assessment** is used here to denote activities for gathering data on which to base instructional plans for individual students. Informal measures provide ongoing assessment, and encompass items such as criterion-referenced tests, teacher-made tests, interviews, behavioural observations, case history information, work samples, and rating scales. Used in conjunction with more formal measures, these tools supply information for planning and revising programs, and report pupils' progress to parents and others. Informal assessment is used to identify areas of strength and weakness within individuals, while formal assessment tends to be used to investigate the precise nature of students' difficulties. Formal assessment plays a part in educational placement, and implies the use of **standardized tests**, instruments commercially prepared by measurement experts, that provide uniform methods of obtaining samples of behaviour.

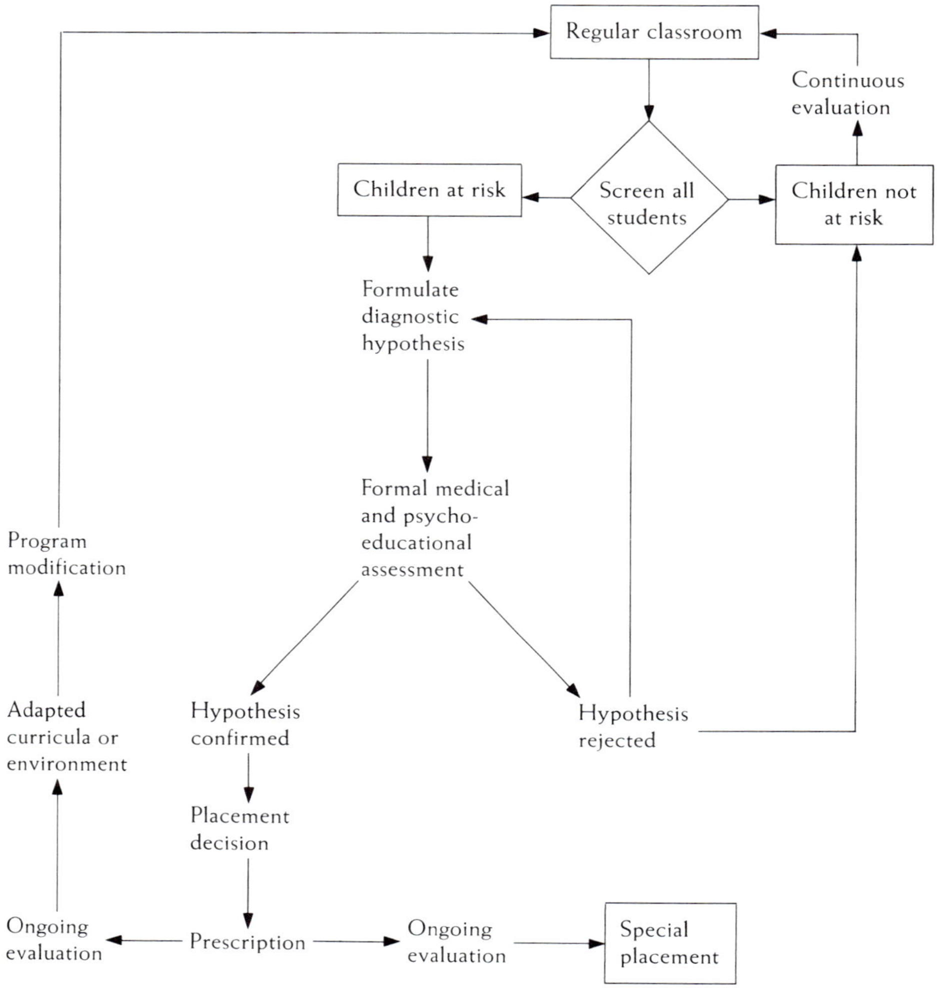

Figure 3–1 Identification of special learners

Standardized tests have a fixed set of questions, the same set of directions, timing constraints, delineated and precise scoring procedures, and are usually **norm referenced**. Some standardized tests may be used by classroom teachers, but others can only be administered by specially trained personnel. Mental ability measures, for example, require very specialized training in administration and interpretation.

There are a number of limitations to standardized tests:

- The scores indicate only a small sample of a child's performance, and provide only a limited measure of ability.
- The statistical validity and reliability of a number of standardized tests have been seriously questioned. The confidence level on some tests is distressingly low.

- There is great variability in a child's daily performance, particularly for exceptional youngsters.
- Examiners, too, may vary daily in patience, their ability to relate to children, and their skills.
- Many standardized tests rely heavily on reading and are unsuitable for any student displaying reading difficulties.
- Standardized tests do not provide information on which to build educational planning.

Because a single measure of a single aspect of functioning provides only the most limited information, the results from standardized tests cannot be used as the sole criterion for determining educational placements; informal measures must complement and supplement the data. The trained examiner then integrates test findings with observations and other relevant information to develop a complete diagnostic picture.

Standardized tests

The word "test" in the term "standardized tests" is rather a misnomer in the context of screening and diagnosis. Strictly speaking, a test is something that you pass or fail. The more correct term in psychology and education is "measuring instrument," because such tools are designed to measure, among other things, achievement, aptitudes, personality, interests, behaviour, performance, opinions, and relationships. Only the first type of instrument — achievement — is really a test; you cannot pass or fail on such things as personality and interests (Allison, 1982). Yet even measurement texts talk about "personality tests" and "interest tests" and so this text adopts the common usage. Whatever the instrument, the same five important criteria apply: objectivity, validity, reliability, comparability, and usability (Allison, 1982).

Objectivity

Because people are so different it is not easy to be objective when measuring behaviours, abilities, and attitudes. An objective instrument clearly defines the attributes to be measured and carefully analyses all their constituent elements. In educational and psychological measurement, objectivity can be operationally defined as a high degree of agreement about test results among qualified observers (Allison, 1982). A test is objective when it contains only one correct response for any given question. Because the scoring procedure is therefore consistent, there is less chance that responses will be incorrectly interpreted.

Validity

Validity refers to the extent to which a test measures what it claims to measure. If a test purports to assess spelling skills, for example, it should be constructed in such a manner that the student actually spells words.

There are a number of ways of looking at validity, depending on the use to be made of the data obtained. **Content validity** refers to the appropriateness of the items in a test, and the level of mastery at which the content is assessed. **Face validity** refers to professionals' general acceptance of a measuring instrument. **Criterion-related validity** is determined by the extent to which a student's success on a criterion-related measure can be predicted from that student's score on a norm-referenced test or subtest. Criterion-related validity becomes important as instruction shifts from mastery of specific knowledge and skills to generalizing and applying those skills. **Construct validity** refers to an instrument's ability to measure variables such as creativity, risk-taking, or intelligence. These variables are called constructs and are used to explain observed interindividual differences. A test measures the construct by measuring the behaviours that the construct describes or predicts. As an example, a test may measure creativity by assessing drawing, one of the behaviours within the construct of creativity. Most psychological tests are designed to measure some construct and, to the degree that they are successful, they have construct validity.

A test is invalid if it has poorly structured items that are inappropriate for the student population being assessed. It may be rendered invalid if it is inappropriately administered or interpreted, or if the data it produces are put to the wrong purposes. A test may be valid for one purpose but not for another.

Reliability

Reliability refers to the consistency of a test, to its ability to produce the same results on different occasions under the same circumstances. Reliability is important because any differences in the two sets of results obtained if students are tested on two different days, or given two different versions of the test, or are retested after a period of time, should reflect changes in the students, not in the test.

Comparability

Measurement results are meaningless unless we have some basis for interpreting them. Most standardized tests are norm-referenced, which means that they supply norms or standards that enable us to interpret the results. The norms are the average scores obtained by the students who took the test when the norms were being established, the standard of comparison by which to measure later scores. A test has comparability if it provides an appropriate standard of comparison.

Usability

The term usability is applied to many of the practical features of measuring instruments. The methods of administering and scoring a test make it usable or not. One must also decide whether the test has appropriate levels of difficulty in reading and vocabulary, whether it provides adequate norms, and whether the instrument is generally accepted. The importance of usability is obvious: some instruments require special training or equipment to administer and score, and if these are not readily available, the tests are not usable; some tests are not feasible because they cost too much or take too long to administer; others look very interesting, but have no basis for interpreting the results. In the latter case, the test has no comparability and local norms have to be developed for it to become usable.

Administering tests

The results of assessment are used to make important decisions, and it is critical that standardized measures be properly applied. A good test becomes bad if it has little relevance for the student to whom it is given, or when it is poorly administered, scored, or interpreted. If the tester deviates from the time limitations, the procedures for presenting and scoring a test, or the method of recording responses, then the validity, reliability, and objectivity of the instrument are violated, and errors in placement or gaps in instructional units will result. Incomplete test information may lead to inaccurate findings; inaccurate findings to erroneous conclusions; erroneous conclusions to false labels; and false labels to inappropriate class placement (Hirshoren & McGuigan, 1984).

Even with instruments that require only simple administration and scoring, some practice is necessary. The following procedures are helpful to develop confidence and expertise in administering tests:

1. Secure a copy of the test manuals, materials, and record forms.
2. Read the material carefully, and highlight the statements and questions that the examiner is to give orally.
3. Learn the acceptable and unacceptable student responses, as well as if and when prompts and cues are permitted.
4. If possible, observe a competent examiner in the process of administering and scoring the test.
5. Practise the test by administering it to adults until you feel comfortable with the procedures, materials, and scoring. In presenting the test, use the exact wording, adhere to the time limits, give the materials in the prescribed manner, and follow the scoring rigidly.
6. Practise on children of different ages and levels. If possible, have an experienced person oversee the administration or else videotape the process for later review. At least have an experienced tester examine your scoring and interpretation of the results.
7. Use the test with children as part of the assessment process only when you feel secure in all aspects (Faas, 1976; Mandell & Gold, 1984).

Levels of assessment

The assessment process is best viewed as containing three interrelated levels—**screening**, **diagnosis**, and intensive or medical testing—all of which employ many different kinds of measures. Each level of assessment builds on and supplements the others, although not necessarily in a fixed order. Screening, for example, provides an initial overview, but not every student will require screening before diagnosis. A student with an easily demonstrable, severe physical or mental handicap obviously will not need to be screened. The three levels do not really constitute fully separable activities. Observation begins the screening process, but is also a necessary part of any ongoing assessment. The levels are diagrammed in figure 3-2.

The process and value of early identification

Early identification employs all three levels of assessment. When combined with early intervention, it exercises a powerful appeal in today's special education and is receiving a great deal of attention. The idea that handicapping, and potentially handicapping,

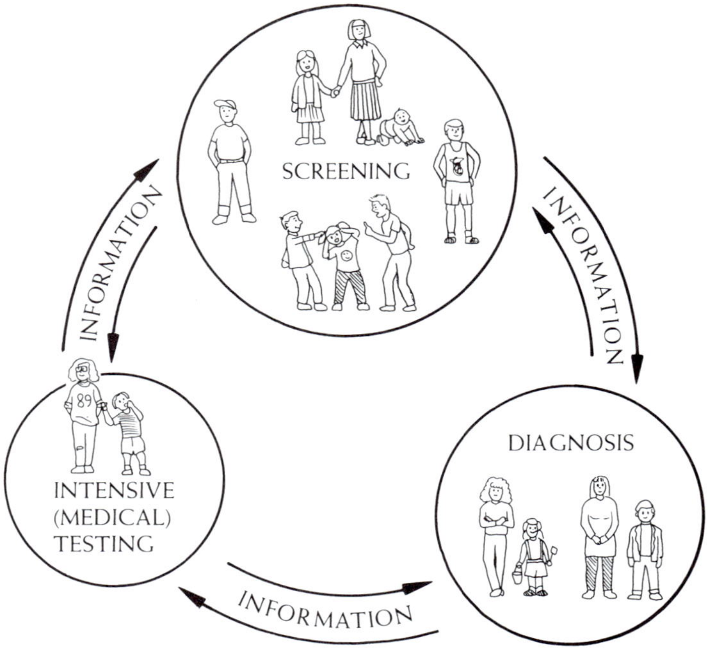

Figure 3–2 Levels of assessment

conditions can be detected, prevented, or at least partly ameliorated, is both logically and intuitively attractive (Keogh, 1983). Early identification and early intervention are founded on a preventative service model, which assumes that if problems are detected early on, programs can be developed that will prevent more complex difficulties from evolving later in life. Assessment can then be used to evaluate the success of a program by determining a child's changes over time.

Proponents of early identification suggest that the behaviour of very young children is capable of positive change and that early development is therefore important to later progress. As well, families require early assistance in order for their children to adjust to handicaps in the best possible way (Hayden, 1974). Early identification and intervention constitute an area of education that cuts across all categories of disability.

Developmental screening is employed to identify infants and preschoolers who are at high risk for certain conditions. Nevertheless, testing infants and using the results as a basis for predicting achievement in the future should be viewed with great caution. Single variable measures cannot be considered consistently reliable as predictors of school achievement for young children (Murray, 1981). Apart from developmental and motor criteria, it is difficult to identify factors to distinguish mildly handicapped individuals at a young age. The negligible correlation between early and later intelligence in non-handicapped children is well documented (Honzig, 1976), and the problems are carefully reiterated by Clarke in this chapter's opening letter. Infant testing only describes accurately how well a child is performing in a particular functional domain at a particular time with a particular tester, and whether the appropriate developmental milestones are being attained within normal limits.

Kindergarten screening is used to identify children who do not have the required readiness skills to perform adequately in a classroom. Still, it is difficult to diagnose many learning problems in kindergarten or first grade pupils who have not yet been taught how to read and write. During kindergarten, only vulnerable or high-risk children who may or may not develop problems as they proceed through school can be identified. Even so, a huge range of measures exists for the assessment of preschool and very young school-age children. Some are used for screening, while others involve more formal diagnosis.

Screening

Educational screening is typically a classroom procedure. Whole age groups of children are tested in order to identify those performing below the norm in certain areas of behaviour or intellectual achievement, or both (Lewis, 1980). The procedures follow from surface clues that the child may have problems or risks developing them. Screening provides an overview; it is the first step in the diagnostic-prescriptive cycle and provides only enough information to determine whether further diagnostic study is needed.

Before and when screening children, it is important to ask whether the problem identified has an effect on the educational well-being of the child being screened. As well, will the screening and identification process be followed by diagnosis, and is there an available treatment designed to correct or modify the problem (Salvia & Ysseldyke, 1978)? If the answer to any of these questions is no, then screening becomes a futile process. Screening must lead to more exhaustive assessment, in which the existence of a problem is confirmed or discounted. Further, the data generated must lead to appropriate treatment of the difficulties.

Because screening begins in the classroom, classroom teachers hold the primary responsibility for it. Teachers are adept at focussing on problematic behaviour and poor patterns of learning. Indeed, teachers' observations have been found to be one of the most valuable and practical elements of the assessment process (Zukow, Zukow, & Bentler, 1978). The teacher may observe a child underachieving, withdrawing, becoming hyperactive, or having inadequate peer interactions. Although they are excellent critics of unusual and poor behavioural and learning patterns, it should be noted that teachers are not nearly as proficient at identifying gifted youngsters, although training can develop this skill.

Specific classroom screening procedures, which are described later in the chapter, include observations, developmental checklists, inventories, rating scales, measures of adaptive behaviour, interviews, case histories, and past records. A primary screening instrument should be short, open to use by a variety of professionals with a minimum of training, and have a quick and simple scoring method.

Diagnosis: assessing present levels of performance

In the classroom, teachers must develop skills in observing and rating children's functioning in areas such as attention, listening, reading and comprehension, computation, oral and written expression, memory, and visual motor capabilities. Measures to assess students' progress include general achievement tests, informal educational skill inventories, work samples, and criterion-referenced instructional batteries. With screening tools, these instruments identify and assess specific educational needs that require intervention. Some of the measures overlap with those used in screening. Again, particular types of instrument are discussed later in this chapter.

Diagnosis is best viewed as an outgrowth of the screening process: while screening focusses on a potential difficulty, diagnosis moves from suspecting a problem to precisely delineating the difficulty, its etiology, the prognosis and developmental consequences, and the most effective intervention. Diagnosis, then, is the aspect of psycho-educational assessment that involves an acute examination of various problematic functional areas. Some diagnostic procedures are administered by classroom teachers, who may then refer students to other professionals for further diagnostic assessment.

The diagnostic process is both complex and time-consuming. Tests at this level of assessment are longer, and their scoring procedures more detailed, than those employed in screening. In order to assess the cognitive, developmental, linguistic, perceptual motor, social, and emotional status of an individual student, many different personnel lend their expertise. Diverse measures cover a spectrum of developmental domains, and skills within those domains, thus providing a profile of abilities and deficits.

Diagnosticians aim at **differential diagnosis**, the precise specification that a given set of symptoms is indicative of one disorder rather than another. The term **diagnostic-prescriptive teaching**, often used in conjunction with differential diagnosis, refers to the practice of formulating instructional prescriptions on the basis of differential diagnostic results (Arter & Jenkins, 1979). Diagnostic-prescriptive teaching is synonymous with the diagnostic-remedial approach (Bateman, 1967). Other terms include prescriptive teaching (Peter, 1956), ability and process training, psychometric phrenology (Mann, 1971), and even **task analysis** (Johnson, 1967).

Generally, a psycho-educational assessment should provide information about

- physical growth and development, including medical history and status
- intellectual ability
- academic functioning in a variety of areas
- skills in communication and language
- social and emotional development, including self-help skills
- fine and gross motor skills
- perceptual and sensory motor skills
- vocational interests and skills

This assessment, coupled with information from teachers and parents, helps to confirm or discount the existence of a problem, and to pinpoint the areas requiring special intervention. In order for teachers to translate diagnostic data into educational goals and objectives, however, results should be reported in educational terms. To say, for example, that a child has a particular learning disability in visual processing may be specific, but it provides very little prescriptive information. To note also that the child

Assessment is an essential prerequisite to identification and placement.

demonstrates reversals and mirror writing, poor visual memory for spelling words, and severe difficulties with word recognition in reading, provides the first step on the road to effective educational intervention.

Diagnosticians will also present tentative predictions regarding a child's future development. While this information is important in arranging the best possible placement for the child, assessment does not allow definitive predictions because conditions may alter rapidly; if immutable decisions are made they may very well preclude educational opportunities for a youngster.

Tests of mental ability

Tests of mental ability, or IQ tests as they are more commonly called, are a type of standardized test that first appeared in 1904, arising from the seminal work of Alfred Binet and Theodore Simon in France. They are formal measures administered only by trained personnel. Teachers will sometimes be presented with the results of mental ability tests, and should be aware of their purpose, and the significance of the scores.

Tests of mental ability are based on a normal distribution: a continuum of scores that vary from the average score by standard deviations, or predictable amounts. The tests provide an intelligence quotient, which is the relationship between a child's mental age and chronological age. The intelligence quotient reflects the differences between a child's performance on a test and the normative performance for the child's age level. IQ tests are designed to assess global aspects of intelligence. They are used primarily to determine **interindividual differences**, those that exist between members of an age group or grade level, and **intra-individual differences**, the variations in performance that are observed as an individual performs several different sorts of task.

The most widely used test of mental ability is the Wechsler Intelligence Scale for Children, Revised [WISC-R] (Wechsler, 1974). Teachers are very likely to be presented with psychological reports on exceptional students that contain results from this measure. The Verbal and Performance scales of the WISC-R each contain five subtests, with an extra subtest to be used if the examiner requires more information. Each subtest explores certain domains. Short-term memory, for example, is tested by the digit span test, but is also involved in coding; long-term memory is tested with the subtests for arithmetic, comprehension, vocabulary, and similarities. Responses on each subtest are first given a raw score, which is then converted to a scaled score according to the child's chronological age, by using a table in the manual. Scaled scores range from one to nineteen, with an average score of ten; there are three standard deviations in either direction. If a student receives a scaled subtest score of fourteen or above, the score is therefore regarded as above average. Conversely, a score of seven or below is considered to be below the average of that age group.

The psychologist's report to the teacher should contain scores from both the Performance scale and the Verbal scale as well as the Full scale score. The Full scale score is not an average of the other two but is computed on a formula. Table 3–1 explains the significance of the separate scores within the WISC-R, and case studies 3–1 and 3–2 present extracts of psycho-educational reports, which focus on WISC-R scores and interpretation. Complete reports would contain additional information on the student's previous school performance, health history, and family climate, as well as the results of a battery of tests, observations, and the presenting behaviour of the child.

Table 3–1 Skills measured by the WISC-R subtests

Verbal scale	
Information:	Information from experience and judgment, common sense, reasoning
Similarities:	Logical and abstract thinking abilities, conceptualization
Arithmetic:	Concentration, arithmetic reasoning, auditory memory, visualization, mental alertness, education, social awareness, associative thinking
Vocabulary:	Word knowledge from experience and education, fund of information
Comprehension:	Practical knowledge and social awareness
Digit span (supplementary test):	Attention, rote memory, auditory perception
Performance scale	
Picture completion:	Visual alertness, visual memory, recognition of detail, conceptual and perceptual abilities
Picture arrangement:	Interpretation of social situations, social intelligence, attention to details
Block design:	Analysis and formation of abstract design, ability to perceive patterns and whole parts, visual motor co-ordination, abstract thinking, ability to plan and organize
Object assembly:	Putting together concrete forms, perception of whole, relationship of parts, visual motor co-ordination, spatial relationships
Coding:	Speed of learning and writing symbols, visual perception, manual dexterity
Mazes (supplementary test):	Planning and following a visual pattern, eye–hand co-ordination

Case study 3–1

Extract from a psycho-educational report

Name: Barry School: Canada Elementary
D.O.B.: 12 January 1983 Grade: 1

Reason for referral:
Barry was referred by the classroom teacher because of concerns about his lack of academic progress in all subject areas. He is reported to be inattentive in class, with a short attention span, and much out-of-seat and disruptive, aggressive behaviour. Classroom screening indicated no beginning in reading and severe deficits in number skills. The teacher also noted that Barry's behaviour is relatively recent, quite different from that displayed during his kindergarten year.

The school psychologist presented Barry with a battery of measures. The following scores are for the WISC-R:

Information	11	Picture completion	8
Similarities	12	Picture arrangement	6
Arithmetic	5	Block design	8
Vocabulary	13	Object assembly	7
Comprehension	13	Coding	5

Verbal scale: 105; Performance scale: 79; Full scale: 91

Barry's WISC-R Full scale IQ of 91 (±6) places him in the slightly low category. Nevertheless, it is important to look at the scales singly and to note the wide discrepancy in scores. On the Verbal scale, Barry demonstrated relative strength but with an area of deficit in arithmetic problems presented orally. Success in oral arithmetic depends on attention and past learning, both consistent areas of weakness for this child. On the Performance tests, Barry had difficulty in attending and in manipulating and interpreting visual stimuli. He was unable, for example, to distinguish between the letters *b* and *d* when either writing or reading them. The examiner believes that the weaknesses are reflective both of his failure to concentrate and of deficits in the skills involved.

Case study 3–2

Extract from a psycho-educational report

Name: Miyuki School: Maple Leaf Elementary
D.O.B.: 1 March 1979 Grade: 5

Reason for referral:
Miyuki was referred for intellectual assessment by the principal since she is a new student in the school and placement in an appropriate class was in question. She approached the testing situation somewhat cautiously and expressed concern over the need for special testing since she had always done "okay" in school. She accepted

the explanation regarding placement and was obviously relieved to know that she was not to be graded on the basis of this test. Miyuki worked attentively and co-operatively throughout the testing session and eventually stated her enjoyment in doing most of the tasks.

Miyuki's WISC-R scores were:

Information	13	Picture completion	9
Similarities	13	Picture arrangement	10
Arithmetic	11	Block design	12
Vocabulary	14	Object assembly	11
Comprehension	12	Coding	12
(Digit span)	11		

Verbal scale: 115 (± 6); Performance scale: 105 (± 7); Full scale: 112 (± 5).

The numbers in parentheses provide the confidence bands for each score. Thus, for example, we can be reasonably certain that Miyuki's Full scale IQ falls between 107 and 117. All three scores fall within the average to high average IQ classification or roughly between the seventieth and the ninetieth percentile. The difference between the Verbal and the Performance scales, while not large enough for significance, suggests functionally better verbal than non-verbal skills.

On the basis of these results, there is no indication that special programming is needed. Since the WISC-R is known to predict academic success, we could predict that Miyuki will be an average or above-average student.

Although the WISC-R is one of the best and most widely used instruments available, it is not perfect and problems do exist. On IQ tests, estimates of reliability are based on statistical analyses of groups of children; this kind of analysis masks the fact that an individual IQ can change dramatically. Researchers have shown that in a group of middle-class normal children there was an average shift (in one direction or another) of 28.5 IQ points between the ages of 2.5 and 17 (McCall, Appelbaum, & Hogarty, 1973). Moreover, all IQ tests are culturally biased to some extent. Children from minority groups, largely because of differences in language and expression, are more or less at an immediate disadvantage when judged on such measures. Box 3–1 presents some cautionary points to keep in mind when examining diagnostic results from any instrument.

In the past, intelligence tests were used as the sole criterion in the assessment and placement of exceptional children, especially those designated as mentally retarded or gifted. Today, we have adopted a less cavalier stance as we come to realize that intelligence is a multifaceted and virtually indefinable construct. We now present children with a battery of measures, of which IQ tests are only one component.

This is especially true for exceptional youngsters. Traditional measures to describe levels of intellectual functioning are often inappropriate when used with children who show dysfunctions in motoric ability, hearing, vision, communication, or behaviour.

Box 3–1 Some general reminders regarding test results

Do . . .	**Don't . . .**
. . . remember that IQ tests measure only a small part of human intelligence.	. . . think of the IQ as an immutable number to be fixed forever on a student's record.
. . . become familiar with the behaviours measured by psycho-educational tests.	. . . forget that it is a waste of time and money to have tests administered if the results are not used effectively and appropriately.
. . . continue to carry out informal testing.	. . . be satisfied with reports that give only numbers. Ask for observations, the student's presenting behaviours, and subtest results.
. . . use the results as part of the foundation of individual programming.	. . .believe that psycho-educational assessment will tell you all you need to know about a student.
. . . remember that a score is not a precise point, but lies within an interval or band.	

For these youngsters, diagnosticians use instruments that avoid, as much as possible, the restraints on the students' responses that deficits impose.

Intensive testing

Intensive testing is a level of assessment that typically involves medical and paramedical personnel. A complete evaluation of a child's health history and current medical status is a crucial component of any assessment. The child should be referred for a complete medical evaluation, which includes tests of visual and auditory functioning.

Many professionals are involved at the intensive level of testing: the school nurse, the family doctor, the pediatrician, the neurologist, the audiologist, and the ophthalmologist, to mention only a few. A medical evaluation is thus a collaborative effort to arrive at a total picture of a child's health and general physical adaptation to her or his environment. Like other aspects of assessment, medical diagnostic procedures search for assets as well as liabilities. They determine whether the child has potential abilities that he or she can learn to draw upon to function more efficiently.

Screening measures and procedures

As has been discussed, screening is usually a classroom procedure and one in which teachers will necessarily become adept. A wide range of procedures are included; they run the gamut from simple observations to far more structured testing measures, as discussed in the following sections.

Observations

Observation typically forms the starting point for assessment, and indeed is important throughout the diagnostic process. Teachers know their students well and are in a prime position to observe behaviours and performance in various types of situations and settings. The thousands of behavioural events that occur in the classroom every day can provide a wealth of information. Cartwright and Cartwright (1974) suggest a number of areas that classroom teachers should consistently observe for potential or present difficulties: information processing, storage and retrieval of information, language, speech, vision, hearing, and social and emotional functioning.

In observing children, teachers should focus on particular behaviours so that they may determine frequency and search for possible patterns and causes. If they are to be effective, observations should be made in conjunction with other informal measures, to clarify or modify perceptions, and reduce ambiguity in reporting. Measures such as those discussed below help to document and quantify teacher's observations.

Checklists and self-report inventories

Teachers' assessments, preferably through the use of structured checklists, are emerging as one of the most promising methods of identifying high-risk children (Evans, 1977; Glazzard, 1977). Checklists can be used as crude measures of academic and behavioural performance, and may be either prepared by the teacher or commercially constructed. They are actually very simple devices, merely containing a group of statements that are checked off in order to describe the presence or absence of a behaviour. Statements may focus on expected behaviour, characteristics of performance, or subskills of a task. The advantage of checklists is that a great deal of information can be accumulated very quickly.

Teachers can develop their own checklists to serve specific purposes. As an example, table 3–2 presents a checklist constructed to monitor certain aspects of an individual student's behaviour. Pete, a junior high school student, is having difficulty maintaining on-task behaviour, completing homework, and generally following class rules. Pete carried the list to his various classes and teachers filled it in daily by checking off behaviour that was present on the given day.

Commercial checklists are also readily available. The decision to use one kind of checklist over another would be made individually, based on availability, the particular need, and whether one wants to compare the child's behaviour to group norms or not. Commercial checklists are sometimes standardized and can cover a broad range of behaviours. They are typically intended to be filled in by the teacher with the parent or caregiver.

Self-report inventories are also a useful way to gather a relatively large amount of information in a short time. Inventories either record an individual's responses within a set of behaviours or across varying behaviours. They are used for older students, as they are not effective with children below about grade five. An example of a self-report inventory that focusses on homework is presented in table 3–3.

Table 3–2 A checklist for school and homework performance

	M	T	W	Th	F
In class					
1. Completes class assignments.					
2. Stays in his seat.					
3. Follows oral directions.					
4. Follows written directions.					
5. Is attentive to the task at hand.					
6. Works neatly and carefully.					
7. Shows consistency in the quality of his work.					
8. Works well in structured situations.					
9. Works well independently.					
10. Demands appropriate amounts of attention.					
11. Participates in group activities.					
12. Uses class time productively.					
Homework					
1. Attempts assigned homework.					
2. Completes assigned homework.					
3. Homework is tidy and well presented.					
4. Independent in doing homework.					
5. Homework is handed in on schedule.					
General					
1. Alert and responsive in class.					
2. Punctual.					
3. Brings necessary books and materials to class.					
4. Abides by class rules.					
5. Follows class procedures.					
6. Treats teachers and peers with respect.					
7. Takes responsibility.					
8. Consistently seems to work at the level of his ability.					

Rating scales

Checklists indicate the presence or absence of a behaviour; rating scales force the observer to judge the quality of a performance. Instead of using simple yes/no responses, the rater marks the presence or absence of a behaviour on a scale, usually from 1 to 5. If an item asked whether a student was punctual, therefore, a notoriously tardy student would be rated as 1, an average student as 3, and a very punctual student as 5. Most rating scales contain a selection of items that cover behaviours readily observed by anyone involved with the student. They can be routinely administered by an examiner with limited training to many different pupils in a relatively short period of time and at modest cost (Winzer & Malarcyzk, 1985). Rating scales are used to

- assess students in classroom settings so that behaviour is measured at the time and place of its natural occurrence
- determine at what level of school adjustment students are functioning
- compare an individual student's behaviour and performance with that of a group
- predict possible learning problems

Table 3–3 Self-report inventory for homework

Homework	Yes	No
1. I find homework interesting.		
2. I understand that completing homework assignments will make me a better student.		
3. I often start homework, but quit if it is too long or too hard.		
4. I usually do the written part of the homework, but not the reading.		
5. The reading is interesting, but I don't usually complete my written homework.		
6. I dislike certain teachers and won't do homework for them.		
7. Even though homework is dull, I usually finish it.		
8. I often forget to write down the homework assignments.		
9. My parents help me with my homework.		
10. I put off doing assignments until the last minute.		
11. My teachers don't explain the homework clearly enough.		
12. I get behind in homework because I have too many other things to do.		
13. When I study, the radio or TV is turned on.		
14. I only study before a test.		
15. It is almost impossible for students to complete all their homework.		

Rating scales are most valuable in assessing behaviour. They overcome the subjective nature of definitions of behavioural disorders, at least to some degree, and objectify and quantify data. A particular rating scale can be selected to measure overt behaviour, personality, social adjustment, giftedness, the behaviour associated with learning disabilities, or other aspects of functioning. Student self-report inventories can also be used as rating scales. Students assign a specific rating to each statement or question. Table 3–4 shows a scale devised to assess attitudes towards mathematics.

Measures of adaptive behaviour

Historically, the phenomenon of mental retardation has only been understood by aligning it to the concept of intelligence and intelligence has come to mean that which can be measured by IQ tests. Such a restricted conception of mental retardation is no longer considered appropriate. Not only must students demonstrate performance two standard deviations or more below the mean on measures of mental ability, but they must also clearly show deficits in **adaptive behaviour**. This may be construed as the behaviour that is appropriate in specific situations and settings for a particular individual's age and culture. Using language to express basic wants and needs is appropriate adaptive behaviour for a three year old, for example, but by the time the child reaches the school years, he or she should also be able to use language for meaningful interaction with peers of both sexes.

Table 3–4 Self-report rating scale

Statement	Circle the number that corresponds to the statement. Circle 1 for a completely false statement, and 5 for a completely true statement.				
1. Math is fun.	1	2	3	4	5
2. Nobody should do math unless they have to.	1	2	3	4	5
3. Doing math is boring.	1	2	3	4	5
4. There are too many chances to make an error in math.	1	2	3	4	5
5. Math is needed in everyday life.	1	2	3	4	5

Source: Adapted from *Teaching Mathematics to Children with Special Needs* by C. Thornton, F. Tucker, J.A. Dossey, and E.F. Bazik, 1983, Menlo Park, CA:Addison Wesley.

Mildly handicapped children often encounter problems in social interactions. Scales of adaptive behaviour, closely related to behavioural rating scales, are used to measure the ability of individuals to cope with the natural and social demands of the environment. Scales of adaptive behaviour are not as reliable as IQ tests chiefly because definitions of what is actually being assessed remain imprecise. Nevertheless, their use is particularly important for placement, because the child with a low level of adaptive behaviour is especially likely to present problems in the regular classroom.

Scales of adaptive behaviour constitute a general level of assessment designed only to identify the global strengths and weaknesses of a target learner. The measures incorporate various categories, such as interpersonal relations and self-help skills, and allow professionals to rate learners on a graduated scale. The person using the scales must either interview someone who knows the child intimately or else have contact with the learner in observable situations.

Interviews

Interviewing is not a simple procedure. The interviewer must develop considerable skill in establishing rapport with people and in drawing out the most relevant information. Some interviews are conducted by using a predetermined set of questions; others are less structured, being guided by the interviewer's sensitivity to areas of questioning that suggest themselves in the course of the interview.

Interviews with parents provide important information about a child's developmental background, health history, and behaviour in the home. As well, such conferences allow the interviewer to discern the behaviours and responses that are important to the parents, and the attitudes of the parents toward their child's learning and behavioural problems. For example, a family of professionals who have a daughter with a severe learning disability may possess different attitudes than those inspired by a daughter with a similar problem in a traditional family that does not place a high priority on education for girls. Procedures for parent interviews are fully discussed in the next chapter.

Interviews with students are also potent sources of information. Casual questions such as "What's your favourite subject?" or "Why don't you like math?" can reveal a great deal about students' perceptions of their world and their place in it, their hopes, their problems and means of coping with them. Not only can the interviewer gather data about a learner's integration of information, recall, language, and reasoning level, but the youngster's own cognizance of problems becomes clear. Yet student interviews are far from easy; school-age children have a self-conscious aversion to self-revelation (Levine, 1981) and it takes patience, empathy, and time to draw usable information from young children.

Case histories and past records

Nearly all children come to school with some type of records available to the classroom teacher. These may include results of psychological tests and updates, audiological, ophthalmological, and dental information, or occupational and physical therapy reports. Folders may also include achievement test results, teacher-made tests, checklists of attainments, self-report inventories, anecdotal records, observations, interviews, case studies, and samples of past work, both corrected and uncorrected.

Without some historical information, it is not possible to understand present functioning adequately (Salvia & Ysseldyke, 1978). A case history provides a picture of the interplay of experiences and attitudes that have gone into the making of an individual; it focusses on developmental data, fashioning environments, and manifest behavioural and learning problems.

School records provide valuable information about a youngster's learning patterns over the years and pinpoint persistent areas of weakness. When constructing a profile of academic skills, it is particularly important to note the age that marked the onset of learning difficulties (Moran, 1979). If the records show that a child had learning problems on entering school, then the individual probably has a **developmental disability**. Learners whose deficits do not appear until later generally demonstrate problems resulting from other sources, external factors such as problems at home or too many lessons missed because of illness.

School records will also show a student's rate of progress. They often specify the type of help received in the past and the ways in which the learner was able to benefit from special intervention. For older pupils, it is essential to discover how they functioned in elementary school and whether they have exhibited any sudden changes in behaviour or achievement. Changes can reveal problems such as dislike of a teacher, or alterations in the home environment.

When reviewing past student records, teachers must be careful not to develop a negative predisposition toward a student. Reading previous teachers' comments about how unco-operative, belligerent, or delayed a student has been may lead to unfortunate biases that will only perpetuate the student's prior poor behaviours.

Measures to assess present levels of performance

Teachers are particularly concerned about the level at which their students presently function, the effectiveness of the instructional program, and the rate at which students progress through the curriculum. In order to assess these components of the educational process, teachers may employ a mix of formal and informal measures in both the regular classroom and the resource room. The two kinds of measures supplement one another.

Formal measures: standardized tests and diagnostic instruments

Much data can be generated using formal, standardized measures. The sections below discuss achievement tests, diagnostic tests (a specific kind of test, not to be confused with the general term "diagnosis"), process-oriented tests, language tests, and social measures, all of which form part of the larger assessment battery.

Achievement tests

Unlike IQ tests, achievement tests may be used by a variety of personnel. Diagnosticians use them as part of psycho-educational diagnosis, but regular teachers and resource-room teachers may also employ them, among other tests. Achievement tests may be chosen for group or individual use. Regardless of how and by whom they are administered, all achievement tests are designed to assess students' learning in specific areas of the curriculum.

A huge range of achievement tests is available. Even so, only two achievement tests are standardized for use across English-speaking Canada: the Canadian Test of Basic Skills [CTBS] (Scannel, Haugh, Schild, Ulmer, & King, 1981, 1988) and the Canadian Achievement Test [CAT] (CTC, 1981).

Most achievement tests are norm referenced. Thus, if a child takes a norm-referenced mathematics achievement test, the number of items that are answered correctly will be compared with the scores for other children at the same age and grade level, and the child will be assigned a score reflecting the grade or age level of mathematics functioning.

The most widely accepted measures of achievement, however — the commercially developed, standardized, and norm-referenced tests — have been roundly criticized (Deno, 1985). Jenkins and Pany (1978) argue that the tests are biased regarding curricular content. Frequently, a teacher will have stressed one part of the curriculum and an achievement test will stress another. Achievement tests are also considered technically inadequate for making instructional decisions about individual students (Salvia & Ysseldyke, 1985). Because the tests are timed, for example, they discriminate against some students; the measures may not be accurate if the pupils taking the test are slow workers or poor readers. In addition, they measure only the broad parameters of achievement, not being sensitive enough to assess a student's daily progress or the effectiveness of a program.

Yet the results of achievement tests are not futile; rather, they must be placed in their proper perspective. For one thing, this kind of testing constitutes only a part of ongoing assessment. For another, achievement tests are widely used despite their drawbacks. They are, for example, the most common tests used with learning-disabled students (Hallahan & Kauffman, 1986), because deficits in achievement are the primary characteristic of these children. Finally, achievement tests are useful methods to measure learning rapidly and to identify areas that require more specific diagnostic testing.

Diagnostic tests

Norm-referenced achievement tests do not provide much diagnostic or prescriptive information. On the other hand, **diagnostic tests** are designed to identify students' specific problems perceiving or responding to teaching and to information. Diagnostic tests verify educators' suspicions by probing deeper than achievement tests can, to determine if an academic problem exists, and what its parameters are. The measures furnish a microscopic view of the component elements within different areas of performance, a detailed picture in a relatively short time of a learner's abilities in a particular subject area. Characteristically they are administered to individuals, rather than groups. Teachers can use diagnostic tests to analyse the way that a student functions within a given subskill, to focus on a specific disability, and to observe faulty habits. The tests offer directions for remediation, either by making specific suggestions, or by very precisely delineating problematic areas.

The great majority of diagnostic tests are available for use in the core subject areas: language arts (especially reading) and mathematics. The subtests usually focus on central areas of the given subject. In a diagnostic mathematics test, for example, the questions may cluster around such general areas as basic operations, numeration, time, and money. A diagnostic reading test may cover areas such as word-attack skills, sight words, and reading comprehension.

Process-oriented tests

Process-oriented tests are a recent innovation in special education. First used in the field of learning disabilities, the tests assess the underlying psychological processes or subskills necessary for all efficient learning. They are often administered to students suspected of being learning disabled, because problems in psychological processing are inherent in the many definitions of their disability.

Process-oriented measures attempt to assess how a person integrates, and then uses, stimuli. Areas assessed include auditory processing, visual processing, visual motor functioning, and development of motoric skills. The tester concentrates on those areas that comprise the underlying psychological causes of an individual's learning problems. While many educators have reservations about the usefulness of process-oriented tests, there is no good substitute for them at present. They can be administered by classroom and resource-room teachers or psychologists, depending on the measure, and range from brief, two-minute tests to complex instruments taking up to an hour and a half to administer.

Language tests

The quality and quantity of a child's **receptive** and **expressive language** are vital to school success. Communication disorders cut across most areas of exceptionality and surface in many ways. Language problems can manifest themselves as difficulties with vocabulary, word order, meaning, comprehension, or expression. In assessing language, it is important to distinguish between language comprehension (receptive language) and language performance (expressive language). Because so many areas are to be assessed with language, a huge variety of language tests and language sampling procedures are available. The important subject of language testing will be returned to later, especially in chapters 7 and 11.

Social measures

The measures that diagnosticians employ are designed either to determine academic potential or to reveal aspects of a child's emotional health, personality development, and social maturity. The latter instruments are social measures and may explore areas such as self-help skills, self-direction, socialization, occupation, communication, and locomotion. The scales of adaptive behaviour discussed earlier are social measures that must be completed by the parents or caretakers of a child. Personality tests, on the other hand, are administered directly to individuals by specialists. Personality measures, such as the Piers–Harris Children's Self Concept Scale (Piers & Harris, 1969), require a high degree of sophistication in administration and interpretation. These will not usually be encountered by the classroom teacher.

Projective tests are also administered directly to individuals, and are widely used in the social area. They too are administered only by professionals, often psychiatrists. The tests probe otherwise inaccessible personal constructions of self and the world by presenting the subject with a stimulus and requesting a subjective response. Subjective drawings, picture-story tests, and completion techniques are used.

Informal measures

Much information can be gleaned from informal measures. By correcting students' daily work samples teachers can identify patterns of error and check whether progress is being made, and at what rate. Teachers can also construct tests to assess various aspects of achievement. While informal measures are not reliable on their own, they do provide a great deal of data.

Criterion-referenced tests

A norm-referenced test is one that has been administered to a large group of people so that any individual score can be compared to the average, or norm. IQ tests, as we have seen, are a good example of norm-referenced instruments. Nonetheless, an IQ test or a standardized achievement test is not really useful in developing a program within a given curriculum.

Criterion-referenced tests, on the other hand, were developed to assess a student's progress against criteria set for a number of instructional goals for that student, rather than against group norms. A student's performance is measured against an absolute, or a specific predetermined criterion (Wallace & Larsen, 1978). Criterion-referenced instruments thus assess the extent to which a student has reached the specified objectives.

Because clear statements of these objectives are usually provided before instruction begins, criterion-referenced assessment depends on breaking a task down into its individual subtasks or components. Tests may then include an assessment of all the skills prerequisite to performance within a particular area of achievement. The sequence of skills is identified and the objectives for each subskill are written in behavioural terms.

Many teachers prefer to construct their own criterion-referenced tests. There are three basic steps involved: choosing the skills to be assessed; writing objectives that describe the skills; and delineating methods to evaluate acquisition of the skill (Howell, Kaplan, & O'Donnell, 1979). As an example, a long-term goal — the criterion — for six-year-old Bettina is saying and writing the letters of the alphabet in order. Bettina's progress will be assessed against that particular skill, rather than against the norm for any group, in this case, the rest of Bettina's class. The teacher first breaks the long-term goal into attainable short-range objectives written in behavioural form, and then presents the tasks to Bettina in small, incremental steps. Her attainment is then judged against the individual criterion, learning the alphabet.

To use another example, ten-year-old Andy is unable to decode simple consonant-vowel-consonant (CVC) words. Andy's teacher may set forth an objective that states, "When presented with a list of ten CVC words on flash cards, Andy will decode them orally to 100 percent accuracy," and then use a criterion-referenced test in which the task is to meet that objective.

Criterion-referenced tests are directly relevant to the classroom curriculum. Because basic skills are relatively sequential in nature and the skills to be learned are limited in scope, criterion-referenced tests can be used to assess a student's progress as he or she masters each skill and moves through the curriculum. The measures are more difficult to use after the developmental level of learning, when instruction extends beyond areas of basic skill. At this point, the students are required to use higher thinking skills to learn complex materials. These skills do not lend themselves to assessment by the scope and sequence charts commonly used at the basic skill level.

While many criterion-referenced tests are made by teachers, a number of commercially made ones are appearing. Well-designed criterion-referenced tests of either kind are based on task analysis; they employ instructional objectives that precisely describe conditions, standards, and performance; and they measure each skill in a valid and reliable manner. Good tests make an effective selection of instructional objectives possible and measure progress (Cypher, Hinves, Baine, & Sobsey, 1984).

The main advantage of criterion-referenced testing is that it establishes a criterion specifically suited to the student. If the student does not achieve that goal, it can be presumed that it was not appropriate, or that additional practice is needed. Criterion-referenced tests can be profitably used when teaching groups or team teaching, and for organizing teaching resources. Criteria can easily be set for a small group although they would not be appropriate for the whole class. They can accommodate individual needs, allowing pupils to progress at their own rates, and helping teachers to individualize instruction.

Curriculum-based assessment

Curriculum-based assessment is a new term for a teaching practice as old as education itself — using the material to be learned as the basis for assessing the degree to which it has been learned. Because it is so closely linked to the classroom curriculum, curriculum-based assessment (CBA) provides the most basic and meaningful form of educational assessment.

Curriculum-based assessment procedures determine the instructional needs of students based on their ongoing performance in existing course content. CBA determines each student's entry skills in relation to the course work — the instructional demands made by the various course assignments—and controls the degree of difficulty by adapting tasks to match the student's ability (Gickling & Thompson, 1985). The procedures therefore eliminate the instructional mismatch between the skills of low-achieving and mainstreamed special students and the demands of the regular curriculum. The point is to improve instruction by reteaching where necessary, so that pupils will learn more. By administering a CBA before instruction on a given topic, a teacher is also able to identify those students who already know the material and should be learning at a more advanced level. Because the essential measure of instructional success is a student's progress through the curriculum, CBA, which can be used for any academic subject, enables teachers to "teach to the test." Blankenship (1985) lists some general guidelines for teachers using curriculum-based assessment:

1. List the skills presented in the materials selected.
2. Examine the list to see if all the skills to be learned are represented, and modify the materials if any skills are missing.
3. Decide if the skills are introduced in a logical order.
4. Write an objective for each skill on the list.
5. Prepare materials to test each listed objective.
6. Give the CBA immediately prior to beginning instruction on a topic.
7. Study the results of the CBA to determine pupils' knowledge.
8. Form instructional groups.
9. Readminister the CBA following instruction.

Error analysis

As part of the ongoing assessment process, teachers continually scrutinize samples of students' work. If these work samples are analysed carefully, they can provide a wealth of information about a particular student's progress, ability to handle assigned tasks, and behaviour. **Error analysis** is the process of studying students' work samples in order to discover patterns of errors, and involves a set of teaching procedures to classify and analyse learners' errors (Cox, 1975). It can be applied to any subject in which students produce written work.

Students' errors provide much more useful information to govern teaching than do their successes (Clinchy & Rosenthal, 1971; Reid & Hresko, 1980). Error analysis is based on the assumption that many mistakes are not haphazard but instead indicate that the learner is missing a vital skill, is under a misconception, or lacks information. By analysing a student's behaviour throughout the performance of a task, a teacher will be better able to specify where and why an error occurs. Error patterns can be found by identifying each mistake and asking: "What is the nature of the error?" and "What are the most likely causes of the error?" (Wiederholt, Hammill, & Brown, 1983). This information generates greater acumen about the learning process than does a simple tabulation of the student's responses. It also increases the likelihood of developing appropriate instructional approaches. Of course, error analysis is not new; conscientious teachers have been using it as an informal assessment technique for years.

Students appear to make three major types of errors in their work (Mandell & Gold, 1984). *Input errors* occur because pupils are receiving too much information at one time.

With too much stimuli, students do not scan the material for sequence, sense, and significant points, or attend to all the critical details. *Output errors* are simple mistakes that may result from fatigue or nervousness. *Elaboration errors* occur as students are working through a problem. Bachor (1979) outlines three kinds of elaboration errors. An incorrect rule applied to a complex problem is indicative of *simplification*. A child who spells Wednesday as Whensdae, for example, is applying known, but incorrect, phonic rules. *Omissions* occur when pupils simply ignore rules or omit parts of questions. Third, the term *inappropriate rule errors* refers to using incorrect strategies in performing a task. The young child who says "I goed," is overgeneralizing the rules for past tense.

Listed below are guidelines that have been developed for using work samples as diagnostic tools. Assessments can be designed to expose procedural errors and locate their origin. To carry out an error analysis, the teacher should

- score the student's assignment
- categorize the errors as input, output, or elaboration
- search for error patterns
- summarize the types of errors
- hypothesize about the reasons behind the errors
- reteach or remediate

(Bachor, 1979; McLoughlin & Lewis, 1981)

Teacher-made tests

In addition to the informal measures already outlined, there is also a need for tests that can be administered to the whole class rather than to an individual or a group, and that are prepared and corrected by the classroom teacher. Most educators are well aware of these types of instruments and probably use them daily. Teacher-made tests include numerous measures, from brief daily quizzes to weekly tests, unit-end tests, pretests, and lengthy, formal, end-of-term examinations. These classroom measures are usually of two kinds: objective tests and essay tests. Objective tests can be roughly divided into multiple-choice exercises, true-false exercises, recall exercises with short-answer or completion questions, and matching exercises. Interested readers are directed for more information to Brown, 1976; Fox, 1985; Garret, 1965; Green, 1975; and Thorndike and Hagen, 1978.

Classroom measures for assessing behaviour

Teachers often complain that a child is always indulging in a particular form of misbehaviour, but when the complainant is asked to record the number of times the behaviour occurs over a nominated period, it appears to diminish. This may happen because the observer was unintentionally exaggerating the incidence or nature of the behaviour; or perhaps the child, aware of being observed and responding to the increased attention, behaved more appropriately. On the other hand, the behaviour could indeed have diminished, possibly as a result of some extraneous influence (Bond, 1981).

Teachers are usually the first to identify children with behavioural problems. They are well aware of the frequent inappropriate behaviours that emerge in their classrooms, and are responsible for both screening and ongoing assessment. Behavioural excesses may include physical and verbal aggression, defiance, lying, swearing, temper tantrums, stealing, and classroom disruptions. Aggressive, acting-out, and disruptive children are unlikely to escape attention: such youngsters challenge and frustrate teachers and hinder the achievement of everyone in the environment. Children who are anxious and withdrawn are more likely to be overlooked at the outset, but most teachers will quickly respond to their unusual patterns of behaviour. Many measures, formal and informal, are available to identify and diagnose behaviourally disordered children, some of which have already been discussed. Teachers need informal classroom measures to assess behaviour on a continuing basis, however, and some of the methods available are outlined below. It should be remembered that none of these measures possess the clarity of standardized tests. Bias, however subtle, creeps in and influences expectations and observations in any area dealing with behaviour. Nonetheless, informal procedures are easy to construct, easy to use, and easy to score, and are therefore very helpful if they are not used in isolation.

Direct observation

If he or she is to institute an efficient program for behavioural management, a teacher must assess the data relevant to a child's specific pattern of behaviours. Although some teachers find the idea of collecting data unappealing, it is really very important. For one thing, measuring a specific behaviour precisely may give the teacher an idea of the best way to change it. For another, initial measurement will allow later changes over time to be measured accurately.

Observation is the process of systematically recording social and academic behaviour in order to make instructional decisions. While all effective teachers evolve their own informal tactics for observation, it is a skill that can be honed through practice and variation of techniques. Direct and detailed observations are vital in order to detect the existence of behavioural problems. **Direct observation** is simply observation that takes place within the normal daily routine. By carefully observing children in naturalistic settings, teachers are able to decide which types of material or activity students prefer and which situations induce poor behaviour. Yet some behaviours are more easily observed than others. Children who have learned to write their names can easily demonstrate this newly acquired behaviour. Youngsters who indulge in prolonged, screaming temper tantrums are behaving in an obviously observable manner. On the other hand, the child who has improved in peer relations cannot manifest that behaviour so easily; not only is it more subtle, but demonstration depends upon a particular situation that calls forth the interaction.

The observer should note the frequency, incidence, and duration of an event or behaviour, the preceding or following activities that may be connected with the occurrence, and the frequency with which the undesired behaviour takes place compared to the frequency of selected desirable behaviours. In addition, observers should rate how far the behaviour or event deviates from that of the normal group, the peer group (which shares the student's disability), and from the individual's usual or previous behavioural pattern (Bond, 1981).

There are a number of ways to record behaviour, each applicable to different situations and behaviours. **Event recording** simply records the number of times that a specified behaviour happens over a given period, at least five days. Each day's occurrences are tallied and the totals transferred to a data sheet. Jane, for example, has begun throwing temper tantrums and the teacher records them, as shown in figure 3–3. The graph shows that Jane had a particularly bad day on Tuesday (day 2), while she was relatively calm on Friday.

(a)

Student: Jane Observer: Mr. Leistner

Behaviour: Temper tantrums

Situation and setting: School day, regular classroom

Date of observation	Frequency of behaviour	Number
Jan. 12th	11	2
Jan. 13th	++++	5
Jan. 14th	11	2
Jan. 15th	11	2
Jan. 16th	1	1

(b)

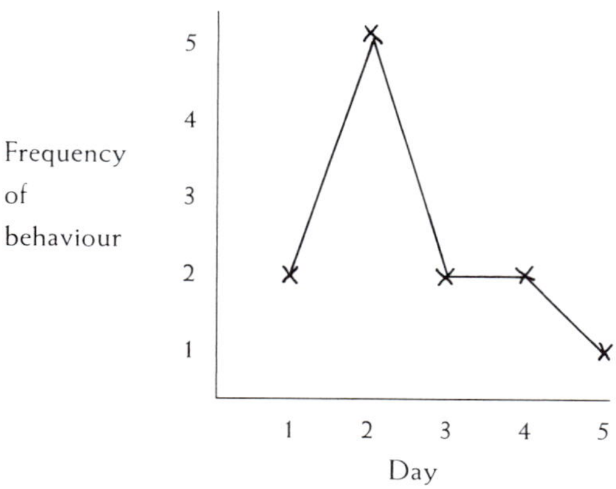

Figure 3–3 Event recording

The teacher may also wish to chart the duration of the tantrums. **Duration recording** measures the intensity rather than the frequency of a behaviour, while **interval recording** allows the observer to chart both the frequency and the duration of a particular behaviour. Over a period of time, for example, an hour, a child's behaviour is charted and the number of times the specified behaviour was apparent is expressed as a percentage of the total time, as shown in figure 3–4.

Student: Glenn Observer: Mrs. Treacy
Behaviour: Out-of-seat behaviour
Situation and setting: School day, regular classroom

Interval number (five-minute intervals)

Date:	1	2	3	4	5	6	7	8	9	10	11	12	
May 10th	+	+	–	–	–	+	+	+	+	+	+	+	75%

Present behaviour: +
Absent behaviour: –

Figure 3–4 Interval recording

Time sampling is similar to interval recording, in which the behaviour is checked at certain specified intervals. Alec, for example, is being observed for out-of-seat and inattentive behaviour at five-minute intervals over a one-hour period. The observer first divides the sheet into intervals, and then records whether Alec is on or off task at the end of each five-minute interval (see figure 3–5).

Student: Alec Observer: Ms Downie
Behaviour: Off-task
Situation and setting: School day, regular classroom

A	A	N	N	N	N	A	N	
5	10	15	20	25	30	35	40	minutes

Attending: A
Not attending: N
Percentage of off-task behaviour: 62.5%

Figure 3–5 Time sampling

In order for the data collected from direct observation to represent a child's behaviour accurately, the observation should be repeated over time, by more than one person if possible, and the student should be unaware of being observed. Observers need to be constantly on guard for bias both in themselves and in the procedures. It is especially important to avoid a "halo effect," consistently under- or overrating a pupil on the basis of an initial impression or a preconception.

Anecdotal reports

Anecdotal reports are simply brief written accounts of the behaviour of a particular student. They are useful for tracking chronic behavioural problems or describing a particular action or set of actions that the student displays quite infrequently or without a discernible pattern. Although informal, the anecdotal report should be expressed as a precisely written narrative. Systematic, periodic anecdotal reporting can hold considerable value: it allows the teacher to observe the environmental antecedents of and responses to a student's behaviour; and it provides documentation that can often substantiate specific behavioural patterns (Stephens, Hartman, & Lucas, 1978). Haphazard reporting, on the other hand, can lead to incorrect assumptions.

Teachers should report incidents that are typical of a recurrent type of inappropriate behaviour displayed by a particular student or, conversely, that are atypical and therefore significant. If behaviours have been selected aptly, a report may warn of future problems or hint at previously undiscovered potential. Teachers may indicate their own feelings, but any subjective reporting must be clearly distinguished from the behaviour itself. Anecdotal reports are brief but as complete as possible, and contain

- the student's name
- the name of the person making the observation
- the time, day of the week, date, location, setting, and activity
- a precise description of the behaviour in non-judgmental terms
- the events that preceded and followed the behaviour
- any information about the behaviour obtained from other sources, such as another teacher or a teacher's aide
- additional comments, perhaps about how the observer perceives that the behaviour made the student feel

The report is most effective when written as soon as possible after the incident. The student must then be further observed in a variety of settings in order to confirm or discount the presence of a chronic difficulty.

Q-sorts

A Q-sort is an assessment tool, developed by Stephenson (1953), that can be used in conjunction with student interviews to ascertain targets for behavioural intervention. The Q-sort is founded on the idea that discrepancies exist between an individual's perception of his or her real self and ideal self. By identifying these discrepancies, one can discover the ways in which a student needs to develop socially. In doing a Q-sort with a student, the teacher or tester adheres to the following process:

1. Give the student two decks of cards. The decks should be distinguishable by colour but contain identical sets of positive or negative descriptive statements. Each card carries a single statement such as "I pay attention to work," "I throw objects in class," "I disrupt my neighbours," "I hand in homework," "I skip classes," or "I'm rude to teachers."
2. Have the student rank the statements from "most like me" to "not like me" in each set, one for the real self and one for the ideal self. With the first set, then, the student ranks the cards as she or he would like to be, and with the second, as he or she really is.

3. After the student has ranked both decks of cards, the teacher copies the responses. The greater the agreement between the order of cards in either set, the better the match between how the individual supposedly behaves and how he or she wishes to behave.
4. The Q-sort reveals both the kinds of behaviour that the student values, and where she or he believes that shortcomings occur. The teacher can then plan intervention to focus on those areas of discrepancy between ideal and real behaviour.

The procedure can be used again at a later date to assess changes in behaviour over time, but the student does need some maturity to use the Q-sort properly from the outset.

The measures discussed in this chapter are useful tools in the initial and ongoing assessment of the student. Before instruction begins for the exceptional student, however, she or he will not only have to be assessed. The school-based team should also draw up an individual education plan, designed to tailor instruction to the individual. Individual education plans form the subject of the following chapter.

4 *Individual education plans*

Dear Reader,

Individual education plans (IEPs), or individual program plans (IPPs), are now used in various forms in most parts of Canada. Loosely defined, IEPs are written plans in which instructional objectives, monitoring procedures, and the responsibilities of involved parties are clearly detailed. Many educators are now expected to take a leading personal and team role developing, implementing, and reviewing these plans, in addition to their teaching duties. To do so, they must possess many interpersonal and administrative skills not routinely required of regular teachers.

The IEP process in Canadian educational policy has not come about in isolation. American legislation, specifically Public Law 94–142, the Education for All Handicapped Children Act of 1975, has greatly influenced Canadian education. The legislation decrees that every American local educational agency *must* maintain an IEP for each handicapped student and that the programs detailed in the IEP be established, reviewed, and revised in accordance with procedures specified in the same law. The primary intentions of the law are to guarantee that special education services are available to those who need them, to ensure that decisions involving the provision of those services are fair and appropriate, and to put in place a system of accountability for the vast federal funds released for the education of the handicapped. Procedural safeguards are legislated, addressing issues such as the language to be used for assessment, parents' rights to see all information, the confidentiality of reports, parental consent to assessment and programs, and the appeal process to be used if parents disagree with test results or proposed programs.

Note that this extremely influential educational legislation was enacted by the federal government of the United States. In Canada this type of federal influence is not possible since the provinces have direct authority over education. Some provinces have chosen to model their legislation closely after Public Law 94–142, while others have not (Winzer, 1982b). Great differences therefore exist among various provinces, and indeed school jurisdictions, over the requirements for individual programming. In my view this should not be seen as a disadvantage, for we are a very diverse people, living in a very diverse cultural and physical environment. It is not reasonable to assume that the same IEP process applies in urban centres, where the services of many different professionals are available to a school, and in remote northern or outport settings, where the teacher is the only consistently available resource. Because in most cases provincial legislation relating to special education is not as directive as Public Law 94–142, we have the flexibility to be creative in our individual service delivery to students with special needs. We can adopt the same laudable goals, such as fair and appropriate special education services to all handicapped children, but use locally developed processes to meet the ideal. As you read this chapter, the information presented will be most helpful if you discern how it applies to your provincial, regional, and school setting.

Two key issues should arise in a discussion of the IEP process. The first is the importance of establishing a prereferral system that requires the regular classroom teacher, with advice from others as deemed necessary, to identify and attempt to rectify the learning and behavioural problems in his or her classroom before referring a student for special services. Research shows that once a student is identified for referral to special education services, the chances are very high that she or he will receive those services. A prereferral procedure can help to ensure that only those whose learning difficulties cannot be fully accommodated within the regular classroom are referred. It also emphasizes the responsibility of regular classroom teachers, thus circumventing the attitude that special services are a dumping ground.

The second issue is the balance between teaching and paperwork. View all standard forms as working copies; change them to suit your individual needs and preferences, as long as the intent of the forms remains intact. If your teaching approach stems mainly from a cognitive perspective, for example, and your IEP forms are based on a behavioural model, modify the forms. The spirit, not the letter, of the law applies here. As a teacher, insist on having a say in the entire IEP process used in your school. Paperwork and endless conferences can be very frustrating and destructive. Remember, the most important charge of the teacher is effectual instruction. The IEP process can support, and indeed promote, this function.

David Peat
Cognitive Education Project
University of Alberta

François has been sitting in the grade six classroom for four months now: sitting, occupying a desk, marked in on the register, occasionally joining in the games on the playground, and even less frequently participating in classroom activities.

The grade six teacher expects all the pupils to keep up: to pass through the curriculum at about the same pace and to produce more or less the same results on tests and assignments. Of course, she is aware that some class members learn faster than average, while others require extra drill and practice. She accommodates these differences by dividing the class into groups at the beginning of the year and then providing each group with instruction and assignments at its own level.

Even if this immutable grouping system is working with some students, it is not accommodating François. When the other children read, he daydreams, because his reading is at about a grade two level and the class texts are far beyond him. He doodles when the other pupils write, because his spelling is so poor and his handwriting so laboured that writing becomes an exercise in frustration. Even copying from the board is painful for him: he sometimes has trouble deciphering the letters and he cannot remember enough of the words or configurations to ease the task.

In the regular classroom, under a regular curriculum, François is not really achieving anything. Indeed, he seems to be sliding backwards as he becomes more enmeshed in a web of failure. Yet this need not be. It is probably not too late to help him by creating a program that takes into consideration his unique pattern of strengths and weaknesses, his age, history of school failure, and mounting level of frustration. François needs special education, that collection of special forms of education designed for pupils who are unable to profit sufficiently from regular instruction.

If we think of learning as a process in which practice and experience result in a change of behaviour that is not due to maturation or growth, then we realize that many patterns of learning exist. Each individual will respond to some methods of instruction better than to others. Similarly, individualization is not a concept with a single meaning. To some people it evokes the image of children seated at individual work stations using self-paced workbooks, perhaps helped by an aide. To others, individualization implies instruction in small groups, or perhaps it suggests a process in which pupils select their own learning tasks. Probably the most pervasive picture of individualization is that of the teacher sitting and working with a special student on a one-to-one basis for large portions of the school day.

Yet, individualization for special students does not necessitate individual instruction at all times. Most exceptional students in regular classrooms will learn skills in common with their peers, but at their own pace, perhaps with different materials or content, or with extra drill and practice. **Individualization** is thus a process or series of decisions — about the learner and about programming — that reflects the most effective ways to accomplish goals and objectives set for each student. Ongoing evaluation is built into the process.

When the regular curriculum and mode of instruction are judged to be unsuitable in some way for specific students, individual plans of action are formulated. An **individual education plan** (IEP) is one of the most useful tools for meeting the needs of exceptional students. It supplies teachers with a set of goals and learning outcomes that will define the student's progress, and delineates the instructional route to those goals. Teachers therefore have a standard by which to organize instruction and evaluate

Small-group instruction is an important part of individualization.

exceptional learners' progress. Careful individual planning will also naturally engender more efficient organization for groups and for the entire class to the extent that teachers have specific goals and can communicate clear expectations. As Peat points out in the opening letter, IEPs also provide a measure of accountability for teachers, administrators, parents, and the school system.

There is nothing revolutionary about IEPs. Many educational systems have engaged in similar, formal instructional practices for years. Teachers today, however, are assuming more central roles in the mainstreaming movement, and must become acutely aware of the processes involved in individual plans. Regular classroom teachers are vital members of the team that devises these plans, and are responsible for putting them into practice.

The main objectives of this chapter are to

- describe the purpose, benefits, and difficulties of the IEP process
- explain the steps taken to formulate IEPs
- discuss the methods by which diagnostic data are translated into educational objectives
- explain the role of the classroom teacher, the special educator, and support personnel in the team responsible for educational planning for exceptional pupils
- discuss the role of parents and parent–teacher interaction in the diagnostic and IEP process
- examine the components of IEPs, with particular emphasis on **goals** and **objectives**

Individual educational planning

Most students do not need individual planning and curricular modification to succeed at school, but the regular curriculum can snare many exceptional learners in failure: it asks too much, too soon, and is too varied. These youngsters need individualized instruction. Individual plans can best be viewed as prescriptions for preventing or treating a student's learning or behavioural problems at a level that is individual and child-oriented. While plans may vary in length and complexity, in the personnel involved, and the format employed, it is essential that an individual plan be written for every exceptional learner. The plans may be given slightly different names, but individual education plan (IEP) is the most common.

An individual education plan is a written document delineating a special education program that may be provided in any type of educational setting, ranging from the regular classroom to very specialized segregated situations. It also sets out the related services required, naming the support of such people as speech therapists, audiologists, physical and occupational therapists, psychologists, physicians, counsellors, and others. Regardless of the nature of a particular plan, three fundamental elements are inherent. Abeson and Weintraub (1977, p. 5) observe that *individual* refers to the educational needs of a single student rather than to a class or group of students. *Education* in the context of an IEP refers only to those elements of the pupil's education that specifically require special education and related services. The term *program* (this text uses *plan*) refers to a statement of what will actually be provided for the student, as distinct from general guidelines.

The IEP is a management tool, used to ensure that when a student requires special education, the designed program is appropriate, implemented, and monitored. Simply, it can be viewed as a map routing the learner's progress. It contains the final destination of the learning process — the long-range academic goals for an individual — and the stages, or the short-term objectives, that must be passed to reach those goals. The IEP also describes the vehicle for learning — the methods to be used — and enumerates the personnel who direct the way, each responsible for a specific facet of the program.

Providing each exceptional individual with a basic educational program involves the consideration of many elements critical to a student's growth. The development of a meaningful plan is first of all contingent upon accurate educational assessment, and those involved in placement and planning must seriously address the student's handicap, concomitant learning and social problems, and individual pattern of strengths and weaknesses. Program planning, therefore, is founded on the full range of diagnostic data collected. Armed with this information, the team can select the educational offering, goals, strategies, materials, and evaluative procedures.

Developing an IEP is a complex and time-consuming procedure. In addition to the time and numerous personnel required for the initial assessment, considerable staff time and paperwork are needed to develop a draft plan, hold meetings, finalize the plan, maintain the necessary records, and conduct continual monitoring and an annual review. The advantages for exceptional children, however, are obvious and these should form the paramount consideration. Yet too often those benefits have been overshadowed by the inherent difficulties. Admittedly, not all the promises of IEPs have been realized, but to some extent, at least, we are still in an experimental stage of mainstreaming and individualization, in which philosophy has far outstripped practice. Box 4–1 outlines some of the pros and cons of IEPs.

Individual educational planning is founded on two important premises (Pijl, 1986). As pointed out in box 4–1, diagnosis must be linked to instruction: a successful IEP

Box 4–1 Pros and cons of individual education plans

Pros	**Cons**
IEPs translate diagnostic results into educational planning.	It is not always easy to translate data into goals and objectives.
IEPs involve an ongoing process. Educational planning is linked to actual instructional practice, which is constantly evaluated.	Special education teachers do not perceive a clear relationship between the IEP and what actually happens in the classroom (Morgan & Rhode, 1983).
IEPs require teachers to have a wide repertoire of instructional alternatives.	Teachers tend to prefer one way of teaching and do not possess a range of alternatives (Brophy, 1982a; Peterson & Clark, 1978).
IEPs involve a more planned way of teaching.	Many teachers think that they can teach just as effectively without IEPs; they view the paperwork as an administrative or clerical task (Morgan & Rhode, 1983).
IEPs necessitate individualized planning.	Teachers prefer to make group plans; they favour group instruction and like to admit pupils to already established groups (Pijl, 1986).
IEPs stress *what* is to be taught to a target pupil.	In the past decade, and even up to the present, the mainstreaming debate has centred on *where* mildly handicapped students should be taught and this may have clouded the vital issue of what to teach (Gottlieb, 1982).
IEPs are formulated and evaluated by a team.	Special education teachers indicate that they receive too little support in the development and implementation of IEPs from other teachers, ancillary personnel, and program administrators (Morgan & Rhode, 1983).

depends upon translating diagnostic data into educational planning and practice. Second, teachers must be committed to a more planned way of teaching, involving greater individualization and a fund of instructional alternatives. Individual planning serves many purposes; it can

- clarify and articulate good educational practice by defining expectations, assigning responsibility, and allocating instructional resources
- provide a basis for consultation and reporting
- elicit the commitment of staff and material resources to special education, and guide administrators in allocating them
- form the foundation of educational management and consistent monitoring
- facilitate communication between the parents and the school

The IEP process under Public Law 94–142

In the United States, IEPs are legislated under Public Law 94–142. For many reasons, they have been a continual source of controversy and difficulty. The prescriptive nature of the IEP process as set out in Public Law 94–142 in the United States has been one of the great pitfalls in its implementation and has tempted some educators to rename it "the impossible education plan" (Turnbull, Strickland, & Hammer, 1978). American teachers are concerned about the amount of time that must be devoted to planning and fear that they are drowning in paperwork. They have complained that they spend too much time meeting detailed technical requirements that interfere with teaching, that there are increased demands on their personal time, that they must share the responsibility for classroom activities, and that they have to acquire new skills (Katzen, 1980; Morgan & Rhode, 1983; Morrissey, Kaufman, & Lewis, 1978).

Price and Goodman (1980) found that teachers devoted an average of 6.5 hours to developing each IEP, of which 68 percent was school time and 32 percent personal time. Different categories of children required different amounts of time. Preparing IEPs for hearing-impaired students used the most hours; that for trainable mentally retarded youngsters the least. No time differences were found between preparation for elementary and for secondary students. Gathering diagnostic data and actually writing the document took most of the time. Experienced teachers, however, needed less time to write IEPs, and training in IEP preparation also cut down the amount of time spent.

Some American teachers are reluctant to write optimistic goals for exceptional students because there is no way to identify how much a student will change over a period of time. It depends on such variables as the student's age, degree of handicap, maturation, motivation, and the teaching environment. One pupil may attain all the prescribed long-term goals in six months while another in the same diagnostic category will proceed much more slowly.

Administrators also have grave concerns about accountability, due process of law, and litigation. When a student does not meet the long-term goals set forth in an IEP, teachers and school boards may be held legally accountable. School personnel have therefore attempted to develop a fail-safe method for developing IEPs, which seems to do more to protect the educational establishment than the rights of children with exceptional needs (Bosno, 1981).

The difficulties that American teachers have encountered with IEPs should not stop Canadian educators from adopting the concept. On the contrary, the American experience presents reasonable cautions and realistic guidelines that may be adapted to Canadian education. Competent teachers already do almost everything required in an IEP, but tend to be intuitive in their instruction. They have global goals about where activities will lead and do not generally make plans by stating goals and objectives and then explicitly choosing materials and methods to match them (Clark & Yinger, 1979).

Steps to develop individual education plans

After screening, five main steps are taken to formulate and implement individual educational planning: referral, diagnosis, developing the IEP, implementing the IEP, and finally monitoring, evaluating, and revising the plan. Each step is detailed in the remainder of the chapter, focussing on the teacher's perspective and those aspects of individual planning of particular importance in the regular classroom. Figure 4–1 first gives an overview of the entire IEP procedure, while case study 4–1, part 1 introduces Sally and the experiences of her classroom teacher from referral to evaluation of the IEP.

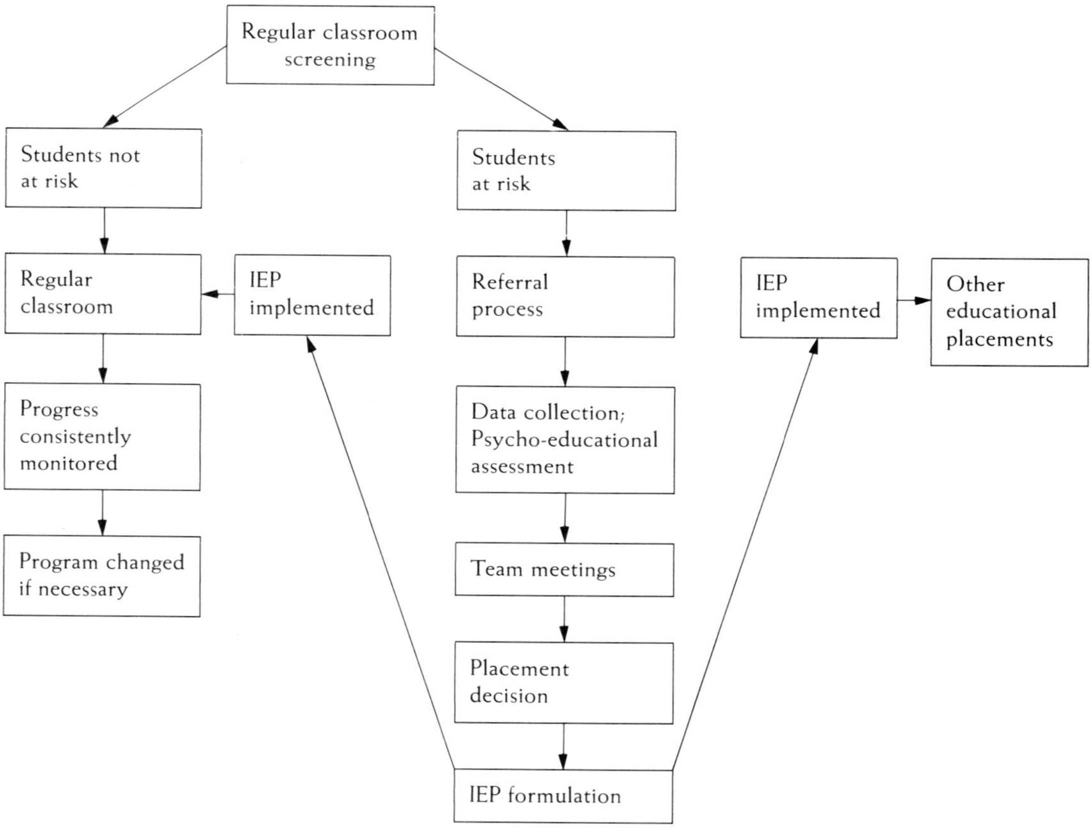

Figure 4–1 An overview of IEP development

Case study
4–1, part 1

Steps to develop an IEP

Name: Sally School: Prairie Elementary
D.O.B.: 3 February 1979 Grade: 3

Step 1: Referral
Ten-year-old Sally attends a large elementary school in Saskatoon. She is in her second year in grade three with the same teacher, Ms Davy. A strong bond exists between the child and the teacher and Sally is motivated to achieve success in this classroom.

Yet, even though Ms Davy has, with the assistance of the resource-room teacher, modified and adapted Sally's educational program, the child is becoming increasingly frustrated as she lags behind the rest of the class. Her lack of success is manifested in withdrawn behaviour, and a growing dependence on the teacher, punctuated by increasingly frequent temper tantrums.

Ms Davy carefully documented Sally's academic achievement and used behaviour rating scales, baseline observations, and anecdotal reports to detail the mounting behavioural problems. She discussed the problems with the special education teacher and the principal and then formally requested that Sally be given a full psycho-educational diagnosis.

Step 2: Diagnosis
Working through the principal, parental permission was obtained to initiate psycho-educational assessment. Sally's parents also took her for medical assessment, which included tests of vision and hearing.

Based on the classroom teacher's referral, the psychologist selected a battery of measures for Sally. In two sessions she administered the WISC-R, the Woodcock Reading Mastery Tests, the Durrell Analysis of Reading Difficulty, the Key Math Diagnostic Arithmetic Test, the Beery–Buklentica Test of Visual-Motor Integration, and the Wepman Test of Auditory Discrimination. From these, and other supplementary measures, the psychologist derived a broad profile of Sally's functioning and potential. She reported that Sally's general intellectual ability fell within the average range, although on the WISC-R she tended to perform much better on the Verbal than on the Performance scale.

The psychologist also noted that Sally demonstrated relative strengths in understanding through listening, concept development, and the use of oral language. Her understanding and generalization of mathematical concepts was at grade level, but her performance was hindered by poor memory for number facts.

It was found that Sally's major weakness was in reading. She had a very limited sight-word vocabulary and appeared to have missed the basic skills for word attack and phonetic decoding. In addition, her handwriting was poor, showing many deviations and malformations, at least partly due to her left-handedness. She had great difficulty with the additional mazes subtest on the WISC-R and scored below average on the Beery–Buklentica Test of Visual-Motor Integration. The psychologist pondered whether the weaknesses noted in visual motor skills would be contributing to Sally's lack of handwriting skills as well as to her problems with near and far point copying.

Step 3: Developing the IEP

The school principal organized a meeting of those involved in Sally's diagnosis and education, in order to assess the diagnostic data, determine her current levels of performance, and begin to formulate an individual education plan. Present at the meeting were the psychologist, the school principal, the resource-room teacher, Ms Davy, and the educational consultant. The parents were unable to attend but forwarded medical reports.

The report from an ophthalmologist indicated that Sally suffered from myopia, and recommended prescription lenses. Even though the team agreed that the medical problem could have contributed significantly to Sally's academic problems, they also felt that special education services were vital to provide the skills necessary for average academic achievement. Remedial work was necessary to close the gap between Sally's functioning and that of the rest of the class.

The service-delivery placement recommended was a combination of the regular classroom and the resource room. Sally would remain in her classroom for all subjects except reading, which would be taught by the resource-room teacher. Ms Davy would provide Sally with special instruction for handwriting skills. Both teachers would consult each other frequently on the two curricular areas requiring special help — reading and handwriting — and both would monitor Sally's progress.

The resource-room teacher and Ms Davy would be jointly responsible for writing the IEP, with help from the educational consultant. They approached the task by first carefully determining Sally's present levels of functioning, specifically in reading and handwriting. They then decided upon long-range goals and from these listed short-term objectives. Finally, they selected appropriate strategies and materials and incorporated evaluative methods into the plan. An extract from Sally's individual education plan is shown later in this chapter.

Step 4: Implementing the IEP

Implementation of the IEP began immediately. Ms Davy designed a new schedule for Sally so that her resource-room sessions coincided with reading periods in the regular classroom. To improve Sally's handwriting skills, the first step was to alter the materials used; rather than using an exercise book with its restricted surface, Sally began with large paper on an easel. This was done in the regular classroom.

Step 5: Monitoring the IEP

Once the IEP was drawn up, Ms Davy and the resource-room teacher used it to monitor Sally's attainment of the set objectives. Consequently, the plan was revised often. Ms Davy found, for example, that using large pencils on an easel was beneficial to Sally but that an even larger surface was better. Handwriting instruction was therefore done at the chalkboard in an attempt to teach Sally the correct letter formations.

Screening

In any classroom, the teacher continuously and consistently evaluates students' progress and the success of the program. As well, teachers are responsible for identifying students who display educationally disabling conditions and those whose performance indicates that they may be at risk for such conditions. Screening will identify about 85 percent of those students who need help (Lerner, Mardell-Czudnowski, & Goldenberg, 1981).

As stressed in the previous chapter, screening is the essential prerequisite to referral, diagnosis, decision making, program planning, and program implementation, and teachers are integral participants in the screening process. If teachers suspect that a student has a learning problem, they will find it necessary to compile and analyse a comprehensive body of information documenting their concerns and derived from observations of classroom performance, reviews of the pupil's performance on classroom assignments, teacher-made measures and achievement tests, and any relevant information from the parents.

Referral

Following screening, the teacher has several alternatives. She or he may

- refer the student to the school-based team
- consult other professionals about the student's problems and try to make curricular and instructional modifications within the classroom
- continue to gather information with the assistance of support personnel
- decide that there is no genuine problem and maintain the student under current conditions
- make a referral for psycho-educational assessment

If the teacher decides that the problem is indeed of a serious nature he or she elects the final option, which allows more exhaustive diagnosis to confirm or discount the presence of learning or behavioural difficulties. Referring a pupil does not indicate weakness in teaching or an inability to individualize instruction. Rather, teachers fulfil an important responsibility when they identify exceptional youngsters so that especially designed instruction can be provided for them.

Referrals are not initially very formal processes. A regular education teacher may at first simply approach the specialist teacher in the teachers' lounge to talk about the student, but after this point she or he should follow the guidelines prescribed by the particular school board. Usually, school board policy requires notifying the parents that a referral is being made. The reasons for referral, the process of evaluation, and the goals of the procedure should be carefully explained to the parents, and no diagnosis should be initiated until they have given their written permission.

Documentation for referral is generally not elaborate; it provides a simple record of problems, and lists the strengths, weaknesses, and general areas needing improvement. Many school systems have developed special referral forms to summarize and organize data, such as the one shown in figure 4–2. The information filled in refers to François, the grade six student whom you met in the opening paragraphs of this chapter.

Psycho-educational diagnosis

The diagnostic process identifies the problem more precisely, suggests possible causes, and provides ideas about prognosis and individual treatment. Psycho-educational diagnosis was fully discussed in chapter 3. It generates data used to determine the type of setting most suitable for the student, to plan a program, and to ascertain the necessary support services. Pijl (1986) points out that criterion-referenced tests seem to be the most useful measures for program planning, while norm-referenced instruments are valuable for placement decisions.

Translating diagnostic data into educational objectives

It is crucial to use the diagnostic process to formulate educational goals and objectives. To build a link between assessment and the curriculum, personnel will need to take the following steps:

1. Identify those developmental deficits that require more intensive diagnosis.
2. Match assessment devices to the characteristics and content of the curriculum. In other words, choose a device that contains items similar to the types of objectives in the curriculum.
3. Determine the student's developmental levels in the major areas of functioning.
4. Identify the developmental ceilings in each domain; find the point at which the learner begins to fail consistently.
5. Match the tasks that represent the developmental ceilings to the objectives in the curriculum for each developmental domain (Cartwright, Cartwright, & Ward, 1984)

Different people are likely to make different inferences from a set of behaviours. It is therefore essential that teachers and diagnosticians present their findings in terms of specific behaviours. A psycho-educational report should include adequate information about the procedures used in assessment, so that the people using the results know exactly what the scores mean. Being told that a child scored fourteen on a certain subtest, for example, means virtually nothing unless the reader knows what the test was designed to measure, what behaviours were sampled, and how the results are to be interpreted.

The IEP is a direct outcome of the diagnostic process. It describes a student's individual differences and then identifies the objectives that form the basis of the instructional plan. Teachers have extensive contact with their students in a range of settings and situations; they are also intimately acquainted with the goals of the instructional program and can assess their pupils in relation to those goals. Classroom teachers are therefore invaluable, first in assessment and then in linking diagnostic data to planning.

Developing the individual education plan

When all the assessment data about an individual is collected, the student's current level of functioning and special needs are determined in order to establish those areas of instruction that should be given priority. The student's level is compared to that of her or his chronological peers to discover how great a lag exists. For example, in case study 4–1, part 1 you met Sally. After determining Sally's current status in reading, it may be said that her reading skills are at about a grade 1.6 functional level, showing a delay of approximately two years behind other children of the same age. This discrepancy means that Sally will encounter great difficulty participating in the language arts and content areas in her grade three classroom.

Student's name: *François* Referred by: *K. Wong*
Age: *11 years 2 months*
Present class: *Grade 6*

Reason for referral: *Increasingly poor academic functioning; withdrawn behaviour*

General classroom behaviour: *Passive; rarely participates; rarely volunteers.*

Situation specific behaviour: *Daydreams constantly; never finishes his work.*

General classroom performance:

a) Strengths *Participates better in non-academic subjects such as art and music.*

b) Weaknesses *All core and content areas.*

Functional levels in specific areas:

a) Reading (oral, silent, comprehension) *At grade 2 level: poor word attack, recognition, and comprehension*

b) Spelling *Often spelling shows little relationship to word.*

c) Language (receptive, expressive, written) *Poor usage: incorrect syntax, restricted vocabulary*

d) Handwriting *Full of malformations; often mixes upper and lower-case letters on one page*

e) Mathematics *Behind class, but not as much as in other areas*

f) Other *Lacks in reading and spelling adversely affect content areas.*

Curricular modifications or strategies attempted: *Working in slower group for reading and spelling.*

Degree of success: *Seems to be falling further behind*

Summary: *François is encountering problems in all areas of school performance.*

Signature: *K. Wong* Date: *9 November*

Figure 4–2 Pupil referral form for classroom teachers

The decisions on which an IEP is based arise from several different sources of information, of which the most important is diagnostic data on the pupil. Other relevant considerations, referred to as **boundary conditions**, include the classroom situation, the wishes of the parents, the teacher, and the pupil, and the characteristics of the school-based team (Yinger, 1978). These are important because the plan cannot rest exclusively on pupil-bound data. Considering boundary conditions ensures that a certain teacher, working in an existing classroom situation, is in fact able to conduct the planned implementation for an exceptional student. In other words, giving credence to boundary conditions addresses the careful balance between individualization and practicality (Pijl, 1986).

The team approach

The assessment of an exceptional student is the responsibility of a team of people (see figure 4–3). The most successful IEPs are those drawn up by experts who pool their knowledge in order to place a special learner and construct a program for him or her. If an effective program is to be developed, the team must also ensure that the student's parents or guardians are consulted and that the placement is flexible.

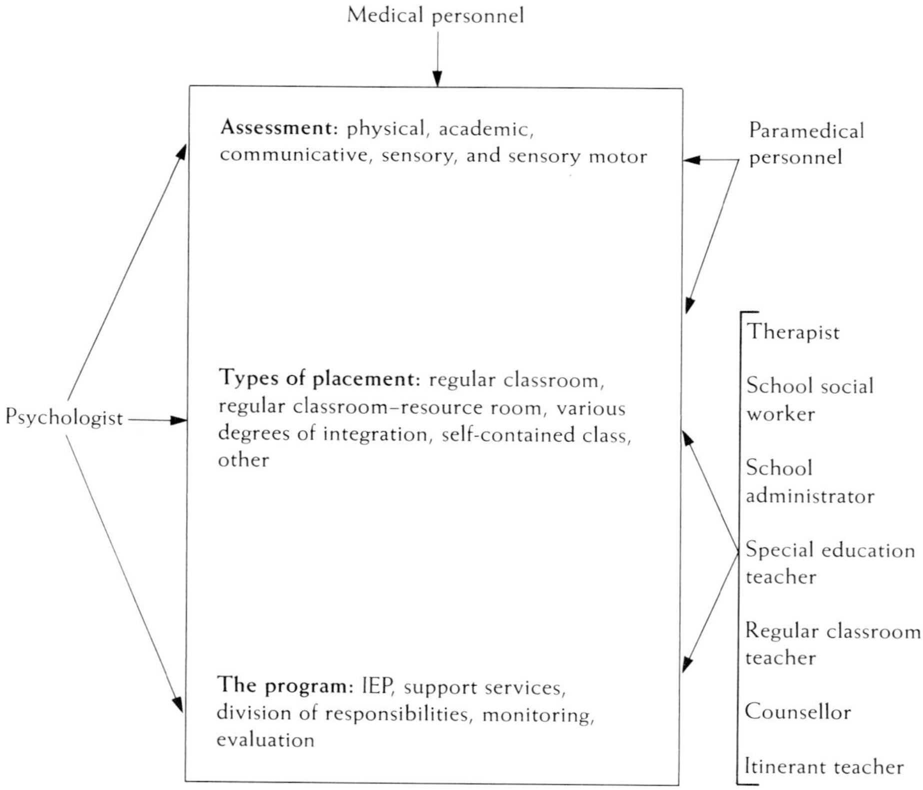

Figure 4–3 The school-based team and its areas of responsibility

Ideally, the **school-based team** is responsible for co-ordinating the entire special education planning process, including the important step of evaluation. The most efficient procedure is to use a multidisciplinary team, the exact composition of which will vary, for both evaluation and programming, according to the needs of the specific student. As an example, the team for a hearing-impaired youngster may include an audiologist and a speech therapist. By contrast, an ophthalmologist and an orientation and mobility specialist may be involved with a visually handicapped student. Certain core members will usually be included on any team, however:

- teachers: the individual teacher who was responsible for the initial referral and the receiving teacher who will be largely responsible for implementing the individual education program
- special education personnel: teachers, itinerant teachers, and educational consultants
- the school psychologist or person responsible for the psycho-educational diagnosis
- the principal or administrator responsible for providing support services

It is not easy for a relatively large and fluctuating group of people to meet regularly to discuss thorny issues in a consistently amicable manner. Clear communication among members of the team is therefore critical. In a team that functions efficiently, each member respects the perspectives of professionals in his or her own and other disciplines, and can embrace other points of view (Mandell & Gold, 1984). The participation and interaction necessary for effective teamwork are dependent upon team members who are prepared with data, upon proper distribution of leadership functions, adequate and complete coverage of the agenda, an accepting, non-threatening climate, and upon a continual evaluative process for the group (Hill, 1977). When team members know themselves, and establish trust and empathy, they will be able to engage in profitable discussion. They can do so by listening actively, with a sense of other people's feelings, being honest, and avoiding value judgments. The team should also try to promote the importance of both sending and receiving messages (Fiscus & Mandell, 1983). Team personnel must feel that their contributions are valuable and that all have equal status in the group. There must be a clear definition of the role of each member and available times for communication among them. As long as the interests of the student under discussion are held paramount, professional territoriality should disappear and communication remain open.

Parental participation

It is often helpful to have parents involved in the discussions and decisions of the school-based team. (Students, especially adolescents, may also be present on occasion.) New legislation has created an unprecedented opportunity for parents to participate in the process of making educational decisions. They should, however, be allowed to choose whether or not they involve themselves. Usually, parents will not attend early sessions at which team members share information, but they may certainly take part in later discussions.

Although important, parental participation in educational planning remains tenuous, at best, and a number of barriers to wider participation have been identified. Parents themselves see difficulties arising from logistical problems (such as taking time from work to come to the school), communication problems, lack of understanding about the school system, feelings of inferiority, and uncertainty about their child's exceptionality. Teachers view parental apathy, professional time constraints, and lack of expertise as obstacles to full participation (Turnbull & Turnbull, 1986). It is vital to the educational and social well-being of the exceptional student, however, to establish good relationships among the school, parents, and classroom teacher.

At the infant and preschool level, parents are ideally placed for early intervention. They know their children, spend more time with them than anyone else does, and can work with them on a one-to-one basis, thereby reducing the costs of instruction and other services (Stile, Cole, & Garner, 1979). Parental participation often decreases as the child reaches school and grows even less as he or she proceeds through the system; by the secondary level, it is not a predominant feature. Nevertheless, the expectations held by parents of school-age children match those held by teachers. Whatever the age of the student, parents are natural sources of reinforcement in the educational process (Allen, 1980).

Teachers should never think of parents as critical outsiders, but instead as extra resources. Parents can contribute knowledge and discernment about their children that can help teachers to improve educational programs. Parents ought not be seen merely as passive receivers of information: they have a viable role to play in the formulation of educational policy for their children, in classroom visits and activities, and in ongoing evaluation.

A number of approaches have been used to expedite parents' participation in the educational process, although all tend to fall into three broad categories (Beale & Beers, 1982). The *parental education* approach, most prominent at the infant and preschool levels, focusses on teaching parents what they need to know in order to stimulate and maintain progress in their children at home. *Parental involvement* implies bringing parents into educational situations and putting them to work. The third approach involves simply *communication* between educators and parents, which can be encapsulated as "I talk, you talk, we talk." The feelings and attitudes of all involved family members should be considered as far as possible in any planning for special learners. When professionals are aware of all the relationships within a given family circle, they are more likely to make realistic decisions for both the home environment and the classroom (Winzer, 1989).

Parents rely on teachers to provide them with relevant information concerning their child's education. Professionals have the responsibility to share this information and to keep abreast of current issues in order to serve all pupils in the best way. To bring parents comfortably into the educational process, information must be presented in terms that they readily understand. Educators love jargon and few parents will be assertive enough to question the meaning of technical terms. If professional jargon must be used, then it should be explained in terms of how it relates directly to their child and to the teaching situation.

When working with parents, teachers frequently find themselves in the role of counsellor because they are often the first people with whom the parents have developed a trusting relationship concerning the child. It is therefore important that teachers are aware of a good counsellor's characteristics: he or she must both listen to parents and impart to them her or his own desire to work with them, designing and realizing an effective program for the child. Working together helps to build a bridge of mutual trust, but the process is not always easy. Parents often feel angry and hurt when they find that their child has a handicapping condition and they may project their anger onto teachers. This leads professionals in turn to adopt defensive stances; they fail to realize that the parents may be experiencing an array of feelings related to their child's diagnosis, and may also be frustrated in their attempts to obtain special services.

The anxiety that both parties may feel in an interview can be eased if teachers hold clear objectives about the purposes of the conference. Generally, teachers will wish to alert the parents to concerns about a student's learning and behaviour, share information and suggestions about those concerns, and endeavour to establish a co-operative atmosphere in which to search for solutions. The list below presents more specific ideas to facilitate interviews with parents:

1. Begin by explaining the purpose of the interview.
2. Ask the parents if they have any information to share.
3. Adjust the sequence of topics to be discussed to the anxiety levels of the parents.
4. Frame questions clearly, economically, and naturally.
5. Attempt to get beneath superficial answers.
6. Move rapidly through the interview, but allow adequate time for parents to respond.
7. Stress the positive aspects of the student's development.
8. Explain any terms that may be unfamiliar but try to avoid using confusing educational jargon and acronyms.
9. Explain test results in understandable terms and outline the limitations of the data.
10. If the parents are unhappy about results or decisions, support their right to obtain another opinion.
11. Inform parents but don't patronize them.
12. Listen to the parents, solicit their ideas and opinions, and let them know that you want to solve problems with them.
13. Avoid comparing the student to others.
14. Be sensitive to the individuality of both the student and the parents.
15. Be perceptive and honest about the limitations of your own knowledge and ability.
16. Handle emotional scenes tactfully but firmly.
17. Prescribe solutions for the present.
18. Avoid long-term predictions about the student's functioning and achievement.
19. At the close of the interview, ask the parents if there is any other pertinent information that they wish to share.
20. After the interview, record all relevant information immediately, inform appropriate persons of any decisions, and ensure that plans are carried out as agreed.

The format of the individual education plan

An IEP identifies only those parts of the curriculum for which the student requires special education and/or related services. The document typically authorizes a modification of the standard school curriculum that may include changes in content, methods of instruction, materials, or expected rate of progress. The items included in the IEP need not be restricted to academic areas, but can also encompass social adjustment, vocational education, physical education, adaptive behaviour skills, and so on. Two different typical formats are presented in figures 4–4 and 4–5.

School district: School:
Grade or current placement: Date of birth:
Date of meeting(s):

Persons present:
Individual program beginning ______________ until ______________

Recommended placement:
Reasons for recommendations:

Related services required:

Curricular areas requiring special education:	**Mathematics**	**Reading**
Present levels of functioning		
Annual goals		
Short-term objectives		
Strategies		
Materials		
Division of responsibilities		
Evaluative methods		

Figure 4–4 Suggested format for an individual education plan, no.1

As can be seen, the first plan is far more comprehensive than the second, a variation characteristic of IEPs from one place to another. Most, however contain some or all of the following components:

- a statement of the placement, or educational setting, considered most appropriate for the exceptional student
- a summary of the student's present level of performance across a range of domains
- long-range, or annual goals
- short-term objectives for each annual goal
- a description of the specific educational and support services needed to attain each educational objective
- a list of the personnel who will hold primary responsibility for specific long-range goals and short-term objectives
- the date for the beginning of special education services
- the anticipated duration of the services
- the level of the student's integration into the regular classroom
- the strategies and materials necessary to fulfil the educational objectives
- unbiased evaluative procedures for each objective to determine whether or not it has been reached
- procedures for re-evaluating the complete IEP document

A. School information:

B. Student information:

C. Present levels of functioning:

D. Annual goals:

E. Short-term objectives:

F. Educational services required:

G. Personnel:

H. Evaluation:

I. Placement:

Figure 4–5 Suggested format for an individual education plan, no. 2

Each of the above components is discussed in the remainder of the chapter, with emphasis on drawing up goals and objectives. From the classroom teacher's perspective, goals and objectives are the most important part of the IEP because they provide specific instructional direction.

Assessing present levels of performance

The student's entry-level skills and concepts establish the starting point for planning goals and objectives. The highest level of skills that the student currently possesses in each functional area is considered to represent an accurate statement of present functioning, and is determined by close scrutiny of the diagnostic data.

In conjunction with diagnostic data, school-based reports form an important aspect of the IEP documentation (see box 4–2). School-based reports are usually compiled by the classroom teacher and contain information specifically related to the student's classroom performance. They are prepared with the intent to provide sufficient information to be useful for programming recommendations, and are therefore more comprehensive than the earlier referral forms. School reports should, however, be concise, summarizing only those factors pertinent to program decisions, rather than attempting to reconstruct an entire case file.

Box 4–2 Suggested format for a school-based report

A. School history:	Chronological listing of school and class assignments, with notes on unusual or discrepant patterns of performance and behaviour.
B. Physical, medical, and health factors:	Description of any physical accommodations, medications, or special physical considerations.
C. Family and social factors:	If the parents will share the information, these factors should be included but only so far as they are relevant to instructional planning.
D. Behavioural factors:	Description of any unusual behaviour as it relates to teachers and peers in the classroom and the school environment.
E. Diagnostic information:	Description of observed classroom strengths and weaknesses, as well as the results of teacher-presented assessment measures.
F. Programming intervention:	Brief description of intervention strategies to date, with comments on the degree of success.
G. Other considerations:	Any other relevant information that may be important in placement and programming decisions.

Determining educational placement and related services

The first decision that the educational team makes after gathering and assessing all the data determines the course of all further discussions and decisions: they must decide if the student is exceptional and in need of special education and related services. If the answer is yes, then the team must consider the best placement for the student. Determining the least restrictive environment for each exceptional student is not easy, because it involves so many different factors.

The IEP document should specify the amount of time that the pupil will spend in the regular classroom (expressed as both a percentage of the total instructional time and the number of hours) and in which subject areas. The needs of the regular classroom, and the availability of related services, must also be considered. Regular classroom placement is not warranted if there is potential harm to other class members. Very aggressive, acting-out children, for example, can totally disrupt a classroom and hinder everyone's learning. Their placement in regular settings may convince other children that highly aggressive behaviour is tolerated, if not acceptable. As well, unless support services are at hand, the regular classroom may not be the most suitable environment for an exceptional student. Braille-reading blind students, for example, can usually function adequately in regular classroom settings, but to place the learner with a teacher who has no knowledge of either blindness or the necessary educational adaptations may be inappropriate. Support services must be available to help the teacher to adapt the curriculum and use the technical equipment. A specialist in orientation and mobility, as well as someone well versed in special reading devices, will also need to be available for the blind pupil.

Chapter 2 outlined some very general conditions for integrating mildly handicapped students into regular classrooms. These criteria generally reiterate those of Schubert and Glick (1981), who believe that children considered for integration should

- be capable of doing work at grade level, to some extent
- be capable of doing work in the regular classroom without too much assistance, special materials, or adaptive equipment having to be provided by the regular classroom teacher
- be capable of staying on-task in the regular classroom without as much attention and feedback from the teacher as was available in the special education setting
- be able to fit into the routines of the regular classroom
- be able to function socially in the regular classroom and to profit from the example of appropriate behaviour modelled by their peers
- be able to adjust physically to the regular classroom, perhaps with some adaptations, so that the setting does not interfere with the student's functioning
- be given a flexible schedule to accommodate various classes as well as changes in the student's progress

Whatever the decision made about placement, it should not be viewed as immutable. Exceptional children must be given a variety of educational placement options, as necessary. As the IEP is reviewed, placement decisions are scrutinized for possible changes.

Setting educational goals and assigning priorities

Once the school-based team has reviewed the student's levels of performance and determined how different they are from the rest of the class, it establishes goals and objectives. These are the heart of the IEP. They represent the content or substance of a student's educational program, and are chosen for their relevance to the student's present functioning and current and future needs. The skills selected for the student to master must provide the pupil with a functional behaviour that will directly enhance his or her ability to live independently, a priority that should direct all goal-setting activities.

The individual education plan demands two types of commitment: long-range goals and short-term objectives. Both of these are necessary constituents in order for the plan to be functional and effective. A **goal** is really a general, long-range aim or direction, whereas an **objective** is a very specific statement derived from the general goal. A long-range goal represents an estimate of accomplishment, based on the identified needs of the student and defined in terms of her or his growth and development. A goal may state, for example, that a particular student "will demonstrate skills in writing job applications," whereas the short-term instructional objectives will delineate the particular skills to be covered in order to attain the general goal, and will specify the level of mastery required.

Goal setting is important for several reasons: it involves teachers in the ongoing evaluative process; it encourages motivation, participation, reinforcement, and feedback, all of which are essential to learning; and it provides unambiguous, measurable results. Setting goals has another benefit: it engenders good communication between the evaluator, who assesses the student, and the teacher, who must translate the goals into actions. Finally, goal setting is consequential because it begins the process of sorting learning objectives into their order of priority.

There are certain principles that should be adhered to in setting goals:

- Goals should be few in number. Too many will render the process unwieldy and make writing objectives an arduous task.
- Goals should be significant. Those that are of most importance to a student at that particular time in his or her educational career take priority.
- Goals must represent a needed change in behaviour or a challenge for the student, focussing on areas of learning and behaviour that require attention and improvement.
- Goals should be specific and measurable even though they are much broader than objectives.
- Goals need to be realistic and attainable. It is futile to set goals that students can never reach. A poorly motivated grade eight student, for example, who reads at a mid-grade two level, is unlikely to attain the reading standards of a regular grade eight student in one school year.
- Goals must be clearly stated in writing, in terms readily understandable to professionals and parents.
- Goals should be modified as necessary. They are not written in stone and should be altered as the student's progress indicates.

Long-term goals cover an extended period, sometimes up to five years; the usual span, however, is one year. The duration of services is based entirely on the needs of individual pupils. Some students require special education for only a short period, while for others it is a continuing process throughout their school careers. Although there is no set model, an IEP typically includes three or four annual goals for each selected area (Schultz & Turnbull, 1984). Because of their breadth, they do not deal with the minutiae of the instructional program; it is the short-term objectives that add specificity (as can be seen in the example below). These are statements of intent or expectation, to be achieved within a specified period of time. They should cover at least three months, and are generally written in monthly or weekly installments. The objectives are obtainable, but tentative, and must be consistently appraised in light of a student's changing needs.

The IEP extract reproduced below contains some goals and objectives used by a teacher's aide working with a severely reading-retarded ten year old. The aide was not responsible for the entire reading program but extracted specific long-term goals and short-term objectives, and then broke them down into a progression of activities for each session. In other words, daily lesson plans were drawn from the short-term objectives. Immediately following each session, the aide wrote an evaluation to determine whether the objective had been attained, so that the student's progress could be discussed with the teacher.

Goals and objectives for a reading-retarded ten year old

Long-term goals:

- to create an interest in books that will motivate Chris to want to read
- to introduce books that are high in interest and low in vocabulary
- to show Chris that reading can be fun and enjoyable

Short-term objectives:

1. We will cut out pictures of interest and paste them on paper (put together a book).
2. Chris will give me a sentence to describe what is happening in the picture. We will then paste this sentence at the bottom of the page.
3. Chris will complete the book by giving it a title and below the title he will print his name.
4. He will be able to read the sentences in his homemade book.
5. He will draw a picture and give a sentence to tell what is happening in the picture. Then he will print the sentence at the bottom of the picture. (This picture will also be put in his homemade book.)
6. After reading a page of a story, he will tell me what happened in his own words.
7. After reading a small book he will tell me the main points of the story.

Objectives for today October 7th	What happened?
1. To read a simple story to Chris. After each page he will relate to me what has taken place in his own words.	Chris was aware of the events of the story and has no problem telling me the story in his own words.
2. Once the story has been discussed page by page, ask Chris to restate in his own words the main points of story.	I tried to get him to read each page before discussing it but he had trouble with some words and I helped him with the words. After trying to read we then discussed the story.
3. After looking at a Winnie the Pooh story and discussing the pages, Chris will give me a sentence to tell what is happening in at least three or four pictures.	Chris enjoyed the pictures of Winnie the Pooh because he said "they were funny."

October 9th	
1. After discussing "objects that fly" Chris and I will construct objects such as an airplane, bird, clouds, sun, moon. Each object will be drawn on an individual sheet.	Instead of using the topic "objects that fly" we discussed a book about dogs. Different dogs were discussed and Chris chose at least six of his favourite dogs. Chris and I drew a picture of each of the six dogs on separate sheets of paper.
2. After drawing the object Chris and I will make a sentence to tell about the object.	Then Chris gave me a sentence to describe each dog.
3. These pictures will then be put into another homemade book.	Next day we will paste each picture on construction paper and make a homemade book.
October 14th	
1. Chris and I will paste pictures of the dogs we made last day on construction paper. Under each picture he will tape the sentence describing the dog.	The objective was achieved but Chris's interest tended to wander.
2. Chris and I will make up a simple poem (about four lines) about our book of dogs.	With some encouragement we made the poem and put it in the book.
3. We will complete our book and decide upon an appropriate name for it.	The title "My Special Dogs" was chosen.
4. Chris and I will discuss what animals would make good household pets. Chris will print two lines about two of these pets.	Did not attempt this Oct. 14th.
5. Chris read his new book "My Special Dogs."	He did not have much trouble with most of the words in his new book.

Source: D. Squires, 1987 (unpublished).

Preparing instructional objectives

All learning is goal-directed and instruction therefore needs stated objectives. It does not matter whether or not instruction takes place in a formal classroom setting, nor whether the instructional level is preschool or secondary. What *is* important is that the person offering the instruction knows the direction that learning should take, and is clearly able to communicate these expectations to the students.

Precise objectives are necessary in order to establish an exact sequence of instruction. The objectives should be arranged in sequences from simple to more difficult, and from high to low priority. Although there is no single method to do this, the general rule here is that the more the student needs a skill, the higher the priority assigned to the corresponding objective that will meet the long-term goal. Teachers must be able to write good instructional objectives if they are to individualize instruction effectively. These objectives each describe a specific behaviour, indicating what the pupil should be able to do following instruction.

Objectives should be presented in behavioural terms, as explicitly as possible. Basically, they describe what to teach, how to evaluate skill acquisition, and what materials and activities to employ. The specific elements of an objective are: a condition, a criterion, and a terminal behaviour (see table 4–1). The **condition** refers to the situation in which the student is to perform the desired task. Conditions frequently include the materials used, the amount of verbal direction given, and the setting in which the behaviour is to be performed. Conditions vary depending upon the behaviour desired and the intent of the objective. The **criterion** dictates how well a student must perform the behaviour before the performance is considered sufficient to proceed to the next objective. It also specifies the number of opportunities that the student will have to perform the behaviour, for example, every session for three or four sessions, or on each of three or four consecutive days. The **terminal behaviour** denotes the performance that the child will produce; in other words, the student will be able to complete a specified act (the terminal behaviour) under certain conditions and to a particular criterion.

Some objectives, however, especially those in the social areas, do not lend themselves to behavioural phraseology, but should nevertheless be stated in terms of anticipated student outcomes and supplemented by the criteria that will be employed to determine the degree of accomplishment. If the goal, for example, is for Peter to increase his interaction with peers, the objective may state, "Peter will work with another student on an art task for fifteen minutes." The amount of time is the criterion. It introduces too many intangible factors, however, to state, "When seated at a table with another student and presented with an art task, Peter will interact appropriately for fifteen minutes."

Different objectives will stress different qualities in the performance of a task. In helping a student to improve in spelling, for example, the teacher may be most concerned with accuracy. The objective could be: when presented with twenty consonant-vowel-consonant (CVC) words orally, Jim will write them to 90 percent accuracy. In another instance, the instructor may be interested not only in the accuracy of a performance, but in the fluency and speed with which the student performs the task. Fluency, correct speed, and accuracy are components of good oral reading, for example. Again, as a student becomes more automatic with number facts, the time taken and accuracy exhibited on a work sheet in arithmetic becomes important.

Selecting an objective as close as possible to the student's present level of functioning requires separating the skill to be learned into precise, graded steps that build toward a larger goal. It is a good idea to begin a little below the student's existing competency level. This ensures success and builds motivation at the outset, as the student has already mastered the first two or three objectives.

The first step in writing an instructional objective is to determine who is going to complete the action stated by the objective: the student, the teacher, the parent, or some other person involved in the educational process. The second step is to decide upon the action. Because it must be measurable, vague terms such as understand, know, appreciate, try, discover, think, and enjoy should be avoided. More measurable terminology includes words such as arrange, dramatize, pick, choose, draw, point to, or circle. With the actor and the action set down, it is then necessary to state the object of the action. As an example, Maria (the actor) will write (the action) ten CVC words (the object). As well, conditions are imposed to make the task easier or harder: Monique (the actor) will hop (the action) for thirty seconds (the object) on her right foot (the condition). The final step is to develop an evaluative criterion. This should be flexible, and is generally set at somewhere below 100 percent.

Table 4–1 details the format of instructional objectives, indicating the different terminology that they may employ. Further examples of "objectives in action" can be found in case study 4–1, part 2, which presents an extract from the IEP prepared for Sally, the student introduced at the beginning of this chapter.

Table 4–1 Preparing instructional objectives

Who	Does	What	When	How much
	Terminal behaviour or learning outcome		Condition	Criterion
The student	◆ names ◆ identifies ◆ spells ◆ selects ◆ repeats ◆ explains ◆ chooses ◆ restates ◆ operates ◆ draws ◆ records ◆ quotes	◆ three words ◆ all red items ◆ the long rods ◆ a reading passage	◆ when directed ◆ from among a group ◆ when presented with flash cards	◆ to 100 percent accuracy ◆ to 90 percent correctness ◆ in twenty seconds ◆ on three consecutive days

Case study 4–1, part 2

Extract from an IEP

Present level of functioning:

Mathematics: Sally's skills are at grade level, but she has a poor memory for number facts.

Reading: Her functioning is at a mid-grade one level, with a limited sight-word vocabulary and no real beginning in basic skills for word attack and few phonic skills. Sally does, however, show relative strengths in understanding through listening, concept development, and the use of oral language.

Handwriting: She is left-handed, which may contribute to the problems. Her handwriting shows many deviations, malformations, reversals and difficulties in near and far point copying.

Social skills: At the moment, Sally is regressing socially and emotionally, displaying withdrawn behaviour punctuated by increasing numbers of temper tantrums. It is felt, however, that if Sally can be helped to achieve some academic success, her poor behavioural patterns may be reversed. It is therefore important to focus on her strengths while improving her deficits. Sally's oral comprehension is a strength that she could use by listening to a story, and then retelling it to the class, or taking part in a dramatization activity.

Suggested placement:
A combination of resource-room and regular classroom time appears to be the most appropriate option for Sally at the moment. She will go to the resource room for remedial reading work, which will then be integrated into regular classroom programming.

Long-range goals (one school year):
- to provide Sally with beginning skills in reading by teaching a sight vocabulary of two hundred words from the basic Dolch word list (Dolch, 1936)
- to provide beginning word-attack skills by reviewing all sound–symbol associations and extending those to the use of a word-family approach (see chapter 8 for more information)
- to stimulate interest in reading by using an enactive approach
- to help Sally improve her handwriting by introducing cursive writing
- to practise near and far point copying
- to employ writing skills copying enactive stories (see chapter 11 for more information)

Short-term objectives (one month):

Objective	Techniques
1. When presented with stimulus words, Sally will recognize and say the words to 100 percent accuracy.	Use groups of five sight words on flash cards with a look-say method.
2. When presented with simple sentences incorporating the sight words, Sally will read them orally.	a) Use flash cards to have Sally make sentences. b) Present Sally with whole sentences to read out loud.
3. When presented with word families using a short *a* in the medial position, Sally will say them accurately 90 percent of the time.	a) Have Sally match words to pictures on a chart. b) Using families and initial consonants, have Sally make words such as b-at and c-at.

4. Using an enactive setting, Sally will give a series of four sentences after manipulating the objects.	a) Have Sally manipulate objects. b) Prompt her to produce sentences. c) Write the sentences in the correct form and have Sally copy them. d) Read the sentences; have Sally read them.
5. Using chalk, a large paint brush, and then a large pencil, Sally will produce the beginning looped letters for cursive writing.	Present Sally with patterns such as *eee*, *lll* and *iii* to copy on the board, on an easel, and then on paper taped to her desk.
6. On demand, Sally will reproduce practised, separate cursive letters accurately on large, folded paper.	Give Sally oral directions to follow while she writes cursive letters on large, folded paper.
7. Using a large pencil and paper taped to her desk, Sally will copy the patterns and join different letters.	Have Sally copy from the board and from paper to produce cursive joins, such as *eil* and *lie*.

Task analysis

Objectives have two major characteristics: they stress the pupil's behaviour rather than the teacher's, and they specify precisely what the student is expected to be able to do following instruction. Each skill taught should either be in itself a functional behaviour or a building-block skill that forms an element of a functional behaviour. To ensure that skills are taught in an appropriate sequence, it is often necessary to undertake a **task analysis**, to break a skill into its smallest components.

Task analysis is actually something that we all do daily. When we go to a restaurant, for example, we first look at the menu, decide what we would like to eat and how much we wish to pay, then match the two considerations and, finally, place an order. It would obviously be illogical to call the waiter before going through the early sequence of steps. Educationally, task analysis is used for assessment and instruction. It is not a casual process; the ability to develop high quality task sequences involves a logical thought process and the aptitude to perceive the fine details of how a task is completed.

Task analysis of a particular area of skill is a blueprint for assessing behaviour, teaching new skills, and subsequently modifying the program (Langone, 1986). Because analysis breaks a task down into its smallest components, a teacher can locate exactly the point at which a student encounters difficulty. For the same reason, the approach provides an instructional sequence that works very well for exceptional learners. By analysing objectives and teaching the material in small building steps, teachers can help students to grasp the information more quickly. Once the elements of a task are mastered, they can be synthesized into the complex level required by the complete task. Two examples are shown in box 4–3.

As can be seen, a task analysis describes the subskills necessary to accomplish a given objective by breaking a task into its behavioural components and prerequisite skills. The steps are then taught in a linear progression and a subsequent step is not attempted until the former one has been mastered.

Box 4–3 Task analysis

Objective: Leslie will tell time by five-minute intervals.
Prerequisite skills: number knowledge, counting by fives, some concept of the passage of time
Task analysis:

1. Given a clock face with no hands, but with marks for the numerals, the student will print the correct numerals.
2. Given a clock face with numerals and only an hour hand, she will read the hours when directed.
3. Given a clock face with hour and minute hands, the child will read time by hours and half hours.
4. Given a clock face with hour and minute hands, and with the hour hand held still, the student will count by fives in order to give minutes by five-minute intervals.
5. Given a clock face with hour and minute hands, Leslie will read time by five-minute intervals.

Objective: Peter will print his name legibly without the use of a model.
Prerequisite skills: ability to hold a pencil, ability to draw straight lines and circles, knowledge of the letters of the alphabet
Task analysis:

1. Given a printed model of his name, Peter will trace over the letters.
2. Given only dotted lines, the student will trace over the letters.
3. Given a model missing the final letter, he will trace the first letters and complete the final letter without help.
4. Given a model with two letters missing, Peter will trace the letters and complete the model.
5. Given a model with only the first letter available, the student will trace the first letter and complete the name.
6. Peter will write his name without the use of a model.

Task analysis plays an important part in helping teachers to adapt the content level of the curriculum to determine pupils' readiness, teach groups of students with varying skills, and produce instructional alternatives that avoid failure. It individualizes the demands that a task will make on students, and allows them to meet each demand (Junkala, 1972). The amount of material presented is directly related to the accuracy of the student's response (Blake, 1976).

There is no unique analysis for any given objective: a special education teacher may identify fifty steps for one task and a grade two teacher identify a dozen. The learner's classroom performance determines the size of the steps. Yet there exists a range of techniques for preparing a task analysis of intended objectives. It is not always obvious which techniques provide the most effective analysis and more than one may be used in a program.

Slicing is particularly useful in areas of academic skill such as reading, spelling, and arithmetic. To teach a student CVC words, for example, the teacher may "slice" the skill into the following tasks:

1. Read aloud twelve CVC words with a short **a**, such as b**a**t.
2. Read aloud twelve CVC words with a short **e**, such as b**e**d.
3. Read aloud twelve CVC words with a short **i**, such as b**i**t. (This would continue until all the vowels are mastered.)

Chaining breaks an objective into a number of component behaviours that can be performed separately and that have a fixed order. These are taught individually and then linked or chained together. Although the chaining technique is more frequently used in areas such as self-help skills and motor development, it is occasionally useful in academic subjects such as spelling and language correction. A teacher may use chaining to help a language-delayed child with syntactical development and use. To stress the structure *noun phrase* + *verb phrase* + *noun phrase*, for example, as in "John caught the ball," she or he would present most of the sentence, "John caught the...," and the student would complete the chain. Then the teacher would present, "John caught...," for the student to complete, and so on.

Shaping is most useful in analysing tasks that involve fine motor control rather than for academic skills. The same action is used in all the objectives, but the materials change. A student experiencing difficulty with letter formation, for example, may practise patterns on the chalkboard, then move to a paint brush and easel, and finally to a large pencil with folded paper.

When preparing a task analysis for an objective, some points should be kept in mind. Frequently, when breaking a skill down into smaller components, some unnecessary steps will emerge that should simply be deleted. Also, the listed tasks should be taught in the order in which they are performed within the skill. Clearly, when teaching a child to tie her shoes, grasping the laces would come before tying the bow. As well, tasks must be taught from the most simple to the most complex.

Entry behaviours are sometimes necessary before a student can perform the easiest steps in a task analysis. A student learning addition problems that involve carrying, for example, needs prior skills in counting and a knowledge of number facts and place value. Although there will usually be many entry behaviours, there are generally two or three critical ones and teachers may wish to list these in the analysis.

The true test of how well a task analysis works is in the teaching situation. If the student fails then the tasks were too difficult or the appropriate entry skills were not present. This is the time to change the task or restructure and simplify the analysis.

Selecting activities and approaches

The most challenging aspect of the IEP process lies in selecting and adapting instructional approaches, activities, and materials to meet the set of objectives. Because teachers must instruct many children, they must strike a balance between individualization and practicality, but it takes careful planning to develop materials and activities that can be used on many levels at one time. To illustrate the point, a class of very young children using finger paints can benefit in several different ways from the activity. The general objectives are to provide all children in the class with some experience of creative art and to enhance their social skills through co-operative work. The activity could also serve, however, to strengthen the weaker arm of a child with cerebral palsy and to teach colour mixing to a gifted youngster. With sand added to the paint, a visually impaired child can be exposed to a new tactile experience. The teacher can also teach new vocabulary, about colours and shapes, to a language-delayed child (Deiner, 1983).

The teacher must think in terms of the underlying principles of the activities when choosing them for exceptional learners. Teaching begins at the student's level: it ensures that all the stated objectives will be met, and it proceeds in small, building steps. Generally, the less serious the handicapping condition, the more diverse and numerous are the teaching strategies employed.

Good materials individualize and supplement the regular curriculum. The exceptional student may indeed be taught the same curriculum as the others, but be provided with additional materials to teach prerequisite skills or allow more intense instruction and practice over a longer period. The materials selected must be compatible with the needs of the exceptional learner and match the teacher's beliefs. If the teacher sees little efficacy in Cuisenaire rods for arithmetic, for example, then the likelihood that a great deal of learning will take place is reduced. Special materials are discussed fully in chapter 5.

Assigning responsibilities

Classroom teachers are not alone in their efforts to provide efficient programming for exceptional students. When the IEP is formulated, a decision should be made about the relative responsibilities of all those involved in the education of the special learner. This information is entered on the IEP form (see figures 4–4 and 4–5). Often, the classroom teacher and the resource-room teacher will take responsibility for specific areas, co-operating with one another and working in tandem. Itinerant teachers, speech therapists, orientation and mobility specialists, and other personnel may also share the responsibility.

Establishing evaluative procedures

Evaluation is a mechanism to refine the IEP by monitoring a student's progress toward mastery of goals and objectives. If objectives are clearly written, they will contain the necessary evaluative criteria for determining when a student evidences the desired behaviour or skill. Case study 4–1, part 2 specified, for example, that Sally would reproduce separate cursive letters on demand. Evaluation is, of course, inherent, based on whether or not Sally can complete the task after appropriate instruction and practice.

Evaluation should concentrate on three questions: are the set goals appropriate, are the listed services being delivered, and is the student evidencing gains in skill? If the student does not exhibit positive changes in learning and behaviour, the plan should be changed rather than the student blamed. Evaluation is ongoing and should accommodate flexibility in the IEP.

Translating the IEP into classroom practice

The IEP is the beginning point for instruction. From there, the teacher translates the IEP into weekly and daily lesson plans. To do so, he or she needs to decide on ways to adapt the curriculum content. The teacher must determine the instructional strategies that will be most effective and manageable in the context of the whole classroom. Procedures to co-ordinate instruction between different educational settings, to evaluate the IEP, and to assign grades are all also necessary. All of these issues are covered in the following chapters.

5 Classroom management

Lesson plans
Report cards
Materials
  Packaged materials
  Self-correcting materials
  Games
Computers in the classroom

Dear Reader,

Special schools exist in recognition of the following facts: grouping is an essential reality in education; mainstreaming is an ideal and is not yet realizable for many exceptional students; and educational systems continue to need specialized facilities that can focus on the deep-seated disabilities of severely handicapped students. These facts suggest, not that we should avoid reducing the number of special schools in Canada, but that whatever movement we make in this direction should be carefully planned. Philosophical positions such as normalization and mainstreaming are not enough unless those who hold these positions are willing and able to engage in the real work of preparing educational systems to meet the needs of exceptional students.

We need to recognize that the greater the handicap, the greater the need for long-term planning. Before teaching any exceptional students we must identify specific goals and objectives for them, based on input from the students, the parents, and any other appropriate sources. Many exceptional pupils are difficult to teach because they are not focussed, and it is therefore helpful to share the goals with them.

The long-term planning process for exceptional students does initially require much time and effort from staff, but the subsequent benefits outweigh the precursory costs by far. For many exceptional pupils the past represents failure and the present threatens the same. By building bridges into the future, we add a positive dimension to their lives: the pupils learn that the future can be planned, and the plans realized. If they need a great deal of help in this, then that is our job.

For teachers, too, a long-term planning process is decidedly beneficial. Since planning requires teamwork, it reduces the likelihood of breakdowns in communication. Teaching cannot possibly be an isolated activity in this context, and ad hoc measures are unnecessary. Teachers like to work in a planned environment in which directions are clearly articulated. It gives them a sense of purpose and relieves them of the stressful business of having to deal with the unclear expectations of an unplanned work situation.

Clive J. Hodder
Program Director
The Trillium School
Milton, Ontario

Have you ever watched the staff of a fast food restaurant during the lunch rush? Within all the bustle and flurry, everyone behind the counter is actually well organized: they know exactly what to do and where everything is kept. Everything is placed conveniently to cut down the steps in preparation, and a set routine is followed when taking and filling food orders, packing trays, and so on. Often, a manager circulates in order to prevent snags or offer assistance. What could be chaos is actually very efficient.

Like the supervisors in a fast food restaurant, teachers must be excellent managers. They manage the learning and behaviour of students, and the efficiency with which they do so is an important variable in the productivity of the organization — in this case the classroom. Their management style controls students' output in terms of the quality and quantity of work, and determines students' attitudes toward their peers, learning, and school life in general. The teacher must keep class members organized, motivated, task oriented, and productive. Rewards should be made meaningful, and adverse behaviours reduced to a minimum. In order to accomplish these aims, teachers must be acutely aware of what is happening in the classroom (Kounin, 1970). They must demonstrate empathy and understanding and have the ability to communicate effectively with students.

If teaching is conceptualized as the structured presentation of content in order to provide productive school experiences, then the validity of teachers as good managers is obvious. Also, good classroom managers appear to be happier and to suffer less stress. They tend to be perceived by their colleagues as good teachers, especially if they manage students' behaviour well.

Classroom management implies manipulating the classroom environment to facilitate students' achievement of academic and social goals (Englert & Thomas, 1982). The ultimate aim of good management is to ensure that all students will be able to manage their own behaviour and co-operate with others.

Decisions about the use of time and space, the pace of instruction, the manner in which the curriculum is structured, and the way that students are grouped for instruction can directly affect their attainment of basic skills. Classroom control, motivation, and appropriate rewards enhance the process.

Efficient management depends upon several interrelated factors. The *physical environment*, which includes the architecture, furnishings, and seating arrangements in the instructional space, should be well lit, airy, and carefully designed. *Instructional arrangements* include the content and character of the curriculum, teaching methods, educational materials (such as books and games), and instructional media (such as films and overhead projection). Additionally, the effective learning environment requires that the teacher understand each phase of the instructional process and be able to select the instructional approaches and learning strategies best suited to individual students. The third component necessary for good management is the *classroom climate*, the learning atmosphere. This includes behavioural control, discipline, group dynamics, and social relationships among and between the students and teacher. The management style of the teacher forms and maintains the classroom climate. The classroom can be organized or chaotic, supportive or authoritarian, a pleasant learning environment or a difficult place to exist.

Good managers assume an active role in creating a stimulating and orderly classroom environment in which positive learning experiences take place. They also attempt to formulate balanced programs that provide all students with academic, personal, social, and daily living skills. These teachers realize that they are charged with teaching youngsters who can master the curriculum content of a grade two to four times faster than average as well as those whose learning is below the norm. They recognize the individuality of all students and set objectives designed to challenge bright students, foster the abilities of average learners, and overcome the deficits of those with learning difficulties. Effective managers realize that the mix of instructional objectives within and between domains will vary considerably according to the different types and degrees of strengths and functional limitations among students.

In regular classrooms, exceptional pupils require a number of physical and curricular modifications. Generally, the more severe the exceptional condition, the greater the modifications and the fewer instructional alternatives the teacher will have. Instructors are therefore challenged to find innovative ways of enriching the learning environment to accommodate learning differences and behavioural difficulties. Students may need special attention because of limited ability, poor motivation, sensory or physical impairments, specific learning disabilities, or a combination of several factors.

Classroom management, classroom discipline, and individual behavioural control interweave and influence each other. Effective teaching and learning demand a regulated but rewarding milieu in which individual rights are respected. This chapter deals with some general approaches to teaching special learners and planning individualized programs, and then discusses methods for classroom management. The next chapter treats the development of social skills in exceptional learners as well as those most vital of all apsects of classroom management, discipline and behavioural control.

The main objectives of this chapter are to

- discuss some fundamentals of teaching and to draw from them some instructional approaches for exceptional students
- describe those teaching and learning conditions that enable students to develop in the least restrictive environment
- detail aspects of the physical organization of the classroom
- present strategies for record keeping
- describe materials appropriate for exceptional learners
- introduce the use of computers in the classroom

General approaches to teaching exceptional students

Alter and Goldstein (1985) view teaching as a paradigm. They observe that someone (the manager of the learning) teaches something (the content of the curriculum) to somebody (the learner), somehow (with strategies and tactics), somewhere (the learning environment), at some time (according to a schedule, at a particular pace, and with attention to learning variables). This text views teaching as an art, but also as a technology. On a practical level, teaching consists of a number of elements: the curriculum and accompanying documentation laying out goals and desired behaviour; the procedures to be employed in the educational setting; the instructional materials; and the setting itself, which is a unique combination of curriculum, methods, and materials.

Teaching involves a blend of both technical knowledge and interpersonal skills. Good teachers apply principles drawn from the study of learning, teaching, motivation, and development, and combine these with warmth and empathy. They are capable of interacting with students, setting clear rules and procedures, and effectively monitoring group and seatwork activities (Englert & Thomas, 1982).

Box 5–1 Teaching mildly handicapped students

Academic tasks

- Explain skills and concepts in a concrete, realistic manner.
- Avoid digressions.
- Organize material into meaningful segments.
- Use reinforcement and incentives.
- Use plenty of drill and practice.
- Teach children rehearsal strategies.
- Do not teach skills in isolation. Relate teaching to other subject areas, and especially to everyday matters.
- Avoid calling on students unless you are sure that they want to contribute.
- Instruct small groups for only short periods: twenty minutes is probably long enough and never more than thirty.
- Insist on accuracy and ensure mastery at one level before moving to the next.
- Before presenting any materials, assess the level of readability.
- Preface all remarks with a title, or the main idea of the lesson.
- Indicate the important points during a lesson by saying, for example, "Listen carefully," or "This is important," and then changing the volume and tone of your voice.
- Vary presentations, so that both written and visual components are included.
- Use diagrams and visual materials frequently so that the students may grasp ideas without depending solely on language.
- Never assume that pupils have heard and comprehended until you have asked them to repeat the information verbally.
- Give advance notice of each required task by statements such as, "When I blow the whistle, you go to the white line."
- Immediately after teaching an important concept, check students' power of recall.
- Schedule more time for activities than would be required by a normal group.
- Make sure that all paperwork handed out is legible.
- Allow short answers to questions.
- Allow slow writers enough time to finish tests.
- Post all crucial information on the board in note form.
- Provide self-tests and checklists so that students can monitor their own programs.
- Before an examination, provide practice questions.
- Teach students to scan examination papers and to underline key words.
- Modify grades to reflect intra-individual differences.
- Provide for overlearning.

The following discussion centres on those instructional factors and applications that are especially important in teaching exceptional students, and on this topic there exists no universal agreement. The field is so broad and the students so varied that summary generalizations are obviously difficult and often superficial. Among learning-disabled children, for example, diversity in characteristics and functioning is intrinsic to the population and many methods for remediation have therefore evolved. Some stress teaching to strengths (Johnson & Myklebust, 1967); others emphasize teaching to weaknesses (Bannatyre, 1971); and others lean toward multisensory training (Gillingham & Stillman, 1965). Because the evidence concerning any single teaching approach for exceptional students is far from compelling, a number of general techniques are presented here.

Adaptations for many exceptional students lie in the intensity of instruction, the pace of lessons, and the content of the curriculum. There are general guidelines to stimulate and improve learning for special learners in regular classrooms (see boxes 5–1 and 5–2). Although the list may, at first glance, seem overwhelming, a careful reading will reveal many familiar elements.

Box 5–2 Mildly handicapped students in the classroom

Behaviour

- Maintain a supportive emotional climate.
- Be specific and consistent in what you expect and be systematic in following it through.
- Stick to classroom routines.
- Provide structure in the classroom: teach subjects in the same order and have the same adult or peer working with the student each time.
- Guarantee success in academic learning.
- Seat special students near to the front of the room or use carrells if necessary to reduce distractions.
- At least once a day, give students classroom chores that they can successfully complete.
- Demand a reasonable and flexible degree of conformity. The special student may not listen intently when you read to the class, for example, but neither should that student be permitted to divert the attention of others.

Stages of learning

There are a number of crucial stages of learning that apply to all students in all learning situations (see figure 5–1). The first stage is **initial acquisition**, the student's initial exposure to the skill. Since the task is new, it is vital to present it in a logical, organized manner, with much hands-on activity. Teachers have high success when initial instruction proceeds in small steps and pupils practise the new knowledge and skills until they have overlearned them (Brophy, 1982b). This instructional strategy is successful with both older and younger students. For younger children, especially, profitable learning requires a large amount of successful practice. In the first three years of school, the average child spends the time trying to master the basic, well-recognized skills in reading and arithmetic. Learning is enhanced when the basic skills become automatic, and overlearning them is necessary for higher cognitive processing (Beck, 1978).

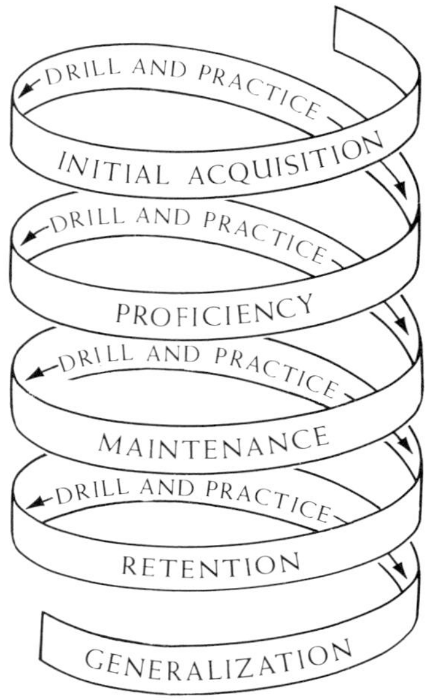

Figure 5–1 Stages of learning

The second stage, **proficiency**, implies building on the original task. At this stage, pupils need to repeat the task over and over again. In mathematics and spelling, automaticity should be the terminal objective. Students who are mildly handicapped need much *drill* (repeating a task) and extensive *practice* (applying the task to similar situations). In mathematics, for example, students may be drilled on number facts by rote repetition, work sheets, and games. They may then practise the skills by performing a task, such as applying the number facts to addition problems. Drill helps students to acquire new information or behaviours and begins their progress toward proficiency; practice brings them to a level at which they can maintain the skill.

The repetition involved in practice and drill can lead to boredom and we can see the effects of boredom in patterns of performance. Bored children show increasing numbers of errors, decreasing fluency, and mounting behavioural problems. It takes a creative teacher to devise ways to make daily practice enjoyable and rewarding.

When students have reached the **maintenance** stage, they perform the skill even after instruction ceases. Students do not maintain a skill when they are not motivated to use it, do not understand its underlying logic, or simply forget the behaviour. Exceptional children need extra help to maintain skills. They may need the skill reviewed many times and should be provided with opportunities to use it in many different contexts.

Retention refers to the proportion of material that students remember over a given period of time. They are likely to have better retention when the material is meaningful. Teaching it in segments and helping students to understand the inherent concepts and relevant language will therefore improve their retention.

Generalization is ongoing throughout any teaching process. It involves developing strategies with which to associate the relevant dimensions of similar stimuli. For example, if a child learns to sound out the word r*a*te using a long *a* rule, then it is hoped that the pupil will generalize the skill by applying it to new stimuli, words such as h*a*te, l*a*te, and m*a*te. With the ability to generalize and transfer skills, learning in one context influences learning in another. Students can then apply skills outside the classroom in a variety of ways.

Components of the instructional process

The general stages of learning are inherent in all classroom activities. In addition, instruction should encompass: daily review; questions, reinforcement, and feedback from the teacher; and seatwork assignments. For daily review, the teacher checks previous work to see if either remediation or reteaching is necessary. Homework, particularly, loses any value if it is not checked and analysed for recurring errors. Every lesson should contain a component that reviews the previous work in an area or, if a new topic, tests the level of students' prior knowledge. Those who have already mastered the material should be allowed to pursue different areas of the curriculum (see chapter 16).

Several different activities are effective for review. Teachers can go over concepts and skills, and correct homework; students may correct each other's papers, and give the teacher their reaction to homework items of particular difficulty. Teacher-directed questioning is the most common effective mode of review at all levels.

When students first practise new skills, they need numerous questions and prompts from the teacher. Teachers influence the way that students think by asking questions that elicit description, explanation, expansion, or evaluation of a topic. Nevertheless, teachers tend to ask factual questions (Sitko, Bachor, & Slemon, 1980) and this is especially prevalent in classrooms for low-achieving pupils (Brady, 1977). Many educators are embarrassed by a lack of rapid verbal response, even if students are clearly thoughtful. Some teachers, in fact, report a sense of panic when questions are not answered immediately (Gambrell, 1980). The average amount of time that teachers allow for responses is one second (Rowe, 1978). Yet they must be prepared to cope with silence, because some students will abandon their attempts to answer if they cannot construct a response in the time provided (Cacha, 1981).

Certain questioning techniques will help to elicit responses:

- Ask questions that require more than a yes or no answer.
- Ask questions about specific knowledge only when recall is important.
- Allow students sufficient time to deliberate about the question and formulate an answer.
- Try to sequence questions.
- Reword questions when children fail to respond, or respond incorrectly.

- Avoid repeating questions in exactly the same words.
- Be acutely aware of altering questioning techniques for certain class members. A severely language-delayed child may, for example, respond better to questions that are phrased for either a verbal or a non-verbal response.
- Occasionally give a student the question before the lesson begins, to encourage him or her to become organized and attentive.
- Ask questions that require analysis, synthesis, and evaluative skills once pupils have mastered a given task.
- Do not always accept the first response to a question, even if that response is correct.
- Question students' responses in order to elicit a higher level of thinking.
- Direct questions to all students who appear willing to participate, not just volunteers or the brighter class members.
- Generally, do not call the name of a student before asking a question. Directing a question to a specific student sometimes can, however, decrease inattention and off-task behaviour.
- Try to avoid students' constant handwaving by either ignoring it or verbally stopping it.
- Reinforce the behaviour if students use time to deliberate or give a thoughtful answer (Belch, 1975; Mandell & Gold, 1984).

Teachers may evaluate how well students understand material by the quality of their oral responses. It is therefore important that all students be given an opportunity to respond and then provided with positive feedback. Figure 5–2 illustrates the possible

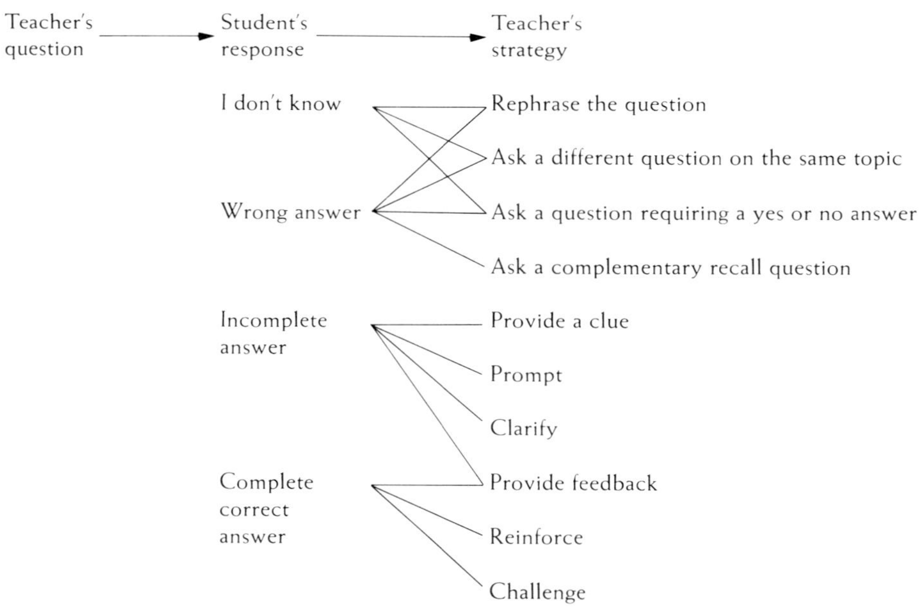

Figure 5–2 Techniques of questioning

reactions to students' responses. It should be noted here that although calling out answers is a poor way for students to make progress, it is best to get low-achieving students to respond in any fashion possible (Brophy & Evertson, 1976).

Throughout the learning process, it is important that teachers provide feedback, especially if the students are correct but hesitant. It is a source of reward and a fundamental learning device, but should not be confused with praise. Praise or special attention is given for a desired behaviour or performance. It is the type of reinforcement that tends to govern interpersonal relationships and can be very effective with exceptional students.

Teachers must be cautious, however: praise alone contains very little supplementary information. In fact, overusing praise can actually have negative effects. Students experience worry and anxiety if they believe that they can not continue to live up to high praise. On the other hand, they can become inured to praise, so that it holds very little value. At the secondary level, praise must be subtle or it may embarrass students and cause the peer group to react negatively.

While praise certainly creates positive feelings, teachers must be careful to identify clearly the behaviour being reinforced. Telling a pupil that his seatwork is "beautiful," provides very little information. For the teacher to say, "I like your work today because you have been very careful in your writing and have very few erasures," gives much more positive feedback. In other words, feedback is different from and more efficient as a learning tactic than praise. It helps students to identify areas that require change. Without precise information from the teacher, students will remain unsure and may constantly repeat errors, thus reinforcing poor learning.

When giving feedback it is best to use objective, measurable terms such as, "You were 80 percent right." For very young children, a consistently used hierarchy of praise related to specific behaviours is most effective. Work and responses could be judged as, "That's a try," "Good," and "Very good," so that children always understand the exact terms of the evaluation, in addition to comment on specific aspects of their work. As well, the wording can be gradually varied and always combined with non-verbal social cues, such as a smile. High praise, such as "Wonderful" or "Wow!" should be reserved for truly outstanding academic or social achievement.

Many, if not all, lessons are completed with some form of application, or seatwork, another component of the instructional process. Seatwork is the most common context for individual practice: students in grades one to seven spend more time working alone at seatwork than doing any other activity, approximately 50 to 75 percent of their time (Fisher, Berliner, Filby, Marliave, Cohen, & Dishaiv, 1980). Seatwork exercises should reinforce the content of the taught lesson. Students can learn more from seatwork if time is spent in lecture, discussion, and guided practice through the first seatwork problems. During seatwork, teachers should circulate actively, asking questions, providing short explanations, and responding to students. Contact should be brief, however: an average of thirty seconds or less. Longer contact suggests that the initial learning experience was not complete and more rehearsal is necessary. Learning is also enhanced when seatwork is broken into small segments, a particularly effective method for difficult material and for slower students (Emmer, Everston, Sanford, & Clements, 1982).

Independent practice with seatwork is intended to develop automaticity. To maintain a skill, students should be provided with weekly and monthly reviews. When planning seatwork exercises, keep in mind the following guidelines:

- Identify the particular skill or concept that the exercises are designed to reinforce.
- Do not rely solely on drill exercises using pencil and paper. Vary the type and format of seatwork.
- Estimate the amount of time needed to complete the assignment.
- Give careful directions, and check that all pupils understand what is to be done.
- If the seatwork takes the form of a group project, ensure that everyone in the group understands the rules.
- Have all the necessary materials ready.
- Remain accessible by circulating during seatwork.
- Decide in advance how feedback will be provided.
- For exceptional pupils, stress only one skill at a time. Challenge them but do not frustrate them.

Individualizing instruction

As discussed in chapter 4, when teachers individualize instruction, they plan programs and manage learning for each student on the basis of that student's demonstrated competence and motivational structure. Mildly mentally retarded students, for example, should progress through about two-thirds of a year's growth in one academic year. At the other end of the spectrum are gifted students, who require rapid pacing, a minimum of drill and practice, and extension of the depth and breadth of learning experiences.

Individualized instruction, in the form of the individual education plan, is not a teaching method but a plan for organizing instruction that may incorporate many methods (Klausmieir, Rossmiller, & Saily, 1977). It does not require any one form of educational service, setting, or teaching, and may be applied to individuals, within groups, or even to a whole class. The following general approach to individualization, however, is helpful:

1. Carefully assess the students, curriculum, and resources.
2. Give students opportunities to build the skills they need for individual learning: making choices about educational objectives, evaluating their own work, and sharing ideas.
3. Teach students the skills involved in co-operative assessment and setting goals.
4. Teach the skills that students need in order to learn in small groups: role playing, peer teaching, group analysis, and discussion.
5. Let the class assume some responsibility for planning and implementing the program.
6. Establish instructional areas that support individual learning, such as interest areas, learning stations, media centres, games areas, and reading and study areas.
7. Encourage students to use resources and alternative thinking activities independently (After Dunn & Dunn, 1975).

Individualization expects certain things not only from teachers but also from learners. Students must take an active part in the process by making some choice of educational objectives, selecting activities from a list designed by teachers, making independent use of instructional materials and media, asking for help when necessary, keeping to a schedule, and finishing assignments (Dell, 1972). Individualization involves learners in the decision-making process to a much greater degree than do other forms of teaching. If students are provided with choices, they will gradually accept responsibility for their own activities and behaviour.

There are a number of ways to incorporate individual programming into the regular classroom, although all imply that students work at their own rate, sometimes alone and sometimes as members of a group. Using one-to-one instruction exclusively is not generally the most appropriate method of individualization; instead the day's activities may be arranged into a combination of individual work, one-to-one tutoring, and large-group and small-group settings. An exceptional student may, for example, receive direct instruction from the teacher within a large-group setting, proceed to individual drill from self-explanatory booklets, and finally, move to a library corner to read something of her choice. Following these activities, the student may engage in a one-to-one tutorial session with a peer tutor. Various methods to individualize instruction in the regular classroom are discussed in the following sections, while others appear in later chapters.

Grouping

Groups can be effectively employed in the core and content areas if instructional objectives and materials are adjusted for each pupil's level of performance. In fact, some research indicates that academic gains are greater when pupils are taught in groups (Dunkin & Biddle, 1974; Medley, 1977).

A group has an internal interpersonal structure: students within the group communicate with each other as well as with the teacher. Membership is based on common learning styles, skill levels, and academic needs. Teachers should, however, allow for frequent shifts among groups during the school year (MacKenzie, 1983). Grouping and regrouping students blunts the stigma that a student may attach to a specific group (particularly if groupings are established on the basis of competency).

Groups work best when they contain approximately five children sitting in a semicircle with easily distractible children in the centre. Within these parameters, students should be trained to function using their own material.

Direct instruction

Direct instruction involves directly measuring a pupil's performance on a learning task and arranging instructional programs and procedures for that student in consequence (Haring & Gentry, 1976). The instructional environment and procedures are set up in such a way that both the learner and the teacher know exactly what is to be learned as well as the criteria by which learning will be judged. The teacher controls the instructional goals, chooses materials appropriate for the student's ability, paces the instruction, and guides the learner through a sequenced set of materials or tasks. The goals of the teaching activities are made clear to the students and the activities themselves are directly relevant to academic progress in the most conducive setting. Ongoing daily instruction covers content extensively. Teachers ask questions at the appropriate cognitive level, so that students can produce many correct responses. They give students immediate, academically oriented feedback, and monitor performances carefully. Direct instruction involves:

- using small-group instruction
- employing specified teaching procedures
- employing specified motivational procedures
- monitoring progress with criterion-referenced tests
- having a common logic in the selected teaching examples and program sequences
- using pretested, daily scripted lessons, designed so that teachers know exactly what to say and do
- training teachers to deliver the scripts in a specified manner (Condon & Maggs, 1986)

Direct instruction is a model that delivers both basic and advanced skills to a range of students, from the severely mentally retarded to those of superior intellect. It was originally applied to instructional programs in the basic academic areas of reading, spelling, language, and mathematics, but has been extended to increasingly complex levels of skills (Condon & Maggs, 1986).

Precision teaching

Precision teaching is a procedure used to make teaching methods more effective; not an instructional method in itself but an adjunct to teaching techniques. It involves making modifications to instructional and other school variables based upon individual diagnosis in order to assist the student's learning. As with direct instruction, precision teaching focusses upon a student's deficits and establishes what is educationally relevant in terms of the handicapping consequences of a particular condition. By concentrating on changes to the curriculum, precision teaching enables the student to have greater success in classroom work. Rather than offering rewards for completing tasks, it renders activities more suitable for the student's functional level. Precision teaching involves a series of steps:

1. The desired student response is identified and specified in behavioural terms.
2. Baseline data is collected and charted: the student is observed to determine how often a behaviour occurs and under what circumstances.
3. A strategy for change is devised and put into effect. The antecedents and consequences of the behaviour are manipulated to make learning more effective.
4. The resulting responses are charted; continuous observation is used to determine the result of manipulation.
5. The process repeats itself.

Task variation

Direct instruction and precision teaching are structured methods for presenting information and evaluating its acquisition. They emphasize bringing students to mastery, the stage at which they have achieved a predetermined criterion to the satisfaction of the teacher. The level of performance is numerically defined, usually as a percentage. Each skill is thoroughly mastered before another is introduced.

Task variation takes a somewhat different approach. The new skill is taught, but presented alternately with already acquired skills so that students consistently gain success. The process of alternating known and unmastered tasks during a teaching session can facilitate learning and heighten motivation for mildly handicapped students (Dunlap, 1984; Dunlap & Egel, 1982). A teacher wishing to employ task variation can follow these steps:

1. Select the new task.
2. Choose the review tasks.
3. Present the new task with known skills randomly.
4. Provide feedback and reinforcement.

Remedial instruction

The word *remedial* means providing a cure or remedy. **Remedial instruction,** therefore, is the process of improving or correcting a skill in a particular area in order to raise the individual's skill levels to normal or near normal standards. It can be used with children up to the age of twelve, at which point compensatory instruction begins. Remedial strategies are not mysterious: they are based on alert diagnosis of learning problems.

Although exceptional learners seldom have one learning deficiency, to which there is a single remedial response, special education teachers now realize that remedial instruction can nevertheless result in marked functional improvement for some of these students. Although remediation does result in new learning, other factors may also intervene. In some cases, students demonstrate substantial improvement because they merely needed a little assistance to fill in gaps in learning. In other instances, learners improve as much as a result of enhanced confidence as from new learning, or because the materials and approaches that induced failure before have been abandoned. For other students, a demonstrable advance in achievement may simply stem from extra attention and the new feeling that an adult is genuinely concerned.

When teachers remediate academic difficulties, they may find some of the following ideas useful:

- Secure the learner's co-operation. An active participant learns better than a passive one and success ultimately depends upon the student's participation in and commitment to the process.
- Set long-range goals and short-term objectives.
- Plan instruction in large conceptual blocks related to the structure of the subject matter and proceed in short steps.
- Begin each lesson with a review and then explain to the student the purpose of the current lesson.
- Guarantee success by beginning each lesson at an accessible level or in an area of strength.
- Vary the teaching techniques if necessary.
- Concentrate on one skill at a time, beginning with the simplest and most concrete.
- Teach pupils how to practise and overlearn the material, so that they will retain it.
- Provide opportunities for pupils to give their responses in verbal or written form, or by manipulating objects.
- Spiral the instruction by returning often to review material already covered.

- Give pupils opportunities to practise the skills under varying conditions so that they learn to generalize them.
- Encourage pupils to discover relationships.
- Give students immediate, positive feedback about their progress, and provide correction.
- Show students their own progress on charts and graphs, to enhance their affective development.
- Be flexible and evaluate strategies constantly.
- Keep tasks meaningful. Do not, for example, use a beginning basal reading series with a twelve-year-old retarded reader.

Remediation cannot counter all diagnosed deficits at once, but it should result in their gradual, steady elimination and a concomitant accumulation of success. Motivation, however, is the essence of remediation. The most interesting techniques and the most colourful materials will fail if the student shows little inclination to participate and learn.

Motivation

Motivation refers to a student's affective response to a problem, which then influences how she or he will solve it. Motivation is an essential ingredient of efficient learning especially for handicapped students, who need to channel their energy, intellect, personality, strength, and dexterity into constructive behavioural and learning skills.

Motivation arises from a number of sources: success, knowledge of results, interest, concern about academic progress, fear of failure, and various other intrinsic and extrinsic forces. Children and youth will only learn new academic and social skills if they are motivated to do so. Yet motivating children, especially those with already battered self-concepts and poor self-esteem, is extremely difficult and a tremendous challenge for teachers. Students who have suffered years of school failure often develop **emotional overlays** — adverse reactions to learning problems — and **outward loci of control** — the tendency to attribute all events, whether good or bad, to outside forces or luck.

Ideally, students would be naturally motivated to learn new skills, but their actual level of intrinsic motivation is often insufficient — exceptional children are young, handicapped, and human. Teachers therefore often rely on external motivators such as rewards, and use a range of techniques subsumed under the general rubric of behaviour modification (see chapter 6). Students need help to develop constructive and socially acceptable responses to frustration and other forms of stress. They must learn how to participate in groups and develop a positive attitude about themselves and others. While it can only be assessed through its manifestations, motivation will definitely increase with success in academic tasks. The old saying that success breeds success is as true for exceptional learners as it is for anyone else.

Compensatory instruction

Although it is difficult to separate remedial teaching from compensatory instruction, we generally look at compensatory strategies for children older than twelve (Wepman, Cruickshank, Deutsch, Morency, & Strother, 1975). **Compensatory instruction** refers to counterbalancing or substituting one skill with or for another. Because some factors

Children work well with peer tutors.

prevent children from acquiring normal or near normal skills, they must be provided with skills in another area and taught to use their best skills to meet the demands of school.

Some types of compensatory education are obvious. It would not be reasonable, for example, to try to take profoundly deaf students through a series of phonic exercises in order to teach reading and spelling. Their auditory deprivation must be compensated by building a strong sight-word vocabulary.

In other cases, for learners with less severe impairments, only a subtle change is necessary in the way a skill is taught. The student may need to be seated in a different place, have the skill broken down into smaller steps, or employ different equipment. The teenager who cannot learn the number facts or the tables may use a calculator. The child who can never remember which hand is which may learn to distinguish by checking for a freckle on the left hand.

Co-operative learning

As the term implies, co-operative learning is a procedure in which students work together in pairs or small groups. The results of co-operative learning have been very successful: students have been observed to increase their productivity and change their attitudes to school. To facilitate co-operative learning, teachers can plan the activities in advance, train students in leadership if needful, observe their interactions, intervening only when necessary, and evaluate work according to predetermined criteria. The rationale and process of co-operative learning are addressed in greater detail in chapter 6.

Peer tutoring

Peer tutoring has proven very effective for mildly handicapped students. Mildly retarded and learning-disabled students tutored in word recognition, spelling, oral reading, word-attack skills, and multiplication have proven to learn more effectively than they do in small groups instructed by teachers (Dale, 1979). The procedure also provides valuable assistance to overworked teachers, and uncovers the potential in peer interactions for constructive educational experiences. Peer tutoring therefore benefits both the tutor and the student.

Students who have peer tutors do not have to wait for help from the teacher. As well, they may very well co-operate better with a peer. The learner who is more relaxed working with a peer than with the teacher is better able to concentrate on learning (Ehly & Larsen, 1980).

The tutor may develop improved social skills, academic motivation, a growing sense of responsibility, and a more positive attitude toward school. Tutoring allows more capable students to move from their usually passive roles into the attractive position of being the teacher, and may prevent them from becoming bored and restless. Peer tutors can experience heightened self-esteem if they feel that they are a valuable and influential part of the classroom environment. They gain status in the eyes of other students, attention and rewards from adults, and respect from younger pupils. Peer tutors may also learn academic skills themselves; the best way to learn the real essence of material is to teach it to someone else.

Even though the impact of peer tutoring programs has been well established, any program can be diminished by inadequate planning and supervision. To ensure the success of a program, it is therefore essential that teachers monitor peer tutors. Although tutors volunteer their services, they should go through an orientation. The learning tasks should be structured beforehand by the teacher. During sessions, tutors must have clear objectives and adequate, familiar materials. Each tutor must demonstrate mastery of the skill before teaching it, and should tutor regularly.

For the teacher instituting a peer tutoring program, the following steps apply:

1. Select the peer tutors.
2. Train the tutors in the skills to be taught.
3. Demonstrate techniques of instruction, reinforcement, and evaluation for the tutors.
4. Observe the peer tutors in several practice sessions.
5. Structure the material to be taught with flow charts (see figure 5–3), which tutors may then follow throughout sessions.
6. Continually monitor the progress of the tutorial sessions.

Classroom management

As was observed at the beginning of the chapter, the most important elements of classroom management are classroom climate, the physical environment, and the instructional arrangements. Classroom climate is dictated in a large measure by the teacher's management style. The following sections therefore first discuss the teacher's classroom approach, then various aspects of the physical environment, and finally, instructional arrangements. This last part of classroom management incorporates many elements, such as scheduling, record keeping, the curriculum, lesson plans, report cards, and instructional materials. A relatively new consideration is the use of computers, and this is dealt with in the final section of the chapter.

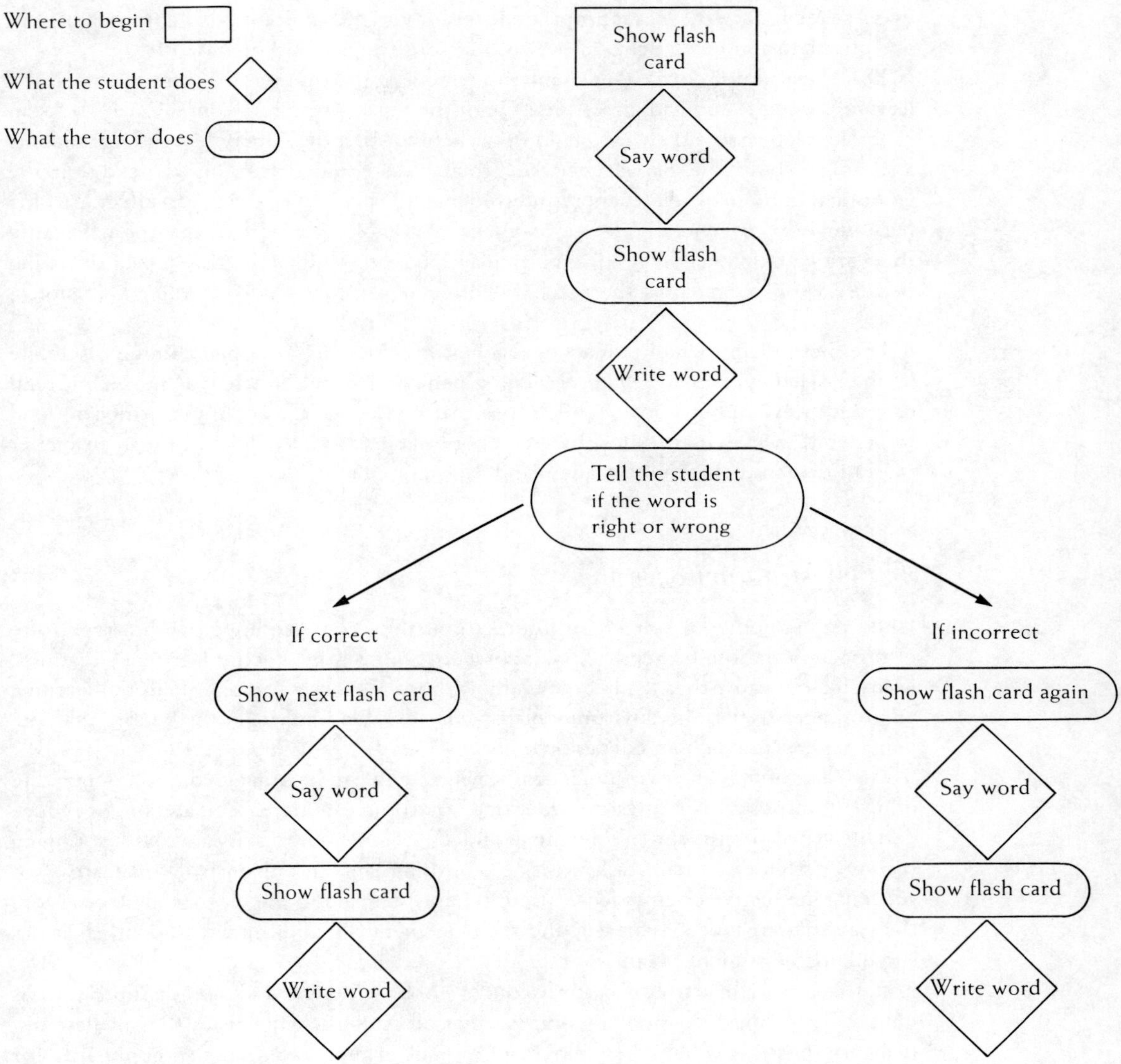

Figure 5–3 Flow chart for peer tutors

The teacher

Teachers can stimulate students' enthusiasm by being enthusiastic themselves, and they must be careful to do so because pessimism is as catching as optimism. Teachers can convey enthusiasm by movements, gestures, variations in voice, eye contact, and overall energy level. They need to position themselves well in the classroom, observe every student directly, use appropriate forms of verbal and non-verbal communication, and circulate among students in between lessons (Englert & Thomas, 1982).

The physical presence, stance, and movement of the teacher are components of the learning process, and can affect the pace of the lesson (Apter & Conoley, 1984). As an example, teachers who always stand or sit behind their desks may be sending students a message about the barrier between them. Since much learning depends on the emotional bond between teachers and students, the act of distancing can affect learning negatively. Even generally active teachers may avoid one part of the room because they are uncomfortable with a particular student. Ultimately this is self-defeating because it only decreases the teacher's influence on that student (Apter & Conoley, 1984).

The methods by which a teacher teaches are also critical in maintaining discipline (Cohen, Medley, & Soar, 1980). Teaching behaviours that enhance achievement tend to reduce deviant behaviour, while those that do not, such as constant criticism, tend to generate negative attitudes toward school. These may be linked in turn to higher rates of deviant behaviour, truancy, and dropping out.

The physical environment

Children are active organizers of information; they come equipped with a repertoire of processes that help them to make correct responses in specific learning situations. Many factors can either facilitate or inhibit those responses, among them the learning environment itself. The environment has considerable impact on the energy that students expend in reaching educational goals.

The classroom is an environment for learning, and can be organized to accommodate different purposes. The physical order of a classroom can increase, maintain, or reduce certain types of student involvement and communication. This involves arranging seating, designing certain task areas, establishing small-group instructional areas, or reducing ineffective open spaces. Attention must be paid to the teacher's line of vision, the way that areas are separated, and the placement of handicapped students. Settings should enable students to interact.

In the classroom, traffic patterns ought to be efficient and non-disruptive. It is important to organize the classroom so that all students will create the smallest disturbance possible when they move into small groups, walk to the cupboards for supplies, or go to their lockers for materials. As well, furniture should be positioned for the utility and comfort of the student. Of course, unalterable factors such as the available natural light and the placement of fixed blackboards and bulletin boards will affect the arrangement.

Bulletin boards should be designed to teach, stimulate, and interest children, and should carry displays of their work rather than materials that appeal to adults. A special message on the bulletin board each day for particular students can enhance their affective development.

It is possible to structure space to increase a teacher's control, thereby circumventing disciplinary problems. Classrooms should be set up to avoid clutter and have as much open space as possible. The teacher must be able to scan the class easily, as this is

A well-organized classroom stimulates learning.

probably the single most effective technique for controlling behaviour. It is also necessary for safety and maintaining on-task behaviour. Really effective teachers are aware of everything that goes on within the confines of their classroom at all times.

Most regular classrooms assign each student a place at a seat or table that constitutes a kind of home base where tasks are done. Straight rows of desks are more conducive to quiet, individual tasks, while less formal seating arrangements usually signal collaborative activities or discussions. Some students are more distractible when seated near certain classmates, or pay more attention when seated near the front of the room. Disruptive students who are grouped with well-behaved students display fewer disruptive behaviours and the group as a whole tends to remain well behaved (Stainback, Stainback, Etscheidt, & Doud, 1986).

For some exceptional students, the physical layout of the classroom is of paramount importance. Someone using crutches should be seated near the door to avoid an obstacle course of desks, feet, and bags; a wheelchair-bound student may require a specially lowered desk or table; and a visually impaired pupil may need more space in which to lay out equipment. These students should be seated as near as possible to the group settings to which they may need to move within the classroom.

Physical adaptations are an additional factor in the physical environment. In certain cases, integrating an exceptional student involves the teacher with some novel technical devices. Teachers of the hearing impaired, for example, may use an FM (frequency modulation) system; teachers of visually handicapped youngsters must develop familiarity with various reading devices. Discussion about specific physical adaptations, types of technical equipment, and prosthetic devices necessary for exceptional learners is embedded in the categorical chapters.

Creating learning areas

The following sections outline some of the general physical and organizational strategies that ease the integration of exceptional pupils into regular classrooms. By establishing specific areas in the classroom, a teacher can improve the environment for small-group work and individualized instruction. He or she can create a social interest centre, for example, simply by stocking an area with games, puzzles, books, and other high-interest activities, to be used as rewards. Reading corners, learning centres, offices, small-group instruction centres, and listening stations are all excellent for individualized work. Obviously, however, not every classroom will have all of the areas described below.

Reading corners

To motivate students to read, one must provide them with interesting books and materials, and a comfortable place in which to read them. They will interact with print better in an environment that encourages literacy. Reading areas work successfully at both the elementary and the secondary level, using the same basic components: shelves of books and comfortable chairs or cushions on the floor. Creative ideas seen in Canadian elementary classrooms include setting up the reading corner as a boat, a space ship, or a bath tub.

This is an example of a learning centre for science.

Learning centres

The learning centre is an area of the classroom that contains a collection of activities and materials to teach, reinforce, or enrich a skill or concept, or stimulate exploration in further subjects. Learning centres are popular structures because they provide an alternative to directed lessons, and are excellent vehicles for activities designed as a sequel to direct instruction. They allow the teacher to provide pupils with self-directed learning experiences that furnish immediate feedback.

Learning centres are particularly successful as vehicles for individualized instruction. Within the centre, instruction can be tailored to different modes and rates of learning. Teachers can devise specific activities to match needed skills and yet allow students a choice of activities. Mildly handicapped children proceed at their own pace while gifted youngsters pursue open-ended and divergent thinking activities and projects.

The area should be a colourful and motivational instructional device. It can contain activity cards, directions, games, and work sheets for students to complete independently. The activities and materials should be related to teaching objectives, and varied enough to appeal to a wide range of interests and abilities. Activities range from simple to difficult and from concrete to abstract. They should encourage learners to observe, classify, and manipulate materials, to use numbers, and to communicate.

A learning centre is most effective when used by one student or by a small group. If it is properly designed, the area will:

- constantly rotate activities and skills to maintain interest
- contain materials and activities relevant both to the student's everyday classroom instruction and to the teacher's philosophy
- be a prime method for individualizing programs
- promote socialization as well as academic learning when used by small groups

- be relatively independent of assistance from the teacher
- have a built-in evaluative component

Within the classroom, a learning centre can be organized as a separate area at a table or in a cubicle. The centre may be time-consuming to construct, but it can have a life span of many years. It is a good idea to let students help plan aspects of the learning centre. They can further their own needs and interests and so help to individualize activities. They may also overcome any negative attitudes they hold about certain curricular areas. When preparing a learning centre:

1. Select a topic limited in focus so that the students are not overwhelmed.
2. Write objectives on which the activities will be based.
3. Collect inexpensive or free materials for the centre.
4. Prepare materials such as task cards, work sheets, student record forms, and decorations to attract interest.
5. Use every available resource, such as film strips, rewards, and puzzles to stimulate interest.
6. Create activities that take into account students' different characteristics, levels of sophistication, and modes of expression, so that they can all participate.
7. Place the centre in an area of the classroom where it will not disrupt traffic patterns or other activities.
8. Schedule times for students to work at the learning centre, to avoid confusion.

In order to evaluate the success of a learning centre, prepare record forms to keep track of students' participation and the results of all completed work. To assess work, use spot checks, observations, pupil–teacher conferences, assignment sheets, and individual and group testing.

Offices

For students with attention deficits, cubicles or carrels offer a useful means of reducing incoming stimuli. It is easy to construct individual cubicles from large cardboard boxes or even chart stands. A distractible pupil may work in the "office" but join the rest of the class for group activities. Students are responsible for the appearance of their own offices.

Small-group instruction centres

A small-group centre allows the teacher proximity to students when they are engaged in reading groups or other small-group lessons; it provides cohesiveness between the teacher and the students. The area may be defined by tape, a round table, or a rug. Students with mobility problems should be seated as near as possible to their own instructional area.

Listening stations

A listening station is a specialized learning centre that presents instruction by using headphones, tapes, records, and other forms of audio equipment. It can be useful for remedial or developmental work, or for enrichment.

Scheduling

The foundation of efficient teaching is efficient classroom organization, particularly for new teachers. The day will proceed much more smoothly and more will be accomplished if the teacher is fully aware of what is to be done, when, by whom, how, and why. **Downtime**, when little or no instruction occurs and the students have little or no knowledge of what to do or what comes next, contributes significantly to poorly managed programs in which various inappropriate behaviours can occur (Laycock, 1980b).

Careful scheduling is an intrinsic component of organization, since it is necessary both to manage time and to keep track of pupils moving in and out of the classroom. Elementary school teachers generally plan their own timetables, keeping in mind provincial policy regarding the various percentages of time to be devoted to different subject areas. At the secondary level, timetables are extremely complex and usually planned at the administrative level for the entire school.

By weaving exciting creative activities into the daily schedule and alternating the types of activity, teachers can plan enjoyable, interesting, and profitable programs. It is particularly important to keep blocks of time short for exceptional pupils. For all students, active sessions should be varied with quiet periods. Generally, for younger children, academic subjects such as reading, spelling, and mathematics are better taught in the mornings when the children are fresh.

Timetables should be flexible enough to accommodate changes in the students' moods. Trying to teach a new mathematical procedure when the class is excited after a recess game of touch football is not likely to be terribly successful. They will need a quiet period to calm down. Sometimes, the best planned lessons must be abandoned or delayed because of sudden changes in the learning environment. One Vancouver teacher, for example, was avidly trying to interest a class of very small children in a language experience story when it began to snow. Even though the teacher tried to ignore a somewhat unusual Vancouver weather pattern, the children lost any interest in the activity. Not only did a well-prepared lesson fail but a wonderful incidental learning opportunity was lost.

Schedules can be used as learning tools as well as organizational aids. When a schedule has been established, teachers should initially keep to a strict routine as far as possible. They can then plan deliberate changes to promote flexibility in the pupils (Hart, 1981). Planned changes teach students how to deal with sudden alterations in schedules in an appropriate and orderly fashion.

Strict schedules constitute an area of potential difficulty for mildly handicapped students at the secondary level, where they are expected to adhere to timetables independently. The responsibility may result in tardiness and even truancy. Other students arrive in class on time but armed with the wrong books or missing materials and homework. Secondary pupils should keep a timetable taped to the inside of the door of their locker and another one in a folder that is always with them. Some students may need assistance organizing their lockers: keeping books for the morning on the top shelf, for example, and afternoon books below, or colour-coding books by subject.

At several times during the day scheduling problems are likely to arise. Vulnerable times include the start and finish of the school day, transitional times when students arrive and leave a classroom, and the time between one activity and another. With exceptional students who need time in the resource room or with special personnel, classroom scheduling can be difficult. If their time for special help always clashes with art or physical education or a favourite subject, they may become resentful and apathetic. It is better to stagger times out of the classroom so that different areas are missed, or to schedule the help on alternate days. Of course, the schedule for exceptional students must remain consistent or it can be disconcerting to both student and teachers.

With students moving in and out of the classroom and going to various activity centres, it is often difficult to ensure that they follow their particular schedules. For younger pupils, display an enlarged version of the class timetable with different periods of the day marked in different colours. Individual schedules can be drawn up on a second large timetable or on individual sheets.

In addition, a teacher needs some method to keep track of students' whereabouts. Figure 5–4 illustrates an effective and easily constructed device for elementary pupils. Trip tickets are also useful to monitor students' movement. The ticket goes with the student and the teacher notes the time of leaving and returning (see figure 5–5). A master schedule for all students is posted in conjunction with trip tickets (Bullock & Mintz, 1979).

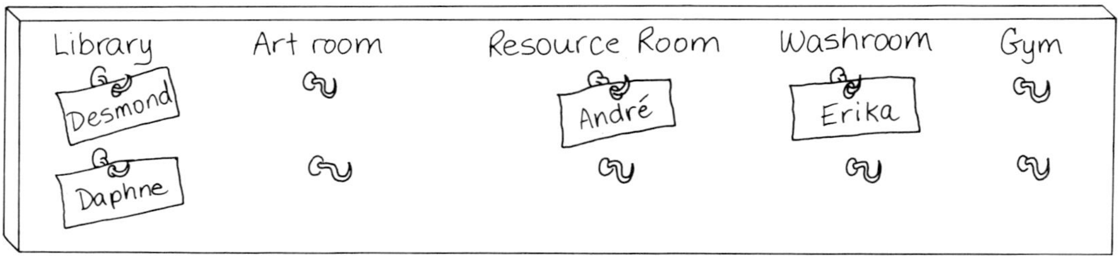

Use a piece of light wood with cup hooks

Figure 5–4 Keeping track of elementary pupils

Routines constitute a form of scheduling by providing firm expectations about coming events. They help children to know what they should be doing at a certain time. This is especially important for exceptional children and it is a good idea if teachers use cues or prompts before changing an activity, to help to make routines firm.

Particularly in the early stages of learning, children respond best to well-planned and highly structured regimes in which programming decisions are made on the basis of objective data. Teachers should therefore be very specific in instructions. Rather than saying, "Do ten math problems," it is better to specify, "You have twenty minutes in which to do these problems." Similarly, homework directions must be very clear, given in phrases such as "This work must be in on Thursday, in two days," or "This must be in the work basket at nine o'clock in the morning."

Figure 5–5 Trip tickets

Ancillary personnel in the classroom

Scheduling other personnel in the classroom is a vital step toward developing an efficient instructional system. Some teachers are lucky enough to have the benefit of a teacher aide or a volunteer, whose time must be deployed in an efficient classroom routine.

Chapter 2 mentioned the significant role that teacher aides and volunteers can play in the classroom. It is important, however, if aides are to be used to the best advantage, that they be given only tasks of which they are capable. It is a misapplication of resources to assign tasks beyond the aide's level of confidence, expertise, or training. As well, teachers should ensure that aides' responsibilities are of a supportive rather than a direct nature. They should not be expected to perform tasks that are parallel to the teacher's own responsibilities, such as teaching a whole class. The teacher is the primary designer, developer, and evaluator of the instructional program.

A second person in the classroom complicates discipline and it is therefore vital that the teacher and the aide show absolute consistency in all aspects of classroom management and instruction. This is in fact the most important point to remember when using a teacher aide. The teacher and aide can plan a schedule together that meets the needs of students and with which they are both comfortable. Any problems that arise should be discussed openly and frankly.

Supervising and evaluating another adult is often a new experience for teachers and can therefore cause some concern. Once the aide's help has been enlisted, the teacher often asks, "Now what can I do with this person?" The list, however, is considerable, as can be seen in box 5–3. The presence of a teacher aide creates a variety of different options for service delivery.

Box 5–3 Tasks for teacher aides

- assisting students with school work
- helping students to make reading and study booklets
- helping during art periods so that students can use more media
- assisting in group and science activities
- supervising activities in the learning centre
- arranging and adding to the materials in learning and resource centres
- assisting with language arts activities, by such tasks as story telling and leading discussions and reading groups
- helping children to record and copy experience chart stories
- helping individual students to correct written assignments
- correcting workbooks
- helping some students to stay on-task while the teacher works with others
- helping children to learn more appropriate social skills and expressions
- helping with fine motor skills such as tying bows and using scissors
- collecting library books and specific materials for lessons
- ordering and returning filmstrips and other materials
- operating audio-visual equipment
- displaying pupils' work
- helping students to keep desks and storage places neat and orderly
- keeping records of the books that students read
- completing non-confidential records, bringing information up to date, and filing paperwork
- making arrangements for and assisting on field trips
- helping with games during physical education activities
- arranging and supervising indoor games on rainy days
- handling commonplace interruptions such as notes, messages, telephone calls, and deliveries
- telephoning parents about routine matters

Record keeping

A simple but efficient system of record keeping is an essential component of an effective teaching program. Record keeping demonstrates whether the program is effective, and helps to monitor individual progress through all curricular areas. Good record keeping also allows the teacher to share a consistent view of the teaching program with aides, parents, allied professionals, and the student (Lund, Schnaps, & Bijou, 1983).

Instructional standards are tightening in an effort to increase accountability in the school system. Record keeping is therefore becoming an important issue, although often uniform recording techniques do not exist in school districts and individual teachers are left to develop their own systems.

In the broadest sense, there are three types of records. Documents concerned with the school structure, classroom organization, and scheduling are the first type and include attendance registers, timetables, and schedules for various school and extra-curricular duties and activities. Second, records are used to track and evaluate individual students. A teacher may hold files containing formal and informal test results, psycho-educational reports, data from team meetings, copies of report cards, anecdotal records, notes on parent interviews, and the like. Documentation that helps teachers to prepare, present, and evaluate instruction is the third component of record keeping. This includes the curriculum, unit plans, lesson plans, day books, and IEPs. Table 5–1 presents some of the most common types of records that may be kept in the classroom.

Table 5–1 Classroom records

Structural records	Records for tracking students	Teachers' records
Attendance register	Results of teacher-made tests	Curriculum for each subject
Class timetables	Standardized test results	Monthly plans
Resource-room schedules	Anecdotal records	IEPs
Individual schedules	IEPs	Instructional units
Details of yard and bus duty	Data from team meetings	Day books
Schedules of extra-curricular duties	Data on medical and physical accommodations for special students	Lesson plans
	Details of interviews with parents	
	Report cards	

Curriculum

The definitions used in the field of curriculum tend to be rather vague and global because different people hold different views on the relationship of the curriculum to the teacher and the learner. The terms curriculum, instructional program, course of study, curriculum guide, and many others, are generally used interchangeably (Gickling

& Thompson, 1985). Basically, a **curriculum** is a document written for a grade level and designed to benefit the greatest number of students. Hewett and Taylor (1980) define curriculum as "any activity, lesson, or assistance given to children which is directed toward assisting them in achieving competence in one or more of the six levels of learning—attention, response, order, exploration, social roles, and mastery" (p. 108).

Gickling and Thompson (1985) point out that curricula make explicit demands on users: they set standards of progress by designating a certain volume of material to be covered day by day and week by week. They also assume previous experience, because their developmental format is founded on what the student has learned before. Moreover, curricula are inflexible, placing the same demands on all students and therefore failing to respond to individual needs. Finally, they promote comparisons among peers. The inherent nature of curricula discriminates between students who succeed and those who fail.

The content of instruction is built on educational goals set forth by provincial and local educational agencies. In spite of Canada's regionalism and vast geography, a reading of provincial curricular guidelines reveals substantial similarity in both the images of educated persons and the means to educate them. Curricula are composed of sequences or strands that combine to describe the skills that students are expected to master. Where exceptional students are concerned, additional curricular decisions fall to the classroom teacher, who must break curricular goals into explicit performance objectives. Performances or tasks are themselves broken into lists of behavioural objectives, against which attainment can be measured. Such objectives then become the content of the lesson plans. This process, as we have seen, is often called task analysis.

The curriculum should stretch far enough to include the upper and the lower boundaries of skills likely to be exhibited by the students in the classroom. These upper and lower boundaries are used to establish lists of those skills to be acquired by the entire group. To individualize a curriculum for a certain class, the teacher must prepare courses of study or syllabi for each subject, founded on the level and aptitude of the average pupils in that class. The course of study describes which areas of the general curriculum will be taught to that group of students.

Teachers must know how to modify educational materials and curricular guidelines in order to teach logical skill sequences. In other words, they must know what material students should be taught, in what sequence, across a variety of levels. Although curricula specify learning outcomes, teachers are generally free to use their own instructional methods and to select most of the supplementary instructional materials. This allows teachers to establish their own general teaching style.

Integrated units

Unit teaching is a flexible approach to organizing the form and content of instruction. There are many ways to plan units, which may be organized around a central theme or around independent study. Teachers have long used unit teaching in specific academic areas. These units integrate skills, concepts, and information drawn from the curriculum, and are therefore known as integrated units.

The various experiences to which pupils are exposed within the unit are organized around a single theme, problem, or area of interest, presented in a series of lessons on related subjects. As an example, an integrated unit with the theme "people of other lands" could use mathematics to estimate distances across the ocean, art to draw pictures related to a particular country, social studies to make maps, and so on. As they progress, these units permit the teacher to evaluate students' understanding and achievement continuously. They incorporate all or many of the subject areas taught in the regular school day. The theme and the skills are taught in a variety of contexts so that students will reach mastery and be able to generalize them.

Using integrated units allows teachers to concentrate on teaching specific skills in a structured and logical progression while individualizing these skills for exceptional pupils. Units capitalize on the student's background and experience and allow teachers control over the instructional content of lessons. The teacher chooses appropriate material from the curriculum to include in the unit. For exceptional students, specific work on vocabulary and language should be part of all unit planning. When planning a science unit on animals, for example, the teacher would plan to teach needed vocabulary, semantic structures, and idiomatic expressions beforehand.

There is no single, formal pattern for constructing integrated units, but teachers may:

1. Select the theme.
2. Set attainable goals. Only include material that can be covered in three or four weeks, as a unit longer than this begins to pall.
3. Determine the content area around which to structure the unit.
4. Prepare an outline of essential information.
5. List the learning outcomes and objectives for the unit.
6. List the logical progression of core activities within the unit.
7. Note the materials and resources to be used and collect them.
8. Decide on a particular content sample for students to study first.
9. Design projects and small-group work.
10. Devise an exciting activity with which to introduce the unit.
11. Add additional learning outcomes as necessary.
12. Evaluate students' progress.

Lesson plans

A lesson plan is an important tool in education. Teachers of all ages and all degrees of experience devise and use lesson plans. A plan involves actually writing out the environmental events related to learning. It can be seen as an individual teacher's model of how to produce learning because it provides evidence that the teacher has thought about the lesson in terms of review, pretesting, the progression of steps, aids and materials, seatwork, evaluation, and individualization. Written lesson plans direct the efforts of both teachers and students by bringing the sequence and continuity of learning into clear focus. They provide a reference point for teachers during the lesson and a record afterwards.

Lesson plans are a valuable resource for teachers. While plans must be reviewed and updated from year to year to meet the needs of different classes, old plans serve as valuable starting points for new ones. The teacher can evaluate a lesson after presenting it, to reveal its strengths and problems and lay the foundation for future lessons.

Systematic planning involves making a specific set of decisions about ways to attain goals. It therefore ensures that academic deficits will receive attention and reduces the probability of overlooking behavioural or environmental events related to specific deficits. A plan guides the progress of a lesson, outlining the steps toward individual lesson goals. Yet lesson plans should never inhibit teaching or a teacher's creativity. Plans may be formal or informal, simple or complex, but they should be flexible enough to adapt to students' interest and responsiveness where feasible.

Report cards

Grading schoolwork by letters or percentages began in the early twentieth century in an attempt to rate education more effectively. It persists because education still needs a way to compare teachers' expectations with students' performances. The teacher evaluates a product, an attitude, or a strategy for solving problems to decide if it is good, worthwhile, desirable, or undesirable; in other words, to determine its value (Kinnison, Hayes, & Acord, 1981). The end product of evaluation in this sense is a grade.

Grades are assigned by comparing a student's progress with that of others in the peer group. They carry no inherent, stable meaning because they are assigned by various teachers, using informal tests. Teachers often demonstrate inconsistency when marking papers, and different teachers stress different aspects of the work, such as neatness or correct spelling. There is little correlation between school grades and later progress. They do not predict success in careers, living, or level of ability (Clark, 1983).

Although they do not necessarily motivate learning, grades nevertheless assume elevated levels of significance for a great many students, and are also important to parents. Teachers likewise stress grades, and assigning them is always a serious issue involving difficult decisions. In the regular classroom, awarding judicious and meaningful report cards to exceptional students is particularly difficult. Teachers must attempt to individualize instruction and also to keep grade inflation to a minimum.

When exceptional pupils are placed in regular classrooms, grades are usually assigned by the regular classroom teacher. Rather than assigning grades on an interindividual basis, it is more appropriate to grade exceptional students against their own personal set of objectives, to individualize report cards. Students should be marked on achieved minimum competencies rather than on a group norm. Individualized grades may be as appropriate for gifted students as for mildly handicapped students. Grades for gifted pupils can be unfair, misleading, or meaningless and may, as Clark (1983) observes, even penalize the students. Because grades are held in such esteem, pupils may be loath to venture into the unknown or to attempt areas at which they know they cannot succeed, and thus learn inappropriate coping strategies.

Systems employing multiple grades have been used successfully to evaluate the progress of exceptional students. One such system uses the three areas of ability, effort, and achievement. Ability in this context reflects the student's growth in the content area being studied, based on expectations of his or her ability to grasp the material. Effort describes how hard the student tried, and achievement compares the student's achievement with that of others in the same group. An average of ability, effort, and achievement provides the final grade (Kinnison, Hayes, & Acord, 1981).

In a point system, on the other hand, the student accumulates points for specified activities, such as essay writing, over a semester. The activities are given equal weight beside tests in order to accommodate students who may have difficulty reading, writing, or working under time constraints (Kinnison, Hayes, & Acord, 1981).

Materials

Appropriate materials will not make a good program, but it is difficult to mount a strong educational program without them. Materials designed for the specific learning patterns of individual learners are useful tools by which to individualize instruction and provide concrete experience of what is being taught.

Instructional materials are increasingly in demand. As they become more widely produced and disseminated, education is paying attention to materials as an important variable in the teaching process. Although choosing materials may be the first step in instruction for regular students, however, exceptional learners should be assessed first and then the appropriate materials for their programs selected.

Exceptional students may be provided with different materials, or simply more of them. Specifically, they might be given more concrete materials to supply extra practice and drill, stress a new idea, focus on a skill, or extend learning. Yet research has shown that many mildly handicapped pupils can use regular instructional materials (Browning & Regan, 1978). It is therefore advisable to present regular materials to exceptional learners whenever possible.

The most important characteristic of instructional materials is their application to specific deficits and learning objectives. Most published materials — textbooks, workbooks, and even programmed materials — do not clearly indicate their instructional objectives. They often progress in a linear fashion too slow for some students but without enough sequential steps for others. In order to be useful, materials must therefore be field tested.

Instructional materials should allow active responses, give direct feedback, and reinforce behaviour. They should also have easy, immediate methods of correction. The materials must be appropriate to the student's level of ability and maturity, and special, but changing, instructional needs. It is particularly difficult to select materials for secondary level exceptional students. Materials written and colour-coded for younger children are inappropriate and will only create resentment.

It is also important that materials serve the teacher, not dictate what is being taught. Once a basal reading series is adopted by a teacher, for example, she or he makes decisions about how to teach reading that are largely determined by the nature of the basals themselves. In recent years, the number and quality of materials available has increased dramatically, but teachers often pick items from available catalogues at random. Sometimes they rush to select materials at the beginning of the school year or at the suggestions of colleagues. In other cases, they make choices based on a few students' requirements rather than the diverse needs within a classroom, or solely on subject matter.

These practices lead to either overabundance or lack of materials in a particular subject area, since one type of material cannot cover the complete range of learning abilities. When teachers select materials casually they also fail to consider how they may be modified for many different learning needs (Weinthaller & Rothberg, 1970). Table 5-2 presents an evaluation form that can help to forestall these shortcomings in the choice of materials.

Table 5-2 Evaluation of classroom materials

	Yes	No
1. Do the materials teach appropriate concepts and skills?		
2. Do the materials match the objectives of the lesson?		
3. Do the materials help students to attain long-term goals?		
4. Do the materials make sense within the structure of the subject?		
5. Do the materials have a good progression of incremental steps?		
6. Are the materials appropriate for a number of students?		
7. Do the materials match the child's learning characteristics?		
8. Are the materials flexible and can they be adapted to individual needs?		
9. Do the materials require the teacher's direction or are they designed for individual activity?		
10. Are the materials designed so that students can finish them in a reasonable amount of time?		
11. Are the materials self-correcting?		
12. Are the materials bright, colourful, and likely to gain the learner's attention?		
13. Are the materials durable?		
14. Can the materials be reused?		
15. Are the materials cost effective?		
16. Can the materials be easily stored?		

Teachers most frequently use duplicated materials for instruction, then workbooks and finally, readers and other books. Many if not all of these types of instructional materials need to be adapted for individuals and groups if they are to be effective, and this is especially true for special learners. Teachers should not hesitate to alter the scope and sequence of skills presented, the stated goals, responses required, or amount of active participation. It is possible to modify materials in a number of ways to accommodate special needs:

- changing the directions
- rewriting the materials to a more appropriate level (see chapter 8)
- providing study guides that include vocabulary, definitions, and a general outline of the concepts being discussed
- allowing students to respond orally or on audiotapes

- cutting up a workbook to limit the materials or reduce the number of activities on each page
- teaching in advance the terms commonly used, such as circle, underline, and match

Packaged materials

Instructional packages, or programmed instructional materials, are a systematically designed way of teaching. Most often, the term implies a self-contained and portable system. A package may consist of printed materials alone, but can also include slides, cassette tapes, videotapes, films, and computer disks. Instructional packages provide a way for students to work individually or in small groups and also be in charge of their own learning. Generally, they include assessment or pretest procedures, so that students can discover their own entry levels. They also have multisensory resources and activities and a self-evaluative or post-test component.

Direct instruction, which was discussed earlier, and programmed instruction, are close kin. Both depend on teaching small units in a logical sequence through very small steps with a great deal of repetition, a process that often uses packaged materials. Programmed instruction is simply instruction that uses these materials. Many of them are self-correcting, which is important for reducing failure, providing practice and repetition, and increasing attention to tasks (Mercer & Mercer, 1985). These programmed instructional materials also offer the advantages of being cost effective, individualized, and self-paced. They are therefore useful for many students with mild and severe learning problems. The materials may be linear — a series of structured statements and questions that require a response from a student — or branching, in which an incorrect response means going to easier material or another place in the booklets.

Special education packages are also available. These are relatively inexpensive printed materials that provide precise practical instructions for teaching specific skills to given populations of special education students. Even these, however, may need modifications to suit the needs of particular students.

Self-correcting materials

For students in individual programs, it is essential that materials be as self-correcting as possible. The materials must provide rapid, corrective feedback to prevent students from practising mistakes as they work through the activities. Taping a flap containing the answer to the question card or making question and answer cards in the form of simple jigsaws, as shown in figure 5–6, will make materials self-correcting. A colour code (green for right, red for wrong) on the back of question cards is also effective.

Games

A **game** may be defined in an educational context as a pleasure-invoking, rule-based interaction between two people or more that involves moving toward a terminal goal, dependent on the mastery of academic skills and agreed upon in advance (Salend, 1979). Students at all levels prefer games to classroom activities because everyone loves a challenge. Games provide excitement while stressing the concepts of teamwork and fair play. Players who hold no hope of success, however, because they do not understand the rules or possess the basic skills to play the game, will become frustrated, unable to learn, and will probably stop playing. Yet if the players have a chance of either winning,

Make jigsaws out of question and answer cards.

Tape a flap to the back of the card with the correct answer underneath.

Figure 5–6 Self-correcting materials

achieving something, or just having fun, a game can promote learning and keep them interested. To encourage social integration as well, teachers should stress co-operation over competition at all times.

Classroom games are excellent vehicles for motivating pupils and improving their memorization skills. Games can often circumvent the boring process of learning by drill, but are equally suitable for teaching complex conceptual systems such as trade relations, government institutions, or family relations. They can also promote individualization in the classroom. Students with varying levels of ability can interact with one another if the game demands different skills from each participant. A mathematical game, for example, may require players to give number facts in order to move their counters. The facts required can be adjusted to match the aptitudes and learning objectives of individual students.

When choosing classroom games, ask first, "What skills are to be taught?" and "Can learning be structured in this game?" Games take a multitude of forms; they may also be made by teachers or commercially produced. In either case, the teacher controls the academic component of the game and the learning outcomes.

The most common, and the easiest type of game to make, use, and adapt for many functions is the track game (see figure 5–7). The board can be adapted to any level of ability or subject area and is used to reinforce basic skills. The same board may be used for several games with different playing counters or cards. Track games should always go from left to right. Chance sequences such as free turns, lose a turn, or go to jail may be used to add interest. Card games in which players try to collect as many sets or pairs as they can, can also be used in the classroom. A card game for practising concentration skills is presented in figure 5–7. All the cards are initially placed face down. Players then turn them over one at a time and try to match pairs. If a player makes a pair, he or she turns another card over. Other widely used games are based on formats found in popular amusements such as bingo or snakes and ladders.

Track games

Card games

Ladder games

Climb the ladder

Climb the tree

Figure 5–7 Games for drill and practice

Games are a good method of promoting learning.

Computers in the classroom

By now, everyone knows that microcomputers have come to school. The possibilities for both exceptional and non-exceptional learners seem infinite and many have not even been identified yet. It is clear, however, that microcomputers will play an increasingly crucial role in the education of exceptional students.

In mid-1984 approximately 27 000 microcomputers were in use in Canadian schools, with 33 percent in Ontario, 6 percent in Quebec, 49 percent in the West, and 12 percent in the Atlantic provinces, the Yukon, and the Northwest Territories (Allan, 1984). Across the country, however, no national policy regarding computer use exists. Provinces and school districts are still formulating their policies about acquiring software and hardware. The attempts by Quebec and Ontario to design their own microcomputer systems are perhaps the best known. Ontario had planned to have a microcomputer system available to every one of its classrooms by 1990, with 10 000 teachers using the system (Allan, 1983).

Computers cannot replace classroom teachers, but they are consistent and accurate teaching tools, in contrast to television, which promises only entertainment. It is a mistake to equate computers with visual aids (Wright, 1981); they must be used to do more than display information or add colour and interest to a lecture. In a non-threatening manner, computers can ensure that students master new skills or knowledge without failure, or they can reinforce prior attainments. Computer programs provide instruction, drill, and practice in modes that match the learner's requirements to the task.

Although there is relatively little information available about optimal learning outcomes with computers, educators must nevertheless seriously address the benefits of the new technology. Of course, not all educators have greeted technological innovations with open arms. Many reject computers because of what has been called technophobia, an anxious reaction to the presence and use of the new technology (Blank & White, 1974; Touchings, 1989). These teachers and administrators tend to view the rapidly developing technology as dehumanizing.

Although such concerns should certainly be considered, they can be effectively answered. Educators must begin to reshape their instructional approaches thoughtfully to prepare all students to use current and future technology as vocational, educational, recreational, and prosthetic tools. It is their responsibility to take advantage of the potential of computers and of systems developed by combining computers with other traditional and future media equipment. If we arbitrarily dismiss computers from the classroom we will limit the access of exceptional students to teaching devices of potentially enormous benefit. Luckily, the mystery that has surrounded computers is gradually dissipating, as every new generation of computers is easier to understand and operate.

Generally, the potential and management of computers in the classroom are categorized into three broad areas: computer literacy, computer-assisted instruction (CAI), and computer-managed instruction (CMI). Computer literacy refers to introducing students to computers; that is, giving them at least a minimal understanding of computers. Courses are intended to prepare students of all ages to become literate citizens of a computer-based society, in much the same way that they become literate with language (Ife, 1982).

Computer-assisted instruction (CAI) denotes any method of instruction in which the computer is the primary delivery system (Burke, 1982). The student will usually have direct interactive instruction, on-line with the computer. Compared to traditional instruction, CAI results in equal or better achievement, in less time (Thorndyke & Symmach, 1982), although it is better used as a supplement than as a replacement (Burns & Bozerman, 1981). It is particularly helpful to students with special learning needs who need to review materials or go through a lot of drill to master concepts or facts. In fact, low-aptitude or deprived students seem to profit more from CAI than do average or high-aptitude students (Ragsdale, 1982).

The vast majority of educational software to date has provided drill and practice, the most commonly used mode of computer-assisted instruction (Maddux, 1987). Programs are available for language, reading, spelling, science, social studies, and other content subjects. Although computers were never intended for reading instruction, they can also fill a variety of needs in this area (Biltz, Detweiler, & Grant, 1983). Many programs have been devised to impart reading and comprehension skills and to focus on areas such as word attack, letter recognition, word-recognition skills (Kolich, 1985), word decoding (Torgensen & Young, 1983), syllabication, sentence recognition, sentence sequencing, cloze procedures (see chapter 8), and so on. Computer programs can also teach spelling efficiently. The child can play a game of "hangman" against the computer, for example. As well, computers are particularly appropriate for computation and mathematical applications. Because mathematics requires so much drill and practice, a wide variety of software is available in the area (see Bachor & Crealock, 1986).

Drill and practice, though valuable, do not realize the full potential of computers. Other types of programs for computer-assisted instruction are now emerging. Many simple, linear drill-and-practice programs designed to supplement a teacher's instruction are still being produced, but tutorial programs are also taking their place in the classroom. These are self-contained courses of instruction with the capability for machine decisions and program branching. As well, there are dialogue or inquiry programs, which enable students to interact with the computer and control the pace and level of instruction (Mason, Blanchard, & Daniel, 1983).

Computer-managed instruction (CMI) is somewhat different. It includes the systematic management of instruction by the computer, characterized by testing, diagnosis, learning prescriptions, and record keeping (Burke, 1982). Computer-based testing is a significant area of use for CMI, in which computers code and score students' responses to questions from a program and then, based on results, prescribe or branch to needed instruction. Teachers can either use computers as testing devices or administer tests on paper and then use the computer to score and record the results. Researchers Hasselbring and Crossland (1981) have, for example, prepared a version of the Kottmeyer Spelling Test (Kottmeyer, 1970) for microcomputers — the Computerized Diagnostic Spelling Test — that reduces scoring errors and the time taken by the examiner. Computers may also be employed to help teachers manage daily tasks such as keeping records and developing IEPs.

All students, of course, love to play games on the computer. Not only do the games appeal to students (Kennedy, 1984), but unintended applications have surfaced. Computer games can provide insight into a child's motivation, interests, and co-ordination. Game-playing time on the computer may be sparingly used as a reward or to ameliorate motivation. The paddles used in many of these games exercise fine motor skills, and even playing games improves students' computer literacy.

Technology has opened the doors for educators to devise exciting and useful methods of instruction. Computers possess unlimited appeal and high motivational value for children (Splittgerber, 1979), and hold enormous benefits for the special needs population. The colour, sound, and motion from a computer screen can gain and hold a student's attention. Some of the advantages of incorporating computer technology into classroom instruction are presented in box 5–4.

As non-critical and efficient teaching aids, computers are of value to all students. Using a computer may improve a student's skills significantly, partly because computers require a great deal of interaction. They are not a passive medium: computer programs present a stimulus, demand a response, present appropriate feedback and reinforcement, and then move on to the next instructional segment. This pattern may encourage students to explore new ways of thinking, help them to develop logic patterns, and stimulate their imagination and creativity (Papert, 1980). Much software uses graphics to heighten interest.

Microcomputers can provide a solution to many problems facing exceptional students. They can bring simulated speech to the non-vocal, allow the deaf to use telephones, and provide braille or synthesized voice for the blind and environmental control for the physically handicapped (Hagen, 1984). For students who cannot read, microcomputers and associated technologies offer an important innovation — the reading machine (see chapter 14). Physically disabled students and cerebral palsied youngsters who have trouble keeping pace with their classmates or with communication, can

Box 5–4 Computers in the classroom

Computers can provide:

- direct individual instruction
- instant feedback and reinforcement in a variety of forms
- drill and practice, using animation, sound effects, and games
- games for individual, pair, or group competition, which encourage co-operative learning, developing strategies, and following rules
- a multisensory approach to learning
- remedial, developmental, or enriched instruction depending on the learner's needs
- progress reports to which both students and teachers can refer
- diagnostic and prescriptive information for the teacher

Computers are user friendly. They:

- present self-pacing instruction with unlimited repetition in a non-threatening correction mode
- do not possess human impatience, irritability, or fatigue
- allow students to learn at their own rate
- are suitable for use with a diverse student population
- eliminate writing problems for very handicapped children
- can be used to teach a wide range of subject matter
- can introduce new material as well as monitor instruction and evaluate progress
- "remember" students' responses
- have a high motivational value and may induce students to work for longer periods and to repeat exercises if they find them fun
- stimulate students by enabling them to take part in activities or processes, make decisions while learning, and see the results of that learning
- allow students to learn by discovery
- stress methods of analysing problems and developing solutions in various ways
- allow children some sense of power and self-esteem as they learn to master a highly complex technological device

use computers to type easily, or produce messages with voice synthesizers (Foulds, 1982). Recent programs now provide computerized talking Blissboards that allow users to communicate with a greater number of people, including those who are not trained to understand Bliss (Bennett, 1982). Similarly, students with muscular dystrophy experience great fatigue in writing and typing, which can be alleviated by using computers. Most of the microcomputers found in schools can be used in some way by visually impaired students if the computer can be connected with a device that gives speech or tactile information to the user. Transcription programs produce direct braille transcription of material (Mellor, 1981).

Learning-disabled youngsters may find that the computer reduces their errors in mathematics by inserting numbers in the right place in a column or by simplifying the display of materials to one problem at a time (Johnson, 1982). As well, computers are becoming more prevalent in classrooms for mentally retarded children (Hagen, 1984) to provide immediate reinforcement and feedback, allow self-paced instruction, and motivate students (Rupley & Blair, 1983).

For gifted and talented students who require instruction that is advanced in both content and process, microcomputers will play an increasingly important role. The computer allows gifted youngsters access to instant advanced instruction through complex, multilevel branching programs. They encounter phenonema outside the realm of their experience but not beyond their level of ability (Dover, 1983). This topic is readdressed in chapter 16.

Even though computer technology offers much to students, there are drawbacks. In the classroom, the computer can be a Jack-of-all-trades: a workbook page, a science laboratory, a four-dimensional model, a teacher, or an administrator (Ife, 1982). It can also be frustrating. A printed workbook is always there to rely on; a laboratory experiment gone wrong is usually explicable; a teacher can respond with sensitivity to a student's learning problems. No such certainties yet exist with computers. The single guarantee is that the computer always interacts with its user — either it does what is expected, or it sends back a message that says it cannot complete the function, or it repeats the previous message (Ife, 1982).

If students use computers too often, teacher–student interaction decreases (Clarke, Chow, & Winzer, 1988), and the technology may also lose its appeal. In addition, using computers does not eliminate the need to learn the fundamentals of a subject. Further considerations are cost, which will not yet allow a computer for each student, and the quality of currently available educational software. Of course, teachers also have to take the time to learn something about the technology themselves. Teachers can get the most from computers if they understand some of the basics of programming, although it is not a prerequisite for using CAI. They do, however, need to know something about the hardware (the monitor and the drive) in order to care for the equipment.

Even the most efficient and modern hardware will be of little use without effective software. Care must be taken that the programs do not merely present the illusion of instructional individualization by virtue of their sophisticated, electronic medium. Software must meet academic goals to be educationally relevant, and must engage the student if it is to be effectual. Today an ever increasing variety of software is available. This text therefore does not point to any specific programs. Between the time of writing and of publication it is quite likely that much of the software mentioned would become outdated at best, or obsolete at worst.

Selecting appropriate software for special learners requires special considerations. Many educational software packages are more technically than educationally sound (Hannaford & Taber, 1982). Some are too narrow, some are poorly sequenced, some do not match instruction to skills appropriately, some give negative feedback, and others force answers requiring too much guesswork. These weaknesses all have particular relevance for exceptional students. Finally, programs may present material in a way that is visually inappropriate for special learners. The size of the characters, for example, may be too small.

Software is expensive, and a number of investigators have identified considerations for evaluating it. Table 5-3 draws from a number of writers (Hannaford & Sloane, 1981; Ife, 1982; Kamil, 1984; Norman & Malicky, 1986) to devise an evaluation form for software.

Table 5–3 Evaluation form for microcomputer software

	Yes	No
The learner's needs		
1. Does the program reach the population for whom it was designed?		
2. Will the program motivate students to learn?		
3. Is the content relevant to the instructional needs of the students?		
4. Will the material be effective with individual learning styles?		
5. Will the format appeal to students?		
6. Is the material relevant to daily living experiences?		
7. Does the user have control over the operation of the program?		
8. Are instructions for the program clear and acceptable?		
9. Are the screen displays effective?		
10. Is the program easy for students to use?		
11. Does the program make appropriate use of the limited computer resources available?		
12. Does incidental, supplementary learning result from using the program?		
13. Is the program more effective than non-computer instruction in the area?		
The teacher's needs		
1. Is the program compatible with the teacher's instructional style, goals, and classroom organization?		
2. Is the teacher able to use the software?		
3. Are supporting materials available?		
Instructional integrity		
1. Does the program state instructional and behavioural goals?		
2. Does the program match established curricular goals?		
3. Is the content accurate?		
4. Is the teaching/learning mode—drill, practice, diagnosis, tutorial, inquiry, game, solving problems—suitable for enough members of the class?		
5. Is the teaching/learning mode identified?		
6. Is the program organized and presented in an appropriate developmental sequence?		
7. Does the program have fast and flexible methods of data retrieval?		
8. Does the program take longer than fifteen seconds to retrieve files?		
9. Does the computer do the work that it is supposed to do?		
10. Do disks need to be continually shuffled?		
Operating the program		
1. Can the software be modified to meet individual students' requirements?		
2. Is the software package self-contained or does it require a teacher's intervention?		
3. Does the program tap a variety of learning modes?		
4. Is the program free from bugs?		
5. Is the material reusable?		
6. Is the initial cost reasonable?		
7. Can the program be easily and safely stored?		
8. Does the program handle users' errors efficiently and flexibly?		

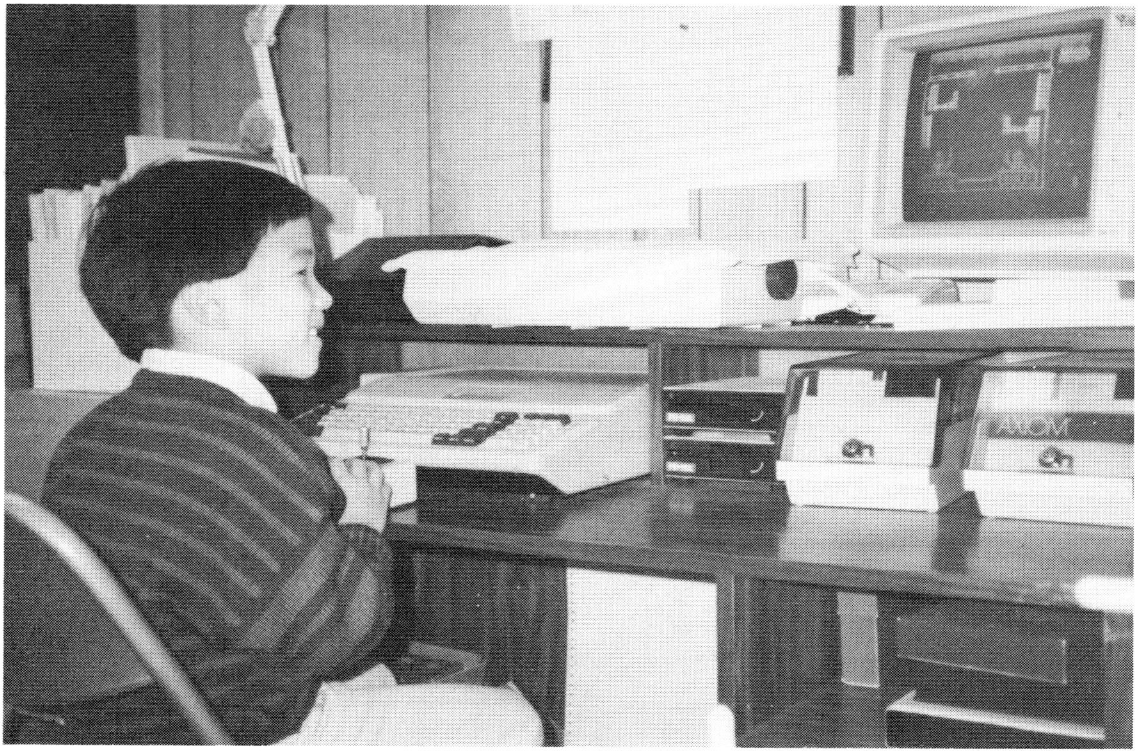

Computers possess high motivational value.

Although the cost of computers is steadily decreasing, not every classroom is yet equipped. Computers are only one possible component of an effective learning environment, and some combination of the ideas presented in this chapter is necessary to produce the best classroom climate for all pupils. Good management must also be matched by social integration and acceptance, the subject of the next chapter.

6 *Social integration and behavioural management*

- Changing behaviour
  - Bibliotherapy
  - Play therapy
  - Music therapy
- Behavioural approaches
  - Principles of reinforcement
- The behavioural management program
  - Token economies
  - Contingency contracts
  - Daily work contracts
  - Daily report cards
  - The punch-card technique
  - Cognitive behaviour modification

Dear Reader,

Classroom management and socialization have always been a concern for teachers, whether the teacher is just beginning, is teaching regular or special classes, is of a humanistic orientation or a behavioural one. In fact, one of the most consistent comments from novice and experienced teachers alike is that they need better training to manage or socialize the behaviour of their charges so that they can get on with "teaching" them something or other. It seems that no matter what we try, or how we set up a situation, something can happen or someone can do something to torpedo our efforts to establish that ideal learning climate we study about in textbooks.

We must remember, of course, that the classroom is a unique environment in itself, quite unlike anything the teacher or the students experience anywhere else. Frankly, some students are, at best, only marginally suited, by nature or needs, for that environment and its inherent demands for self-control, attention, and application. Although elements of the classroom setting are similar to the real world, we know, as the students know, that the classroom is little like the real world that we or they know and have experienced. The corollary may be that if we use approaches that make the classroom more like the real world, we just might make it easier even for children with "difficult behaviours" to adapt to, even flourish in, that environment.

When I look back on how certain teachers made me flourish, I am sure that much of what they did came naturally, not from a textbook on behavioural management in the classroom. They managed children with behavioural disorders, learning disabilities, and hyperactivity, as well as genuises and the mentally incompetent even before research pointed out that all these categories of students existed. Many of these students, in their own way, at least learned, if not flourished, under some teachers' management. In retrospect, I can identify a few of the techniques these teachers used.

For one thing, they did not apply their techniques to certain behaviours, but rather to individuals who happened to have certain behaviours — a big difference. They cared more for the behaver than the behaviour and were able to communicate, by word or deed or both, with everyone. They showed concern for the reasons why particular students behaved or felt the way they did; they applied what they knew about children and their social situations and needs, and worried less about measuring "relative frequencies" and "valences" and "the suitable application of appropriate reinforcers."

These teachers all had a sense of humour although they never made fun of anyone but themselves. They always took what they were doing as serious business but they never made the fundamental error of taking themselves too seriously. That way, they didn't have to be perfect, and their students lost much of their defensiveness too. Isn't defensiveness in children really at the root of a great many "behavioural problems," such as speaking back to the teacher, fighting, and daydreaming?

These teachers knew, or sensed, when a student needed privacy, or closeness. Their classroom management techniques were subtle, even gentle at times; there were no screamers in the lot. They used physical proximity (simply moving closer to the sources of disruption) and eye contact. My feeling is that the less verbal interaction used to control behaviour, the better. Non-verbal control is so much less likely to bring on confrontations. A quick way to quiet any group down, at least for a moment, is to lower your voice or even whisper.

Occasionally, these teachers would say something nice to a particular student; they gave personal and public recognition when it was deserved. So much of what a teacher, even a good teacher, says to a student is negative — as much as 70 percent of verbal interaction.

Finally, these teachers did not create behavioural problems by setting impossible restrictions or by not letting their classes know what was expected of them. I remember that classes were flexibly structured. We had rules, but the rules were there to help us to learn and we knew it; they weren't there simply to fuel the teacher's authority. We even determined some of the rules ourselves.

All these qualities are part of being a good teacher. If you bear them in mind, you can offer a great deal to your students, and enjoy their qualities too.

Lee D. Klas
Professor
Department of Educational Psychology
Memorial University of Newfoundland

Everyone needs other people: our social, emotional, and psychological health largely depends on positive interactions with others in our environment. Exceptional youngsters are no different. They need to be accepted, to make friends, to join in games, and to feel part of a group.

A handicapping condition can, however, affect a child's social development in a variety of ways. The condition can implicitly or explicitly limit specific behavioural interactions. Physically handicapped youngsters, for example, may lack the motor movements for waving and smiling. Blind children may not look toward other people and typically will not smile. Deaf children experience a delay in communication that often inhibits social relationships and interactions. Mildly retarded youngsters may be deficient in social skills: they may not recognize greetings or respond appropriately to requests. The disorders in the verbal and social skills of learning-disabled children have likewise been well documented (Bryan, 1978); and, typically, the behaviour of emotionally disturbed children is intimidating and socially unacceptable.

One purpose of teaching is to transmit the curriculum, the material considered important for children to learn. Another aspect of school life is the hidden curriculum, the provision of rewarding social experiences that will instill in children the values and skills necessary to function successfully in society. Given that the overall goal of education is to prepare students for life and for work, mainstreaming is the process through which many, though not necessarily all, special learners will best achieve this goal.

As exceptional learners are ceded the rights of the regular classroom, they must simultaneously assume certain responsibilities. They must follow class rules and routines and behave within acceptable social limits. Before entering the regular class, these pupils must be taught positive social skills and helped to correct inappropriate behaviour (Kehle & Barclay, 1979). Discipline and behavioural management are therefore prime considerations in the process of integration. Some teachers believe that managing a class of students with diverse needs will be too difficult. Often they worry that exceptional youngsters will disrupt the classroom and halt or hinder effective learning for non-handicapped pupils.

It is far from given, however, that children with learning problems will automatically display behavioural disorders. Behavioural management for these students is not necessarily problematic, and curricular adaptations are not necessarily time consuming. Rather, the real challenge for educators is to teach children socialized behaviour as opposed to mere school compliance. Nevertheless, there is no question that managing students of any age, grade, or functional level can be a challenging and often frustrating task. Even though teachers may prefer not to concern themselves with classroom control, they have to devote some effort to it, typically about 10 percent of their time (Crealock, 1983).

Classroom behavioural problems constitute the most common reason that students are referred for special education (Ysseldyke & Algozzine, 1982). Too much or too little motor activity, inattention, excessive talking, not completing assignments, not doing homework, and other such problems are often listed on referral forms. Mild behavioural problems such as these are faced by most teachers daily. At the same time, teachers may meet students who demonstrate persistent and chronic behavioural problems that extend far beyond the norm. These youngsters move the process of behavioural management from a task to a preoccupation, and seem intent on satisfying impulses that are not compatible with the kinds of classroom control or academic activities that the teacher has in mind.

Terms to refer to these students include mildly emotionally disturbed, behaviourally disordered, and conduct disordered, usually used interchangeably. However they may be labelled, the disorders encompass any behaviour that causes difficulty or disruption in the student's relationships with family, teachers, or the larger community. The subjectivity of such a definition is obvious. In fact, the implications of a certain behaviour or set of behaviours are largely defined by the teacher's expectations and the teacher's view of what constitutes acceptable behaviour.

Behaviourally disordered children are not rare. Many years ago Bower (1961) discovered that, in an average classroom, there were three pupils who warranted the label of emotionally handicapped. The behavioural disorders of these children, including aggression, bizarre statements or actions, disruptive violations of rules, and the like, impeded the productive performance of the whole class, of groups, and of individuals. Today, ever increasing numbers of students are being identified as emotionally disturbed. The best available evidence indicates that 6 to 10 percent of school-age children exhibit serious and persistent behavioural problems (Kauffman, 1981).

The vast majority of children who are in conflict with themselves and who exhibit behaviour that is personally distressing to others in the environment fall into the mild and moderate categories of disturbance. Boys outnumber girls in all classifications from mild to profound by at least two to one (Kelly, Bullock, & Dykes, 1977). They exhibit more aggressive disorders and conduct disorders than do girls (Quay, 1979), with estimates as high as twelve to one for the more serious forms (Cummings & Finger, 1980). First-born males are more likely than those born later to exhibit serious behavioural disorders and to be rated by teachers as anxious and aggressive toward their peers (Lahey, Hammer, Crumrine, & Forehand, 1980).

Behavioural disorders are usually identified during students' middle childhood or early teen years. They have a low prevalence in the early grades, a peak in the middle years, and a drop in the last years of high school (Morse, Cutler, & Fink, 1964). Some disorders only show up in school, where they are precipitated by the demands of school routines, teachers, and forced social interactions. Behavioural problems are clearly associated with low ability and achievement (Oliver, 1974). Conduct-disordered students are usually substantially behind in reading, arithmetic, and spelling (Kauffman, 1981).

Behavioural control is of paramount importance. In fact, instructional success is often directly proportional to a teacher's ability to use appropriate management strategies. A punitive classroom environment is not conducive to learning, but neither is a chaotic one. Even the most interesting and well-prepared lesson will fail if students are misbehaving.

As Klas points out in the opening letter, there are many, many ways of handling students who display problematic behaviours. This chapter deals with the social integration of exceptional students into mainstreamed educational settings, and then discusses behavioural management in the regular classroom. The main objectives of the chapter are to

- discuss procedures to integrate exceptional pupils socially
- outline the special needs and difficulties of mainstreamed students at the elementary and secondary levels
- present some general and specific methods to instill discipline in the classroom
- discuss some therapies for behaviourally disordered students

The social integration of exceptional students

Social integration involves the student's interactive behaviour, assimilation, physical proximity to, and acceptance by, non-handicapped classmates (Kaufman, Gottlieb, Agard, & Kukic, 1975). Only when the social intent of mainstreaming is met will the anticipated benefits become possible. Stereotypes will be destroyed, differences valued rather than rejected, and the classroom environment enriched for all students and the teacher. When handicapped students are liked, accepted, and chosen as friends mainstreaming becomes a positive influence on the lives of both exceptional and regular students.

Mainstreaming is based on the assumption that exceptional children will be accepted in the regular classroom with contact and familiarity, and will naturally model the appropriate behaviours of their non-exceptional peers. Unfortunately, there is little to support these beliefs. Regular classroom placement alone does not produce these benefits, and preliminary training for both regular class members and potential mainstream exceptional students is necessary to ease the transition (see figure 6–1).

Obstacles to social integration

Studies to determine how well handicapped students have been accepted in regular classrooms have not presented encouraging findings. Interaction between non-handicapped and handicapped students occurs at extremely low rates and is generally negative in nature. Exceptional students are perceived by their non-handicapped peers in negative and prejudiced ways (Gottlieb & Budoff, 1973; Porter, Ramsey, Tremblay, Iaccobo, & Crawley, 1978), are less likely to be named as friends, and more likely to be named as someone "I don't like" on sociometric measures (Gottlieb & Leyser, 1981b).

Many of the studies on acceptance and rejection in the regular classroom have been conducted with mildly intellectually handicapped students and have concentrated on the preschool and elementary levels. Generally, both peers and regular classroom teachers hold negative attitudes toward children thought to be retarded (Ballard, Corman, Gottlieb, & Kaufman, 1977; Copeland & Weissrod, 1976).

By the same token, learning-disabled students are not positively perceived by their peers (Bryan, 1978). They have been described as having poor self-esteem (Bruininks, 1978), poor self-concepts (Lerner, 1981), external loci of control, and poor motivation (Deshler, 1978). Learning-disabled students suffer a range of social problems, specifically in interacting appropriately and in establishing positive relationships with parents,

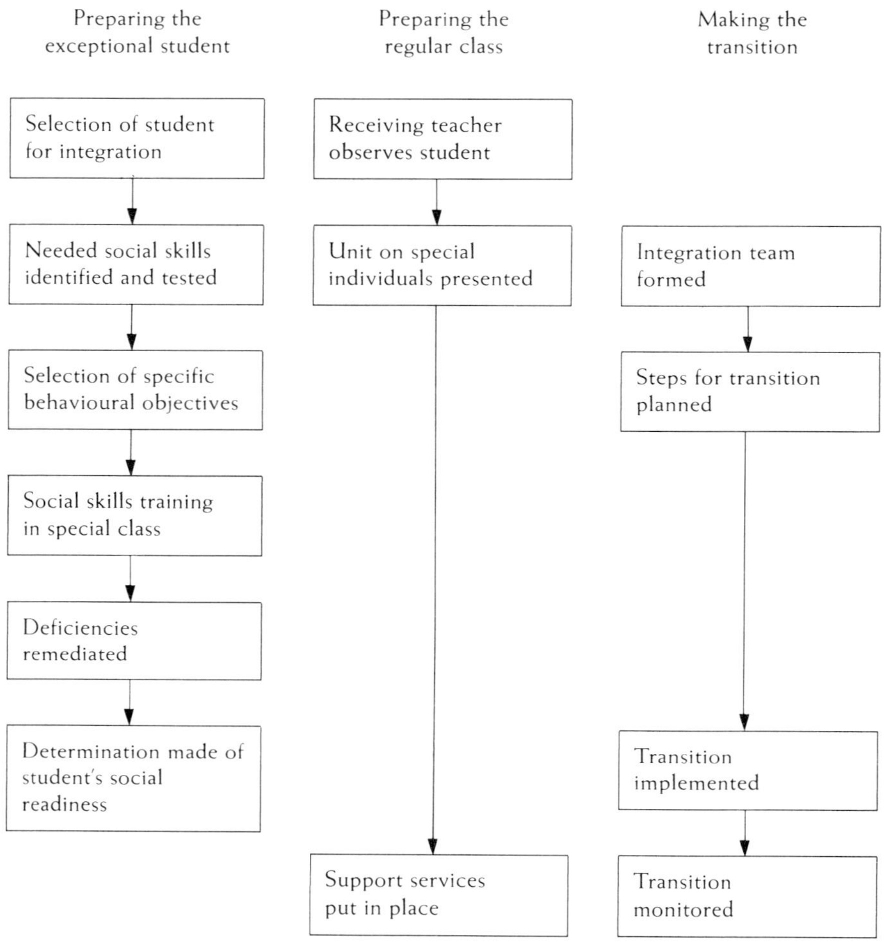

Figure 6–1 Social integration of exceptional students

siblings, peers, teachers, and the general community. Behaviourally disordered youngsters also tend to invoke negative reactions and rejection (Shores, Hester, & Strain, 1976). The majority of these youngsters are deficient in social skills and do not fit either their peers or the teacher's expectations for classroom behaviour.

Similarly, hearing-impaired children are not well accepted in regular classrooms, although they may occupy a position of social neutrality rather than rejection (Justman & Maskowitz, 1957). For hearing-impaired students, at the secondary level, at least, acceptance may be an evolving thing. One study (Ladd, Munson, & Miller, 1984) discovered that over a two-year period interactions became more frequent, reciprocal, and social in orientation.

Classmates may accept handicapping conditions that are visibly evident more readily than others (Jones, Gottfried, & Owens, 1966; Justman & Maskowitz, 1957). Blind students, for example, tend to be better accepted than those who have low vision. There is even evidence to suggest that non-integrated handicapped children are better accepted than are those placed in regular classrooms (Gottlieb & Budoff, 1973; Iano, Ayers, Heller, McGettigan, & Walker, 1974).

If acceptance is difficult to achieve at the elementary levels, then the problems may be even worse for older students, for whom social success is of the utmost importance. Handicapped teenagers thrust into the demanding and competitive environment of secondary school may be at a great disadvantage. For students at any level who are less well accepted in the regular classroom than in a special class, the regular classroom is the more restrictive environment, unless interventions are planned to develop constructive relationships among pupils. These interventions stem largely from the regular classroom teacher, who should be involved in placement decisions from the outset.

Promoting integration between special and regular classes

For integration to work successfully, all staff members should co-operate to ensure that exceptional students follow the same rules as everyone else and are treated in the same way within the school and on the playground. Making special disciplinary provisions for exceptional pupils will only cause resentment among their regular peers and point to differences in functioning.

Special class students can be made integral parts of the day-to-day operation of a school. Depending on their skills, they can carry messages, serve on the safety patrol, and assist in the kindergarten. Affective development and interaction are promoted when special class students join school clubs and help to organize and participate in all the social and cultural events such as school dances, sports events, and music programs. Exceptional students will also find themselves becoming socially integrated if they are actively involved in collaborative, non-academic tasks with non-handicapped peers. Research has indicated that social outcomes may be improved by using structured, co-operative learning arrangements. It is important, however, to exclude elements of competition or laissez-faire from the interactions (Peck & Semmel, 1972).

Special classes and regular classes can maintain a connection with one another through peer tutoring programs, which benefit both parties. The regular class may also "adopt" the special class. They can take field trips together, co-operate on fund-raising ventures, and so on.

Preparing regular class members for integration

Non-exceptional pupils can be instrumental in determining the success or failure of mainstreaming. By interacting with their exceptional peers, modelling appropriate behaviours, and providing assistance to physically handicapped and sensorily deprived youngsters, they can make the integration process a fulfilling one. Indeed, full integration is not possible without a heightened level of acceptance and understanding in the regular peer group.

Regular children may hold fears and prejudices that prevent them from accepting the exceptional student into the regular classroom. They may attach a stigma to the handicapped student and believe him or her to be disqualified from certain activities. It should be noted, however, that unfounded fears and misunderstandings are characteristic of handicapped as well as non-handicapped children. Indeed, handicapped youngsters often have difficulty accepting students with handicaps different from their own (Dewar, 1982).

It is a good idea to ready regular students for the mainstreamed pupil by teaching them specifically about children with differences. Instruction will help them to use appropriate terms when discussing disabilities, and to act more naturally around exceptional individuals. As well, such programs promote more positive attitudes toward disabled persons and increase understanding of the feelings of handicapped people (Popp, 1983).

Programs to inform students about handicaps employ various techniques, depending on the age of the children being instructed. Successful approaches have included simulations of disabilities, group discussions, books, films, videotapes and filmstrips, classroom visits from disabled people, direct teaching about disabilities, and, very rarely, analysing the nature of prejudice (Heinisch, 1981).

Units on handicapping conditions should include a progression of activities:

1. books and audio-visual material to introduce the topic
2. simulation activities
3. exposure to the handicap, preferably by inviting a classroom speaker
4. discussion and follow-up

A unit plan for teaching about visual impairment is detailed below. The lessons described are for children in grades three and four but can easily be modified for older or younger students.

Unit on visual impairment

Grade level: 3 and 4

Learning outcomes:

- to prepare the class for the integration of a visually handicapped student
- to establish positive attitudes about the disability and about the potential of disabled persons

Objectives:

1. The class will be introduced to a variety of handicaps.
2. The special education teacher will present concrete information about visual impairment.
3. Using blindfolds, children will simulate the experience of visual impairment.
4. Using specific devices, pupils will experience the tools used by visually impaired people to cope with orientation, mobility, and reading.
5. An older, visually impaired student will speak to the class to explain about visual impairments and the manner in which visually impaired people wish to be treated.

Steps:

1. Assess the pupils' level of understanding to determine their needs. Ask them to respond to statements such as
   a) "I am scared to play with handicapped kids."
   b) "A handicapped child would be welcome in my classroom."
   c) "Handicapped kids like to be alone most of the time."
   d) "A handicapped person could be my friend."
   e) "Handicapped kids can do a lot of things."
   f) "Handicapped kids are sad most of the time."
2. Encourage "sanctioned staring" using books and films about handicapped people.
3. Present concrete information that focusses on some causes of visual impairment, how people see, and the developmental consequences of visual impairment.
4. Have the children use blindfolds to simulate the experience of blindness. Follow the exercise with a discussion and ask students to write about the experience.
5. Provide the children with blindfolds and white canes to demonstrate a mobility device.
6. Have the students use the Optacon, the Kurzweil Reading Machine, magnifying glasses, and lenses to gain experience of how visually impaired children can be helped to read.
7. Invite a visually impaired older student to speak to the class.
8. Throughout the unit, students should record information in written exercises and book reports.
9. Conclude the unit with a discussion. Answer final questions and draw conclusions. (Adapted in part from Binkard, 1985.)

Probably the best method to introduce a unit on handicaps is by using books and audio-visual materials. Children can first read about the effects of a handicapping condition and discuss them with each other. The greater benefit of audio-visual materials is the opportunity to watch handicapped people, to use "sanctioned staring." This is important to reduce the discomfort that children may feel in the presence of a disabled individual (Donaldson, 1980). Given opportunities for staring, children may avoid disabled people less (Langer, Fiske, Taylor, & Chanowitz, 1976).

Puppet shows using large puppets to tell and show the experiences of various groups of exceptional children have also been found most effective (Binkard, 1985). They dispel myths and fears, and students are consequently less likely to feel alienated from handicapped individuals when encountering them for the first time.

Simulations are very popular. Typical activities include having students take turns to use a wheelchair for part of the day, or blindfolding them and letting them feel their way around the classroom. Pupils may go about their daily activities with a book or metre-stick attached to one arm; use crutches for the first time; wear mittens while writing reports; or try to tie their shoelaces with one hand (Dewar, 1982). A lesson plan for teaching students about physical handicaps is outlined below. Although it is designed for young children, it can easily be modified for older students.

Lesson plan to teach a class about physical handicaps

Grade level: 3 and 4

Learning outcome: to prepare students for the arrival of a physically handicapped student in the classroom

Objective: to allow the children to experience the isolation felt by people in wheelchairs

Materials:
- large classroom area
- conversation starters on flash cards, such as "My favourite television show is...."

Steps:
1. Arrange the class into small groups, with four or five children to a group.
2. Have one student from each group choose a conversation starter.
3. Place a chair in the middle of each group. Tell the group that this chair will serve as a wheelchair and that one of them will have the opportunity to experiment with it.
4. Ask one student to sit in the chair and have the others in the group remain standing.
5. Have each group discuss their selected topic in turn, with the rest of the class observing.
6. Afterwards, lead the discussion with questions such as
   "Did you include the person in the wheelchair in the discussion?"
   "Did you sometimes forget?"
   "How does it feel to be excluded?"
   "Did you [the person in the chair] feel uncomfortable?"

Simulation activities can rapidly teach students about the restraints imposed by a handicap. Simulations of physical and sensory handicaps are not difficult to devise, but illustrating how mildly handicapped children learn is far more difficult. Rasche and Dedrick (1986), however, have devised simulation games that focus on learning difficulties. They suggest using a special game of Simon Says to demonstrate the frustrations suffered by children who have learning handicaps. The activities stress processing skills and mathematical computations and are deliberately designed to cause frustration in the participants. They are best suited to junior high school pupils.

Simon Says is played in the traditional manner except that two directions are changed: left becomes right and over becomes under. If Simon says, "Put your left hand under your right foot," the players would put their right hands over their left feet. The difficulties with rapid auditory processing and motoric translation become obvious in this activity.

In the second game, Rasche and Dedrick (1986) use simple number facts, but with altered terms. As an example, "times" becomes "trugs," "minus" becomes "brugs," and "divide" becomes "grubs." Hence, six grubs six is one and six trugs six is thirty-six. Memory, auditory processing, and automaticity of number facts are of course necessary prerequisites for playing the game.

After going through the activities, pupils should be led in a class discussion to talk about their feelings and the frustrations they experienced. It is important, however, that tactics for coping with the handicap form an integral part of simulation exercises. Children should be shown the ways in which disabled people learn to adapt and to manage problems, as well as the adverse effects of the handicap (Wright, 1980).

Group discussions, led by an individual comfortable with the difficulties of a specific exceptionality, provide information and may help to develop positive attitudes among the students. If a mentally retarded child is to be integrated, for example, a teacher can make the class aware of the problems that mentally retarded children have in learning and the reasons for any anti-social behaviour. Children who understand the difficulties are usually far more tolerant.

Visits by disabled people to the classroom can be a rewarding experience, but should occur after the students have had ample experience with visual materials. Short, structured contacts are best to induce positive changes in attitude. The most successful speakers are handicapped children themselves (Dewar, 1982). Peers are an excellent source of relevant information about what it is like to be handicapped, and how handicapped people prefer to be treated (Donaldson, 1980).

Preparing exceptional students for integration

The social aspects of the school curriculum are especially important for exceptional youngsters. An individual's culture establishes the patterns of daily life and shapes the way in which people interact with each other. Every classroom has a culture too, not represented simply by what is taught there, but also by the ways in which it is taught and in which children and teachers interact.

Students who have been in special education programs and are entering mainstream settings have two major adjustments to make. They must meet the teacher's behavioural and academic standards, and they must learn to interact with a new peer group. If they cannot, then they will remain, to a greater or lesser extent, outsiders. Skills such as co-operation, positive peer interaction, greeting people, asking for and giving information, and making conversation, all promote social acceptance (Asher & Hymel, 1981). Yet handicapped children are more likely to exhibit hyperactivity or hypoactivity, distractibility, attention disorders, impulsiveness, perseveration, disorganization, and social imperception. Not only do they often start out with poorer social skills, but the school experience itself may exacerbate social and emotional problems if the students' self-concepts are continually battered. There is therefore considerable agreement among professionals that mainstreamed students must be adequately prepared for the behavioural and academic demands of the regular class for the transition to be successful (Gresham, 1982; Hundert, 1982; Salend, 1984).

Both social skills and adaptive behaviour fall under the broader construct of social competence and constitute crucial areas of development for all school-age children (Reschley & Gresham, 1981). Social skills have been defined as "those responses, which within a given situation, prove effective; or in other words, maximize the probability of producing, maintaining, or enhancing the positive effects for the interactor" (Foster & Ritchey, 1979, p. 626). Social competence is the ability to understand and use the culturally accepted and contextually specific behavioural patterns of an environment (Hymes, 1974). Exceptional children may also need to learn appropriate social interactive behaviour, the verbal and non-verbal communication that occurs between them and their non-handicapped peers, as well as the behaviours listed below:

- acceptable habits of cleanliness
- the ability to stem inappropriate outbursts by inhibiting reactions to stimuli
- the ability to select appropriate choices based on probable consequences
- values involving loyalty, honesty, truthfulness, and dependability
- positive ways of dealing with social conventions
- ways to deal with personal feelings and the feelings of others
- methods of dealing with stressful situations and conflicts
- ways to handle teasing
- ways of greeting people
- ways to extend and receive invitations
- the ability to give verbal and non-verbal compliments and positive responses to others
- conversational skills, such as asking about other people's interests, responding to others' questions, and maintaining an extended conversation by taking turns to comment on a topic
- listening skills
- proper ways to ask questions
- appropriate methods of gaining the teacher's attention
- some measure of academic success
- understanding the rules and routines of the regular classroom (Cartledge & Milburn, 1980; Goldstein, Baker, Bruce, & Jamison, 1980; LaGreca & Mesibov, 1979; McGinnis, Sauerbry, & Nichols, 1985; Mesibov & LaGreca, 1981)

Assessing social skills

Because it is so vital that exceptional children acquire social skills, ways to assess these skills have recently gained much attention (Asher & Hymel, 1981; Asher & Taylor, 1981). Social assessment usually includes naturalistic observations, sociometric measures, and teachers' ratings. All three may be carried out by different observers at different times and should include a variety of settings and situations. Both assessing and teaching social skills are the responsibility of special and regular teachers, before and after a student's transition to the regular class.

Naturalistic observations correlate to sociometric measures and teachers' ratings to a certain degree (Greenwood, Walker, & Hops, 1977; Gresham & Nagle, 1980). The observer watches a student's social performance in settings such as the classroom, the playground, and the school cafeteria, and records the occurrence or non-occurrence of specific behaviours, such as verbalizations to other children and compliance with teachers' requests.

Sociometric measures include peer nominations and peer ratings, both of which have been widely used in mainstreaming research (Asher & Taylor, 1981). With peer nominations, the students are asked to specify or select a certain number of classmates who fit a particular criterion. They may be asked, for example, "Name three people you like to play with." Peer ratings use the same type of questions but ask students to rate their peers on a scale of one to five. They could be asked how much they like to play with the particular child. Peer nominations tend to assess "best" friendships, whereas peer ratings assess a child's overall acceptance within the peer group (Hymel & Asher, 1977).

Teachers' ratings include formal reports on social skills. These may include commercial measures, such as the Social Behavior Assessment Scale (Stephens, 1977), a six-point scale designed to help teachers assess social behaviour. Behaviour rating scales and measures of adaptive behaviour, which were discussed in chapter 3, may also be employed effectively here. Adaptive behaviour is a vital component of social competence.

Teaching social skills

Learning problems can result in a constellation of behaviours: a conscious refusal to learn, overt hostility, negative conditioning to learning, displacement of hostility, resistance to pressure, clinging and dependency, discouragement, the attitude that success is dangerous, extreme distractibility and restlessness, and absorption in a private world (Harris & Sipay, 1975). Many youngsters with learning and behavioural difficulties have reduced motivation. Undoubtedly, these behaviours and attitudes affect a student's interactions with peers. Generally poor self-concept and inappropriate attitudes make it difficult for children to socialize.

Many mildly handicapped children lack systematic and organized judgment. Because of this, they have poor conversational skills and unco-operative behaviour, and have difficulty interpreting the affective reactions of others in the environment. As well, they are impulsive, and unable to adjust their behaviour or to learn from mistakes. These youngsters may be inattentive to others and insensitive to the general atmosphere of a social situation. They will interrupt conversations, ignore turn-taking conventions, and laugh or cry inappropriately. Their understanding of non-verbal cues may also be deficient (Bryan, 1978).

Mildly handicapped students therefore reap direct benefits if they receive social training both prior to placement and within the regular classroom. Training lessens their frustration and averts potential problems. Coaching in social competence and communication also increases social interaction and acceptance for mentally retarded and low-status children (Kelly, Furnam, Phillip, Hawthorn, & Wilson, 1979; Oden & Asher, 1977). Social skills instruction begins by recognizing the specific problems. It identifies solutions by determining realistic and appropriate social skills, and helps children to evaluate and monitor their own behaviour. Coaching works best as a sequential process involving modelling, rehearsal, feedback, and generalization (Cartledge & Milburn, 1980). Quite a few commercial programs are available, most offering a variety of skills in communication and courtesy suitable for any setting. Programs are available for all age groups and usually provide guidelines, activities, and materials.

Whether teachers choose to follow a commercial program or to write their own objectives and plans, the essential thrust of social skills training will be the same. Throughout training, teachers should stress reducing the behavioural patterns that stem from academic failure and negative responses to school. The main objective is to improve students' self-concept, in their school setting, peer group, and neighbourhood. Although it is important to deal with specific social skills, teaching mildly handicapped children isolated skills and hoping that they will carry them into their everyday lives is not sound educational practice. Instruction must occur across a variety of settings that are as close as possible to those in which the skills will be applied (Goldstein, 1981).

It is reasonable to assume that mildly handicapped students realize that their social relations lack richness and will not reject efforts to improve their social interactions. A unit on social skills may be introduced by telling them that they will learn "the skills to get along with people." Throughout the life of a unit, instruction should last for twenty to thirty minutes, three days a week. On the other two days, place the students in situations in which they can practise and generalize the skills learned in the classroom. They may record their own social progress on a form such as that shown in figure 6–2.

Figure 6–2 Self-recording form for social skills

It is essential to identify individual needs and objectives before beginning training. Some youngsters may need to learn how to co-operate, or share possessions, and others how to control and redirect aggressive urges.

Modelling

The initial step in the actual training is to model appropriate social skills. Modelling is a form of imitation; the teacher presents a stimulus behaviour for the student to duplicate. Because both instructional and social skills are strongly influenced by examples of socially acceptable behaviour, modelling is a particularly practical and effective technique. This is especially true for children who have difficulty understanding verbal instructions or remembering a series of instructions. Modelling is useful in the motoric, linguistic, and social domains.

The live model, in which the teacher demonstrates — or has one of the student's peers demonstrate — certain behaviours that she or he wants to inculcate, is the most widely used. Symbolic models are also effective. These include such materials as videotapes, filmstrips, written stories, and pictures of people performing the selected behaviours appropriately. Modelling behaviour does not come about by exposure alone, however. Exceptional youngsters must be exposed to relevant stimuli, retain the information that was modelled, and be motivated to perform the behaviour.

Modelling is most effective when performed by someone helpful and friendly, of the same sex, age, and social status. Models should be rewarded for the behaviour (Goldstein, Sprafkin, Gershaw, & Klein, 1980). When the exceptional student sees a model being rewarded or showing pleasure in the behaviour, he or she is more likely to want to participate in the same activity. The behaviour will appear to be fun and to have positive consequences. Modelling is most appropriate for young pupils, whereas role playing is suitable for any age group.

Role playing

Children learn social behaviours by interacting with people and other parts of the environment. Role playing involves performing a skill in a certain context through some form of play-acting. It allows students to solve problems while at the same time expressing feelings and emotions. With role-playing techniques, students can practise appropriate skills in a non-threatening environment and explore the feelings associated with some situation or event, to develop a sense of social awareness. Role playing is conducted under a teacher's supervision; both the teacher and the other class members provide feedback.

Role playing has proven an effective technique in social skills training when an instructional component is included in the process (Bornstein, Bellack, & Hersen, 1977). It best follows modelling techniques in the sequence of a unit's activities. When incorporating role-playing techniques into a unit, the following steps should be taken:

1. With the students, identify the problem or conflict. This may follow an actual situation, such as an argument on the playground, or may be a remembered or imagined event.
2. Establish roles and assign students to specific parts.
3. Introduce the play with a short narrative and then prompt the students to continue with action and dialogue.
4. Following the role playing, the class discusses both the action and the outcomes.
5. If it is necessary to discover further solutions to the problem, repeat the process, assigning different students to the roles.

Group meetings

Older students may attend group meetings to improve their social behaviours. Small groups discuss issues of interest to them, such as how to handle ridicule, how to get along with peers, or how to initiate conversations. Behavioural control, teacher-pleasing behaviour, and study skills are all essential topics of discussion for exceptional students.

Similarly, values clarification is a suitable process for secondary pupils. It involves giving students topics to open a conversation, such as "how I think others see me," "ten things I like to do," "memories of success," "my ideal twenty-four hours," or "my ideal person." The process helps handicapped adolescents to learn about themselves, make decisions, and understand and accept their own behaviour and that of others. Through the discussions they achieve personal growth.

Specific activities

As well as the general methods to develop social skills already pointed out above, teachers may incorporate specific activities into their daily teaching routine, such as the ones below.

Objective: to heighten children's awareness of the affective status of others

a) Divide the class into small groups. In each group, the students will weigh and measure each other using a scale and metre stick. Write the results on a chart and discuss differences in a positive manner.

Kindergarten (K) to grade 6

b) Collect pictures of faces. Help the children to sort them according to expressions or moods.

K to grade 9

c) Discuss the meaning of various natural gestures, such as placing a finger over the lips to indicate "Be quiet."

K to grade 12

Objective: to build an awareness of the social uses of language

a) Use traditional fairy tales to stress how different moods may show up in voices. For example, Father Bear was angry, the little pigs were frightened, and so on.

K to grade 6

b) Read short pieces of writing to the class. Have them discuss whether they are fact or fiction. Extend the exercise to deal with the differences between fact and opinion.

Grades 4 to 12

The transition to the regular class

The social nature of a regular classroom can be upsetting to a child who is not functioning as a member of the group. Placing a special learner in a regular classroom must be accomplished gradually. Integration may begin with only one period a day and increase slowly from there. The teacher can ease the student's transition by following certain guidelines:

- Carefully point out the rules and regulations of the regular classroom to the student.
- Do not ask the student to read aloud or speak alone at first.
- Use peer tutors and cross-age tutors (Leyser & Gottlieb, 1980).
- Use role models and role playing.
- Pair exceptional and non-exceptional students for structured activities such as preparing and presenting a skit to the rest of the class (Chennault, 1967).
- Dispel competitiveness. Assign joint projects and emphasize sharing materials (Antia, 1982).
- Place students in small groups to work on multimedia projects (Ballard, Corman, Gottlieb, & Kaufman, 1977).
- Be tactful, and show respect for exceptional students by not talking down to them.
- Encourage students to talk. Listen carefully to what they have to say, and try to discover their hopes, aspirations, and fears.
- Keep a positive outlook. Negative feelings are as catching as optimistic ones.
- Avoid comparing exceptional students to others; see them as individuals and praise their accomplishments.
- Make special learners feel part of the regular classroom by assigning them responsibilities and chores.
- Reinforce behaviours that extend beyond academic areas. Good manners, friendliness, and co-operation deserve positive notice.
- Encourage success rather than winning. Stress to all students that participation, fun, and co-operation are more important than competition.

Both the physical layout of the room and the schedule of activities will affect a student's experience of integration. It is practical, for example, to seat visually impaired students very close to the chalkboard at a desk or table large enough to hold any special equipment, but such an arrangement may discourage contact with other students. To enhance social integration, a visually impaired pupil should therefore be encouraged to change desks for certain subjects and activities. Similarly, exceptional learners have to leave the regular classroom for special help, but this reduces their opportunities to become an integral part of the class. Stagger times so that students do not always miss favourite subjects or co-operative activities.

The classroom teacher must create an accepting environment for the exceptional student, matching his or her teaching style to the learning style of the pupil. A shy, timid student who is somewhat reluctant concerning the new placement may not be comfortable in a classroom with a traditional, structured environment and an authoritarian teacher. She or he may adapt more readily to a climate in which the teacher encourages group work and learning by discovery, at least at the outset.

Co-operative learning activities

Tasks involving peer interaction require students to work in a co-operative manner. Research suggests that such activities lead to more positive interactions between non-handicapped and special learners (Jones, Sowell, Jones, & Butler, 1981; Leyser & Gottlieb, 1980), and also teach children to value diversity (Johnson & Johnson, 1981), by instilling better attitudes toward both exceptional learners and students from minority groups (Aronson, Blaney, Sikes, Stephens, & Snapp, 1975; Martino & Johnson, 1979). Co-operative work also improves all students' levels of learning and helps them to retain and generalize skills.

Co-operative learning does not absolve the teacher of instructional responsibility. On the contrary, the teacher must establish heterogeneous groups of appropriate size, determine instructional goals for them, and set evaluative criteria. Groups should be kept small. In fact, for younger children, pairs or group of three probably work best. Assigning students with differing levels of ability to the same group ensures heterogeneity.

The classroom should be arranged so that members of each group are close to one another and can reach materials easily. Provide the appropriate materials at different levels, and include any adaptations necessary for exceptional students. Explain the activity and its evaluative criteria to the students before they begin. During the activity, observe the way that they interact, and note any problems they encounter in functioning co-operatively. Intervene if necessary to help all members work together effectively. The teacher's involvement should be kept to a minimum, however, since it usually decreases interaction among students (Antia, 1985).

The activity should be structured so that co-operation is not only desirable, but necessary, and should continue for a sufficient period of time for the students to get to know one another. Evaluate all members of the group together, on the basis of their performance as a group, and each member individually. Provide both the group and its members with feedback (Johnson & Johnson, 1978, 1980).

Co-operative learning activities can be employed for all school subjects. They are most successful when students must manipulate concrete materials, as in mathematics or a science project. It is also possible to use the activities in less structured areas, such as games. Pairs of students might act out an event in pantomime, for example, increasing their level of co-operation as skills develop. Pairs of students can also conduct interviews in which they obtain information using a predetermined set of questions. These can focus on academic or social areas, the application of knowledge, or questions about values. Another co-operative activity involves *peer helping*, in which one student gives directions while the other performs the activity. *Skill sharing* is a procedure that allows exceptional students to be seen as competent individuals with interesting skills to demonstrate or teach. As an example, a student who collects stamps might show the collection to the class and explain the hobby.

The transition from elementary to junior high school

Any major change in curriculum, placement, or routine can confuse students who are meeting problems in learning or behaviour. One of the most difficult times for many exceptional students is the transition from elementary to junior high school, with its increased curricular demands and change of routine. Not only are handicapped teenagers experiencing their own physical growth at this time but they find it extremely difficult to cope with the effect of their handicaps on the new pressures of adolescence.

They are also moving into situations that require them to function more independently. They are expected to assume responsibility for many activities and to impose their own structure on both behaviour and learning.

Secondary settings differ in physical design, instructional format, teaching styles, behavioural expectations, and patterns of socialization. In this situation exceptional students, at least initially, may be frightened and bewildered. Difficulties may surface in such practical areas as moving from room to room. Punctuality can pose a problem: there are stricter schedules and students need to be on time. Gym classes may be new to students and they may have trouble changing their clothes, or coping with combination locks. Similarly, many junior high schools have cafeterias which, by their very novelty, can present difficulties to exceptional students.

Success in secondary school depends largely on the skills needed to study and to take tests. Special learners may be deficient in both. They can have trouble planning a daily schedule, reviewing material frequently, and understanding the difference between familiarity with and knowledge of the required material. They must learn how to ask for help, and whom to ask. Elementary teachers cannot prepare them for all the difficulties of a complex new environment, but they can certainly help special learners to acquire some of the necessary skills. The extract below, for example, presents part of a unit on training students to find their way from room to room in a more complex school plant.

Unit on transition to junior high school

Topic: finding the way from room to room in a new school.

Objective: Each student will read a map of the new school in order to locate specific classrooms.

Activities:

1. Give each student a map of the classroom that indicates the location of specified objects and ask students to search for the objects.
2. Extend map-reading exercises to the playground.
3. Supply students with maps of their entire school and send them on specific errands.

Follow-up: Arrange a field trip to the junior high school and provide each student with a map.

The transition from junior to senior high school

As the move to junior high school can be traumatic for exceptional pupils, so the first year of senior high school is an important and potentially problematic transitional period. High schools have different administrative processes and a more complex organization than elementary schools. They are also usually much larger, drawing students from a broader catchment area. They offer a wider range of programs and each teacher specializes in only one or two subjects. Students must negotiate diverse teaching styles and demands and become familiar with a far wider array of services and professionals than they are used to.

Senior high school is highly structured: classes are often presented in the form of lectures; there is a great deal of written work; the school day is longer; a great weight of content is covered; and unique terminology is employed. The level of the work is more demanding and encompasses a higher level of figurative language. Students must be able to read rapidly and with good comprehension, and to take notes quickly. As well, students require a wider range of social skills.

In senior high school exceptional students may very well miss the secure and flexibly structured atmosphere of the elementary school. Gone too are the teachers who knew all the children from their kindergarten year. If they are to succeed at the high school level, exceptional students should therefore receive counselling and instruction to help them

- acquire the social competencies necessary to reduce social isolation
- master aggressive impulses
- learn about such adolescent problems as using illegal drugs
- develop a sexual identity
- learn to assume other people's perspectives
- learn about educational achievement and career possibilities
- understand their own needs, abilities, responsibilities, and obligations to the community at large
- acquire the skills necessary to make a smooth transition to greater independence

Classroom discipline

Discipline is a form of behavioural management, a type of habit training. It encompasses those methods used to maintain an environment conducive for learning and for managing students' behaviour (Cartwright, Cartwright, & Ward, 1984, p. 383), and is essential to the integration process. Discipline must be taught, learned, and internalized if it is to be effective, but it is important to remember that discipline and punishment are by no means synonymous. Students need consistency: they need to know what to expect of the teacher, what is expected of them, and what consequences success and failure have. Most authorities agree that whatever system of classroom management teachers use, it can be successful only if they implement it in a systematic and consistent fashion.

There is no question that discipline is a problem in the educational system. It is an imperative concern to parents and administrators. For many teachers too, especially those at the beginning of their careers, discipline and classroom management are matters of concern. They are expected to manage most of the behavioural problems that arise in their classrooms, and most of them do. An interested teacher with a flexible curriculum, organized plans, and a realistic marking system is well equipped to provide the structure, motivation, and control essential to learning. The teacher's authority, however, depends upon students' perception of their instructor as an efficient director of teaching and discipline. When pupils do not comply, teachers have no control. Without control, teachers cannot establish an environment in which it is possible to teach, and clearly, without instruction, students cannot learn (McGuigan, 1985).

Virtually every teacher has at least one student who might be described as having a behavioural problem. Inattentive, hyperactive, acting-out, or disruptive children and youth who fail to comply with simple or complex requests pose special problems for educators. Some of these students seem totally unresponsive to external pressure, whether it is in the form of a reward or of punishment. In fact, it seems as though they behave worse and learn less the more they are rewarded and, conversely, the more they are punished.

Exceptional students often use inappropriate strategies to solve conflicts or cope with frustration. The demand that they share materials, wait their turn, and co-operate with others over such issues as who can play what game, can cause these pupils stress. Some exceptional youngsters become too reliant on the teacher; others develop aggressive behaviour. Behaviourally disordered students characteristically display underachievement or poor quality achievement, and inconsistent performance from day to day.

No behaviour occurs in a vacuum, and students misbehave for many reasons. They may have troubled self-concepts, and feel inadequate or insignificant. If they are unable to reach their goals by appropriate behaviour, they seek out other, less acceptable means. Acting out brings attention from teachers and peers and makes the student feel significant. Sometimes they may try to mask academic inadequacies by poor behaviour. Visibly deficient skills in mathematics, reading, and the content areas may be covered up by students who present themselves inappropriately, skip classes, or avoid developing a sense of responsibility about classroom interaction and tasks. Hence, laziness, arrogance, and irresponsibility may be hiding poor academic, communicative, social, or adaptive skills.

Misbehaving students have been described in many terms, some downright unsavoury. Yet whether the problem is a mild annoyance, or severe enough to disrupt classroom routines, most of these students can remain in the regular classroom. They can be helped as long as support services are provided (Kauffman, 1981; Kelly, Bullock, & Dykes, 1977). Essentially, educators want students to learn that it is more rewarding to complete academic tasks and behave appropriately than it is to misbehave. Many learners labelled as behaviourally disordered, however, need to acquire certain social skills before they can benefit from instruction.

Teachers have been found to concern themselves chiefly with behaviour that hampers achievement and management in their classrooms. Passive behaviours such as anxiety and withdrawal are less obvious than overt, aggressive, acting-out behaviours. Children who scream, steal, and destroy property are harmful to themselves, intimidating to other children, frustrating to teachers, and cause massive disruptions to programs. Teachers consider certain areas of behaviour to be particularly likely to cause problems (Gropper, Kress, Hughes, & Pekich, 1968), and these are shown in box 6–1.

Nearly all teachers develop their own personal methods of behavioural control. Some hark back to the manner in which they were disciplined in school and adopt those principles. Other teachers discuss the problems with colleagues and adapt their methods. Some teachers glean ideas from reading or from courses, and quite a few

Box 6–1 Potential areas of trouble

Area	Manifestations of non-compliance
Attention to classroom activity	Inattention, daydreaming, withdrawal
Interest in work	Playing, doodling, drawing
Meeting work requirements	Self-criticism, giving up, not working
Physical activity	Restlessness, hyperactivity, noisiness
Reaction to tension	Emotional upsets
Appropriateness of behaviour	Telling tales, collecting objects
Getting along with others	Name calling, fighting, passivity
Consideration for others	Impatience with others, interrupting others, talking out of turn
Degree of independence	Seeking praise, currying favour, seeking attention
Regard for school rules and conventions	Smoking, swearing, truancy, tardiness, destroying property
Integrity	Cheating, tattling, stealing

simply use intuition. Teachers need both knowledge and practice to develop their own techniques of management. If they plan instruction and maintain classroom organization, they should become aware of those techniques that affect students' behaviour and reinforce a stable learning environment.

Teachers need to be flexible enough to adopt or adapt various techniques to deal with behaviours that range from inattentiveness to aggression. People are so complex that no method will work every time with a particular student, nor indeed suit every teacher. Interventions must match the teacher's personality, teaching style, and pedagogical philosophy. If a teacher does not feel secure with a particular intervention, it will not be successful.

In general, in order to maintain good relationships with their students, and thus maintain effective discipline, teachers need to be well informed and understanding about the emotional development of children. Setting tasks that assume a level of social development beyond the students' may create disciplinary difficulties. Probably at no stage is understanding more important than during early adolescence. In the younger grades, behavioural problems usually take the form of attention-seeking and acting-out behaviour, but are more likely to involve peers, peer pressure, and interpersonal relationships as children reach adolescence. The opening years of adolescence are highlighted by the conflicting attractions of independence, especially in relation to parents and teachers, and of the security promised by more childish activities.

The uncertainty and unpredictability of early adolescence make discipline challenging for junior high school teachers. Often, by the time they reach this level, students are frustrated by continuous failure and have developed negative attitudes toward the environment in which that failure occurs. They often hold remedial work in low esteem, and removal from the classroom for specific resource-room periods may cause embarrassment and resentment. As well, teachers possess a declining influence. Adolescents are capable of making more objective and less flattering evaluations of their teachers. They are quick to notice and condemn hypocrisy.

Behaviourally, late adolescence is a stage of greater equilibrium and relative stability. Students are capable of accepting constructive criticism with more grace. They have developed more adult social skills, more stable and reciprocal friendships, and are better able both to control their feelings and to display fewer emotional extremes.

At any level, the way that the teacher perceives and treats particular behaviours can modify inappropriate acts. Negative perceptions and treatment have the potential to escalate behaviours to produce even more serious problems. Repeatedly admonishing a special student for not listening, or being unmotivated, may ignore the underlying problem that, at least in part, the initial instructional demands were incompatible with that student's learning style and needs. Good discipline is synonymous with well-planned and interesting lessons. The class will rapidly become bored if a teacher presents repetitive lessons or assigns work simply to keep students occupied. When the teacher rushes to class with only a vague idea of what is to be taught and tells the students to open their textbooks and do the next set of exercises, then behavioural problems emerge. If students are repeatedly subjected to such unproductive sessions discipline becomes very difficult.

Assessing behaviour

Behaviour is particularly difficult to quantify. It is not possible to obtain a behaviour score as we can for hearing acuity or for IQ. Assessing behaviour is a much more subjective enterprise. Knowing when and what to report and when to seek help can therefore be difficult. Gropper, Kress, Hughes, and Pekich (1968) suggest that teachers view poor behaviour within specific parameters:

- *Intensity:* Does the student's behaviour disrupt other activities?
- *Appropriateness:* Is the behaviour a response to a certain situation?
- *Circumstances:* Is there an obvious reason for the behaviour?
- *Comparison:* How does the behaviour compare with the general level of behaviour in the class?
- *Duration:* How long does the behaviour last?
- *Frequency:* How often does the behaviour occur?
- *Manageability:* Is the behaviour improved or eliminated by management efforts?
- *Contagion:* Do other students copy the behaviour?

If, in the teacher's view, the behaviour exceeds many of these parameters, the student may need special help, in the form of psycho-educational diagnosis, therapy, counselling, special education, or specific behavioural techniques within the regular classroom.

The approaches used by educators to identify behavioural problems have been determined by various philosophical and pragmatic considerations. Informal methods are the most widely used. In the classroom, these include observations, direct observation, and rating scales, all of which were discussed in chapter 3. Observational data are drawn from measurable behaviours in a normal environment. The behaviours are recorded using a variety of measurements, such as frequency and duration.

Informal measures must take precedence over others, given the subjective but complex nature of human behaviour. There are probably no psychological tests that measure personality, anxiety, or social adjustment well enough to be useful in determining behavioural disorders (Reeve & Kauffman, 1978).

Counteracting behavioural problems

As with all procedures for remediation or intervention, different techniques for counteracting problematic behaviour apply under different conditions. Discipline may at times include punishment. More often, it will incorporate praise, attention, feedback, privileges, or tangible rewards. Some students need a systematic and carefully designed program of rewards. Teachers may intervene before a crisis happens (preventative techniques) or at the time it occurs (crisis intervention). Undoubtedly, prevention is more acceptable than intervention, although not always feasible. The following list presents some fairly broad ideas for establishing and maintaining an environment suitable for effective behavioural control:

- Establish supportive relationships with the students. Create a warm atmosphere characterized by acceptance without permissiveness.
- Develop mutual respect. Neither be a tyrant nor allow yourself to be tyrannized.
- Establish routines and rules, setting consistent and clear limits. Teachers do not convey legitimate authority if they are confusing and arbitrary.
- Organize the classroom by keeping only those supplies that are immediately needed within reach, so that students do not have too many alternatives.
- Balance the timetable. Follow a work period that demands much from the students with a period in which nothing new is required.
- Establish a structured atmosphere by allotting regular times to each type of task, so that students learn to anticipate demands. If a certain schedule seems to be a problem, however, rearrange it.
- If students do not find an activity exciting, assign it first but follow it with another that has high interest.
- Avoid being discouraging, but do not praise a student too much. Praise is not the same as encouragement: it can engender anxiety, fear, and growing dependence.
- Stress co-operative, non-competitive behaviour, not winning.
- Always separate the actor from the deed. Make the student understand, "I like you, but I don't like what you did."
- Do not allow past misdeeds to form the basis for present interactions.

- Accept students as individuals and work toward realistic improvements, not perfection.
- Stimulate and lead students rather than pushing them.
- Communicate expectations to students and allow them to suggest ways to change their own behaviour.
- Display goals publicly. The technique often prompts behaviourally disordered students to do better (Lyman, 1984).
- Chart progress to reinforce behaviour.
- Be explicit about both the positive and negative consequences for behaviours, and do not use empty threats.
- Do not allow students choices unless you plan to abide by them.
- Be objective and impersonal when giving directions to the group.
- Speak slowly, firmly, confidently, and clearly, without anger or impatience. If the teacher loses control, students will feel threatened and blame the teacher.
- Keep commands short, simple, and explicitly related to the task at hand.
- Insist that a task is carried through to completion, as long as it is within the student's capability.
- Reinforce behaviours. Remember that in the classroom there are three main sources of reinforcement: the peer group, the work activity itself, and the teacher.
- Remove any tangible results of poor behaviour, such as broken glass, immediately.
- Avert crises by directing the student to a different activity.

The general approaches outlined above must of course be supplemented by techniques that take students' individual behavioural problems into account. Box 6–2 describes a number of inappropriate behaviours often exhibited by exceptional learners. Each entry in the box contains a brief suggestion about how to cope with the specified behaviour.

Preventative techniques

Preventative discipline is an integral component of classroom discipline. It is designed to prevent poor behaviour from happening by organizing the classroom, setting up consistent rules and routines, and providing appropriate rewards for correct behaviour. Teachers can do a great deal to establish the type of behaviour that they desire in a classroom by calling attention to behaviour when it occurs, especially when it provides a model for the type of conduct wanted. "I like the way that David is sitting," for example, is a more effective comment than, "Jennifer, be quiet now."

Effective teachers will find that they already employ some of the following practical techniques for controlling surface behaviour in the classroom. Classroom meetings, classroom rules, positive reinforcement, and so on, are all extremely useful for the day-to-day management of a classroom. They will not be sufficient, however, for the more serious difficulties that arise from time to time. These problems require the more structured techniques of crisis intervention or behaviour therapy, which are discussed later in the chapter.

Box 6–2 Techniques to manage specific behavioural problems

- *Careless performance:* Ignore the student or provide rewards for accuracy.
- *Classroom disruption:* Ignore the disruption if it is not dangerous. Restate classroom rules. Praise or reward appropriate behaviour.
- *Disinhibited behaviour:* Behaviour that lacks self-control is found among exceptional students. Set definite behavioural limits and help the student to understand the consistent consequences for overstepping social bounds.
- *Disorganization:* Some special learners are unable to make appropriate choices and cannot decide when to start or stop an activity. Adhere closely to routines, and structure the environment so that it contains few choices.
- *Distractibility:* This is a problem for some exceptional learners, who cannot block out extraneous stimuli. Try to keep the classroom as quiet and free of distractions as possible. Use offices or carrels.
- *Domineering behaviour:* Use a predictable order when calling on pupils, or ask a question first and then call a name. Pause after asking a question.
- *Frustration and failure:* These may manifest themselves as behavioural problems. Present tasks that have entry levels below the student's level of functioning in order to ensure success.
- *Hyperactivity:* Give specific tasks with a specific time limit.
- *Inattention to instructions:* Refuse to repeat instructions. Praise and reward good listeners.
- *Lack of attention:* Pause and look around before asking questions. Indicate that a specific person will be chosen to answer the question. Walk around the classroom, and stand close to the inattentive student.
- *Off-task conversation:* Ignore the behaviour or in some cases use conversation as a reward for completing work.
- *Overdependence on the teacher:* Use student tutors, reduce the complexity of tasks, and gradually decrease the amount of attention paid to the student.
- *Perseveration:* Verbally cue the student. Have the student practise alternative responses with a peer tutor.
- *Poor recall:* Review material, slow down the presentation, and spiral instruction.

Classroom meetings

The most common preventative technique is the classroom meeting. In this procedure,

1. Children sit in a circle.
2. They have a discussion, led by the teacher, that focusses on promoting improved self-images.
3. Students are encouraged to concentrate on the nature of the gathering rather than on a set of rules. The only rules for the meeting are: raise your hand before you speak; listen to the speaker; and do not mention private or family concerns.
4. By discussing problems, the students develop the skills they will need to solve future issues.

Positive imagery

The purpose of an exercise in positive imagery is to increase the number of positive feelings that students experience in the classroom, on the assumption that they will then have less reason to misbehave. To use this procedure, the teacher first prompts the students to imagine that they are in a beautiful place. Then they share their images with each other during a class discussion. They talk about good feelings and being happy.

Classroom rules

Any decision about what may or may not be done in the classroom constitutes a rule. Different age groups and grade levels need different rules. Classroom rules provide a framework for behaviour. They will not reduce all poor behaviour, but they do establish and maintain behavioural limits in a clear, straightforward way. Good rules are definable, reasonable, and enforceable. They should be short and concise, and focus on positive rather than negative behaviour: "Walk in the classroom," rather than "Don't run in the classroom." Students may be more co-operative if they are allowed to plan classroom rules jointly with the teacher.

Teachers should formulate a basic set of rules and post them in the classroom. Occasionally, students should be reminded of the rules, especially if they have been breaking them with any frequency. As well, specifying the rules and reviewing them occasionally may prompt students to rehearse them to themselves, and perhaps remind others of them (O'Leary & O'Leary, 1977). In very young classes, the teacher can introduce rules by using modelling. As well, pictures to accompany the written rule are effective devices.

Logical consequences

The term *logical consequences* applies to a group of methods for classroom control that concentrate on personal interactions between the pupils and the teacher. Students are seen as part of a social system comprising peers and adults, and as such must learn to respect the rights of others. The methods help students to judge the value of their behaviour and to elect alternative, more reasonable action.

Dreikurs (1968), who defined the type of method, has identified four mistaken goals that appear to motivate children's behaviour: attention-seeking, power, revenge, and disability. Children who adopt attention as their primary goal do so because they feel that the group does not value their contributions; they therefore constantly seek affirmation that they belong by drawing attention to themselves. Other children see the position of "boss" as having the highest social value. As a result, they attempt to assert power and establish authority. By engaging the teacher in a power struggle, these students are able to see themselves as equals. If successful, they can view themselves as superior to the authority figure. Many children who do not see their needs being met by getting attention or asserting power adopt the goal of revenge. They see that they are recognized most by their ability to hurt, and therefore attempt to solidify their positions by being as rebellious and hurtful as possible. These children need to be convinced that they can be loved, accepted, and valued regardless of their behaviour. The fourth mistaken goal, disability, is evident when children feel that they have failed in all their attempts to gain recognition and are incapable of contributing to the group.

At this point, they may decide to become helpless. These children are so discouraged that they give up trying. To them, their only alternative is to define their own value by how much they are pitied.

In a sense, logical consequences are classroom rules structured by social sanctions. In setting up a system of logical consequences, it is more effective if the whole school is involved. Students will then always know the consequence of a behaviour, no matter where it occurs and with whom. It is also a good idea to give students a say when establishing logical consequences. This links the behaviour to a natural consequence and to the wider society, thereby strengthening the effectiveness of the approach. For students who choose to misbehave, the consequences should be logical whenever possible. Students who waste time when they should be working, for example, should forfeit their free time during some other part of the day.

Positive reinforcement

Rewards, or positive reinforcers, constitute one of the most valuable tools that teachers have at their disposal. They apply to all students because all students need ample rewards in order to behave and achieve success in school, and positive reinforcement can often improve behavioural patterns. In the classroom, there are three main sources of reinforcement: the peer group, the work itself, and the teacher. Reinforcement from any source will be of little value, however, unless it is used properly. Rewards must match the needs and maturity level of the learners. A gold star for a sixteen year old would probably be as futile as a period delving into an encyclopedia for a prekindergarten child. Social reinforcers, such as a few words of encouragement, must always accompany tangible rewards. So many rewards are available in the regular classroom that box 6–3 presents just a sampling, after Clarizio (1976).

Crisis intervention

There will be times, even when a good preventative program is planned, that crises will arise. These can be grouped into three categories: routine management problems, a student's expression of strong emotion, and other, potentially serious crises.

Routine management problems occur daily in any classroom. Some possible problems and solutions were shown in box 6–2. Not every instance of misbehaviour needs an involved response. Many simple techniques exist that may be employed without even stopping the lesson or activity: planned ignoring, signal interference, proximity control, restructuring the activity, and direct appeals. If minor behavioural problems are really only a bid for attention then they are best ignored. Most teachers soon develop an unfailing nose for poor behaviour, however, and the process of planned ignoring is very difficult for them, requiring rigorous self-control. Responding to certain behaviours can strengthen them, whereas ignoring them avoids arguments and removes the incentive: attention from the teacher or peers. Of course, if a behaviour causes harm to others, disrupts the lesson, or sets off a chain reaction of similar behaviour from other students, the teacher should definitely intervene.

The term signal interference alludes to non-verbal cues, such as making eye contact, raising an eyebrow, and so on. Proximity control simply involves standing near a student to help him or her maintain composure. Both of these methods act as effective checks on minor disturbances. An alternative method of intervention is to restructure the

Box 6–3 Rewards in the classroom

Approval from adults
- The student's name written on the board
- Non-verbal reinforcement, such as a wink
- A good behaviour note sent to the principal, parents, or both
- A message of respect, such as "No one else thought of that"
- The principal's signature on students' papers of a certain calibre

Status and respect
- Being first in line
- Giving the weekly spelling test
- Being class librarian for the day
- Being a peer tutor

Approval from peer group
- Receiving a citizenship award
- Placing stars on other students' papers

Activities
- Putting head down to rest
- Library period
- Learning-centre period
- Drawing pictures
- Games

activity. Teachers should be flexible enough to vary the lesson in response to the tone of the class. Also, if teachers recognize how students will react to specific frustrations, they can prepare themselves to avert behavioural problems. Finally, the teacher may also make a direct appeal to students to behave appropriately, invoking class rules, peer reactions, or personal relationships. Just mentioning to some students, "Your behaviour today makes me feel uncomfortable (unhappy, angry, disappointed)" can induce more appropriate behaviour.

More serious behavioural problems naturally demand more serious measures. When a student shows a strong emotional reaction, teachers should not take it personally. They may help the student to control the tantrum through direct interventions and then actively listen to the student's problems. For other, potentially serious crises, teachers may have to resort to the stronger interventions discussed in the sections that follow, such as punishment or time out. It is important to develop one behaviour at a time, to keep rigorous documentation, and to involve parents and other teachers. Use notes to maintain communication between the school and the student's home. The most important factor in crisis intervention, however, is the teacher's composure and self-control (Coleman, 1986). If the teacher is prepared for the crises that inevitably arise and has a plan of action, she or he will remain controlled.

Punishment

Punishment has been widely used by parents and teachers to extinguish undesirable behaviours. Although the term has acquired many negative connotations, punishment is still used in classrooms. Teachers cannot tolerate all situations, and rewards will not work all the time. Punishment notifies the student that the behaviour or set of behaviours is unacceptable, usually by removing possible pleasant events. Sometimes punishment is used to eliminate a behaviour more quickly. At other times, a student will be punished for a behaviour that is simply too disruptive or extreme to be ignored. Some children respond to punishment if they are accustomed to it at home and may react poorly when the teacher uses positive reinforcement alone (Gardner, 1974).

Punishment may, however, produce undesirable side effects and can be a poor deterrent to unwanted behaviour for several reasons. First, the fear of punishment generates anger and may produce greater conflict. Often, too, the student will associate the punishment with the punisher. Second, punishment does not answer two crucial questions: do students know that they are breaking the rules and are they interpreting social cues correctly? Third, punishment in the classroom may suppress the problem but reinforce other unwanted behaviours and even teach aggressive behaviour through modelling (Polsgrove & Reith, 1983). It neither indicates correct behaviour nor stops the poor behaviour from returning.

Paying attention to the following guidelines, adapted from Gardner (1974), will produce the most desirable behavioural effects and the smallest number of negative side effects:

- Define precisely the inappropriate behaviour, the conditions under which it occurs, and its strength.
- Use punishment infrequently. Using time out or response costs is preferable to punishment.
- Administer many positive reinforcers, in addition to punishment, to prevent the student from associating the punisher with the punishment.
- Make explicit the circumstances under which students will be punished, and use clear procedures when administering punishment.
- Put the rules about punishment into effect consistently and immediately.
- Identify, and then reinforce, alternative, more acceptable behaviours to replace the punished behaviours.
- Present the maximum aversive event from the outset. In other words, do not increase the punishment.
- Ensure that the punishment is, in fact, unpleasant to the student. Giving a student a detention on a very cold day may actually reinforce the behaviour if it is more unpleasant to be outside than in.
- Do not threaten or nag about punishment.

Time out

Successful programs for behavioural change place great emphasis on rewarding positive behaviour and less on attending to poor behaviour. But some behaviour simply cannot be ignored. The consequences, however, vary in degree and complexity.

Time out is a flexible procedure in which the student is removed from a desirable activity for short periods of time (Gast & Nelson, 1977). It is therefore an immediate consequence for persistent, unacceptable behaviour. The idea is that the brief period of removal will help the student to learn which behaviours cannot be tolerated and to regain enough composure to participate in the rest of the learning activity.

Life-space interviews

Life-space interviews were first used in residential settings as part of a therapeutic intervention for behaviourally disordered students, but they may also be used in regular classroom situations (Redl, 1966). The purpose of an interview is for the student to identify and discuss inappropriate behaviours with an adult, usually a counsellor or teacher. Life-space interviews should be used sparingly as the situation demands. They are only conducted if both the teacher and the student are in the right mood: neither should remain angry or resentful over the behavioural incident. The interview covers present issues: short-term strategies that will ultimately lead to long-term improvement. During the interview, the student states his or her own perception of an incident rather than being immediately criticized by the teacher. The teacher then attempts to show the student how the behaviour affected the group. The student is not punished but is required to identify alternative ways of coping with the type of situation that provoked the incident (De Magistris & Imber, 1980). The teacher helps the student to do this, and to devise a plan to avoid repeating the problematic behaviour.

The process must be an interview, not a discussion. It should be conducted in a private setting away from the classroom by an adult who plays a strong role in the student's life. The interview should occur as soon as possible after the troublesome event and as close as possible in physical proximity to the setting where it took place (Coleman, 1986).

Changing behaviour

Ideally, all children should develop self-control. Unfortunately, many need help to develop efficient and effective coping strategies. Although teaching aggressive children to be less obnoxious is no simple task, a number of therapies have evolved for intervention with mildly handicapped youngsters who exhibit behavioural problems. It must be pointed out, however, that therapies are not a substitute for instruction in social skills. Personal insight into behavioural patterns does not provide enough motivation to change those patterns.

Although classroom teachers are not necessarily responsible for presenting or supervising the therapies, they should be aware of some of the processes involved and the many varieties available: art, music, play, drama, group, behaviour therapy, and so on. For a full discussion of various therapies the interested reader is directed to Newcomer (1980).

Bibliotherapy

Bibliotherapy can be used successfully in the regular classroom. It is based on the idea that students can discover specific resolutions to personal problems by reading literature. It is hoped that they will then learn strategies to solve their own problems and begin to understand the problems of others. Selected readings range from books and magazines chosen by the student to passages selected by the teacher and designed to stress a particular topic, trait, reaction, or moral.

The readings should produce identification, catharsis, and insight. If the readers share the attitudes, motivations, values, needs, and desires of the characters they read about then identification has taken place. They will then express an empathetic emotional response (catharsis), which leads to the discovery (insight) of personal motives, desires, and wishes, and helps the readers to arrive at the solutions to their own problems.

Play therapy

In this procedure, children are encouraged to express their pent-up feelings by playing with toys (Schaefer, 1979). The sessions take place in private, where the therapist can control the environment. In non-directive play therapy the child directs the play and the therapist clarifies the child's feelings (Axline, 1977). In directive play therapy the play is highly structured and follows a developmental pattern (Burt & Myrick, 1980).

Music therapy

Music can be used to produce both physiological and mental effects (Charlesworth, 1982). In music therapy, different types of music are selected and played, depending on the desired mood. It is hoped that the music will help children to verbalize their feelings, or calm them so that they will work better.

Behavioural approaches

The primary goal of education is the acquisition of behaviour — or learning. As educators, our role is to teach students new behaviours such as reading, writing, and attending. To accomplish this, we apply knowledge from learning theory and experimental psychology.

Students who are hyperaggressive and highly disruptive constitute the major portion of those identified in schools as emotionally disturbed (Kauffman, 1981), and for these students the presence of deviant behaviour interferes with their ability to acquire the behaviours that educators are endeavouring to impart. Structured behavioural programs have been used successfully with such students.

Behavioural approaches to classroom management and discipline arose from the seminal work of J.B. Watson and B.F. Skinner. The approaches were originally developed to treat maladaptive situations, usually phobias, stuttering, and infantile autism, for severely retarded children. Behavioural approaches have been employed successfully in both regular and special classrooms. A number of investigations have indicated that behaviour modification techniques can improve the social and academic behaviours of both non-handicapped and exceptional youngsters.

Behaviour therapy, or behaviour modification to use the more common synonym, has three steps. First, the behaviours that need to be changed are identified. Second, the behaviours are monitored and reinforcers are identified. Third, the alternative, appropriate behaviours are modelled. The simplest way to remember the sequence is to think of it as the ABC of behaviour modification: the antecedent, the behaviour, and the consequence.

In its broadest sense, the term behaviour modification refers to a set of principles that specify the conditions under which behaviour is learned, altered, maintained, or eliminated. Behaviourists believe that all behaviour is learned and that the conditions controlling the learning process exist outside the individual. The behaviour has a cause and can therefore be changed by altering the conditions in the environment that cause or maintain it. This applies to all behaviour, deviant or otherwise, thus making it both possible and reasonable to talk about attending behaviours, reading behaviours, spelling behaviours, and so on. There are a variety of approaches subsumed within behaviour therapy, just as there are many behavioural terms (see box 6–4).

Box 6–4 Behavioural terms useful for classroom teachers

Aversive: unpleasant, painful, annoying, or uncomfortable.
Baseline: the strength or level of behaviour before any procedure is introduced. Baseline measures are applied to assess a type of performance until it has stabilized and can be used as a basis of comparison to assess the effects of intervention.
Behaviour: any action a person performs that may be observed and measured.
Behavioural objective: a precise specification of a goal, which includes the behaviour, the situation or condition under which it is to occur, and the standard of acceptability, or criterion.
Chain: a learned sequence of behaviours usually performed in the same order; once the first behaviour in the chain is performed all the others tend to follow.
Consequence: any action or event that occurs as a result of a behaviour.
Contingency: a statement of the dependent relationship between two events.
Contingency contract: an agreement between two or more parties that stipulates the responsibilities of each with regard to a specific item or activity.
Extinction: the process of removing reinforcement until an inappropriate behaviour returns to low levels.
Modelling: providing examples of appropriate behaviour after which students can pattern their own.
Positive reinforcement: a response to a performance, given to students to encourage them to maintain or increase the level of the appropriate behaviour.
Premack principle: a precept that, given two responses, one can be used to reinforce the other. In other words, the probability of a less enjoyable task being performed is increased by making a more enjoyable task contingent upon its completion.
Response cost: the penalty of losing a token, in a token economy, as a punishment for inappropriate behaviour.
Terminal behaviour: a behaviour within a developmental or curricular dimension or subdimension of instruction that represents reasonable progress or change from past behavioural patterns.
Time out: the process of reducing inappropriate behaviour by removing the student from the situation to a place where reinforcement for that behaviour is not available.
Token economy: a system in which the student receives tokens for performing a predetermined behaviour, which she or he may later exchange for a reinforcer.

Principles of reinforcement

Behaviour modification explicitly states that behaviour is caused and controlled by external environmental events. If we therefore assume that reinforcement — reward — is necessary for, or at least enhances, learning, then the student must be rewarded for mastering a task. For a student who has met with failure, the task will not be inherently rewarding and in fact may be aversive and thus inhibiting. It is therefore important to make the completion of a task meaningful to the student by establishing a reinforcing climate. If the completed task is immediately met with the reinforcer, task mastery will itself eventually become reinforcing. To be educationally effective, behavioural techniques must not only provide immediate rewards for a single pupil if necessary, but must also encourage the entire class or peer group to support the situation.

The success of a behavioural program depends upon the effective use of reinforcers. Of these there are two major classes, primary and secondary. In either case, of course, the reinforcer must be of value to the student. Primary reinforcers are biologically satisfying to the individual. Food, such as cereal or candy, is generally used. Secondary reinforcers, on the other hand, have a learned value. The tokens used in a token economy are a good example. It is preferable to use secondary reinforcers because the goal of behaviour modification is eventually to remove any external reinforcement for appropriate behaviour. Always therefore accompany them with social reinforcers, such as a smile or nod, so that students gradually cede less importance to the secondary reinforcer itself and learn to respond to positive feedback.

To illustrate how reinforcement is used in a behavioural program, box 5–5 outlines the steps involved in managing a particular behaviour, temper tantrums, in the classroom.

The behavioural management program

The school-based team determines the specific components of a behavioural management program from detailed information about the behaviour being changed, the physical and social setting, the people who will administer the program, and the student's individual characteristics and age. The most successful strategies for adolescents, for example, seem to be those that employ home-based reinforcement, **group contingencies**, or self-determined reinforcement (Martin & McLaughlin, 1981). When planning a program, the teacher must ask several questions. What behaviour is lacking or maladaptive? What behaviour should be increased or decreased? What contingencies in the environment support the behaviour? What may be manipulated to reinforce good behaviour?

The behaviour to be modified should first be clearly defined. Aggressive behaviour, for example, might include fighting, kicking, throwing objects, or indulging in verbal abuse. Once the behaviour is defined it must be measured using the techniques explained in chapter 3, such as direct observation, event recording, and time sampling. After assessing the inappropriate behaviours, the teacher selects behavioural methods to use in the program.

As a general rule, a specific behavioural management plan should be developed with well-defined objectives covering numerous behavioural dimensions for each student. The plan should include procedures for evaluating its usefulness and for revising

Box 6–5 Managing a temper tantrum in the classroom

1. Define the behaviours that made up the temper tantrum. Note the time, place, and social setting in which the tantrum occurred. What produced or precipitated it?
2. Obtain some measure of the strength of the behaviour. How many tantrums occur during a day? An hour? How long do they last? How intense are they? Does the child lose all control?
3. Describe what happens in the child's environment during the tantrum? How do the other children react?
4. Inform the child that reinforcement will only be provided for specific behaviours, for example, remaining seated for specified periods of time.
5. If the temper tantrums are likely to occur at certain times or in specific sitations, attempt to involve the child in another behaviour at that time to reduce the possibility of frustration and the resulting tantrum.
6. Do not reinforce the tantrum once it is under way. Let it run its course. After ensuring that the child cannot hurt himself or herself, or anyone else, ignore the behaviour. Even acknowledging the tantrum may increase its intensity and duration.
7. Reinforce the child at other times when appropriate behaviour is displayed.
8. Especially reinforce the child's behaviour at times when she or he experiences frustration but does not indulge in a tantrum.
9. Inform the child of the consequences of the tantrums. Tell him or her, for example, "You cannot join the class for art unless you choose to stop crying."
10. Do not let the child arouse sympathy or guilt. Instead help him or her to develop personal responsibility for all behaviour.
11. Never give in. Eventually this will only prolong the tantrums.

Source: Adapted from *Children with Learning and Behavior Problems: A Behavior Management Approach* by W.I. Gardner, 1974, Boston: Allyn and Bacon.

strategies if the original ones do not work. When devising a plan and putting it into effect, consider the following suggestions:

- Set realistic objectives that aim for improvement, not perfection.
- Draw up the program in small steps that introduce changes slowly. Concentrate on only one behaviour initially.
- Give the student time to adapt to the new situation; don't expect change to occur immediately.
- Success depends upon the student's involvement. Discuss the whole process with him or her.
- Plan reinforcement for positive behaviours.
- Describe the behaviour being reinforced to the student at the time of the reinforcement.
- Demonstrate the new behavioural requirements.
- State requests positively.
- Give the student success from the outset.

Some of the following behavioural techniques require only very minor classroom adaptations; others imply greater modifications in teaching practice and time management. All, however, are geared to helping behaviourally disordered students attain appropriate educational and social standards in the regular classroom.

Token economies

As with many types of behaviour therapy, token economies can be used either with the whole class or with individuals. Essentially, the term implies rewarding students for appropriate behaviours with tokens that they can later redeem for a larger reward, or reinforcer. To institute a token economy:

1. Select the behaviours to be rewarded and those to be extinguished. Be sparing.
2. Select the students whose behaviour needs modifying.
3. Select tokens. These are small rewards of no intrinsic value, such as poker chips, gold stars, or check marks. Be sure to change the tokens often as the program proceeds.
4. Specify the number of tokens needed to earn a reinforcer, to increase over the duration of the program.
5. Discuss the program with the class or student. Explain exactly what happens and why. Allow students to have a say when choosing reinforcers. These should be school-based activities such as an hour in the library, an art period, or free time.
6. While the program is underway, keep a master list of transactions. You may wish to use response costs also, taking back a token as punishment for poor behaviour.
7. Present reinforcers at specified times.

Contingency contracts

Many teachers find contracts to be especially useful for working with students with behavioural and social disorders (see figure 6–3). Contracts appear to have a special attraction for many adolescents, possibly because they realize that both partners signing the agreement have obligations. In addition, contractual agreements are a real feature of the everyday world (Bond, 1981). The technique involves carefully identifying the troublesome behaviour. The teacher then draws up a contract specifying behavioural goals, the criteria for reaching them, and rewards. Both parties sign the contract in the presence of witnesses who have explained the obligations entailed. The contracts must be honest, positive, fair to both parties, and used systematically. On the contract include:

- the date that the contract begins, the date that it ends, and the date that it is to be renegotiated
- the behaviour to be changed
- the amount and kind of reward or reinforcer to be used
- a schedule for delivering reinforcers

A schedule for reviewing progress is optional but recommended. Also optional are a bonus clause for sustained or excellent performance and a statement of the penalties imposed if the specific behaviour is not performed.

This is an agreement between Harry (student) and Mr. Yu (teacher).

The contract begins on January 21st and ends on June 27th

It will be reviewed on every Thursday.

The terms of the agreement are:

The student will come to class on time, with all his books, and present his completed homework to the teacher at the beginning of the class.

The teacher will - allow Harry one spare period every Friday
- notify Harry's mother to allow him to go to the movies once a week.

Bonus clause: For exceptional behaviour, Harry will earn $2.00 extra spending money.

Penalties: If Harry breaks the contract he will not be allowed free time or movies.

Signed by:
(student) Harry Vermeer
(teacher) Mr. Yu

Figure 6–3 A contingency contract

Daily work contracts

Daily work contracts lay out clearly and specifically all the tasks that a student must perform during the day. Each teacher signs the contract or checks off the tasks listed, as shown in figure 6–4.

Date April 2nd

Student Cameron

Today Cameron must complete the following tasks:

	Yes	No
1. Write a story	✓	
2. Complete a science experiment at the learning centre.		✓
3. Practise mathematical facts.		✓
4. Answer questions about the story.	✓	

Figure 6–4 A daily work contract

These students are conferring about their report cards, which reflect both behaviour and performance.

Daily report cards

Daily report cards are designed to increase communication among students, teachers, and parents. By responding to a student's behaviour and performance, the report gives information about progress not usually available to the parents. Daily report cards should point out success as well as problems.

The punch-card technique

Crow, Johnston, Meeks, and Wilson (1975) report that using a punch card to keep track of earned points for behaviourally disordered youngsters is a successful approach. Students are daily presented with the cards when they arrive in class. As the day proceeds, students are assigned points and have their cards punched if they perform certain activities. At the end of the day, the teacher and students together count the earned points. A specified number of points then earns a reward.

The flexibility of the punch-card system meets the needs of individuals, the group, and the teacher. The cards may be used with chosen individuals and events are quickly and easily recorded. The system thus accommodates a number of goals and can be useful in the regular classroom.

Cognitive behaviour modification

A variety of methods fall under **cognitive behaviour modification** that have in common the aim of prompting students to learn to think about their feelings and behaviour. The methods are based on the assumption that students who are taught to think first will be less likely to behave impulsively. Thinking and self-vocalization (inner speech) act as a buffer between feelings and behaviours. Students are trained to use inner speech for their own benefit. Although the procedure is used in academic tasks (see chapter 13), it is also successful for self-monitoring (Hallahan & Sapona, 1983). In this process, the student monitors his own behaviour and keeps a record of the evaluation.

One method is to teach students to ask themselves questions such as, "Was I paying attention?" every time they hear a tone on a tape-recorder set by the teacher at random intervals, the average interval being about forty-five seconds. If the student can answer "yes," she enters a checkmark on the evaluation sheet, while a "no" gains a mark in the negative column.

As chapters 5 and 6 have stressed, efficient organization underlies successful teaching. The well-organized teacher is more likely to have a smoothly running classroom with well-disciplined students, at which point she or he will be able to present a range of academic content. The next part of the text delves into numerous approaches for presenting various subjects to special learners.

PART

3

Presenting instruction

7 Teaching language arts

Grammar, syntax, punctuation, and capitalization

Teaching grammar, syntax, punctuation, and capitalization

Creative writing

Assessing creative writing

Teaching creative writing

- Journal writing
- Publishing students' stories
- Poetry writing
- Descriptive writing
- Story writing
- Expository writing
- Creative writing activities

Dear Reader,

Why is it that for some children learning language is extremely difficult and for others so easy? The question has been raised many times by both parents and educators. We do know that most young children learn to understand and speak their language in a very short time. It is when they begin school that they encounter difficulties in the language areas, especially in reading and writing.

Language is neither innate nor learned only by imitation. Instead, the young child must try out the rules of language. Parents and siblings do not teach language, although they help to shape its development. If children do not have the opportunity to interact, then they may come to school with a limited experiential background. If teachers keep language natural, however, and remember that its primary purpose is communication, these problems become more manageable.

Keeping language natural (or whole, in the popular terminology) means allowing all children to use their language. Teachers should provide lots of opportunities for children to interact with one another, to discuss things, to listen, to explain, to give their opinions, and to hear those of others. This is how we build on what they know and help them to progress.

Children need to develop their expressive skills in writing as well as in speaking. They need to experiment by scribbling, printing letters, and copying words. Soon they learn sound–symbol relationships and begin writing down messages. Those children who don't learn this at home go through the stages at school. Children perfect their writing skills not by filling in words on a notebook page but by writing, editing, and then sharing with their classmates what they have written.

Reading, the other component of receptive language, is a source of frustration for many children. Before they come to school, they can read signs such as Stop and Exit, and can identify their favourite cereal package at the supermarket. They are getting meaning from the printed word. When children begin school, their teachers must build on this rudimentary knowledge about reading. First and foremost, they must realize that when children begin to read they expect to make some immediate sense out of what they're reading. Too often, so much emphasis is placed upon decoding each word that students begin to think of reading as a word-by-word process in which getting each word right is the primary concern and getting the meaning, secondary.

Perhaps the most important thing for the classroom teacher to remember is that each child, including each exceptional child, is unique. The teacher must be aware of what the child knows and what he or she needs to know, and proceed from there. It is not an easy task, but it can be done.

Beverly Lee
Remedial Instructor
Memorial University of Newfoundland

Acquiring language is probably the most important single learning experience in an individual's life. Communication with others is one of the most complex activities that humans undertake. Effective communication is vital to our daily existence and social progress, yet learning language demands so much from the human organism that the process is vulnerable to all the problems that affect children.

Language is a dynamic interplay of sound, syntax, and semantics, developed by interaction among people. The growth of communication is cumulative, not linear. Development should not be conceptualized as a ladder or stepping stones, because these metaphors imply that the student leaves behind old learning as he or she acquires the new. In language, as in most models of mental growth, learning is continuously transformed into more advanced skills and knowledge.

Language begins and develops in a social setting. Although researchers are still trying to understand the processes involved, it seems clear that competence in communication must be learned within the course of everyday transactions between children and their caregivers. Attempts to classify experiences of the world and of language are reflected in the development, between two and three years of age, of a personal variety of grammar. By the age of four, most children have achieved a great deal of linguistic maturity: they have usually mastered the basic structures of their language. By the time they arrive at school they have a firm linguistic base, with a sophisticated grasp of semantic and syntactic rules, and an ever-expanding vocabulary.

Some people seem to have a talent for learning their native language. Early in life, and almost without effort, they learn to understand speech and to make themselves understood. They learn reading, writing, and spelling in the early grades of school or before. They easily acquire the skills necessary to present their thoughts clearly by word of mouth or in writing. For many exceptional pupils, however, acquiring and using language are difficult tasks. Among most special learners, language is the class of behaviour that most clearly carries the mark of exceptionality. Language difficulties traverse many areas of difficulty; one problem influences another and can have a progressive, debilitating effect on behaviour and academics.

There is a correlation between deficits in speech and language and lower intelligence, although there does not exist adequate evidence to state that mental retardation is the cause of linguistic impairment (Miller & Yoder, 1972). Cognitive development and language are interactive in nature, however, since the comprehension and expression of ideas are mutually dependent. It is typical to find a higher rate of speech impairments among mildly mentally retarded children than among the general population. As well, the linguistic levels of mentally retarded pupils are below their general mental age (Smith, 1974). Deficits in certain cognitive abilities, such as short-term memory, may explain the lag.

Mentally retarded children tend to use poor grammar and syntax, improper speech sounds, and poverty-stricken meaning. They demonstrate delays in the development of sentence length, sentence complexity, and speech-sound discrimination. Their expressive language tends to be less complex than average, often revealing a lower percentage of nouns and difficulty generalizing the rules of grammar (Cramer, 1978). Yet although many mildly mentally retarded children possess vocabulary and language that are limited in academic contexts, their skills are usually adequate for most ordinary situations.

An increasing number of researchers are suggesting that learning disabilities are related to facility with language (e.g. Bryan, 1978). Learning-disabled students may manifest difficulties in oral expression, listening comprehension, written expression, basic reading skills, and basic comprehension. Perhaps 50 percent of learning-disabled students have speech and language problems (Marge, 1972). **Language disorders** are the most common learning disabilities noted at the preschool level, and may result from lags in the normal maturational patterns of learning (Slingerland, 1971). Usually, it will be noted that the child does not use language in the same way as other young children. Specifically, learning-disabled youngsters will often demonstrate quantitative delays in morphology, limitations in their comprehension of syntax, impairments in abstractions, generalizations, oral syntax, and finding words, and significant misunderstanding of linguistic concepts in which logical relationships are expressed between two or more verbal elements (Semel & Wiig, 1975).

Once these children reach school, their difficulties may be manifested in all areas of the language hierarchy. If left unrecognized, the problems will intensify, becoming increasingly difficult to overcome. Mildly learning-disabled children, however, do not hold a monopoly on language deviations and difficulties. The condition of a child's basic sensory and motoric systems will have much to do with the adequacy of her or his linguistic repertoire. A child with defective hearing can not learn language effectively, and a child with motoric dysfunctions may encounter difficulties with speech. On the other hand, gifted children may demonstrate precocious development in all areas of the language hierarchy.

The **language hierarchy** contains the four areas of listening, speaking, reading, and writing, as shown in figure 7–1. The relationships among the different areas are close and vital; as skills are acquired, each builds on the preceding one. Listening and speaking are referred to as primary linguistic activities because most children learn them naturally, early in life. The secondary linguistic activities, reading and writing, must generally be taught and are the prime focus of school programming, especially in the early grades. As well, listening and reading are known as decoding activities because they interpret an incoming message, and speaking and writing are encoding activities, since they formulate messages for someone else to decode. The language hierarchy, of course, is founded firmly on an experiential base.

English is very difficult to learn, and its complexities are compounded by the largest vocabulary of any language in the world. English has twenty-six letters representing forty-six sounds, both variant and invariant, silent letters, and three hundred different letter combinations for seventeen vowel sounds (Allred, 1977). Little wonder that many children encounter severe difficulties acquiring the rules and innumerable exceptions that comprise spoken and written English.

Some exceptional youngsters have difficulty with the earliest parts of the language hierarchy, receiving and expressing oral language. They may have trouble following directions, interpreting messages and "wh" questions correctly, and adapting their style of communication to their listeners' needs. Children with these kinds of difficulties have problems with everyday communication, not just in language-based school tasks.

Without question, however, reading problems constitute the most prevalent linguistic deficits found among the population of exceptional students. Reading disability is related to general facility with language (Abrams, 1975; Vogel, 1974), and may compound, be

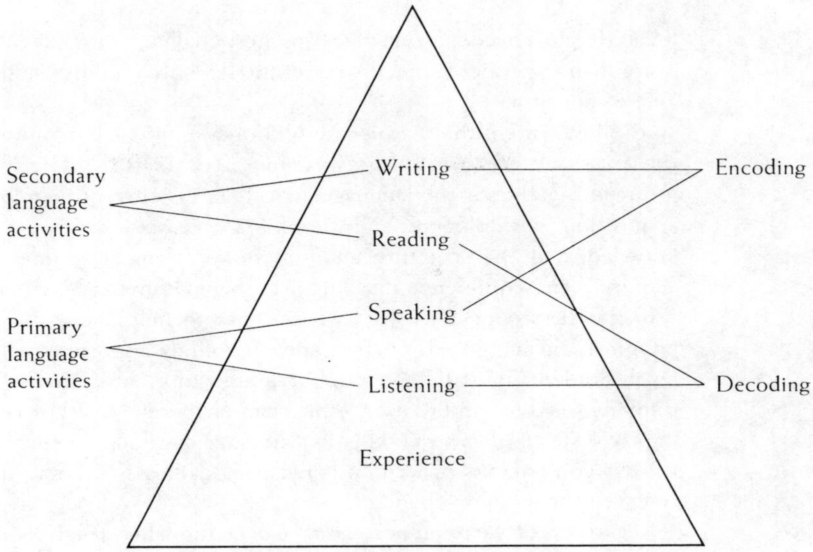

Figure 7–1 The language hierarchy

a component of, or cause deficits in other linguistic areas. Compared to normal readers, poor readers show less verbal fluency, smaller speaking vocabularies, poorer organizational and integrative skills, and inferior syntactic ability. Differences between normal and disabled readers are seen in the broad areas of semantics, syntax, and phonology (Vogel, 1975, 1977).

Writing, the ability to put thoughts down on paper, is the highest form of communication and the last to be mastered. Many children and adults write poorly and even incomprehensibly. Writing actually refers to a variety of interrelated skills, chiefly spelling, handwriting, and composition, or creative writing, as this text terms it. It also rests on underlying prerequisite skills such as facility in oral language, reading, some knowledge of the rules of written usage, and a flexible and usable vocabulary.

Teaching is, above all, a linguistic activity, and as children progress through the school system, they will encounter ever-increasing ways of using language. Instruction in the early years, from kindergarten to grade two, centres on the basic skills in reading, spelling, and arithmetic. Teachers employ many pictures and concrete materials. In grades three and four the demands on language increase considerably. Emphasis shifts to the content areas and the development of reasoning skills. By the time pupils reach grades five and six, language becomes the main instructional vehicle. Materials are more abstract and symbolic and students are expected to demonstrate their ability to learn from written and spoken sources. Grades seven and eight place still heavier emphasis on developing expertise in written and oral language. Students are required to develop more advanced strategies for solving problems and issues. The high school curriculum tends to be based almost exclusively on language, and students who suffer deficits in any area of the language hierarchy are at a severe disadvantage. At secondary levels, English becomes one of the greatest challenges for exceptional students. English, more than any other subject, stresses the skills that mildly handicapped pupils are least able to perform.

It follows, then, that within the school system teachers must be concerned with all the areas related to language. Listening, speaking, reading, and writing are usually grouped together as the language arts. There is currently an increasing interest in the acquisition, development, and use of language. Teachers are demonstrating expanded knowledge of the structure and function of language, interest in how language is acquired, and confidence that linguistic behaviour can be taught.

In the classroom, it is the teacher's task to help each student to learn the words, grammar, meaning, and correct speech sounds appropriate for each developmental level. Students must be given opportunities to practise their skills in communication, thinking, reading, and writing. This chapter therefore discusses teaching techniques to improve special learners' skills in listening, speaking, spelling, handwriting, and the further components of written language. Reading is such an important area that it is reserved for the next chapter.

Regardless of the pupil's category of exceptionality, teachers should be eclectic about choosing ideas for teaching language arts. The main objectives of this chapter are therefore to

- outline approaches and activities for teaching language arts to exceptional students
- discuss methods to assess receptive and expressive language, spelling, handwriting, and written language

Learning language

Children learn language through meaningful interaction with the adults around them. As they develop competence in the various forms of communication, their skill in receptive language precedes and exceeds their skill in expressive language. Learning-disabled and mentally retarded students generally reach a plateau in their linguistic development (Tarver & Ellsworth, 1981). Students with severe language problems may need special instruction into their mid-teens (Menyuk, 1971).

While educators agree on the importance of language in the curriculum and its basic nature in all teaching and learning, Dever (1978) points out that it is relatively rare for the goals of linguistic instruction to be made specific, because the instruction is very complex and involves so many diverse tasks for the student. When developing individual education programs for exceptional students who are meeting difficulties with language, educators must create behavioural objectives that centre around language programs within the ongoing curriculum. The programming should also be firmly rooted in actual experiences provided for the students within the context of instruction.

Assessing language

Communicative competence is measured on the basis of an individual's ability to use semantics, grammar, syntax, phonology, and pragmatics—the effective use of language in social interactions. The purpose of language evaluation is to establish a baseline by which to describe an exceptional student's typical pattern of skills in language and communication. Further, evaluation seeks to identify the factors that facilitate or inhibit those skills and to obtain the information necessary to formulate individual language instruction goals for the individual. Children should be screened when they first begin school. Critical points, at which children are at risk for linguistic disorders and should be evaluated, occur in the transition from grade three to grade four, from grade six to grade seven, and from grade eight to grade nine (Shames & Wiig, 1982).

A comprehensive language evaluation includes data from two main sources: formal and informal measures. Formal assessment procedures, employing standardized tests, identify specific structural and communicative deficiencies. They do not, however, yield information about a student's functional use of language. Formal measures to assess syntactic complexity and diversity of vocabulary do not do justice to children's language competencies as reflected in their spontaneous interactions (Wilkinson & Dollaghan, 1979). These instruments should be supplemented by behavioural observations and qualitative analysis of spontaneous language samples.

Language samples are examples of children's natural and spontaneous language, collected during periods of social interaction. They provide the material for the most realistic and comprehensive assessment of children's communicative competence. Language sampling procedures are fully discussed in chapter 11.

Stimulating and improving language

Language stimulation and improvement are intended to provide children and youth with a framework on which to build the sentences that they need to communicate freely and easily. Daily experience in putting thoughts into words is an essential part of acquiring and practising the rules of language. Good instructional approaches use children's own language and stories, and familiar material such as nursery rhymes, jingles, songs, and fairy tales to stimulate language and to teach early reading. On a more general note, some points to keep in mind about teaching language are given below:

- Language instruction goes on all day; be a good language model, and ensure that children are bathed in a stimulating linguistic environment.
- Instigate many interactions between language-delayed pupils and their non-handicapped peers. There is strong support for mainstreaming communicatively disordered children on the basis that they will tend to imitate desired linguistic behaviour (Ross, 1978).
- Integrate all areas of the language hierarchy into instruction carefully and consistently.
- Give students many opportunities to practise language. As an example, schedule a short daily period devoted to developing conversational skills.
- Reword or repeat a message if students do not understand it; use much verbal redundancy.
- Without overenunciating, slow down speech slightly for language-delayed youngsters.
- Use many non-verbal cues for children with language problems. Always accompany a direction with a gesture.

- Provide labels when possible for actions, things, and feelings. Constantly repeat the names of key objects and allow children plenty of "hands-on" experience with the labelled articles.
- Allow auditory training (listening skills) a crucial place in the curriculum.
- Recognize that understanding precedes expression.

For older students:

- Develop a flexible system of small groups, arranged around subject interests and writing needs.
- Use peer tutors.
- Reduce the length of assignments for students with writing difficulties.
- Allow these students more time to complete tasks.
- Use assignments and materials appropriate to the students' age.
- Allow language-delayed students to take tests in alternative ways; by tape recorder, for example.

Language instruction should not be compartmentalized. Although formal teaching may take place during one particular period in the timetable, usage, generalization, correction, and reinforcement should be consistent and continuous. One way of ensuring continuity is to employ unit approaches (see chapter 5), which review and reinforce instruction in some or all curricular areas throughout the school day. If, for example, a teacher has been stressing the correct use of adjectives, this emphasis can easily be incorporated into several curricular areas.

A whole language approach

Traditional approaches to language have tended to fragment instruction. Instead of dividing the language arts program into separate subjects, however, the **whole language** approach (sometimes referred to as language across the curriculum) operates on the principle that reading, writing, speaking, and listening are closely related linguistic processes rather than autonomous units.

Many researchers and educators interested in ways to instruct exceptional students who have reading and language difficulties advocate a whole language approach because it emphasizes meaning over form, and uses children's own language in instruction. Lessons are structured so that a specific activity includes all the language arts, allowing children to make use of the natural relationships among linguistic components as they learn. Language is used in a meaningful manner that can be transferred and generalized to other situations.

A language experience approach

Language experience is particularly effective in the earlier school grades but can also be used very successfully with older students. The approach involves all aspects of the language hierarchy. Language experience may be thought of as a child-centered program that capitalizes on children's own language patterns and experiences. The approach encourages them to express their own ideas, feelings, and emotions so that they can hear their ideas and see them in written form.

Although there are many ways to stimulate language through language experience, the approach should include planned and continuous activities. Pupils can, for example, dictate stories (as a group or an individual activity), illustrate them and maintain notebooks of the stories, create individual word banks, and complete handwriting and creative writing exercises. On the teacher's part, the approach incorporates such activities as reading prose and poetry out loud each day with the students, assigning time in the learning centre, guiding reading and thinking sessions, and keeping records of pupils' progress.

A language experience approach is especially appropriate for exceptional children because it is both individualized and diagnostic. It allows flexibility in the size and ability of groups and employs open-ended questions demanding diverse and individual responses. Using a language experience approach, a teacher can readily identify the special needs of an individual pupil and then plan the direction of future teaching and learning.

In fact, for all students, regular and exceptional, the effects of using a language experience approach are positive and varied. The approach enhances children's self-concepts by making them aware of the importance of their own thoughts and experiences. It involves them in learning and fosters a natural pride in their own work because their ideas are accepted. It also helps to bridge the gap between oral vocabulary and reading vocabulary. Finally, language experience develops co-operation by teaching children to appreciate the ideas of others, and extends their concepts and language by encouraging them to share ideas and have discussions, which then generate new ideas.

Language experience techniques hold inherent advantages for teachers, as well as benefiting students. They encourage teachers to be creative and accommodate flexibility in programming. The approach also impels teachers to individualize instruction to a greater extent. The manner in which language experience is presented is determined only by the needs and interest of the students, and the inventiveness of the teacher. One example of a language experience lesson is presented below.

Language experience lesson

Age level: Kindergarten to grade 3

Objectives:
- to develop a permanent record of the language connected with a child-centred experience
- to improve expressive and receptive language
- to practise sight-word recognition
- to extend vocabulary by using the names of different kinds of fruit, and their comparative sizes, shapes, textures, and colours

Materials:
- large bowl
- knives
- an assortment of fruit

Developing the activity:
Place the various types of fruit in a large box or bowl. Ask one child to come and take a fruit, and then supply the appropriate language, such as, "Adrian has a big green apple." Have the children select the fruits in turn, cut them up, put them in the bowl, and stir. Throughout, prompt them to provide the appropriate language for their actions.

Developing the chart story:
Following the activity, compose a chart with the class to describe the experience. Elicit sentences, reword them if necessary, and record them on the chart (figure 7–2). When the chart is complete, read the sentences, and then have the children read. Illustrations or even photographs may be added to the chart. If children are old enough, they copy the story into their books; if not they draw pictures of the experience.

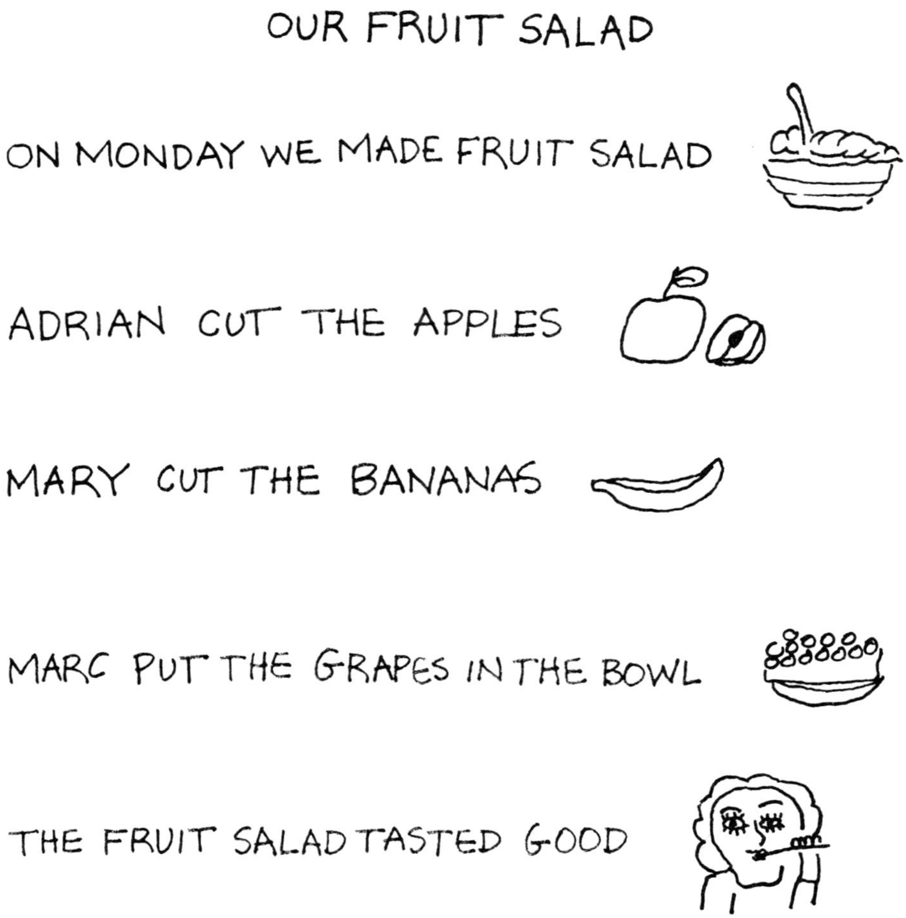

Figure 7–2 Language experience chart

Follow-up activities:

a) Write the sentences on heavy cards, and then cut them into word units. Have the children place the words in the correct sequence to form sentences.
b) Place the names of the fruits in one column and descriptions in others. Ask each child to select an entry from the columns and to write her or his own sentence.

oranges	orange	tangy
apples	red	crisp
bananas	yellow	soft
grapes	green	sweet
pears	yellow	juicy

c) Use the same vocabulary as above, but have the children match the fruit to the description of their choosing.
d) Print the chart story sentences on a single sheet. Have different children illustrate each sentence. Bind and add the book to the class library.

Vocabulary

Vocabulary refers to the total supply of words that an individual uses. Children need instruction designed to develop their vocabulary systematically and extensively if they are to communicate effectively, write adequately, and read well. *Word usage* refers not to a person's supply of words but to the appropriateness with which the individual selects them. Take, as an example, the teacher of deaf children who introduced her class to the new word, disintegrate. She taught the meaning as "to break up," but discovered that the class had internalized a strange usage when they reported, "Joe and Colleen disintegrated last night."

Roughly speaking, the reading vocabulary of an average high school graduate should consist of about 40 000 basic words, including all their variations. Add to these proper nouns, places, and idioms and the total is doubled. This says something about children's ability to acquire new vocabulary. If the average high school graduate is 17, he or she must have learned 80 000 words over a period of 16 years; that is 5 000 words a year or roughly 13 or 14 words a day (Miller & Gildea, 1987).

Language-disabled children acquire vocabulary more slowly. For these students, vocabulary expansion should form a part of the language arts program, the component that helps them to learn more about familiar words, to learn new words, and to become aware of the multifarious meanings of words. Research conducted into the processes involved in learning words suggests that a teacher's best friend in this endeavour is the student's motivation to understand the language (Miller & Gildea, 1987).

Young children need activity centres and play centres where they can handle, discuss, and experiment with a range of objects. The activities will lead to naming, describing, forming sequences, and using qualitative words such as big, tall, wide, thin, hot, and rough. Children should be supplied with paint, paper, and scrap materials, and be encouraged to discuss their activities with peers and teachers. Structured play of this kind also develops appropriate interactions among pupils, such as taking turns, asking questions, and completing tasks co-operatively. Story telling that involves children in both responses and dramatization also spurs the development of language and vocabulary, as do carefully selected songs and plays.

For older pupils, a language program should provide continued, systematic attention to words and word acquisition. A game-like atmosphere that fosters incidental learning will often stimulate vocabulary (Manzo & Sherk, 1971). As far as possible, teach words that are useful and relevant to the pupils. The teacher's attitude toward vocabulary development is contagious and rapidly acquired by the pupils (Manzo & Sherk, 1971). As well, almost any technique that draws attention to word parts or meanings can positively influence word acquisition, although studying a few words in depth results in greater usage than does exposure to a large number of words (Manzo & Sherk, 1971). Students are stimulated to acquire vocabulary when teachers point out words in different contexts, and teach dictionary skills and word derivations.

Dictionary skills build and expand vocabulary and improve word usage. Picture dictionaries are useful up until about grade three, at which point more formal dictionaries can be introduced. Using dictionaries may not be beneficial, however, if the demands placed on the student are too great. Some dictionaries are just too complicated in format and provide more definitions than the students can grasp. Care should be taken to select dictionaries that present information in ways commensurate with the cognitive levels of the students.

For some learners, too, simply being given a word and asked to find its meaning in the dictionary is not enough. Many pupils need to apply new words and concepts actively in order to acquire them thoroughly (Donlan, 1975). Pictures, concrete objects, labels, and discussions must supplement dictionaries. Sometimes illustrative sentences are more informative than definitions or pictures. When given a relevant sentence, some students interpret it as a puzzle to be solved and are led to spend more time thinking about the meaning of the word. They will therefore ultimately remember it better (Miller & Gildea, 1987).

Teaching vocabulary

Objective: to increase students' oral vocabulary

a) Teach pupils to repeat an incomplete sentence on request, such as "This is a very nice. . . ." Pointing to specific objects, have the children repeat the stimulus sentence and add the name of the object.

Kindergarten (K) to grade 4

b) On a large piece of paper draw a circle and divide it into eight sections. Write new words in each section. Ask pupils in turn to close their eyes, move a pointer, and locate a word in the circle, which they then say, and put into a sentence.

K to grade 4

c) Riddles and jokes stress the nuances of the language. Collect riddles from books and magazines and write them on cards. Have pupils read riddles to the class.

Grades 2 to 8

d) Have students find and write down as many words in a word family as possible by attaching different consonants to the beginning of the initial word. *Ill*, for example, becomes h*ill*, p*ill*, f*ill*, and so on.

Grades 2 to 8

e) Create a "word-a-day" display on the bulletin board. To maintain pupils' interest, relate new words to special days, seasons, and classroom themes. Allow students to add words.

All levels

f) Have students use forms of the same word as different parts of speech. Ask them to create sentences using *fire*, for example, as a noun and then a verb, or forms of the word *success* as a noun, a verb, an adjective, and an adverb.

Grade 4 and up

Objective: to stimulate functional language and vocabulary

a) With the pupils, list all the things that elephants can do, such as trumpet, run, flap their ears, and eat.

K to grade 4

b) Say a word, such as *dairy*, and have the class respond with as many words as they can that are relevant, such as *milk*, *cream*, and *butter*.

K to grade 6

c) Ask students to explain how they accomplish everyday tasks: brushing their teeth, getting dressed, or coming to school.

K to grade 6

d) Have students write lists of instructions for games or treasure hunts for other children to follow.

Grades 3 to 8

e) Set aside a "discussion corner" on the board for pupils to note down anything that they would like to talk about. The class discusses the topics, after which the pupils can write about them, to present their own opinions.

Grade 4 and up

f) Use such materials as menus, telephone books, and so on, as shown in the unit below:

Unit on functional language

Objectives:
- to stimulate language by using everyday items
- to improve functional reading

Materials:
- a menu for every student
- individual work sheets

Procedure:
1. Discuss the menus with the class.
2. Present individual menus and work sheets and ask the students to complete them.

Work sheet:
1. The name of my restaurant is ____________________
2. My favourite food on the menu is ____________________
3. The most expensive item on the menu is ____________________
4. Five words that describe the food are ____________________
5. If I could order from this menu I would have
   sandwich ____________________
   dessert ____________________
   drink ____________________

Grade 4 and up

Objective: to expand students' use of descriptive vocabulary

a) Sketch a picture on the board (see figure 7–3) and write a simple sentence, such as "The woman is wearing a dress." Ask students to expand the sentence by adding modifiers.

K to grade 4

Figure 7–3 Expanding descriptive vocabulary

b) Use description posters to extend students' knowledge of adjectives. To create a positive learning experience, stress that the students should use only "good" words. Have them print their names down one side of a large sheet of paper, and ask them to place descriptive words beginning with the appropriate letters opposite each letter of the name. The adjectives can be chosen either by the individual or after group discussion. As an example, Philip's poster might look like this:

I AM

Patient
Happy
Interesting
Lucky
Impulsive
Pleasant

Grade 4 and up

c) Obtain a set of restaurant menus. Ask the students to underline all the adjectives and then to choose the foods that sound best.

Grade 4 and up

Objective: to expand students' use of antonyms or synonyms

a) Cut out a large piece of cardboard in the shape of a mitten with small "mittens" that fit into slots on the larger one, as shown in figure 7–4. Write antonyms (or synonyms) on each pair of mittens. Ask the students to sort them into correct pairs on the large mitten chart.

Grades 1 to 3

b) Present sentences orally for students to complete, such as "The skin of a pineapple is rough, but the skin of an apple is. . . ."

K to grade 6

c) Cut short articles from the newspaper and give them to individual pupils or small groups. From the articles, the pupils choose ten words, write them down, and then think of synonyms for the words.

Grade 4 and up

Objective: to introduce new and unusual words

a) Use compound words in exercises to extend vocabulary and improve spelling. For example, on a worksheet present parts of compound words such as snowb__ __ __, snowfl__ __ __, snowf__ __ __, snowdr__ __ __, and ask students to fill in the endings.

Grades 3 to 8

b) Ask the students to check the television guide or the newspaper for unusual words. A student writes a chosen word on the board and the class discusses meaning and usage.

Grade 4 and up

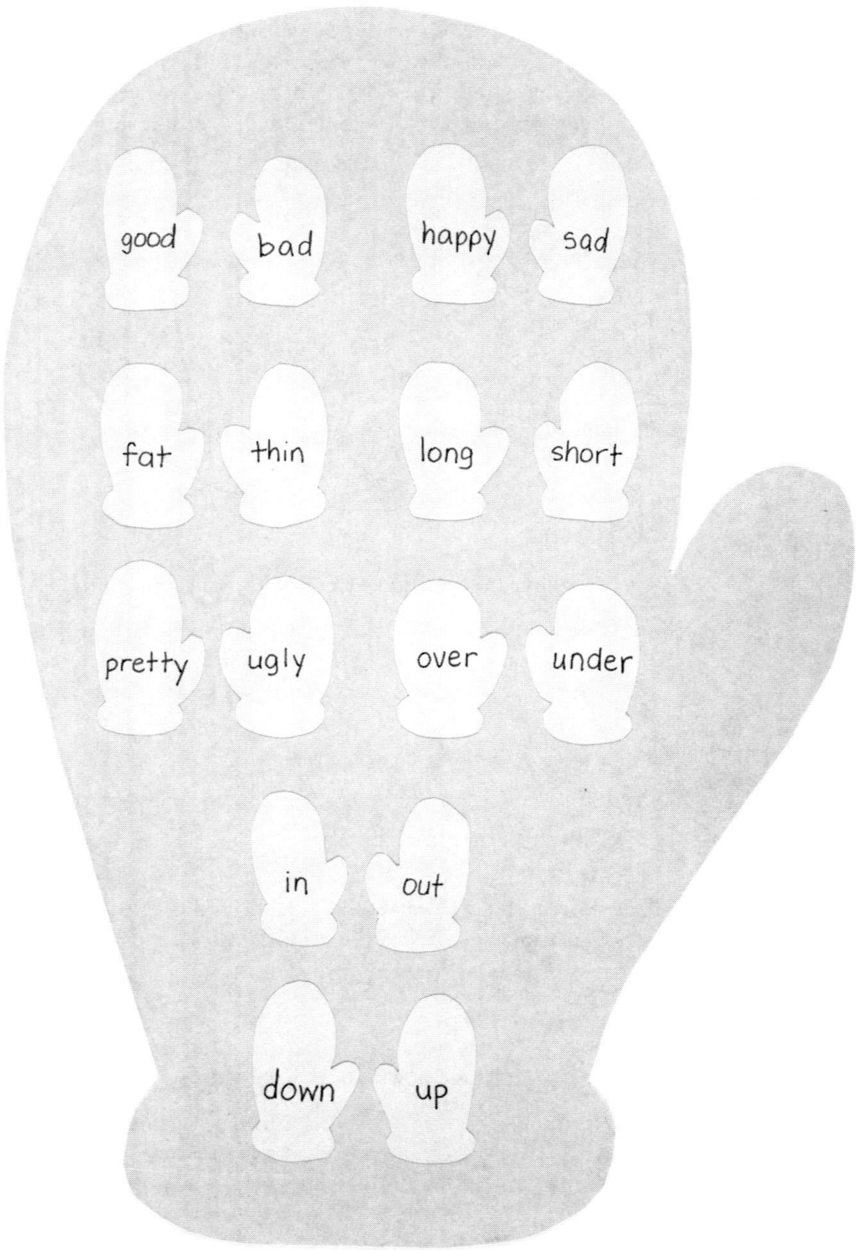

Figure 7–4 Vocabulary matching game

Objective: to demonstrate how the dictionary is a guide for spelling, pronunciation, and meaning

a) Divide the class into teams. The teacher, or a pupil, pronounces new words one at a time. The players find the word in their dictionaries and call out the page number and the column. A point is scored by the first team to find the word.

Grades 4 to 8

b) Give students groups of words and ask them to circle the word that comes first in the dictionary:

soap	soapy	soapsuds
pattern	patty	patter
budge	budgie	budget

Grade 4 and up

c) Ask the students to find several meanings in the dictionary for common words such as *board, blow,* or *bridge* and to write the words in sentences to illustrate the different meanings.

Grade 3 and up

Objective: to improve word memory

a) Early in the day, give a student a "special sentence," a personalized message such as "You have a pretty blue dress on today." Have the student repeat the message aloud and ten minutes later ask for another repetition. In the course of the day gradually extend the interval between repetitions to about an hour.

K to grade 4

b) Place common articles found in the classroom behind a screen and then arrange the class into two teams. Students take turns to name the articles as they are displayed. Those who make mistakes are removed from the team until only one person is left.

K to grade 4

c) Use rapid naming drills, asking the students to name, for example, all the things in a pet shop or in an ice-cream parlour.

K to grade 6

d) Teach sentence transformations by providing students with a kernel sentence — "John enjoys school," for example — and having them add elements to create new sentences such as "John enjoys school very much," and "Does John enjoy school?"

Grades 3 to 8

e) Spell words orally that the students cannot spell and ask them to spell them back from memory.

Grades 2 to 8

f) Play oral games that employ compound words. Ask students to change a watch into an animal (watchdog), or change ice into something good to eat (ice cream), for example.

Grades 1 to 8

g) Ask the students to write down new words as they come across them in their textbooks or other reading. Gradually, the students create personal dictionaries, as shown in figure 7–5.

All levels

h) Have each pupil divide a piece of paper into three columns and head them "people," "places," and "things." From a newspaper article pupils then find ten words for each column.

Grade 3 and up

Objective: to give students practice verbalizing abstract material

a) Ask children to close their eyes and describe what they are wearing.

K to grade 6

b) Divide the class into small groups and ask them to discuss a specific problem cooperatively, such as taking turns at classroom computer terminals. Peers will stimulate each other's vocabulary.

Grade 4 and up

Objective: to improve students' visual memory for pictures, words, phrases, and idioms

a) Use flash cards containing common pictures, words, phrases or idioms. Flash them for five seconds, have the students wait for five seconds, and then ask them to repeat the information on the cards or to write it down.

Grade 3 and up

Listening

Listening is a fundamental element of the communication process, essential for both social and educational endeavours. School success is partly predicated on the ability to listen and to process messages correctly, and a large part of every school day is occupied with oral interchanges. Within the classroom, students require good listening skills in order to follow directions, record information, and appreciate words and music. As they develop, children must learn to listen in order to evaluate messages for the main point, discover hidden messages and feelings, judge authenticity or contradictions, and gain specific information. The importance of good listening skills for productive living and learning cannot be overemphasized.

Very often, mildly handicapped youngsters demonstrate lacks in their listening skills. When listening, they tend to misperceive phonemes requiring very fine discrimination (Wiig & Semel, 1976), which can cause problems in reading and spelling. They will also sometimes fail to process an entire message, or be unable to retain oral information and follow directions.

Becoming a better listener involves developing an awareness of listening and listening techniques through structured classroom practice. Auditory training can be integrated

Figure 7–5 Page from a personal dictionary

into all instruction involving oral components. The teacher's role is to maintain an appropriate climate for listening, use exercises to practise listening, and establish a rapport with students. Most importantly, the teacher, as the communication leader in the classroom, must model appropriate skills for students.

Listening involves listening to the message within the words, listening to the feeling behind the message, and listening to word choice and usage. Underlying these elements are a number of subskills, such as auditory comprehension, auditory discrimination, auditory closure, auditory memory, and auditory sequential memory (Winzer, Rogow, & David, 1987). A number of instruments are available to assess receptive language and the underlying subskills.

Teaching listening skills

The strategies and games outlined below are not designed to be taught as specific lessons. Rather, they can be incorporated into other lessons or used as a break between activities. More than a short period of specific auditory training activities can be very tiring for youngsters, so the exercises should not be overused.

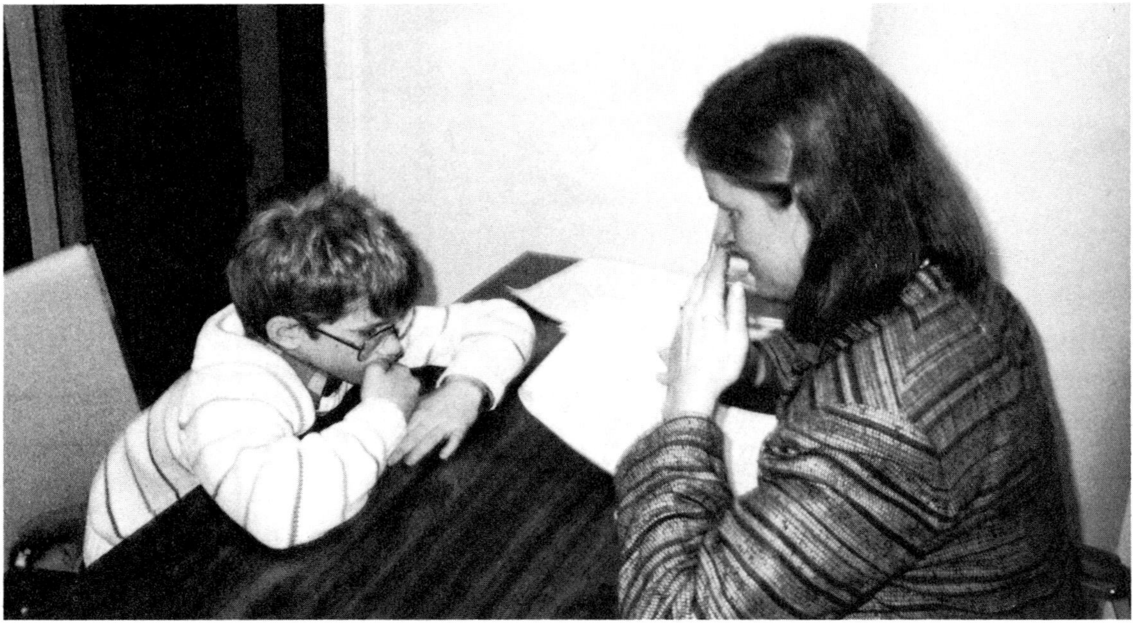

Auditory training is particularly helpful for many exceptional children.

Objective: to practise listening for environmental sounds, vocal sounds, and the location of sounds

a) Draw a circle with chalk on the floor and place a small object, such as an eraser or a block, in the chalk circle. Place a child, the "puppy," facing away from the circle. The object is the "bone" and children are then chosen to get the bone. If the "puppy" hears someone trying to take the bone, the response is "bow-wow." If someone manages to get the bone then he or she becomes the puppy.

K to grade 3

b) Tell the children to close their eyes and listen. Make various sounds, such as dropping a pencil, bouncing a ball, sharpening a pencil, or using a stapler, and ask them to identify the sounds.

K to grade 6

c) Place a chair at the front of the room to represent a train station. One child waits for the "train," which is made up of three children who chant "choo-choo-choo." They begin at the back of the room and increase the volume of the chant as they near the station. The first child joins the train, which then circles the room with decreasing volume.

K to grade 3

d) Fill drinking glasses with water to different levels, and then strike the glasses gently with a spoon. Have pupils identify high and low sounds.

K to grade 4

e) Play a tape of common household sounds for the class to identify.

K to grade 6

f) In the game of "Tick-tock, where's the clock?" a clock with a loud tick is secreted somewhere in the room. Children search for it and the finder is permitted to hide it for the other children.

K to grade 4

g) Tell the children to close their eyes. Move to one part of the room and call a child's name. If the child can identify the approximate location of the sound, then he or she calls another student.

K to grade 4

Objective: to practise following sound patterns and discriminating the pitch and tempo of various vocal, environmental, and musical sounds

a) Tell the children to close their eyes. Present a short pattern or rhythm by clapping hands, bouncing a ball, tapping on blocks, or beating a drum, and then ask the children to clap out the rhythm.

K to grade 6

b) Tell a story such as "Goldilocks and the Three Bears," or "The Three Billy Goats Gruff," stressing pitch differences in the voices, and ask children to identify the character from the pitch.

K to grade 6

c) Present multisyllabic words to the class and ask them to clap through the words to identify the number of syllables in each.

K to grade 4

Objective: to increase the ability to listen for, and discriminate, vocal sounds

a) Say three words, two of which begin with the same consonant, and ask the students to identify the odd consonant.

K to grade 4

b) Assign each child a specific consonant sound. Read a list of single consonants aloud and have the students call "Stop" when they hear their particular sound.

K to grade 4

c) Ask the class to listen for specific sounds in words in order to identify whether they are in the initial, medial, or final position.

K to grade 4

d) Have the students say the exclamation "Oh" in various tones that apply to different situations, such as receiving a new bicycle or falling and getting hurt.

K to grade 6

e) Tell the class a story and ask them to stand up every time they hear a certain word, such as *apple,* whether or not it is used correctly. As an example, the story could begin, "On apple, Jimmy played outside. For lunch he ate an apple sandwich. He played with his dog and tried to skate on the apple."

K to grade 6

Objective: to stimulate receptive language skills

a) Begin reading a story, but then pause to establish the purpose for the remainder of the reading, as in "Listen carefully now to find out what the princess says."

K to grade 6

b) Say four sentences, only one of which makes sense: "The cat barked. The dog sang. The bird chirped. The cow danced." Have the students identify the proper sentence.

K to grade 6

c) Say a line of a familiar rhyme such as "Jack and Jill went up the. . . ," and have the students respond by first marking the word on a sheet that has a choice of pictures, and then saying the word aloud.

K to grade 6

d) Ask students to identify their own addresses and telephone numbers from a tape listing several.

Grades 3 to 8

e) Give the students directions such as "Stand up," "Go to sleep," or "Bounce the ball," keeping your voice inaudible. The students must get clues from facial expression and gestures.

K to grade 6

Objective: to practise comprehending oral messages

a) Place four or five small objects in front of a child and give specific directions such as "Pick up the red ball," gradually expanding directions to, for example, "Pick up the red ball and put it on the blue chair."

K to grade 3

b) Give children simple directions, but tell them that you want them to carry them out later. After ten or fifteen minutes have a child carry out the directions.

K to grade 4

c) Give directions for tasks involving physical activity, such as "Touch your nose and clap your hands"; "Put your hands on your head and cross your legs"; "Go to the cupboard and get a ball and some blocks."

K to grade 4

d) Read a description and then ask students to draw the person, landscape, or animal that was described.

K to grade 8

e) Pick out several headlines from the newspaper. Read them to the class one at a time and ask the students to work out the content of the articles.

Grade 4 and up

f) Read a passage of about one hundred words to the class. Have them identify the main ideas and the supporting arguments.

Grade 7 and up

g) Have the students listen to the sound track of a film and tell or write what happened. Then show the film with the picture. Discuss similarities and discrepancies between the real film and the students' versions.

Grade 7 and up

Objective: to practise identifying the feelings behind emotionally laden material

a) Line up several pictures. Say a sentence that conveys the mood in one of the pictures and ask the students to point to the one described. Extend the exercise by using less descriptive sentences.

Grades 4 to 9

b) Use pictures illustrating different emotions such as sadness, happiness, and anger. Tell students to make up sentences that express the emotions of each picture.

Grades 4 to 9

c) Play an excerpt from a recorded speech and have students identify the feelings expressed.

Grade 4 and up

Objective: to develop students' ability to listen carefully, to make judgments, and to evaluate what is being said

a) Use flannel board figures while telling a story but make obvious errors in what is being said and done. Children should correct the errors.

K to grade 4

b) Say a sentence that includes illogical choices of word or phrase, such as "The sun shone brightly in the middle of the night." Children then identify and explain the incongruencies.

K to grade 4

c) Select a short, interesting article from the newspaper. Read the article to the class and tell the students to listen to the details. On the board or on individual sheets of paper list the questions, "Who?" "What?" "When?" "Where?" "Why?" and "How?" and ask them to provide the appropriate information.

Grades 4 to 9

d) Have the students listen to advertisements to determine how the advertiser is trying to induce the listener to buy the product.

Grade 4 and up

e) Prepare a rating sheet and have the pupils rate news, anchor people, public affairs programs, and so on.

Grade 7 and up

Oral language

The language that children bring to school at five or six years of age is grammatically advanced, but their strong oral background is largely neglected in an educational system that places a greater emphasis on the receptive modes of language. In schools, we tend to talk at children, rather than letting them talk to us. Yet frequent oral interaction among children, and among children and teachers, is an invaluable learning tool. It enables youngsters to practise their familiar language and allows teachers to perceive any problems.

Children's linguistic behaviour reflects, in one way or another, all of the physical and environmental factors that influence them, and will often reveal their disabilities. Exceptional youngsters may display all kinds of oral language problems, such as immature speech patterns, mild irregularities, or general unintelligibility (Morris, 1970). Some students are unable to speak with good syntax or grammar, probably because they cannot make the connection between the speech that they hear and the speech that they try to form themselves. Learning-disabled children, especially, may make syntactical and grammatical errors and meet difficulties with semantics (Bryan & Pflaum, 1978; Denckla & Rudel, 1976; Vogel, 1974; Wiig & Semel, 1974). Pragmatics, the social use of language, presents another potential area of difficulty (Bryan, Donahue, & Pearl, 1981; Noel, 1980).

Effective oral language depends upon the child's ability to remember linguistic patterns, to be agile in selecting the parts of speech and to produce the necessary vocal motor movements. Children are active constructors of language. They learn not simply by being guided through a predetermined set of hierarchical skills or acquiring a specific amount of linguistic information. Teachers can arrange events that make it easier for students to practise the rules and functions of language for themselves.

Teaching oral language

All genuine learning involves discovery and children can learn by talking as well as, if not better than, they can by listening. Teachers must provide an environment that exploits the process of discovery through language, as the surest means for children to master linguistic skills. To improve their oral language, students first need to build a speaking vocabulary, then to learn linguistic patterns, and finally to practise how to formulate sentences (Alley, 1977). For exceptional students, prone to problems in any of these areas, teachers should emphasize learning and using oral language. The activities that follow promote several different aspects of oral skill.

Objective: to increase children's ability to describe objects and events

a) Have a bag of toys and ask a child to select a toy and describe it, first by touch and then by sight.

K to grade 4

b) Invite a "Martian" to the classroom. Have the children explain how they perform various simple activities, such as brushing their teeth or answering the telephone. This is also an excellent activity to improve oral sequencing.

K to grade 4

c) Give students hand puppets and ask them to provide a dialogue. Either supply a theme in advance, or have the class make one up.

K to grade 6

Objective: to practise oral sequencing

a) Say the names of animals and have the children respond by making the animal sounds in the correct sequence.

K to grade 3

Objective: to develop conversational and thinking skills

a) First make simple statements such as "Puppies are young dogs," and then have pupils respond rapidly to "Puppies are. . . ," "What are puppies?" and "A puppy is. . . ."

K to grade 4

b) Clip headlines from the newspaper and put them in a hat. Individuals draw the clippings as subjects for brief impromptu speeches.

Grade 4 and up

c) Read a question and answer from an advice column in the newspaper. Then read only a question and ask the students to present their solutions to the problem.

Grade 7 and up

Spelling

Spelling is based on the interplay of many factors: experience, auditory and visual comprehension, discrimination, memory, sequence, word knowledge, phonetic and morphemic rules, and a kinesthetic sequence of motor actions. Because it is such a complex skill, spelling presents difficulties not only to children but also to many adults. Both the public and the educational community stress the importance of spelling by often associating the development of this skill with academic achievement, neatness, accuracy, and level of intellectual ability (Graham & Miller, 1979). Learning to spell is a tedious business, especially for children who have problems with the concepts and mechanics of sound–symbol relationships. Moreover, spelling does not encourage creativity; there is usually only one correct arrangement of letters (Lerner, 1981). Spelling difficulties are common among handicapped youngsters (Bryant, Fayne, & Gellinger, 1980; Reynolds & Birch, 1977) and their spelling achievement usually lags behind their grade placement (Carpenter & Miller, 1982). Spelling is therefore likely to be an important component of remedial emphasis.

Unlike reading, spelling requires concentration on each letter of each word. Good spellers, however, have internalized correct spelling to such an extent that they rarely have to direct any mental energy to the actual writing of a word. Before children can spell, they must possess certain prerequisite skills. They must, for example, be able to scan visually from left to right, possess spatial skills, good fine motor co-ordination, visual motor skills, motivation, and organization. When they actually come to spell a word, they must perform several tasks in close harmony: saying the word to themselves; mentally breaking off the first sound; matching a letter to the sound mentally; remembering how to write the letter; deciding where it should go on the page; and performing the motor activity. They must then remember the word again, and repeat the process over to the end of the word.

As every teacher can attest, problems in spelling are manifested in many ways. Some examples of common sorts of spelling errors are found in table 7–1, with possible explanations for the different types. Of course, innumerable spelling errors are matched by innumerable causes and a single table cannot do justice to them all. Apart from learning deficits, carelessness, fatigue, and lack of motivation can all induce errors.

Out of the vast number of spelling errors, three primary categories emerge. Errors may be non-phonetic and bizarre; they may show a high proportion of phonetic equivalents; or the student may demonstrate low-level skills when spelling on both phonetic and non-phonetic words. Spelling problems also spill over to affect other academic areas, and have a negative impact on all forms of written language. Students may write simplistically if they have to change words to accommodate their spelling ability, and the simpler words selected may affect the clarity of written expression. As well, there are some students who are convinced that they cannot write because they cannot spell. Good readers may or may not be terrible spellers, but bad readers are almost certain to spell poorly. Ability in spelling is associated with general intelligence and reading ability, although reading may result in new vocabulary more than in improved spelling.

Assessing spelling

Formal and informal procedures are used to assess spelling competence. Teachers often employ informal inventories and checklists based on words needed or taught at a specific grade level. They can evaluate students' skills on informal spelling samples and checklists by asking the following questions:

1. Can the students recall the letter and sound symbols quickly and accurately?
2. Can they produce them correctly on paper?
3. Can they fuse the sound parts of words together into whole words?
4. Do they reverse letters within the sound parts of a word?

5. Can they remember what the teacher has written on the board a few minutes after it is erased?
6. Do the children learn words by hearing the letter sequence rather than writing it?
7. Do they appear to block out or not hear sounds?
8. Can they write the correct symbols for single sounds when the sounds are dictated orally?
9. Can they identify sounds such as *b* and *d*, or *f* and *v* (Linn, 1967)?

Table 7–1 Common types of spelling errors

Error	Example	Possible explanation
Adds letters	paturing for party; farard for farm	◆ mispronunciation ◆ reflection of dialect
Omits letters	tword for toward	◆ mispronunciation ◆ poor auditory discrimination
Whole word reversal	saw for was	◆ poor visual discrimination ◆ mirror writing
Vowel–consonant reversal	gril for girl; dnace for dance	◆ poor visual discrimination ◆ poor auditory memory ◆ consonant confusion ◆ poor grapheme–phoneme knowledge
Syllable reversal	hpype for happy; leepant for elephant	◆ poor auditory discrimination ◆ phonetic spelling of non-phonetic words
Unrelated letters	junkped for jumped	◆ poor listening ◆ dialect ◆ mispronunciation ◆ guessing
Phonetic spelling of non-phonetic words	enuf for enough	◆ inappropriate application of a rule ◆ poor memory
Incomprehensible spelling	silac for special	◆ poor memory ◆ no knowledge of word
Misplaces silent *e*	rosed for rode; gose for goes	◆ poor application of a rule ◆ poor visual memory
Transposes silent letters	rian for rain	◆ poor visual memory
Omits syllables	aftnoon for afternoon	◆ poor listening ◆ poor visual memory
Rotates letters	tup for tub; buck for duck	◆ poor phoneme–grapheme correspondence ◆ unsure letter formations
Wrong association of sound with given set of letters	charp for sharp	◆ learned incorrectly

A simple procedure for assessing a student's level of spelling is to use a basal spelling series and select fifteen words from the grade one list, and twenty words from each successive book up to grade six. To present the test, the teacher says the word, says it in a sentence, and then repeats the word as the students write. This is continued until the students miss seven consecutive words (Mann & Suiter, 1975). Error analysis may also be used effectively (see chapter 3). The basic error classifications are omissions, additions and repetitions, transpositions and reversals, phonetic substitutions, non-phonetic substitutions, and unrecognizable or incomplete words (Brueckner & Bond, 1967). Informal spelling measures should be supplemented by diagnostic spelling tests. As well, spelling subtests are included in many of the more popular achievement batteries.

Teaching spelling

In today's classrooms, the popular methods for teaching spelling are founded on traditional practices rather than on research (Fitzsimmons & Loomer, 1977), even though spelling is one of the most thoroughly researched areas of the language arts (Allred, 1977). Teachers tend to rely on spelling texts, which ordinarily offer a set pattern of instruction without any allowance for individual differences (Dietrich, 1973). Traditional instructional practices involve drill activities and memorization of assigned spelling lists. Nevertheless, two approaches have evolved from traditional spelling instruction, each with its own advocates, materials, and methods: the linguistic approach and the word frequency approach.

The linguistic approach to spelling uses a phonetic or sound–letter method. It stresses phonic generalizations, structural analysis, and linguistic patterns. While remaining acutely aware of the masses of irregularities that occur in English, proponents of the linguistic approach still focus on predictable spelling patterns and on the underlying morphological and phonological regularities. Spelling words are selected on the basis of their structural patterns, in order to help children form linguistic generalizations. If, for example, the digraph *ow* was being taught, the teacher would include all of that word family: h*ow*, n*ow*, c*ow*, and so on. Advocates of the word frequency approach point out, however, that English spelling is so irregular that spelling should be taught without rules or with only a few general rules. Children should initially learn the words that they will use most frequently in written language. Irregular words are then taught as they become necessary.

In spelling, as in all areas, children have different skills and needs. Exceptional children, however, are likely to encounter many difficulties at all levels of learning to spell, and require both extended drill and practice in spelling, and an individualized spelling program that relates to other curricular areas, especially reading. Teachers should motivate special learners to upgrade their spelling standards by presenting them only with functionally relevant or interesting words (Rubin, 1980). Older students especially may need help to overcome years of frustration and failure. Exceptional students need to expand their spelling vocabulary, and improve their auditory, visual, phonemic, and dictionary skills. They must increase their ability to detect and correct errors and gain automaticity in learned spelling words.

Although direct spelling instruction is the best way to ensure success, few materials specify direct teacher involvement during spelling instruction. There are many ways to modify the spelling program without investing large amounts of the teacher's time or making massive revisions. Individual instruction, diagnostic-prescriptive teaching, or peer tutoring may improve spelling ability for some exceptional pupils, and media such as instructional packages and computer drill and practice programs are especially helpful. Combinations of computerized and conventional spelling instruction may produce higher achievement than either instructional method alone (McDermott & Walkins, 1983).

Teachers should introduce new spelling words slowly to exceptional learners, only three to six words at a time, and teach confusing letters, such as *b* and *d*, as far apart as possible. Short, frequent spelling periods of about fifteen to twenty minutes duration are the most useful. Often, visual or auditory knowledge of a word is not enough. Mildly handicapped children need many experiences in which the spelling words are related to objects. Teachers will find it necessary to provide for overlearning, and to evalute progress consistently. Charting their own progress will motivate many students.

Poor spellers are often hindered by an inability to detect their own errors, even if the teacher points them out. They can improve their spelling, however, if they are taught to analyse their errors. Research findings suggest that the traditional practice of writing words several times without intervention does not, in fact, help to ensure spelling progress (Blair & Rupley, 1980).

Rather than rigidly adhering to one method, teachers should endeavour to match materials and techniques to the individual needs of exceptional learners. An eclectic approach is the most satisfactory in spelling instruction, and the following techniques offer some variety.

Objective: to strengthen children's knowledge and use of letter and sound sequence

a) Abbey (1979) suggests that spelling can be improved by an intensive focus on the letters, sounds, and syllables within words. For each student, prepare pages with specific headings and words, as shown in figure 7–6. Instruct the students to count the letters of a word, enter the number, write the sounds separately and enter the number, and then write the syllables and their number. Once they have filled in the page, the students then copy the whole word, write the word in syllables, and write the word saying it aloud. Finally, they write the word again. Test the students' retention of the spelling and then write the words on individual cards and file them to be used for review exercises. Review any incorrect words the next day, using the same sequence.

Grades 3 to 8

b) Use visual closure exercises in which children fill in missing letters in words, as in pota__o or or__nge.

Grades 3 to 6

c) On work sheets, write sets of spellings such as *geen, green, neegr, grene*. Ask the students to circle the correct spelling and to write the word in a sentence.

Grades 3 to 6

Word	Number of letters	Sounds	Number of sounds	Syllables	Number of syllables
basket	6	b as k et	4	bas ket	2
happy	5	ha ppy	2	hap py	2
swimming	8	sw imm ing	3	swimm ing	2
lesson	6	l ess on	3	les son	2
jolly	5	j oll y	3	joll y	2

Figure 7–6 Spelling book

d) Cut up flash cards that contain single words and ask the children to sort them into the correct letter sequences.

Grades 2 to 6

e) Present children with flash cards containing long words such as *transportation, Massachusetts*, or *rollicking*. Ask them to find and write all the small words contained within each word, as in trans*port*ation.

Grades 3 to 8

Objective: to enhance auditory and visual memory

a) Say a word and write the initial letter on the board. Ask the students to look at the letter, erase it, and have them write the letter. Repeat the word but now write the first two letters on the board, allow the children to look, erase the letters, and ask them to write. Continue the chaining until the students can write the whole word from memory.

Grades 2 to 6

b) Adapted from the Fernald multisensory approach, the following method is effective with students from grade four onward who display problems in their visual memory of irregularly spelled words (Armitage, 1978a). Carefully explain the procedure in advance to the pupils and emphasize the importance of completing all aspects of the exercise.

1. Decide on a core group of commonly used words that the pupils should know how to spell.
2. Dictate some of the words until the pupils make five consecutive errors.
3. Write the five errors in a special spelling book.
4. Write the first misspelled word on the board, in letters approximately eighteen inches high. Explain to the pupils that there is a rhythm in learning to spell and that the rhythm will be marked for each word. For words of two or more syllables, draw a curved line under each syllable or part, as in be cause. For one-syllable words, draw a line under the parts that go together naturally, as in lau gh. The

purpose is not to teach syllabication but to break the words into simpler parts to aid retention.

5. The pupils trace the word five times with chalk, repeating the names of the letters aloud, and holding each one vocally until ready to begin tracing the next one. They also vocalize the rhythm, as lau (pause) gh.
6. After tracing the word, the pupils turn to the teacher and spell the words orally but without looking at the written symbols. If the word is spelled incorrectly, the whole procedure is repeated.
7. If correct, erase the word and have the pupils rewrite it in their books.
8. At the end of each period, give the words to the pupils in dictated sentences, so that they can practise them in context for the most effective learning.
9. Only work with a maximum of five words at a time and allow pupils to attain mastery before continuing.

Grades 4 to 9

c) Some children, especially those who have experienced failure in the past, are threatened by traditional spelling instruction. Spelling games that use music or graphics are useful to reinforce these youngsters' skills. Teach them to spell *snake*, for example, by writing the actual word in a snake shape.

Grades 4 to 9

Objective: to develop automaticity in spelling

a) *Imitation training* involves systematic direct instruction in spelling. First select the words to be taught for the individual student. Say each word, give it in a sentence, and then spell the word out loud. Show the student the word on a flash card and ask him or her to point to each letter as you respell the word. The student then initiates the procedure of saying the word, placing it in a sentence, and using the card to spell. Then, with no prompts available, the student spells the word orally and writes it on the board. It is vital to give positive reinforcement during this procedure.

Grades 3 to 8

b) The cover-and-write method is especially good for pupils who require a great deal of repetition before they master a skill. The pupil

1. looks at the word and says it
2. writes the word twice
3. covers this and writes the word once
4. checks the word
5. writes the word again twice
6. checks the spelling again
7. writes the word three times
8. covers this, and writes the word once
9. checks the spelling of the word (Gajraj, 1983)

Grades 3 to 9

c) The "coach's spelling approach" stresses studying words as a whole rather than in syllables, and has students correct their own work. It is most appropriate for students in the nine-to-fourteen age range because the techniques parallel a football coach's steps in preparation for a big game:

1. In the scouting step, students get to know the opposition. They read the words to be learned and divide them into groups of phonetically regular and irregular spellings and words with common patterns. They also sort them into piles of easy and hard words.
2. In the practice step, the students outline study procedures with the teacher and then practise the words until they achieve mastery. For words with regular phonetic spellings, the students look at and say the words slowly, trace them while stressing each sound, cover and write the words, and finally check the spellings. For non-phonetic words, the procedure is the same except that the students say the name of each letter when tracing the words.
3. The final step involves keeping statistics. Here the pupils record the number of words spelled correctly and adjust their practice based on successes (Dangel, 1987).

Grades 4 to 9

Objective: to improve spelling ability by studying word meanings. There appears to be a relationship between the ability to spell a word and the ability to understand its meaning (Mangieri & Baldwin, 1979). The following strategies use dictionary skills and word study.

a) Have students locate and define spelling words by using the dictionary (Urbani, 1978).

Grade 3 and up

b) Allow students to design their own lists of spelling words (Wilson, 1979).

Grade 3 and up

c) Allow students to design their own strategies for learning spelling words (Harris, J., 1978).

Grade 3 and up

d) Use exaggerated oral pronunciation and syllabication when giving spelling words (Parke, 1978).

Grade 2 and up

Objective: to increase motivation among students with mild spelling problems

a) Establish a special spellers' program. At the beginning of the week, tell the class all the assigned words for that week. Students can "challenge" and, if they know all the words, can use spelling periods for related activities such as doing puzzles, using words in sentences, making up rhymes, and playing spelling games.

Grade 2 and up

b) Draw up spelling contracts by selecting groups of words with the individual students. On the contract, specify procedures for studying the words. A certain student, for example, may learn best by writing the words on cards, writing and defining them in a vocabulary book, and then writing them in sentences. The spelling contract also specifies the reward for the student if all the selected words are learned correctly.

Grade 3 and up

Handwriting

In recent years, educators have grown concerned over the inadequate handwriting skills demonstrated by exceptional pupils (Kaminsky & Powers, 1981). While many factors contribute to poor handwriting, too often it is not regarded as a vital aspect of the curriculum. Instruction often does not follow a hierarchical developmental progression and is only fitted into the daily schedule when extra time is available. Such pervasive neglect has led some researchers to refer to handwriting as "the neglected R" (Milone & Wasylyk, 1981).

Handwriting is a necessary tool for expressing thoughts, the highest priority of which is legibility, rather than aesthetics. If a student's writing is so illegible that the message is not communicated effectively, intervention is necessary. Perfect copperplate is no longer considered essential, although handwriting style may change again with the advance of word processing, since the new media presents new styles of, for example, spacing, slant, and letter formation.

Good handwriting remains important, however, and demands efficient eye–hand coordination, form perception, and memory for sequences. Although, unlike spelling competency, handwriting does not seem to be related to IQ (Seifert, 1980), difficulty in handwriting may reflect many underlying deficits or reveal a lack of systematic instruction and practice. Patrick's writing (figure 7–7) indicates many deviations and is below the standard that one would expect of a ten year old.

Handwriting problems are manifested either in the product, or in the student's behaviour. The writing itself may demonstrate illegibility, poor formations, transposed letters, mirror writing, or inconsistent slant and spacing. On the other hand, the student may write legibly, but exhibit elevated amounts of stress and anxiety over handwriting tasks. The list below notes examples of both types of handwriting difficulty:

- "death grip" on the pencil or pen
- incorrect pencil grip
- awkward positioning of the body, squinting, or bending too close to the paper
- symptoms of premature muscle fatigue
- use of delaying tactics and other measures to avoid writing tasks
- sparse written output in relation to the student's age, reading ability, and verbal ability
- numerous eye fixations from far to near point during a copying task
- excessive number of erasures
- frequent referral to an alphabet chart to check the formation of letters
- confusion in directional orientation, such as mirror writing and reversals

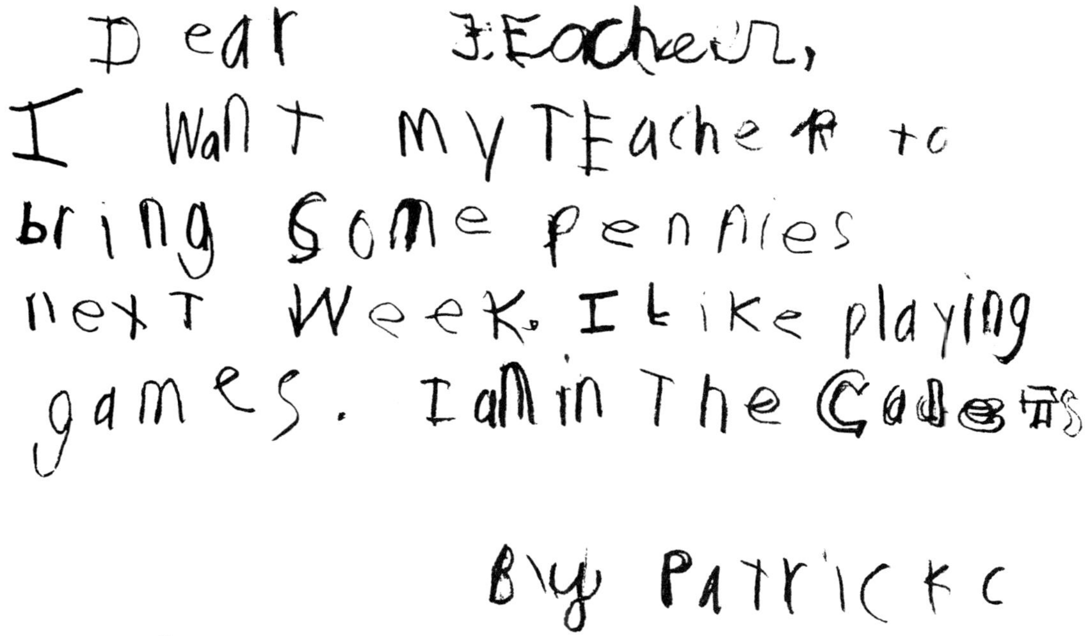

Figure 7–7

- poor use of space as observed in sprawling or cramped writing
- inadequate space between letters and words, inappropriate letter-size relationships, and inability to stay within head and base lines
- poor letter connections and illegible letters
- inaccuracies, such as omissions, perseverations, lack of punctuation, and line skipping
- slow motor speed in comparison with that of peers
- hesitation and difficulty in generating letters in a non-copying writing task, particularly capital letters
- difficulty in keeping up with dictation tasks because of a breakdown in the integration process (Armitage, 1982; Kaminsky & Powers, 1981, pp. 21–22)

The causes of poor handwriting are as varied as the number of students in a classroom, but can be broadly categorized as problems lying within the student and those arising from poor instructional practices (Kaminsky & Powers, 1981; Milone & Waseylyk, 1981). Students who experience problems from within may simply not understand the letter formations as quickly as the teacher presents them. Others need much more time then they are given to practise and internalize the motor movements required for particular letter formations. Children with perceptual problems may see individual letters inaccurately, while those with visual memory difficulties simply cannot remember the formation of the letters without a great deal of repetition. Some students may be unable to execute the motor movements efficiently that are required to copy letters and forms. They cannot transfer the visual input to an output of fine motor movement (Lerner, 1981). Fine motor co-ordination difficulties produce poorly shaped, jerky, and uneven writing. Some students may be poor in other visual motor functions, such as discrimination or figure-ground, and in activities requiring motor and spatial judgments. Lack of a well-developed sense of layout can hamper them, but projects are improved if attention is paid to the manner in which the work is laid out and presented. Finally, left-handedness often hinders a student from learning legible handwriting. It is important that writers position the paper correctly and maintain a good writing posture. If writers sit improperly they gain a distorted view of what is being written and fail to correct mistakes. Encourage children to sit upright in a comfortable seat, with both feet on the floor, and the non-writing hand helping to anchor the paper (Lerner, 1981). If necessary, tape the paper to the student's desk in the correct position.

Assessing handwriting

Handwriting is the most tangible of the basic skills: samples can be easily analysed and saved to compare with others over a period of time. Simply looking at a student's work will suffice for a general assessment of handwriting strengths and problems, but in order to discover the specific difficulties, individualize planning and instruction, and increase competency, more rigorous measures are necessary.

Samples of the student's handwriting, drawn from a number of sources, are the most appropriate material for assessment. The collection should include typical classroom work, a near point copy book, a far point copy exercise, a dictated paragraph, and a self-generated paragraph (Kaminsky & Powers, 1981). Alternatively, Armitage (1982) suggests a sample sentence format as a basis for handwriting assessment:

1. Write a simple sentence on the board, such as "The quick brown fox jumps over the lazy dog," which uses all the letters.
2. Have the pupils read the sentence until they are familiar with the words.
3. Ask the pupils to write the sentence five times in their "everyday" writing.
4. They then rewrite the sentence five times in their "best" writing, taking as much time as they need.
5. Collect the writing samples, underline each error, and note them on a diagnostic sheet (see table 7–2), using one sheet per student.
6. Compare the "everyday" and the "best" sample. If letters are inconsistently formed or other problems are noted in both samples, then remediation or reteaching is indicated.

Using these different types of sample, teachers can analyse errors using a diagnostic checklist. Filling in each area of the checklist will provide an overview of specific handwriting errors and malformations.

Some students write legibly, but so slowly that their writing resembles tracing or drawing. To meet the demands of the regular classroom, children must maintain good handwriting speed. Pupils in the elementary grades should write at approximately the following speeds: grade three, forty letters a minute; grade four, fifty letters a minute; grade five, sixty letters a minute; grade six, sixty-seven letters a minute; grade seven, seventy-four letters a minute; grade eight, eighty letters a minute (Currie, 1981; Freeman, 1954). To establish the writing fluency rate of older students have them write the letter *e* for one minute, and then count the number produced. There should be about

Table 7–2 Diagnostic interpretation of handwriting samples

	Yes	No
Letter formation		
letters formed inconsistently		
letters formed incorrectly		
letters too round		
letters too thin		
beginning strokes of letters correct		
connecting strokes correct		
loops correct		
upper case letters properly formed		
lower case letters properly formed		
Letter size		
half-space letters too large		
half-space letters too small		
letters too large		
letters too small		
Slant		
slant not uniform		
too much slant to right		
too much slant to left		
Spacing		
spacing correct between letters		
spacing too wide between letters		
spacing too narrow between letters		
spacing inconsistent between letters		
spacing correct between words		
spacing too wide between words		
spacing too narrow between words		
spacing inconsistent between words		
words and letters arranged properly on page		
correct use of left margin		
correct use of right margin		
Alignment		
letters resting on lines		
letters and words in writing space between the lines		
Line quality		
lines too heavy		
lines too light		
line quality variable		

Sources: Adapted from Armitage, 1982; Kaminsky & Powers, 1981.

one hundred. Then ask them to write *q*s for one minute. The count here should be about fifty. An *e* is the easiest letter to write and a *q* the most difficult, and so all the other letters will fall somewhere between the *e* and *q* speeds. If students write below these standards, they are clearly going to meet problems getting information down in time to keep up with seatwork assignments, class lectures, and audio-visual presentations.

Teaching handwriting

An interest in writing surfaces very early in children. At the age of eighteen months infants love to scribble on almost any surface. By twenty-four months they scribble on paper, but go off the edges. By the time they are thirty months old, toddlers are beginning to develop a sense of laterality, can handle a writing tool, and have mastered the circle. At forty-eight months preschoolers can draw more complex shapes and can complete two or three sides of a square correctly. By five years of age most children are able to draw a true square and are ready for formal writing instruction. Children also usually arrive at school with the ability to recognize their own names in print, and to print their names in some form. As well, most children have come to the realization that print relays information and are motivated to learn to read and write.

A child's success in learning to write largely depends upon the quality of the instruction provided. Handwriting instruction is generally straightforward, materials are inexpensive, and student motivation is unusually high. By following a careful progression of steps, insisting upon accuracy at every step, and instilling proofreading habits, teachers can help children to write legibly. Instruction must be individualized, however, to accommodate the many differences within a class. Left-handed children may need special help orienting the paper; other youngsters require assistance overcoming reversals or letter misorientation. Still other students may need a sequential program for keeping between the lines, forming letters, and spacing them properly.

Handwriting instruction must be systematic and should constitute a formal component of the curriculum. Lessons should be short, no more than fifteen to twenty minutes at a time. A daily short lesson is more effective than less frequent, longer instructional periods (Calman & Freeman, 1976). Teachers may find the suggestions given below useful for successful handwriting instruction:

- Individualize lessons to produce the highest degree of legibility.
- Use rhymes, finger plays, and memory strategies, especially with children just learning to print.
- Spend fifteen to twenty minutes daily on direct handwriting instruction, and supervise practice sessions closely.
- Use consistent and relevant terminology.
- Use half space interlined paper for initial cursive instruction; later change to one-third space interlined paper. Overline paper for special students.
- Make sure that paper is clearly lined. For special students, trace over lines to darken them.
- Children may be more comfortable with some writing tools than with others. Experiment to find the implements most suitable for particular children.
- Provide writing samples for the students to trace.

Small children enjoy experimenting with paper and crayons.

- Omit unnecessary loops and curls from letter forms.
- Teach lower-case letters first, and emphasize correct letter formation, slant, and space.
- Initially, have pupils write with the paper in a vertical position. Introduce slant in cursive writing after pupils have mastered vertical letter formation.
- Have all pupils evaluate their own work for correct letter formation and uniform spacing and slant.
- Prominently display model letter forms in the classroom.
- For students with severe difficulties, adapt written assignments when necessary.
- Reduce the length of assignments and allow more time for completing tasks for secondary students with handwriting problems.

Very young children need a great deal of readiness work involving fine and gross motor co-ordination in order to develop a firm foundation for printing and writing. Finger plays, finger painting, painting with large brushes, modelling, and the like are employed to improve fine motor skills. At the same time, children should experience wide exposure to print, to establish the value of the printed word as a form of communication.

As children discover all forms of language they gain a working knowledge of the alphabet. They learn that letters are symbols with specific names, shapes, and sounds that come in two forms, upper and lower case. At least some children will find that some letters have more difficult formations than others. When teaching children to print, present letters in the following sequence, overlapping one segment of instruction with the next, and repeatedly returning to the earlier letters:

1. circle letters: *o* and *c*
2. most commonly used letters: *e* and *s*
3. stick letters: *i*, *l*, and *t*
4. circle and stick letters: *a*, *d*, and *g*
5. curved letters: *r*, *f*, *m*, *h*, *u*, *n*, and *j*
6. other circle and stick letters: *y*, *b*, *p*, and *q*
7. other stick letters: *k*, *v*, *w*, *x*, and *z*

The transition from print to cursive writing

At the moment, there is some debate about whether children should be taught print or cursive writing from the outset of instruction. Most Canadian schools begin with print (manuscript writing) and then shift to cursive writing, usually during grade three.

The advantages of manuscript writing are that the letters are easier to learn (since they consist only of circles and straight lines) and that the form is closer to printed text. Manuscript writing has fewer changes of letter forms; as an example, in cursive writing the *n* in *no* has different stroking from the *n* in *on*, a variation that does not occur in print. Advocates of manuscript style see the ease of letter formation as more appropriate for all young children (McGinnis, 1977), and believe that printing provides a natural foundation for later cursive writing. Some educators argue that it is not important for children to move to cursive writing at all since print is both legible and rapid (Lerner, 1981).

On the other hand, there are educators who believe that teaching only cursive writing is more appropriate, at least for handicapped children (Graham & Miller, 1979; Heyman, 1977), since it can prove easier than print. Cursive is seen as a less time-consuming and more personal form of writing that develops fine motor skills and a sense of rhythm that cannot be duplicated by printing. Because the continuous movement of cursive writing permits the writer to feel an entire word, it promotes tactile-kinesthetic and visual feedback. Cursive may thus foster the automatic aspects of writing, which are vital if a student is to reach the stage when she or he can concentrate on expressing thoughts rather than forming letters. Moreover, cursive writing may minimize problems with spatial judgment and specific letter confusions, such as the common difficulty with *b* and *d*.

Dubrov (1968) developed a sequence for teaching cursive letters based on the number of movements involved. For the lower-case letters, the sequence is

1. swing-up letters: *i, u, w, t, r,* and *s*
2. swing-up and over letters: *n, m, v,* and *x*
3. swing-up and turn-back letters: *e, l, b, h, k,* and *f*
4. swing-up and over and turn-back letters: *c, a, g, d,* and *q*
5. more swing-up letters: *o, p,* and *j*
6. more swing-up and over letters: *y* and *z*

Some cursive letters require special attention. Because the letters *a, e, r, t,* and *d* form nearly half of the most common errors in handwriting, their formations should be carefully taught and practised (Armitage, 1982).

Since students use their handwriting throughout the school day, remediation becomes more difficult as time goes by. Incorrect formations are particularly tricky to unlearn. After intervening to improve handwriting, teachers must check written work throughout the day to ensure that students are generalizing corrections.

Alternative writing strategies for secondary students

By the time students reach secondary school, poor handwriting will prove much more difficult to remediate. Not only will they have internalized incorrect formations, but remedial instruction holds little joy for adolescents.

Taking notes is an essential skill at the secondary levels. It clarifies classroom procedures, reinforces reading and study skills, and provides information on current events and materials. If secondary students demonstrate severe handwriting difficulties, if their writing is illegible, or if they cannot achieve the speed and fluency necessary for taking notes, teachers may need to adopt alternative strategies. Students may be allowed to tape-record work that would otherwise be written. Those who write slowly may use the lunch hour to copy notes from the blackboard or bulletin board. Others may need the help of note takers, other students, who actually take the notes for their disabled peers. The principles of note taking are discussed in chapter 12.

Alternatively, a typewriter may be the answer. Students with handwriting problems can learn to type reasonably well. Lovitt (1973), for example, has taught typing skills to learning-disabled pupils. Typing has certain advantages, especially for individuals who experience difficulty in the visual motor skills required for handwriting. Once the student has learned the basics, typing is faster than writing and produces a consistent, legible script. Students who learn to type also appear to develop a better sense of the sequence of letters in words (Lerner, 1981). Motivation is not usually a problem as children generally find typing an intriguing activity.

Word processing has proven to be a remarkable aid for those who meet difficulties in handwriting and has been particularly useful in teaching handicapped students. It is superior to traditional typewriting because the text can be revised on the screen easily before printing final copy (Maddux & Johnson, 1983).

Teaching left-handed students to write

From 12 to 17 percent of the population is left-handed. Left-handed children have special problems with handwriting, and more than any other youngsters they suffer from the dearth of handwriting instruction so common in today's schools (Harrison, 1981). Handwriting problems characteristic of left-handedness have varied causes. A lack of a firmly established sense of laterality, pushing the pen rather than pulling it, or receiving instruction from right-handed teachers using methods suitable for right-handed children can all induce problems.

Left-handed pupils require handwriting instruction geared especially for them. They are generally slower at writing (Burns, 1968), hold themselves in more awkward and uncomfortable positions, and are more likely to become fatigued after extended periods of writing (Clark, 1957). They are more likely to write with irregular slant, reversals (Enstrom & Enstrom, 1970), and illegibility.

It may be helpful if a left-handed adult teaches handwriting to left-handed students who are having difficulty, especially when skills are first being established. During formal handwriting lessons, left-handed children should be grouped together, so that they provide models for each other, and seated away from light sources that will cause them to shadow their own work with their hands (Bachor & Crealock, 1986). Left-handed writers should slant the top of the writing paper toward the left side of the desk at about a forty-five-degree angle, and hold their pens or pencils up higher than right-handed writers do, to make it easier to see the paper. A piece of tape or elastic on the writing instrument can mark the spot. A ballpoint pen with a longer than normal point is easier for left-handers to use.

Handwriting activities

Objective: to practise the prerequisite skills necessary for writing

a) Have children make lines, geometric shapes, and patterns on the blackboard.

K to grade 3

b) Cut out geometric forms, letters, and numbers for children to trace around with large pencils, crayons, or felt-tipped pens.

K to grade 3

c) Use closure exercises (see figure 7–8) to prepare children for formal handwriting instruction.

K to grade 3

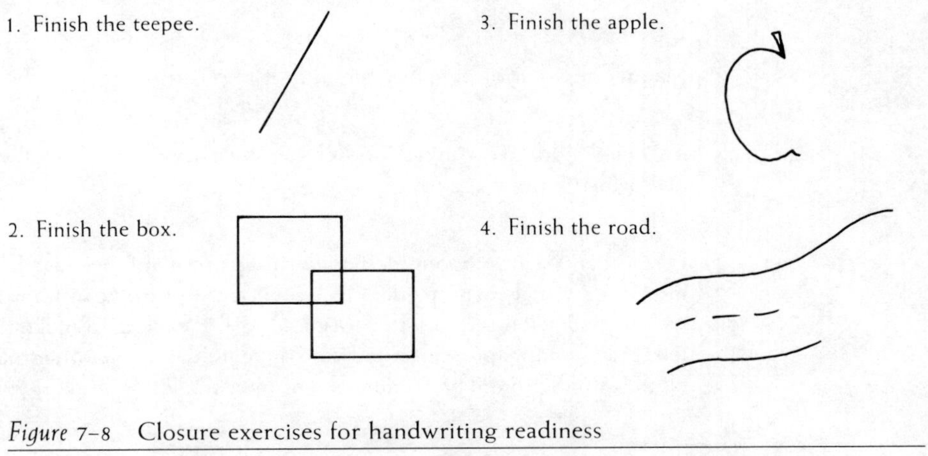

Figure 7–8 Closure exercises for handwriting readiness

Objective: to practise correct pencil grip. Pencil grip is a learned skill that must be both demonstrated and reinforced. The thumb and the middle finger should be at the sides of the pencil with the index finger in the front, and all the fingers above the sharpened point (Lerner, 1981).

a) Once in a while a student may have a great deal of trouble learning a suitable pencil grip. A wire writing frame to hold the pencil firm can help to establish a proper hold. Alternatively, a rubber pencil gripper may help the fine muscle control needed for maintaining a tripod grip on the pencil.

K to grade 6

b) Push the pencil through the holes in a practice golf ball. Have the child place the middle finger and thumb around the ball to practise the correct grip.

K to grade 6

c) Mark the child's thumb, index, and middle finger in the appropriate places with different colours of felt-tipped marker and have him or her match the marks to a piece of tape stuck to the pencil. As the child gains confidence, take away the cues gradually (Mendoza, Holt, & Jackson, 1978).

K to grade 4

Objective: to teach, remediate, or practise letter formations

a) Have the pupils create montages out of print in different typefaces cut from the newspaper and magazines, to develop an awareness of various forms of print.

K to grade 6

b) A dot-to-dot technique may help students who have difficulty forming letters. Write a letter and then outline it with dots. Have the pupil connect the dots (Gajraj, 1982).

K to grade 4

c) Write a complete letter or word and have the pupil trace it. Then write the first part of the letter or word and have the pupil trace this and complete the rest. Reduce the cues until she or he can write the entire word or letter (Lerner, 1981).

K to grade 4

d) Make letters out of pipe cleaners. Have pupils trace around them.

K to grade 4

e) To help children to avoid poor letter formations, present them with a sheet of malformed letters to correct.

K to grade 6

f) For students who encounter handwriting problems because of perceptual, visual motor, or visual memory deficits, using tactile cards can improve their quality of writing and retention of letter formations. On each card make the shape of a single letter from sandpaper, sprinkled sand, glue, felt, or some other material that provides tactile stimulation. The student traces over the letter while saying the sound aloud.

After using the cards, the student can repeat the procedure on a different surface, such as a desk top, and then write the letter on the chalkboard or on paper while saying the sound.

K to grade 6

g) Print letters and words on the board in white chalk and then ask pupils to trace over them with coloured chalk.

K to grade 6

h) Provide pupils with overlays of correctly formed letters or words that they can use to check their own letter or word formations.

K to grade 8

Objective: to help students who are encountering problems with directionality

a) Use physical prompts and cues when children demonstrate problems with directionality. Arrows, for example, guide the direction and order in which letter strokes are made.

K to grade 4

b) Tape directional devices, such as an arrow indicating writing flow from left to right, onto pupils' desks.

K to grade 4

c) To help children who demonstrate many reversals in their handwriting, talk them through each step of the letter formations until they are automatic.

K to grade 6

Objective: to overcome improper spacing and slant

a) Use graph paper.

Grades 3 to 6

b) Draw spacing and slant guides on the writing paper, as in figure 7–9.

Grades 3 to 6

Figure 7–9 Guide for proper spacing and slant

Objective: to regulate the speed and fluency of handwriting

a) Using a metronome helps to control speed and rhythm in movement drills and in writing letters and figures, although it should not be used for word or sentence writing (Calman & Freeman, 1976). Increase the pace of the metronome until students reach the required standard.

K to grade 6

b) Select a letter and then take students through the formation bit by bit. The letter *i*, for example, can be taught as "up the hill, down the hill, throw a stone." Repeat the process with the student on different surfaces before moving to paper.

K to grade 4

Objective: to practise joining cursive letters

a) Children can develop flowing strokes for writing if they first draw two large circles on paper, then trace over the circles with the palms of both hands simultaneously. They then trace the circles with a crayon, developing a steady rhythm. The process can also be used with letter strokes, isolated letters, and connected letters.

Grades 2 to 6

b) After isolated letter practice, dictate letters embedded in larger contexts: syllables, words, phrases, and sentences. For example, the *o* and its connectives may be practised in a sentence such as "The moose and goose are in the caboose."

Grades 3 to 8

c) Calman and Freeman (1976) suggest using print letters as a crutch when making the transition to cursive writing. Children print a line of selected letters, and then write a line of cursive letters under the print line.

Grades 3 and 4

Grammar, syntax, punctuation, and capitalization

Grammar formalizes the conventions of language so that communication is consistent throughout a society. It refers to the rules, or systematic structure of language, as opposed to usage, which deals with the word choices made within the grammar. The child who says, "I ain't going to do it," has perfect grammar but questionable word usage, whereas the child who talks about a "Ball, big red here," is using incorrect grammar.

In order to express their thoughts effectively on paper, students need to know the rules of grammar, punctuation, and capitalization, and correct syntax and paragraph construction. The writer uses punctuation to communicate mood and present a logical progression of ideas. Syntax refers to the appropriate arrangement of words within sentences, and is a crucial element of good grammar. Paragraph organization depends on well-developed topics, supportive facts, examples, and conclusions. Students must learn to locate the main idea in a topic, put their points in logical order, provide details, take notes, construct outlines, and make generalizations (Hall, 1981).

Exceptional students encounter innumerable problems in all areas of written language. Their written work is replete with syntactic and semantic errors, run-on sentences, sentences that are too simple, confusion of tense, and overuse of conjunctions for complex sentences. They may demonstrate poor use of pronouns and prepositions, inconsistent use of time, and adverbs and adjectives missing or used incorrectly.

Many regular class students learn these skills of written expression incidentally (Smith, 1974), but exceptional children may not pick up the rules easily. They therefore require planned instruction, although they do not need as much stress on the formal aspects of grammar (Kolstoe, 1976; Smith, 1974) as they do on writing conventions such as paragraphing.

Punctuation, capitalization, and grammar are straightforward to teach. Teachers can usually remediate errors in the context of writing done for other purposes. Although pupils need a great deal of writing practice, they will learn more easily if they are motivated and allowed to generalize skills to a wide variety of real situations. Capitalization, for example, becomes more important for the pupil who wants to write a letter asking for information for the class than it is when he or she completes exercises from the board. The exercises that follow are designed to improve students' use of grammar, syntax, punctuation, and capitalization.

Teaching grammar, syntax, punctuation, and capitalization

Objective: to teach, practise, or remediate punctuation and capitalization

a) On the overhead projector, present sentences lacking capitalization and have the pupils correct them.

Grades 3 to 9

b) Present a written passage lacking any punctuation or capitalization and ask pupils to read aloud and punctuate as they read.

Grade 3 and up

c) Allow students to work in teams directly from the computer screen to correct passages that have been stored on disk (Maddux & Cummings, 1987).

Grade 3 and up

d) Teach students how to proofread by having them read their work aloud to a teacher or peer.

Grade 3 and up

Objective: to improve syntax and grammar

a) Present a declarative sentence and ask pupils to respond in the interrogative. Thus "Today is Thursday," becomes in response "Is today Thursday?"

Grades 3 to 8

b) Use word-picture cards, with each picture representing a language function as shown in figure 7–10, to make sentences more concrete. Have pupils sort the cards to make sentences.

Grades 3 to 8

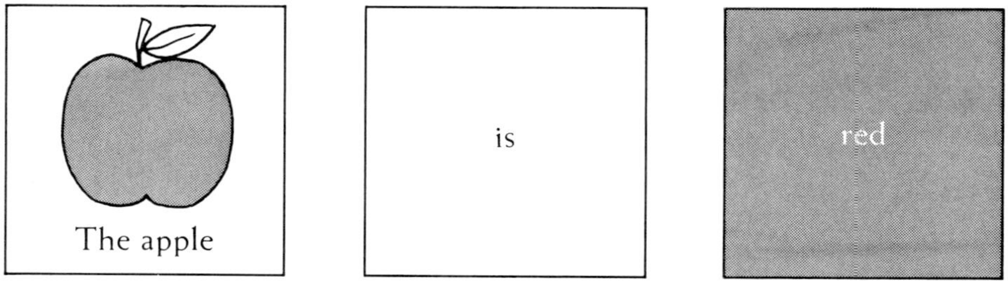

Figure 7–10

c) Present simple written or oral sentences with the words out of order and ask pupils to place the words in the proper order. Similarly, write a series of sentences that tell a story but present them out of sequence.

Grades 3 to 9

d) Write sentences and ask the pupils to rearrange them to produce a different meaning, as in "In the forest the trees are tall" and "The tall trees are in the forest."

Grades 3 to 9

e) Write two columns of scrambled sentences on the board. Divide the students into two teams; each team takes one column to unscramble, and the first team to finish wins.

Grades 1 to 6

f) Present a list of sentences with errors in tense for students to correct.

Grades 3 to 9

g) In order to teach style, flow, and form, ask the students to "hide" their own sentences in an existing passage of writing and to challenge others to find them.

Grade 7 and up

Objective: to improve sentence and paragraph construction

a) Give students a list mixing phrases and complete sentences and have them sort the material into two groups.

Grade 3 and up

b) Present short paragraphs and have the students underline the topic sentences. Then give only a topic sentence and have the students complete the paragraph.

Grade 4 and up

c) To help students organize stories and papers, teach phrases that lend meaning to paragraphs, such as *to begin with, next, after that,* and *finally* (Mercer & Mercer, 1985).

Grade 4 and up

d) Construct learning packages graded by level of ability (see chapter 5). A package on capitalization, for example, could contain work sheets, each of which stresses one of the following areas: people's names; the first word of sentences; rules for capitalizing *I*; days, months, and holidays; proper names; addresses; personal letters; common product names.

Grade 4 and up

Creative writing

Traditionally, the process of teaching children writing skills has been referred to as *composition*. Today, *written language* is the more accepted term because it encompasses all aspects of the writing process from writing a note to the papergirl to composing a poem. This text prefers the term *creative writing*, however, because writing is not simply a tool for communication, but also an avenue for personal, social, and intellectual growth (Moffet, 1978). Writing must therefore be taught in ways that recognize the writer's individuality and allow him or her to progress at a comfortable rate.

In the past, writing instruction emphasized product over process. Teachers would ask students to submit compositions for a grade, correction, and comments. The work was seldom shared with classmates, and educators seemed to view composition as a skill rather than a form of expression (Hammill & Bartel, 1975). Rather than encouraging clear, vivid language, they required writing free of errors, and used workbook exercises, drill, and analysis of existing prose. Negative correction and prescription often replaced instruction. Lately, however, classroom practices have been changing. Increasingly, writing is taught as a process, and correctness is subordinated to invention.

Written language poses great difficulty for mildly handicapped students. It incorporates all the elements of the language hierarchy in which they are likely to encounter difficulties. As well, written language is far more complex than oral language, which allows the speaker to repeat words and statements without loss of communicative power. Writers, on the other hand, must communicate ideas directly, succinctly, and without the benefit of intonation, gestures, and audience response. They must be aware of the organization underlying sentences, descriptions, passages involving comparison and contrast, and expository prose (Meyer, 1979).

Exceptional students show a wide range of problems with written language, from grammatical errors to dysfluencies, and can meet problems with content: getting knowledge and giving order to it (Bereiter & Scardamalia, 1982). The most frequent manifestations of difficulty are word omissions, distorted word order, incorrect verb and pronoun usage, and lack of punctuation. Lerner (1981) suggests that poor writing skills are the most prevalent communicative disability among learning-disabled students. In fact, at the secondary level there may be a lag of six to eight years between a student's speech and linguistic skills (Weiner, 1979), and these students often show gross disorganization and disconnected thoughts in their written expression. A study of creative writing skills at the secondary level also revealed that learning-disabled students detected only one-third of their own errors (Deshler, 1974).

Students with learning problems may write poorly as a consequence of other deficits: poor reading, difficulty expressing themselves well orally, an inability to remember cogent arguments, keep to the point, follow sequence and logic, and gauge their audience. Some students cannot express themselves in writing because they cannot classify information or they lack experience. Others do not understand linguistic rules and therefore cannot produce syntactically correct sentences (Wallace & McLoughlin, 1979). Many mildly handicapped students use ungrammatical forms in their speech, which they then incorporate in their written compositions (Bachor & Crealock, 1986).

Assessing creative writing

Assessment attempts to identify students who are unable to write well enough to meet the minimum standards necessary both in and out of the classroom. The inherent complexity of written language makes it difficult to assess in a comprehensive manner. Assessment, both formal and informal, can encompass several areas, including grammar, handwriting, and spelling (Cohen & Plaskon, 1980), capitalization, punctuation, written composition, and creative expression.

Informal assessment involves comparing samples of a student's work to checklists and inventories of skills necessary at a particular level, or using evaluation forms (see table 7–3). Teachers can also use direct observation to assess students' creative writing skills. They may observe how long it takes students to begin to write, how much they produce once they begin writing, and how much they protest when asked to write (Bachor & Crealock, 1986).

Table 7–3 Evaluation form for creative writing

Name:	Date:	
	Yes	No
1. Content: Does the work keep to the subject?		
2. Appropriateness: Is the work appropriate for the age and grade level of the student?		
3. Organization: Are the ideas coherently connected and does the piece have a recognizable and logical beginning, middle, and end?		
4. Paragraphing: Is the work unified and does it develop the theme effectively?		
5. Sentence structure: Does the work exhibit proper syntax and grammar?		
6. Language: Does the work use language at a level appropriate for the student?		
7. Punctuation and spelling: Does the work demonstrate consistent use of logical punctuation and correct spelling?		
8. Originality: Is the work original in theme and purpose?		

Some of the formal measures discussed earlier can be applied to creative writing. Many general achievement tests have subcategories that assess writing skills. As well, many commonly employed language tests assess written competence.

Teaching creative writing

The natural way to teach writing is to have students write, and yet students just learning to write spend less than five minutes a day completing writing of any kind. Much more of the day is spent filling in the blanks on work sheets (Bachor & Crealock, 1986). Daily writing practice should include a spectrum of activities other than using workbooks and dittos, copying notes or letter formations by rote, underlining, filling in the blanks, or circling the right word. It implies that students write their own thoughts, in the form of stories, a diary, research, or letter writing. Daily writing may include taking notes, if the student first absorbs the information mentally and then writes it down in a changed, personalized manner.

Exceptional youngsters, especially those who have experienced failure in the past, must develop positive attitudes if they are to improve their writing. Teachers should remain optimistic about students' progress and emphasize the creative process involved in a piece of work, rather than its structural defects. They must be encouraging and enthusiastic, conveying that writing is fun.

As students write, they go through certain processes; prewriting (planning), drafting, revising, editing, and sharing their work with others. Prewriting generates ideas and sharpens them. The student collects information on the chosen subjects, reads, takes notes, conducts interviews, observes people, makes drawings, deliberates, talks with other students, and maps out the topic. Even this stage can present severe problems to handicapped learners. Eventually, their difficulties lead them to avoid writing and to lose sight of its function. They therefore need many varied opportunities for observing things around them, making sensory explorations, interviewing, and mapping their topics (Tompkins & Friend, 1985).

Once they begin writing, mildly handicapped students and disabled writers often produce very little, possibly in part because they are unclear about the inherent value of the process. In general, there are three aspects of written language: the writer's attitudes toward language, the content of the written product, and the technical forms needed to express thoughts correctly (Alley & Deshler, 1979). Too often, teachers fail to address the question of why writing is important and do not separate the form from the content.

Deficiencies in production constitute perhaps the easiest language subskill to remediate (Morsink, 1984). Even asking students to write more can almost double their output (Scardamalia, Bereiter, & Goelman, 1982) and improve techniques (Kraetch, 1981).

Pupils may be reluctant to write if they know that the teacher places emphasis on copying, as opposed to editing their own work, or habitually marks every error. Certainly, however, their creative efforts must be corrected in some way; errors in grammar, syntax, and spelling must not be reinforced by being ignored. Students may demonstrate heightened performance if they are assured that only one particular type of error, punctuation for example, will be marked, and that content holds priority.

For exceptional students who encounter immense difficulty in presenting their thoughts in written form, word processing has proved effective. Electronic writing makes it easier to correct errors, delete mistakes, rearrange words in a sentence, and generally spend both less time on the mechanics and more on the content of a piece. Students can use spelling and grammar checkers to relieve the anxiety of searching for a word within their own spelling vocabulary.

Older students who have met recurring failure in the past may prove particularly hesistant to commit themselves to paper. Teachers can ask these students to create stories orally at first, thus building on speech strengths while limiting cognitive demands. Instructions that have initially been introduced orally and have required oral responses from the student can also gradually be transferred to written presentation and written responses (Dugues, 1986).

The main objective of creative writing is to help students to express their ideas on paper. Instruction should stimulate and motivate students: asking them, "Write a composition about your summer vacation," for example, is unlikely to elicit a great deal of creativity. The ideas presented below stimulate creative writing in a variety of contexts, and are adaptable for most grade levels and most age groups.

Journal writing

Journal writing, with its focus on personal thoughts and feelings, teaches writers about themselves as well as about writing. It can clarify students' feelings, and provide them with a meaningful writing occasion on which they are free to decide the topic and mode of expression (Yinger, 1985). In journals, students are able to express their own purposes and concerns privately, giving priority to meaning over form (Staton, 1985). Students write every day in their journals and the teacher responds daily in written form. The continuing written exchange allows teachers to engage students in the natural, purposeful use of written language. Completed journals can be bound and kept.

Publishing students' stories

Publishing is essential for writers, and teaches students to share their creative efforts. By interacting with others, students come to express their feelings; by writing stories, they learn to articulate and clarify their thoughts, and to explore their own identities. The stages in the classroom publishing procedure include planning, composing, revising, editing, and finally, "publishing." Students benefit from involvement in every aspect of the process.

Manson (1985) suggests marking off specific areas in the classroom for different stages of publication. The first area contains a display or a picture file from which students generate ideas or topics. They may also contribute toys and belongings from home. In the draft writing area, the students find blank paper on which to begin their work. It is not uncommon for some students to spend two or three weeks writing a draft, revising it, conferring with the teacher, and meeting in small groups to improve specific skills, such as developing a story line. The planning stage results in a rough outline and then a first draft, which may be characterized by many crossed-out sections, erasures, and misspellings as pupils alter their work. Teachers offer assistance on content but ignore punctuation and spelling. In the editing area the teacher works with the students to polish the stories. Content and syntax are improved, mechanical errors eliminated, and, finally, the story is rewritten.

Finished work may be typed. The students can then bind their books and illustrate their own work. It is essential that students share published stories with classmates, or the purpose of the exercise is destroyed. A small group of students may gather in a writers' circle afterwards to listen to each other's work and discuss how the stories were produced.

Poetry writing

Poetry has been used effectively in the classroom both for its intrinsic qualities and as a vehicle for other subject matter (Natheson, Cynamon, & Lehman, 1976), because it uses language in expressive and unique ways to present ideas to an audience. It therefore teaches students to play with language.

Poetry can be introduced in the following manner:

1. Go for a walk, either real or imaginary, with the class.
2. Collect objects for the classroom.
3. Ask students to describe the objects in the following manner, to create a poem:

Name the object. ______________________
Two words that describe it (adjectives or adverbs) are ______________________
and ______________________
Three action words (verbs) that describe what it does are ______________________
and ______________________ and ______________________
Write a four-word statement that describes what this object does.
____
Another word for this object (synonym) is ______________________

The result might look like this:

Deer
Brown, Small
Leaping, Running, Standing
Swift as a thought
Doe

Another method to introduce poetry is to ask each student in a group to write a single line, and then pass the poem on to the next student.

Descriptive writing

Students can be helped with descriptive writing if they are first given many opportunities to discuss the specific characteristics of objects, people, places, and so on. Picture descriptions can stimulate the process. To supplement the exercise, the teacher can design lists of prepositions, possessives, and adverbs.

A picture description is an essay in which the students describe a picture in the present tense. Although the procedure should be used sparingly, it does help students to build and review vocabulary and linguistic principles. The teacher displays a picture and questions the students about it to stimulate discussion. New and difficult words and phrases are listed on the board. The students derive ideas from the questions, and add new expressions to their vocabularies. Through questioning, the teacher helps them to develop a logical sequence of sentences. The students then write their own descriptions, using the key words and terms listed on the board as aids, if necessary. Some students may be helped by a chart to prompt their descriptions:

Tell about the object (person, event, thing, place)

Colour:
Size:
Shape:
Feel or texture:
Smell:
Taste:
How it is used:

Story writing

Writing stories is extremely difficult for some children. They find it hard to come up with an idea, to organize their thoughts, and to get them on paper coherently, with reasonable grammar, spelling, and writing. Well-developed stories follow a basic four-part structure (Stein & Glenn, 1978). The *setting* establishes the characters, date, and location. The *problem* confronts the character or characters and the *response* describes how they behave within the given situation. Finally, the *outcome* describes the resolution of the problem. Students need to understand this structure to improve their own writing techniques. Teachers can read stories to the class and then discuss the relationship of its characters or parts to one another, or define the story structure in diagrams with the students, as shown in figure 7–11. A webbing technique is also effective. The student begins with a theme, and writes it down in the centre of a piece of paper. She or he then lists themes that branch off from the central one, placing them on the page in a web pattern that illustrates the connections among them (see figure 7–12).

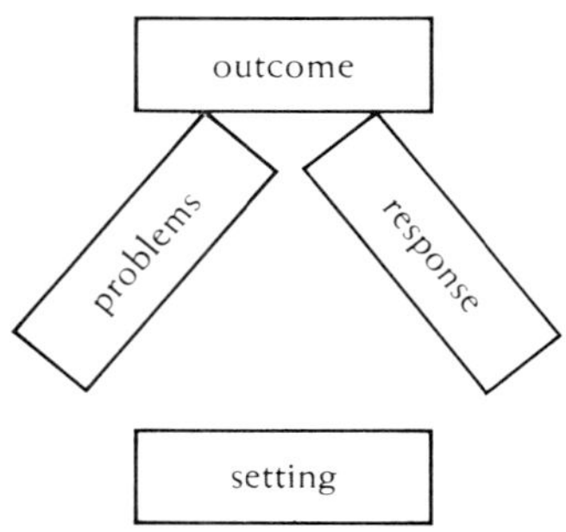

Figure 7–11 Defining story structure

Source: Adapted from "An Analysis of Comprehension in Elementary School Children" by N.L. Stein and C.G. Glenn, 1978, in R. Freddle (Ed.) *Discourse Processing: Multi-disciplinary Perspectives*, Hillsdale, NJ: Ablex.

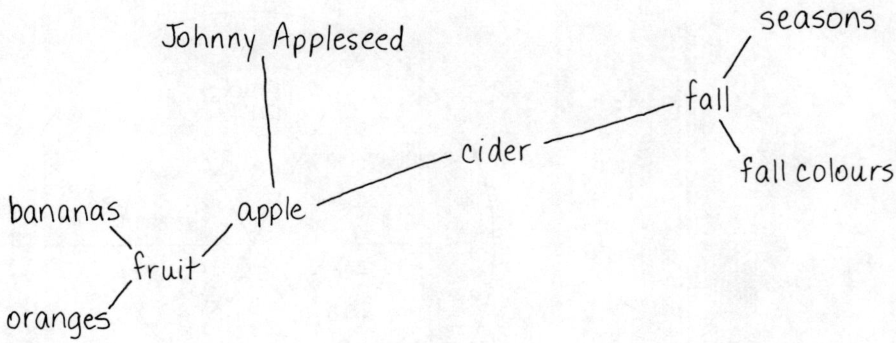

Figure 7–12 Webbing technique

Story guides are another way of introducing structural analysis prior to writing. Students who are encountering difficulties with the writing process find them useful to give shape to ideas, because the guides determine the information to be included and transform loosely related ideas into an organized framework of information (Graham, 1982; Yatvin, 1981). The story guide should be presented on large paper and may include the following elements:

Setting: where does the story take place and who are the characters?
Problem: what is the problem and what is its cause?
Response: how do characters feel about the problem, what will they do, who will help to solve it, and who will obstruct the solution?
Outcome: how does the story end and how does everyone react?

Expository writing

To help students write, use the idea of the paragraph pie (see figure 7–13). The main idea of the paragraph is designated as the first slice and the supporting statements become other slices. With this in mind students can start their paragraphs in an organized fashion with a statement of the main idea, and then add supporting details. The pie helps them to gain an understanding of the relationships among statements. The same model is useful for teaching students to discern the main idea in what they read.

Creative writing activities

Objective: to motivate students and to stimulate the writing process

a) Show students a picture and discuss it, noting key words and phrases on the board. Ask them to write a description of the picture. Alternatively, use a picture but have the class write about characters in the scene and what might happen next.

b) Ask students to draw a picture of something that happened at home. They then exchange their pictures and write stories to match them.

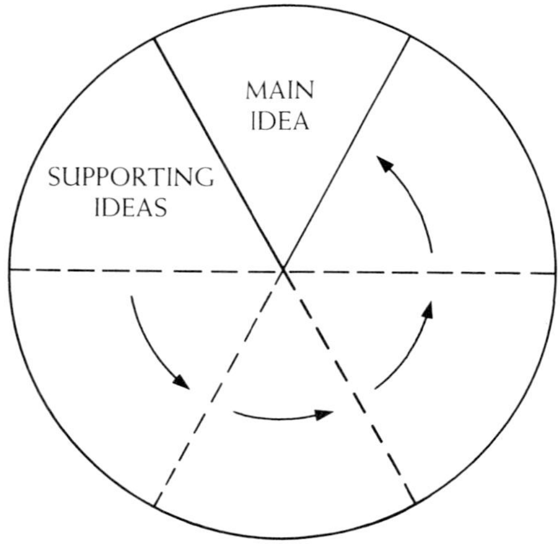

Figure 7–13 The paragraph pie

c) Ask pupils to write a story around a word or a phrase.

d) Show a videotape of a short story, except for the ending. Have the students write their own endings and then watch the end of the tape and discuss the different ideas.

e) Ask students to write book reports or movie reviews and to include their opinions of the work.

f) Discuss a piece of art with the class and ask them to give it a caption.

g) Allow students to use different kinds of writing instruments, such as a typewriter or a computer.

h) Publish a class newspaper.

i) Assign sentence-combining exercises, to help students to produce sentences more automatically, thus freeing them to focus on the substance rather than the mechanics of writing (Flower & Hayes, 1980).

j) Provide students with support sentences, such as "I feel . . . because. . . ."

k) Have the students search through the "Articles for Sale" section of the newspaper to find something that they would like to buy, and ask them to write a composition describing the article and explaining why they want to own it.

l) Copy a comic strip onto an overhead transparency or onto individual work sheets, making sure that all the dialogue is erased. Have students write in their own dialogue. The idea can be expanded by having the students listen to a short story or a joke, and then draw their own comic strip, placing appropriate dialogue in word balloons.

m) List five nursery rhymes or fairy tales on the board and have the students write an interesting headline for each one. They can then "report" the story.

n) Write a list of words on the board that could fit together in a story, such as *moon, earth, rocket,* and *astronaut.* Pupils begin to write their stories, but on a predetermined signal they each pass their papers to another pupil who continues the work. Do this four or five times, telling the final writers to conclude the story. Read the stories aloud and discuss the efforts.

o) On small index cards write unfinished sentences suitable for story beginnings, such as, "It was a dark and gloomy night and . . ." or "Jim answered the doorbell and was surprised to find. . . ." Each student draws a card and uses the sentence to start a story.

p) Provide students with a list of words and ask them to write a short story incorporating the words in the list. The story can be structured by providing a title in advance.

q) Show photographs to the students and ask them to write a story. Add structure by asking them to answer specific questions, such as "Where are you?"(setting); "Why are you there?" (justification); "What are you doing?" (action); "What are you looking at?" (details); and "What will you do next?" (resolution or implications).

Objective: to use logical sequence and story structure

a) Prepare a sequence of pictures and have the pupils write a story based on the pictures.

b) Show students only one picture. Ask them to discuss it and to write a complete sequence around it.

c) For beginning writers of any age, put up a poster with questions in large print that ask Who? What? When? Where? and Why? The poster serves as an effective story outline.

Objective: to use writing for everyday purposes

a) Present students with a topic and have them write the information out in the form of a telegram.

b) Have the students analyse advertisements of their choice and then create their own advertisements.

c) Ask students to identify words relevant to a theme and to compile a list of synonyms. List these on the board.

Objective: to use writing for personal communication

a) Encourage students to write letters to penpals.

b) Discuss the students' favourite television shows. Help them to write letters to a television magazine asking questions.

Objective: to report factual information in written form

a) Have students write thumbnail sketches of people, or descriptions of objects.

b) Have pupils provide directions for puzzles, recipes, games, and so on.

c) Stage an event in the classroom with another teacher or a student. The event should be surprising, fast, and loud. A student may burst in, for example, point to the teacher, shout, "You won, you won," and then rush out again. Following the action, ask the students to write a newspaper account of the event including as much detail as possible. They may also editorialize and discuss motives and outcomes.

d) Have the pupils prepare shopping lists, fill in forms, or write notes for the classroom bulletin boards.

The activities just described have dealt with written language in a broad context, and the chapter as a whole has addressed several aspects of language. Reading, however, is another large topic in its own right, and forms the subject of the following chapter.

8 *Teaching reading*

- Guided reading
- Previewing
- Repeated readings
- Fernald method
- Neurological Impress Method
- RATE method
- High-intensity reading practice

Reduced reading and non-reading curricula

Reading activities

Dear Reader,

I frequently receive inquiries such as "What is the best way to teach reading?" "Is this reading material good?" "How do I help a child who has dyslexia?" All these questions share an underlying assumption that one method or material will be effective for all learners, or at least for all learners who are experiencing difficulty learning to read. They fail to take into account both the complexity of the reading process and the wide variation in how people learn to read. They seek a simple solution to a very complex problem, largely as a result of the high level of significance attached to reading.

Parents and teachers know that a reading deficiency will have an impact on a child's progress through school and on his or her quality of life beyond school. Being able to read is necessary to be as good as, not better than, other members of our society. It is a means of entry into the culture of the literate, and failure to gain entry carries high personal and social costs. Reading is so vital that we often feel we must find "the best way," although, of course, there are as many different best ways as there are children and adults in our reading programs. Educators need to know how to determine the needs of students with reading problems and to be aware of a wide range of techniques and materials to help these students learn.

Planning programs for reading-disabled students has few absolutes, but it is certain that material must be adjusted to the level at which the students read or else they will continue to be frustrated by their interactions with print. Little learning will occur and in fact, inappropriate strategies for reading may be reinforced. Perhaps of even greater concern is the impact that daily frustration can have on students' attitudes and their concepts of themselves as learners and readers, creating a vicious cycle of reading failure and low self-confidence. While adjusting material is not sufficient to remediate most reading difficulties, it is certainly a necessary component of the remedial program and critical to break the cycle. One important goal of a diagnostic battery, then, is to determine each student's instructional reading level.

Another absolute is the need to focus on "reading as communication" as the basis of all programs for problem readers. Many traditional remedial materials and approaches teach word identification as an end in itself rather than as a means of facilitating communication between a reader and an author. They do so on the assumption that breaking the complex task of reading down into discrete pieces will make it easier. Proponents of whole language dispute the claim that small is easy, suggesting instead that learning is easier when it is whole, meaningful, relevant, purposeful, and belongs to the learner. The movement toward whole language in Canada has had more impact on regular than on special education classes but it is hoped that this will change. While I would not suggest that we stop teaching students strategies for basic word identification and comprehension, it is important that these strategies be taught in the context of meaningful reading experiences. For many at-risk children with little understanding that reading is communication, an early focus on isolated letters and words is confusing rather than helpful.

Finally, because we are so concerned that our students make rapid progress, educators often create an imbalance between the time that students spend in class receiving reading instruction and the time that they spend actually reading. We often assume that practice occurs outside of school hours but in fact, research shows that the gap between the amount of reading done by good and poor readers widens rapidly across the elementary school grades. We must make sure that children with reading problems have opportunities at school every day to read, read, read. Again this may not be sufficient to overcome a student's problem, but it is certainly necessary to ensure progress.

Grace Malicky
Director
Reading and Language Center
University of Alberta

Reading skills are one of the most important academic goals for children. In spite of the role that non-print media play in presenting messages, life lacking adequate reading skills is uncomfortable and full of closed doors. In our daily activities we read instructions, signs, packages, television guides, telephone books, newspapers and magazines, and a host of other materials that keep us in tune with society.

Reading is a highly complex process, much more than just "talk written down." It is not simply a discrete set of skills, but a cognitive, linguistic, cultural, pragmatic, and emotional interaction with print (Ewoldt, 1982). Although reading is an extension of natural language development, reading and speaking are actually two different modes. A reader needs to associate ideas with words, to understand fine shades of meaning that go beyond informal conversation, and to recognize the effects of grammatical structures on meaning. Yet the process of reading—how it actually works—is not well understood and many different descriptions have been suggested.

Acquiring literacy should be a natural process, like learning to speak or listen, because reading draws heavily on an already established linguistic base (Gillett & Temple, 1986). By grade three, reading should have progressed to a communication skill that children can apply to tasks in the content areas. Most pupils can fulfill the oft-quoted teacher's criterion, "Children must learn to read so that they can later read to learn." Yet most of them do *not* learn to read automatically; they must be taught.

Children differ greatly in their readiness for learning to read and in their acquisition of reading skills. As students advance through the grades, individual differences increase, and may span a noticeably greater range in a class of intermediate pupils than in a primary class. Nor do all children learn to read in the same manner. No single approach can be effective to promote efficient reading skills in all children, and not every pupil in a class has to read at the same level, although they must have fairly good reading skills for all school learning and for later adult living. It is important too, that children discover reading as an end in itself. They should experience the joy and fun of reading.

Almost every classroom teacher has met students who cannot, will not, or do not read. Some of them appear limited in their ability, others seem confused, or resistant. Indeed, of all areas of the curriculum, reading forms a stumbling block to the greatest number of students. It is estimated that 10 to 15 percent of all school-age children suffer from reading disabilities that hamper their academic achievement (Harris & Sipay, 1975).

Reading retardation is probably the earliest and most common sign of academic difficulties, and one of the most reliable preliminary indicators of poor scholastic achievement. Failure often begins in grade one when a child demonstrates an inability to master basal texts or other instructional materials. As they proceed through school, students may continue to show poor responses to typical teaching methods and fall progressively behind the rest of the class.

Reading-disabled pupils are not necessarily included among the population of special learners, but, not surprisingly, reading difficulties abound among exceptional children and youth. Of all the areas in which exceptional students experience failure, reading is the most prominent and receives the most attention. Two-thirds of mildly handicapped learners are referred for reading problems (Wiederholt, Hammill, & Brown, 1983). Most students in programs for learning disabilities are handicapped by poor reading skills (Kirk & Elkins, 1975), and mentally retarded students do not achieve levels of reading commensurate with their intellectual ability. Eighty-five percent of learning-disabled students suffer reading disabilities (Kaluger & Kolson, 1978), their most common academic deficit (Norman & Zigmond, 1980).

Some children may learn the skills in the elementary grades and still encounter problems in the higher classes when they must apply those skills to other learning. By this stage, students need to think actively about the content of material, to be familiar with, and responsive to, different linguistic structures in the text, to retain new words encountered in reading, and to develop study skills.

Teachers devote the greatest percentage of instructional time to reading, which is also the academic subject most commonly studied in research (Kirk & Elkins, 1975; Torgesen & Dice, 1980). While reading forms the major component of instruction, especially in the early school years, educators are currently showing increasing interest in reading instruction for the middle and senior high school levels. Although elementary teachers are responsible for developmental reading, in reality every teacher, even at the secondary level, should be concerned about reading, and must be aware of students' different levels of reading comprehension.

A teacher makes crucial educational decisions when selecting both an instructional approach and reading material. Success in reading is related to the degree to which instructional procedures match the attention, processing, and response styles of the learners (Ratekin, 1979), and therefore avert inappropriate reading habits. Over the years, instruction has alternated between pure look-say and pure phonic approaches. Today, to meet the needs of more students, modern methods combine the best aspects of the traditional reading systems with linguistic systems that concentrate on spelling patterns. The methods chosen depend upon the material available, the teacher's preference, and, most importantly, the school's orientation.

Given the complexity of the reading process, continuing controversy over instructional approaches, and the wide variety of developmental and remedial reading techniques available, this chapter can only touch on the reading process. The approaches selected for discussion are those that have proven successful with exceptional learners, but the general superiority of any single approach has not been conclusively proven.

The main objectives of this chapter are to

- discuss reading disabilities
- discuss some widely used assessment measures
- discuss the different types and purposes of reading and the ways in which teachers can include these in the classroom
- discuss a range of instructional methods and materials appropriate for exceptional students

Reading disabilities

The underlying causes of reading disabilities are complex, the educational implications far-reaching, and the social costs disturbing. The poor reader has a 50 percent chance of not finishing high school (L'Abate & Curtis, 1975), but this may only be the beginning of the student's problems. Reading is a key to obtaining employment, participating fully in society and culture, increasing the options for leisure activities, expanding personal horizons, and becoming independent at home, work, and in the community.

Reading is a blend of many separate skills working in harmony; if one is missing, the entire process breaks down. Reading problems are inappropriate patterns of behaviour that people use when they encounter print. A number of terms have evolved to describe reading problems, among them **dyslexia**, which has been adopted, often inaccurately, into the common parlance. Too often, the term dyslexia is used synonymously with learning disabilities. The word comes from the root *dys*, meaning poor or inadequate, and *lexia*, meaning speaking, and simply implies a disorder in reading. It therefore encompasses a broad range of students, both learning disabled and not.

The term **specific reading disability** denotes an inability to learn to read with the rapidity and skill required of an individual's mental age. *Retarded readers* possess a reading capacity considerably greater than demonstrated reading achievement. *Slow readers* demonstrate problems in word recognition and comprehension, or read word by word, because of ingrained bad habits, low IQ, excessive use of phonics, inadequate sight-word vocabulary, or ignorance of phrasing and punctuation, to mention a few factors. *Non-motivated readers* sometimes display a blasé facade, but are often trapped in failure. They say "I won't," when really then mean, "I can't."

Reading problems have various levels of severity. A mild disability describes readers whose overall achievement levels are either less than a year below expectations for the grade in which they are placed or whose difficulties have lasted less than a year, and who are responsive to remedial procedures (Morsink, 1984). Conversely, serious reading disabilities place the reader more than one grade level below expectations, have lasted longer than a year, and require extensive remedial work.

One way to determine reading grade expectancy is to subtract five from the mental age of the child. A youngster with a mental age of seven, for example, would have a reading expectancy age of grade two (Kirk, Kliebhan, & Lerner, 1978). Reading grade expectancy levels are shown in table 8–1, with samples of reading material appropriate for the grades shown.

Reading disability may be functionally related to instructional, socio-cultural, psychological, neurological, or attitudinal factors, or a combination of these. In fact, large reading problems usually turn out to be made up of a collection of small problems, exacerbated by other intervening conditions. Students with hard core reading problems may have difficulties with word recognition, or with reading comprehension — the ability to weave ideas together and draw inferences from the context. While many students will demonstrate deficits in both areas, comprehension problems tend to dominate in secondary level reading-disabled readers; more adolescent learning-disabled students, for example, are affected by comprehension problems than by any other reading disability (Lindsey & Kerlin, 1979). These students are unable to answer questions about what they have read or to state the main topic of a paragraph.

Some children exhibit slow cognitive and perceptual development, and their reading performance will be characteristic of younger students (Gredler, 1978). Other reading-disabled students are distractible; they seem confused by letters and words that look alike and are unable to follow a line of print from left to right. Reading disability can also result from deficits in perception, laterality, directionality, visual scanning, decoding, discrimination, memory, or abstract reasoning.

Table 8–1 Reading grade expectancy

Mental age	Reading grade expectancy	Typical material
6.0	1.0	Jim ran to school.
6.5	1.5	He saw a big dog.
7.0	2.0	He wanted to take the dog home. One day Jim saw another big dog. He wanted to feed the dog.
7.5	2.5	He walked over to the dog and tried to pat him.
8.0	3.0	Jim's father bought Jim a dog. Jim called the dog Ruff because he had such a loud bark. Jim always takes Ruff to school with him.
8.5	3.5	One day Jim took Ruff for a long walk in the woods.
9.0	4.0	It was great fun and Jim and Ruff enjoyed it very much.
9.5	4.5	Ruff ran from tree to tree looking for birds and squirrels. Once he saw a fat old bumble bee and began to chase it through the tall trees.

Learning-disabled students tend to read one to six times more slowly than do normal readers (Critchley, 1975). They demonstrate dysphonic problems: deficiencies in sound–symbol integration and decoding phonetics, substitution of words or letters, wild guessing, reversal of letters or syllables, and incorrect pronunciation of vowels and consonants (Boder, 1970, 1971). They may also have dyseidetic problems: deficits in the ability to perceive whole words, manifested by a lack of sight vocabulary, omitting small words that change the meaning of a sentence, and difficulty gaining meaning from long sentences and paragraphs (Boder, 1970, 1971).

Mentally retarded learners are significantly behind other students in reading, and the gap widens as they get older. Boys tend to be below girls in all facets of reading and more erratic in performance. The final reading status for mentally retarded readers falls somewhere between grade two and grade six. Specific achievement is determined by their degree of intellectual impairment, associated learning characteristics, the quality of the educational environment, and the functionality and relevance of instruction for the student.

In general, mildly handicapped students show the whole spectrum of reading problems. They may have failed with traditional reading methods and developed an entrenched dislike of the reading process. They often have inferior word-attack skills, make less use of contextual clues, mispronounce more vowels, and make more omissions of sound. Their failure may not be due to reading deficits alone. Students may have poor language foundations, listening comprehension, study skills, and motivation, or an inability to select important facts, organize ideas and materials, and memorize information. Many retarded readers have unproductive learning strategies that impinge on their reading achievement (Gredler, 1978).

Personality plays a part in learning to read. Some children arrive at school lacking incentive while others already look upon reading as an important part of life. The child who lacks interest in reading, or who sees no purpose in it, is unlikely to progress satisfactorily. On the other hand, highly motivated children who fail to learn reading may begin behaving aggressively. Indeed, behavioural problems seem to increase as reading level decreases (Graubard, 1971) and poor readers have more social and emotional problems than average (Gillespie & Johnson, 1974). Children's first reading experiences may determine their later progress. Confronting children with reading instruction before they are ready for it can frustrate and antagonize them. Eventually they may profess a dislike for books.

Older students who have reading difficulties will experience academic deficits and, perhaps, deeper emotional problems. Secondary students who read at a grade two level are almost certain to fail in most other academic efforts. Soon, they feel defeated by and perhaps prejudiced against the reading process. A teacher at the secondary level who attempts to improve students' reading habits will have to consider their needs and goals carefully.

Assessing reading

Reading assessment takes many different forms. Prior to or during psycho-educational assessment, it is routine to check students' hearing and vision; uncorrected sensory problems will render reading an almost insurmountable task. A broad range of general and specific skills are evaluated during an assessment. Global skills include: general comprehension and vocabulary; recognition of key concepts; recognition of the reading rates and strategies appropriate for different reading tasks; and ability both to apply critical analysis and to cope with unfamiliar words (Vaughan & Gaus, 1978). More specific skills include: basic word-attack skills; phonetic and structural analysis; directional habits; and level of comprehension, recall, and vocabulary. It is equally important, however, to assess study skills, reading tastes, reading needs in the content areas, and the student's rate of learning.

Formal measures

The teacher or reading specialist can draw upon several sources to assess students, although fewer measures are available at the secondary level. Standardized reading achievement tests are most commonly used and include both tests that are components of a standardized achievement battery and tests expressly developed as separate measures of reading achievement. Reading sections appear on most of the major achievement tests, such as the Metropolitan Achievement Tests (Prescott, Balow, Hogan, & Fan, 1978), the Wide Range Achievement Test (Jastak, Bijou, & Jastak, 1965), and the Canadian Test of Basic Skills (Scannel, Haugh, Schild, Ulmer, & King, 1988).

Although these measures provide a general estimate of reading ability, their vocabulary and content seldom match that found in specific subject areas. Inventories and cloze procedures can more effectively assess the relationship between reading ability and the demands of print used in secondary areas (Summers, 1984). Extended examination using formal measures should, however, provide a clear picture of the specific nature of reading retardation. It reveals an individual's deficits in concept development, perception, and spatial relationships and development, as well as disturbances in receptive and expressive language (Rourke, Young, & Flewelling, 1978).

Informal measures

While formal measures are widely used to assess achievement and to diagnose difficulties, they have relatively little value for instructional programming. Numerical scores do not yield specific information about what a student can and cannot do (Gillett & Temple, 1986). Informal procedures more closely resemble natural reading in the classroom; teacher-made measures seem to have the most validity because they use material found in the students' textbooks (Wiederholt, Hammill, & Brown, 1983).

The measures look at reading behaviours qualitatively rather than quantitatively. They take place in natural situations and are basically exploratory in nature. Inventories and checklists, miscue analysis, and cloze procedures are all informal reading measures. If a student is lagging behind, demonstrating reading difficulties, or losing motivation, the teacher can use whichever procedures are best suited to that individual.

Inventories and checklists

Reading inventories and checklists are quite simple both to construct and to use, and flexible enough to assess many aspects of reading, from interests to specific skills. Checklists, whether made by the teacher or commercially prepared, usually consist of a series of letters, graded word lists, or reading passages presented in order of difficulty. As an example, a teacher may decide to make an alphabet checklist for beginning readers. Letters are typed in random order, triple spaced on sturdy paper, in lines containing about three letters each. The teacher then simply points to each letter and asks the child to name it. Knowing the names of letters is a prerequisite for reading, and most educators believe that children who do not know the alphabet cannot make a start in reading. In fact, Chall (1967) found that letter knowledge predicts early reading ability better than do the various tests of intelligence and language ability.

Children between the ages of seven and nine confuse lower-case letters most commonly (Dunn-Rankin, 1968). They also find letters with similar features difficult to distinguish, particularly letters containing diagonals (Gibson, 1969). The most frequently confused letters fall into four groups: *a c e o s*, *m n v w*, *b d p*, and *f h i k l t*. Children often muddle letters in the same group but do not mix them with letters from other groups (Dunn-Rankin, 1968), a factor that should be taken into account when interpreting data from checklists. Early on in reading instruction, teachers need not be very concerned about children's occasional difficulty discriminating among letters. Children often miss *b*, *d*, and *p*, or *q* and *a* on the alphabet list because of directional confusion, but will usually identify them correctly in text. Children who have difficulty with letters other than these, however, are not likely to be reading soon. They need more exposure to letters and print (Gillett & Temple, 1986).

Inventories have been found particularly useful as screening devices to assess reading levels (Summers, 1984). They use materials commonly employed in the classroom and are therefore readily available and inexpensive. Inventories may ask questions about specific areas of reading, such as phonetic rules, or they may relate to more general areas (see table 8–2).

Table 8–2 General inventory of reading problems

	Yes	No
Word recognition problems		
1. Skips or slides over words that should be familiar.		
2. Substitutes words with familiar meanings for unfamiliar ones.		
3. Repeats words before the word causing the problem.		
4. Fixes on one part of a word.		
5. Confuses similar configurations, such as *bond* and *board*.		
6. Demonstrates difficulty with sound blending.		
Comprehension problems		
1. Lacks expression in oral reading.		
2. Cannot interpret or retell material in own words.		
3. Unable to answer various types of questions, such as details of story sequence.		
4. Cannot state main point of a paragraph.		
5. Substitutes words that destroy the meaning of a sentence.		
6. Cannot follow simple written instructions.		
7. Shows excessive physical activity during reading, such as squirming and fidgeting.		
8. Demonstrates faulty study habits, such as failure to read and summarize material. (This applies to older students.)		

A pupil's ability to respond quickly to the words in a given list reflects sight-word recognition. A graded word list can be used to arrive at a quick estimate of the level at which the pupil begins to experience difficulties, while his or her attempts to analyse unknown words can reveal where basic weaknesses lie in word-attack techniques.

To construct a basic word checklist, select words at random from the glossary of the basal reader, type them on a master sheet, and also print them on individual flash cards. To administer the test, present the flash cards to the student and note responses and specific areas of difficulty on the master sheet. Continue the procedure until the student misses three words consecutively. Lerner (1981) suggests that the student who misses one word functions at an independent reading level with the material, two words, at the instructional level, and three, at a frustration level. Word lists also provide some data about the student's reading comprehension. Because recognizing the words and understanding the text are normally closely related, word-recognition rates can predict comprehension fairly well (Gillett & Temple, 1986).

Estimates of reading ability may vary considerably with the student's interest in a particular passage. Interest inventories of the type presented in table 8–3 are useful to assess a student's reading interests, and therefore discover how to motivate him or her to read.

Table 8–3 An inventory for reading interests

1. The kind of reading I enjoy most is
   a) poetry
   b) stories
   c) comics
   d) newspapers and magazines
2. I prefer to read
   a) orally
   b) silently
3. I like to read about
   a) animals
   b) adventure
   c) mystery
   d) romance
   e) real people
   f) inventions
   g) history
   h) science fiction
   i) sports
   j) television and movies
   k) everything
4. The last three books I read were
   a)
   b)
   c)
5. I read the newspaper
   a) often
   b) occasionally
   c) rarely
   d) never
6. My favourite magazines are
   a)
   b)

Cloze procedures

Cloze (or close) is an abbreviation of the term *closure* which, in this case, implies completing a pattern that is missing a part. Cloze procedures are used to determine if students are capable of completing a particular text and to assess their ability to use contextual clues (Bormuth, 1968; Jongsma, 1971). Cloze may measure a student's reading level, help to determine placement, diagnose specific problems, provide insights into a student's language competence, and teach students to read in context. The emphasis on meaning inherent in cloze is particularly recommended for older pupils.

Pleasure in reading is the ultimate goal of the reading program.

Cloze requires students to replace words that have been left out of a passage with logical substitutes. Readers are forced to use the syntactic and semantic information available to predict what is missing. The tester first selects three passages of about one hundred words each, from the beginning, middle, and end of a story suitable for a particular student or group of students. The passages are clearly typed or printed with roughly every fifth word omitted, until there are fifty blank spaces altogether. (The pattern can be varied.) Words from the first or last sentence of each passage are not deleted, and nor is the first word in a sentence unless it is an article. Neither proper nouns nor numbers are omitted and the tester selects the next word instead.

The tester prepares students by leading them through a short practice exercise at the board. Before students begin, testers should encourage them to read the entire passage first and to use the words that make the most sense. Synonyms are acceptable if the cloze procedure is being used for instructional purposes, although Miller and Coleman (1967) suggest that to determine placement the most valued scoring system is to accept only the exact word, and the cloze exercise should therefore be constructed to avoid guesswork. Each response that lends a correct reading to the passage is given a mark of one. (The total number of marks can be doubled to give a final score out of one hundred.) The higher the final score, the easier the book or the story will be for a student. Table 8–4 outlines the implications of different scores using cloze procedures.

The cloze maze is a variation of the cloze procedure suitable for very young or very disabled readers (Guthrie, Seifert, Burnham, & Caplan, 1974). Instead of blank spaces, students are provided with three alternatives for the word: the correct word, an incorrect word from the same class of words, and an incorrect word from another class.

Miscue analysis

Goodman and her associates view reading as a "psycholinguistic guessing game" (Burke & Goodman, 1970; Goodman, 1972). By this they imply that the reader's thoughts and language ability interact with what is written and to come in the text. The reader must learn to select the fewest and most productive cues necessary to guess about the words (Lerner, 1981). All readers, both proficient and disabled, make errors in reading, but the errors of disabled readers tend to be of a different kind (Lerner, 1981). Analysing a reader's errors therefore provides insight into the ongoing psycholinguistic process. The method is called miscue analysis, a **miscue** being an unexpected response to print.

Miscues occur when the reader, using semantic, syntactic, or graphemic cues, makes an incorrect prediction about what will come next in the text (Ewoldt, 1982). If the reader does not correct the mistake, the sentence becomes meaningless. Miscues are thus judged by whether they disrupt the meaning of the sentence.

Ewoldt (1982) outlines a procedure for using miscue analysis. The first step is to select an interesting, well-formed, and cohesive story about one reading level above the student's usual one, that is likely to be familiar to her or him. The tester introduces the story and then asks the student to read it through aloud, close the book, and retell the story orally. If the student has trouble retelling the story, the tester may use prompts and open-ended questions such as "Tell me more," or "What happened then?" The entire session should be videotaped or audiotaped, and the tape transcribed in order to complete a miscue analysis checklist, as shown in table 8–5.

Miscue analysis examines errors in terms of remediation; that is, to see if they are due to phonic, grammatical, semantic, or dialectical problems, or deeper language deficits. The tester scores the passage by marking each miscue, but not the student's corrections, pauses, and repetitions. The total number of miscues is then expressed as

Table 8–4 Scoring for cloze procedures and miscue analysis

Reading level	Implication	Cloze score	Miscue score
Independent	The student can read the material with high interest and without help.	80 +	97 +
Challenge	With a minimum of instruction, the student can read and enjoy the material.	60–80	96–97
Instructional	The student can read the material but requires prior or simultaneous instruction in vocabulary and comprehension.	40–60	90–96
Frustration	The material is too difficult; the student will falter and read so poorly that comprehension will be inadequate.	40 –	90 –
Listening	The student may understand and enjoy the story when it is read by someone else.	20 –	_____

Table 8–5 Miscue analysis marking

dog The little boy fell on the steps.	Substitution of a word or phrase
down The little boy fell ^ on the steps.	Insertion of a word
The little boy fell (on) the steps.	Omission of a word
The little boy fell on the (steps.)	Word given by the teacher
The little boy fell on the steps.	Miscue spontaneously corrected
The little boy fell on the steps.	Repetition of a word
The little boy fell on the steps.	Reversal of words
The little boy ‖ fell on the steps.	Pauses too long
feld The little boy fell on the steps.	Mispronunciation of word
The little boy fell on the steps X	Punctuation ignored
W The little boy fell on the steps.	Hesitancy
F The little boy fell on the steps.	Unknown word

a percentage of the total number of words in the passage. If a student miscues fourteen times in a passage of a hundred words, for example, then the miscue rating is 14 percent, which provides a level of eighty-six (see table 8–4).

To assess the retelling, the tester has an outline of the story and on it records the information that the pupil retells freely. All prompts and open-ended questions are also included. Testers should look for discrepancies in recall of sequence, of main characters, of feelings and relationships, of actions and events, of the plot, and of the theme of the story. Ewoldt (1982) suggests scoring a retelling by assigning 25 percent for characters, 25 percent for events, and 50 percent for sequence. The criteria for analysing miscues are set much higher than they are for cloze procedures because miscue provides the benefit of sentence context. Once the student's reading level is established, it can be closely matched to reading materials.

The listening level is the highest level a reader can comprehend when listening to another person reading aloud. It provides a rough estimate of a student's potential for reading improvement. The frustration level indicates that the material is too difficult in vocabulary and concepts. The student has poor comprehension, forgets or misunderstands the main ideas, and shows laboured silent and oral reading with frequent stops to analyse unknown words. The instructional level represents the desired reading level. The pupil is comfortable with the material and demonstrates good comprehension but will benefit from instruction. Although the student has fairly rapid silent reading and smooth, accurate oral reading, the material is challenging and he or she will need help with some concepts. Students who score at the challenge level read well but must still apply themselves, whereas those at the independent level can read the text easily, showing good comprehension. The reading is not challenging and more complex material should be introduced.

Approaches to reading

Generally, reading programs for mildly handicapped students are not very different from those used with other students but may contain more stress on subskills such as perceptual motor training, visual motor training, and auditory perception. It is important also that they avoid materials that have brought failure in the past. The programs use the same scope and sequence as for non-handicapped children, but base the activities very directly on the relevance of the skills being taught. Mildly mentally retarded pupils, for example, are primarily taught functional, informational, and recreational reading. Many remedial reading methods can be incorporated into the regular reading program. In addition to these, there are several general points to bear in mind when giving special learners reading instruction:

- A reading program for special learners should include functional reading, or reading in a practical situation; informational reading, for knowledge; recreational reading, for fun; and instructional reading, to develop the student's ability to gain information and understand the purpose of print.
- The reading program should begin at a student's level of language development, based on demonstrated language performance.
- Students must be able to gain meaning from print at a literal level before they can be expected to use critical reading skills.
- Reading stories to pupils stimulates their interest in the printed word and expands their experiential backgrounds.
- Children are motivated to read if the material interests them.
- Children benefit most from instruction when they are fresh. Do not follow vigorous play times with formal reading instruction.
- Slower reading groups usually work best at the beginning of the reading period, so these students should have priority.
- Retarded readers need consistent daily work with the teacher. Since their attention span is usually short, it is better to plan two brief sessions than a single long one.
- Create appropriate materials that focus on the students' interests and use them as the core of the program at various stages of reading instruction.
- Try a variety of instructional approaches, if necessary, in order to find the ones that match individual learning styles and interests.
- Help students to evaluate their own progress, perhaps by using individual graphs to record achievements such as the number of sight words learned, questions answered correctly, or books read.
- Calling on students in ordered turns when they are reading in small groups ensures

that they all have an opportunity to participate and to practise skills, and also simplifies group management (Anderson, Evertson, & Brophy, 1979; Brophy & Evertson, 1976).

- Teach one skill at a time, both in isolation and immediately in context, and ensure that students attain mastery before you teach the next skill.
- Often, mildly handicapped students are sated with drill and practice exercises, and have had little opportunity to read for natural purposes. Find many different ways for them to practise each skill.
- Supplement instruction for students with visual difficulties with activities that use other modalities; for example, listening to stories on tape.
- Children will interact with print better within an environment that encourages literacy and demonstrates the variety of purposes and forms of written language. Teachers can, for example, place illustrated poems on the walls, the lunch menu by the door, and the daily schedule on the board.

Reading in the classroom

Reading is an active process, founded in experience and based on linguistic competence. It is also used for different purposes and in different contexts, although the line separating reading purposes is not clear. Figure 8–1 illustrates the blend of elements involved in reading: beginning attitudes, reading skills, and the actual type of reading being done. The following sections discuss the various kinds of reading and reading instruction.

Reading readiness

Without doubt, it is better to prevent reading difficulties than to remediate them. Ideally, appropriate beginning reading instruction should reduce the number of students suffering from reading disabilities, but no clear agreement exists over the exact nature of the most appropriate instruction or the best mental age at which to introduce it if failure is to be avoided. Most children, however, are introduced to formal reading at the age of five or six.

Readiness is the initial stage of reading, and refers to a stage of development necessary before a skill can be learned, in which the child is able to process the skills and abilities of the preceding stage. Readiness is a product of environmental and maturational factors, but is concerned with prerequisite skills rather than with an assessed maturational level.

Very young children need to develop social, cognitive, linguistic, physical, and motor skills, all of which add up to readiness. At the preschool level, they need exposure to many language-oriented activities, and especially to stories and oral language. Children who have heard a variety of stories eventually develop a set of expectations about how stories unfold. They learn to understand story structure and to recall plot. As well, children must first understand the purposes and meaning of print before they can read, and must learn to follow a line of print. After they have had many experiences with oral language and print they are ready for a more formal reading process. They can now develop sight-word skills, comprehension, and knowledge of phonics, word structure, and the use of context (McClure, 1985).

Developmental reading

The developmental aspect of a reading program deals very specifically with developing students' reading skills in a sequential, hierarchical manner. The process, which is necessary at every academic level, uses the methods and materials of the regular classroom that are designed for children who are learning to read at a normal and expected rate. Regardless of the nature of a given reading approach (phonics, language experience, and so on), developmental reading must involve learning both phoneme–grapheme association and sound blending. If pupils fail to acquire these skills, it is unlikely that they will become fluent accurate readers (Samuels, 1981).

Skills should be presented together, so that they operate in combination as children develop a working vocabulary of sight words, word-attack skills, comprehension, and a strong desire to read independently. Sight words are best taught by demonstration, prompting, and practice (Stevens & Rosenshine, 1980). Yet merely recognizing words is insufficient for receiving communication from the printed page; teachers must stress "bringing meaning to print" (Smith, 1978, p. 2).

Figure 8–1 Elements of reading

Comprehension, the reader's ability to construct meaning by integrating textual information and background knowledge, is the heart of the reading program. Rather than relying entirely on visual text, readers use all they know about language and the world to gain an understanding of the author's message. The depth of their prior knowledge and the extent to which they are able to relate it to visual information from the page determines the depth and extent of comprehension (Goodman, 1976).

To develop effective skills in reading comprehension, children must learn to grasp the main thought, to distinguish between important and unimportant elements, and to discover the critical details used to support thinking. They must also infer meanings and recognize the author's plan in presenting material. Exceptional students often demonstrate underachievement in comprehension (Dunn, 1973). Pupils may indeed decode words, but then lack the insight to obtain meaning from their efforts. They do not have the ability to place the ideas in proper relationship to each other.

Basal reading materials

Developmental reading will most often use a basal reading series as one of the main tools of instruction. Basal series have been used for the past forty years, and generally contain four main elements: a reader, a workbook, a teacher's manual, and tests. They are usually ordered in a hierarchy graded according to degree of difficulty and the skills needed, and therefore provide organized methods of planning instruction although they are not committed to any one teaching procedure. Teachers tend to like basals because they are structured, have comprehensive teachers' manuals that list objectives and supplementary activities, and are self-contained (Langone, 1986).

It is not surprising that teachers with large classes have often limited their reading instruction to basal series, but to include all children on a series and expect progress at the same rate is contrary to the notion of individual differences. Indeed, for exceptional learners, adhering solely to these series can induce serious problems. Basals are designed for average children and often present a scope and vocabulary too broad for special learners. As well, while normal and above-average readers can overcome the vagaries of basals' typically inconsistent readability, low achievers may face disaster. They may be confused by the format of basal texts (if both narrative and poetry are used, for example), the unfamiliarity of the material, and the sequence of stories. Basal readers sometimes use language and syntactic structures that do not match those used by children, will often emphasize phonics, and can have inappropriate story content and pictures (Winzer, 1985a).

The manuals so assiduously followed by many teachers have also come under attack. Page (1978) found that teachers' manuals cannot be easily followed in any kind of step-by-step method that results in effective learning. Even though many activities are offered, there is only time to use a few, which results in a lack of sequential skill development. What is more, the materials can turn teachers into little more than presenters and recorders. A diligent route straight through the manuals, the basal texts, and the supplementary materials actually does most of the preparation and instruction, and over-reliance on basals may limit a teacher's willingness to develop innovative activities.

Although the problems created by using basal programs for exceptional students integrated into regular classrooms may appear overwhelming, the prospect of completely individualizing reading programs may appear equally dismaying to teachers.

Story telling enhances students' interest in reading.

Nevertheless, although no set of instructional materials is likely to be suitable for an entire class, it is not always necessary to abandon the basal series completely. For one thing, it is important that exceptional students read commercial print as soon as possible. For another, these pupils should, as far as they are able, read the same materials as the rest of the class. The teacher may use a basal series as the core of the reading program but supplement it with other methods, or else introduce readers gradually as exceptional pupils develop competence and confidence in their reading skills. There is nothing sacrosanct about the readers; they can be adapted at will to suit individual learners. It is not essential, for example, to read all the stories in the basals, or to follow all of the objectives or activities.

Remedial reading

Remedial reading is intended to support readers' strengths while teaching them skills that they have not acquired; to help them develop a balance in their learning strategies; and to bring their skills to a level that enables them to use reading for functional and recreational purposes. The job of the remedial reading teacher is to teach reading to children for whom it is a difficult and sometimes threatening task. The idea is not to push pupils laboriously through practice exercises but rather to help them see function and meaning in reading. Some students have never grasped the real reason for reading and they should be helped to realize that reading generates ideas and enjoyment. Remedial programs therefore stress motivation and comprehension over word-attack skills.

Remedial reading is important for non-readers, slow readers, and non-motivated readers. It may deal with a specific problem that a student experienced during the developmental reading process, or may be carried out independently of other materials and activities. In either case, the remedial component of a program should provide drill for very specific reading skills. Remedial reading is based on careful diagnosis and classroom observations, and uses methods and materials geared especially to the individual's needs.

With their long history of failure, exceptional students need to experience success in remedial programs. It is essential to divide the initial activities into small steps that students can master quickly. Mildly disabled readers need to overlearn specific skills. Different severely retarded readers demonstrate vastly different rates of acquiring subskills and reading comprehension. They require significant adaptations in the program, probably accompanied by extensive resource-room tutoring. Classroom adaptations include matching instruction to specific reading levels, remediating skill deficits, individualizing programs, and increasing motivation. The following general procedures are effective in remedial reading programs at all levels:

1. Try to establish a student's confidence. Tell the pupil that you are going to try a different method of learning to read.
2. Establish realistic goals and explain them to the student and the parents.
3. Allow repeated practice of skills spread over a long period of time, and include more thorough scope and sequence than in a regular program.
4. Use charts, graphs, tests, and rewards to show pupils their own progress.
5. If one approach does not work, try another. Remember that the process is more frustrating for the student than it is for the teacher.
6. Although teachers should be eclectic, be aware of how many different techniques an exceptional student can handle. Some pupils who have experienced failure in the past may be confused about what reading really is and need the security of one, consistent program.
7. Have secondary level students tutor younger problem readers. Cross-age tutoring, with weekly discussions on techniques, has been shown to improve secondary disabled students' reading levels and self-image (Lane, Pollack, & Sher, 1972).

Functional reading

The term functional reading describes the component of the reading program in which students apply their reading skills to practical situations. It is of strategic importance to exceptional students because it provides them with the skills necessary to undertake the reading involved in daily living. Recipes, newspapers, job applications, safety words, menus, and street signs all have functional vocabulary. To teach functional reading, teachers use real objects such as packaged food, facsimiles and photographs of street signs, store names and addresses, supermarket aisle signs, menus, and other public print. Functional reading skills also apply, in a sense, to classroom materials, since they are required in order to understand what is being asked on a mathematics problem or a test question or to report on current events in the newspaper.

It is important to teach students how to recognize the circumstances under which the various functional materials are used. Encourage them to keep a personal file of functional reading materials helpful to them. The materials have a huge variety of formats, linguistic structures, and uses, and include, among other things: signs, telephone books, movie listings, television guides, classified and other advertisements, weather reports, dictionaries, encyclopedias, titles, letters, postcards, greeting cards, coupons, posters, labels, package directions, tickets, timetables, regulaticns, job applications, questionnaires, charts, graphs, maps, calendars, guarantees, warranties, budgets, receipts, logos, and game rules.

Functional reading skills are taught with the same methods as other reading skills. The uniqueness of the approach lies in the type of vocabulary chosen (Polloway & Polloway, 1981). To illustrate a functional reading approach, the written assignments below apply to business cards and to the telephone book.

Functional reading assignment no. 1: Using business cards

Objectives:

- to introduce new functional reading materials
- to practise alphabetical order and locating information

Materials:

- set of business cards for each pupil
- newspapers

Procedure:

1. Give each pupil a set of ten business cards to place in alphabetical order.
2. Ask the pupils to copy any abbreviations from the cards and then to write them out in full.
3. Ask the pupils to find the classified section of a newspaper and to match the people described on the business cards to the jobs described in the advertisements.
4. Ask each pupil to design a logo for one of the business cards.

Follow-up: Give each pupil a blank card to design, complete with logo.

Functional reading assignment no. 2: Using the telephone book

Objectives:

- to introduce pupils to a source of information
- to practise locational skills

Materials:

- telephone books
- individual work sheets

Procedure: Present each pupil with white pages, yellow pages, and a work sheet.

Work sheet:

1. What is the address and telephone number of ______________________________ ?
2. What listing in the white pages come after ______________________________ ?
3. What are the addresses of ____________________ and ____________________ ?
4. How many people with the name of ______________________________ are listed?
5. Find the telephone number of ______________________________
6. In the yellow pages what heading would you use to find an Italian restaurant? ______________ What heading would you use to find a car dealer? ______________
7. In the yellow pages, find a place that gives dance lessons. The number and address is ______________________________
8. Look in the front of the telephone book to find out how to dial long distance. Write out the steps.

Informational reading

Informational reading is the process by which students read to gain knowledge, understanding, and insight. The form and content of this component of the reading program must be carefully considered, since it should allow students to use what they already know to learn the new material. Informational materials include: atlases, yearbooks, dictionaries, reference books, magazines, bulletin boards, notebooks, pamphlets, reports, circulars, notices, directions, petitions, catalogues, captions, language experience charts, and puzzles.

When reading for information, students should first learn **locational skills**, how to scan the material rapidly to locate a specific piece of evidence for an argument, fact, or event, or a phrase that defines new vocabulary. Locational reading is a prerequisite for outlining skills; it implies reading a passage without reading every word, but taking mental note of titles, headings, illustrations, italics, boldface, summaries, and the like.

Teachers should help students to assess the kinds of information that can be found in specific sources, to use their own notebooks as sources of information, and to use reference materials. Teachers should also build up a classroom collection of materials based on students' interests. Yet informational reading need not be restricted to academic texts. Nearly all children, for example, watch television and are very familiar with programming and guides. The television guide is not only a good vehicle for functional and informational reading but comes with built-in motivation. The extract from an integrated unit, presented below, is designed to teach students how to locate specific information using the television guide.

Unit on informational reading: the television guide

Objectives:

- to introduce a source of informational and functional reading
- to motivate interest by using television guides
- to practise locating information, skimming, and recording specific information

Materials:
- television guide for each pupil

Oral discussion:
With the class discuss the parts of the television guide, such as the cover picture, articles, letters to the editor, the best movies and their ratings, sports schedules, and so on.

Mathematics:
1. Have the students graph the number of hours that they watch television each week.
2. Have the students use a stopwatch or a watch with a second hand to time all the advertisements during a specific show.
3. Use word problems, such as "Jim watches television for three hours every day. How much is this in one full week?"

General information:
1. Have the students read the guide to answer questions such as "How many different channels are there?" "How many cable channels are there?" "What time does the first show come on in the morning?" "How late do shows run?"
2. Have the students answer questions such as "What is your favourite show?" "What is your favourite show on Monday?" "What show do you like to watch on Wednesday?" "List the time, day, and channel of your favourite show," and "Find one movie in the guide. List its title and rating."

Creative writing:
Have the students choose one show that they have watched, and write an essay that answers questions such as "Describe the plot of the show," "Describe the characters," "Explain how they act," and "Explain why you enjoy this show."

The daily newspaper is a particularly valuable instructional tool for all students, not only for teaching academic skills, but as a source of practical information for daily living, career education, developing reading skills, and generalizing mathematics skills. The lesson presented below makes use of the newspaper, and could be extended over several lessons.

Informational reading lesson(s) using the newspaper

Objectives:
- to introduce a source of informational and functional reading
- to practise locating, summarizing, and rewriting information
- to practise sequencing skills

Materials:
- daily newspaper

Procedure:

1. Select a short newspaper story and ask the students to read it to identify the *who*, *what*, *when*, *where*, *how*, and *why*, information typically found in the lead paragraph.
2. Ask the students to use the newspaper to answer a series of questions, assigned in advance and related to a specific section. They may choose the movie section, for example, to answer questions about the name of a film, the stars, the theatre, the rating, and the general theme. They may include information from reviews.
3. Select a news story and have the students read it, close the paper, and write a summary. This exercise improves comprehension, recall, and sequencing.
4. Cut comics from the newspaper into frames and have the students place them back in the proper sequence. Alternatively, present all frames but the last and have students present their own ideas about the "punch line."
5. Read and discuss questions submitted to an advice column. Then read a question and have the students write their own answers.

Recreational reading

The ultimate objective of any reading program is to teach students to read well enough that they will continue to read for both information and pleasure. The recreational component of a reading program aims to inspire, interest, and motivate readers, and may use contemporary and classic literature, stories using fantasy or realism, historical fiction, science fiction, books of records or lists, joke books, magazines, or comics. Teachers can guide the students' choice of materials, expose them to a variety of topics, and monitor the frequency with which they read. Storytelling should be widely used at all levels to introduce new materials and stimulate interest. As well, reading materials that the students have made themselves encourage reading.

Reading at the secondary level

By the time students reach the secondary level teachers must change their tactics not only to accommodate specific reading deficits but also in response to the students' personalities and the behavioural implications of reading retardation. Pressing sound–symbol associations on adolescents is likely to produce aversive reactions to the whole reading and remedial process. In secondary reading programs, teachers should present a combination of meaning-oriented techniques that allow students to apply several different strategies to reading tasks. In many cases supplementary materials are necessary, but the lack of appropriate materials at this level is a constant source of frustration for teachers.

Literal comprehension is an area of stress for reading-retarded secondary students because the ability to recall facts is necessary for academic competence. They must be able to recall both written and orally presented material in order to participate in class, take examinations, and generalize concepts (Burmeister, 1974). They must also learn to summarize, restate, and draw inferences from material, and to evaluate what they read.

Individualizing reading materials

Just as basal readers can present problems at the elementary level, printed instructional materials designed for secondary classes can also contribute to students' reading problems. Many of today's secondary texts are conceptual in nature and possess vocabulary and sentence structure that require extensive and precise reading. Often too, business, industrial arts, home economics books, and vocational texts are overwhelmingly verbal in nature and beyond the appropriate level of readability. Aukerman (1972) found that literature anthologies for secondary students range in readability as much as nine grade levels. Some texts have unreadable material (Aukerman, 1972), others are comprehensive but complex, and some at least are poorly written and organized (Gagne, 1970).

At some critical stages, retarded and disabled readers may require alternative or supplementary approaches that incorporate different reading materials. Materials should be chosen according to certain criteria: they should not remind students of past failure; they should be popular and avoid formats that induce boredom (Gallagher, 1979); and students should be able to relate the materials to the real world.

In general, commercially available textbooks are of limited use for retarded readers, and it is often necessary either to write original material using topics of interest to the class or to simplify the language in existing texts and stories. Rewritten material can motivate students, develop or remediate reading, present information, and build specific skills. The materials are particularly useful in remedial reading programs. The main steps to rewriting are as follows:

1. Determine the skills to be stressed.
2. Choose the material and apply a readability formula (for example, Fry, 1977).
3. Rewrite the story paying attention to syntax, semantics, idiomatic language, and the particular skills for which the story is intended. Limited amounts of material may certainly be written in more sophisticated language, with complex sentences and difficult vocabulary. Very simple sentences convey only a restricted amount of information and are fairly certain to bore older readers. A varied style will also challenge the stronger readers among the reading-disabled students and strengthen their skills further.
4. Illustrate the story, matching the print to the pictures precisely, by drawing, tracing, copying, or photographing pictures. They may be coloured or left black and white.
5. Print or type the rewritten material. For young children limit each page to a small amount of print. If necessary, leave some pages with print only, as long as they contain only a few sentences. (The photograph opposite shows a page from a book rewritten for younger students.)
6. Laminate the finished product. It will last longer and be a valuable addition to the class library.

For secondary students who must glean information from a variety of textbooks, highlighting can be extremely helpful. If the school allows it, the teacher highlights the main points of the text for the students, using a yellow felt marker. Notes are also especially useful to older pupils. The teacher summarizes textual materials and then prints or types the notes to serve as reading material for students.

It is sometimes necessary to rewrite materials for children with reading disabilities.

Individualizing reading instruction

Trying to define programs, goals, and objectives for every retarded reader would simply be an impossibility. Instead, this section uses a number of short case studies to illustrate the ways in which programs can be individualized.

Case study 8–1

In her grade two glass, Helen is lagging behind her peers in all aspects of reading. She has only a small repertoire of sight words, little knowledge of word attack, and poor comprehension of written material. She has adequate listening skills, however, and does seem to understand that the printed word relays a message.

As Helen is not reading retarded by more than a year, the teacher has decided to retain her in the regular classroom with modifications to the reading program. Helen works with the slowest classroom group, but not for the whole reading period. She spends more time on drill and practice for specific skills. If the teacher introduces ten new vocabulary words for a story to the group, for example, Helen is exposed to two and then leaves the group to work with a peer tutor on recognizing the words, using and reading them in context, and answering simple comprehension questions. Although Helen uses the basal workbook, the teacher cuts down the number of exercises.

Case study
8–2

Clare is in grade four and although she seems to have acquired enough basic reading skills to work with the other pupils in the slower reading group, she is lagging further and further behind. Her silent reading is slow and halting and when she reads orally the recitation is marked with stops, repetitions, and miscues. Her comprehension is suffering, making it difficult for her to read for information in other class texts.

To strengthen Clare's oral reading fluency and give her more confidence, the teacher has decided to initiate a Neurological Impress Method, as detailed later in this chapter. Although Clare works with her own reading group, she sits with the teacher for ten minutes each day and they read aloud together.

Case study
8–3

Brian is in grade six. Ever since he started school, Brian has met immense difficulties with reading and the other language arts. By this stage of his school career, he is reading at only an early grade two level and appears to find the entire process distasteful. Mrs. Pohorecky, his classroom teacher, believes that she must meld reading instruction with techniques to teach Brian the value of reading and to overcome his reluctance.

Mrs. Pohorecky has therefore presented Brian with an entirely new reading program rather than requiring that he struggle along with the regular grade six curriculum. First, she discovered his main interests. Finding that he enjoys watching television, she devised the first reading unit around the television guide. Working with a peer tutor, Brian found and recorded specific information from the guide. As the year has progressed, Mrs. Pohorecky has kept Brian on an individual reading program, constructing reading units built on his interests and needs. After the television guide, Brian worked on a Canadian Tire catalogue, the yellow pages of the telephone book, a simply written book about dinosaurs, and take-out restaurant menus. Mrs. Pohorecky often asks him to present his findings to the rest of the class.

Case study
8–4

Jason, a grade eight student, has faced so many years of frustration and failure in the reading process that he dislikes reading and refuses to participate. His academic work is suffering greatly, even though he is an extremely capable student when he is able to circumvent reading. In mathematics, especially, Jason demonstrates very good conceptual development.

At the beginning of the school year, Mr. Graham, the classroom teacher, taped material for Jason so that he could acquire information without the strain of reading, but has decided to make another attempt to teach him this necessary academic and social skill. Rather than stressing Jason's weaknesses, Mr. Graham has built a reading program around the mathematics curriculum. In other words, the mathematics text has become Jason's reader. While the other students are engaged in seatwork, Mr. Graham works with Jason for about ten minutes daily on reading problems and explanations from the mathematics text. He also devises written assignments to take advantage of the "math" reading. Other mathematics texts can soon form part of the lessons.

Methods of reading instruction

The methods outlined below attempt to cover a number of different situations. The shared-book approach can be used with the whole class, for example, while repeated reading and the Fernald method are suitable for either groups or individuals and are particularly effective when peer tutors work with the reading-disabled students. A procedure such as Neurological Impress demands that a pupil work individually with the teacher. The RATE method is an effective individual exercise for both reading-retarded and gifted students.

Listening, reading, speaking method

Similarities exist between this method and the language experience approach. Although an experience determines the language and reading material used in the listening, reading, speaking method, however, it does not form the initial step. New material is introduced in the following manner:

1. The teacher writes a story in the present tense concerning a proposed experience and then reads the complete story to the class, using good intonation and indicating phrasing.
2. As the teacher reads through the story a second time, the students imitate the teacher's phrasing and intonational patterns for each sentence. The teacher clarifies new vocabulary with pictures, explanations, and oral questions.
3. The students then undergo the actual experience that the story described, perhaps by using books and games, going on a field trip, or undertaking projects or units of study. The purpose of the activity is to generate spontaneous language, using the new vocabulary already presented.
4. When the experience is complete, the teacher and the group review the story and change all the tenses to the past.
5. To review new language, students answer oral and written questions based on the story.

The shared-book approach

Children's literature is predictable: it is repetitive, rhythmical, and cumulative. The shared-book approach models bedtime stories within the classroom using books with rhyming, repetitious structures. The material is effective because it allows children to predict what is coming next and is familiar enough that they can use their experiential background to decode the written material. The cumulative patterns extend vocabulary, assist memorization, and provide success (McClure, 1985). The vocabulary should be enriching, natural, memorable, and predictable.

The steps to follow in the shared-book approach are as follows:

1. The teacher reads aloud to the class or group from a large book, showing them the print and pictures.
2. The teacher reads the story a second time, and the children read along. The teacher points out new words and phrases.
3. The children then read the book alone or with partners.
4. After they have developed familiarity with the whole story, children match word cards to phrase cards that are missing a word (McClure, 1985).
5. The teacher includes the new vocabulary in classroom activities (McNeil, 1981).

Using cartoons

Most of us still chuckle at the antics of cartoon characters who find themselves involved in ridiculous or thought-provoking situations. Cartoons are an excellent medium for beginning reading because they show most of the action and humour in the pictures. From cartoons, young children can learn to use eye movement from left to right, to tell a story in a logical sequence, and to respond to picture clues (Hoover, 1972). For older students, cartoons stimulate reading, develop language and conceptualization, and teach them to translate ideas from pictures into written and oral thought. Teachers should follow these steps to use cartoons in the classroom:

1. Choose a comic strip and make transparencies of each frame, mounting them on cards.
2. Show the students the frames one by one in sequence on an overhead projector, without offering any help or suggestions. Students will respond to the pictures in several ways, focussing on entirely different aspects or ideas.
3. Ask the students to discuss their own ideas about each frame in the sequence.
4. Help them to read the cartoon balloons.
5. Follow the exercise with activities such as drawing and captioning the next frame in an incomplete sequence, or answering questions about the cartoon story.

Guided reading

Guided reading is an intensive activity and should therefore be used selectively. The procedure helps students to remember and organize content, and to establish relationships among ideas. Readers incorporate strategies to make hypotheses, find proof, suspend judgement, make decisions, and express findings (Stauffer, 1975). The students are responsible for establishing a purpose for the reading. The teacher's job is to guide them through the material in order to reconstruct the author's message. The students predict the outcome and purpose of the story, first from the title and pictures, next from the first page, and then from one or more subsequent pages. They also make a final prediction at the point just prior to the climax of the story.

The specific steps involved in guided reading are as follows:

1. Prepare the students for the assignment by presenting something related to the reading, for example, by displaying the title picture and title page to a story and telling the students: "These pictures go with our story for today. Can you guess anything about the story?" Encourage them to speculate on the story, and then write their predictions on the board. The object here is not to get a right answer but to get students involved in the material (Maxwell, 1974).
2. The students read the story silently, in segments, and then retell it orally, adding to or eliminating some of their predictions based on the new information. The procedure helps them to process their thoughts and then express them.
3. Question the pupils in order to guide them as they organize the remembered information. By furnishing proof for their assertions they learn to establish relationships among concepts. As they keep returning to the material for new information, continue to question them to stimulate discussion.
4. Once the students have gained an understanding of the story, there is no necessity for extra work. Written questions will not materially aid the reading process (Maxwell, 1974).

Previewing

Previewing also introduces students to reading material and helps them to define its purpose. The teacher presents students with the basic vocabulary, concepts, and format of the selection, however, before they read it. He or she chooses the key words, concepts, and applicable non-textual information, and presents them in a systematic manner. Students then apply the previewed material to the selection as they first read and then discuss it. Previewing is most effective when combined with purposeful silent reading.

Repeated readings

Because students must have extensive reading practice to become fluent and to increase their repertoire of sight words, it is useful to have them read the same passage repeatedly (Samuels, 1979). The method motivates students and improves their reading skills (Neill, 1980). Students read short, simple passages out loud, and the teacher times and scores each reading on an individual reading graph. Students are therefore actually competing against themselves. As they gain fluency, they can tape-record their own readings. Neill (1980) lays out a series of steps for repeated reading procedures:

1. The student and teacher select a passage of one to two hundred words from a basal reader at an appropriate level.
2. The student reads the selection while the teacher times the readings and counts the number of words pronounced incorrectly.
3. The teacher gives the student an opportunity to look over the selection, reread it, and ask for the correct pronunciation of any word. The student may later use a list of the words that caused problems as a study guide.
4. With the help of the teacher, the student decides on the reading time and percentage of words correct that she or he wishes to attain.
5. The student repeatedly practises reading the selection.
6. After reaching the predetermined goal, she or he may make a new selection and repeat the procedure.

Fernald method

The Fernald method combines the *v*isual, *a*uditory, *k*inesthetic, and *t*actile modes of learning in a multisensory (VAKT) approach to spelling and vocabulary instruction for language-delayed children. It thus attempts to use these modalities in conjunction with one another rather than to develop them as separate skills. The Fernald approach is most effective with disabled readers who are having difficulty with visual perception and recognition. Essentially, it is a word-learning technique that stresses directionality, syllabication, and word meaning within reading.

The word as the smallest unit of meaning is basic to the Fernald method. Words are therefore always written as a whole, never as separate letters, and are always presented in cursive script, to provide a continuous pattern and flow. The student never copies a word, but always writes it from memory, and the teacher always stresses the correct word form.

The Fernald method is the chief among VAKT methods, which all employ every major learning modality. For the specific steps involved, the reader is directed to

Winzer, Rogow, and David (1987). The Orton–Gillingham method is also often used, and is discussed in chapter 11 with reference to students who have speech and language problems.

Neurological Impress Method

The Neurological Impress Method (NIM) was first developed in 1952 by Heckelman for students ten years old and above with severe reading deficits and in particular, with visual discrimination defects (Heckelman, 1969; Langford, Slade, & Barnett, 1974). The procedure is based on the theory that the auditory process of feedback from the reader's own voice and the voice of someone else reading the same materials establishes a new learning process.

No preliminary preparations are made with the reading material before the pupil sees it. The object is simply to cover as many pages as possible within the time available without fatiguing the student. During reading, the student sits slightly in front of the instructor and they read together rapidly. The instructor speaks into the student's ear at fairly close range, and points to each word as it is spoken. As the reading proceeds, the student should gradually take the lead. Throughout, problematic words are reviewed.

Some research has indicated that students who received this type of instruction made no significant gains in word recognition or reading comprehension, although the researchers did note improvements in fluency, oral expression, and students' confidence in their ability to read (Lorenz & Vockell, 1979). Armitage (1978b) mentions, however, that although no improvement may be seen for three or four weeks, dramatic changes are often manifested by the end of seven weeks. The Neurological Impress Method should supplement the reading program to develop fluency. Hoskinson (1979) suggests that it be used initially, but followed by more systematic instruction once the student has become more fluent.

RATE method

Reading progress depends upon motivation and satisfaction (Kranes, 1980). The more highly motivating a remedial reader is, the greater the student's progress and success (Harris & Sipay, 1975). RATE stands for *r*ead *a*nd *t*hen *e*valuate. The students share their own judgments and help others to choose recreational reading material (Bamberger, 1976). The method is valuable because it helps students to gain confidence in themselves as readers. The teacher gives students review forms on which they include

- the book title and the author
- a colour-coded rating scheme: green for books highly recommended for all readers; yellow for books recommended with some reservations; and red for books that are poorly rated or considered too difficult for most class members
- a sentence giving the reason for the rating (Jamison & Shevitz, 1985)

High-intensity reading practice

High-intensity practice involves setting aside a specific time every day for students to read. USSR, an acronym for *u*ninterrupted *s*ustained *s*ilent *r*eading. The teacher sets the stage by giving appropriate instructions, organizing the room, providing materials, and modelling the task. As the students read, no one interrupts another person, no one asks about a word, and no one exchanges books. If a student does interrupt, then the USSR is ended for everyone.

Reduced reading and non-reading curricula

It may seem pessimistic in a chapter about reading to discuss reduced reading and non-reading curricula, but it is best to acknowledge that, despite our best efforts, there remain some students who cannot read or seem incapable of responding to remedial instruction. Because so much information can only be acquired by reading, non-reading interferes with progress in all areas and creates the need for a non-reading curriculum.

Many handicapped learners can actually learn complex information if their skill deficits are avoided or the effects lessened. While some students need to have reading levels reduced, as discussed earlier, others suffer such severe deficits that their curricula must circumnavigate reading altogether. A non-reading curriculum, initially described as a bookless curriculum (Blau & Blau, 1968), uses videotapes, films, slides, lectures, tape recording, and various forms of television.

Tape-recorded readings, for example, allow students to stay current with class assignments and to supplement the information presented in lectures (Deshler & Graham, 1980). Not everything need be taped, only the salient sections of material. The teacher can scatter assignments and activities to develop study skills throughout the tapes. Alternatively, a peer may read into a tape-recorder or to the student. As another example, a student who is not able to read a novel for English class comfortably may nevertheless understand the subtle interaction of characters and events in a film.

Reading activities

The following section addresses some of the more common skill deficits and presents specific techniques for various age levels that may be helpful in correcting the problems. Teachers should choose the activities that suit their students' needs best.

Objective: to develop beginning readers' readiness skills

a) Have youngsters classify pictures and objects according to size, shape, colour, or direction such as up and down.

Kindergarten (K) and grade 1

b) Cut pictures from magazines and help the pupils to make up captions for them.

K to grade 3

c) Have children identify the letters on a page of print.

Grades 1 to 3

d) Have children imitate speech sounds, and discriminate speech sounds made by other people.

Grades 1 to 3

Objective: to improve phoneme–grapheme association

a) Give pupils word cards as shown in figure 8–2. Have them connect each initial consonant to the rest of the word to read the word out loud. They may also write the words in their notebooks and draw pictures of them. This exercise works well for pairs of students.

Grades 1 to 3

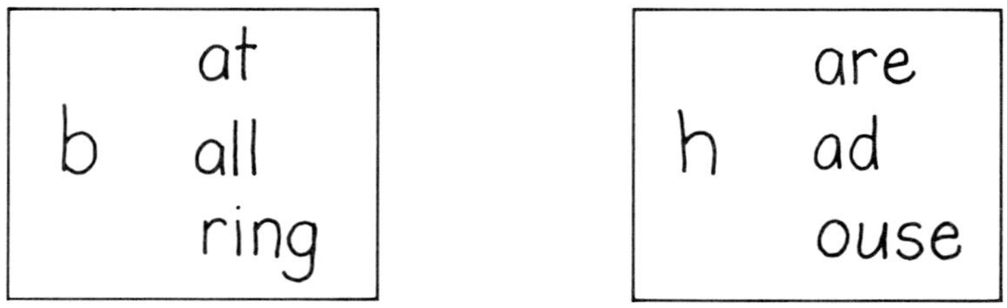

Figure 8–2 Word-building exercise

b) Present children with the wheel game, in which they spin the wheel and say the word (see figure 8–3).

Grades 1 to 3

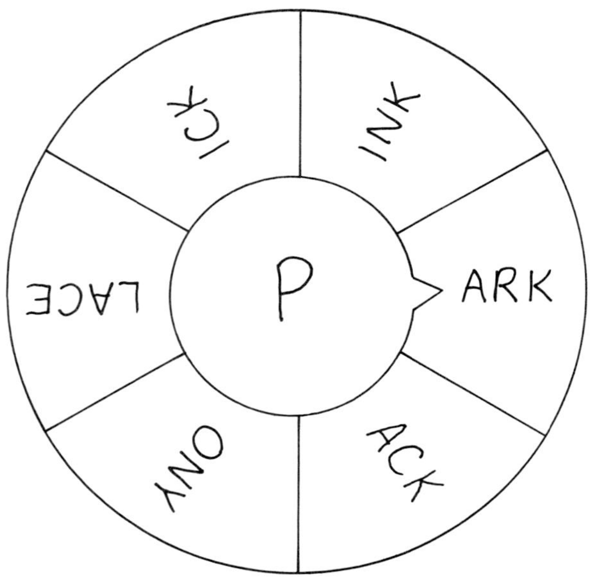

Figure 8–3 The wheel game

c) Make jigsaw cards containing word fragments, and have pupils make whole words (see figure 8–4).

Grades 1 to 3

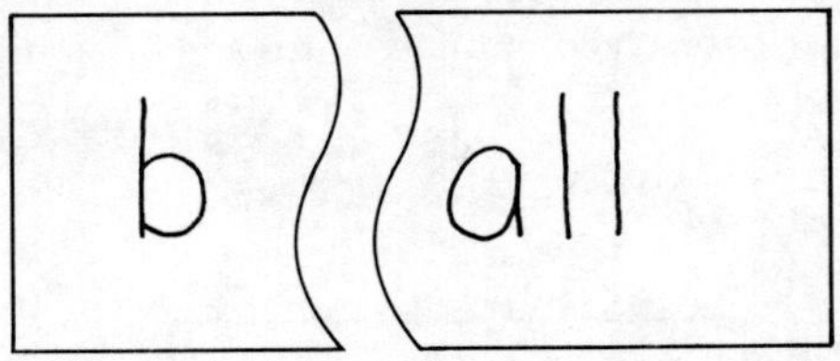

Figure 8–4 Word jigsaws

d) Present words by using cards, each with a single letter written on it, to help pupils divide words into initial, medial, and final sounds.

Grades 1 to 3

Objective: to improve word-attack skills

a) Show the pupils pictures, some illustrating a single object and others illustrating more than one. Ask them to place word cards under the appropriate pictures (see figure 8–5).

Grades 1 to 6

Figure 8–5 Word-matching game

b) Ask pupils to complete written sentences such as "The cat sat on a rug/reg/rog" by circling or saying the right word.

Grades 1 to 6

c) Give pupils groups of picture cards and word cards to match together, as in figure 8–6, to teach compound words and other forms of structural analysis, such as prefixes and suffixes.

Grades 1 to 6

Figure 8–6 Making compound words

d) Ask students to find all the compound words in a newspaper article.

Grades 3 to 6

e) Kaluger and Kolson (1978) suggest teaching suffixes in the following order: *en, ent, ly, ish, ful, less, our, er, ous, ation, al, able, ance, ence, ate, est, ity, ic, ist, like.* While it is advisable to keep to this order as much as possible, it is also useful, however, to teach those suffixes first for which pictures or dramatization can be used, such as care*ful* and care*less*. Have the students act out the words or match them to pictures.

Grades 1 to 6

Objective: to develop speed and fluency in sight-word recognition

a) Have the students climb the word ladder quickly to reach the star (figure 8–7), or identify all the words on the word octopus (figure 8–8). In the first activity, the ladder is usually drawn on the board, while the star is detachable, so that the student can actually take it.

Grades 1 to 4

Figure 8–7 The word ladder

b) Give students written lists of words, and have them group the words by categories such as families, foods, fruit, animals, and so on. Extend the exercise by asking students to group words within each category by features such as initial consonants

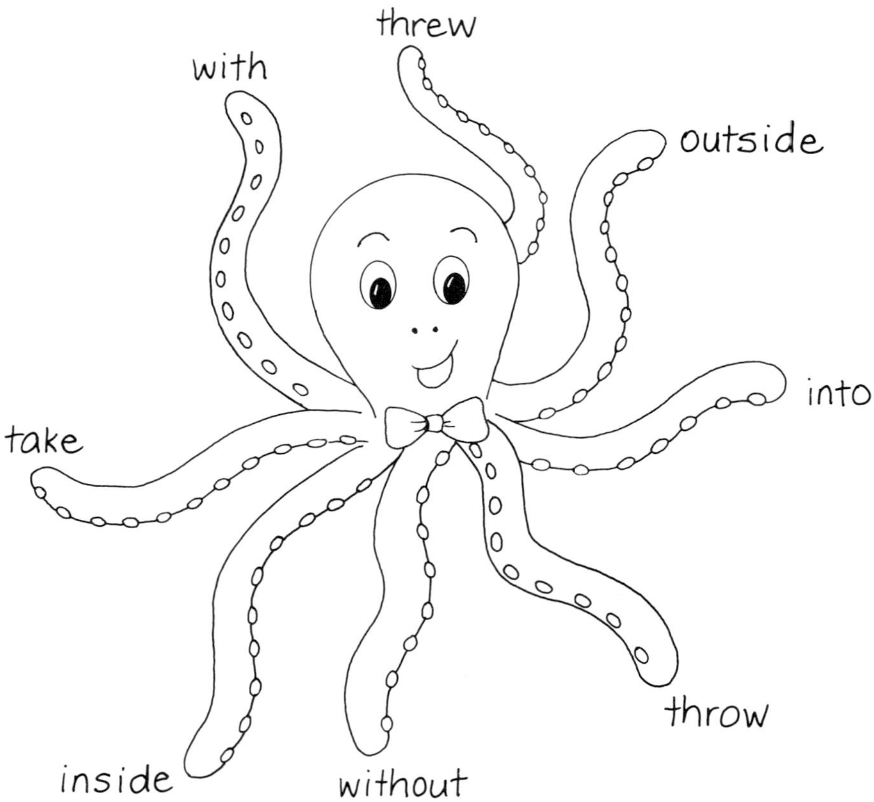

Figure 8–8 The word octopus

or syllables. They can also match the words to pictures. As well as pictures of objects, use some that illustrate descriptive and quantitative phrases such as "a big ball" and "two dogs."

K to grade 3

c) Ask the student to draw or select a picture and to describe it. Write a caption based on the student's description and read it aloud. Ask the student to read and then reread the caption, and then to copy it down.

Grades 1 to 6

d) Have pupils read simple verbs such as *run* or *jump* from flash cards and without saying the words, follow the commands. Once they can follow simple one-word commands, move on to simple phrases and sentences. Students can then write commands for other students to follow.

Grades 1 to 6

e) Present groups of flash cards that go together in some way, perhaps by sharing a common initial consonant, sound, or number of syllables, and have students identify the commonalities.

Grades 1 to 6

Objective: to practise using contextual clues

a) Present incomplete sentences with pictures (see figure 8–9) and ask students to complete them.

Grades 1 to 4

Mary is wearing a blue ____________

(dress, bless, class)

Figure 8–9 Sentence completion

b) Have the students match cards containing sentence fragments such as:

I am . . . .   a cat
I have . . . .   happy

K to grade 3

c) Write a sentence with a word missing on the board or on paper. Use the following type of sequence until the students can guess the word:

The cat is in the ________
The cat is in the g________
The cat is in the g______ge.
The cat is in the g___r___ge.

Grades 1 to 4

Objective: to improve oral reading fluency

a) An imitative reading strategy can have positive effects on the pupils' reading with no disruption of normal routine. Read the first hundred or so words of a story aloud, to provide pupils with a model to imitate. Then read it again as the pupils read along. It is also possible to break the procedure down further, reading only phrases at first for students to imitate, and moving on to sentences (Henk, Helfeldt, & Platt, 1986).

Grades 1 to 6

b) Give one student in a group the "script" of a radio news story and ask him or her to "broadcast" the story after first silently scanning the material (Searfoss, 1975).

Grade 4 and up

c) A readers' "theatre" allows students to participate in drama without the burden of learning lines. Prepare reading materials in the form of scripts at the students' own reading levels and have them practise in advance. They then read from the scripts while in a group. Emphasize both fluency and the need to convey ideas and feelings from the script.

Grade 7 and up

Objective: to develop phrasing and expression in oral reading

a) Phrase reading or "chunking" is used to expand units of analysis beyond the single word (Brozo, Schmelzer, & Spires, 1983). Select a passage and divide it into "chunks" using slashes to indicate phrasing, as in "The silly boy/jumped/in the puddle." First present the sentences on cards, one sentence per card; as students become more fluent, gradually remove the slashes.

Grades 3 to 9

b) Pair students of the same reading ability to read aloud together.

All levels

c) Have pupils read along out loud with a tape-recorded reading.

Grades 3 to 9

Objective: to improve reading rates

a) To motivate students and improve their reading rates, give them graduated materials to read, to prove that they can read some materials faster than others. Have them time themselves, and discuss efficient reading rates with them. Allow them to practise with easy material and use graphs to illustrate improvement.

Grade 3 and up

b) Have students read headings, topic sentences, introductions, and end paragraphs, either silently or orally.

Grade 3 and up

Objective: to reduce the percentage of miscues in students' reading

a) Write several words on the board for students to use as examples, and then ask them to
   - find three things in the room that begin with the same letter as a word on the board
   - use their readers to find three words with the same number of letters as a word on the board
   - find three words in their readers with the same vowel sounds as a word on the board
   - write two sentences using one of the words
   - find synonyms for the six words that they have already chosen from the reader

- find three words in the reader that end with the same letter as a word on the board

Grade 3 and up

b) Epstein and Lynch (1974) suggest that the following procedures reduce miscues:

1. Tell the student the miscued word.
2. Have the student put a finger on the word.
3. Read the sentence up to the miscued word.
4. Stop and tell the student to read the word.
5. Have other pupils repeat the word after the student has read it.

Grades 3 to 9

c) Occasionally, allow students to play a game of spaghetti and meatballs, to read for fun. The student reads aloud and substitutes the word spaghetti for every word beginning with *s*, and meatballs for every word beginning with *m*.

Grades 3 to 9

Objective: to improve skimming and locational skills

a) Give students a list of words and ask them to circle the words whenever they find them as they read a passage. Alternatively, ask them to skim the passage to find specific information such as "the girl's name," "the place where the hydroplane is defined," or "the section in which the graph is discussed."

Grade 3 and up

Objective: to practise finding the main idea in reading materials

a) Ask students questions about the material using a multiple-choice format, as in the following example:

This story is about:
a) a girl named Kate
b) a carpenter
c) a mother

Grade 3 and up

b) Have students read a story, select a title, and underline the most important sentences in each paragraph.

Grade 3 and up

Objective: to practise discerning the details in reading material

a) Give students specific directions to follow; for example, directions to find a buried treasure.

Grade 3 and up

b) Have the students dramatize characters in stories (Jenkins, Stein, & Osborn, 1981).

Grade 3 and up

c) Give students story summaries that they can match to stories they already know or have read, to teach them about plot. They can also match headlines cut from the newspaper to the news stories.

Grade 7 and up

Objective: to practise recalling previously read information

a) Make a puppet to represent one of the characters in a book and let the students use it to recount the events that occurred in the story.

K to grade 6

b) Have students make a poster to advertise a book that they have read.

Grade 3 and up

c) Give students organizational devices, such as an outline of main headings, before they read material. Organization in advance stresses the important concepts and information, and helps readers to take an appropriate approach to the material. They can then relate previously learned information to the new material and, conversely, link new information to previous experiences.

Grade 7 and up

d) Encourage students to take notes of class lectures and discussions and to mark key words and phrases. They can then meet in small groups to edit their notes. Ensure that they pay attention to spelling, noting important points, writing outlines and summaries, organizing notes, formulating questions relating to the main point, and inventing trial examination questions.

Grade 7 and up

Objective: to teach sequencing skills

a) Ask the students to read a short article. Make incomplete statements and ask them to "fill in the blanks" orally, as in "First, Mary . . . ," "then she . . . ." and "after that. . . ."

Grades 3 to 9

b) List the major events from a story on the board in random order and ask the students to read the story and then write about the events in the correct order.

Grades 3 to 9

Objective: to improve functional reading and introduce sources of information

a) Give students reading material that pairs pictures with written directions, as in recipes, and have them match the directions to the illustrations (Hargis, 1982).

Grade 3 and up

b) Choose an article from the newspaper, give each student a copy, and write questions about it on the board. Students skim the article for the responses. Their answers should be factual, for example, names, places, and dates. Students could read a sports article and list the name of the sport, the team names, the final score, and something unusual or interesting that happened in the game.

Grade 7 and up

This chapter and the one that precedes it have dealt with different parts of a very large topic, teaching language arts, concentrating on useful instructional techniques for the regular classroom teacher. The next chapter also focusses on a curricular area, mathematics. Although the mathematics curriculum has a very different type of content from language arts, language is integral to the process of teaching mathematics, as the following chapter shows.

9 Teaching mathematics

Dear Reader,

How often have you heard your students make remarks such as "I'm dumb," "I hate math," "I can't do math," or "It's my worst subject"? The implications of such comments are extremely serious for teachers. In today's society, literacy refers to both language and mathematics. The mathematical component of literacy is often referred to as numeracy, but I prefer the term mathematical literacy since it emphasizes that literacy has a dual nature and that the mathematical component involves more than just knowledge of numbers.

The chapter that follows concentrates on identifying students' problems in mathematics and on remedial procedures for teaching mathematics to special learners. I will therefore address the general issue of the goals of mathematics education for these students, and leave the diagnostic and instructional questions to the chapter.

Students are classified as exceptional for various reasons. In some cases they have severe handicaps; they may be slow learners; they may have problems in just one or two subject areas; and so on. With such a variety of rationales, in a period when individualized programs for special learners are the vogue, it is critical to determine the needs of the student. Deciding what mathematics to teach is therefore crucial. One of the major objectives of any program is to develop all students, exceptional and non-exceptional, to their full potential. Mathematics plays a key role in this development and is of critical importance for many careers.

Teachers hope that, wherever possible, their exceptional students will complete as full a program as possible. Because mathematics is so hierarchical in nature, gaps in students' backgrounds will prevent them from continuing their studies. When designing an individualized program, the school-based team should consider that the student may eventually return to a regular mathematics program. Excluding parts of a program will limit the student's future options and the decision that a particular student cannot cope with the regular program should be delayed as long as possible. Basics are not enough. Special learners will need not only basic skills but also comprehension of the concepts within a program and the ability to apply them.

Teaching mathematics to special students is a complex task; there are no simple answers or "correct" methods. Once you have decided what is appropriate for your students, then the following chapter contains many good ideas on how to meet those goals.

Lionel Mendoza, Ph.D.
Department of Curriculum and Instruction
Memorial University of Newfoundland

The acquisition of number sense is one of the basic milestones of learning.✧ Long before children come to school they have accumulated meaningful experiences on which to base number symbols. As they play and explore the physical attributes of materials, small children become aware of such complex concepts as size, balance, symmetry, shape, mass, number, and measurement. They begin to develop number sense as early as one year and express their knowledge in phrases such as "all gone," "no more," "more," and "too much."

The surprisingly sophisticated mathematical strategies that young children gain through informal everyday experiences underlie the development of a strong number sense. Number sense is, in turn, a prerequisite to quantitative thinking, particularly in dealing with relationships of space, form, distance, order, quantity, and time. Even before formal schooling begins, children typically acquire impressive counting and number knowledge (Fuson & Hall, 1983). By the time they are five, most children can count orally to twenty-nine (Ginsberg & Baroody, 1983), have efficient object counting skills (Gelman & Gallistel, 1978), and can count out a specified number of items (Wang, Resnick, & Boozer, 1971). Moreover, most children can automatically recognize number patterns to at least sets of four without counting them (Gorman, 1977), can automatically represent numbers with their fingers (Siegler & Robinson, 1982), and can estimate the equivalence of two sets by counting (Gelman & Gallistel, 1978).

Although most children acquire an adequate number sense — which teachers can build upon as they teach mathematical computations and concepts — the movement into school mathematics presents considerable difficulty to many children, difficulty that becomes compounded in subsequent years. Their problems appear to stem from two causes: some children do not easily translate the early richness of mathematical experiences into the symbols and procedures of school mathematics; and the connections between the form and procedures, between mathematical algorithms and naturally acquired problem solving strategies, are not always clear (Ditchburn, 1987). Many mildly handicapped students have difficulty with such beginning skills as counting, writing numerals, and learning basic associations, and they are unlikely to follow systematic strategies for solving word problems. In fact, few learning-handicapped children are competent even in the basic addition and subtraction facts (Connor, 1983).

Compared to language and reading instruction, little attention has been paid to systematic diagnosis, instruction, and remediation in mathematics. Especially for handicapped students, available instructional time tends to be given to improving language and reading skills. The same is true in the research literature. In speaking specifically of mathematics education for the learning-disabled population, for example, Cawley (1981) noted that "information is so sparse in this area that there is not enough of a history to generate issues and controversies. The virtues and values of one intervention approach versus another are virtually unknown" (pp. 89–90). The lack of research information and of appropriate intervention affects other exceptional populations. Deaf students, for example, acquire mathematical skills to grade seven level only, on average (Messerly, 1986). This is at least partly because the majority of programs are not offered

✧ This chapter was co-authored by John Percevault, whose significant and invaluable contributions the author of the text would like to acknowledge.

under the direction of trained mathematics educators and rely on commercially produced materials that are seldom, if ever, selected by mathematics educators (Johnson, 1977).

Yet with the rapid technological advances occurring in society, students, exceptional and regular, will be called upon to use more arithmetic skills than ever. As well as the traditional daily tasks of telling time, changing money, and reading recipes, it is now necessary to learn how to use instant banking cards, calculators, and computers. Ditchburn (1987) points out that we must re-examine beliefs, values, and teaching strategies in the field of mathematics. Educators must decide just what constitutes mathematical thinking for students and in what manner they can provide experiences that encourage students to think mathematically.

For many learners, deficits in mathematics will accompany problems in other subject areas. Mathematical proficiency requires students to understand different concepts from those associated with other areas, however, and some students who are behind in mathematics may actually perform adequately in, for example, reading and spelling.

Students who demonstrate deficits in mathematics as their sole disability do require intervention. As well, many exceptional students mainstreamed into regular classrooms are at a significant disadvantage in mathematics and are likely to need adaptations to the program in order to achieve maximum gains. A model program for mathematics instruction must include both developmental and remedial components. A diagnostically based remedial component will serve the students who manifest clear and specific disabilities in mathematics only, while a developmental program that systematically corrects deficits in a structured, hierarchical manner will meet the needs of students who are disabled in a number of academic areas.

Mathematical disabilities exist at all age levels. During the preschool and primary years, some children cannot sort objects by size, match objects, understand mathematical language, or grasp the concepts involved in rational counting. Later, these children will have problems with number facts and computational skills and, as they progress through the grades, such areas as measurement, decimals, fractions, and percentages will present particular difficulty. By the time pupils reach the secondary level, they face complex algebra, geometry, and trigonometry and are expected to bring a package of basic mathematical skills to subjects such as physics, chemistry, drafting, and woodworking. The mathematical deficits exhibited by many secondary students, however, are similar to those of younger children, such as difficulty with basic number facts and place value. In fact, one study found that students with deficits in mathematics were generally functioning at a grade three to four level (McLeod & Armstrong, 1982). Over 60 percent of secondary level respondents indicated that they had major deficits in areas such as division, fractions, decimals, multiplication of whole numbers, percentages, place value, measurement, and the general language of mathematics.

Teachers need to look at both the disabilities that contribute to learning difficulties and the appropriate methods to help students overcome them (Cawley, 1981). Remediation of arithmetic problems requires step-by-step instruction, beginning at or just below the level at which the student is performing and moving onward only at a rate that allows the student to learn successfully. Instructional adaptations in mathematics usually focus on modifying the scope or difficulty of the content. Wherever possible, concrete materials should be used. Organization games are also valuable tools, especially those that provide multisensory experiences and emphasize sharpening visual perception skills within the framework of mathematics (Swett, 1978).

Because of the complexity of the mathematics curriculum, the discussion in this chapter is restricted to basic arithmetic with an emphasis on functional mathematics. Students who understand the basics will clearly encounter fewer problems than those who do not comprehend place value or number facts.

The main objectives of this chapter are therefore to
- identify some of the major problems that special learners meet in mathematics
- describe various methods of assessment
- discuss the diagnostic/remedial process as it applies to mathematics
- offer general and specific suggestions for teaching key basic mathematics topics

The mathematics curriculum

Mathematics may be conceived of as a symbolic language that allows human beings to think about, record, and communicate ideas concerning quantitative elements and the relationships among them. The scope of mathematics includes the operations of counting, measurement, arithmetic, calculation, geometry, and algebra, as well as the ability to think quantitatively (Lerner, 1981).

Especially in the early grades, arithmetic is developmental, a hierarchy of skills that build on one another. The major areas of arithmetic taught from kindergarten to grade six are presented in table 9–1.

Table 9–1 Major areas of arithmetic

Number systems	**Operations (computation)**	**Applications**
Numeration	Addition	Word problems
Notation	Subtraction	Interpretation of
Whole numbers	Multiplication	graphs and tables
Counting	Division	Money
Place value	Fractions	Measurement
Decimals	Decimals	Time
Fractions	Percentages	
Geometry and symbols		

A reading of provincial curricula from across Canada (Curriculum Committee, 1979) shows that the same basic skills are taught to all students although the emphasis may vary. There are minor differences in the age level at which a topic is introduced, in how it is developed, and in the order of subtopics. Greater differences are seen at the secondary level; for one thing, the amount of time students spend each day in mathematics instruction varies from thirty to seventy-five minutes a day across the country.

The term *mathematics* encompasses more than the term *arithmetic*. Mathematics is the study of the properties, measurement, and relationships of numbers; arithmetic is simply the computational problem solving taught in schools (Laycock & Watson, 1975).

There are many ways to conceptualize mathematics instruction. Greenwood and Anderson (1983) see it as a mixture of two domains—the operational and the conceptual. The operational domain encompasses basic skills and algorithms, the procedures for performing operations. It therefore involves the execution of mathematics. The conceptual domain consists of understanding when and where various number properties apply and how to use those properties to solve problems. It therefore involves the "Gestalt" of mathematics: an understanding of the total structure or pattern of skills and processes that can be used to solve problems. The conceptual domain also includes communication, in terms of the ability to describe observations and to paraphrase the solutions to problems in understandable terms. Finally, the conceptual domain encompasses an appreciation of mathematics and its values. Greenwood and Anderson feel that the two domains are equally important where effective problem solving is concerned and that both should be developed concurrently.

Mathematics is presented to youngsters at different conceptual levels, as shown in figure 9–1. The *concrete* level involves the manipulation of objects. For example, as they learn addition problems at this level children may manipulate blocks or counters. The *pictorial* level involves working with illustrations while performing mathematical tasks. Line drawings and other pictures are included at this level. The *linguistic* level, or the language of mathematics, consists of oral and written vocabulary that has specialized meaning in a mathematical context; for example, words such as plus, times, and remainder. The *abstract* or *alphanumeric* level involves working only with numerals and mathematical symbols to solve problems.

Mandell and Gold (1984) present the following example to illustrate how the meaning of fractional parts could be presented at each developmental level. At the concrete level, the teacher uses three-dimensional objects, such as clay models representing fruit cut into various fractional segments. Using an apple to illustrate the concept of one quarter, for example, the teacher divides it into four equal parts, counts each with the student, and shows one part saying, "I have one of four parts; I have one fourth or one quarter." At the semiconcrete, pictorial level, the teacher uses similar instructional procedures but the materials that illustrate the concepts are two-dimensional; pictures of pies, for example. At the abstract level, the teacher uses numerals to communicate the concept of fractional parts, with little reliance on two- and three-dimensional examples. Throughout, the teacher stresses the language of mathematics.

Teaching mathematics involves two basic considerations: what to teach and how to teach it. In the past twenty years, these two questions have created heated controversy among mathematics researchers and teachers. They disagree on the relative emphasis that should be placed on developing students' comprehension of the structure of mathematics and on developing students' mastery of basic skills. Traditional teaching has stressed a regime involving rote memorization, drill, and practice to acquire skills, but such an approach finds few supporters in contemporary mathematics education. Today, it is believed that other goals are more important, none more so than understanding. It is more essential, for example, that a student understand what decimals are, why they are used, and how they relate to money, fractions, and percentages, than that the student be able to divide decimals by rote.

The goals of the mathematics curriculum are not noticeably altered for special learners. For mildly handicapped students especially, however, functional mathematics

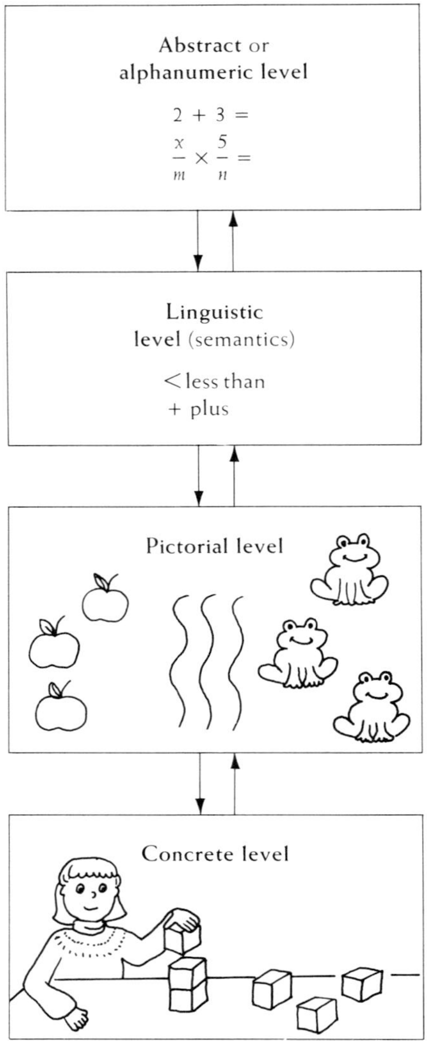

Figure 9–1 Levels of mathematics instruction

is essential. Students with special needs require an emphasis on number meaning (at least through three digits), number sequencing, and its practical application — for example, finding house and page numbers and understanding the terms "more," "less," and "enough." They also need much practice in all areas of handling money, including budgeting; in the basic operations of addition, subtraction, multiplication, and division; in measurement, especially of money and time; in simple fractions; in simple problem solving; and in using percentages in functional situations. At all times, the language of mathematics must be stressed.

Difficulties in mathematics

There are many reasons why some students fail to learn how to comprehend and manipulate numbers: inferior or inappropriate teaching, poor materials, generalized mental incapacity, or dysfunction of the central nervous system. For some students, deficits in mathematics constitute their sole academic disability. For many exceptional pupils, however, specifically those considered to be mildly handicapped, mathematical disabilities go hand in hand with deficits in other subject areas.

Many of the characteristics attributed to mildly disabled learners are related to arithmetic deficits. Problems of perception, directionality, abstract thinking, memory, and reading, for example, are frequently typical of these students and each of these is closely aligned with mathematical difficulties. Children with spatial problems, those who do not fully comprehend left–right and up–down, and children with temporal problems, those who do not understand first, last, today, tomorrow, and yesterday, are likely to encounter difficulties with formal mathematics in the classroom. Difficulty with abstract or symbolic thinking interferes with a youngster's ability to conceptualize the relationship between numerals and the objects represented by them. Mildly disabled students who lag in abstract thinking abilities may meet problems in such areas as place value and understanding the relationships among units of measurement. Students with memory problems will forget number facts, the steps in the four basic operations, and even mathematical terms. They may be particularly slow or inefficient in arriving at answers to problems. There is no question that many arithmetic skills are founded on a good memory. For some students, poor reading contributes to difficulties in mathematics. They may be unable to read word problems, to learn mathematical language, or to understand the directions in texts and on work sheets.

In the context of the mathematics curriculum, Guerin and Maier (1983) have identified certain variables related to arithmetic problems: difficulty in recognizing and recalling computational words, symbols, and numerals; lack of opportunities to use a new skill repeatedly until its performance becomes automatic; a poor foundation of basic arithmetic skills; reading comprehension insufficient to complete arithmetic word problems; and poor use of checking skills, especially in estimating whether answers are reasonable.

Students often perform poorly on teacher-made tests even if they have learned the information. They may be unable to demonstrate their knowledge because they have inadequate reading skills, reasoning, and comprehension, fine motor and visual perception problems, and other related deficiencies (Miederhoff & Wood, 1988).

If mathematics is presented in ways that fail to interest students, then further problems ensue. Teachers of young children usually employ a variety of concrete materials but teachers in the upper grades do not. Instruction becomes geared toward textbooks and lectures, and instructional goals at the upper elementary levels often concentrate on students' mastery of algorithmic processes in place of the earlier stress on comprehension. Even at the upper levels, it may be more efficient to introduce new mathematical topics to special learners by using concrete materials. If students are learning how to find the area of a quadrilateral, for example, they may understand the concept more clearly if they have opportunities to manipulate pieces of cardboard, cutting them into quadrilaterals of different sizes.

The quality and degree of instruction has a direct bearing on mathematical disabilities. In fact, Spoder (1985) suggests that the way mathematics is taught, rather than the nature of the subject, creates learning difficulties. Carpenter (1985) found that resource-room teachers spent one-third of their instructional time on mathematics instruction, yet one resource-room teacher in four was uncertain of his or her ability to assess students' mathematical skills through the use of scope and sequence charts. Teachers often do not feel competent to teach higher mathematical skills, to assess students' attitudes to mathematics, to use error analysis, to assess verbal problem solving, or to use non-traditional conceptual approaches to mathematics instruction (Bachor & Crealock, 1986). Too frequently, teachers are unaware of the basic **axioms** that underlie mathematics, the intuitive rules that arise from a study of numbers. Because of this, mathematics is in some sense "the silent subject." Too often, it is taught by teachers who say "Open up your textbook. Get to work. Don't talk."

Experienced teachers have probably encountered students displaying a huge variety of mathematical difficulties, ranging from the subtle to the bizarre. Blaney and Thornton (1981) have, however, identified five types of students experiencing problems in mathematics:

- the student who presents unsatisfactory homework assignments because of unsatisfactory copying
- the student who does well on isolated facts but cannot apply these to word problems or complex computations
- the student who seems not to pay attention or to comprehend oral presentations; or the one who does not answer in class
- the older student who "refuses" to learn basic facts
- the student who performs wrong procedures or skips steps in some random fashion

Diagnosis in mathematics

As in other academic areas, a comprehensive assessment battery in mathematics includes both formal and informal procedures. Frequently, formal tests are used to identify global problem areas while informal measures permit teachers to identify a student's specific skill deficits and learning style. Both formal and informal measures are, of course, necessary for effective programming. Readers are urged to review the general topics of formal and informal testing in chapter 3 as background to the information presented below.

Formal measures

Formal arithmetic tests tend to cluster into two general types, achievement tests and diagnostic tests. Achievement tests address numerous arithmetic subskills and yield information about a student's general arithmetic ability. Typically, these tests produce a raw score that is converted to an approximate grade-level ability. Achievement tests are often best used as screening instruments.

Mathematics instruction can be enjoyable.

The Key Math Diagnostic Arithmetic Test (Connolly, Nachtman, & Pritchett, 1979, 1982) is perhaps the most widely used formal assessment measure for mathematics. A teacher can administer the measure without much training and it has a practical structure. The test also has Canadian norms. The Test of Early Mathematical Ability (Ginsberg & Baroody, 1983) includes subtests on concepts, counting, and calculations. It is designed for children from age 4 to 8 years 11 months, and identifies those who are at risk. The test has a practical format and is easy to use. Canadian norms are not available.

Informal measures

Before a teacher can hypothesize about appropriate remediation procedures for a particular student, he or she must find out what that student knows about specific mathematical topics. Commercial tests are sometimes used to collect this information but the results are often of a very general nature and the student's specific strengths and weaknesses are unlikely to be identified. Additional data are necessary before remediation can begin.

Informal measures are crucial in mathematics diagnosis. Since the measures do not draw comparisons among students, teachers do not need specialized knowledge in order to interpret them. More importantly, informal tools offer opportunities for teachers to explore students' thought processes, to estimate their potential as well as achievement, and to have students use materials other than paper and pencil. Moreover, informal measures are also practical, since teachers can design them to fit the needs of particular classes or individuals and there is room for latitude in the procedures and language they use. Finally, informal measures have the merit of demonstrating to non-specialist mathematics teachers that students vary widely in their approaches to mathematical situations, and that many students are very creative.

When employing informal assessment measures, teachers must ensure that students are allowed time to get used to the tests. Teachers should administer the measure over several days and evaluate performance as soon as possible. As well, it is up to teachers to develop their own assessment instruments based upon local curricula, and to obtain suggestions from other professionals on how to improve them (Plata & Calvin, 1984).

Observation and interviews

Teachers can gain a great deal of information about the way that students approach mathematics and process arithmetic problems, simply through observation. They may also be able to deduce patterns of error by studying students' work. More rigorous methods are needed as well, however, to allow teachers to discover the logic behind errors.

The oral interview — known also as the Piagetian interview or the clinical interview (see Liedtke, 1982) — is an effective observation technique. Not only do interviews pinpoint errors and incorrect procedures but students seem to like them because of the individual attention (Liedtke, 1983). An interview is not simply an oral test to see whether a student can perform a task. Rather, within the context of the interview the teacher asks the student to describe the process that he or she uses to solve a problem. The teacher is then able to explore how the student thinks and to determine **cognitive competence**; that is, what the student could do, as opposed to what he or she characteristically does (Ginsburg, 1977).

Interviews can vary widely in their structure. Specific data can best be collected in a one-to-one setting. Typically, the teacher prepares a work sheet of three to five problems of the type on which the student makes errors. These are called **probe sheets** because they focus on a specific skill, tentatively identified as one in which the student is having difficulties (Mandell & Gold, 1984). To get at the student's thinking, the teacher then prompts either an introspective or a retrospective response to each problem. To elicit introspection, the teacher asks the student to comment on his or her thoughts while performing the task; if responding retrospectively, the student comments on his or her thoughts only after completing the task (Ashlock, 1986). Each of the teacher's questions is contingent upon the student's previous response. Evidence of a student's faulty understanding of processes can be pursued by further questioning or noted for a later occasion. Interviews reveal not only errors but also the different levels of sophistication in students' problem solving strategies.

Checklists

Although they have many forms, all checklists are constructed around the logical sequence of skills within particular mathematical concepts. Commercial checklists are available, but should be modified in order to make them relevant to the specific curriculum. Many teachers make up their own checklists. A properly constructed checklist, designed by a teacher for a given topic, can be one of the most valuable tools available. It should contain a hierarchy of skills and include tasks at the concrete, pictorial, and abstract levels of thought. As the teacher poses questions, the student should verbalize his or her thinking and illustrate it with objects or drawings whenever possible. When the teacher makes notes about the session, he or she should keep statements about the *results* of performance, such as "could perform subtraction computations with three-digit numbers," separate from observations about the student *during* performance, such as "seemed very tense within the testing situation."

Attitude scales

As was pointed out in chapter 3, attitude scales for arithmetic are available; they are not, however, widely used since teachers are not always aware of them (Fennel, 1981; Suydam & Trueblood, 1974). They are useful to gauge either motivation or attitudes toward specific mathematical areas. In the Test of Mathematical Abilities (Brown & McEntire, 1984), a standardized test containing a subtest on attitudes, children are asked to agree or disagree with statements such as "Math is tiresome and boring." Dunlap (1976) devised a scale that has been used successfully with children in grades one and two; the scale includes facts already taught in class and therefore shows attitudes to particular areas as well as to mathematics in general.

Criterion-referenced tests

Criterion-referenced tests in arithmetic are often developed in conjunction with the skills listed on scope and sequence charts and are designed to measure how well a student performs a specific skill. On a criterion-referenced test, the student must complete a group of related problems rather than just one representative problem in each area as in a norm-referenced test. The information provided by the test therefore permits the teacher to determine whether a student's skill performance is consistent or whether it occurs by chance.

Although informal measures such as criterion-referenced tests can include a wide variety of skills, it is probably more efficient to limit the number of skills tested in any one session. By focussing on specific skills, teachers are better able to analyse performance in a comprehensive manner.

Teacher-made tests

Teacher-made tests are the most widely used method of evaluation in school mathematics classes (Miederhoff & Wood, 1988). For most students, tests may be a bit of a nuisance, but for many mildly handicapped learners, tests remind them of earlier failures and feelings of inadequacy and doubt. It is not always necessary for teachers to lower their expectations, however, or even to alter course objectives. They can simply prepare two versions of tests, one with minor alterations in the procedures (see table 9–2). A few changes can mean the difference between success and failure for mainstreamed students.

Error analysis

While a number of commercial error analysis measures are available, teachers can create their own equally useful tools. With a minimal investment of time, error analysis provides valuable information about individual or class performance that can be used to improve instruction. Bachor and Crealock (1986) and Radatz (1979) have identified general error patterns that teachers may use as a basis for categorizing errors (see table 9–3).

Table 9–2 Teacher-made tests

All students	Extra modifications
◆ Keep directions simple. ◆ List directions in a logical sequence. ◆ Divide the test into sections, with specific directions for each section. ◆ List only one direction in each sentence. ◆ Avoid using words such as *never*, *not*, or *always*; underline them if they are used. ◆ Avoid mixing different problem formats in the same section of the test. ◆ Use problems that are relevant to the students' experience.	◆ Define any unfamiliar or abstract words. ◆ Give an example of how to respond. ◆ Read directions orally to the students in advance, as well as writing them on the test. ◆ Supply visual prompts (see figure 9–2). ◆ Explain symbols and mathematical language (see figure 9–2). ◆ Underline or circle key words. ◆ Use no more than five word problems on a test. ◆ Adjust the level of readability. ◆ Prepare the test in short sections that can be administered separately if necessary. ◆ Place only one type of question on each page. ◆ Use graph paper for students who have difficulty aligning digits. ◆ Modify time requirements, by giving the test over two sessions, for example.

Source: Adapted from Miederhoff & Wood, 1988.

Visual prompts	$\overset{\quad R}{26\overline{)523}}$	□□ 326 $-\underline{127}$ ___
Symbols	$<$ = less than $>$ = greater than	
Formulae	Length × Width = Area L × W = A	

Source: Adapted from Miederhoff & Wood, 1988.

Figure 9–2

To construct an error analysis measure to check, for example, the addition of whole numbers, the teacher first applies task analysis. She identifies all the component subtasks involved in adding whole numbers, such as being able to add two single-digit whole numbers with and without regrouping ones and tens. She then creates a number of problems for each skill and arranges them randomly on a test. By assessing students' answers, the teacher can discover patterns.

Table 9–3 Error analysis

Language difficulties	The student misunderstands the semantics of a mathematical statement such as "How many are left?" or interprets instructions too literally.
Insufficient mastery of prerequisite skills	The student has been given problems in an inappropriate order; problems in division, for example, before he or she has mastered multiplication and subtraction.
Use of irrelevant rules or strategies	The student repeats an algorithm that has worked in the past.
Incorrect association	The student has not been taught relevant cues for applying the appropriate algorithm.
Difficulty in obtaining spatial information	The student has been presented with materials that limit illustration of a mathematical concept to the pictorial or symbolic level.
Poor alignment of numbers	The student copies a question incorrectly or aligns it wrongly on the page.
Saving face	The student puts down anything in the answer space.

Some examples of error patterns are shown below. In each of the examples it is clear that the errors were caused by systematic application of some faulty procedure; they were neither arbitrary nor careless.

Example 1

$$\begin{array}{r} 62 \\ -\underline{18} \\ 56 \end{array} \qquad \begin{array}{r} 55 \\ -\underline{28} \\ 33 \end{array} \qquad \begin{array}{r} 70 \\ -\underline{24} \\ 54 \end{array}$$

Subtraction: no regrouping in units

Example 2

$$\begin{array}{r} 627 \\ +\underline{\ \ 39} \\ 6516 \end{array} \qquad \begin{array}{r} 834 \\ +\underline{\ \ 58} \\ 8812 \end{array} \qquad \begin{array}{r} 831 \\ +\underline{\ 48} \\ 879 \end{array}$$

Addition: no regrouping in units

Example 3

34	75	64	94
+ 22	+ 68	+ 93	+ 37
56	116	112	113

Addition: regrouping, but adding left to right

Example 4

$\frac{17}{75} = \frac{1}{5}$ $\frac{21}{42} = \frac{1}{4}$ $\frac{4}{30} = \frac{4}{30}$ $\frac{16}{256} = \frac{1}{25}$

Fractions: cancelling similar numbers

Case study 9–1, part 1 introduces Jan and illustrates how some of the informal measures just discussed helped the teacher to pinpoint Jan's major deficits in mathematics.

Case study 9–1, part 1

Nine-year-old Jan arrived at her new school in September. Because Jan was a shy, timid little girl, the teacher decided to observe her behaviour and performance rather than administer any assessment measures before she was used to the new school. Reports from the previous school were sparse, merely indicating that Jan had no medical problems, was a little behind in some areas, and should be placed in a grade four class.

During the first few weeks of school, the teacher observed that Jan was reading a little below grade level. Her spelling showed many errors and she was still printing rather than using a cursive script. Although the teacher determined early that some remedial work was needed in the language arts, she was primarily concerned about the level of Jan's achievement in arithmetic. Using only general observation of Jan's daily work, the teacher soon discovered that the child demonstrated major deficits. She did not know basic addition and subtraction number facts, appeared to have little knowledge of the multiplication tables, and was deficient in all of the four basic arithmetic operations. While Jan sometimes obtained the correct answer to addition and subtraction problems, albeit slowly and haltingly, she was unable to generalize rules that had been learned by rote. In addition, even though Jan could read word problems, she was usually unable to identify the correct process by which to arrive at a solution.

Taking into account Jan's natural timidity, the teacher decided not to use a standardized survey test to identify general areas of strength and weakness further. Rather, she made a careful error analysis of Jan's daily work that confirmed her initial observations. She found that Jan's errors in using operations were not random but seemed to have two sources: Jan was often confused about the steps in using an operation and she often copied or aligned the work incorrectly.

To assess Jan further, the teacher prepared a short written test that focussed only on the operations of addition and subtraction up to three digits. As well, the teacher prepared concrete materials and pictures to be used as necessary. Through a series of questions, responses, and clarifications in a one-to-one interview, she worked with Jan to try to understand how the child was conceptualizing problems. When given enough time, Jan could perform addition and subtraction computations with numbers up to three digits long, including zeros, and with one regrouping performed by rote. Her explanation of the approach she used, however, revealed it to be unorthodox. On the question 846 + 597, for example, Jan obtained the correct answer although she had to draw the equation in order to work out the number facts. When asked about regrouping and adding, Jan explained, "You always write down the big number and carry the little one." This prompted the teacher to check Jan's comprehension of place value by using pictures. When Jan presented sketchy responses, the teacher moved to concrete materials — bundles of popsicle sticks — and found that Jan could explain place value and even some regrouping when she had items available to manipulate physically.

Following the interview session, the teacher made a number of decisions. She decided to discuss Jan with the resource-room staff so that they could recommend any necessary further testing. With the resource-room teacher, the classroom teacher then prepared an individual plan that focussed on arithmetic to be presented within the regular classroom. Because of Jan's deficits, the plan stressed activities at the concrete and pictorial levels, word problems, and the language of mathematics. An extract from Jan's IEP appears later in this chapter.

General instructional approaches

Certain principles are applicable to all types of mathematical learning and are essential for effective teaching (Lerner, 1981). Students best understand a concept when instruction moves from the concrete to the abstract. They need plenty of drill and practice to develop automaticity about facts and operations. Finally, they need the opportunity to see mathematics as part of the real world. Teachers must consider the quantity, level, pace, and mode of mathematics instruction. The pace will affect students' attention spans and levels of fatigue. The mode of presentation determines whether symbols or pictures are used, what amount of drill the students undergo, and so forth. Some general tips for teaching mathematics to special learners are presented in table 9–4.

Teachers must bear in mind that mathematics is a tool for handling problems that originate in the physical world. Whenever possible, students should be presented with realistic problems related to the concrete world. These problems attempt to go from the simple to the more complex, both syntactically and conceptually, and should be in keeping with students' language and cognitive development.

Educationally handicapped students have two basic needs with regard to mathematics instruction. They must learn how to perform basic arithmetic operations and subsequently how to apply arithmetic skills to everyday problems. Students must be able to apply skills to many different situations in order to function adequately in daily life.

Table 9–4 Teaching mathematics to special learners

Use concrete materials.	Familiar, concrete items are best to illustrate mathematical concepts, facts, symbols, or processes.
Use charts.	Use wall charts to illustrate algorithms.
Use patterns and associations.	As an example, when students are learning to multiply by fours, relate the lesson to wheels on an automobile.
Use visual prompts.	Visual prompts such as those shown in figure 9–2 help students to solve computational problems.
Use visual cuing.	Use colour coding to point out the beginning of each problem or the proper sequence of steps in a series of instructions.
Use spatial cuing.	Use circles, boxes, and lines to focus on separate parts of work or align work properly. For students who have problems with spacing or with directionality, use graph paper or add guidelines to regular paper.
Use tactile cuing.	Use textured numerals, for example.
Use realistic materials.	As an example, when teaching students to make change, use real coins and bills.
Make mathematics functional.	Mathematics should be associated with the student's own world and daily activities.
Explore alternative materials and methods.	Choose instructional materials different from those that have caused failure in the past.
Give students a stake in the learning process.	Let the students choose from the available materials.
Encourage the students to appraise their own work.	Help students to detect their own mistakes.
Teach students how to estimate.	If they know how to estimate, students can make educated assessments of their answers in mathematics.
Emphasize careful penmanship and proper alignment of digits.	Correct alignment will eliminate some errors.
Eliminate copying.	Use prepared work sheets rather than having students copy from the textbook or the board.
Employ technology.	Explore the numerous drill and practice programs available for computer-assisted instruction.
Base corrective instruction on diagnosis.	Test carefully.
Adapt instructional sequences.	Use smaller steps and precise sequencing.
Adapt seatwork.	Present seatwork in small amounts interspersed with instruction.
Modify assignments.	Assign fewer problems.
Keep homework brief.	Brief homework assignments, routinely corrected, solidify learning.
Provide more practice and review.	Use games, self-correcting materials, tape recorders, and so on.
Provide review items.	Provide folders that contain information such as vocabulary, definitions, and restatements of algorithms. Always review thoroughly.

Sources: Ashlock, 1986; Bachor & Crealock, 1986; Burton & Meyers, 1987

Children learn about symmetry and beginning geometry from their environment.

The first consideration when developing an individualized instructional program is to identify a student's level of conceptual understanding. Some students demonstrate their need for, or reliance on, concrete activities by counting on their fingers when requested to complete a simple addition problem. Such students require more instructional time at the concrete and pictorial levels of conceptualization. In fact, some low-achieving students need concrete presentations well into their secondary years (Case, 1982), but materials should match the students' ages. While a very simple balance is appropriate for young children, for example, a properly calibrated scale is more suitable for high school students.

When teaching mathematics to mildly handicapped youngsters, teachers should allow more exploratory and consolidating activities. Consolidating activities help students to visualize a new idea, verbalize a useful rule, see a relationship between two ideas, agree on terminology, or relate what is seen to what is written (Thornton, Tucker, Benny, Dossy, & Bazik, 1983). Students also need much drill and practice to overlearn mathematical facts and concepts, since these must be used automatically. Techniques for providing practice include work sheets, flash cards, games, and computer-assisted instruction.

Peer tutoring is especially helpful in mathematics, although here groups of four seem to be more appropriate than pairs. Some investigators who used a class-wide peer tutoring approach found that students' weekly mathematics quiz scores increased by about 20 percentage points during the peer interventions (Maheady, Sacca, & Harper, 1986; Sacca & Harper, 1986).

Approaches for gifted students

Mathematics is an area in which gifted students should be able to proceed at their own pace but often do not because of the constraints of a hierarchical curriculum. Gifted students require enriched and expanded curricula that emphasize a higher order of thinking skills, non-traditional topics, and the application of skills and concepts in a variety of contexts (National Council, 1986). Ellis (1987a, 1987b) suggests that teachers use the following guidelines when presenting mathematics to gifted students:

- Provide a context for applying mathematical concepts or skills that allows more than one correct answer to a problem. As an example, ask students to find ways to measure how high a ball bounces.
- Have students explore imaginative ways to apply mathematical concepts to the world around them. They might, for example, find all the ways that they can make triangles with their own bodies.
- Have the gifted students use mathematics in unusual contexts or for unusual purposes. Tell them, for example, that they must describe themselves to a new pen pal by using twenty-one sentences, each of which includes numbers or arithmetic in some way.
- Use the manipulative objects from a mathematics lesson in a following creative lesson. After adding and subtracting pieces of macaroni, for example, students can use the pasta for an art project.

Functional mathematics

Wherever possible, mathematics for mildly handicapped students should be functional. Classroom instruction in basic operations and problem solving should be related to real life skills involving money, time, and measurement. Students should, for example, be taught comparative shopping skills to enable them to select the best value on a given item. As another example, since banking is an important part of our lives, teachers can help students to learn banking procedures and vocabulary by creating a classroom banking system in which students receive privileges through checks. In other words, good behaviour or performance earns them a credit at the bank, while unacceptable behaviour results in a withdrawal of funds (see figure 9–3).

Handling money is another important skill. Ibbitson (1987) stresses that real money is the best medium through which to teach students about money. She notes that play money is lighter and feels different from real money, and that students seem to show more respect for real money. Ibbitson also suggests making packages of coins for each student containing 4 quarters, 10 dimes, 10 nickels, and 20 pennies. An introductory unit on money would then explore the money's size, shape, pictures, and value. Not until the students are extremely familiar with the coins should counting begin. When counting, begin with only one type of coin. Once students have become familiar with the coins, they can be taught to make change. Making change is an important idea that can be conveyed by creating a classroom store in which students take turns being the shopkeeper or the customer.

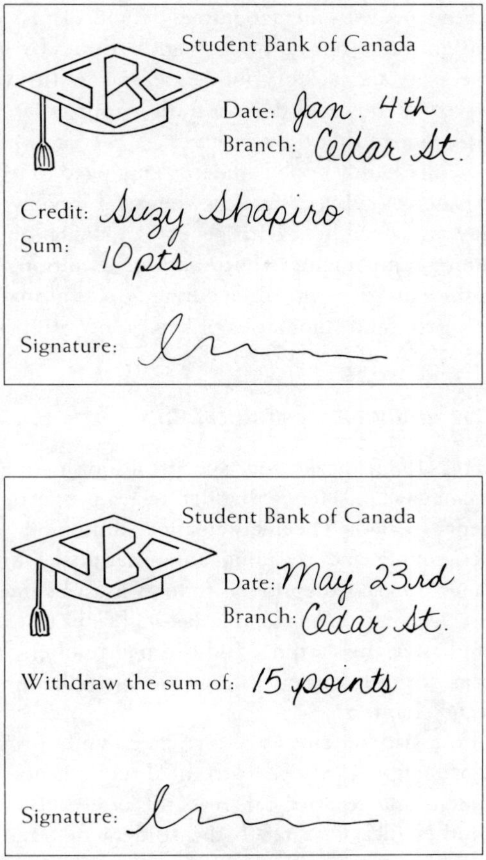

Student Bank of Canada

SBC

Date: Jan. 4th

Branch: Cedar St.

Credit: Suzy Shapiro

Sum: 10pts

Signature:

Student Bank of Canada

SBC

Date: May 23rd

Branch: Cedar St.

Withdraw the sum of: 15 points

Signature:

Figure 9–3 Classroom banking system combining functional mathematics and behavioural control

Metacognitive strategies

Mildly handicapped students are often deficient in metacognitive strategies. Slife, Weiss, and Bell (1985) tried to identify the metacognitive strategies used by learning-disabled students and their non-disabled counterparts. Cognition was measured by how well students did on a set of arithmetic problems and the regulation of cognition was measured by having the students indicate whether they thought their attempted solutions were right or were wrong. The actual results from the learning-disabled group were significantly below those of the other group. In addition, while both groups overestimated the number of correct solutions, the learning-disabled students' predictions were considerably less accurate than their normal peers' predictions, suggesting that there were metacognitive differences between the two groups.

Students with metacognitive deficits display a range of behaviours. They often show inattention to relevant information, difficulty in changing from one activity to another, insecurity and lack of confidence, and confusion with respect to time and space. Chiefly, however, they will demonstrate inappropriate learning for the amount of instruction and practice that they receive.

Mildly handicapped students may need to be taught specific strategies for mathematics, such as subvocalization, rehearsal, review, estimation, and cues for memory. They may also need help with general organization. Students can keep special folders containing supplementary information: definitions of terms, algorithms or formulae restated in students' own words, accurate copies of material that was on the board or overhead projector, and summaries of key points, prepared by the teacher or classmates.

The language of mathematics

Bangs (1982) speaks very specifically of mathematics as a language. She notes that it is "a language of science that deals with properties and relations of quantity and measurement" (p. 54). The mathematical difficulties of many students stem from problems recognizing and recalling computational words, symbols, and numerals (Guerin & Maier, 1983). Exceptional students must be taught, for example that words such as *sum*, *plus*, *total*, *add*, *addend*, and *addition* all refer to the + symbol. Teachers will also need to emphasize the cardinal and ordinal numbers, the language for measurement, and the terms for different operations, as illustrated in the extract from Jan's IEP presented later in the chapter.

To assist students in recognizing symbols used in the operations, it may be helpful to present work sheets with the directions noting operations circled. Alternatively, the student and teacher can read the question and mark the relevant language together. Another idea is to teach the student to trace the sign with his or her finger before beginning the problem, especially on pages of work with mixed problems. Another cue to students is a wall chart with each operation sign in a distinct colour. Then if all seatwork is keyed to that colour, the student has an additional indication of how to proceed (Bley & Thornton, 1981).

Number facts

If the facts involving ones and doubling are not included, then there are fifty-six facts to be mastered in each of the four modes of arithmetic computation (Otto, McMenemy, & Smith, 1973). Edge (1984) points out that the optimal recall time for addition and multiplication facts is three seconds and five seconds for subtraction and division.

Most teachers agree that students should know the basic number facts. Teachers usually aim for students to have automaticity of basic number facts by the end of grade three. Building on those facts, they can then provide students with strategies — such as doubling numbers, halving numbers, skip counting, and so on — to generate unknown facts from known facts. Learning number facts and strategies should be relevant to students' experiences and initially based on manipulation of objects. A wide variety of materials can be used, including, in order from simple to complex: multicoloured counters, ten-centimetre blocks, base ten blocks, graph paper, number boxes, and number lines.

Manipulative and pictorial materials help students to understand mathematics. (Curriculum—Math #1, 1964)

Place value and numeration

Most children are able to read numbers with several digits but a great many have difficulty expressing those numbers in alternative ways; that is, renaming them. Renaming activities are central to all algorithms — since understanding renaming is part of learning place value — and should therefore be stressed in students' early years. Any materials that can be grouped into ones, tens, hundreds, and so on can be used in activities to teach place value and renaming. Counters, bundles of sticks, and other similar materials are helpful to teach two-digit numbers but sets of base ten blocks are more effective to convey larger numbers, since large numbers of sticks or counters can be unmanageable. During the early stages of learning, the student should be given many concrete aids. To teach place value the teacher could, for example make boxes that contain slots for 9 sticks or rods, as shown in figure 9–4. When students have 9 rods in the box, they move to a box designed for the next unit; that is, for the tens. This box also fits only 9 sticks, but of a larger size. Students may learn place value more easily using a number box (figure 9–5) than a number line, since counting the *spaces* rather than the *points* on a number line will lead to errors. More abstract aids such as an abacus or a pocket chart may be delayed with exceptional learners until grade three (Liedtke, 1982).

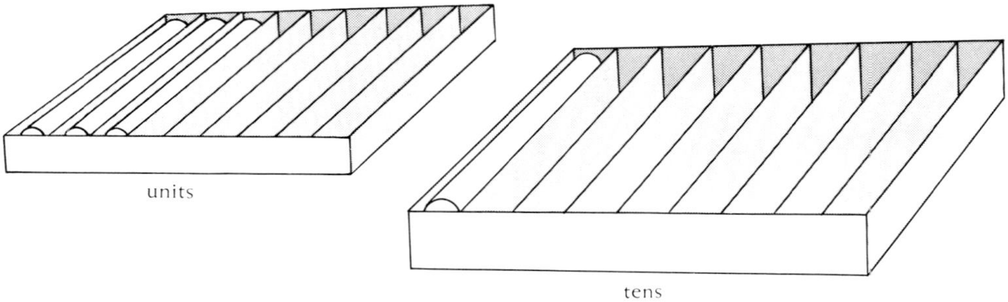

Figure 9–4 Place value boxes

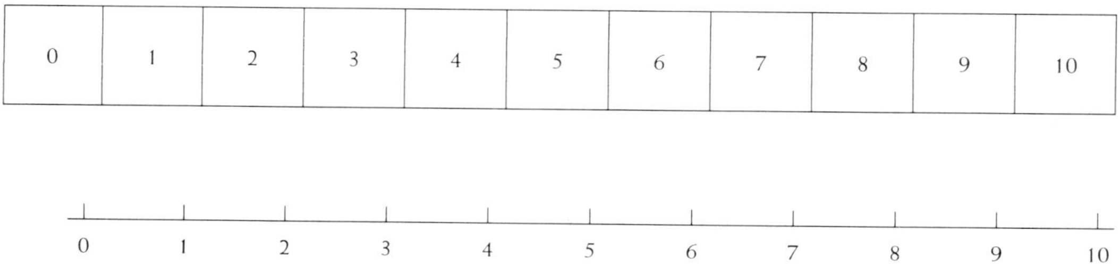

Figure 9–5 Number box and number line

Operations

The fundamental operations of arithmetic are usually taught as a chain of rules. The simplest rule is taught first and entrenched by drill and practice; more complex rules follow in a logical order. Students then work through the learned chain to find the correct rule. They often cannot make intelligent decisions or verify their choices, however, because they do not possess a sense of the logic underlying mathematical rules (Jencks, Peck, & Chatterley, 1980). Jencks and his colleagues interviewed a number of students and found that they

- had no meaningful referents for the symbols and rules that they used
- frequently applied rules that would have been correct in different situations
- believed that the incorrect methods they were using were the ones that their teachers had taught them
- could not verify for themselves whether or not the rules they used were correct

As the study shows, it is important to stress the meaning of operations and the relationship between operations and the algorithms that use them. The teacher must spend time building connections between manipulation of concrete objects, verbalization of the manipulations, and manipulation of symbols if students are to understand that those symbols have meaningful referents. Additionally, mathematical processes should be introduced by having students make up problems using their own experience. Facts and computational skills then arise from students' own needs.

Word problems

Certain components of the arithmetic curriculum are sequential; for example, a knowledge of place value is necessary for efficiency in the four basic arithmetic operations. Problem solving strategies, however, should be taught to students regardless of their age or skill level. Instructional programs tend to emphasize computation at the expense of word problems. Yet in order to complete arithmetic tasks successfully, all students must be able to recognize the essential cues in any given problem; in other words, what to do in order to solve the problem.

There is no question that special learners encounter severe difficulties with word problems. Some are unable to compute with numbers or have trouble understanding the meaning of number operations and the relationships between them. They may lack the special types of reading skills required in problem solving or the ability to sense quantitative relations within verbal problems. They do not always possess a knowledge of essential facts, rules, and formulae, of the uses of arithmetic in social situations, or of vocabulary to express ideas quantitatively. The amount of practice needed to solve verbal problems may also present difficulty (Mandell & Gold, 1984). Finally, Bachor (1985) and Levy (1984) have suggested that the level of syntax and vocabulary in many instructions and word problems is too difficult for mildly handicapped students.

As well, difficulties can arise from the word problems themselves. Students may confront insufficient information, information that must be recalled or inferred, information to be determined from a diagram or a graph, or information to be discovered only through research.

A wide variety of techniques are available to teach students how to develop effective problem solving strategies, and most have two aims in common: making word problems relevant to students' everyday activities and stressing the language of mathematics. Much emphasis should be placed on oral problem solving strategies, of the type shown in box 9–1.

When teaching special learners how to solve problems, examples from daily life, such as their own baseball scores or spelling quiz scores, provide suitable and relevant material. It is also important that students be given ample opportunity to develop their

Box 9–1 Example of a problem solving strategy

1. The teacher presents a problem, such as "I am thinking of two numbers. The sum of the two numbers is 13. The numbers are . . . and. . . ."
2. The teacher asks questions and records the students' answers on the board.

Questions	**Answers**
What are we to find?	Two numbers
How are they related? (What is a condition of the problem?)	Sum of 13
Can the condition be expressed differently?	Yes, by subtraction 13 − 1 13 − 2 13 − 3, etc.
How many addition facts are there that have two addends for the sum of 13?	14
Can we develop an organized list of addition facts?	Varied answers
How will we organize the list?	Varied answers
Can you see patterns in the list?	Yes 13 + 0 12 + 1 11 + 2, etc.

3. The teacher encourages discussion on how the problem was solved.

Source: Adapted from Percevault, 1985.

own equations from problems that they have made up themselves. The students may say, for example, that Team A scored 7 runs and Team B only 4. The teacher can then help them to write this information in the form of various types of problems, from which they derive equations:

1. Who scored the most? (no operation)
2. What were the scores of both teams together? $(7 + 4)$
3. How much did Team A win by? $(7 - 4)$
4. How much did Team B lose by? $(7 - 4)$
5. If there were 9 people on one team, how many were on the two teams? (9×2)
6. If Ron was pitching, and Marita was the catcher, how many people were fielding? $(9 - 1 - 1)$
7. If Pietra was up to bat, Juan was on first base, and Janet on third, how many people were left on their team? $(1 + 1 + 1 = 3,\ 9 - 3)$

As well as having students make up their own problems and write their own equations, the teacher can introduce problem situations that are relevant but use few numbers and that concentrate on the process rather than an answer. To continue with the baseball example,

8. If there are 9 people on a team, how would you find out how many people make up 3 teams?
9. If we know that there are 12 teams in the National League and 14 in the American, how would we find out how many teams there are in both leagues altogether?

The teacher can read problems to the class or group and have students act them out before they solve them. Students may also require much time to read such problems with the teacher, discuss them, underline the key words, and determine the correct operation. When the problem asks "How many were there altogether?" for example, then addition is warranted; when the student is asked "How many were left?" then the process is subtraction. For young children, problems may be presented within the context of a language experience unit, as shown below in box 9–2.

Box 9–2 Language experience unit

1. Choose a place for the class to go on a field trip; the zoo, for example.
2. Obtain brochures describing the zoo; keep them pinned to the bulletin board for some time before the trip; and discuss them with the class.
3. After the class has gone to the zoo, help them to make up a story about their trip, and record it on a chart.
4. Have the pupils invent word problems orally about the experience; for example, "Twenty people went and it cost a dollar each to get in. How much was that?" The class discusses the process and the answers.
5. Have students write down their own word problems and swap them with classmates; each student thus solves a new problem.

Some students' difficulties with word problems are more closely related to reading deficits than to mathematical dysfunctioning. Rewriting material at a simpler level (see chapter 8), reading the material with or to the student, using peer tutors for reading, or tape-recording the material may circumvent reading deficits.

LeBlanc (1977) recommends that teachers present instruction on problem solving strategies in a certain hierarchy:

1. understanding the problem
2. planning the solution
3. solving the problem
4. deciding if the solution makes sense in the context of the problem

To help students develop problem solving skills, Earp (1970) suggests teaching them the following steps:

1. Read the problem or listen to the problem presented orally, in order to visualize the situation that it describes.

2. Reread for the essential facts.
3. Identify technical or difficult concepts.
4. Reread to plan steps for the solution.
5. Reread a third time to compare the nature of the problem with the planned solution.

Blankenship and Lovitt (1975) suggest that teachers categorize problems by their various sets of characteristics and then teach them in a systematic order. Teachers should outline a specific group of instructional techniques for every kind of problem — although it may be necessary to vary the techniques according to each student — and construct several problems of each type in order to give students sufficient practice.

Graphing Helping students to make the connections between their own experiences and the world of mathematics is not easy, but graphs can help them to illustrate and interpret data. A graph may be thought of as a picture that symbolizes some real situation (Gilbert, 1987). When first teaching students how to use graphs, teachers should keep the graphs simple and also remember that producing a graph is not the end of a project. It is as important that students discuss the process with the teacher and their peers. Pictographs should be introduced before bar graphs.

Materials

The most common form of instruction in arithmetic is the developmental approach, frequently used with basal arithmetic programs. Basal programs are often viewed as suitable for all students; they introduce basic skills such as addition and subtraction and stress place value, measurement, fractions, and geometry. Sometimes teachers supplement the basal programs with additional instruction in specific skills in order to remedy special learners' problems, or with specialized mathematics programs that provide more instruction for slow or atypical learners.

If a basal mathematics series and the accompanying workbooks are used, it is often helpful to special learners to cut the pages in order to present a smaller number of problems. Teachers may opt to make their own work sheets and materials. As far as possible, these should be self-correcting (see chapter 5).

Within the mathematics curriculum, it is likely that exceptional pupils will require much drill and practice, for which microcomputers have been shown to be particularly effective. Messerly (1986), for example, used computer-assisted instruction (CAI) for six months with hearing-impaired students in self-contained mathematics classes. When the Stanford Achievement Test was used for evaluation, many students demonstrated more than six months' growth in various areas, including computation, application, and concepts. A study of learning-disabled students in grades four to eight clearly supported computerized instruction in mathematics for these students as a viable alternative to existing instructional methodology (Trifiletti, Frith, & Armstrong, 1984). Most software in CAI is directed toward mathematical drill and practice.

A variety of mathematical materials are available for very special populations. Mathematics makes use of a special braille notation system, for example, which is available on all mathematical implements for severely visually impaired students. Similarly, teachers can obtain magnetized rulers and instruments for wheelchair-bound students.

Many commercial mathematical games are also available. The best are those involving only a few students, preferably of comparable ability (Ashlock, 1986). Games that provide immediate or early verification of mathematical facts should be chosen. Teachers can also allow students to make up their own games or to alter the rules occasionally.

Specific activities

Mathematics is taught in a developmental and hierarchical fashion. If students fail to acquire beginning skills, then the remainder of the program is built on quicksand. The case study below illustrates ways that the regular classroom teacher can give Jan, the student introduced earlier, a solid grounding in mathematics. Following that are some activities for teaching the beginning mathematical skills. It should be pointed out that techniques and games presented elsewhere in this text can be adapted for mathematics instruction.

Case study 9–1, part 2

Student: Jan School: St. Mary's Separate School
Age: 10 years, 2 months

Reason for referral:
At this time, Jan has not been referred for a complete psycho-educational diagnosis. Both the classroom teacher and the resource-room teacher are monitoring her progress closely, however, and carefully assessing the results of intervention in mathematics.

Major areas of deficit:
After informal testing, it was found that Jan was functioning in mathematics very much at a concrete level. By manipulating real objects she demonstrated some comprehension of place value up to the hundreds and some basic number facts. At the pictorial and abstract levels, however, she met severe difficulties, being unable to translate her concrete knowledge into symbolic forms. At the same time, Jan gave little indication that she understood the basic language of mathematics. She appeared to complete operations by a rote procedure based on phrases such as "take away" and "carry the one."

Responsibilities:
- program to be presented by the classroom teacher within the context of the regular mathematics period
- progress monitored by resource-room teacher and classroom teacher
- attention paid by parents to mathematics at home

Long-range goals:

1. Jan will use concrete objects and pictorial representations to gain a thorough understanding of place value.
2. Jan will practise counting, skip counting, ordinal and cardinal numbers, and numeration and notation up to 100, before instruction on the basic number facts is attempted.
3. Jan will become competent in basic terminology and the uses of operational symbols through the teacher's emphasis on the language of mathematics.

Short-term objectives:

1. When presented with materials, Jan will make tens and hundreds and verbalize the process to make equations.
2. With the groups intact, Jan will represent them pictorially.
3. Jan will read and write numbers to 99.

Objective	**Techniques**	**Materials**
1.	Have Jan make bundles of tens with the sticks as she verbalizes the process. Then have her make hundreds.	Popsicle sticks
2.	Have Jan draw her equations and verbalize the numbers.	Stick bundles, pencil, paper
3.	Show Jan numbers on cards and have her read each number, write it, and represent it concretely and pictorially.	Flash cards

Objective: to establish one-to-one correspondence

a) Make a pattern by placing pegs in a pegboard and have children reproduce the design on their own pegboards.

K to grade 3

b) Beat a drum and have the pupil place a peg in a board for each beat.

K to grade 3

c) Present the pupil with a group of objects, such as dolls, and have him or her complete an action with each object; for example, placing a hat on each doll.

K to grade 3

d) Have children undertake classroom chores such as putting out the pencils.

K to grade 6

Objective: to improve counting skills

a) Use regular classroom materials for counting. Have children count drum beats, beads, and so on.

K to grade 3

b) When teaching young children to count, use the terms "greater than" and "less than" rather than "large" and "small." On a work sheet, for example, a student can circle the group that is "greater than three."

K to grade 3

c) Use a hundred board (figure 9–6). Have the students count and colour every second square (or third, fourth, and so on) and look for patterns. Begin with twos and fives.

Grade 1 and up

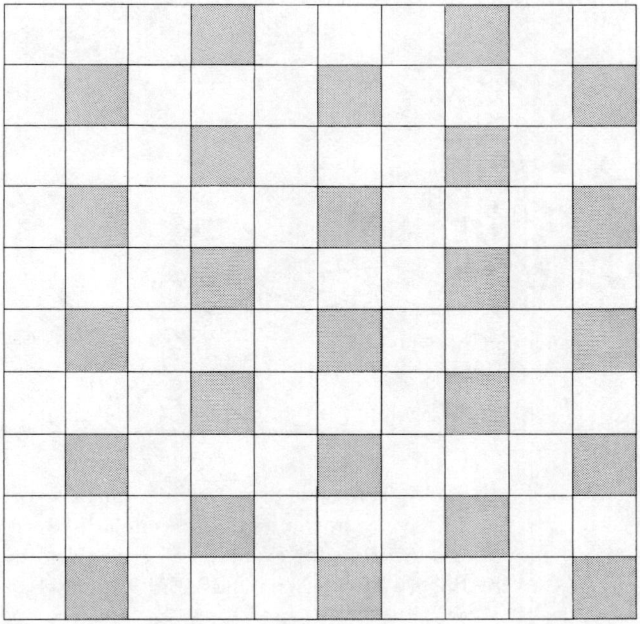

Figure 9–6 Hundred board showing counting by 4s

Objective: to master number facts

a) Use doubling (2 + 2, 3 + 3) as a basis for addition. Zeller (1983) suggests relating doubling to specific objects, such as 2 wheels on a bicycle and 2 + 2 wheels on a car, or 5 + 5 fingers on our hands, and so on.

K to grade 6

b) Have students design a game that uses a specific number in many different ways (Ellis, 1987b).

Grade 3 and up

c) Make counting the basis for learning multiplication facts. Show students the patterns involved in various counts, such as 8, (1)6, (2)4, (3)2, (4)0. If a given counting sequence is written on file folders spread out on the floor, as shown in figure 9–7, a student can walk through the count, stepping on the appropriate file folder each time and therefore using kinesthetic clues as well as the visual and auditory stimuli of seeing and saying the sequence.

In order to illustrate the pattern in a count, the first digit in each two-digit number is omitted from the file folders. The student therefore *sees* the pattern in the units while *saying* the two-digit number. The sequence is written on both flaps of the file folder and the student first walks "up" the count, stepping on only one side of each folder, and then "down" the count, stepping on the other side of each folder.

Grade 3 and up

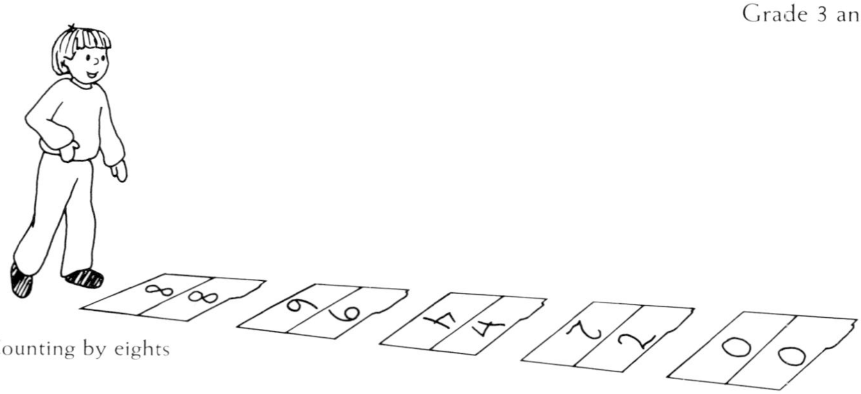

Counting by eighths

Figure 9–7 Walking through counts

d) Teach multiplication facts in order from easiest to most difficult. The tables 5, 10, 9, and 11 have a shorter and more regular pattern than do 3 and 7. Relate the tables to the "real world"; for example, 5 is related to five-minute intervals on a clock, 10 to the fingers on the two hands, and 9 to baseball teams.

Grade 3 and up

e) Use a standard multiplication grid with students who have problems remembering the multiplication facts (see figure 9–8). Begin by marking in all known facts for 0 and 1, and continue counting by marking in new known facts daily or weekly.

Grade 3 and up

f) Some students improve their skills using a tactile mode. Finger-tip mathematics, closely related to the Chisanbop finger calculations, is a human extension of the abacus, based on the decimal system. Each finger represents a number, and various basic number operations can be performed (see Chisanbop, 1978).

Grade 3 and up

	0	1	2	3	4	5	6	7	8	9	10	11	12	13	14	15
0	0	0	0	0	0	0	0	0	0	0	0	0	0	0	0	0
1	0	1	2	3	4	5	6	7	8	9	10	11	12	13	14	15
2	0	2	4	6	8	10										
3	0	3	6													
4	0	4	8													
5	0															
6	0															
7	0															
8	0															
9	0															
10	0															
11	0															
12	0															
13	0															
14	0															
15	0															

Figure 9–8 Multiplication grid

g) Let students play with numbers. They might, for example, make up codes using letters and numbers, assign themselves number names, or make number shapes with their bodies in physical education.

K and up

Objective: to master place value

a) Use Cuisenaire rods. Have children make tens using the unit rods, for example.

K and up

b) Ashlock (1986) suggests using trading games that stress the idea of trading one unit for many units, in order to teach place value. In a dice game, for example, students may throw to earn certain chips: white chips may be worth 1, red chips, 10, and blue chips, 100. Board games can be used in the same way with colour-coded dice that have different assigned values.

Grade 3 and up

Objective: to improve skill with word problems

a) Use problems that do not involve numbers. Ask students, for example, "How could we find the weight of some candy?" or "If we know what a ball costs, how can we find out the cost of many?"

All levels

b) Use pupils' favourite nursery rhymes as the basis for problems. From "The Three Pigs," for example, make up problems with the class about the building materials (Fennell, 1980).

Grades 1 to 5

c) Use a process similar to language experience. Elicit a problem from the class, write it on a large piece of paper and have students use counters or other manipulative materials to solve the problem (Worth, 1987). Then have them read the problem and restate it in their own words.

All levels

d) Dry (1977) suggests that the teacher tell a fantastical story in order to promote a mathematical concept. The teacher should use a student as the central character in the story and sketch pictures on the board to illustrate the action. The story can be outlandish but should include number concepts. Students can then invent their own stories and illustrate them for the class.

K to grade 6

e) Let students work in pairs. One makes up a problem based on everyday activities, and the other solves it.

Grade 3 and up

Objective: to become familiar with the language of mathematics

a) Use visual discrimination activities for students who confuse 6 and 9, 14 and 41, and so on (see chapters 7 and 13 for examples).

K and up

b) On work sheets, have students complete words that are missing letters, such as tri _ _ _ _ _, rect _ _ _ _ _, and so on.

Grades 3 to 8

c) Give students groups of words and ask them to cancel the word in each group that does not belong, such as

triangle circle rectangle banana
plus add divide sum
metre sunshine litre centimetre

Grades 3 to 8

d) To improve students' memory of mathematical language, have them play games such as tic tac toe or bingo. They can, for example, use bingo game boards containing mathematical symbols.

K to grade 4

e) Teach older students to read their mathematics textbooks for information. High school students often consider the text to be an exercise book and ignore its usefulness as a reference book.

Grade 7 and up

Objective: to learn measurement and handling money

a) Have students use restaurant menus to estimate or compute the cost of different meals.

Grade 4 and up

b) Ask students to find different advertisements in the paper for particular items and to compare prices.

Grade 4 and up

c) To introduce geometry and the idea of symmetry, go for a nature walk with the students and collect objects such as leaves. Point out different examples of natural symmetry.

K to grade 6

d) Have students sort collections of everyday objects into circles, squares, rectangles, and so on.

K to grade 4

e) Have students use mathematical instruments such as compasses and protractors during art periods.

Grade 3 and up

f) Have students plan a field trip, sort out the cost, and raise the money.

Grade 4 and up

g) Set students many tasks involving measurement in a familiar context, such as reading a thermometer or estimating and measuring the width of the classroom.

All levels

h) Have students time certain activities, such as the length of time it takes to walk to school.

K to grade 6

i) Mandell and Gold (1984) suggest that cards such as those shown in figure 9–9 help students to understand comparative shopping.

Grade 5 and up

j) Use recipes in the classroom to teach liquid measurement.

K to grade 6

k) Allow students to set alarm clocks to coincide with school bells or special events.

K to grade 6

Purchase card	Pick from		
Bread	\$1.00	2 for \$1.75	3 for \$2.50
Hamburger	\$4.75 1 kg	\$9.00 2 kg	\$20.00 5 kg

Figure 9–9

Source: Adapted from Mandell & Gold, 1974, p. 358.

Too often, teachers see mathematics instruction as a chore, a rather dull curricular area in which students proceed through a set of basic facts and processes. When instruction is approached with creativity, however, mathematics can be stimulating for all students and for their teachers. With the appropriate use of concrete materials, computer programs, and so on, mathematics instruction can be directed toward students' individual abilities without great alterations in the program. Imaginative instruction need not be reserved for the content and creative areas, the subjects of the next chapter.

10 *Teaching content areas and creative subjects*

Dear Reader,

As its title suggests, this chapter deals with the range of subjects that gather under the two headings of content areas and creative subjects. I propose to discuss exceptionality and the science curriculum specifically, as one element of the content areas. Each year thousands of children are barred from participation in science because of their handicaps. Myths have been perpetuated that aggravate the situation and deny help to those who are most in need: the supposed difficulty of science, the increased likelihood of injury and failure, the potential for equipment breakage, the perceived need for exceptional children to spend time learning basic skills rather than science, the necessity for specialized equipment, and for even more specialized teacher training (Thompson, 1980). The objections are soon overcome, however, once these students are allowed access to what can be an important area of study for them, when they are provided with hands-on activities, simple and inexpensive materials, and responsive teaching. Such experiences can often compensate for other deprivations, enhance reading and communication skills, and enable special students to enjoy the study of science.

Accepting special learners into science programs does involve making accommodations within ordinary classrooms. Curricular modifications in science range from slight changes, such as a slower pace of learning, longer periods of time for activities and practice, linking of classroom experiences to real-life experiences, and interaction in small groups, to a totally new science curriculum.

Suggestions on how to accomplish modifications are far fewer for intellectually handicapped than for physically handicapped students, even though the first category far outnumbers the second. The dearth of help in the literature, and the lack of science curricula and materials designed specifically for special students will not, however, be a deterrent to teachers who are already aware of the great potential for learning inherent in science instruction. Science teaching lends itself to adaptation for a diversity of students, because it encompasses numerous approaches that awaken curiosity and the desire for understanding. These involve students in meaningful activities, and are based on the premise that thinking and learning result from actions rather than from words. At all levels, the help given to special learners will also benefit other pupils in the classroom, many of whom learn well from the same concrete experiences and guidance.

Teachers will find many of the tested curricular materials of the 1960s and 1970s helpful. These units are useful for group activities, science projects, and learning centres. Some of the more recent textbook series also provide both a source and a sequence of activities, and help to build concepts gradually. I have used units from a textbook series very successfully with intellectually handicapped children by focussing on the activities and drawing the concepts from the students' experience over a number of related investigations. Interest has been extremely high, and the students' obvious feelings of achievement, enjoyment, and success were very gratifying to witness. When children, through repeated experiences, see a relationship between concepts, they have made a new, exciting, and rewarding discovery.

Successful science experiences begin by students actively observing and manipulating phenomena. Materials and activities should be familiar, concrete, and relevant to everyday living. Such experiences lead to improved communicative, social, motor, and cognitive skills, aesthetic appreciation and interests, and greater ability to solve problems.

As educators, we must try to ensure that what exceptional students learn in science is enjoyable enough to encourage them to keep on exploring; comprehensive enough to enable them to understand and participate in daily activities; practical enough to apply to the problems that they will encounter in the future; and satisfying enough to allow them to appreciate the beauty of the world around them. When these goals are realized, then our science teaching may be deemed successful.

Ruby L. Gough, Ed.D.
Department of Curriculum and Instruction
Memorial University of Newfoundland

The academic part of school learning, especially in the early grades, concentrates on skills in language arts and arithmetic. Given their academic importance, these subjects are often grouped together as the core curriculum (see chapters 7 to 9). Complementing the *core curriculum* are social studies, science, career education, and vocational education, traditionally referred to as the *content areas*. Creative arts and physical education form the third component of school instruction, often called the *creative areas*. This chapter draws together those subjects outside the core curriculum and discusses their relevance for special learners.

In many instances, no curricula exist for exceptional students in the mainstream, and this is especially true for the content and creative subjects. Yet although the content areas present many difficulties for exceptional learners, they can still benefit from these subjects at their own levels, and many adaptations are possible to accommodate their needs. The resulting orientation of the content areas toward exploration, experimentation, and tangible experiences, and away from textbook instruction, is of substantial benefit to all students. Because intellectual skills are by nature interrelated and based on content, social studies, career education, and science are highly effective vehicles for learning. They represent many disciplines and many modes of inquiry, and they provide a far-reaching context in which to develop various combinations and overlapping patterns of intellectual skills.

The arts, however, are equally versatile. They are accessible sources of pleasure because they can be enjoyed at many levels of sophistication. It is only recently that the arts have been recognized as a potent force for learning (Appell, 1979). There has been limited but consistent support in educational literature for the idea of using the arts to improve specific areas of exceptional students' functioning, to motivate learning, and to teach discipline (Rockefeller, 1977). Special educators are coming to view the arts as extremely beneficial, socially and educationally, for children with physical, mental, emotional, and sensory limitations (Behr, Snyder, & Clopton, 1978; Jennings, 1978; Shaw & Stevens, 1979).

The main objectives of this chapter are to

- discuss some useful approaches to teaching content areas to exceptional students
- stress the need for, and the concepts involved in, career education for all students, exceptional and otherwise
- provide an overview of the principles of vocational education and work experience as they apply to exceptional learners
- illustrate, by discussing various instructional approaches, how creative arts can enhance special learners' academic and social functioning
- discuss approaches to teaching physical education to mildly handicapped students

Content subjects within the school curriculum

Integration often begins with non-academic subjects such as music and art. Certainly, the creative, co-operative, non-competitive nature of these areas is particularly apt for exceptional learners. But special learners are often integrated in the content areas as well, on the assumption that they will achieve success more easily here than in reading or mathematics. In reality, the strong conceptual base and ability to generalize needed in the content areas, especially social studies, make them a sphere in which special students may rapidly flounder. Nevertheless, as Gough points out in the letter that opens this chapter, content subjects can provide versatile, exciting, and valuable learning experiences for exceptional learners.

Conceptual understanding, the way to organize and perceive order in the world, often proves difficult for exceptional students. They may be delayed, for example, in developing concepts of time and space, which are necessary for appreciating at least some of the ideas of social studies. They may have deficits in the ability to see cause and effect, which is necessary for science. It is therefore especially important to provide exceptional learners with many examples to illustrate what concepts are and are not, as well as a great deal of concrete and "hands-on" activity. Concept development is readdressed in chapter 13.

Content subjects require exceptional students to absorb information by the traditional methods, such as reading textbooks and taking notes from lectures, although their reading levels are often far below those of many content area textbooks. Indeed, a recent appraisal of elementary and secondary texts (Fitzgerald, 1979) found that not only were the reading levels in high school texts far too advanced for most students, but the general tenor of the material lacked realism. While authors discussed a tangle of social problems, they were simplistically sanguine about the future. Teachers should determine the readability of materials by gauging whether or not the vocabulary, sentence structure, and sentence length are commensurate with students' reading levels. They should also assess the content level to see if the material is overloaded with concepts, or if the concepts are vague or abstract. As well, the organization of the material must clearly emphasize the main ideas and give sufficient examples. Finally, materials should possess interest and motivational appeal (Epanchin & Dickens, 1983).

When teaching particular skills in the content areas, teachers must endeavour to circumvent reading deficits. They may teach key vocabulary prior to lectures and demonstrations, or tape-record chapters of textbooks to provide another learning modality. In addition, it is crucial to give the subject matter as much immediacy and relevance as possible in relation to the students' ongoing daily activities. Newspapers are an asset here. They generally fit in with any school's content area program, and provide a constant, inexpensive, and easily available source of information about events. Newspapers also accommodate a wide range of reading abilities.

Instruction in the content areas must move far from lecture formats to avoid ensnaring students in simple reiteration of facts. For special learners, instruction should encourage flexibility and exploration rather than passive reception of facts. Teachers will find it helpful to use an inquiry, or discovery, method for both social studies and science. A simplified example of inquiry is presented within the model given in figure 10–1. Inquiry is based on questions that the students themselves have asked, such as "How does an airplane fly?" or "How does the heart work?" The teacher then asks leading questions that prompt the students to come up with various alternatives to answer the problem. Gradually, the teacher expands students' own statements to include a new concept. As the model shows, the students then collect further information about the topic, synthesize it, and present it, a process that can take up to three weeks. Student questions that are answered by this method are dealt with as the topic arises, although the teacher will guide inquiry to keep within the curriculum. Because the basic inquiry model is quite a free process, it is most appropriate for older students.

Guided discovery is similar to the inquiry method but is more closely guided by the teacher and is therefore suitable for younger students. As outlined by Gallagher (1975, pp. 215–16), the process begins with a general principle, provided by the teacher, who then constructs examples to illustrate different elements of the concept. The teacher then presents the students with relevant problems to solve. Rather than simply reiterating the concept, however, which can short-circuit the process of comprehension, the students sort and collate information in their own minds first. They might, for example, solve the problem through a project, or within a group discussion. Guided discovery can be applied over the length of the unit, or in a single lesson.

"Brainstorming" should become a part of discovery and learning in the context areas for all students because the sessions stimulate greater fluency of ideas. Students examine a particular problem and are invited to make suggestions. Although the technique has been advocated primarily for gifted youngsters, it is also useful for low achievers because it teaches them the importance of coming up with as many solutions as possible before making a judgment about something. Gallagher (1975) has suggested that no criticisms should be allowed in brainstorming sessions. The more ideas generated, the better; integrating and combining ideas should be encouraged. Teachers evaluate the session and the students only after all the ideas have been presented.

Hands-on work with group projects and in the learning centre also proves effective in the content areas. Group and co-operative learning help students to acquire concepts and information, while a variety of activities in the learning centre allows them to progress at their own rates.

Bachor and Crealock (1986) point out that it may be necessary to teach the students how to initiate projects, complete them, and submit them on time. Special students often require guidance selecting a topic within their interests and abilities, and will almost certainly need assistance locating, collecting, recording, and organizing information. Teachers may also have to help them select the most suitable format in which to present the project. Finally, the project must be subjected to some type of evaluative procedure. Self-evaluation is a vital part of the process and students should be shown appropriate methods.

Students who have difficulty studying because their notes are untidy or disorganized will need special help in outlining, taking notes, and organizing their notebooks. Precise methods of organization may be necessary, such as using a different colour for each notebook, starting each notebook with a table of contents, numbering and titling each page and each note, and labelling all maps, pictures, and graphs carefully (adapted from Bachor & Crealock, 1986). To help students develop consistency when they label material, give them simply worded lists of written directions to which they can refer. For maps, for example, give pupils the following list:

1. Print the title of your map.
2. Indicate the compass direction north.
3. Use a key or legend.
4. Finish the map in ink or crayons.
5. Only use print to label your map.
6. Use map symbols when they are needed.
7. Underline all titles with a ruler.

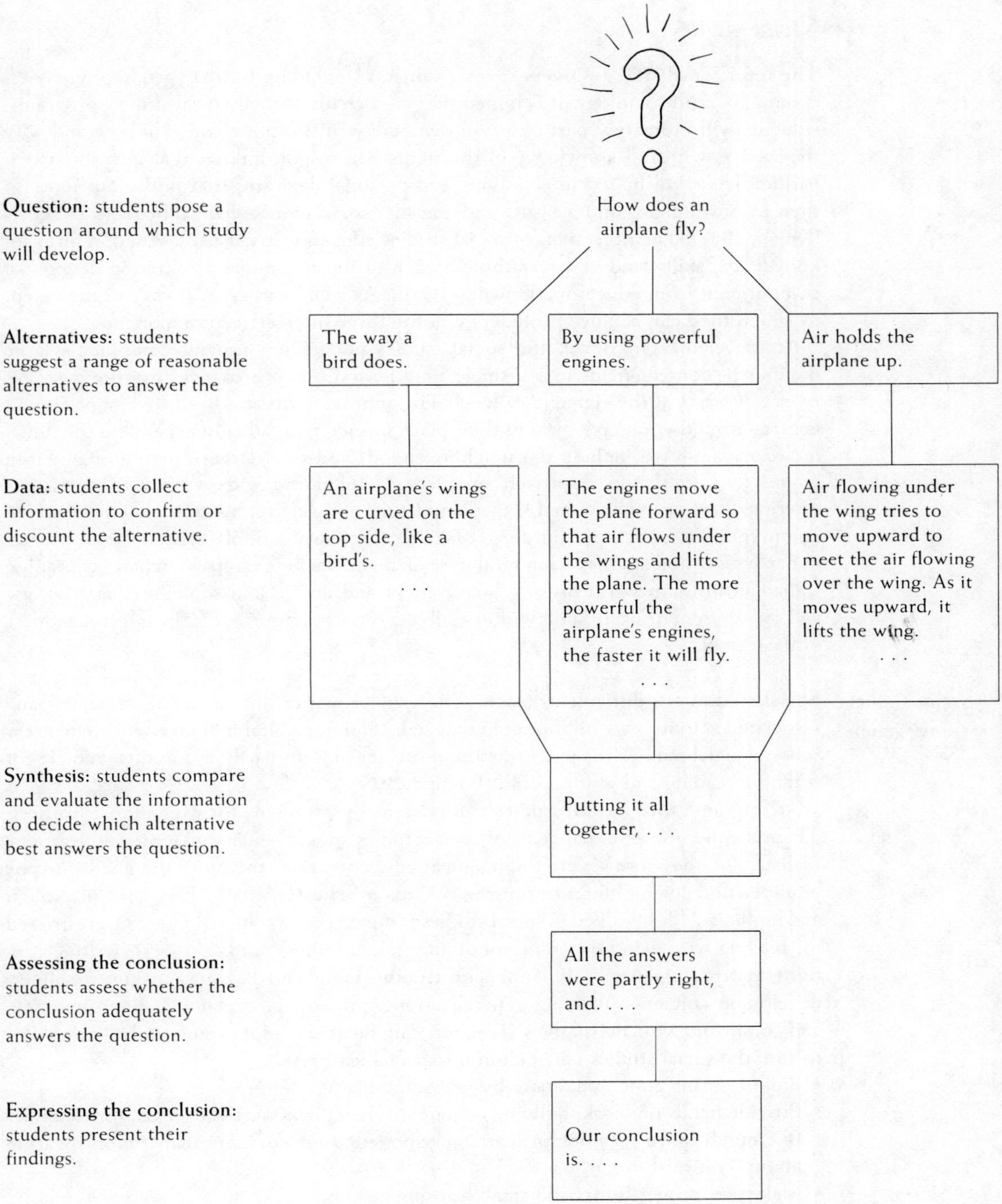

Figure 10–1 Basic inquiry model

Source: Adapted from Ontario, Ministry of Education, 1978.

Social studies

The term social studies covers several subjects, including history, geography, civics, economics, and sociology. It is hoped that, as a result of their social studies programs, students will ultimately participate in democratic institutions knowing how and why they work, with full knowledge of the rights and responsibilities that govern participation. They will be led to economic and personal decisions that both contribute to their own well-being and pleasure and consider social and ecological benefits and costs (Kniep, 1986). The objectives of social studies education are usually stated in terms of knowledge, skills, and values, although each of these commands differing degrees of commitment from educators (Downey, 1986). As well, learners will vary in the extent to which they can achieve proficiency in the three interrelated components.

At the elementary level, the social studies curriculum usually combines a large number of content fields into a single time period. Most provinces use the *expanding horizons approach* at the elementary level. The approach, first outlined by Hanna (1963), centres around young people and their place in society, gradually expanding the initial focus on family to include the neighbourhood, and then larger communities. From grades four to six the approach broadens to include a wide variety of curricular offerings, from provincial and Canadian history and geography, to the study of world communities (Council of Ministers, 1982). In secondary schools, students take courses in particular subject areas. Common core elements include courses such as geography, Canadian history, world history, government and civics, and sometimes psychology and sociology. The list of skills within a subject is not as important as the interrelatedness of those skills.

Social studies instruction

Social studies are difficult to teach. The subject matter, instructional strategies, and associated activities are all too often flat, stale, and unprofitable. Indeed, in elementary school, social studies receive little attention, serving primarily as another vehicle for teaching reading and writing skills (Ponder, 1979).

At the same time, social studies can pose many problems for exceptional learners. Theoretically, the essential goals of social studies should remain intact for all learners; realistically, the more severe the handicapping condition, the more the goals must be modified and given different priorities (Ochoa & Schuster, 1980). The range of explicit and implicit skills involved in social studies is huge. They include, but are not restricted to, reading, reviewing, listening, outlining, taking notes, doing projects, writing captions, interpreting maps, tabulating, constructing tables and diagrams, making timelines, developing concepts, forming generalizations, predicting, explaining, hypothesizing, and coming up with alternatives. Teachers can, however, adopt some general principles to ease the social studies curriculum for special learners:

- Build a strong conceptual base by providing many examples.
- Provide hands-on work. Building a model of the railway across Canada, for example, is a much more meaningful learning experience for students than simply hearing about westward expansion.
- Make use of peer tutors and small learning groups.
- Use the learning centre for small-group projects.
- Dramatize concepts.

- Use visual and auditory communication as much as possible and give students extended opportunities to manipulate objects.
- Explain all new vocabulary and relate it to the lesson content.
- Use simple statements delivered in an organized fashion.
- Repeat concepts.
- Assess the readability levels of all texts.
- Provide an outline of main points for secondary students.
- Use instructional packages to improve specific skills and convey information (see chapter 5).

It is not really possible to isolate one part of the conceptual structure of social studies as it is in science or mathematics. The concepts serve as organizing threads that run through the grades, tying the data together. The concepts of time and space, for example, are integral to social studies but are difficult for many exceptional students to grasp. These children cannot understand the notion of past centuries and events until they have developed a stable sense of time. The past may have little meaning for them except as a collection of stories and unrelated events, and they cannot discriminate between what happened five days ago and what happened five hundred years ago. Even non-handicapped children experience problems developing temporal concepts. Pratt (1983) discussed a study in which half of the thirteen year olds surveyed believed that putting the clocks forward in the spring made them older.

The teacher must therefore develop strategies to help exceptional children understand how people, places, and things are related in space and time. The younger and more handicapped the learners, or the more unfamiliar the subject, the greater the need for students to interact with concrete examples of instructional sequences. Conceptual understanding is built on repeated contact with a variety of real people, places, and events (Kniep, 1986). One successful method to develop a sense of the passage of time, for example, is to have the students collect old photographs from home and mount them on a bulletin board display. The students will then be able to trace changes in clothing, automobiles, and lifestyles visually.

While mildly handicapped students encounter difficulty with the conceptual aspects of social studies, it is an area in which many gifted students shine. They are adept at evaluating facts and arguments critically; they readily recognize relationships and comprehend meanings; and they can therefore arrive at solutions through a process of reasoning. Many of these youngsters are fascinated by historical events and figures, and show a complex appreciation of history.

Social studies provide all students with extensive opportunities to develop skills in reading, writing, language, research, memorization, study, and critical thinking. Through committee work, role playing, creative dramatics, classroom visitors, classroom discussions, and informal interviews, students develop social and citizenship skills. It is also useful to integrate social studies content with art, music, literature, science, mathematics, and environmental studies to help students make connections between their own world and the wider community.

Social studies may examine private as well as cultural values. Questions about how to treat other human beings are as essential as questions about the principles of democratic governance (Downey, 1986), and values should be woven into every level of education. This is especially true where exceptional students are involved, and some of the simulations and activities discussed in chapter 6—such as classroom meetings—are relevant in this context.

Another useful function of social studies is to introduce research skills to handicapped pupils. In an oral history project on Canadian immigration, for example, pupils were asked to interview five individuals, using a list of questions constructed by the teacher. Respondents were asked, "When did you come to Canada?" "Why did you come to Canada?" "Who came with you?" and "How different do you find Canada?" Pupils analysed the collected information and chose one country of origin to study in encyclopedias, atlases, newspapers, and so on. They then presented the project, including a paragraph on their feelings about living in the country surveyed (Winzer, 1982).

Within a modified social studies curriculum, learning objectives must reflect concern for the student's eventual place in the community. Students may find map reading important, for example, in terms of their local environment. To learn the relevant skills, they need experience with concrete props, such as three-dimensional models of familiar buildings. In general, activities need to be varied to account for short attention spans and should include both physical and social involvement, such as role playing and simulations. Both didactic and inquiry teaching models are necessary.

Science✧

There has been a strong move in recent decades to make substantial changes in both the content and the process of science instruction for elementary and secondary students, particularly those designated as gifted. Emphasis has moved from "chalk and talk" teaching to exploration and discovery.

To many curriculum specialists, science is the ideal area around which to develop a total curriculum: it integrates mathematics, movement education, health, nutrition, writing, and aesthetic expression ("Early childhood," 1979). Science is a mode of inquiry, rather than a set of conclusions, used to discover new ideas and systems. Science activities spill over easily into social studies, music, and art, and provide an interesting meaningful experiential base for the language arts.

Environmental studies are also an essential part of the science program, as they concern our place in the natural order of things. The success of environmental activities depends in large measure on the individual teacher's enthusiasm for developing activities that focus on the particular skills and talents of each pupil. In the lower grades, outdoor trips are helpful in providing multisensory experiences.

Preschool children have a natural inclination to explore their environment, and abundant early science experiences can take advantage of their intrinsic interest in themselves and the world around them. These experiences, guided by the teacher, initiate the formation of scientific concepts, and the development of both language and logical thinking.

✧The science sections of this chapter were written by Ruby L. Gough, Ed. D., Department of Curriculum and Instruction, Memorial University of Newfoundland.

It is difficult to understand why science has seldom been included in curricular planning for handicapped children, considering its relevance to everyday living, the concrete nature of scientific experiences, and the innate interest of many topics. Science is vital if we are to teach special learners about the importance of life and about human welfare. Furthermore, science curricula that meet the needs of special students can provide excellent learning experiences for regular students as well. Yet a survey of past and current curriculum guides reveals that most handicapped children, whether in special settings or in public schools, receive little science. What they do learn in science is inadequate to prepare them either for a fuller life or for science-related careers. A general insecurity with the subject matter common among teachers of the early grades aggravates the problem (McNeil, 1981), and the likelihood of exposure to science at the secondary levels is correspondingly low because few high-quality science courses are offered to special learners.

The overriding goal of science education for everyone, exceptional and non-exceptional, is to develop *scientific literacy*. Scientific literacy involves having some knowledge of the concepts and investigative methods of science, and the ability to apply that knowledge to science-related problems affecting human beings and the environment. Harris (1979) has identified four groups of goals, all of which relate to this long-range aim:

- *Personal needs:* Students need to learn about self, health, growth, and change, and to become critical consumers capable of making rational decisions.
- *Societal issues:* Students must recognize how science and technology have changed their lives and be able to use scientific processes to solve problems.
- *Academic education:* Students should develop skills and learn concepts from a variety of topics spanning the physical, life, and earth sciences.
- *Career education:* Students need to recognize that scientific careers are acceptable for both sexes and for handicapped people, and that the sciences allow scope for human qualities.

These goals are broad and must be translated into realizable objectives with appropriate methods and materials for the different levels of schooling. Curricular specialists take into consideration the nature of the discipline and its potential as a vehicle for learning when they establish goals and objectives. In any so-called normal group of students tremendous social, emotional, intellectual, and physical differences will exist to which the instructional plan must adapt.

Handicapped students need meaningful experiences to help them to overcome the limitations that interfere with their ability to learn science. Yet all too often science has been taught as a body of knowledge and all its other dimensions have been disregarded. The scientific enterprise involves investigative methods, co-operation, skill development, and attitudes that stimulate the quest for knowledge, all of which are as important as the knowledge itself. Cognitive, affective, psychomotor, and social goals can form the basis for curricular decisions that not only broaden exceptional and non-exceptional children's exposure to science but also constitute exciting starting points for integration with other areas of the curriculum.

Children learn to observe with all of their senses: they learn the principles of classification as they sort objects gathered on a field trip as living or non-living; they learn about measurement by choosing appropriate ways to measure short, long, heavy, light, fat, thin, wide, or narrow objects. They develop motor skills as they manipulate materials, use magnets and microscopes, and learn to handle a thermometer and a balance. Their communicative skills grow with the need to record observations and make predictions from actual findings in the course of investigations. Children who have mastered these basic processes are tempted, by their need to know, into higher thought levels as they try to develop ways to answer questions and problems. The concept of a "fair test" in elementary school is not very different from the controlled experiment in secondary school, and neither are the outcomes for children's learning. Finally, scientific study develops open-mindedness, scepticism, and willingness to change one's mind as new evidence comes to light.

Probably the most important aspect of science education is that it provides students with opportunities for immediate success in small things, which inspires the will to try again, to become involved in further explorations. The teacher's role is to stimulate and maintain interest and to supply the appropriate guidance and feedback.

Science instruction

Science education encompasses many methods. Exposition can be used to introduce a lesson, to demonstrate an activity, or for review. It is directed by the teacher, and the students only interact at certain points during the discussion. The more new learning is linked to the familiar, the more meaningful it becomes. Exposition with interaction is of course the preferred method of instruction. To maintain interest, intersperse any verbal presentation with audiovisual components, and restrict the length of any verbal introduction for young children. A demonstration, using the actual materials the students will use, is an effective expository approach.

At the other end of the instructional continuum is free inquiry, in which students pursue their own questions and solve problems. The teacher acts as a resource and supplies feedback. In its true format, free inquiry is a very advanced mental strategy requiring formal thought.

Current science teaching combines the best of both extremes and suggests that students learn science well through guided discovery. The teacher guides students who are actively involved in their own learning. Guided discovery is intended to teach students how to learn, as they discover knowledge that is uniquely their own. The method develops scientific literacy; it shows students a way to approach problems that is close to the nature of science. Exceptional students tend to retain material and build their own self-concepts through guided discovery.

Science programs also incorporate inquiry training models well. Scientific inquiry attempts to teach students to analyse the relationship between cause and effect. They learn to deal with questions that give rise to a number of plausible alternatives, which must be evaluated and ranked. To incorporate the inquiry method into science instruction, present students with science material from the world around them and encourage them to experiment. They may, in this way, explore many basic concepts from botany, biology, physics, chemistry, and astronomy.

The science curriculum can be enriched by learning centres that contain activities, resources, and equipment. The teacher may introduce activities with the group and then assign individuals to work in the learning centre. For groups, it may be more appropriate to use a multilevel approach than to separate students of differing abilities. The teacher can, for example, set up laboratory stations and materials for groups of approximately four students and assign students randomly to each group. They can then experiment with such activities as pulleys, magnets, electrical circuits, growing plants, and the life cycles of animals.

In general, science instruction for special learners can be improved if teachers follow some basic guidelines:

- Use visual aids and inquiry techniques to minimize the need for reading skills.
- Use functional vocabulary, and avoid technical terms unless they are useful to the student. Reinforce new vocabulary by labelling actual objects in the science interest centre and frequently repeating necessary terms.
- Keep tasks brief and uncomplicated, proceeding from the known to the unknown and linking the familiar with the unfamiliar. Supplement directions with pictures and print.
- Encourage active involvement by using activities for individuals or small groups. Vicarious experiences such as watching an experiment are no substitute for students actually being involved in the activity.
- Give practice with the processes of science: observing with all the senses, classifying and quantifying materials, communicating, and making inferences and predictions.
- Relate classroom science to the real world.
- Plan a large number of related experiences over a long period of time to teach concepts important in the students' daily lives. Allow plenty of opportunity for students to apply and to reinforce what they have learned.
- Encourage students to demonstrate aspects of their understanding. They can often show something before they can verbalize it.
- Ask questions that demand simple recall, to enable students to respond successfully.
- Allow plenty of practice with manipulative skills: using a balance, making an electrical circuit, or using measuring devices, for example. Psychomotor skills are a necessary accompaniment to science activities.
- Develop teaching from students' natural curiosity: plan experiences around their questions or spontaneous additions to the science interest table (perhaps a shell or a rock picked up on the way to school).
- Incorporate a variety of interesting experiences that can result in overlearning and repetition.
- If visually impaired students are in the group, ensure that they have opportunities for exploration without the use of sight. Increase the repertoire of sensory activities: grab bags for identifying objects by touch, or shells to sort by shape, for example. Include multisensory activities such as making popcorn or cookies, and encourage observation and precise description of changes in texture, taste, smell, and sound.
- For visually impaired students, tape-record instructions, using already familiar terms. At times, have other students record the directions to give everyone the feeling of participation.
- If hearing-impaired students are in the group, provide them with an outline before the class begins, and use plenty of non-verbal feedback.
- Remember that the overall aim is to develop a cycle of success through interest and achievement in science.

Career education

Canada has been, and will continue to be, a work-centred society. The perceived worth of individuals is often based on their ability to hold remunerative employment and to contribute to society at large. Making a wise career choice is, or should be, a topic of concern for all young people. It certainly is for their educators, and career education is attracting increasing attention. Although schools cannot decide students' futures, they can present them with viable career alternatives.

Career education was conceptualized in the 1970s as an educational reform to counter social problems. Essentially, career education tries to give respectability to all jobs. The term "career" encompasses an individual's role not just as a producer or worker but as a learner, consumer, citizen, family member, and socio-political human being (Gordon, 1973).

Career education involves communication among students, teachers, parents, and the community. Students explore career options, learn to make decisions, and develop relevant skills. It is hoped that they will also adopt less stereotypical views of women and men at work, and will aspire to less traditional roles. Additionally, it is hoped that as adults they will practise less discrimination in hiring and supervising, and in their attitudes toward other people's career choices (Labour Canada, 1986).

Because the field of career education is relatively new, it has no fixed definition or delivery model. It can be defined as an opportunity to provide learners with direct work experiences, or as a method to involve individuals more productively in the work force. Others see it as a total effort by the school and the community to help all people become familiar with the values of a work-oriented society (McNeil, 1981). This text holds the latter view. Through career education, students discover the relationship between work values and other life roles. Career education provides students with information about specific careers, in an academic context. It is comprehensive in nature, goes right through school (see table 10–1), uses a non-categorical approach, and is closely related to all areas of the curriculum (Jesser, 1984). Instructional materials are chosen that are personally relevant to the students' career interests. If a suitable career education curriculum is not available, however, a school may adopt an **infusion method**, which maintains the basic curriculum but supplements it with activities and units related to career education (Coleman, 1986).

Because of its social relevance and broad application, career education has garnered strong support (e.g. Brolin, 1978; McNeil, 1981). It applies to exceptional students in the same way as it does to their peers; goals are similar for all students, and any differences are a function of individual needs. Yet in a sense career education has always been a dominant strain in education for handicapped children. Special educators have long emphasized the need to prepare exceptional students to lead productive, personally satisfying adult lives. Exceptional students should learn that all work is valuable and develop a focus realistically guided by their own wishes and limitations.

Career education for special learners may require some extra modifications and considerations, and instruction must involve individualized goals. As students grow older, they will need to develop appropriate expectations about the world of work. Career education at the secondary level should help students to choose careers and prepare them for various types of occupations (Faas, 1980).

Table 10–1 Scope and sequence chart for career education

Grades	Content	Concepts
K to 3	Develops occupational awareness with information about groups of occupations representing the entire world of work.	People have many different kinds of careers. Every occupation contributes to society. Every person can have a meaningful career.
4 to 6	Extends occupational awareness to students' own aptitudes and abilities.	Careers require different knowledge, skills, abilities, and attitudes. Individuals develop their own ways of working.
7 to 9	Explores careers, examining several broad occupational categories, and then groups within those categories.	Explores the relationship between personal characteristics and job requirements. Develops students' ability to communicate, use numbers, interact with other people, and use skills related to a field of interest. Develops positive work attitudes.
10 to 12	Explores a few career groups in depth. Develops entry level skills or specialization in one occupational area by offering prerequisites for further education.	Adds specificity to the concepts introduced in junior high school. Introduces formal knowledge of the value of work and a personal set of work values. Develops saleable skills. Teaches students where to acquire additional training and experience.
Post-secondary	Employment and further training	

Gifted and talented students also need career education, to strengthen their motivation to pursue further education. Because they possess many talents and interests, choosing a career is often complicated. Gifted students hold high expectations, which may ultimately restrict their choices. Although they often need to make an early commitment, as many of them will enter careers that require lengthy training, it should be pointed out that vocational testing is less reliable for gifted students because of their tendency to change career choices often (Willings, 1983). The testing only reveals vocational propensities at a particular juncture.

Integrated with other subject areas, career education constitutes an intrinsic component of the curriculum throughout school life. Very young children, for example, may collect hats worn in certain occupations and then discuss the different jobs. Older students can read the classified advertisements to learn about qualifications, opportunities, and training, or watch the way that job roles are depicted on television and discuss these in class. Reading newspapers will also teach students about social problems, such as day care, that involve certain occupations. Later, they can explore different occupational areas on field trips and by talking to people in those professions.

Vocational training

Success depends not only on academic training but on training for good work habits, appropriate occupational behaviour, independent living skills, technical skills, and knowledge. Career education and vocational training both accept the idea that schools should prepare students to participate in the broader society, but vocational education is a narrower field than career education, since it is designed to impart specific skills, and concentrates on the need for a productive work force. Although different in scope, the two are interwoven within the curriculum (Mori, 1979).

Unlike career education, however, vocational education typically begins in high school. It increases an individual's work options and relates general education to work. Organized educational programs equip the trainees with entry level job skills, including initiative, persistence, and perseverance, the ability to work with others and under pressure, to evaluate oneself, and to use judgement in the care of materials and property.

Vocational education usually follows certain steps. The student acquires some vocational experience in shop; he or she then evaluates vocational preferences, and receives specific vocational training, placement, and follow-up. An individual's abilities and attitudes can be assessed beforehand, using measures such as inventories, written tests, or work samples. The AAMD Becker Reading Free Vocational Interest Inventory (Becker, 1975), provides scores on nineteen different occupations and applies especially to students with low reading levels. The individual must choose from among sets of pictures the one that shows the activity he or she would most like to do. The Social and Prevocational Information Battery (Halpern, Raffeld, Irvin, & Link, 1975) looks at purchasing, budgeting, and job search skills, home management, health care, hygiene and grooming, and functional signs such as "stop," "men," "women," and so on. The Strong–Campbell Interest Inventory (Campbell, 1974) assesses interest in school and leisure activities, occupational preferences, and personality characteristics.

Vocational education has much to offer handicapped learners in terms of training for semi-skilled and unskilled occupations (Sitlington, 1981). It is not enough to teach mentally retarded students social and living skills unrelated to work and hope that they will find jobs successfully (Reiter & Levi, 1980).

The effective delivery of vocational instruction and related services to handicapped students is a matter of great interest in current educational practice. Some handicapped students will require only minor adaptations in the regular curriculum; others will need individual programs and additional work experiences. The specific approach will depend upon the instructional area, the characteristics of the trainee, and the resources available in the school and community. An appropriate program builds on students strengths and abilities while allowing them to meet particular training requirements. It also addresses those social differences that interfere with job performance and acceptability to an employer. Exceptional students require skills in locating, securing, and retaining employment. They are in particular need of good work habits and motivation (Stewart, 1977), dependability, honesty, and the ability to stay on task and co-operate with fellow workers. Mildly handicapped workers also require sufficient language skills to communicate effectively (Fiester & Giambra, 1972).

Finally, it should be noted that mildly handicapped adults are prone to be taken advantage of financially, socially, and sexually. They need assertiveness training, through role playing and other techniques, to be able to defend their wishes and judgment (Bregman, 1984).

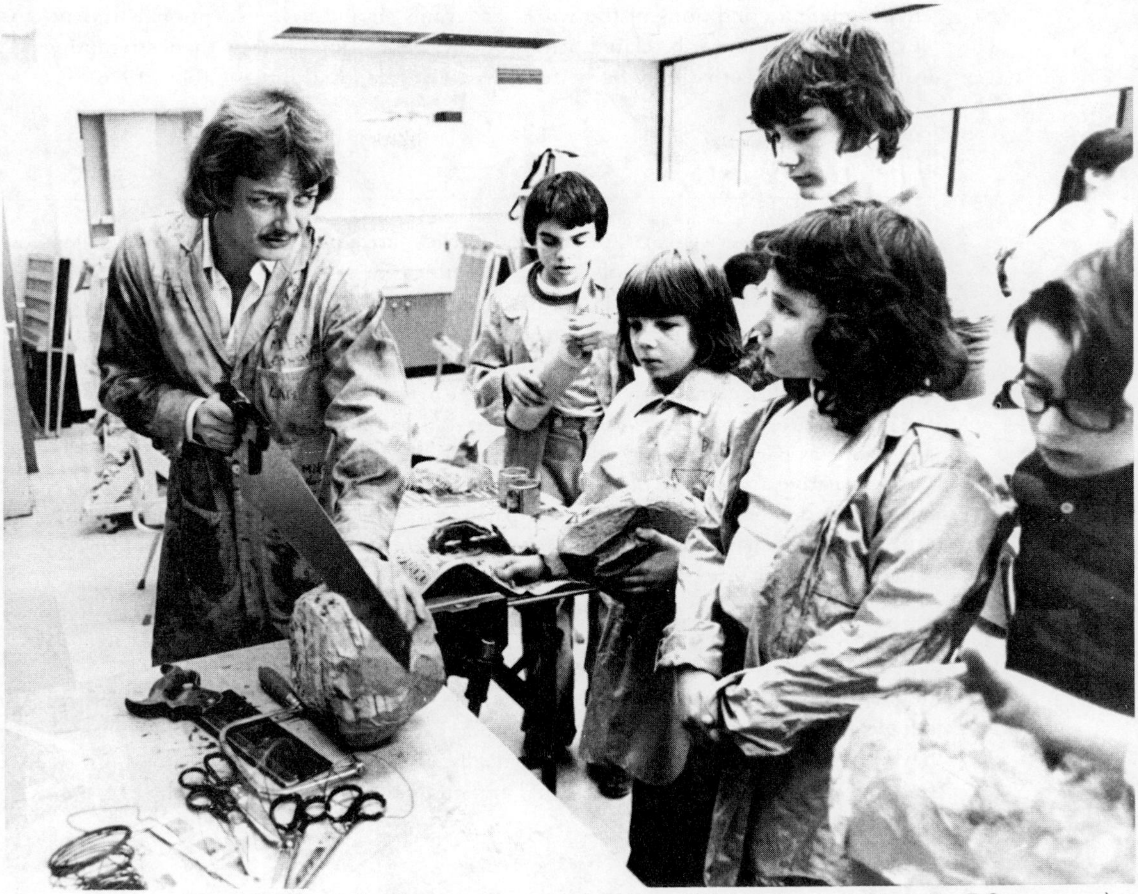

Both boys and girls enjoy vocational subjects. (Graham Bezant, Morse St. P.S. #7, 1979)

Work–study programs

Work–study programs are the practical component of vocational education. Their underlying philosophy states that education should provide a program appropriate to students' abilities, instead of forcing them to adapt to the traditional high school program. Work–study programs co-ordinate the activities of the classroom with actual, on-the-job training. Sequential, planned work experiences help students to learn acceptable work standards, and although students continue to receive basic academic instruction, many classroom experiences are geared to job-related skills. Students discover the meaning and value of employment and begin to understand the relationship between education and the wider world. They also become acquainted with their own strengths, abilities, and interests.

Work–study programs have increased tremendously in both number and variety, although they all generally include in-school work experience, community work experience, and finally, on-the-job training. Before a student receives a job placement, his or her skills and interests are matched to the requirements, physical demands, and environmental conditions of the work. Programs should help exceptional students to develop appropriate job-related attitudes and behaviours, rather than attempting to instill salable skills that may be better learned on the job (Hutt & Gibby, 1976).

The creative arts

The creative arts—visual arts, drama, and music—are a part of arts education, a general term for using the arts in schools, either as a subject or as a method of teaching (Council of Ministers, 1983). They fulfill a basic need to express oneself through, and receive stimulus from, creative media and are therefore important for all students. Elementary schools use either specialists or generalist classroom teachers to teach the arts, depending on the province. In secondary settings, the arts are usually offered as options within the general program. It is possible, however, to include drama in the English curriculum and dance as part of physical education (Council of Ministers, 1983).

The creative arts can be of immense value to exceptional youngsters, both gifted and handicapped. The arts naturally foster participation, communication, exploration, and creativity but remain non-competitive and non-threatening. They also provide excellent opportunities for integration.

The variety of expressive modes available within the arts mediate between self and the world by encouraging children to share experiences and to express themselves. The creative arts also help students to understand a range of subject areas. They may be one of the most effective ways to teach exceptional learners living skills, since all people share affective needs and the desire to express emotions. In fact, many teachers have reported that all students, and especially exceptional learners, respond positively to dance, drama, music, and the visual arts and can concentrate on tasks that involve these art forms (Appell, 1979).

Visual art

When children first discover art materials they explore endlessly. Although the results are often unintelligible to adults, the children are learning to use their own ideas, and begin to feel a sense of pride in what they produce. Because art is highly interactive, it requires children to use all of their senses to deal directly with their environment. In addition, art develops inventiveness and the ability to solve problems. Children learn to gather information, select and modify materials, experiment with alternatives, and come up with solutions. They enjoy the process because they feel under no pressure to achieve anything beyond self-expression, and art provides an acceptable outlet for both positive and negative feelings.

The early years of art education encourage children to appreciate the beauty in their surroundings and to enjoy art. They learn to express personal experiences in basic visual form. By the time they reach adolescence, students find expression in more advanced art forms. Art instruction rises to an increasingly challenging level and uses many more processes. In the senior grades, art is optional; students may elect to study applied, commercial, or graphic design, or art history.

Art allows children to express their individuality.

Art activities hold many advantages for handicapped youngsters. Students learn to recognize colour, design, texture, light, and space, to use different media and to perceive themselves as part of their environment. At the same time, they discover general artistic principles, such as balance and contrast. Art activities develop the perceptual and sensory skills necessary for all academic achievement, and foster creativity and initiative within the students' limitations. Art also nurtures students' social and thinking skills.

The principles of art education do not have to be changed for exceptional learners, although it may be necessary to modify goals and materials in order to accommodate specific handicaps. Pottery and sculpture, for example, bring sensory experiences into closer proximity and are therefore particularly useful for low-vision students. Blind children, however, who rely on their sense of touch to provide information about the world, may balk at using art media, especially finger paints and papier-mâché, because they prefer to keep their hands clean.

Art augments comprehension of other subjects (see figure 10–2 and the unit below). The teacher can, for example, increase language development by encouraging children to touch, name, and describe new materials and colours, and to tell or write stories about their pictures. Art helps children to discern visual and tactile patterns, and spatial relationships. It also teaches them visual discrimination, visual tracking, concepts of directionality, body image, and fine and gross motor skills.

Comprehensive unit based on a high school art project

Topic: constructing masks

Objectives:

- Students will create masks to evoke a particular feeling such as fear, horror, or joy.
- Students will make masks that fulfil a particular purpose such as protection, narration, or symbolism.

Integration with other subject areas: study of a people, drama, literature, Hallowe'en traditions, dance, and movement.

Art instruction

Spontaneity in art occurs, not in isolation, but as a response to the stimulus that the teacher presents before an art activity. The teacher must establish a motivating environment and employ vocabulary that handicapped learners can use to sort out their ideas. When planning art programs, teachers must consider learners' past experiences and present interests and skills. It is important not to exceed their lowest tolerance levels in, for example, attention span or ability to use media (Morsink, 1984) and, although it is desirable to allow freedom of expression, it is also most important that the art program maintains a structure. The teacher will endeavour to strike a balance between discovery and direction. As students undertake art projects, teachers can observe, intervene when necessary, provide fresh stimulus, introduce new materials, or show students how to extend techniques to a broader range of activities.

Many art activities in the regular classroom can give joy, satisfaction, and success to handicapped learners. Nonetheless, Geisser (1985) and others complain that too often art is confined to cutting and pasting, an activity given to students to brighten the burden of learning or else to keep the hands busy while the mind remains passive. To take the best advantage of art education, the teacher should keep a very general progression of overlapping objectives in mind when presenting activities. An early goal of art education, for example, is to teach children to perceive stimuli such as colour. Developing students' appreciation of works of art is an ongoing goal throughout the art program.

For younger children, the most common art activities use paper, crayons, chalk, paint, printing, and modelling materials. Generally, children need little encouragement to participate in art activities. Teachers should mount finished work carefully; children love to see their best efforts displayed. To make displays, prepare sets of reusable backing made from burlap or other cloth glued to cardboard. These add colour and texture to bulletin boards and set off children's work to the best advantage.

Students should be exposed to many different media. They can make exciting works, for example, using crayons, a watery mixture of tempura paint, and construction paper. They first make crayon drawings on white construction paper and then paint them over with a light mixture of tempura paint. The crayoned areas will resist the paint

Processes

Recognize and use appropriate processes such as constructing, carving, moulding, papier mâché, and sculpting.

Materials

Recognize and use appropriate materials such as paper, paint, wood, raffia, clay, foil, found materials, etc.

MASKS

Elements and principles of design

Use elements of design such as lines, textures, colours, and shapes to evoke mood and emotion. Incorporate the principles of design into the project, in terms of contrast, emphasis, balance, patterns, and repetition.

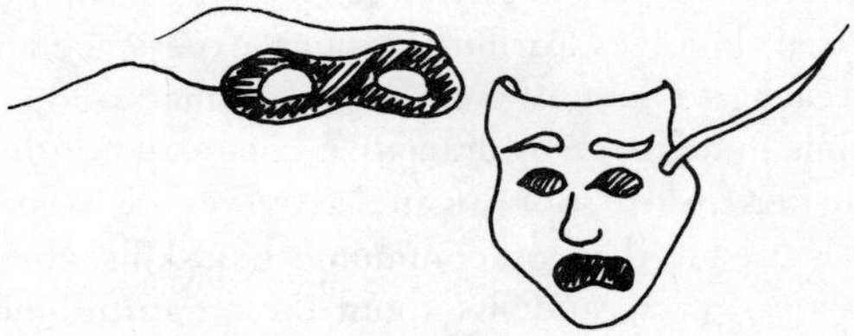

Responding to art

Explore the purposes and functions of masks in our society and others. These might include spiritual or social purposes, theatre, disguise, concealment, and protection. Discuss the important place that masks have had in society through history, and the fact that people have used the power of masks as a means of transforming themselves. Discuss the role of masks in perpetuating rituals and legends.

Figure 10–2 Art unit

Source: Adapted from Goldstein, 1985.

and show through. To extend the activity, try the procedure on paper towels or white crayon on white paper with a coloured wash (Morsink, 1984).

Art activities promote interpersonal skills very well. Each student can, for example, draw a picture of a problem, either serious or funny, and then show it to the class, which tries to find a solution. Similarly, the teacher can promote group work by putting up a large piece of newsprint on which is scattered random dots and having the students, in groups of five or so, take turns with wide-tipped markers to connect all the dots. Lines will cross and curve, eventually forming a design. Following the activity, students can discuss the design, note what they think it is, and then colour the picture.

Heller (1983), discusses an activity in which children worked co-operatively at their own ability levels and pace to create a sculpture from stones, bricks, and rubble. He pointed out that the work produced good co-operation and few behavioural problems because the children were totally engrossed in building the sculpture.

Drama

Drama in education includes a range of activities that aim at self-growth, understanding others, learning to use language well, and moving in ways that communicate significant meaning (Council of Ministers, 1983). Psychodrama, sociodrama, creative dramatics, role playing, and puppetry may all be used as instructional techniques (Necco, Wilson, & Schiedemantel, 1982).

In the early school years, drama education does not involve performance or audiences. Essentially, it is a process designed to strengthen learning in all the subject areas, especially the language arts. It involves learning through experience and improvising movement and language. Teachers employ a great deal of dramatization; as an example, a teacher might select pupils in advance to dramatize characters during a reading of the story, "The Three Little Pigs." More sophisticated activities are introduced in junior high school, where drama is used to develop communicative skills, channel individual resources into group activities, teach students about the art form, and to introduce scripts, advanced mime, and speechwork (Council of Ministers, 1983). Drama at this stage concentrates for the most part on mime, movement, and improvisation, progressing from drama as process to drama as performance. It introduces radio plays and dramatic reading, play writing, and interpretation. In the senior division, drama is optional. Programs involve staging performances, reading, discussing, and attending plays, writing theatre reviews, designing sets, acting, and improvising. Class work is commonly organized on the basis of theatrical skills and experiences (Council of Ministers, 1983).

Drama techniques address a range of social and educational goals. They help students to assume responsibility for their own behaviour, to solve individual social and emotional problems, to make decisions, and to deal with their emotions. (See chapter 6 on role playing, for example.) Through drama, students can experiment with adult roles, explore social and cultural issues, and conceptualize the abstract in meaningful ways (Necco, Wilson, & Schiedemantel, 1982).

Drama activities are as valuable, perhaps even more valuable, for exceptional students, as they are for non-exceptional learners (Behr, Snyder, & Clopton, 1979; Jennings, 1978; Shaw & Stevens, 1979). They can help language and learning handicapped students to find self-awareness, confidence, powers of concentration, and an awareness of body movement. As well, creative drama helps children to use their imaginations and to understand their environment in non-verbal ways—through mime, for example.

For the most part, handicapping conditions do not interfere with drama if the teacher chooses activities carefully. Pantomimes, charades, playing musical instruments, and simple games in which students imitate emotions by their facial expressions make a good beginning since they do not carry the threat of required verbal interaction. The teacher can also narrate original skits or familiar stories, with the students serving as

Drama activities combine spontaneity with communication in a relaxed atmosphere.

actors. These non-threatening activities combine spontaneity with communication in a relaxed atmosphere.

Drama includes a number of techniques that are particularly apt for exceptional students. A student who requires emotional support about an issue can benefit from a *double technique*. While the student plays a role, a member of the audience assists her or him by prompts, verbal encouragement, or physical proximity. In a *mirror technique* a student who has been playing a role cedes his or her place to another player. Watching the other player helps the student to appreciate another person's perspective and to correct distortions in self-perception (Necco, Wilson, & Schiedemantel, 1982). The technique of *future projection* involves having students portray an idealized future event, and following it with a discussion of realistic goals and expectations. A similar technique is to have students act out current events or social problems as "living newspapers" and then discuss the issues. Alternatively, in a *situation test*, volunteers leave the classroom and the class invents a hypothetical situation to which the volunteers must react (Mathis, Fairchild, & Cannon, 1980). At the secondary level, students can use dramatic play to recreate social situations of particular importance to their daily lives and then resolve the conflicts.

Multisensory expressive activities are the core of creative drama, calling into play sight, residual hearing, smell, touch, kinesthetic skills, and so forth. Students invent stories and characters, settings, props, costumes, and movement, all of which exist solely through the creative energies of the participants (Davies, 1984). With the "ball of energy," for example, the teacher creates something imaginary such as a skipping rope or a piece of gum from an invisible ball, and passes it on to a class member to recreate in another form.

To develop communicative competence for older students, Macy (1984) suggests an "add-on pantomime" technique. The teacher creates an empty space — the stage — and asks the students to begin to think of a location, such as a living room, a circus tent, or a car wash. The students then come on the stage and do something to let the audience know where they are. Once they are comfortable with the exercise, students can add to the scene rather than guessing the location. One of them, for example, might begin a scene by miming a cashier and another might join in by being a customer eating lunch, or a waiter, or the short-order cook. Each student is encouraged to watch carefully before coming onto the stage.

Puppetry introduces classroom drama without exposing students directly to physical and verbal communication before an audience. Making and using puppets can integrate various curricular areas, and involve many forms: cloth puppets from simple patterns, sock puppets, paper bag or box puppets, mitten puppets from large woolen mittens, tin can puppets, puppets from styrofoam or cork balls, papier-mâché puppets, shadow puppets from black paper glued to a stick, or clay puppets (D'Alonzo, 1974). Puppetry is an excellent vehicle for speech and language development.

To help students to use simple dialogue appropriately in a social setting, the teacher can make a classroom "store" with goods and a storekeeper. One by one students are told to go to the store, but the storekeeper is always out of the items that they need. Have them talk to the salesperson about alternatives. Older students can augment their language if, following a drama activity, they write out the dialogue. Cast members can then "autograph" the script. Additionally, students can write reviews of a drama production and make a class entertainment page from them.

Many drama exercises encourage co-operation. In the mirror game students work in pairs, one pretending to be the mirror image of the other. The mirror copies all actions, such as pretending to brush teeth or comb hair. An exercise useful for groups of three or four children involves television programming. The groups create productions to present to the rest of the class, in programming areas such as news, documentaries, coverage of sports events, game shows, soap operas, dramas, and commercials. Further ideas for creative drama are presented in box 10–1.

Box 10–1 Creative drama activities for special learners

Introductory (K to grade 3)

Hop like a rabbit.
Be a cow, duck, bird, or pig.
Throw a ball.
Eat ice cream and cake.
Smell some flowers.
Use a vacuum cleaner.
Be a car, bus, airplane, or boat.
Mow the grass.
Wash a car.
Take a train ride.
Walk different ways wearing different hats.
Be a cloud in the sky.
Walk through Jello, mud, cement, or water.
Walk, skate, crawl, and hop.

Advanced (grades 3 to 6)

Be a bear in the zoo.
Be a person locked in a toy shop with a friend.
Be a paper glider.
Be a baby learning to walk.
Give a dog a bath.
Be a balloon.
Be a bubble; float and pop.
Be a seed, sunshine, soil, a farmer, water. Let the seed grow into a flower, be blown in the wind, die, and have the seeds blow away.
Be a snow storm.
With a partner, make yourselves into a statue.

Source: Adapted in part from Davies, 1984.

Music

Music is a basic form of communication, with a special power to evoke and express emotions and mood. Young children react emotionally to the music they sing and play. By adolescence, taste in music may change, but it still forms a vital and emotional component of the young person's world.

The use of music in the elementary school years is well established. Much emphasis is placed upon singing, accompanied by instruments and various types of bodily movement (Council of Ministers, 1983). For adolescents, music education is usually organized around vocal and instrumental classes. Students are taught the social and cultural value of music and learn to understand music as a form of communication. Their musical repertoire is expanded by listening to recordings from their own and other cultures (Council of Ministers, 1983). Like the other creative arts, music is an elective or optional subject in the senior years. It is usually offered on both a performance and a non-performance level, and the non-performance segment involves study of both music history and theory.

Exceptional students derive great benefit from music programs. Music and rhythm have a universal appeal; all children can join in, no matter what their ability. Severely retarded children, for example, have been observed responding motorically to music when other stimuli have failed to elicit observable responses, and autistic children have responded physically, and in some cases verbally, to music when other methods of reaching them were exhausted (Morsink, 1984). Music classes tend to improve handicapped students' self-images and promote socialization (Lee, 1981). Music helps children to discover and explore, to manipulate and rearrange, create, and evaluate, and heightens their awareness of themselves and others. The classes establish an atmosphere of trust in which one student's opinion is as valuable and correct as that of the next. Children are free to express themselves, orally or in movement, without fear of failure or criticism. Ultimately, this may lead them to try something new in another area, such as mathematics or reading (Thursky, 1977). Music also involves practice in auditory discrimination, and because it has a consistent structure, may improve reading, sentence structure, phrasing, punctuation, and expression (Lee, 1981). At the secondary level, handicapped students have just as much potential for increasing their sensitivity to music as do any other students. By adjusting instructional goals, activities, and evaluative criteria, teachers can accommodate mildly handicapped students in junior high school music classes (Lee, 1981).

Unfortunately, too many teachers avoid using music in the classroom because of what they consider to be their own limited musical or vocal abilities. This is doing a disservice to the students and losing an effective avenue for teaching and learning. Young children are not critics and a teacher's off-key singing is not going to worry them overmuch. Regardless of how music is used in the classroom, activities should be interesting, concrete, and structured. High-interest activities guarantee involvement; very young children, for example, are more likely to appreciate and respond to recorded nursery rhymes than they are to Chopin or Bach. Concrete activities are more easily understandable; Peter and the Wolf, for example, relates the sounds of different instruments to the various characters. Structured activities allow the teacher to monitor, evaluate, and reinforce individual responses.

If children cannot participate in singing, they can play musical instruments or engage in other musical activities to foster developmental skills such as co-ordination, sensory motor skills, and auditory perception. The movements of music, the sounds and feel of instruments, and the activities of clapping, stamping, and other rhythmic body movements can be of tremendous help to exceptional learners. Students can construct improvised instruments from materials that they have collected themselves. Maracas can be simply made by filling empty plastic cartons or bottles with dried peas or lentils. To decorate, cover them with papier-mâché and then paint them. Earthenware flower pots, wooden bowls, or tin cans make wonderful drums. Paste two circles of grease proof paper on the opening and then a layer of cheesecloth or muslin and one more circle of paper. Let the layers dry and then give the improvised drum a coat of varnish.

Teachers today are using microcomputers with music synthesizers to create exciting environments in which students can make musical discoveries. Pupils learn to compose, analyse, edit, and play songs, and incidentally absorb concepts related to sound production such as pitch, volume, duration, and transposition (Bachor & Crealock, 1986). Synthesizers can simulate the sounds of orchestral instruments to facilitate learning and playing.

Music develops children's rhythmic sense and listening skills.

Music in the classroom need not, and should not, be restricted to recorded materials and singalongs. It can be combined with other subjects and art forms to provide effective learning experiences. Combining movement or dance, drama, poetry, or art with chant, song, or instrumental music motivates students by allowing success on more than one level, and through more than one avenue of creativity. Musical activities operate by either direct or indirect instruction. Using a song to teach a concept — for example, teaching the colours red, green, and yellow through a song about traffic lights — involves direct instruction. Indirect instruction uses music as part of, or the basis for, another activity. A gross motor activity stressing walking, skipping, running, and jumping could be reinforced, for example, by playing music at various tempos.

Songs and activities selected for exceptional children must provide practice in areas of weakness. Children with speech problems, for example, can practise words in rhymes, chants, and songs. Songs accompanied by a set of actions foster language development. Music lyrics stretch the imagination and often contain new linguistic patterns and vocabulary. A possible language activity is to have each student choose a favourite song and discuss with the class how the song came to be written, the thoughts that it expresses, the names of the composer and lyricist, and how the words and music complement each other. The teacher then selects one of the songs for a game of "Password." One pupil sits in front of the class and the teacher writes the song title on the board in view of the other students but hidden from the selected pupil, who then guesses the name of the song from one-word clues given by classmates.

For language-disabled children who have difficulty discriminating among and producing speech sounds, memorizing songs can be helpful (McDonald, 1975). Students select and memorize a song within their ability level either to say or to sing. Memorization takes discipline and attention to detail; it builds the vocabulary, uses common syntactic patterns, and necessitates structural analysis of elements such as letter patterns and rhyming words (McDonald, 1975). Teachers will find visual cues such as flash cards, word cards, and concrete objects useful aids in teaching songs.

Simple ballads and folk songs are well suited to language stimulation. Their strong rhythms tend to stimulate improvisation and children should be encouraged to create new verses to songs. The selected songs should be easy to learn and have a simple refrain. As well, teachers can effectively use picture song books to teach songs and stimulate language. Focussing students' attention on the specific phonological aspects of each word and verse helps to develop auditory discrimination, pronunciation skills, listening abilities, and increased awareness of language (Bromley & Jalongo, 1983). To improve spelling, teachers and students can spell and chant three-letter words in three-four time, using waltz music, or use marches in four-four time, for four-letter words (Morsink, 1984).

To stress the form and rhythm of music pieces the teacher can place students in pairs and give them each a pair of coloured gloves to wear. As a piece of recorded music is played, the students make up movements with their hands (Morsink, 1984). Alternatively, give them large sheets of newsprint and thick crayons and ask them to draw lines and patterns in response to the music as a selection is played. Musical activities involving listening, looking, moving, and feeling are all important because they develop sensory perception and motor skills.

Music develops children's rhythmic sense and appreciation of the pleasurable aspects of sound. Since it naturally involves listening, it is an ideal vehicle for auditory training. To develop auditory skills, the teacher can divide the class into three groups and give each group a phrase and a rhythm. The students chant the phrase to the rhythm. Alternatively, the teacher plays the piano or a record of a familiar tune and the students follow the notes by raising their arms when the music goes up, and lowering them when the music goes down.

Musical activities are especially helpful to strengthen movement skills and spatial awareness (Thursky, 1977). Abramson (1973) suggests using musical games. The students first follow a piece of music while imitating a given movement, modelled by the teacher, thus learning to integrate movement with auditory and visual perception. In the next stage, they have to react quickly to sudden changes in the music by changing the movement. Their reactions may also be in response to a previously discussed musical, verbal, or visual sign. This helps to develop muscular control, balance, attention, concentration, and memory. Finally, the students learn to sing or play after the teacher or the leader has completed a short singing or playing sequence that incorporates movements. This develops memory and sequencing skills.

Finally, music is also an enjoyable medium to develop cognitive thinking. A well-rounded variety of music can set the mood for creative writing or story telling. If the children have just returned from a trip to the circus, for example, appropriate music will help to revive their excitement and set the mood for writing about their experiences. They can also interpret what they read, and express their feelings orally, by dramatizing stories and experiences to music (Thursky, 1977).

Physical education

Vigorous participation in physical education, recreation, and sports helps individuals to develop socially, emotionally, and psychologically (Carlson, 1982). Physical education comprises a range of goals, such as physical and motor fitness, fundamental motor skills and patterns, and skill in individual and group games, sports, or dance. Dance allows children to explore a wide field of creative body movements.

Physical education should be given a high priority in the curriculum. Unfortunately, schools sometimes treat the physical education period as a recess or present haphazard activities that do virtually nothing for children's development, instead of planning instruction and using equipment appropriate for developmental needs. Expanding and modifying the physical education curriculum is one of the most important components of the mainstreaming process for special learners (Rider, 1980). Educators realize that all handicapped students should receive a sound physical education that mirrors the goals of the normal program yet remains flexible in performance expectations, methodology, and evaluative techniques.

Physical education can provide exceptional learners with opportunities to express themselves, release tensions, and gain a sense of achievement. It therefore enhances social and personal adjustment. The program should give exceptional students tasks that lead in a logical way toward activities socially acceptable to themselves and their non-handicapped peers. Teaching a student how to catch a ball, so that she or he can be on the baseball team, is a good example.

All students can participate in physical education to some extent. (Grant Gibson, Curriculum — Physical Education #51)

The term physical education includes a continuum of program offerings (Klesius, 1981; McClinaghan, 1981; Watkinson & Bentz, 1985): regular physical education with no adaptations; regular physical education with adaptations in equipment or rules, or assistance from support staff; part-time regular physical education; or part-time adapted physical education. A student who participates in some, but not all, regular activities has a part-time regular program; a student who engages in only some activities of an adapted program, with or without the addition of some regular activities, has a part-time adapted program. Adapted physical education programs are founded on individual education plans and involve relatively broad changes. They may include teacher aides, peer tutors, facilities other than the regular gymnasium, and specialized equipment. Currently, more teachers are specializing in adapted physical education for handicapped students (Sherrill, 1982), a trend that reflects growing interest in the field.

Physical education activities should be planned around all students in the class, not just the special learners (Rider, 1980). Mizen and Lineton (1983) suggest that teachers try to prepare an environment in which individual differences are respected and to eliminate practices, such as choosing sides, that unwittingly provoke embarrassment and failure. When necessary, give students individual assistance, or alter programs. Grouping students by ability can be effective to teach activities to mastery. More minor modifications might involve reducing competitiveness or concentrating on individual skills. Adams (1981) suggests reducing the size of the playing area, using lighter equipment, slowing down moving objects, or modifying the rules of a game. Each of these changes involves specific adaptations, such as changing the boundary lines, or increasing the number of players in a certain game.

Students with physical disabilities will obviously require more extensive modifications in physical activities. They may need therapeutic exercises for improving gait or posture, for improving or maintaining their range of motion, or for inhibiting unwanted reflexes, and increasing muscle tone. The special needs of physically handicapped students are readdressed in chapter 15. When planning a program that includes a physically handicapped youngster, teachers will find it helpful first to find out the exact nature of the student's needs (Smoot, 1985) by reviewing notes from the therapist and parents and any other relevant information. The next step is to assess the pupil's present level of functioning and note the significant points on a chart. The exercise program can be written on the same chart, leaving room to indicate increases in the number, intensity, and duration of activities. The teacher should make arrangements for the time and place of instruction, and choose an intervenor, perhaps a peer or an aide, who can supervise the program. The program should be evaluated periodically. Teachers are frequently concerned that they do not have enough time to help mildly handicapped children in physical education classes. Peer tutoring works well in physical education (Folio & Norman, 1981) and teachers can successfully use children from the upper elementary grades to help the younger ones. Their primary role is to assist the physical education teacher with equipment, skill development, record keeping, and help for exceptional children.

In this and the previous chapters, the approaches outlined have been generic instructional methods appropriate for a broad variety of mildly handicapped students in regular classrooms. The next section focusses on students who will need further adaptations, in addition to these, very often in terms of technical equipment.

PART 4

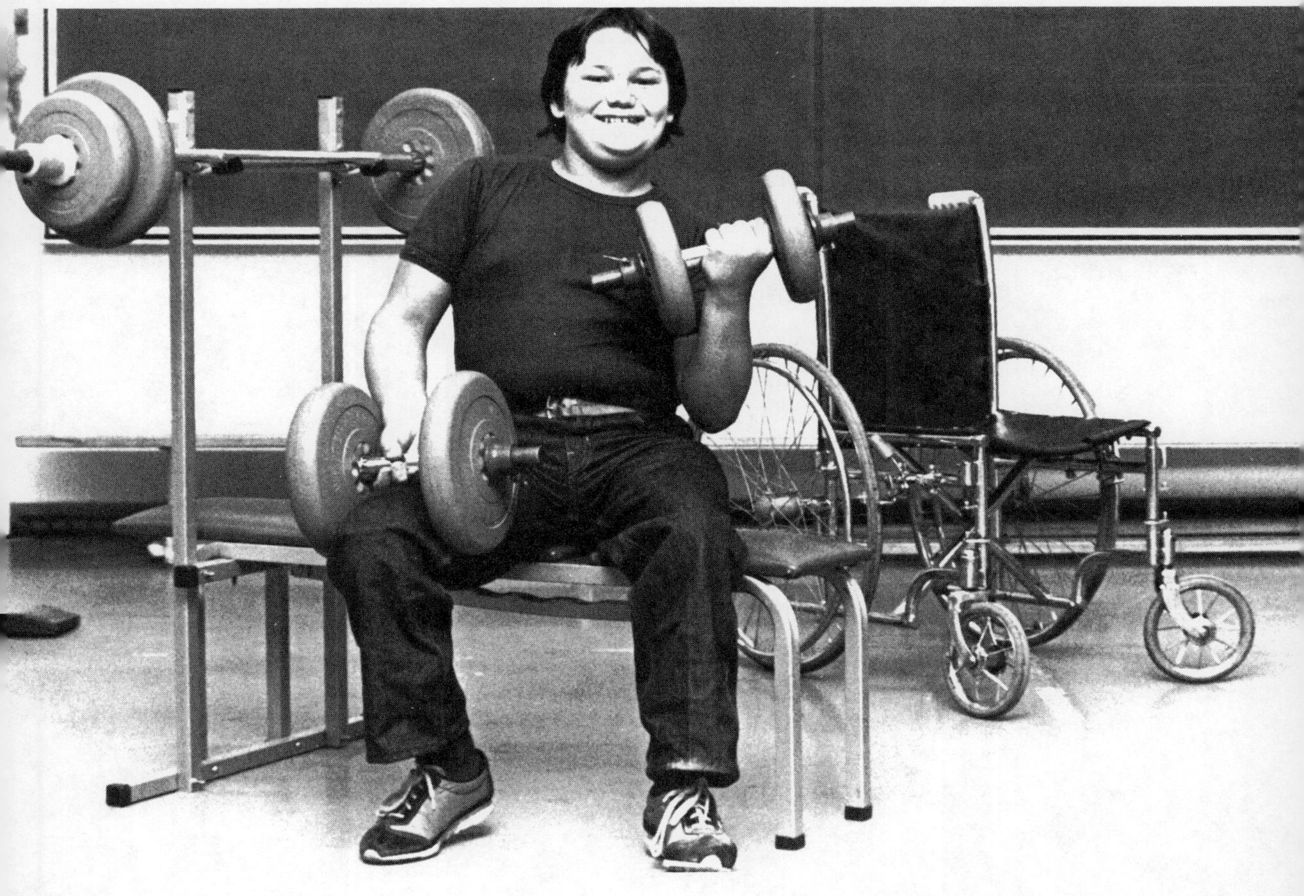

Special populations

11 Students with speech and language problems

Dear Reader,

In recent years, increasing numbers of severely handicapped children have been integrated into regular classrooms. Among them are children who can hear but have difficulty communicating by speech, often referred to as "non-speaking" children. Non-speaking children form one group among those whose needs are addressed in this chapter, under the general subject of speech and language problems, and the one to whom I wish to direct your attention briefly. These children suffer from innumerable combinations of cognitive, neurological, emotional, or structural impairments, and each child presents a very different case (Musselwhite & St. Louis, 1982). Their difficulty with speech may or may not be temporary and can range from severe, when they have no speech at all, to mild, when speech is unintelligible only to strangers. All teachers should be prepared to meet the needs of the non-speaking children who are either in regular classrooms now or are likely to enter them one day. The inability to communicate fully has profound implications for the child's total development.

Until the 1970s, if a child was unable to speak, the only treatment considered, aside from a very limited use of picture or word boards, was speech therapy. Professionals and parents feared that expression by a means other than speech might interfere with the acquisition of speech. Evidence accumulated, however, to indicate that the use of manual communication with deaf children, beginning at very young ages, could have positive effects on linguistic, academic, and psychological development (Moores, 1974; Wilbur, 1976). Equally, it was found that the use of a communication aid or system might actually facilitate speech development (McDonald & Schultz, 1973; Vicker, Schurma, & Kladde, 1974) and have positive effects on social and emotional development in a hearing, non-speaking child (Kates & McNaughton, 1975).

Throughout the 1970s, innovative clinical and educational programs, and research in cognition, language, and communication, led to a new approach for interacting with non-speaking persons (McNaughton, 1982). Teachers, psychologists, linguists, occupational therapists, and speech pathologists came to accept that communication involves more than speech and that augmentative communication systems, such as signing or communication boards, can be beneficial. Language and cognition were seen to have a reciprocal relationship, each interacting with the other in the course of their development, so that deprivation in the area of language might have a damaging effect upon cognitive development (Bates, Beningi, Bretherton, Camaioni, & Volterra, 1977).

Technology is now playing an increasingly important role in augmentative communication, linking physically handicapped people to their communities through telecommunication, giving single-switch access to computers, giving voice to non-speaking individuals, and providing a means of written communication. Increasingly, however, it is the *process* of communication that is considered the central issue: not the system or the technology employed, important though they may be, but the way that individuals use them. Harris (1978) was one of the first to point out that children in the classroom were using their communication boards in a very limited way to respond to questions. It is important for the teacher to view augmentative communication not as a band-aid solution but as a means of building on the base of communication already possessed by an individual.

Jane Green
Department of Educational Psychology
Memorial University of Newfoundland

People use language to transcend their immediate environment: to conceptualize the immaterial world and to become social beings. Language implies the existence of a reference system based on experience common to all members of the linguistic community; to be meaningful, a child's language must conform to established social and linguistic norms. Competence with language also has a direct influence on the child's ability to learn and later to read and write (Polloway & Smith, 1982).

Most children come to school in possession of an intuitive knowledge of language, but they differ in their **language maturity**, their ability with the phonological, morphological, syntactical, and semantic elements of language. The differences correspond to mental age, sensory status, environmental background, dialect characteristics, and previous instruction. Some youngsters do not possess communicative competence commensurate with their age or grade levels. These children are not deaf, not autistic, have no identifiable neural damage, and perform within the normal range on non-verbal tests of mental ability. Yet their language behaviour shows a developmental lag of a year or more. Children who demonstrate significant lags but whose language still progresses according to the stages of normal language development are said to have **delayed language**. A more complex problem resides in children with **deviant** or **disordered language**. (Children suffering from either delayed or disordered language can be said to be language disabled.) Although these youngsters may have the rudiments of a language code and may comprehend language more easily than they produce it, they show large gaps in linguistic development and display little consistency in their various deficits.

Communication disorders are exceedingly complex, are developmentally acquired over a period of time, and vary in numerous ways from the behaviour demonstrated by the average communicator. Nevertheless, most children with these disorders are educated in regular classrooms with their non-handicapped peers. Typically, services for speech- and language-disordered youngsters include regular classroom placement, with or without resource-room help, or services from an itinerant speech and language clinician once or twice a week. The classroom teacher is considered to be the primary language instructor.

While it is completely rational to assume that some degree of intellectual integrity is necessary to acquire language, one should not therefore assume that every child who has not acquired language is mentally retarded. Certainly, mentally retarded youngsters often demonstrate problems in language. They fail to perform at a level commensurate with their intellectual ability in the language area (Smith, 1974) and demonstrate a higher incidence of voice and articulation defects. Learning-disabled and emotionally disturbed children, however, also have many mild and moderate language disorders.

Language and speech are basic components of instruction. (This of course in no way denies the presence and value of non-verbal communication. Teachers and students are continually sending silent messages; students raise their hands, nod their heads, yawn, drum their fingers, or appear confused; teachers smile, shrug, snap their fingers, frown, and so on.) Teaching depends on transmitting and receiving messages and language-disabled children's lack of success in this process jeopardizes their educational achievement.

This chapter is concerned with children who suffer from speech and language problems as their primary disability. Communication difficulties associated with other disorders are addressed in later chapters. Nevertheless, the ideas presented here may certainly prove adaptable for other students demonstrating communication problems, particularly hearing-handicapped pupils. Moreover, the approaches discussed here extend those already presented in chapter 7, and readers are urged to select those that match the needs of an individual learner without regard to any specific category.

The main objectives of this chapter are to

- touch upon the significant characteristics associated with speech problems and language deficits
- discuss methods to identify speech and language disorders
- emphasize the value of language sampling for regular classroom teachers
- present an overview of approaches used with language-disabled students

The field of communication exceptionalities

As children grow, they acquire **communicative competence**, a term referring to an individual's ability to understand and use communication commensurate with developmental levels. Most children in most cultures pass through similar stages as they develop competence, and it is necessary to perceive that progression in order to understand language delays and disorders (see Winzer, Rogow, & David, 1987).

Language and speech are not the same thing. Essentially, language is an arbitrary system of words and word combinations, used by humans to communicate. Learning language, notes Goodman (1982) "is a matter of finding the underlying system, inferring its rules, and then being able to use them to express meaning and to understand it" (p. 88). Of all the language forms we use, spoken language, or speech, is the most common and most useful coin of communicative exchange. It is, however, simply a medium. While language can exist without speech—as is seen in the sign language used by deaf people—speech cannot exist without language, which gives it meaning.

Language disorders may manifest themselves in speech and writing, either at the phonological or grammatical level or both; in the comprehension of specific concepts, or of language structures; or in some combination of these areas. A **speech disorder** is reflected in speech that differs from that of others to the extent that it calls attention to itself, interferes with the intended message, or causes the speaker or listener distress (Van Riper, 1978). Perkins (1977) notes that speech is impaired when it is ungrammatical, culturally or personally unsatisfactory, or injurious to the speech-producing mechanisms.

Most teachers can readily identify children who have difficulty with articulation and are usually aware of the effect on oral reading and spelling. More subtle problems understanding and formulating language may not be so easily recognized (Illerbrun & Greenough, 1983). Language disorders are more complex than speech disorders and consequently more difficult to identify and treat precisely. Much language programming actually focusses on speech, since speech is the most accessible part of language, and also reflects and affects language. Of course, speech therapy can be used to improve speech patterns and deviations, as well as to ameliorate any underlying language disorders. Although speech and language are closely related, speech problems and language disorders are inherently very different, and this chapter therefore discusses them separately.

Students with speech disorders

Although speech disorders are not uncommon, it is difficult to estimate their prevalence because they are often associated with other difficulties. Speech problems are more common among boys than girls, however, especially in the early grades (Eisenson, 1971), and this is particularly true in the case of stuttering. Problems decrease as the grade level rises. Milisen (1971) estimates that between 12 and 15 percent of children in kindergarten to grade four will suffer speech disorders. In grades five to eight the proportion drops to 4 or 5 percent and this remains constant after grade eight unless treatment intervenes. Although many youngsters simply "grow out" of speech disorders, the difficulties that disorders create should never be treated lightly. Problems may spill over to hinder a student's functioning in social and academic areas.

Identification of speech disorders

Typically, the type and severity of a speech disorder is diagnosed in a clinical setting by trained speech therapists. Classroom teachers, however, are responsible for identifying youngsters whose speech does not seem to be developing appropriately. Table 11–1 presents a general checklist to assist identification. Obviously, no child will demonstrate all the problems listed but teachers should listen and observe in order to identify clusters of behaviour.

When using this table, the teacher should take into account the depth or intensity of the student's difficulties, rather than the number. Most children stammer and stumble at times, but problems that seem consistent and chronic need referral. Especially important are the child's own reactions to his or her speech.

Teachers should consider the conspicuousness, intelligibility, and pleasantness of the student's speech as the criteria for making a referral. Articulation errors are present if the sound units considered to be in error are elements of the phonemic system of the child's linguistic community (if the child has heard the sounds), and if it is reasonable to expect that the misarticulated sound elements would be articulated acceptably by most youngsters of the same age (Tomblin, 1978). The teacher's referral should contain notes of any specific deviations of speech production and any available emotional or medical history.

Formal procedures for identifying problems involve articulation tests, which require the individual to say speech sounds. Most articulation tests rely on easily recognized pictures of objects whose names contain the target sound. Although the tests are usually administered by therapists, teachers are often presented with the results. Procedures to produce evidence of phonological processes in a child's language also exist, although they are not used by teachers. These tests are designed to analyse speech within the framework of natural phonology (Grunwell, 1980).

Table 11–1 Checklist for speech disorders

	Yes	No
1. Does the student suffer physically or emotionally when trying to communicate?		
2. Does the student seem embarrassed or express concern about the speech?		
3. Does the speech gain unwanted attention or mimicking from peers?		
4. Is the speech accompanied by any unusual physical mannerisms, such as unnecessary hand or arm movements?		
1. Is the speech dysfluent?		
2. Does the speech have many repetitions of sounds?		
3. Does the speech consistently omit some sounds?		
4. Does the student persist in mispronunciations well past the developmental periods for such errors?		
5. Does the speech contain frequent and recurring misarticulations of one or more sound units?		
6. Are the problematic sound units phonemic elements of the student's familiar linguistic community?		
7. Does the problem involve the production of sounds and rhythms rather than thoughts and ideas?		
1. Are there voice quality problems such as excessive nasality or hoarseness?		
2. Can the speech be easily understood?		
3. Does the speech sound strange?		
4. Does the student have garbled speech even in periods of little stress?		

Mainstreaming speech-disordered students

Speech disorders do not impinge on intellectual development or learning capacity and nearly all speech-disordered children can be successfully integrated into regular classroom settings. In fact, any other placement for students with speech problems only would be detrimental to their educational and social progress. Even students who have additional handicapping conditions, such as cerebral palsy, that necessitate the use of communication boards or other augmentative devices, can be effectively instructed in regular classrooms.

Depending upon the nature and degree of the problem, various related services may be required for the speech-disordered child. Of the professionals involved, the classroom teacher and the speech/language therapist or pathologist spend the greatest amount of time in the school setting with children who have speech or language defects. Speech/language therapists are concerned with communicative development and disorders. They apply the findings of medicine and behavioural science to evaluate speech and language, determine whether problems exist, and decide the best ways to manage them. Articulation, voice disorders, and dysfluency are usually targeted for specialized intervention. Therapists may also be involved in activities that supplement direct services, such as teacher training, curriculum development, selecting textbooks, planning classroom language activities, and participating on school-based educational teams.

Therapy is designed to overcome or compensate for speech deficiencies or disorders. Its main goal is to help the individual achieve the most acceptable speech possible, and treatment may incorporate psycholinguistics, cognitive structures, and behaviour modification. **Voice therapy** attempts to return an individual's voice to normal or near normal. Stimulating vocalization and teaching and correcting speech are complex and demanding tasks requiring very specific skills.

For children at the elementary level, therapy attempts to help them develop good tongue and breathing control, use voice meaningfully, develop a pleasant and relaxed vocal quality, with proper pitch, intensity, and duration, and develop imitative ability with respect to speech production. Therapists also work with children to help them to articulate vowels and consonants correctly in syllables, words, and sentences, and to stimulate the skills necessary for spontaneous speech. Children need to recognize that speech is the most valuable means of manipulating the environment and satisfying their personal needs. It is more difficult to correct speech with secondary level students; some view it as an exercise in special attention. While the goals of correction at the secondary level echo those for younger pupils, older students may also need practice in speech related to vocational expectations and life skills.

The education and therapy of speech-disordered students require a concerted effort by teachers and therapists. Even though most classroom teachers are not trained to remediate speech problems directly, they play a supportive role and should work closely with speech pathologists and therapists. Teachers see children for a significant portion of the day and are therefore in an ideal position to encourage them to use appropriate speech and language daily, to identify those who are not progressing adequately, and to provide students with opportunities to practise speech skills targeted during therapy.

Instructional approaches

Classroom teachers can help youngsters with speech disorders by providing a positive speech environment. Cohen and Plaskon (1980) suggest that they accomplish this by asking themselves specific questions: "How can the classroom environment be adapted to promote oral language?" "How sensitive am I to my own communication, both verbal and non-verbal?" "How can I cope with disabilities and improve the speech of handicapped children?" and "What kinds of approaches and stimuli do I use to encourage communicative encounters among children in the class?" It is incumbent on teachers to stimulate speech production, correct minor deviations, and refer serious problems. The following general tips are intended to help teachers improve students' speech production:

- Establish a relaxed atmosphere in the classroom to allay students' fears.
- Be a good speech model.
- Allow students many opportunities to speak.

- Enrich students' language and speech by consistently naming objects and events, and reinforcing usage.
- Promote good listening skills.
- Face the student when talking in order to provide both visual and auditory cues.
- Keep classroom noise to a minimum.
- Encourage all students to speak clearly in order to provide models for speech-disordered students.
- Do not allow class members to ridicule or mimic the speech-disordered student.
- Do not overemphasize speech patterns for the student. Not only does this draw attention to the speech difficulty but it may actually distort speech. Do not speak louder than necessary; use a natural intensity and pitch with normal intonational patterns.
- Reduce the pressures on the student to speak, by lowering the requirements for oral reading, for example.
- Give speech-disordered students who wish to be involved in oral presentations or activities a chance to practise individually before facing the entire group. Allow them to use visual materials, such as the overhead projector, in their presentations.
- Use activities such as debates and panel discussions, dramatization, role playing, reporting, and practice telephone conversations.
- Reinforce newly acquired skills from therapy sessions.

Games and activities can be effectively employed to improve speech production and usage. In the game "Let's pretend to be teacher," for example, one student gives directions to the rest of the group, and in doing so practises oral skills and sequencing. Children can use puppets to relay simple messages, thereby using speech and practising correct sounds. With the same objective, they can describe objects, people, or seasons using simple phrases such as "My pencil: long-pointed-hard," or describe their feelings in sentences such as "I feel happy because . . . ."

Although remediating speech problems is the bailiwick of speech therapists, teachers can certainly apply simple corrective techniques in the classroom. If a student is encountering problems with particular speech sounds, some of the following techniques may prove helpful:

1. Teach one sound at a time.
2. When referring to a particular sound, use the sound itself and not the name of the sound.
3. Correct problematic sounds through many of the senses. Be sure that the student recognizes if the sound is correct, what is done to produce it, and how it looks when other people produce the sound. Keep in mind that speech is seen as well as heard; a mirror will be helpful to show the student the correct way to produce a sound.
4. Use auditory discrimination exercises. If the student substitutes one sound for another, incorporate both sounds into training, so that the student learns their correct use.
5. Transfer the newly learned sounds to words by first using them in words within the student's comprehension.
6. Use games when teaching sounds to younger children. Practice with specific sounds may also be combined with conversation, reading, and sentence building.
7. Use plenty of praise and encouragement when the student says the sound correctly.

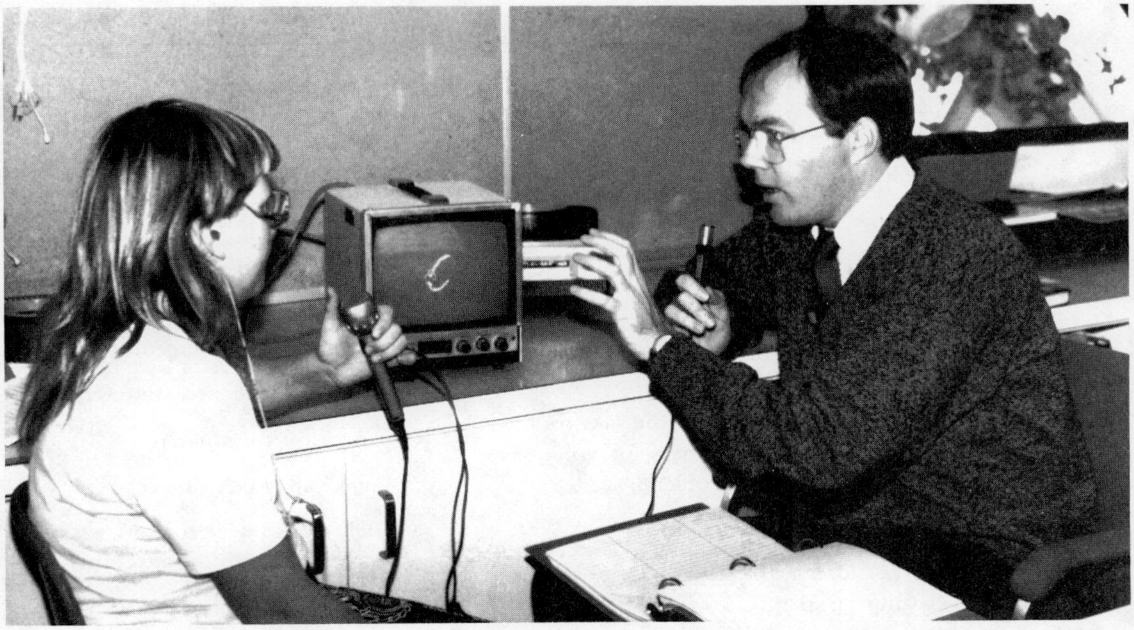

Skills that students learn in speech lessons such as this one must be reinforced by classroom teachers.

To improve the articulation of single consonants, teachers can work with children on labial sounds such as *p* and *b* using a feather held to the lips. The feather will move with the *p* and stay still with the *b*. The *v* and *f* sounds are often difficult for children to produce and distinguish. They can wet their forefingers and then blow them dry with the *f*, or feel the vibration of *v* on the lips. To practise *m* and *n*, children can feel the sides of their noses as they produce the sounds. Hand signals often assist students in simple sound articulation and blending. If a student is encountering problems with blends such as *bl*, for example, the teacher can first have her say the two sounds in isolation. The teacher then tapes a separate letter on either of the student's hands, holds the student's hands in his own, and gradually brings them closer and closer together, until she joins hands and says the blend.

Dysfluency, or stuttering, is often of particular concern to teachers. There are actually two types of stuttering, each demanding somewhat different treatment by the therapist. **Primary stuttering** is characterized by breaks in speech caused by repetitions of syllables and sounds and less frequently by prolongations. It is not usually accompanied by physical signs and is easier to overcome than **secondary stuttering**. Secondary stutterers show terse, non-fluent speech accompanied by facial grimaces, tics, or other forms of spasmodic movement. Both kind of stutterers are, however, very consistent in what they block — when asked to read the same passage more than once, for example, they are likely to block many of the same words (Reich, 1986). Teachers can provide a supportive classroom climate for children with both primary and secondary stuttering. Some suggestions for teachers of dysfluent youngsters are presented in box 11–1.

Box 11-1 Teaching dysfluent students

Do. . .

. . . become adjusted to the student's dyfluency and react unemotionally and objectively.

. . . create an atmosphere of ease and relaxation.

. . . use the student's written work as a measure of achievement.

. . . make visitors in the classroom — aides, student teachers, or volunteers — aware of the problem.

. . . listen to the student.

. . . look at the student's eyes, not lips, during speech.

. . . praise the student's strong points, such as nice handwriting or good manners.

. . . provide opportunities for choral reading.

. . . phrase questions in such a way that they only require short answers.

. . . divert the student's attention to something else after a particularly bad speech block.

. . . allow the student to complete a sentence without prompting.

. . . assign the student duties in the classroom that do not require speech responses.

. . . allow the student to tell stories, to recite verses, and to read aloud in relaxed situations, and encourage participation in dramatization activities.

Don't. . .

. . . show impatience, embarrassment, or boredom.

. . . use rapid speech, loud commands, or strict discipline.

. . . excuse poor work or misconduct because of the speech problem.

. . . label the student a stutterer.

. . . speak for the student.

. . . make an issue of speech.

. . . tell the student to start again, or take a deep breath, or any other such help.

. . . have the student engage in activities, such as speed drills, that only increase dysfluency.

. . . praise the student for fluency.

. . . penalize the student when an abnormality occurs.

. . . try to change the student's handedness.

. . . show sympathy or pity.

Augmentative communication✧

Augmentative communication is a term currently used to describe all communication that supplements or augments speech (Vanderheiden & Yoder, 1986). It encompasses the use of a person's eyes, facial expression, and body movement, in addition to signing systems, graphic systems, technology, or some combination to substitute for or accompany speech. McNaughton and Warrick (1986) also include in the definition the use of technology that enables a person who cannot write with a pencil or use a traditional computer keyboard, to communicate in writing.

Many people who are unable to speak at all, or who have speech that is not functional for their needs, are nevertheless capable of communicating by augmentative communication. "Unaided" augmentative communication requires nothing but the individual's own body, for example facial expression, arms, and hands for signing. "Aided" systems range from communication boards, which can be as simple as a piece of cardboard with pictures, symbols, or words on it, to multilevel computerized technical aids that use visual and voice synchronization. Unaided systems have the advantage of being both portable and available but aided systems tend to have a wider audience because they are more easily understood. Physically handicapped people also find them easier to use. The individual indicates the message by pointing to each picture, symbol, or word on a communication board if he or she is able, or if the disability is severe, by using techniques such as encoding or scanning.

Children with serious speech defects may very well be mainstreamed into regular classrooms, and teachers whose classes include such students will find the following guidelines pertinent:

- Consider the student's potential rather than the limitations of the handicap.
- Inform yourself about the types of augmentative communication that the student is using, such as Blissymbolics, a Canon Communicator, or signed English.
- Become an active part of the multidisciplinary augmentative team who work, when feasible, with both the student and the parents.
- Take time to feel comfortable conversing with the student, and to observe her or his individual methods of communication apart from augmentative communication.
- Give the student non-verbal assignments and responsibilities.
- Do not let the student capitalize on her disabilities; as far as possible, treat her as you do any other member of the class and expect similar behaviour.
- Provide the student with opportunities to participate in groups and interact with other class members.
- Provide many opportunities for oral experiences in the classroom, such as group singing in which the student signs as others sing.
- Inform yourself of the student's special needs in print communication. Is he able to turn pages, write, take notes, and so on?
- Teach the other students about their speech-handicapped peer's methods of communication. They can, for example, learn what the symbols mean on a communication board, learn some signing, become familiar with the communication aid, and recognize idiosyncratic means of communication.

✧The section on augmentative communication and the case study following it were written by Jane Green, Department of Educational Psychology, Memorial University of Newfoundland.

This child is using a communication board.

- If necessary, train other students to help their physically handicapped peer get set up on the computer.
- Expect responses in class from the student using augmentative communication, while being aware of the limited vocabulary that she may have at her disposal.
- Take note of the vocabulary that the student needs, and supply words in context when possible, or else refer the matter to the team member responsible for developing the student's communication system.
- Show an example to others by your attitude when waiting for the student to respond or ask a question in class. As augmentative communication is generally much slower than speech communication, help the student to think of ways to gain time. He may prepare a message beforehand with a peer or volunteer, or use a communication aid to produce and store a written or voice-synthesized message. Often-used sentences and phrases can be included whole in the augmentative communication system.

Case study 11–1 presents the story of John, a cerebral palsied boy with limited speech and mobility. After examining the case study, readers may ask themselves how a teacher could help John to achieve his full potential in an educational setting. Important aspects to consider include sensitivity to John as a unique individual in a particular environment, information and support from those already working with him, and ongoing assessment and programming to accommodate his changing needs. Also important is the type of augmentative communication most appropriate for John. Further discussion on integrating cerebral palsied students is found in chapter 15.

Case study

11–1

John has cerebral palsy, which has affected both his ability to speak and his mobility. His verbalizations are limited to a few single words such as "Mom" and "no." He cannot hold a pencil, nor is it likely that he will learn to walk. His receptive language has been rated as within the average range, however, and early intervention has ensured that he is now entering school able to express his needs, feelings, and ideas in a variety of ways, to use a computer, and to drive his electric wheelchair skilfully. His parents and professionals from a variety of disciplines have prepared John well, but the question arises, "Is the school ready for him?"

John uses Blissymbolics, an augmentative communication system with symbols that have proved easy for children as young as two years old to learn and fascinatingly logical to people of all ages. John's individualized communication board contains approximately three hundred Blissymbols representing all parts of speech, photographs of his family and pet dog, and pictures of his favourite space characters and television shows. Words accompany the symbols and pictures so that anyone who can read can understand John's message as he points it out on the board with his right thumb. He has also been encouraged to use a variety of methods to communicate in addition to his board, including eye gaze, facial expression, gestures (although his range of movement is limited), vocalizations, and the words that he is able to say.

Like the rest of the world, John uses many different ways to express his ideas and feelings, to ask questions, to be rude or loving, or to tell a joke. His communication board helps to fill the gap left by his difficulty in communicating by speech, but it cannot compensate completely. John does not have the vocabulary of an average five year old and using a communication board is much slower than normal speech. His communication partners, whether adults or children, will need to learn that, and although they can speak normally to John, their role as listeners will be more demanding than when two speakers are talking. They will have to remember context, be aware of John's strategies for condensing information, give him time to answer, and react to him as a whole person by watching his face and listening to his vocalizations as well as following his thumb on the communication board.

Students with language delays and disorders

Human language includes both verbal and non-verbal forms. Spoken language, sign language, and communication boards are considered as modes of language that vary in form but have common functions and map similar semantic distinctions (Schiefelbusch & Hollis, 1980). Language usage requires a complex set of mental operations involving learning, memory, and receptive, processing, and expressive skills. In order to communicate effectively, children must first decode the receptive sounds within the linguistic system to work out what the sounds represent; they also need memory of previous linguistic experiences in order to attach meaning to language; and finally, they must be able to encode a response (Naremore, 1980). Difficulties can arise in the areas of sensiromotor processes, cognitive skills, or conceptual knowledge (understanding the environment). Memory deficits will contribute to language disorders and delays because without good memory children will forget the meaning and use of words. An impoverished environment also has detrimental effects. Children may not hear appropriate language or receive adequate responses to their own communicative initiatives, and language production is necessarily the result of an interaction between the skills of the speaker and events in the environment.

Language disorders may be manifested as disruptions in the content, form, function, and use of language. *Content* denotes what the person understands from the message; *form* denotes the shape and sound of the message in terms of acoustic and phonetic qualities, functions, and syntax; *function* denotes the parts of speech or types of sentence in the message; and *use* implies the form the speaker chooses from the available alternatives (Bloom & Lahey, 1978). The disorders are classified as receptive if they interfere with the comprehension of language and expressive if they interfere with language output.

Students with receptive language problems have difficulty comprehending, discriminating, and remembering what was said. This is especially pronounced when the model does not speak clearly or when the environment is loud, as in a noisy classroom. Receptively disabled pupils may appear to understand verbal statements only when the words are accompanied by a gesture. They may not change facial expressions during a conversation or maintain eye contact for the duration of a message. Some receptively disabled youngsters do not seem to understand what is being asked; they may begin to respond to a direction before it is completed, or wait an unusually long time before answering. They may not be able to follow directions that differ from previous ones, a problem that can be manifested as difficulty completing work sheets when the directions are verbally presented (Culatta, Page, & Culatta, 1981).

Children as well as adults can understand more words than they are able to produce, yet when individuals demonstrate an ability to send messages that is significantly below the ability to receive them, or are unable to formulate grammatical sentences, they may have expressive language disabilities. They will use incorrect word order, give grammatically correct responses that make no sense, and often make errors with no consistent pattern. Some students have difficulty using several different ideas in a single sentence, or use an unusually small vocabulary. Expressive language disorders are further manifested when students are unable to find the right words rapidly, a problem referred to as **dysnomia**. They will pause often in order to recall the words or if they fail to do so, may make associations such as "the grey machine and the small wires," for the stapler and staples. These students are prone to frustration and may resort to gestures instead of words.

Many, but certainly not all, youngsters with language disorders will have delayed language although language delays do not imply disorders. About 35 percent of language-disabled children are delayed in both expressive and receptive language; another 35 percent show greater significant delays in receptive than in expressive language; while 29 percent show greater delays in expressive language (Silva, 1980). Delayed is a descriptive, not etiological, term; it refers to the language performance, not the cause, the critical referent being time. Children with delayed language possess linguistic skills and can often be understood by parents and teachers who are used to their simple utterances. The kindergarten child who says "Me eat now," for example, is using an utterance more typical of a two than a five year old, but one that is easily understood.

Other children have more serious problems. Their language disorders imply disturbances in the orderly pattern of language acquisition. Severe linguistic disorders usually involve both speech and language, as well as accompanying handicapping conditions. Deviant or disordered language differs from delayed language in that it is filled with distortions, not simplifications. A language-disordered six year old, when asked to repeat the sentence, "The little boy fell in the water," may respond with "Little fall water." The language-disordered individual does not progress systematically and sequentially in language acquisition or in any aspect of rule-governed and purposive linguistic behaviour (Lucas, 1980). Children with disordered language are aware that their culture has developed a formal symbolic code that represents objects, relationships, and events, but they have either mislearned or not acquired the various structures to organize linguistic information.

A handy rule of thumb to decide whether language content, form, and use are within the normal range is the "rule of six." Children progress in language development roughly by six-month intervals. Not all children attain linguistic milestones at the same time; not all, for example, say their first words at twelve months or begin combining words at eighteen months. Some infants may be three or four months behind their peers, but they can still catch up quite adequately within six months of the typical time for emergence of a language behaviour. If the milestone is not attained within the six months, however, the likelihood is that development will not simply correct itself with motivation and maturation, and cause for concern exists.

The manner in which language develops defines whether it is disordered or delayed, although it can be difficult to distinguish between the two. Figures 11–1 and 11–2 show the work of two children in whom the distinction is clear, however. Compare the letter written by a nine year old displaying a language delay to the piece written by another nine year old with severely disordered language. Given the gross anomalies in the second piece, it is obvious that language intervention with this child will need to be extremely systematic and gradual.

Identification and diagnosis of language disorders

The evaluation of language disorders does not approach the clarity and precision of speech assessment procedures. The disorders are so varied and so complex that it is difficult to obtain specific and valid information about children's skills through an accurate, reliable, and easily applied procedure. The purposes of evaluation are: to establish a baseline to describe a student's typical pattern of language and basic communication skills; to identify the factors that facilitate or inhibit learning; and to gain the information necessary to formulate instructional goals.

Evaluation must measure the student's capacity to understand word meanings, knowledge of structural rules, and ability to use language effectively in social situations. Efficient diagnosis of language delays and disorders endeavours to assess every aspect of language development, including the ability to receive and interpret speech sounds,

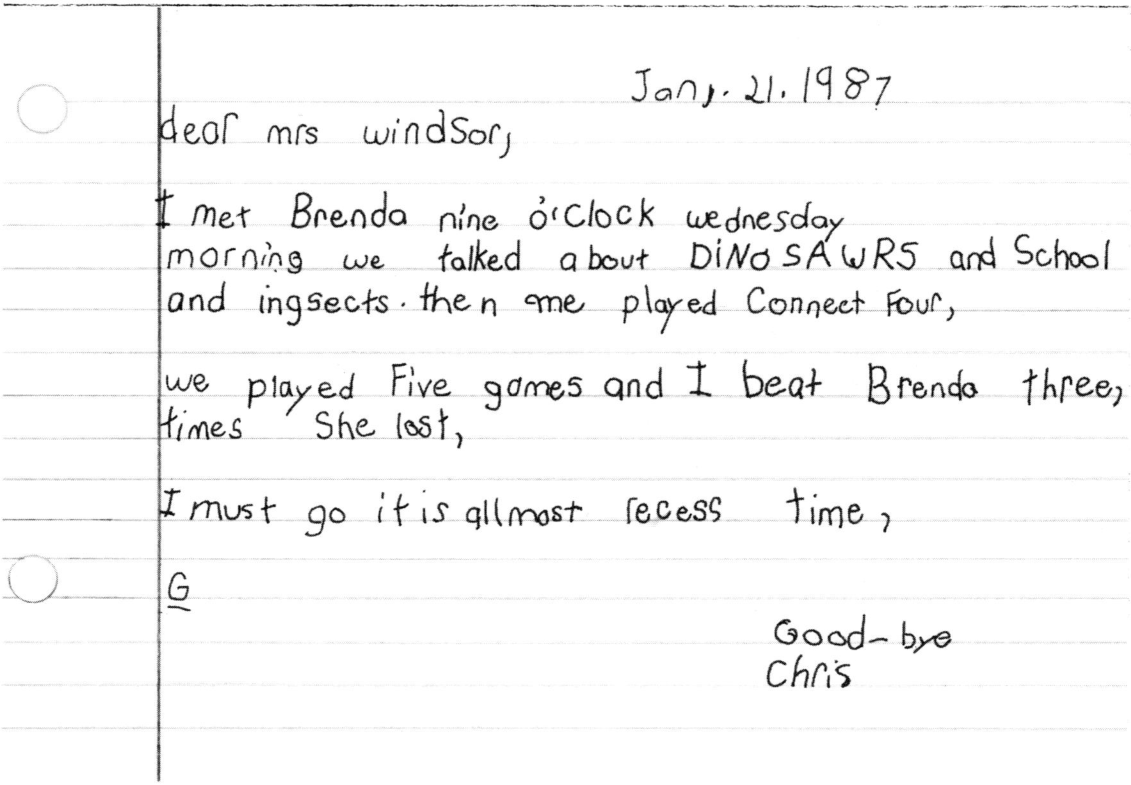

Jan,. 21. 1987

dear mrs windsor,

I met Brenda nine o'clock wednesday
morning we talked about DINOSAWRS and School
and ingsects. then me played Connect Four,

we played Five games and I beat Brenda three,
times She lost,

I must go it is allmost recess time,

G

Good-bye
Chris

Figure 11–1 Language delay

to associate linguistic symbols with past experience, and to encode, imitate, and produce appropriate linguistic responses (Naremore, 1980). It must explore both oral and written production, through syntax, semantics, pragmatics, and vocabulary.

Formal language tests identify specific language delays and disorders. Assessment procedures are complex and time-consuming to analyse, and the average classroom teacher will not find them easy to use without specialized training. (Some courses are beginning to introduce such training.) As employed by trained clinicians, however, formal language procedures add greatly to our understanding of disabled students' language and needs.

Although formal language procedures will identify language-disordered students, they yield little information about the natural language that children use in their daily living. An assessment of a student's functional use of language is best provided through informal measures carried out by the classroom teacher. Gillett and Temple (1986) suggest using a student's dictated account of an experience. The teacher records the language and then analyses it by answering pertinent questions: "Does the student speak in sentences or in single words and word clusters?" "Does the student use descriptive names for objects and events and many ambiguous terms such as 'it,' 'they,' and 'this'?" "Does the

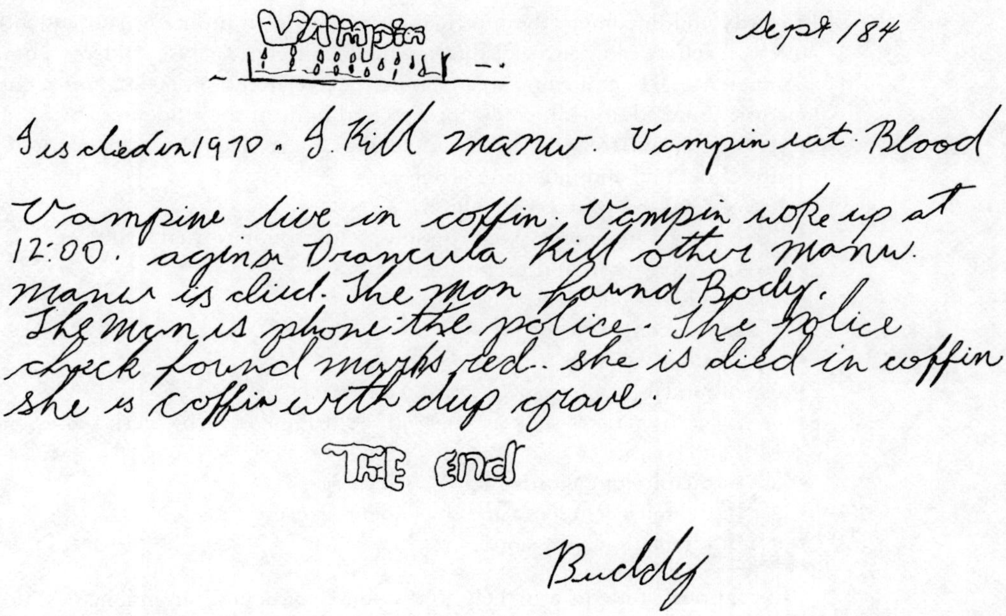
Vampin

Sept /84

Ius died in 1970. I Kill manw. Vampin eat Blood
Vampine live in coffin. Vampin woke up at 12:00. agina Drancula kill other manw. manw is died. The mon found Body. The Mun is phone the police. The police chyck found marks red. she is died in coffin she is coffin with dup grave.

THE End

Buddy

Figure 11–2 Language disorder

student speak slowly, or blunt and mumble sentences and then forget what was said?" and "Does the student either provide information that a person who has not had the experience needs in order to reconstruct the event or ensure that everyone has the same information about the event?"

Language sampling permits comprehensive assessment of pragmatic, semantic, syntactic, and phonologic skills, and provides direction for future instruction (Blau, Lahey, & Oleksiuk-Velez, 1984). Samples should be taken regularly in short sessions that represent as many normal interactions as possible across the entire language program. The samples should each have a minimum of fifty utterances, with at least two morphemes in each utterance. "I see" is acceptable, for example, but "good" is not.

Teachers will need to organize sessions that allow students to use language to describe, state, question, and command. The length of the sessions can be adjusted to the student's skills, and teachers should also vary the topics, the time at which the sessions take place, and the listening audience. Aides and classmates may participate in order to elicit samples of adult–child and child–child interactions. Some teachers will prefer to use several different stimuli to elicit responses, but they should all be at the student's level of cognitive ability and should generate a variety of concepts. The responses should not be prompted or modelled.

Language sampling sessions are best recorded on audio- or videotape, depending on the student's oral competence (a deaf student using sign will be recorded on videotape, for example), and then transcribed and analysed in terms of content, form, and function. Measures such as the Language Sampling Analysis (Tyack & Gottsleben, 1974) and the Teacher Assessment of Grammatical Structures (Moog & Kozak, 1983) are used to quantify and document the information, and to plan programs subsequently. Alternatively, teachers can construct their own checklists to analyse students' communicative competence. The following areas should receive attention, taking into account the age, maturity, and additional handicapping conditions of the student:

- use of appropriate sentence forms such as interrogative or exclamatory
- use of definite and indefinite articles
- use of regular and irregular plurals
- use of pronouns, possessive pronouns, and pronouns used a subject
- use of prepositions and prepositional phrases
- use of adverbs, conjunctions, and negatives
- use of the copula "to be"
- use of auxiliary verbs
- use of modals, such as *could*, *would*, and *should*
- use of verb markers such as -ing and -ed, irregular verbs, verb tenses, and subject–verb agreement
- use of quantitative words such as *more* or *most*
- use of complex sentences and dependent clauses
- use of idiomatic expressions

Exceptional students are likely to encounter difficulties in pragmatics, the social use of language. Assessment should therefore include a student's use of pragmatic functions such as taking turns in conversation or initiating and maintaining a conversational topic. Teachers can observe when and how a pupil changes topics, and the nature of a student's verbal responses to adult utterances (Miller, 1978).

Teachers may also want to assess a student's use of syntax. An intuitive understanding of syntax allows an individual to construct and understand sentences with many components, and conversely, a syntactic deficit will limit utterances and prove detrimental to reading. If children are asked to repeat a sentence more complex than they can produce themselves, they will normally simplify the sentence in the repeated version (Slobin & Welch, 1971). Gillett and Temple (1986, p. 83) suggest using an echo reading procedure to assess syntactic development in both prereaders and older students. The choice of sentences is simply varied according to the individual's age.

To use the echo reading procedure with very young children, the tester selects an eight-line passage from a book at approximately the grade one level and copies the lines so that the student's responses can be marked above each line. The tester then reads each line separately and clearly for the student to echo and the student's responses are recorded as

/ for each correct word

0 for words, word parts, or phrases omitted

______ for substituted words (write in the substitution)

∧ for added words

The sentence, "The little boy skated on the pond near his house," that elicits an echo of "Boy play pond at house," would be marked thus:

0 0 / play 0 0 / at 0 /

The little boy skated on the pond near his house.

In this example, the student has echoed fewer than 80 percent of the words, which indicates the presence of syntactic problems.

Mainstreaming language-disabled students

Few language problems exist independently of other areas of functioning. The results in terms of social interaction and school performance can be devastating, and intervention should be available at all educational levels. Intensive therapy, usually conducted by a speech/language therapist or pathologist on a one-to-one basis, can supplement regular classroom instruction. It is not appropriate as the sole vehicle for language instruction and practice, however, since language is a social medium. In the regular classroom, language-delayed and -disordered students can benefit from appropriate language models and linguistic interaction.

Case study 11–2, part 1 describes Christine, a nine year old with a language delay that is affecting other academic and social areas of functioning. An extract from Christine's individual education plan appears later in this chapter.

Case study 11–2, part 1

Christine, a nine year old attending school in Halifax, already has a history of school failure. When she first arrived in school, the difference between her language and that of the other kindergarten children was noticeable. She seemed to have a restricted vocabulary, poor grasp of grammatical rules, and many misarticulations in her oral language. These problems have largely corrected themselves and her speech is now almost wholly intelligible. Now in grade three, Christine continues, however, to display delayed language.

By the grade three level, language difficulties become more complex, manifested in a small vocabulary, incorrect structures (such as misuse of pronouns and ignorance of verb endings), and difficulties in the pragmatics of language. Christine, for example, rarely seems to understand jokes and riddles because linguistic nuances pass her by. She needs to be instructed in greeting behaviours and conversational skills. Because of her "baby" language, Christine is increasingly subject to ridicule from her peers.

Her receptive and expressive language difficulties have naturally affected other areas of the language arts adversely. Her reading is about two years below the rest of the class and her spelling shows little relationship to the words. Analysis of written language samples shows, apart from poor penmanship and ill-formed letters, difficulty in putting any ideas on paper and serious misuse, indeed, an absence of, grammatical rules such as verb markers, verb agreement, pluralization, or pronoun and prepositional use.

Although a psycho-educational diagnosis indicated that Christine is of average intelligence, her language delays constitute such a hindrance to her effective learning that they could prove devastating to her future school career. The school-based team believes that a combination of instruction in the regular classroom and resource room will prove the most effective. Christine will follow a structured program in the resource room, designed to improve her expressive and receptive language, while the classroom teacher will create as many opportunities as possible for language usage. Reading instruction will take place in the resource room, with the entry levels set very low to give Christine an initial feeling of success. Both the classroom teacher and the personnel in the resource room will monitor the program continually.

The mainstreaming team

The team responsible for assessing and placing language-disabled students will generally include a speech/language therapist, the classroom teacher, special education personnel, the school psychologist, and others. Two approaches to team work have been identified for speech- and language-disabled children in the school system. In a reactive approach, the classroom teacher tries to carry out what the student has learned from the therapist while the therapist tries to extend what the student is learning in class. In a proactive approach, the teacher and the therapist share a common base of information with each other, each providing input into the other's activities. This implies greater participation between therapist and teacher in the interests of the disabled student.

In either case, the IEP will focus on providing a rich language environment in which the student is stimulated to develop language abilities. Within the classroom, language-disabled students should participate in the full range of activities. Language instruction must encompass the entire school day if language is to become the student's interactive tool in all settings.

Instructional approaches

The initial step in language instruction is to reduce any factors that may be causing or influencing the language problem, such as hearing loss, poor health, or poor parent–child interaction. When setting up educational programs, it is also important to remember that although delayed children benefit from a stimulation approach in a functional context more than from a remedial approach in a clinical setting, disordered children may first need to develop prerequisite skills in clinical settings. For both groups of youngsters, intervention is most effective if it begins as soon as problems are noted.

Without perceptibly altering the program, the regular classroom teacher can provide support for the language-disabled student. No special materials are needed to develop the classroom contexts and tasks in which pupils can use language. Students need stimulation in the use of *functional communication* — language used to communicate in everyday settings with both peers and adults—and in language used to regulate others, to let needs and wants be known. Programs should train students in language that has immediate utility for them, as well as teaching them the standard grammatical forms of adult language. The goal is not perfect grammatical construction but effective communication. The list of general ideas below is designed to guide the regular classroom teacher who is faced with teaching a language-disabled student.

- Be aware of the student's specific language problems and the manner in which they affect both academic areas and self-concept.
- Do not give the student special treatment.
- Avoid communication pressures, such as asking the student to read in front of the class.
- Be a good language model.
- Match language instruction to the student's experiences.
- Provide opportunities for the student to give commands or ask for information.
- Prompt the student to use language, by making suggestions such as "Tell Sam what you want."
- Give the student a role as classroom helper.
- Use words and ideas that convey the student's own needs, interests, and experience in simple language.
- Acknowledge and reinforce the student's attempts to communicate.

- Be aware of the limits of the student's comprehension.
- Accept "slow motion" language processing.
- Explain new concepts briefly, clearly, and with many definitions.
- Listen carefully to everything that the student has to say.
- Set a special time aside for oral language activities.
- Allow the student to participate in group activities.
- Keep extraneous noise in the classroom to a minimum.

On a very general level, programming for language-disabled students has evolved in two distinct directions, the **grammatical approach** and the **natural approach**. Many types of intervention have arisen, of course, but most hark back to one of these two approaches. The grammatical approach to language teaching is sometimes called the skills-based approach, the behavioural approach, or syntax-based programing. It is behavioural in the sense that it approaches language as a learned and skill-based process and therefore attempts to provide direct instruction in those skills in which a student is identified as being deficient. In order to develop syntactic skills, the student is taught specific language structures such as subject, verb, object, and word order. Interventions are direct and systematic; the teacher reinforces accurate usage and corrects mistakes.

The grammatical approach uses chaining, prompting, imitation, expansion, and modelling. When using a **chaining** technique, the teacher presents all of a sentence except the last word and has the student say the sentence; then gradually presents less and less of the sentence until the student can respond fully (see chapter 4, p. 114). **Prompting** implies giving the student a clue, such as pointing or touching an object, in order to elicit a correct response. **Imitation** simply involves presenting the correct structure for the student to repeat. A little girl who comes in from recess and says, "Me cold," for example, would be given the structure, "I am cold," and asked to repeat it. **Expansion** involves acknowledging and reinforcing the student's utterances, and **modelling** in this context is similar. To model the sentence, the teacher may add more in the hope that conversational interaction will continue. A dialogue might therefore run as follows:

Child. Me cold.
Teacher. I am cold. [expansion] Can you say that?
Child. I am cold. [imitation]
Teacher. Yes, you're cold. Did you forget your mitts? [response and model]

The Fitzgerald Key (Fitzgerald, 1934), a linear representation of sentence patterns, is an example of a teaching technique that uses the grammatical approach (see table 11–2). Students learn the parts of speech, represented as headings on the Key, and are taught to visualize the grammatical relationships among words, phrases, and clauses. Elements are slowly added to the Key as students achieve mastery. A very young language-disabled child might practise the first two elements of the Key, for example, while an older student could work with all of them. Communication boards are built on the key.

The natural language, or nativistic, approach views language as an innate ability. It regards the developmental sequence of linguistic acquisition as a progression from simple to more complex structures expressing similar communicative functions. Natural

Table 11–2 Fitzgerald Key

Who	Verb	What	Where	When
John	ran.			
The boy	liked	the dog.		
Jane	threw	a ball	over the fence	during recess.

language training programs therefore de-emphasize the importance of direct teaching and stress the value of innate abilities, learning by discovery, and interpretation through listening. Naturalistic intervention duplicates the process of normal language development, but in a more systematic, simplified, and stimulating manner. Instruction uses syntax, word structures, and word meanings appropriate to the student's mental age. The teacher creates a good atmosphere for communication and stimulates students through prompting and modelling. Students then respond to the teacher's use of language. Teaching is often developed from sentence patterns and their transformations, presented in the order in which children learn language naturally (as given in table 11–3).

Table 11–3 Simple sentence patterns

Pattern	Sample sentence	Activities
NP + VP(+ adverb)	The horse neighed. Mother is cooking (happily).	Describing pictures; making experience chart stories
NP + VP + NP(+ adverb)	The boy eats the cookie. Martina is slicing the banana (neatly).	Making collages with string, paper, and so on; making a fruit salad
NP + state verb + NP	Mrs. Jones is the boss. That dog is a beagle.	Discussing pictures
NP + state verb + adjective	Tom is sad. The pumpkin is orange.	Describing objects, events, and people
NP + state verb + adverb of place	The cat is inside. Tim is outside.	Hiding objects; playing games

Source: Adapted from Blackwell, 1978.

Advocates of the natural approach believe that all children learn language in the same way and in the same order, and that children with delays and disorders will follow the natural progression, albeit at a slower and more restricted rate. Teachers attempt to develop the communicative potential in everyday activities, using new vocabulary and constructions within activities that are of interest to the students. As they begin to experience success in communication, the students are sure to develop confidence.

A number of methods have developed around the natural language approach. The language experience approach, which was discussed in chapter 7, is one of the most widely employed. For students with delayed or deviant language, teachers may also consider an enactive method or multisensory methods.

Several commercial materials are available that follow either a grammatical approach or a natural approach and are effective with language-disabled students in regular classrooms. Programs using the grammatical approach go beyond a purely analytical grammatical base to embrace the principles of transformational grammar. Interested readers are directed to Lindfors (1987) for further information.

Below is an extract from the IEP for Christine, the language-delayed student introduced earlier. Note that the extract deals with language only and incorporates elements of the Fitzgerald Key, as Christine requires an extremely structured program.

Case study

11–2, part 2

Name: Christine School: Maple Street Elementary
D.O.B.: 1 September 1980 Diagnostic category: Language delayed

Current levels of functioning:
Christine's current levels of functioning in various academic and social areas were evaluated from collected data. Her major area of deficit appears to be in receptive and expressive language. She uses syntactic structures appropriate for a child at the five-year-old level, has a restricted vocabulary, and problems with the pragmatic functions of language. Articulation per se shows no deviations.

Christine has barely made a beginning in reading; she recognizes a few sight words and has some basic sound–symbol association but experiences great difficulty reading words in context and understanding the message. Her written language is virtually non-existent and her handwriting shows malformations and ignorance of both upper- and lower-case letters. Christine also has difficulty comprehending oral messages. She will listen to stories but cannot recall the characters or the sequence of events.

Suggested placement:
Christine should remain in the regular classroom for language stimulation but will go to the resource room for two hours daily, for a structured language program and extra help in reading. The regular classroom teacher will provide opportunities for language use.

Starting date: immediately

Proposed length of program: one school year initially

Persons responsible: regular classroom teacher, resource-room personnel, educational consultant

Long-range goals:
1. Working on a structured language program, Christine will say simple sentences with correct verbs, subject–verb agreement, and irregular verbs.
2. Christine will use pronouns and possessive pronouns correctly orally.

3. Christine will use prepositions and prepositional phrases correctly orally.
4. Christine will develop the listening skills to follow instructions involving three steps.
5. After listening to stories, Christine will correctly answer questions, identify characters, and describe events in sequence.

Short-term objectives:

1. When presented with pictures of objects and actions Christine will order them to produce sentences that have the patterns NP + VP and NP + VP + NP, and then say the resulting sentences.
2. Given captioned pictures that use nouns and verbs, Christine will make, say, and read sentences.
3. When presented first with pictures, then captioned pictures, then captions alone, Christine will learn to use the prepositions *over* and *under, in* and *out,* and *to* and *from* in phrases.
4. When an oral direction is given to Christine, she will repeat it accurately and carry it out.
5. After listening to short, familiar stories, Christine will list the characters.
6. After listening to short, familiar stories, Christine will place events in sequence using picture cards.

Objective	**Techniques**	**Materials**
1.	Give Christine pictures that represent one verb and a number of nouns. Have her generate sentences from the pictures and say them aloud. Extend the exercise by adding verbs that use different tenses.	Fokes Sentence Builders
2.	Repeat the exercise, using captioned pictures of nouns and verbs.	Captioned pictures using different verb tenses
3.	Present pictures, captioned pictures, and then captions to Christine. Have her generate prepositional phrases. Read the phrases together and then have Christine read them alone.	Pictures, captioned pictures, and captions using prepositions
4.	Give Christine a command to perform an action and then have her answer the question, "What did you do?"	

5.	Read a familiar story out loud to Christine. Ask her to give the names of the characters.	Story book
6.	Read the story again, stopping periodically to ask Christine what will happen next. Give her picture cards of the events in the story to sort into correct order, and have her retell the story.	Picture cards

The enactive method

The enactive method has a number of areas of similarity with the language experience approach. Both are dynamic and flexible methods by which to teach language and both hold many benefits for exceptional students. The enactive method includes all aspects of the language hierarchy and uses small-group work and co-operative learning. To enact means "to act upon," and indeed, the method actively involves students, ensuring that they are processors of the material that they read, rather than passive consumers. It stimulates them to generate sentence forms spontaneously. Wesenger (1980) observes that the enactive method is child-centered because it capitalizes upon children's own language and experiences. By simulating natural situations and stimulating creative thinking, the method helps students to make sense of written information in terms of their recent experiences.

The teacher chooses a setting and materials and either constructs a model of the setting or has the class construct it. The setting represents a selected situation, such as a park, a playground, an Indian village, a camping scene, a castle for King Arthur, an aquarium for treasure hunting in the sea, or a racing circuit for a steeplechase. The materials might be based on a story, a poem, a class outing, a special treat, a theme, television characters, or special days. The objects selected should be of an easily manipulated size and of sufficient number both for the objectives of the activity and for the maturity and needs of the students. (Wesenger, 1980).

The teacher may wish to stress the language and vocabulary that a certain student needs in the park, for example, in which case the setting would be a simple portable model of a park, constructed on board or heavy card and containing "grass," "trees," benches, and a wading pool. The objects to be manipulated within the setting may include a slide, swings, and toy figures. The teacher introduces more objects as the lessons proceed and the student's vocabulary and language expand. Wesenger (1980) has outlined a series of lessons that use an enactive approach for language and reading (see box 11–2).

Although the enactive method is chiefly used to stimulate language in young children, it can be successfully adapted for older pupils. It is possible to integrate the settings and objects with other subject areas; variations depend only upon the creativity and interest of the teacher.

Box 11–2 Using an enactive approach to develop language

1. Select a setting of interest to the student that is within his or her experience and presents good possibilities for the objects to interact.
2. To introduce the lesson, present the setting with a few objects, and then manipulate the objects while discussing them with the student. Describe the action and record the description a chart until there is a sequence of three or four sentences. Read the sentences with the student.
3. On the next day, ask the student to manipulate the objects and to make a series of statements, and then record them on a new chart. (The previous chart might be used for review and then discarded.) Help the student to read the material, and then ask him or her to copy the material into a reading book for enactive material and to illustrate all or part of it.
4. Follow the procedure for about ten days. As the lessons proceed, slowly introduce new objects.
5. Have the student record the full story in his or her enactive book to serve as further reading material for that student.

Multisensory methods

Many individual language programs use multisensory methods (Slingerland, 1971). (Chapter 8 discussed multisensory approaches, specifically the Fernald method, with reference to reading programs.) The Orton–Gillingham remediation technique, for example, is a multisensory alphabetic/phonic approach to teaching language skills. Orton and Gillingham, followed later by people such as Slingerland, created a program designed to remediate not only reading problems but also related difficulties in spelling and handwriting. Children learn the associations between letters and their sounds in all of the modalities required by reading, writing, and handwriting tasks (Gillingham & Stillman, 1965). The Orton–Gillingham method focusses on fusing small units (letters, sounds, and syllables) into more complex wholes (words). Presented below is part of a multisensory language lesson based on the method.

Multisensory language lesson

Objective: to teach the letter *b* in a variety of ways using a multisensory approach

Materials:
- flash cards
- picture cards
- work sheets

Procedure:
Recognition: Ask the students to pick out all the cards showing objects whose names begin with *b* from a box of picture/word cards. The students say the names of the objects.

Auditory memory: Say three words beginning with the letter *b* and have the students first clap out the rhythm of each word after it is presented and then repeat the three words in the same order.

Auditory recall: Say a group of words and instruct the students to put their hands up every time they hear a word that begins with *b*.

Oral production: Have students say the sound *b* and feel it on their lips.

Auditory blending: Say words that begin with *b*, such as *b*at, and have the students blend the sounds into the whole word.

Visual-motor activity: Have students trace the letter *b* and words beginning with *b* in the air, on paper, or on a friend's back.

Motor activity: Have the students write the letter *b* a number of times.

Visual discrimination: Have the students circle all the *b*s and all the words beginning with *b* on work sheets.

Chapter 7 presented a range of techniques for stimulating and improving language, all of which are appropriate not only for mildly handicapped students in general but also for language-delayed and -disordered students in particular. The reader is therefore invited to turn to these for specific instructional suggestions. Of course, different activities work for different students, since language-disabled children form such a heterogeneous population and teachers have their own instructional preferences. The next chapter discusses a different population, yet one whose needs and characteristics have some relation to those of the students discussed in this chapter.

12 *Hearing-impaired students*

Dear Reader,

Last year, the Ernest C. Drury School celebrated its twenty-fifth year serving deaf students in Ontario. Those years have seen profound changes in approaches to educating deaf students. The prevailing philosophy in the early 1970s was one of total isolation from the regular education system. Deaf education was presumed to involve such specialized approaches and techniques that it had little in common with what went on in regular classrooms. During the late 1970s and into the 1980s, the emphasis swung sharply toward mainstreaming, particularly with the introduction of Ontario's special education legislation in 1980. The three provincial schools in Ontario became centres for students requiring a Total Communication approach, while school boards operated programs for students who could profit from oral programs.

In 1980, a very significant event happened in the education of the deaf. At that time, because of the impact of mainstreaming, the population at E.C. Drury School had declined dramatically. Conversely, the population of Milton had grown to the extent that a second high school was desperately needed. Negotiations between the Ontario Ministry of Education and the Halton Board of Education resulted in an agreement to build the new high school on the property occupied by E.C. Drury. This historic agreement created a unique complex that now meets the needs of a wide range of hearing and deaf students. The agreement safeguards the quality of programs for deaf students, while providing them with opportunities for integration into a regular school setting, social experiences, and full use of the extensive campus facilities.

Although there were a few teething problems during the early years, recent times have seen the development of considerable benefits for students at E.C. Drury. In order to facilitate integration, it was decided to join the new building to the existing one and to adopt common school names and colours.

The integration of the two schools in a single complex has provided a wider variety of options to deaf students than would have been the case prior to 1980. Deaf students have the opportunity to play on a number of sports teams. They can also choose from a broad spectrum of program options and models. While most deaf students receive their education in segregated classrooms, a few have chosen to take some of their credits in integrated classes in the high school with the help of a full-time teacher intervener. Another small group of deaf students are taking a full course load in integrated classrooms with the assistance of teachers of the deaf, who monitor their progress. There is also a large group of hearing students who are taking sign language courses for credit that are offered by teachers from the E.C. Drury staff. Several technical facilities, such as Food Services and Autobody, are shared by E.C. Drury School and the high school.

In addition to these programs, every opportunity is taken to promote social integration. Several integrated dances are held during the year, an integrated sports banquet winds up the sports season, and a highly polished integrated drama is held every two years.

E.C. Drury schools give the 1 300 secondary students on campus access to a wide variety of unique integration opportunities. It is a demanding but exciting environment in which to work.

Ron Dodds, Ed.D.
Program Director, Secondary Program
Ernest C. Drury School
Milton, Ontario

From their earliest days, hearing infants begin to master the sound, shape, and sense of language. They monitor their own and other people's utterances to reinforce the process of learning correct speech and language. Hearing impairment poses a serious threat to children's learning. The greatest single handicap of defective hearing is its effect on the development of communication skills, because hearing loss interferes with both the reception and the production of language.

For the normally-hearing person, it is almost impossible to obtain a true simulation of either hearing loss or language deprivation. Turning off the sound on the television may give some feeling for hearing loss, and remembering how difficult it is to learn a foreign language suggests to some degree the effects of speech and language problems. Remember how tired you became trying to learn the vocabulary and grammar, and getting your tongue around the different pronunciations? The same types of problems are encountered by hearing-impaired students, who have to remember the meaning, use, shape, feel, and look upon the lips, of individual words. Our language is also conceptually complex. Imagine a student who has never heard the spoken word trying to learn a word as simple as "run." Demonstrating the word by running around the classroom is easy but conveys only one of the word's meanings. It does not explain a run on the bank, running into a friend, or into debt, and it has little bearing on the word's idiomatic use in double verbs such as *run after*, *run away*, *run off*, or *run afoul*.

Providing the most appropriate educational, medical, and social resources for hearing-impaired youngsters is a challenge. Their identification, evaluation, habilitation, rehabilitation, and education involve the diverse fields of child development, education, linguistics, psychology, counselling, acoustics, electronics, pediatrics, otology, and genetics. The four professional groups most intimately involved are audiologists, educators, speech/language pathologists, and physicians.

In the past, few children with known hearing impairments were admitted to regular classrooms, and provincially operated residential–day schools still educate many of Canada's hearing-impaired students, although enrolment is decreasing. The current emphasis on appropriate integration has resulted in new locations for programs and a greater possibility of regular class participation for hearing-impaired students. Students with severe and profound hearing losses require a great deal of special help and are likely to receive their education in special classes or schools. Those with moderate losses, however, can usually be successfully integrated with periodic help in the resource room or from an itinerant teacher; and students with mild and marginal losses need little extra help when integrated in regular classrooms, although teachers must accommodate their problems and ensure that they progress adequately. Once in the mainstream, hearing-impaired students demonstrate many different rates of progress and achievement, just as hearing children do, but integration greatly enhances their prospects. Many of these youngsters do develop acceptable language and intelligible speech; they do achieve academic success, build solid social relationships, and learn to function successfully as independent individuals.

The increase in local educational programs for hearing-impaired students has created a special need for information and materials that will make the educational process more effective. An increasing number of teachers with no formal training in the education of hearing-impaired children are now faced with the challenging task of integrating these students. Many regular classroom teachers are very anxious about communicating with hearing-impaired students, and ask themselves, "How do I speak to the student?" and "How will I understand what the student is saying?" They worry about physical adaptations, curricular modifications, and using technical equipment. The main objectives of this chapter, therefore, are to

- outline some issues in the field of education for hearing-impaired students
- illustrate how hearing-impaired students, their peers, and their teachers can communicate with one another effectively
- examine the approaches that are valuable to regular classroom teachers who are integrating hearing-impaired students
- describe valuable technological devices for hearing-impaired students in the classroom

The education of hearing-impaired students

Currently, the whole area of education for hearing-impaired students is undergoing profound and far-reaching changes because of technological progress, a more rational view of communication modes, new information about teaching methods, and a flood of linguistic research on what language is and how it is learned. Several new trends have emerged: re-evaluating communication methods; extending work–study programs; extending educational programs up to the post-secondary level and down to the preschool level, including infant stimulation programs; using technology extensively; and providing both more specialized teacher training and more integration using interpreters. The medical community has been examining the causes and prevention of hearing impairment closely, while in the social arena the deaf community is demanding greater influence in the education of deaf children.

The 1960s witnessed a significant growth in programs for hearing-impaired children, which has increased dramatically in the 1970s and 1980s. Not only are mild and moderately hearing-impaired students being drawn into the mainstream of education, but so too are some severely and profoundly deaf students. Much remains to be done, however. The special needs of hard-of-hearing youngsters, programming for hearing-impaired children with multiple handicaps, and curricular modifications to enhance language acquisition and learning all require further research.

Assessing hearing impairment

Hearing impairment has been called the invisible handicap because of its insidious nature. Too often, adults overlook a child's hearing loss, and attribute his or her behaviour to other causes. Teachers and parents should be sensitive to behavioural and physical signs of hearing impairment (Winzer, Rogow, & David, 1987), although audiologists are responsible for the actual diagnosis of hearing acuity, the physical aspects of hearing impairment.

The individual needs of hearing-impaired students are determined by assessing the academic, psychological, and social impact resulting directly or indirectly from impaired auditory functions. Evaluation gives the highest priority to language assessment measures because deficits in speech and language development so often follow hearing impairment. Psycho-educational assessment of hearing-impaired children is fraught with frustration. Few measures have been normed on the hearing-impaired population, and most psychologists are neither trained nor prepared to work with these youngsters. They rely almost universally on standard spoken English in the assessment procedures and frequently administer tests that presuppose standard language skills (Moores, 1986).

The Wechsler Intelligence Scale for Children, Revised (Wechsler, 1974) is the most widely used test of mental ability for both hearing-impaired and hearing students. To test hearing-impaired youngsters, the Verbal scale is often omitted and an IQ score calculated on the basis of the Performance scale only. Recently, the Performance scale of the WISC-R was standardized on hearing-impaired children (Anderson & Sisco, 1977).

Mainstreaming hearing-impaired students

The similarities between hearing and hearing-impaired students are greater than the differences, and integration reduces those differences. Mainstreaming enables hearing-impaired youngsters to interact with hearing students in ways that will prepare them for real-life situations. A mainstream setting provides appropriate models of speech and functional language and daily opportunities to practise imitation (Northcott, [1984]). It also motivates hearing-impaired students to use speech and helps them to develop good speech attitudes.

The mainstreaming process can, however, have a negative side. Competition with hearing students places greater strain on the hearing-impaired student's personality. If the family is not strongly supportive, the student's level of frustration may exceed his or her level of tolerance to withstand such competition (Northcott, [1984]). Hearing-impaired students may also experience social rejection, and some researchers therefore believe that integration can have an adverse effect on the mental health of some of these youngsters (Dale, 1972). This text argues that socially injurious aspects of classroom integration can be overcome in many cases with sufficient attention (see chapter 6).

Case study 12–1, part 1, presents the story of Bruce, a hearing-impaired student integrated into regular classes in junior high school. An extract from Bruce's IEP appears later in this chapter.

Case study 12–1, part 1

Thirteen-year-old Bruce suffers a moderate bilateral sensironeural hearing loss. The impairment was identified during his preschool years and Bruce has been using amplification since that time. Early intervention ensured that Bruce began school with some speech and language, although at a lower level of acquisition than would be expected for a hearing five year old.

From the outset, Bruce was placed in regular classrooms and received assistance in language, speech, speech reading, and auditory training from itinerant teachers for two or three hours weekly. As the demands of school increased, Bruce began to go to the resource room for one hour daily for extra help in reading and the other language arts. By the time he graduated from elementary school, Bruce was within a grade level of his peers in academic subjects. Language, especially reading, caused some concern, and he seemed slower than the other students in completing assignments that required comprehension of reading materials. With consistent instruction, his oral language showed acceptable articulation and production, although it was a little restricted in vocabulary. Bruce interacted well with his peers and seemed pleased with the prospect of moving into junior high school with them.

The adjustment from elementary to junior high proved particularly difficult, however. Bruce was confronted with a new building, new rules, new peers, and many new teachers, who all had different ways of speaking and sometimes forgot that Bruce relied on speech reading for information. At the same time, Bruce began to reject his hearing aid, feeling that it made him look too different from the other students. For the same reason, he ceded low priority to sessions with the itinerant teacher and eventually stated that he "would rather stay in class" with his friends.

The increased demands of the junior high school curriculum meant a greater emphasis on literal and inferential reading skills, which Bruce was expected to apply to learning in other academic areas. Even the classroom situation seemed to militate against him. The noise of the film projector and the fan on the overhead projector brought all sorts of extraneous noise into his hearing aid and hindered his use of residual hearing. He was constantly cut off from speech reading by classroom lights being turned off for films and slides, and by teachers who walked around the classroom or talked to the blackboard. As well, Bruce missed large amounts of information because he could not take notes and speech read at the same time.

Given the complexity of the effects of hearing loss, it is not easy to integrate hearing-impaired students. The degree of hearing loss is only one of the several variables related to successful mainstreaming into both the educational environment and the community. Students considered for mainstream placement should be emotionally balanced and socially mature, with adequate academic and communication skills. The most important requirement for academic integration is the possession of reading skills at close to normal levels, certainly within one grade level of average students the same age. The communication levels demanded of students will depend on their primary mode of communication and on the availability of interpreters. Table 12–1 outlines some important educational and social criteria for mainstreaming placement. This list must be viewed with great caution; each student is an individual and should be judged on his or her own strengths and weaknesses.

Table 12–1 Selected criteria for integrating hearing-impaired students

Elementary	Secondary
Hearing loss (marginal to profound)	
◆ Availability of interpreting services for students who acquire information through the visual mode	

Table 12–1 continued

Elementary	Secondary
Classroom teacher	
◆ Sensitive to the problems of hearing loss ◆ Able to communicate well orally ◆ Prepared to use a great deal of written material and many visual aids ◆ Willing to modify the curriculum and to provide alternative learning experiences ◆ Willing to co-operate with support personnel	
Communication	
◆ Uses connected sentences, generally with correct structures ◆ Has verbal skills in turn-taking and adaptive dialogue ◆ Uses speech reading effectively ◆ Intelligible speech	◆ Expressive and written language within acceptable limits for the class ◆ Willing to participate in learning experiences in and out of the classroom ◆ Understands the pragmatic functions of language
Academic criteria	
◆ Reading at or near grade level ◆ Good reading comprehension skills ◆ Adequate in content areas	◆ Good previous achievement from report cards and tests ◆ Reading at or near grade level ◆ Reads a variety of material for information ◆ Appropriate writing skills at grade level in most areas ◆ Good general knowledge
Social criteria	
◆ Strong self-image ◆ Motivated, responsible, and mature ◆ Establishes relationships ◆ Works independently ◆ Adjusts to new social and academic situations ◆ Has family support	◆ Strong self-image ◆ Mature, adaptable, independent, and responsible ◆ Enjoys the integrated setting ◆ Responsive to peers ◆ Aware of own strengths and problems ◆ Has family support
Support services	
◆ Resource room ◆ Itinerant teachers ◆ Educational consultant ◆ Speech therapist ◆ Oral or manual interpreters ◆ Audiologist ◆ Guidance counsellor ◆ Psychologist	◆ Resource room ◆ Itinerant teachers ◆ Educational consultant ◆ Speech therapist ◆ Oral or manual interpreters ◆ Audiologist ◆ Career, academic, vocational, and guidance counsellors ◆ Psychologist

The mainstreaming team

For mainstreaming to be truly successful, the teacher must be an integral member of a team that will include many different people who are directly or peripherally involved with the student. Team membership may encompass the school principal, guidance counsellor, school psychologist, educational consultant, itinerant teacher, resource-room staff, speech and language therapists, audiologist, otologist, and otolaryngologist. As well, the classroom teacher may have to work with an oral or manual interpreter, a classroom aide, and professional or student note takers.

Curricular objectives and adaptations

Generally, curricular objectives are identical for hearing and hearing-impaired students. The severity of the hearing loss, the age of onset, and the student's mode of communication determine placement and educational methods. Many large school districts have developed a combination of service alternatives: special classes, resource rooms, and itinerant personnel. Special curricula for hearing-impaired students might include hearing aids, auditory training, speech work, speech reading, special media services, and captioned films. For instructional purposes, the regular classroom teacher is usually concerned with the acquisition of a language base, communication skills, and the ability to use alternative learning modalities (such as strong speech reading skills), all of which require specific effort from the student (Caccamise, 1974).

Acquisition of language

Hearing-impaired students are not a homogeneous group. Receptively, hard-of-hearing students usually learn to make effective use of whatever hearing they have. Deaf individuals use other channels, chiefly the visual, to establish and maintain contact with the people around them. Expressively, deaf students use a smaller, more concrete vocabulary with shorter and less complex sentences than do other youngsters. They demonstrate difficulties in the use of grammatical structures, especially verb usage, and tend to omit plurals, possessives, prepositions, and determiners (see box 12–1).

Box 12–1 Syntactic structures generated by deaf students

Structure	**Sample sentence**
Verb system	The girl a ball.
Negation	Beth made candy no.
	I amn't tired.
	Bill willn't go.
Complementation	John goes to fishing.
Relativization	I helped the boy's mother was sick.
	John chased the girl and he scared.
Question formation	Who TV watched?
Conjunction	Beth threw the ball and Jean catch it.
	The dog chased the girl had on a red dress.

Source: Adapted from Quigley, Power, & Steinkamp (1977).

Hard-of-hearing children encounter a great variety of problems. If the voiced sounds of conversational speech remain audible, mild hearing impairment may have minimal effects, although it can still hamper language development. Brannon (1966, 1968) found that hard-of-hearing children tend to use fewer adverbs, pronouns, and auxiliaries than do hearing pupils. Some children display deficiency in the use of several syntactic structures essential for producing grammatical sentences (Brannon, 1968; Brown, 1981; Davis, 1977). Yet hard-of-hearing children seem to use grammatical morphemes and to develop them in a normal, but delayed, sequence. A mild hearing loss may not result in aberrant language, and Ling and Ling (1978) stress that language delays can be prevented if the loss is diagnosed and treated early.

Hearing-impaired students are taught language by methods derived from either the natural or the grammatical approach (see chapter 11). The main differences between their instruction and that of hearing students lie in the degree of intensity and of systematic presentation. Instruction may also employ communication modes that bypass the hearing loss, and it is very likely that students will be fitted with some type of amplification.

Hearing-impaired students must painfully learn and remember every word and construction, and will require intense practice, review, and reinforcement. Teachers must always be ready to interpret, to introduce and reinforce meanings and usage, and to alert pupils to new vocabulary. Hearing-impaired students have difficulty concentrating on long and detailed sections of material, explanations, or instructions. They must reconstruct a large portion of spoken material from contextual clues and by retaining familiar words that they have seen many times on the speaker's lips. They also have to extrapolate new meanings if concepts are new. Teachers can keep students in touch by providing simple lesson outlines before the class, or hand-outs of key points. Page numbers and homework assignments should be written on the board. Oral tests are a real obstacle; teachers should give written tests when possible, making sure that these are at the students' level of reading comprehension.

Communication modes

Although most integrated students will be proficient in speech reading and able to learn through oral/aural methods, the number of students in regular classrooms whose major communication mode is manual is increasing. The communciation mode used by the student has tremendous classroom implications. Total Communication and the oral/aural method are the most common modes employed in Canada today although the spectrum extends from the unisensory, or acoupedic approach, which uses residual hearing only, to American Sign Language. In between are the various multisensory approaches, such as Cued speech and the Rochester method.

Educators believe that the unique needs of each student should largely determine the communication mode. Generally, individuals designated as hard-of-hearing process information auditorally and will be educated entirely through oral/aural methods. For deaf children, modes that incorporate manual ingredients are gaining in popularity. Discussed below are a number of procedures that teachers can adopt in the areas of speech, speech reading, language arts instruction, and amplification to assist students using oral/aural communciation. The option of manual or oral interpreters is also addressed. Even if regular classroom teachers are not expected to have skills in manual communication they may work with an interpreter in the classroom.

Speech Speech acquisition is extremely difficult for hearing-impaired students. Normally-hearing children develop *feedback skills* (the ability to monitor what they are saying and how they are saying it) through *auditory encoding* (hearing what they say) and *articulatory encoding* (physically feeling what they say). All speech sounds feel just as different to speakers when they make them as they sound to listeners when they hear them (Ling, 1986). Hearing-impaired students cannot monitor their own voices or model their speech on incoming stimuli, and instead must remember the shape and feel of every sound that they utter.

A number of systematic methods have evolved to teach speech to hearing-impaired youngsters, as have a number of tools, such as vibrotactile devices, to help students achieve better speech (Erber & Cramer, 1974). Nevertheless, deaf children's speech is often unintelligible, even with optimally effective intervention. Not all the speech sounds have the same strength: vowels and diphthongs carry more acoustic energy and lower frequencies, and consonants are roughly ten to fifteen decibels weaker than vowels and diphthongs. Hard-of-hearing children may not hear and therefore not produce such high-frequency sounds as *s*, *sh*, *th*, and *p*. There are, however, few published studies examining the spoken language of hard-of-hearing children (Brown, 1984).

Correcting defective speech and enhancing appropriate articulation are generally the responsibility of speech therapists or specially trained itinerant teachers. While classroom teachers will not be called upon to alleviate serious speech problems, they can, however, assist hearing-impaired students by employing the general approaches discussed in chapters 7 and 11. Additionally, teachers can always expect appropriate speech at the student's level and provide non-threatening opportunities for her or him to use oral language. It is important that teachers become good listeners and withhold responses until the student completes the entire message.

If a student's speech is unintelligible on a particular occasion, it is not helpful for the teacher to simply indicate understanding; it is demeaning and discouraging and may hinder the pupil from attempting further communication. If it is not possible to understand what a pupil is trying to say, try these suggestions in the following order. First, repeat the message to get the kinesthetic feel of it. If this fails, simply guess at the message, and have the student confirm or reject the guess. Third, have the student write, draw, or dramatize the message. If the message is still unclear, you may have to resort to asking someone who might know.

Speech reading Because they suffer deficits in auditory processing and functioning, hearing-impaired students place greater, if not sole, reliance on their sense of vision. Hard-of-hearing students who typically acquire information auditorally are likely to supplement the auditory signal with **speech reading**, and deaf students will use speech reading as their primary means of gathering information.

Speech reading only supplements spoken language, relaying about 20 percent of the information that an individual receives through normal hearing (Jeffers & Barley, 1971). Moreover, the development of speech-reading skill is particularly difficult, indeed, more difficult for hearing-impaired than for hearing people. More than 30 percent of English words are **homophones**; they look the same on the lips. Speech reading will

Teachers may work with an interpreter in the classroom.

not help the student to distinguish, for example, the words red, green, and white, which are homophonous. Lip movements are also fleeting and hard to see, so the speech reader needs a high degree of concentration and guesswork to reconstruct the message from the visible clues. Finally, good speech reading demands the one skill in which hearing-impaired students are most often deficient: an adequate language base from which to obtain contextual clues.

There is very little data to suggest how best to teach speech reading or to explain why some youngsters are good at it and others are not. Measured intelligence and other factors relevant to successful instruction do not seem to be closely related to success with speech reading. The teacher can, however, make minor adjustments in the classroom to facilitate a hearing-impaired student's comprehension:

- Attempt to maintain a distance of two metres from the student while teaching the class. Giving the student a centre seat in the second row is ideal. In a one-to-one situation, keep your face at the student's eye level.
- Speak naturally, but remember that hearing-impaired students may miss short words or words with a similar appearance, and thus lose the context of the message. If the student seems confused, repeat the message, or rephrase it into shorter, simpler sentences if necessary, placing the key words at the end of the sentences whenever possible.

- Speak only when the student can see. During discussions, ensure that he or she has located the speaker and allow the hearing-impaired student to move as necessary. Use the overhead projector instead of the blackboard whenever possible in order to face the class and project information more effectively.
- Recap discussions briefly and note key points on the board.
- Use consistent phrases to command attention, such as "Watch now" or "Listen carefully."
- Use cues or key words to tell the student when you are about to introduce a new topic. It is very difficult for hearing-impaired students to adjust to topic changes quickly.
- Always keep the light on a speaker's face and behind the hearing-impaired student.
- Try to get a classroom with a white ceiling. This reflects light better and therefore makes speech reading easier.
- Films and audio tapes will be especially frustrating to the hearing-impaired student. Assign a buddy to act as an oral interpreter and keep enough light on the interpreter's face to make speech reading efficient. In a darkened room, use a flashlight.
- Have peers repeat to the hearing-impaired student any messages that come over the public address system.
- In assemblies, a microphone can be annoying if it covers the speaker's face; speakers should be reminded to stand a little to one side.

At the secondary level, the hearing-impaired student faces a new set of obstacles to speech reading. She or he has to contend with the communication habits of several teachers in different subject areas. Panel discussions, questions and responses from students in all parts of the classroom, committee meetings, and assembly programs all become part of a complex communication environment that can be extremely taxing. In addition, note taking plays an increasingly important part in secondary classroom activities but keeping his or her eyes on the page denies the hearing-impaired student many non-auditory clues.

Note taking

Note takers, drawn from volunteers, paraprofessionals, or students from upper classes, are invaluable for hearing-impaired students. Choose individuals who are knowledgeable about the subject matter, above average in academic achievement, and sensitive to the problems of hearing impairment. Note takers need to be self-confident in dealing with teachers and willing to accept criticism and direction (Wilson, 1981). It is helpful to assign a note taker to the student as soon as reading skills are established. While elementary pupils benefit from this system, it is vital to the secondary student's progress. At the high school level, classes have a faster pace, more discussion, and more technical vocabulary.

Those taking the notes should use carbon paper to make an immediate copy for themselves. They can write the name of the class, the date of all notes and written work, and the dates when assignments are due or tests will be given, to help the hearing-impaired student remain organized. The notes should contain as much description as possible of classroom discussions as well as definitions of new terms or ideas (Wilson, 1981).

Language arts

Deaf students are educationally retarded by three or four years, most noticeably in all areas of the language arts, although they are no less capable than hearing students. No relationship exists between the degree of hearing loss and the level of intelligence, but significant correlations are found between degree of loss and the ability to acquire language, to read, and to write. Most hearing-impaired students fail to acquire reading skills comparable to those of hearing children of the same age (Balow, Fulton, & Peploe, 1971) and it is not common for deaf children to read beyond the grade four level (Trybus & Karchmer, 1977). Deaf children also show relatively rigid, immature written patterns, with many grammatical errors and an absence of sentence complexity (Moores, 1986). They tend to do better on more mechanical pursuits such as spelling and arithmetic computation. Similarly, hard-of-hearing children may not perform at the level of their hearing peers (Fisher, 1971; Peckham, Sheridan, & Butler, 1972). Quigley (n.d.) found that this held true even for children with marginal losses in the 16 to 26 decibel range.

The major goal of any reading program is to develop literacy and to help students to read commercial materials for information and enjoyment. It is not really known how deaf children learn to read (Clarke, Rogers, & Booth, 1982), and there exists no agreement over the best way to teach them. Given the difficulties that hearing-impaired students meet in reading, however, it should be the prime area in which to modify the curriculum and instructional approaches. When teaching reading to hearing-impaired students, consider these suggestions:

- Use the whole-word method rather than any type of phonics approach. Phonics approaches to reading instruction are directed to the least reliable sensory system of hearing-impaired pupils.
- With younger children, use an enactive or language experience approach to enhance word recognition and comprehension.
- Explore the special materials devised for hearing-impaired students such as the *Reading Milestones Series* (Quigley & King, 1980).
- Analyse the important concepts, key words, and new constructions within new reading material in terms of students' prior knowledge (paying particular attention to question forms, idioms, and words with more than one meaning).
- Teach new vocabulary and sentence structures in advance, perhaps by planning a class activity that uses words and sentences that will appear in the upcoming reading material (Carlsen, 1985).
- Use many visual media and much dramatization to illustrate new words and concepts.
- Limit the number of new words and sentence structures in a reading assignment.
- Rewrite books to the appropriate level, especially for older students.
- Question students constantly to check their comprehension. It is easy to be misled about how much hearing-impaired students understand, as they may read a passage orally with few errors. By using word matching (context clues) and good instincts about probabilities, they may even score well on objective tests without fully grasping the meaning of what they have read (Carlsen, 1985).

Case study 12–1, part 1 earlier introduced Bruce, a hearing-impaired junior high school student, integrated into a regular classroom, and experiencing increasing difficulty in the setting. Part 2, presented below, includes the team's recommendations and an extract from Bruce's IEP, concentrating on objectives and strategies in reading.

Case study 12–1, part 2

Name: Bruce | School: True North Junior High
D.O.B.: 5 June 1976 | Grade: 7

Present levels of functioning:
Bruce is falling behind academically. Lacks in reading comprehension are affecting other academic areas, specifically English and social studies.

Recommended placement:
Both Bruce and his mother were present at the second meeting of the school-based team to discuss his placement and program. While Bruce openly discussed his dislike of being pulled out of class for additional resource-room help, he was not averse to spending a good part of his school day in the special classroom for hearing-impaired students. The team therefore recommended placement in the regular classroom with four periods daily in the special class for assistance in reading, language arts, and any other areas that Bruce identifies as problematic.

Long-range goals:
1. Bruce will increase his comprehension of written material.
2. Bruce will improve his locational and skimming skills.
3. Bruce will improve his skills in outlining, summarizing, and note taking.
4. Bruce will understand the major concepts and information related to the social studies curriculum by using notes prepared in advance of the lessons.

Short-term objectives:
1. When presented with short passages, Bruce will predict (infer) what will follow, first orally and then in writing, and will sequence sentences within the passages.
2. When presented with short paragraphs, Bruce will identify both the main idea and the supporting arguments.
3. Given short paragraphs, Bruce will skim them for the main idea.
4. Given lists of headings and subheadings, Bruce will sort them and then write a short paragraph for each heading.

Objective	**Techniques**	**Materials**
1.	a) Read short passages to Bruce orally. Ask him to answer the question "What might happen next?" first orally and then in written form on work sheets.	Short passages on individual work sheets
	b) Ask Bruce to read a short passage and sort sentences from the passage in to the correct order.	Sentence strips cut from the written passage
2.	a) Present Bruce with a short paragraph, and ask him to identify the main idea and the supporting ideas and to write them on a "paragraph pie."	Written paragraphs, a "paragraph pie" (see chapter 7)

	b) Have Bruce read paragraphs drawn from his school books. Ask him to underline the main idea and identify the supporting arguments orally.	Textbooks
3.	Have Bruce skim material in order to answer specific questions or locate specific information.	Readers with high interest and low vocabulary
4.	Present Bruce with headings and subheadings drawn from newspapers, or written on flash cards, and mixed together. Ask him to sort them into headings and subheadings and to write a short paragraph for each heading from the resulting outline.	Newspapers, flash cards

Career counselling

Hearing-impaired students will require counselling throughout their school careers, and particularly at the secondary level, when career development is essential. A number of occupations are simply not viable for people with defective hearing. Propp (1973) points out that hearing-impaired adolescents need a school-wide process of career education that offers information and training separately and provides a solid background for making a career choice. Counselling and guidance should be viewed as integral parts of career development programs, as should building students' functional communication skills, favourable work attitudes, and sense of self-worth. Educators and administrators must heighten hearing-impaired students' expectations and standards of performance.

Technical devices for hearing-impaired students

Very few individuals are totally deaf; most have some residual or usable hearing. Perhaps the most important single development for hearing-impaired people was the invention, in the 1920s, of the electronic hearing aid, which can greatly ameliorate the effects of an impairment. Deaf children need amplification, but hard-of-hearing children can also benefit from it. The decision whether or not to equip a hard-of-hearing child with an aid is made by an audiologist, based on the severity, type, and duration of the hearing loss. If a child wears only one aid, it should be placed in the better ear.

Amplifying devices do not, however, fully overcome defective hearing. The user must do more work than the aid in order to understand the spoken message. Energetic and persistent efforts are crucial to adequate comprehension of the aided sound.

All young deaf children, and some young hard-of-hearing children, should use appropriate amplification, monitored by teachers and parents. Adolescents, however, may

FM systems are a useful form of amplification in group situations.

balk at being forced to wear aids. They occasionally feel that the aid identifies their impairment to other people. Others believe that they derive no benefit from amplification, or are distressed by the amount of extraneous auditory stimuli channelled by the aid. By the secondary level, a student's aid can be functioning as well as ever, but communication demands may have increased so dramatically that the student questions its continued use. Teachers and parents must balance the value of amplification and the wishes of the young person; each solution will be individual. Teachers also need to understand the operations, limitations, and maintenance of amplification devices so that they can become allies in the student's efforts to use amplification effectively.

Frequency modulation systems

Frequency modulation, or FM, systems are the most popular form of amplification for group situations, either for a hearing-impaired student in a hearing group, or for groups of hearing-impaired students. The **FM system** is really a miniature radio broadcasting system with two basic components: a microphone worn by the teacher and a receiver worn by the student (Staab, 1978). Because individual aids provide optimal amplification between one and less than two metres from the speaker's voice, and amplify both speech and environmental noise (Van Dyke, 1982), an FM system is a valuable alternative in a classroom setting where noises and reverberation levels may be high (Crum & Matkin, 1976).

FM systems are relatively easy to use. Teachers should remember to check that the microphone and receiver are on the same frequency range, and that the antenna is free.

The plastic tubing on the microphone of many FM systems is the antenna and should not be cut, wound through a belt, or otherwise hampered. Because the microphone picks up all sounds, teachers should be careful of jewellery around the neck that may bang on the microphone, and should make sure to turn the microphone off before doing such things as sharpening pencils. In small-group settings, the microphone can be passed around to each speaker as long as the students realize that it is not a toy but a valuable instrument to help the hearing-impaired student. The system usually requires recharging overnight.

Individual hearing aids

Hearing aids are available to fit all types and degrees of hearing loss. Currently, the four main types are behind-the-ear aids, body aids, eyeglass aids, and custom, in-the-ear aids. Most children will be fitted with behind-the-ear (ear-level) models (see figure 12–1).

Hearing aids consist of a number of parts. The microphone receives sound waves from the air and converts them into electrical impulses. The amplifier increases the strength of the electrical impulses and the receiver changes them back into sound waves. In a body aid, the microphone is found under a grid. The microphone in ear-level aids is usually behind a small opening in the case. Switches and dials vary from aid to aid. The position switch may be set at T for telephone, M for microphone, B for both, or O for off if the aid has an O setting. Often the volume control also acts as an on-off switch. In the classroom, the position switch should be set at M or B. Some aids also have an outer tone control switch but this should not be adjusted.

On a body aid, the receiver is a button that clamps to the ear mould. The receiver cord is connected to the hearing aid case and to the receiver button. The receiver on

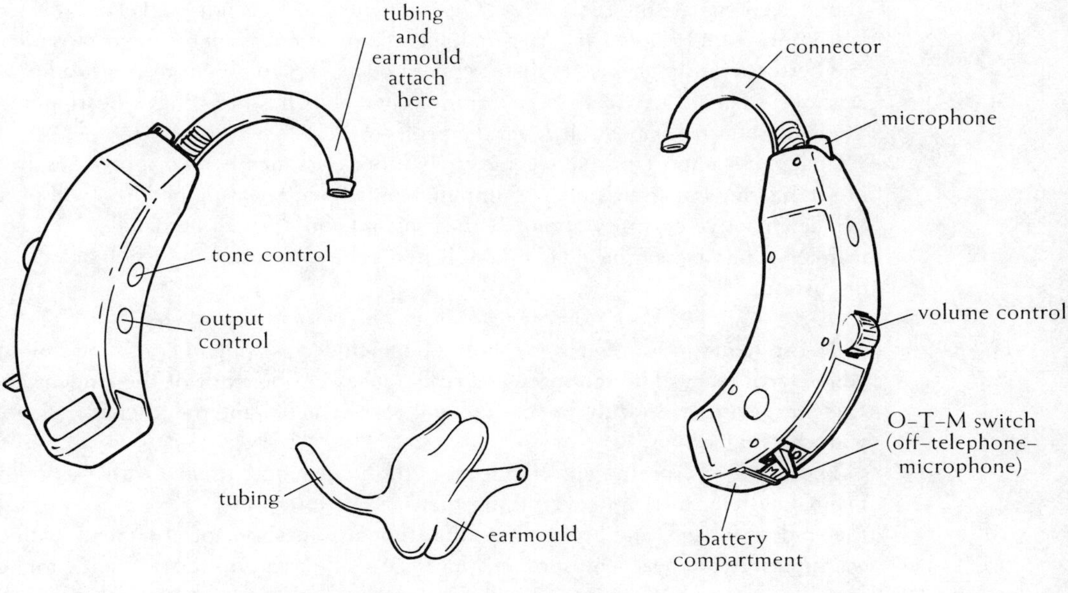

Figure 12–1 Ear-level hearing aid

an ear-level aid is built into the case. Ear-level aids have plastic tubing connecting the aid to the ear mould, which directs sound into the ear. The case protects the inner parts of the aid. Batteries fit right into the case.

Although hearing aids are complex electronic devices, they require only simple care and maintenance. They must be kept dry, clean, away from high temperatures, and should not be dropped. Ear moulds are made individually; they must be kept clean and fit properly. If the mould is loose, feedback, a high static noise, will alert listeners. Moulds can be cleaned with pipe cleaners in warm sudsy water.

Of course, it is the student who wears the mould. Children over the age of five should know how to put the ear mould in, turn the aid on and off, adjust the volume, recognize a dead instrument, and handle the aid. The tip of the mould fits about half-way along the outer ear canal, and does not touch the drum. A teacher may help the child to insert the mould by placing the long piece of the mould gently in the ear canal and at the same time pulling the top of the external ear gently upwards and backwards. The mould can be inserted and sealed by twisting it back and forth.

Just because a student is wearing a hearing aid is no guarantee that it is working. A teacher should perform a daily listening check to ensure that the aid has batteries, and keep an extra supply of batteries on hand. To perform the check, the teacher snaps off the ear mould and listens to the aid's receiver. He or she should also take care that the controls are set correctly, in an *on* position, to M (microphone), at the usual volume setting. Table 12–2 illustrates some of the problems that may arise with hearing aids, and their causes.

Teachers can capitalize on the benefits offered by hearing aids by maintaining a good communication environment, in which the speaker is close at hand, many non-auditory cues support the spoken message, and a minimum of extraneous sound competes with the speech signal (Stassen, 1973). One way of lowering noise levels is to have the classroom soundproofed and carpeted. If carpeting is not available, then a wooden floor has better acoustic properties than a concrete one. Try to obtain an overhead projector without a fan, to use in the classroom. When showing films, have hearing-impaired students sit as far as possible from the projector.

Finally, it is important that teachers help other class members to appreciate the value of the hearing-impaired student's amplification. Young hearing children will probably evince an active curiosity about the hearing aid and this can be handled in a positive manner. A pupil's hearing aid is a suitable item for a show-and-tell session or a classroom discussion.

Interpreters

A deaf student's interpreter is, or should be, included as a member of the school-based educational team. The interpreter is really an extension both of the student and the student's relationship with the teacher, and of the teacher and the teacher's relationship with the student.

The *manual* interpreter will sit in front of the student and, usually with a school-based manual system, interpret everything that is said. Interpreters repeat the message for the student in sign, and also present the student's questions or comments orally. The *oral* interpreter repeats the speaker's message while at an optimal distance for speech reading. During a film, for example, the oral interpreter would face the student and quietly repeat or rephrase the dialogue.

Table 12–2 Problems with the hearing aid

	Battery: dead, run down, wrong type, inserted incorrectly	**Plugs:** not fully inserted	**Mould:** poorly fitting, plugged with wax	**Receiver:** loose parts	**Microphone:** too close to receiver	**Switches:** in wrong position	**Tubing:** cracked or collapsed
Hearing aid dead	X			X		X	X
Hearing aid working, but weak	X	X	X	X			
Hearing aid works, but only intermittently	X	X		X			X
Feedback, a whistling sound			X	X	X	X	
Sounds noisy, raspy, or shrill	X	X		X	X	X	
Sounds hollow, mushy, or muffled	X		X	X		X	

Of the integrated hearing-impaired students in Canadian schools, only 1 percent are provided with manual interpreters (Canada, Health and Welfare, 1984). One reason is cost. Another is that the student interacts entirely with the interpreter who relays the message, and may therefore be *in* the class but not *of* it. The entire situation may be simply too contrived to be superior to a special class with a teacher using sign language.

Deaf students are the most difficult of the special populations to integrate into regular classrooms because their severe auditory deprivation affects speech, language, reading, and writing. With technological equipment, support personnel, and additional assistance from the classroom teacher, however, at least some deaf students can achieve well in regular settings. Integrating hard-of-hearing students depends on their level of hearing loss, and some will function very successfully in the regular classroom.

13 Students with attention problems and perceptual disorders

Dear Reader,

My task now is to speak to you on the subject of "mildly disabled" learners or "learning-disabled" youngsters. These terms are much too easily tossed around, and I need not remind you of the real dangers to young people from the loose use of such labels. The children about whom I am speaking are those whose learning skills deviate from "the norm." In fact, all children differ from the norm, which is simply a hypothetical construct. The average Canadian family contains 1.73 children. It is that .73 of a child who is "mildly disabled" or "learning disordered" or just a little less good at learning some things than you might like.

I speak from experience, not alone as an educational psychologist and researcher, but as someone who has learning disabilities and is also related to people who have them. May I thus share some of my experiences as a learning-disabled person, a parent of children exhibiting, at one time or another, so-called learning disabilities, and a teacher of both the learning disabled and non-learning disabled?

All people learn at different speeds, learn some things better than other things, and better or worse than other people do. It is when you move out toward the extremes of human performance (so-called exceptionality) that you start to notice certain individuals, especially when they have difficulty learning things that others find easy — tying one's own shoes, blowing one's own nose, or learning to read simple sentences. Why do people have trouble doing such things? There is no one reason, but for any particular child, emotional factors, health factors, genetic background, cultural issues, and the interactions of these all influence the degree of learning. Probably the most significant factor that influences the quality of learning for any individual is what that person has already learned. Experienced teachers and parents know this intuitively, but it does help to be reminded of it from time to time, and of its instructional implications.

I mentioned that I was learning disabled. Well, I am. I am lucky to be seated today in front of a word processor. Although I know how to think and to express myself more or less clearly, I cannot write legibly and I never could. I joke about it, as lots of learning-disabled adults do, or deny it, or cover it up. I can't ride a bicycle either. Fortunately I had (mostly) good teachers when I was a pupil. They understood exceptionality in that they treated each student as unique and of equal worth. To this extent they understood morality too. I am not of low intelligence but my patterns of skill strengths and weaknesses are different enough from those of typical people my age to be noticed by others. As a child I was teased and as an adult I still get strange looks when I decline to go bicycle riding or have to write a note to someone by hand. If you have never had this experience, you might have difficulty appreciating how it feels. Take my word for it. All children deserve to have "good" teachers and "these" children deserve it even more.

A number of years ago, being fair to all students meant setting up special schools for each type of disability — objective (physical) and subjective (psycho-emotional) — so that every pupil could have her or his own tailor-made instruction. It sounded good, it was expensive, and it resulted in many different types of schools. Today, being fair involves integrating all students in the same schools and wherever possible in the same classrooms. That is being fair to the child and to the broader society within which she or he must live and work. It is expensive too, since more teachers need special education training, and research must be done to evaluate the effectiveness of the new integrated programs. Fairness requires nothing less. What then is my message to you? Read this chapter with an open mind about the children and about yourself as a future teacher of them. Fairness also requires that all children receive the best teaching available.

Stephen F. Foster, Ph.D.
Department of Educational Research
Faculty of Medicine
University of Limburg
Netherlands

In almost every classroom across the country there are one or two pupils who fail to achieve adequate levels of performance despite conventional and consistent instruction. These students often bother and frustrate teachers with their unpredictable behaviour, their impulsiveness, their emotional lability, their hyperactivity, their lack of attention, and their widely varied achievement in academic subjects.

Sometimes these youngsters have been screened and referred for psycho-educational diagnosis in their early school years. Reports are, however, often contradictory and may be larded with labels such as learning disabled, mildly handicapped, and even emotionally disturbed. As discussed in previous chapters, however, categories are less important than behavioural manifestations. Many texts offer full descriptions of mildly handicapped children: their etiologies, learning and behavioural characteristics, and the developmental consequences of their conditions. The interested reader is referred to Day (1986), Hallahan and Kauffman (1986), Hallahan, Kauffman, and Lloyd (1985), and Winzer, Rogow, and David (1987). The policy in this text is to draw non-categorical and categorical approaches together.

As a general rule, teaching methods for mildly handicapped pupils will not vary greatly from conventional instruction, but the goals will receive very different emphasis. To contemplate completely distinct programs and techniques for various categories of mildly handicapped students, however, is not reasonable, given their functional similarities. Students will need modified programs that stress functional academic skills, language and communication, personal and occupational skills, and skills for independent living. As well, however, their programs must address underlying areas of dysfunction frequently exhibited by these children, specifically attention, memory, perceptual functioning, and concept development, and these are the focus of this chapter.

We have tended to assume that students who received special help in the elementary grades will automatically be cured by the time they reach secondary school but this is patently untrue. Many students will need extra support throughout their school careers. Whatever the age of the pupils or the setting, intervention for mildly handicapped students concentrates on preventing learning failure and providing individualized education programs. The main objectives of this chapter are therefore to

- discuss deficits in attention, memory, organization, perception, and concept development, any of which may inhibit mildly handicapped students from learning efficiently
- present instructional approaches to remediate these areas of dysfunction

Mainstreaming mildly handicapped students

Although many children could be included under the category of mildly handicapped, this discussion is limited to the three groups traditionally labelled as learning disabled, mildly mentally retarded, and behaviourally disordered. These are the youngsters for whom mainstreaming and non-categorical approaches will have the greatest impact. Their disorders are usually categorized as mild because, given special help, these students can function quite adequately in regular classrooms. On the other hand, they frequently have histories of school failure and any set of deficits that can so thoroughly disrupt students' school careers should never really be considered in less than a serious light.

The criteria for accepting mildly handicapped students into regular classrooms are elusive to grasp, and may be different for intellectually handicapped and behaviourally disordered students. Intellectually handicapped and learning-disabled students should have adequate social skills, be prepared for the transition, and be placed in classrooms where physical, intellectual, and social integration is assured. Beyond these very general minimum criteria, however, the elements that will lead to successful integration are a matter of debate. Behaviourally disordered children respond to the environment in socially unacceptable or personally unsatisfying ways, but they can be taught more acceptable and satisfying behaviour. They may be placed either in the regular classroom or in the special class with a reasonable hope of quick reintegration with their peers. For these children, social skills and affective experiences are as crucial as academic competencies (Hallahan & Kauffman, 1986).

To determine whether a particular student is eligible for mainstreaming, it is important to scrutinize both the student and the boundary conditions. The behaviourally disordered student has the potential to disrupt the learning of everyone in the environment and may even leave other students with the impression that bizarre behaviour is tolerable, if not acceptable. Within the regular classroom, all students must learn that aggression and disruption carry serious social penalties. The teacher must also be considered. If a student's behaviour causes behavioural management to become a preoccupation, then a mainstream setting is not appropriate. Regular placement may also heighten behaviourally disordered students' distress and lower their self-esteem. Research on the acceptance of these youngsters in mainstream settings indicates that they are disliked by most of their peers (Drabman & Patterson, 1981; Newman & Simpson, 1983). Yet some behaviourally disordered students do successfully learn to participate in the regular classroom.

It is almost impossible to be certain in advance which students will function successfully in integrated settings and which will not. There are, however, some very general criteria to consider when making decisions about integrated placement (see tables 13–1 and 13–2), although these are certainly not hard and fast rules.

Rather than list criteria for mainstreaming behaviourally disordered students, it is appropriate to outline the factors, especially boundary conditions, that may call for temporary removal of a student from the regular classroom. Temporary separation from regular peers may be justified when:

1. A stable, productive educational environment, otherwise threatened, is preserved in the regular classroom for non-handicapped students.
2. The segregated student is provided with appropriate instruction in academic and social skills.
3. The change in behaviour that the student is able to make in a segregated environment is socially validated and consistent with social and academic expectations in the normal environment.
4. The option of conditional reinstatement is maintained (Kauffman, McCullough, & Sabornie, 1984).

Table 13–1 Selected criteria for integrating mildly mentally retarded students

Elementary	Secondary
Classroom teacher	
◆ Sensitive to the problems of intellectual handicaps	
◆ Wants the student and is willing to adapt programs	
◆ Able to provide alternative learning experiences	
◆ Willing to work closely with special education personnel	
◆ Willing to adopt differential grading systems	
◆ Agrees with the philosophy of integrating mildly handicapped students	
Academic criteria	
◆ Able to handle academic stress	◆ Able to handle academic stress
◆ Can follow oral and written directions	◆ Can comprehend material presented in various forms
◆ Developing sight vocabulary	◆ Attempts homework
◆ Comprehends and uses oral language	◆ Possesses basic reading and mathematical skills
◆ Attempts to remain seated for independent work	◆ Shows continued development of skills
◆ Can work independently	◆ Willing to accept remedial help
◆ Retains general concepts	
Social criteria	
◆ Demonstrates acceptable behaviour	◆ Demonstrates appropriate behaviour
◆ Interacts with peers	◆ Interacts with peers and is accepted by them
◆ Developing social skills	◆ Has good communication skills
◆ Adheres to class rules and routines	◆ Has a good self-image
Support services	
◆ Resource room	◆ Resource room
◆ Speech/language therapist	◆ Guidance, vocational, and career counsellors
◆ Guidance counsellor	◆ Psychologist
◆ Psychologist	

Instructional approaches

The special problems of students who demonstrate deficits in memory, attention, and perception have spawned a variety of approaches in the last decade, far too numerous to be covered in a single section. Educators endeavour to formulate balanced programs that will include academic skills, personal and social skills, daily living skills, and prevocational skills. They also try to relieve as much as possible the external pressure of grades, competition, and social animosity manifested in teasing or ostracism.

Generally, intervention falls into three broad categories: ability or process training,

Table 13–2 Selected criteria for integrating learning-disabled students

Elementary	Secondary
Classroom teacher	
• Willing to accept the student	
• Willing and able to adapt and modify programs	
• Works co-operatively with other professionals	
Academic criteria	
• Developing reading skills	• Able to derive the main concepts of material if they are presented in alternative forms
• Able to copy from the board or a book with some accuracy	• Possesses basic reading and mathematical skills
• Understands and uses oral language	• Able to organize materials and learning, with some help
• If hyperactive or distractible, attention deficits must be amenable to intervention	
Social criteria	
• Relates to peers	• Accepted by peers
• Communicates with peers	• Accepts help from peer tutors and note takers
• Adapts to class rules and routines	
• Can follow her or his own schedule	
• Developing ability to work independently	
Support services	
• Resource room	• Resource room
• Speech/language therapist	• Guidance, career, and vocational counsellors
• Guidance counsellor	• Psychologist
• Psychologist	

the skills approach, and a combination of the two methods. Ability training is founded on the assumption that the cause of a learning difficulty is found within the student. Training procedures are therefore designed to overcome deficits in language, discrimination, attention, thinking, and memory. In the process, some teachers prefer to base instruction on the students' strongest learning modalities while trying to improve weaker learning areas. By contrast, the skills approach sees learning problems as external, the result of some discontinuity in instruction or learning. Instead of trying to remediate faulty learning processes, teachers using the skill model will concentrate on improving students' academic performance, and aim instruction at the areas of academic weakness (see Winzer, Rogow, & David, 1987). The combination skills–process approach uses academic materials but also involves the sensory system.

Education today gives greatest credence to a skills approach, but regardless of which approach regular classroom teachers prefer, they can make use of the general tips presented in boxes 13–1 and 13–2, which supplement the suggestions already presented throughout this text.

Box 13–1 Tips for helping young mildly handicapped students

- Use activities that incorporate a number of curricular areas in order to broaden learning skills.
- Relate teaching to previous learning. Introduce a new lesson with a picture, for example, and tell the class first, "See the picture of. . . ," and then, "Yesterday you saw a picture of. . . ." Simple recall questions or statements also relate ideas to one another. Ask the students, "Is it the same?" or tell them, "Yesterday I had . . . and today I have. . . ."
- Ask students to repeat directions, to ensure that they understand them.
- Reduce the amount of written work or allow students to use other response modes, such as tape recorders.
- Use a variety of multisensory materials. Clarify new information with visual aids.
- If a student seems to be having visual or spatial problems on written work, use unlined paper.
- Use graph paper for mathematics exercises, to help students align their work.
- Tape multiplication tables to students' desks.
- Introduce only two or three new words at a time for reading or spelling.
- Teach students how to write tests and complete workbook exercises.
- Praise small accomplishments.

Box 13–2 Tips for helping older mildly handicapped students

- Put notes on the board before class.
- Post class rules, due dates for assignments, and other reminders and leave them for as long as they apply.
- Allow students to tape lectures for future reference, or to photocopy the notes of a reliable student.
- Provide homework study schedules. Do not overwhelm students with the amount and complexity of homework.
- Teach students how to review reading by first checking titles, captions, subtitles, and summaries.
- Put lengthy reading passages on tape, so that students can follow the tape while reading.
- Use diagrams and visual material whenever possible.
- Use rewritten materials when necessary.
- Provide hand-outs listing specific questions before laboratory exercises. For some students, trying to do an experiment while making notes is an impossible task.
- Allow students with memory problems to use fact tables or calculators.
- For students with spatial organization difficulties in geometry, draw the problem on paper in dark marker. Trace it over with the student, taking her or him through the steps one at a time.
- Grade papers for content first and modify report cards to reflect intra-individual improvement.

Attention disorders and hyperactivity

Attention deficits are prevalent in mildly handicapped students, and are considered to be the most serious problem of learning-disabled children (Bryan & Bryan, 1978; Keogh & Margolis, 1976). Some mildly handicapped pupils have great difficulty attending selectively, are distractible, and demonstrate accelerated rates of motor activity. They become distracted by other objects in the environment or by irrelevant aspects of a task. Deficits in attention span, especially if accompanied by hyperactive behaviour, clearly inhibit learning in school-age children. As students grow older the problems tend to decrease, but not always sufficiently for the long class periods common at the secondary level.

Attention span is the length of time an individual can remain actively involved in an activity before becoming bored and restless. There are two types of attention. **Selective attention** refers to the ability to focus on the relevant features of stimuli. Once students have located the relevant stimuli, they must develop **sustained attention** in order to attend to the stimuli over a period of time. Teachers must be careful to distinguish between students with intrinsic attention problems and those who have simply learned to distract the teacher. The pupil who, in the middle of a mathematics lesson, for example, says, "My finger hurts," or who begins talking about something quite different may really be sending the teacher a message. "I don't understand what's going on," says the student, "and therefore to protect myself, I'm changing the subject."

Attention problems are often associated with hyperactivity: while hyperactive children will have attention deficits, children with attention problems are not necessarily hyperactive. **Hyperactivity** should not be confused with children's normal ebullience; the behaviour is characterized by abnormal patterns of inattentiveness, impulsivity, overactivity, extreme agitation, and overresponsiveness to stimuli. The physical activity seems driven beyond the child's control. The manifestations of hyperactivity alone do not disable the child; it is the impulsive, uncontrollable quantity of the behaviours that are inappropriate for the social norms of school and home life (Goldstein, Baker, Bruce, & Jamison, 1980). Consequently, hyperactive children have difficulty getting along with peers, and experience academic problems because of sudden aggressive outbursts and the inability to concentrate. As a result, they tend to display lower self-esteem and self-confidence than other children of the same age (Goldstein, Baker, Bruce, & Jamison, 1980).

For hyperactive children, attention problems usually surpass the problems created by their excessive movement. Many interventions have been employed to control attention problems and hyperactivity, such as drug therapy, stimulus reduction, cognitive strategy training, and behaviour modification, which was addressed in chapter 6.

Classroom techniques to reduce attention problems

As teachers recognize that, in many cases, attention problems are cognitively based rather than deviously controlled by students, they can learn systematic management and instructional techniques to teach students to increase their attention spans. One method to help children with hyperactivity and attention problems involves the removal of all distracting stimuli. This means having students clear their desks, providing quiet areas, and setting clearly defined units of work. Some pupils will respond more appropriately with a simple change of seating, either away from distracting classmates and close to good role models or at the front of the classroom with distractions behind them. Others may work better in individual carrels, an arrangement that has been shown to increase attending behaviour although not necessarily academic performance (Haubrich & Shores, 1976).

Remediation should focus on a single problem at a time. Teachers should limit the amount of new information presented at any one time and avoid an overreliance on discussion. Attention-disordered and hyperactive children need continuous success through instruction presented in sequenced steps. They should be given a great deal of verbal rehearsal and modelling during both instruction and application. During instruction particularly, their attention should be focussed on consistent clues. Stress the relevant aspects of a task initially and increase the novelty of positive stimuli as the lessons proceed. With application work it may help to have the students head each page in capital letters in order to focus attention on the task at hand.

Learning is enhanced and attention improved when verbal information is accompanied by visual props. Teachers must remember, however, to display materials one at a time and to keep other materials out of the students' visual field. Objects tend to be more effective than pictures. It is vital to prepare materials in advance, as students will certainly lose attention if the teacher has to leave to collect materials.

Teachers should try to vary the presentation of tasks, and make the information relevant to the students' everyday activities and interests. Students with short attention spans require specific tasks with specific time limits. They may also perform more adequately using teaching machines and programmed instructional materials. Although individual work and computer technology may be extremely helpful to a hyperactive student, however, it is important to evaluate the software carefully beforehand. If computer-based drill and practice is to be employed the program should not have a command waiting time longer than five seconds.

Using alternative forms of media can combat attention problems and auditory perceptual problems. Some young learners, for example, may need to spend some time saying or identifying sound blends while they listen to a tape-recorded activity through ear phones and receive appropriate visual stimulation, such as flash cards (Blackman, Burger, Tan, & Weiner, 1982). Some students respond well to the use of a frame with a window in it placed over the book during silent reading to focus attention on the print. For written work, a coloured placemat under the notebook serves the same purpose.

Children with intrinsic attention problems are difficult to handle in groups, and teachers may consider reducing the amount of time these students spend in group settings. Proximity control — seating the student near the teacher — may also help to sustain her or his attention. Of course, students must always be provided with feedback that enables them to assess their own progress and thus realize the importance of their work (Pointkowski & Calfee, 1979).

Attention problems do not simply disappear at the secondary level, although they may be manifested in different ways. Students who constantly shuffle papers, open their desks, drum their fingers, and so on, can distract everyone in the environment. It is possible to hold their attention, however, by using proximity control and by facing the student in order to establish eye contact. Concrete aids remain important and teachers can use many visual aids, such as flow charts, flip charts, and overhead projectors. Students may exhibit better attention if they are provided with a lesson outline or a glossary of key terms prior to the lesson.

Thinking skills

As they progress through school, students are expected to develop skills in logical reasoning, abstract thinking, and working out problems. These are the areas, however, in which mildly handicapped students are likely to be most seriously affected. Thinking skills are rarely taught within the school curriculum. It is assumed rather that they are a by-product of basic skill learning and the acquisition of information. Thinking skills have long been emphasized for gifted and talented students, however, and there is no reason why they cannot be a part of all students' education.

Using visual material will stimulate mildly handicapped students to grasp ideas because they will not have to rely wholly on language. They should also be given opportunities to verbalize abstract material until the vocabulary is familiar. Finally, the students will need to be systematically taught the process of defining the nature of an issue to be solved and then examining the steps necessary to reach the solution.

Memory

Memory is one component of what are known as executive thought processes, or executive strategies. A learner's repertoire of strategies are a set of tools that help him or her to activate and regulate effectively such important activities as attending, comprehending, retaining and retrieving information, thinking, and reasoning.

As well as *internal* executive strategies there are also *external* executive strategies, called mediators. Mediators are processes that connect the stimuli in, and responses to, the learning task. In this sense, the teacher is a mediator because he or she mediates between the learner and the outside world (Mulcahy, Marfo, Peaf, Andrews, & Clifford, 1986). Verbal mediators — the teacher rewording something in order to clarify it, for example — facilitate the student's acquisition, storage, and retrieval of information and are therefore necessary for memory. Teachers must be aware of their role as mediators and reword, reiterate, and review information as necessary.

Mildly handicapped students have trouble employing efficient learning strategies such as organization, and many encounter difficulties with both long- and short-term memory. It therefore takes them longer to learn a skill. The more complicated the learning task, the more memory problems mildly handicapped students will encounter. To ameliorate memory difficulties, at least to some extent, students can be taught to use verbal rehearsal, in which they label aspects of the task and rehearse aloud or silently as the task is performed. N.R. Ellis (1970) and his associates consider the short-term memory problems of mentally retarded students to be due primarily to their inability to use adequate rehearsal activities and strategies. Students can also be helped to employ image rehearsal, in which they associate aspects of a task with pictures or events (Ellis, 1970). They may require assistance in learning to group information, especially for concept development and abstractions.

Increased motivation, continual assessment, and precise, immediate feedback will improve short- and long-term memory functions. In addition, reducing stimuli improves not only attention but also short-term memory. All extraneous stimuli that may distract from the task at hand should be removed and pupils rewarded for attending to the task (Mercer & Payne, 1975).

Simple memory devices, of the type with which most of us are familiar, work well with children. There are five basic types of device: rhyming devices, such as "Thirty days hath September . . ."; associations, such as "The principal is our pal"; grammatical devices, such as acronyms or coined words; linking devices, in which words are placed together to form a mental image; and location techniques, in which the learner mentally pictures where the information required was located on the written page (Criscoe & Gee, 1984). Most people employ some of these techniques when trying to remember facts, matching the device to the type and complexity of the material. This is not true of mildly handicapped youngsters, however, who need to be taught how to use them. Currently, educators are assessing a number of structured methods for improving students' memory, retention, and ability to retrieve information.

Cognitive strategy training

Mildly handicapped learners often do not understand the relationship between learning strategies and successful performance. Recently, educators have focussed on the need to teach these students *how* to learn, by developing instructional programs that stress methods of processing and applying information, organizational and study skills, and strategies to work through problematic issues (Towle, 1982). Cognitive strategy training, or metacognitive training, forms part of the process. It is used to help mildly handicapped students to organize their thought patterns, social behaviours, and learning behaviours through self-assessment, self-verbalization, self-instruction, self-guidance, self-monitoring, self-recording, and self-reinforcement. The executive thought processes, and some of the techniques just discussed to improve memory, are also used in metacognitive training. Various studies have demonstrated that training can have dramatic effects on school performance when students generalize the strategies to natural environments (Ellis, 1983; Schmidt, 1983).

Metacognition refers to one's own cognition and the regulation of one's cognition. Palincsar (1986) explains the process to her students with a football metaphor. Every good team has a number of strategies and can select the one that best fits the play. The coach and players continually evaluate how effectively the strategies are working and select new ones as necessary. Metacognitive processes are the strategies that we select to direct our learning, such as planning, revising, and evaluating. There are many strategies: Wittrock (1983), for example, has identified no fewer then thirty-two that one might teach to enhance reading comprehension.

Metacognitive training teaches students first to consider the variables involved in solving a problem; second, to regulate the processes that they use to solve it; and third, to apply specific cognitive skills to the task effectively (Ellis, 1986). When they first begin to acquire metacognitive strategies, students need to have the benefits of the various strategies explained to them, and should be given demonstrations of how and when to use them. The teacher establishes an academic problem, identifies the strategies to be used, and assesses the prerequisite skills by using task analysis.

One important learning strategy is self-talk, or self-instruction. Meichenbaum (1981) suggests that teachers implementing self-instruction programs should first listen for the strategies that a student is presently using, to determine whether or not they are appropriate, and then make a careful analysis of the behaviours to be changed. Prior to training, the teacher can ensure that the student possesses the necessary skills to use self-instruction (such as memory and sequencing), and should collaborate with the student to devise a routine. Once training begins, the training tasks should reflect the target behaviour as closely as possible.

To initiate the procedures, an adult first performs the specified task while verbalizing aloud: addressing questions about the task, guiding herself through the several steps, and evaluating her own performance. The student then performs the task while the adult instructs him aloud. He then performs the task, first, while verbalizing aloud, second, while self-verbalizing in a whisper, and, finally, while using subvocalizations. Throughout, the teacher should give the student feedback about the utility of his particular self-instructions for performance. To increase the efficacy of the procedures, teachers can point out situations in which self-instruction will be useful, and use a variety of trainers, settings, and tasks to encourage the student to use self-instruction successfully outside of the training session. Students should be trained in the techniques until a reasonable criterion for performance has been reached, and then given occasional booster sessions to maintain the skills.

It is critical that training make use of relevant academic materials. Self-instruction should also be specific: students must be taught to use particular sets of instructions that apply to specific situations, such as problem solving in mathematics (Hallahan, Kneedler, & Lloyd, 1983; Hallahan, Lloyd, Kauffman, & Loper, 1983).

Organizational skills

Educators often assume that students know how to organize material for efficient learning, but mildly learning handicapped youngsters rarely do. In fact, one frequent symptom of mild handicaps is an inability to organize studies and time. Organizational difficulties aggravate whatever other deficits a student has, partly because of the student's inability to understand, manipulate, and make decisions about the specific material being learned, and partly because of the effect that this disorganization has on adults who are trying to help the student learn effectively (Bachor & Crealock, 1986). It is often difficult not to lose patience with poorly organized students.

There are a number of relatively simple ways in which teachers can help mildly handicapped students to improve their organizational skills. Many of the methods have already arisen throughout the text. The benefits of organizing lockers, for example, have been discussed earlier, but for some students, the lockers and locks themselves present real difficulties; the students forget the location of the lockers and cannot manipulate the locks. It may help to allow seriously disabled students to carry all their equipment in a large gym bag. With the inside compartments, the bag can be organized so that students can keep all their possessions in one place and carry them around with them.

Mildly handicapped students may lack test-taking skills, and should be taught to focus on the types of questions likely to arise, to answer the easy questions first, to allot time properly during a test, to answer all the questions, and to check their work. Similarly, teachers will find it necessary when assigning homework to ensure that students understand the instructions. Memory deficits and handwriting problems, compounded by difficulty in following directions, can make noting homework assignments confusing for some mildly handicapped students. They require extra time and prompting to copy assignments accurately.

Not only do mildly handicapped students not organize their belongings and time efficiently, but they are characteristically deficient in study skills, the broad complement of skills used by students to organize their learning environment. Too often a neglected area, study skills are vital for efficient learning. As an example, taking good notes is particularly important because the material that students take in notes is seven times more likely to be remembered than the material to which they only listen (Woolfolk & Nicolich, 1984).

What Do I Need For Classes?

- Binder
- Hilroy Notebook
- Pencil Case
- 1 Blue Pen
- Lined Paper
- 1 Red Pen
- 1 Highlighter
- 1 Eraser
- 1 Ruler

Before I Leave For and From School

- Make sure I have binder and textbooks.

During Self-Improvement Time

1. Check **Advance Planner** for assigned homework.
2. Look in Hilroy notebook for homework instructions.
3. Finished homework early? Go over your notes and:
   a) read today's notes for each class
   b) put titles on **all** notes, maps, drawings, graphs
   c) underline all titles in red
   d) put dates on every page
   e) repair ripped pages
   f) put all pages in order by dates
   g) complete any unfinished notes
   h) get a magazine or a novel to read

Homework Policy

- Students **will** have homework daily from 1 class.
- Students **may** have homework from more than 1 class.
- Students **may** have homework on weekends.

Advance planners and organizational tips can assist students with time management and promote good study habits. The illustration here and the one on the following page show two pages from a specially designed planner.

PROJECTS			
SUBJECT	DATE ASSIGNED	DATE DUE	STEPS TO FOLLOW WITH DATES

To promote good study habits, teachers can assist students with time management, memory, taking notes and tests, and methods to streamline the process of comprehending new material (Bragstad & Stumpf, 1982). Sets of questions directly related to material yet to be presented are especially helpful. They not only reveal students' prior knowledge to the teacher, but also alert the students to important points that will be made during instruction.

Prior to and during instruction, teachers can present brief overviews of important terms and principles. *Overviews* are particularly useful to familiarize students with loosely organized material. *Outlines* are similarly effective, and assist with reading. Students can be given partially completed outlines to finish. As another study aid, *advance organizers* provide a broad conceptual framework focussing on the processes that students are to use throughout the unit.

The survey, question, read, recite, and review method also improves study and note-taking skills (Criscoe & McGee, 1984). With this technique, the students survey the material to locate the main points. They then convert the main points to questions in order to improve their comprehension, and read to answer the questions. They then recite the answers, and finally review all the questions. Translating diagrammatic material into English — for example, matching sentences to the appropriate table or graph — is a comparable study exercise, and should be given emphasis.

Perceptual problems

Perception is the process by which an organism becomes aware of objects, qualities, and events stimulating the sense organs. It forms a link between sensation and cognition. To perceive, an individual selectively attends to stimuli, organizes and interprets the sensory information, and thus gives it meaning. Perception and conceptualization are inseparable, although they are not synonymous. Perceptual abilities develop fairly early in life, and are critical for school learning because they affect the total organism to a much greater degree than functions such as colour, vision, or pure tone discrimination. There is hardly any academic activity that does not require a student to engage in some type of perception.

Perceptual difficulties in mildly handicapped students, especially those labelled as learning disabled, represent a constellation of behavioural abnormalities rather than a single characteristic. Descriptions of these problems have included the visual, auditory, motor, and haptic systems, and consequently involve a great many manifestations. Students may have problems with discrimination, the ability to locate relevant dimensions of a given stimulus. The ability to discriminate the words "cat" and "car," for example, requires the person to locate the relevant stimulus, the last letter of the word. If they cannot discriminate symbols, students may exhibit reversals in their printing and drawing. They may not be able to reproduce information received visually or auditorally, and will have difficulty identifying the letters of the alphabet, reading from left to right, and keeping their writing on the ruled lines.

Students with perceptual problems may be unable to sort foreground from background. They may have difficulties with closure, spatial relationships, and form perception. Problems in spatial relationships are interconnected with directionality and therefore frequently result in confusion concerning basic mathematical concepts. Children with directionality problems may not be able to see a number line, understand positive and negative numbers, or compute problems with more than one row of digits.

Students with deficits in auditory processing possess normal hearing acuity but often seem unable to interpret verbal messages correctly. A student may hear the teacher say "Get your math book," for example, but comprehend the instruction as something quite different. Auditory processing impairments are often manifested in oral language, in locating sound, in detecting voice and gross sounds, and in identifying environmental sounds. When listening to speech, students may not be able to discriminate clearly among consonant or vowel sounds, or determine subtle differences among words. Children with auditory learning problems often ask for instructions to be repeated.

Motor problems have received declining attention in recent years. The efficacy of motor training has been seriously questioned although it still retains a place in the education of learning-disabled students. Gross motor co-ordination problems are demonstrated as clumsy, unco-ordinated behaviour. Children sometimes appear to be at war with their environments and cannot compete with their peers in athletic activities. Fine motor co-ordination problems affect such things as cutting and buttoning, stacking and stringing, or reproducing designs. Motorically disordered youngsters have poor body image, confused laterality, and a lack of directionality.

Classroom techniques to improve perceptual functioning

Teachers should be aware of the role that auditory and visual processing play in learning. Case study 13–1, part 1 illustrates the profound affect that perceptual disorders can have on a student's educational progress. Part 2 presents an IEP extract for the same student, offering suggestions that the regular classroom teacher can use to assist a perceptually disordered student. Following the case study is a set of activities to develop perceptual skills.

Case study 13–1, part 1

Since the day seven-year-old Jamie arrived in school he has presented difficulties to his teachers. Although Jamie is only in grade two, the school already has a thick file of his assessment results. He has been given quite a number of labels in the past three years, most consistently that of learning disabled. The grade two teacher, however, is primarily interested in designing an appropriate program that will help Jamie to modify his erratic behaviour while teaching him the basic skills of reading, writing, and mathematics.

Jamie has good receptive and expressive language. He listens and remembers well and has little difficulty following directions or responding to material presented orally. His spoken language is articulate and even somewhat more advanced than his peers in vocabulary and language structures. Yet when Jamie puts pen to paper or tries to read, difficulties emerge. He seems unable, or unwilling, to learn basic words by recognition and has developed minimal word-attack skills. His spelling

Fine motor co-ordination affects such activities as stacking objects.

shows little relationship to the words and written language of any type is almost non-existent. A lack of graphic skills exaggerates his difficulty in getting thoughts down on paper. Printing presents a particular obstacle, not only because Jamie is left-handed but also because he has not internalized the formation of the letters or the differences between upper- and lower-case letters.

As a general rule, Jamie's classroom behaviour is adequate, but during periods of stress, such as when he is asked to read or do seatwork, Jamie will passively refuse the task. Recently, his objections to these activities have become more pronounced as he manifests them in tantrums. The teacher sees Jamie as a child with great intra-individual differences, one who has many strengths but also many weaknesses. She referred Jamie to the school-based team again in an attempt to gain assistance in devising a program especially designed to concentrate on his pattern of peaks and valleys in learning.

Case study

13–1, part 2

Name: Jamie — School: Island Elementary
D.O.B.: 1 December 1982 — Diagnostic category: Learning disabled

Following the teacher's referral, the team met to discuss Jamie and an appropriate placement and program. Certainly, the child and his problems were not new to the team and previous interventions, of an ad hoc nature, had been attempted without great success.

It was decided to present Jamie with another psycho-educational assessment, but with the measures weighted heavily toward achievement and perceptual functioning. As well, Jamie's presenting behaviours, and the observations of the psychologist, were considered an important aspect of the assessment. During the assessment, Jamie participated happily until a reading measure was presented, when he balked and refused even to attempt the test. He eventually confided to the psychologist that "reading was too hard" and that he'd prefer to have a story read to him.

No question developed among the team regarding Jamie's placement. It was decided to retain him in the regular classroom with resource-room assistance for reading and writing skills. Although he would miss reading and writing periods in the regular classroom, opportunities would be provided in the classroom for Jamie to practise and apply skills learned in the resource centre.

Suggested placement: regular classroom with resource-room assistance for one hour daily

Responsibilities: regular classroom teacher and resource-room personnel

Starting date: immediately

Duration of services: one school year

Long-range goals:

1. It is important that Jamie both forego his distaste of the reading process and understand the purposes of reading. Methods already attempted in the classroom

will be eliminated and Jamie will be placed on a program that focusses on his strong auditory skills.
2. To help Jamie learn sight words, a modified Fernald approach will be used. He will learn to recognize two hundred sight words.
3. Word-attack skills will similarly be founded on his strong auditory modality through a word family approach.
4. Rewritten materials at a very basic level will be employed with Jamie.
5. Handwriting instruction will begin with patterns on large surfaces, and Jamie will be taught cursive script.

Short-term objectives:
1. When presented with flash cards of sight words outlined in sandpaper, Jamie will trace the words, say the words, and then write the words from memory. Learning will incorporate vision, hearing, touch, and kinesthesia.
2. Using the same letters and words as in the first objective, Jamie will be presented with exercises to strengthen his visual discrimination, visual figure-ground, and visual closure skills.
3. Traditional fairy tales will be read to Jamie and followed by oral questioning on characters, sequence, and so on. Once he is familiar with the story he will be given a rewritten version of it as his own reading material.
4. At the board, Jamie will practise simple patterns leading to cursive writing.

Objective	**Techniques**	**Materials**
1.	a) Present Jamie with sight words and ask him to say, spell, trace over, and write the word. b) Present him with sight words and have him say them aloud to 100 percent accuracy.	Flash cards of sight words in sandpaper
2.	Using the same words, have Jamie complete exercises designed to strengthen his skills in visual processing (see figure 13–1).	Work sheets
3.	a) Read a story orally to Jamie and have him answer questions on the characters, events, and sequence. b) Present him with a rewritten story book using the words taught in the first objective, and ask him to read the story aloud and then answer questions orally and in writing (see figure 13–2).	Traditional fairy tale book Rewritten story book

4.	Have Jamie practise simple patterns at the board and then move to an easel with a large paintbrush (see figure 13–3).	Blackboard, easel

a) Visual discrimination

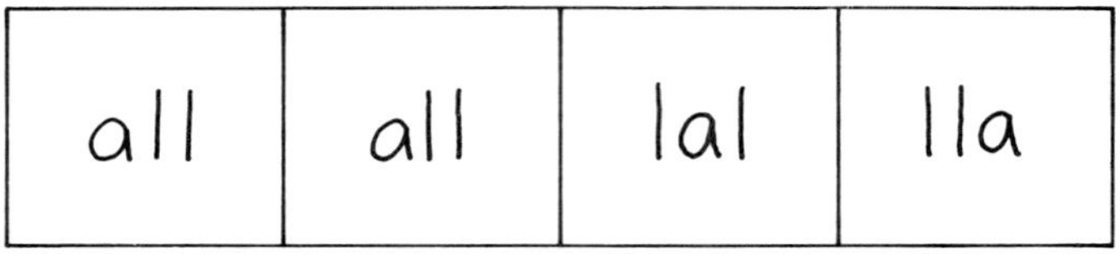

Circle the same.

b) Visual figure ground

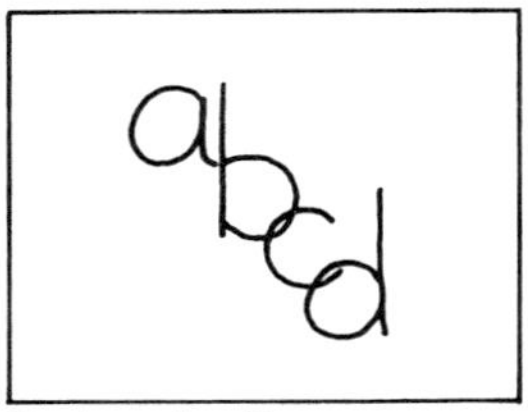

Outline the C.

c) Visual closure

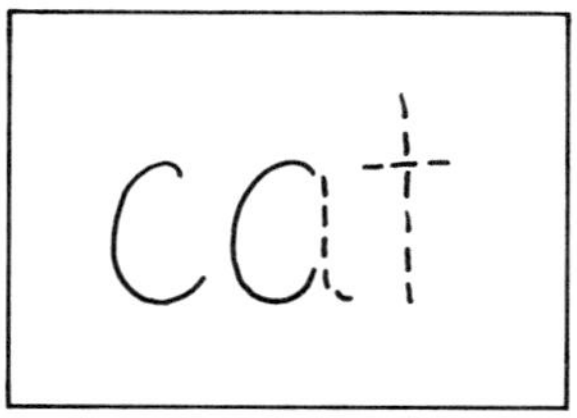

Finish the word.

Figure 13–1

Objective: to improve visual perception

a) Have the children match words to pictures and sentences.

Grades 1 to 3

b) Mount pictures on cardboard and cut them into simple jigsaws for the pupils to put together.

K to grade 3

c) Ask the class to locate all the objects of a certain shape or colour in the classroom.

K to grade 3

See Goldilocks. Goldilocks goes into the house.

a) Colour Goldilocks.
b) Goldilocks goes __________________________
c) Where does Goldilocks go?

Goldilocks sees the three bowls. Papa's porridge is too hot.

Mama's porridge is too cold.

a) Colour Goldilocks.
b) Colour the porridge bowls.
c) Papa's porridge bowl is __________________________
   Mama's porridge bowl is __________________________
d) What does Goldilocks see?
   Why didn't Goldilocks eat Papa's porridge?
   Why didn't Goldilocks eat Mama's porridge?

Figure 13–2

Figure 13–3

Objective: to develop visual memory

a) Open a small picture or story book to a given page and have the pupils scan it for a few seconds. Close the book and ask the children to find the page again.

Grades 3 to 6

b) Have pupils describe in detail what they had for breakfast, how the principal looks, what game they played at recess, and so on.

Grades 3 to 6

c) Project a picture or pattern and ask the students to draw it from memory.

Grades 3 to 9

Objective: to develop visual figure-ground skills

a) Have the pupils sort buttons, pieces of fabric, cardboard, and so on according to a specific attribute, such as size, texture, or colour, and then according to a combination of two attributes.

K to grade 6

b) Give the students a written paragraph and have them circle, for example, all the *g*s.

Grades 1 to 6

c) Use the dictionary, book indexes, and telephone books for students to practise skimming and figure-ground skills. As they read, they scan for specific facts or particular words.

Grades 3 to 9

Objective: to develop skills in visual closure

a) Present pupils with a picture with parts missing and have them point out and then name the missing parts.

K to grade 3

b) Have the students match incomplete pictures to complete pictures, or ask them to complete pictures themselves (see figure 13–4).

K to grade 6

Figure 13–4

c) Ask the students to supply the missing words to complete sentences.

K to grade 6

Objective: to develop laterality and body image

a) Have the students trace their hands and label them as left and right.

K to grade 3

b) Play "Simon Says."

K to grade 6

c) Find examples of directions given in pictures or symbols only and help the students to translate them into English.

Grades 3 to 9

Concept development

A concept is a mental embodiment of an object, an event, a relationship, a thought, or an opinion, derived from previous experience with the thing for which the concept stands. Concepts can refer to the attributes that a class or group of things have in common. In this context, concept formation is represented by the ability to classify objects and events; for example by recognizing a boat, a car, and a train as modes of transportation. Concepts bring order into our environment. When small children discover that an orange belongs to the larger classification of fruit, which in turn is food, they have learned a concept. Teenagers experience more sophisticated concept development when they learn about historical ideas such as nationalism or apartheid.

Concepts are learned inductively; from their experiences, children gradually define what a particular concept is, and is not. The best method to teach a specific concept is therefore to present it in a variety of situations, each illustrating the common attribute. To teach children to conceptualize the word *chair*, for instance, show them kitchen

Classification is an important part of concept development.

chairs, lawn chairs, rocking chairs, doll chairs, and so on. Until they have developed this stable conceptual base, they will not be able to talk about the concept in words.

There are two basic types of concepts, concrete and abstract. The example of chairs just given is, clearly, concrete. Defined or abstract concepts, on the other hand, are learned by rules relating to simpler concepts; in other words, by definition. Children learn rules about place value and word function, for example, which impart mathematical and linguistic concepts. They usually learn the relative concepts of big and little by thirty months of age and from there gradually develop further abstract concepts.

Special learners — not only learning-disabled and mildly mentally retarded children but also visually or hearing-impaired students — often have trouble with concept development. Teachers must use many examples when teaching exceptional students a new skill, whether dealing with a concrete or an abstract concept. Concepts can be taught using a combination of direct experiences, direct verbal explanations, and conceptual explanations. Examples must be carefully assembled, matched, and managed. Because conceptual rules vary in difficulty, teaching and practice time will vary also.

Classroom techniques to teach concepts

Objective: to categorize objects by attributes

a) Begin with an actual object, such as a toy horse or toy elephant. Have the children match the object to a picture, then the object to both the picture and the word. Extend the exercise by asking them to match the object to the word used in a sentence.

Grades 1 to 6

b) Make large cards with pictures of objects that contain smaller objects. A house, for example, contains chairs, tables, beds, and so on. Make small cards of these objects and have the pupils place the correct small pictures on the larger cards (see figure 13–5).

K to grade 3

Figure 13–5

c) Have the pupils search through magazines to cut out pictures of articles of clothing. Ask them to make charts listing different categories, such as clothing worn by people in different jobs, or clothing worn in different seasons. The children stick pictures on the charts according to specified attributes.

K to grade 6

d) Use groups of real objects or pictures and have children find the ones that can be used for the same thing. A cup and a glass, for example, are both used for drinking.

K to grade 3

e) Write out lists of words such as

cereal bread nail potato
wool wood milk ivory leather

Children circle the word that doesn't belong.

Grades 2 to 6

Objective: to seriate objects or ideas according to specified characteristics

a) Hang a clothesline in an area of the room where it can be left for a few weeks. Construct sets of small cards, each set containing a sequence. Children hang the cards on the line in the correct sequence, as shown in figure 13-6. Begin the exercise with simple sequences, such as size, and advance to a higher level of skills, such as sequencing numbers, or letters of alphabet.

K to grade 3

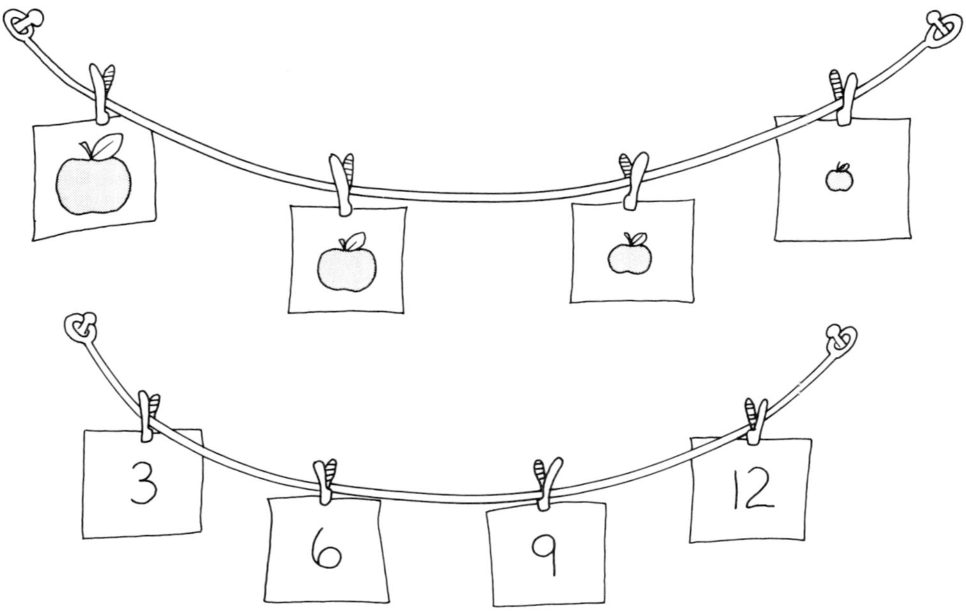

Figure 13-6

b) Give students a series of directions one at a time, gradually adding to the original direction, as follows:
"Draw a castle on the board."
"Draw a lake in front of the castle."
"Draw a tree beside the castle."
"Draw a flag on the roof of the castle."

K to grade 6

c) Provide series of pictures for students to continue, as shown in figure 13-7.

K to grade 6

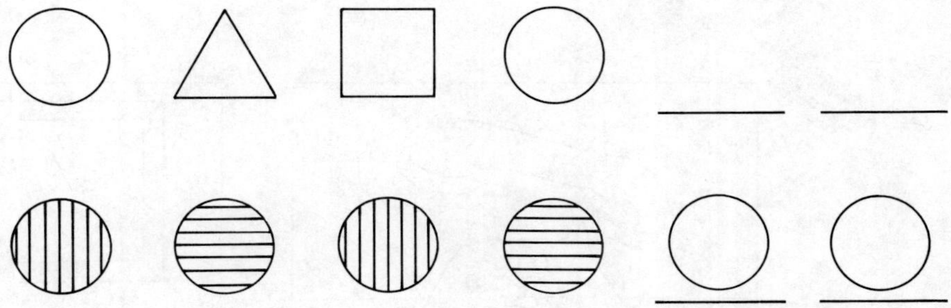

Figure 13–7

d) Ask students to fill in a "concept chart," relating objects to one another. The attributes of musical instruments, for example, can be listed as follows:

A: Musical instrument	B: Part of band	C: Types
guitar	string	electric steel
clarinet	reed	soprano alto

Grade 6 and up

Objective: to develop concept formation and memory using vocabulary

a) Present children with incomplete sentences that require classification, as follows:
"Bluejays, cardinals, and sparrows are all. . . ."
"Joy, anger, and sorrow are all. . . ."

K to grade 9

b) Make up rhyming riddles and encourage the class to think of others; for example, "I rhyme with look and you read me. What am I?"

K to grade 6

Katy turned on the light switch and. . . .

The telephone rang and. . . .

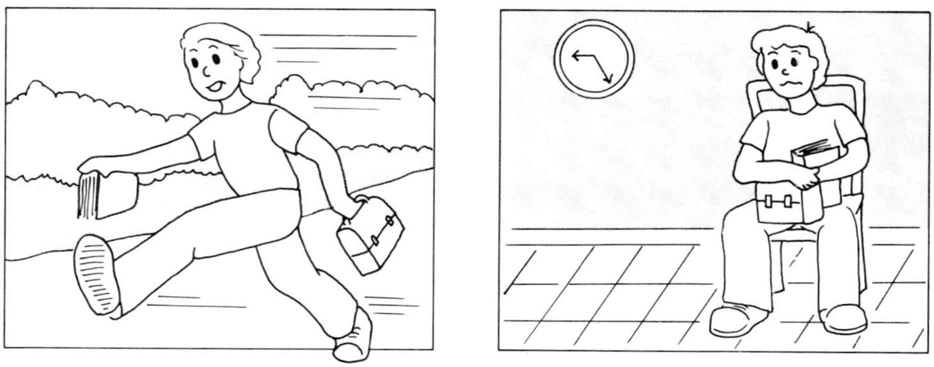

Isaac was late for school so. . . .

Figure 13–8

c) Ask the pupils to complete word analogies, such as "Bat is to baseball as racquet is to. . . ."

Grades 3 and up

d) From real objects, pictures, or word lists, have children select items that satisfy two or more requirements. They could choose an apple, for example, from the requirements *round* and *crunchy*, or *round* and *red* and *crunchy*.

K to grade 6

e) Teach students to think about cause and effect by having them complete pictures and phrases, as shown in figure 13–8.

K to grade 6

f) Use cryptograms to develop reasoning and logical thinking. In the message 8/15/23 1/18/5 25/15/21 20/15/4/1/25, for example, the 1 stands for a, 2 for b, and so on. Set students the task of deciphering or writing code messages. Before using this exercise, ensure that pupils understand both the sequence of the alphabet and counting.

Grade 3 and up

As has been seen in this chapter, mildly disabled children may show lags in specific developmental tasks in various areas: memory, organization, attention, perception, and concept development. The discussion about visually impaired students in the next chapter reveals that they too may encounter difficulties in perception and concept development. Although it is very difficult to pinpoint the root of the problems in mildly handicapped students, however, visually impaired students' difficulties relate chiefly to their physical problems.

14 *Visually impaired students*

Dear Reader,

The organization of formal education for visually handicapped students began in 1784 in Paris, France, when Valentin Häuy instructed his first blind student. Since that time, trends in and attitudes toward the education of blind people have reflected changes in society in general. The issues that are being debated today in this field have been with us for some time: whether students should use braille, large print, or tapes, and whether they should be educated in special schools or local schools.

Legislation in Canada has given parents the right to choose the programs that they believe are most appropriate for their visually handicapped children. Historically, Canada has served its visually handicapped students in residential schools, but more and more provinces are offering programming within their regular school systems. The most popular local service delivery model seems to be that of a specially qualified teacher acting in an itinerant capacity to teachers and students enrolled in neighbourhood schools. Residential schools provide consultative services for local programs, education for teachers and parents, and concentrated courses in specialized areas of the curriculum for students. Some parents still choose to have their children attend the provincial schools for at least some of their education.

Each visual loss creates specific needs, and the multitude of placements, methods, and aids now available (including a wide variety of highly technological equipment) provides new opportunities for students to acquire the necessary skills to reach their highest potential. Among the many alternatives for program delivery, one fact remains constant: specialist teachers trained in the education of blind and low-vision students are needed to design and deliver programs. Full courses to qualify teachers to become specialists are offered by various universities throughout the country.

Deaf-blind students are also now being served both in residential and integrated settings. Integration into the local school setting is an option if the deaf-blind child has a trained intervener and is provided with an individual program.

The best educational process for visually impaired students allows them access to programs appropriate for their needs at different times throughout their entire educational experience. Time spent in both integrated and special school settings offers students a well-rounded program with their sighted peers and with other students who are visually handicapped.

E.J. Chorniak
Program Director
Resource Services
W. Ross Macdonald School
Brantford, Ontario

The generic terms *visually impaired* and *visually handicapped* encompass all students who require special education services because of visual problems. The conditions covered by the terms include a range of degrees and types of visual impairment. Visually impaired students have just the same needs as their sighted peers, and so the aims and content of their education are not essentially different from those inherent in all education. Teachers can use the same teaching methods and the same forms of lesson presentation: group work, individual work, direct experience, and behaviour modification.

Visual impairment does not affect intelligence or language development. In general, visually impaired students are perhaps more easily integrated into regular classrooms than children with other physical defects because they usually do not exhibit accompanying physical characteristics. They are primarily deficient in the motor areas, simply because visual handicaps impair mobility. Multiple handicaps are common among the visually impaired population, however, and while many students can function successfully in regular classrooms with help from itinerant teachers or resource-room personnel, some will need special placements. The education of partially sighted students is much less of a problem than that of blind pupils. In fact, many partially sighted children are integrated into mainstream settings without support help and need only minor modifications in classroom schedules, such as an exercise class in place of physical education.

It is true, however, that visually impaired pupils do differ from their sighted peers in some areas, of which educators must be aware. The differences range from understanding spatial concepts to a knowledge of the general properties of the world, as assessed by Piagetian tasks (Warren, 1977). The main challenge for educators of visually impaired students is to provide either an adequate alternative method of gathering information or an adequate method of developing the student's visual ability to its fullest potential. Braille reading and writing, large print, reading devices, audio aids, concrete materials, and embossed maps, graphs, and geometric designs all allow the visually impaired student to receive information. As well, orientation and mobility training, designed to increase the student's control of the environment, is becoming an integral component of special education for visually impaired students. Orientation and mobility are the most important elements of successful adaptation for severely visually impaired students since they allow students to function independently.

Good educational programs meet students' physical, psychological, and educational needs by using expertise from many fields. As well, classroom teachers should be aware of the physical, social, emotional, and learning characteristics of visually impaired students in order to plan effectively. They must be cognizant of ways in which to adapt regular classroom practices so that students, regardless of how severe their visual losses are, can receive the same chance at education that normally sighted pupils have. The main objectives of this chapter are therefore to

- discuss the special educational needs of visually impaired students
- describe the adaptations that can be made to accommodate visually impaired students in the regular classroom
- discuss the technical equipment that may be required by visually impaired students in the regular classroom

The field of visual impairment

Dramatic changes have occurred in the education of visually impaired pupils in recent years. Increased understanding of the effects of visual impairment on learning has broadened the category of students who can benefit from intervention. This means, for one thing, that more attention is being given to milder visual problems; for another, residential programs for more severely visually handicapped students are much less popular, as are special classes. Many more students are integrated into regular classrooms as more adaptive materials and techniques make it possible for those with visual impairments to participate in practically all aspects of school activities.

Currently, educators are giving less attention to the legal definition of visual handicap than to functional characteristics, which are now being used as the criteria for classification and placement. This parallels an increasing emphasis on the development of residual vision, as it is now understood that residual vision improves with use. Many students demonstrate the ability to read ordinary print with reasonable efficiency and are therefore able to progress in regular classes with the help of vastly improved optical aids and recent technological innovations. Braille is consequently taught less frequently than in the past.

Identification and diagnosis

The identification and diagnosis of visually impaired students is fraught with difficulties; measurement must cover a range of deficits, skills, and behaviours. Generally, medical personnel and diagnosticians will assess visual acuity, visual functioning, sensory abilities, other handicapping conditions, motor performance, language, mental ability, and achievement. Youngsters with mild but potentially debilitating problems may be overlooked and their lack of academic progress attributed to other causes, because they often have no outward appearance of anything wrong with the eyes. Teachers should therefore be aware of certain behaviours, indicative of defective vision, that the student may demonstrate in the classroom (see box 14–1).

Formal testing of any type is particularly difficult with visually impaired students. Any measures used to assess a pupil's learning and achievement must be manipulated to circumvent the visual deprivation; psychologists will often use a variety of tests and combine subtests from the different measures (Barraga, 1976).

Mainstreaming visually impaired students

As with any exceptional youngsters, it is extremely difficult to pinpoint the factors necessary for visually impaired students' successful integration in regular classrooms, but it is possible to make some broad generalizations (see table 14–1). Some modifications and additions to the regular classroom program are necessary, usually to develop students' skills in orientation and mobility, spatial relationships, and conceptual ability.

Box 14-1 Classroom signs of visual impairment

- makes errors while copying from the blackboard or from a paper
- squints to see the board or asks to move closer
- avoids all near-centred tasks
- quickly becomes fatigued when reading or copying
- too frequently omits words, rereads or skips lines unknowingly, shows persistent reversals after grade two, or confuses like letters
- loses place while reading, or uses finger as a reading guide
- says words aloud for auditory reinforcement
- has difficulty remembering reading material
- has difficulty remembering, reproducing, or identifying basic geometric forms; or difficulty with sequential concepts
- uses unusual or fisted pencil grip; frequently breaks pencil; or frequently rotates the paper when copying
- spidery, excessively sloppy, or illegible handwriting; writing that becomes progressively smaller or more crowded, or is inconsistent in size
- irritable doing work
- short attention span
- frequent daydreaming
- low frustration level
- withdrawn
- difficulties with peers

The mainstreaming team

The special educators who work co-operatively with classroom teachers must ensure that visually impaired students are taught to use special equipment such as magnifiers, large print materials, or braille. Special educators also play a part in monitoring students' progress and finding solutions to any problems that arise, and will often work with orientation and mobility specialists to provide training in the classroom and school grounds as needed. Special education personnel, therapists, medical personnel, and orientation and mobility specialists, all form part of the school-based educational team for the visually impaired student.

Case study 14–1, part 1 presents one possible classroom situation, by detailing the history and progress of Jeanne, a severely visually impaired high school student. An extract from Jeanne's IEP appears later.

Case study 14–1, part 1

Jeanne's visual loss was discovered very early in life and during the preschool years she was given a great deal of assistance in language, concept development, and orientation and mobility. Consequently she entered school in a regular classroom with her regular peers. Throughout elementary school, Jeanne worked through the curriculum adequately, although her severe visual impairment hindered her in some areas. She is a print reader, however, and with adapted materials can function well.

Although Jeanne is well accepted by her peers and seems to have adapted to her visual loss, high school has proved difficult for her. She is managing in academic areas, but the stresses of adolescence and her growing realization of the implications of her disability have combined to affect Jeanne's social and emotional development negatively.

She was brought to the attention of the school-based team because her home room teacher believed that extra counselling in both personal and career matters would be beneficial. The teacher also felt that Jeanne required extra assistance in some general social and life skills, specifically grooming and dressing. An IEP focussing on these areas was therefore devised, with responsibility assigned to the school guidance counsellor working in tandem with the home room teacher.

Table 14-1 Selected criteria for mainstreaming visually impaired students

Elementary	Secondary
Teacher	
◆ Wants the student in the classroom	
◆ Understands the implications of visual impairment	
◆ Willing to adapt programs and materials	
Student	
◆ Nature and extent of condition	◆ Nature and extent of condition
◆ Developmental history	◆ Developmental history
◆ Degree of additional handicaps	◆ Degree of additional handicaps
◆ Emotionally stable	◆ Socially and emotionally stable
◆ Accepted by peers	◆ Interacts with peers
◆ Follows classroom rules and routines	◆ Accepts responsibility for own progress
◆ Developing reading skills	◆ Uses appropriate optical aids and technical devices
◆ Shows potential in other academic areas	
Support services	
◆ Guidance counsellors	◆ Career, guidance, and vocational counsellors
◆ Special education personnel	◆ Special education personnel to assist with materials and reading skills
◆ Orientation and mobility specialist	

Classroom adaptations

Visually impaired students tend to lag behind sighted students in school achievement. There is no necessary correlation between achievement and visual impairment, but gaps are likely to occur because visually impaired students tend to enter school later, and may begin in inappropriate programs, or miss segments of school for surgery or treatment. Inadequate opportunities to explore the environment contribute to their academic delays (Scott, 1982), as does their slower rate of reading. Blind children, on average, are two years older than sighted pupils in the same grade (Ashcroft, 1963).

It is estimated that ordinary educational experiences are 85 percent visual (Alonso, 1967; Telford & Sawrey, 1981) but partially sighted students are unable to learn fully through imitation and, of course, totally blind pupils cannot be visual learners. Instruction must shift therefore from the visual mode to auditory, tactile, and kinesthetic modes. Information received in this manner is intermittent and fragmentary. The student synthesizes information to make a whole, and may consequently have a distorted mental image.

Three main educational principles should therefore be kept in mind when teaching visually impaired students. Teachers will find it necessary to make room in the program for learning by doing, for concrete experiences, and for unifying experiences that help students to fit ideas together (Lowenfeld, 1973). Following these principles, the adaptations for visually impaired students presented below can be incorporated into regular classroom routines.

General:

- For the seriously visually handicapped student, physical contact carries the same warmth that eye contact does for the sighted student. Touch helps to lessen the detachment that accompanies defective vision, but remember to speak to the pupil before touching her or him.
- Announce comings and goings in the classroom to keep the student in contact with the environment.
- Speak to all students by name when calling on them in class.
- Make directions specific, and use precise, clear wording. Don't use terms such as "this one" and "the other one." The younger the student, the more often he or she will need to hear the names of objects, and the more precise the directions need to be.
- Expect the visually impaired student to share in classroom duties.
- Try not to overprotect the student.
- Expect the visually impaired student to be responsible for looking after his or her own special equipment.
- Encourage the student to participate in extracurricular activities such as dramatics and debating.

The classroom setting:

- Keep the student as near to other students as possible.
- Allow the student more work space and storage space. Leave things where the student put them since she or he must find them again by remembering the location. If things must be moved, tell the student.
- Follow the student's preferences about lighting.

Academics:

- Alternate periods of work needing close visual application with less visually demanding tasks.

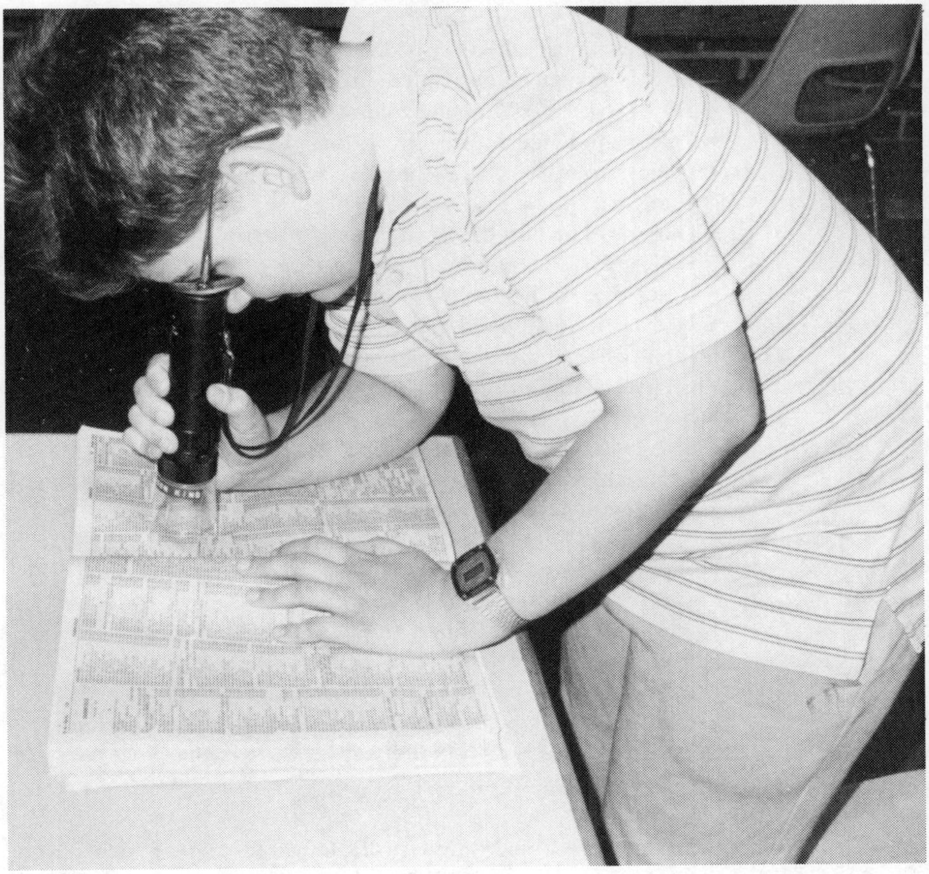

Telescopic devices are common optical aids.

- Encourage the student to use residual vision for large print and the broad details of large pictures.
- Allow students to hold their books in the manner that best suits them for reading.
- Check that the print in workbooks and texts is large enough for the student.
- Use volunteer readers to read assignments to visually impaired classmates.
- Use tape recorders, records, and individual film strip projectors.
- Use real objects as models rather than pictures whenever possible.
- Allow the student to touch equipment, models, and objects.
- When writing on the board to illustrate points, verbalize the writing so that the student can follow the lesson.
- Talk normally and do not be embarrassed to use words such as *look* and *see*.
- Pair the student with a peer for group work and to help the visually impaired student's orientation and social integration.
- Have students work in small groups.
- Don't place time limits on tests that use large print materials.

Assignments and work sheets:

- Visually impaired students do not necessarily lose their sense of colour, but some may. Eliminate colour-coded directions for those students who are colour deficient.
- Adapt written assignments to oral whenever possible for seriously impaired students.
- Provide individual instruction in handwriting and other concepts that are generally taught from the chalkboard but are especially difficult for the visually impaired student.
- Dark print on buff-coloured paper is best for work sheets because buff colour reduces the glare. Use one side of the paper only.
- Trace over all hand-outs with black felt markers.
- Use clear, uncluttered pictures on hand-outs.
- Limit work at the board and keep assignments short to circumvent eye fatigue.
- Prepare work in students' exercise books so that they will not have as much copying to do.
- Use exercise books with wide rules.
- Expect good work, whatever the assignment; lowered expectations may foster feelings of resentment and inadequacy. Do allow the student to type or tape assignments, however.

Social:

- Help other class members to understand their new classmate, by providing information about the causes and nature of the student's impairment, and ways of compensating for it.
- Indicate to sighted children when special help is appropriate — with mobility, for example — and how to volunteer it. Warn them, however, against doing more than is necessary.

Modifications made for visually impaired students depend on the severity of the condition as well as the individual's use of functional vision. Students with borderline vision need to sit nearer the board and in good light, and to move when necessary to be nearer to charts and wall displays. Partially sighted students need materials that make effective use of colour, have good contrast, an efficient and clear page layout, and appropriate type size and spacing. More severely visually handicapped students require special assistance in the form of magnifying devices and books with large type. Other necessary materials may include book markers and book stands, braille writers and braille books, the Cranmer abacus, tactile science materials, tactile maps (or enlarged and simplified maps for the partially sighted), dark pens and pencils, and dark-lined writing paper. Visually impaired students also require many audio aids: tape recorders, record players, and talking book machines will prove helpful in the classroom. The particular devices used will vary from student to student.

It is important to set realistic expectations for visually impaired students, as demonstrated in the case study below. Lack of vision should not be accepted as a reason for non-conformity. Teachers should insist on the same standards of conduct, responsibilities, work assignments, and levels of performance as they do other students. Case study 14–1, part 1, introduced Jeanne, a high school student. In part 2, Jeanne's IEP focusses largely on behavioural aspects of performance.

Case study
14–1, part 2

Name: Jeanne
D.O.B.: 12 May 1973

School: Canada Secondary School
Diagnostic category: Severely visually impaired

The home room teacher is sensitive to the needs of teenagers and has noticed that Jeanne is withdrawing more and more into herself and alienating herself from her peers. Jeanne seems to realize that her personal grooming is different: her hair style, make-up, and clothes, so important to teenagers, are not the same. As well, Jeanne has discussed career choices that are not consonant with her disability. She says that she hopes to becomes a flight attendant but that does not seem feasible.

To assist Jeanne, the team has devised a series of long-term goals. The behavioural nature of the goals does not lend itself to short-term objectives at this time.

Long-term goals:

1. Working with the counsellor, Jeanne will be introduced to career choices that are consonant with her strengths and deficits. The classroom teacher will provide extra reading materials on appropriate careers.
2. The counsellor will urge Jeanne to join in extracurricular activities and give her support as she does so.
3. Jeanne will be provided with extra assistance in matters of personal grooming to improve her confidence in choosing clothes, using make-up, and so on.

Academic areas

Concept development

Visually impaired students' concept development is affected by the restrictions resulting from visual loss, not from the loss itself. Students may not possess an adequate understanding of abstract concepts or things that cannot be touched, and they may have difficulty grasping spatial relationships. The same principles for concept learning apply to visually impaired students as to other children, and these were described in chapter 13. All initial training must be related to the concrete, and should introduce abstractions only after the student has developed concepts that will allow her or him to comprehend relationships.

In addition, however, visually impaired students must use their tactual sense or their knowledge of distance and time in order to learn spatial concepts. Vision allows us to take in large objects all at once, whereas touch provides only piecemeal information. Blind children have to focus their tactual exploration on the critical features of an object and then put the pieces together to form a concept. Not only does touch require more conscious effort on the part of the individual but, since it yields different information than that available with sight, the visually impaired person necessarily obtains a different construction of reality.

Little is known about the tactual sense and how to develop it. It is clear, however, that visually impaired students need a variety of exploratory activities that involve immediate contact. They can be helped to attend consciously to tactile and auditory clues that sighted children do not use, and then to hold the material in immediate

Visually impaired students can use tactile maps to study geography.

memory. When sighted children use pictures, for example, the teacher can provide visually impaired pupils with comparable experiences by letting them feel real objects or models. The teacher should also make generous use of verbal explanations and help the students to relate current learning to past learning.

Mathematics

Mental arithmetic is used extensively in the education of visually impaired students, although most classroom modifications rely on equipment rather than special teaching strategies. Adapted calculators, rulers, slide rules, and geometric equipment are available as aids. The braille writer and the Cranmer abacus are also used in arithmetic calculations, in place of pencil and paper.

Content areas

Visually impaired students may need to employ a variety of techniques, materials, and equipment to obtain information for research projects. Teachers are advised to offer a choice of topics and to recommend alternative sources of information, such as records and sound tracks, when necessary. Time extensions or reduced assignments may be necessary because of students' slower reading speeds. For studying earth science, geography, and biology, students will find tactual devices such as three-dimensional raised surface landforms, maps, and plastic models highly discriminable. It is particularly important to provide clear colour contrast on aids for partially sighted students.

Language arts

The greatest strength of visually impaired students lies in their knowledge of language and of auditory clues. Although they may have problems with concept development, they encounter little difficulty with the language they acquire through hearing. Yet non-verbal communication, such as facial gestures and body language, can elude them and students therefore need to be taught the emotional component of language through role playing, dramatization, practice, and imitation.

This text has stressed the necessity of listening skills for all special learners, and they are especially important for visually impaired students. Activities planned to develop severely visually impaired students' listening skills require adaptations. The sounds used must be relevant to the students, and teachers will need to point out the sounds that familiar things make: the squeak of the classroom door, the squelch of the principal's shoes, the sound of the fan, and so on. Sounds of which the student has no knowledge should be avoided. The listening games and activities described in chapter 7 are particularly relevant for visually impaired pupils.

Visually impaired braille readers need extra assistance in spelling because they rarely see the words spelled out fully. They require frequent oral spelling practice that does not use contractions. If words are presented in braille on flash cards, teachers may cut the upper right-hand corner of the card, so that students can keep them the right way up. Visually impaired children should receive spelling instruction both in the basic word lists used in the classroom and in particularly relevant words. They will need to be taught the spelling of trade names that other children pick up incidentally. Additionally, they require training in auditory discrimination. Finally, before presenting new units for content subjects, it is useful to teach students the core vocabulary.

Modifications for writing and reading

Visually impaired students have problems using tools—pencils, eating utensils, and so on — and will usually need special training to use writing materials properly. Blind braille users learn to use braillers and the slate and stylus, and print readers are taught to write using dark pens and paper with bold rules. For visually impaired writers, the size of the letters is less important than letter formations. Typewriters ease the burden of print output for blind and partially seeing students, and help the teacher who has tried to decipher illegible products. A program of touch typing is usually introduced for visually impaired students late in grade three or in grade four. Regardless of the writing device used, however, all visually impaired students should be taught to write their own names in script so that they will have a personal signature.

Today's students are confronted with an overwhelming mass of printed materials, and reading is clearly problematic for visually impaired pupils. Partially sighted students can read print if it is presented to them appropriately. The best size of type for a child will probably be between twelve and twenty-four point (see figure 14–1). Most large-print books are in eighteen-point type. Some students with borderline vision will find it advantageous to know both braille and print, working in braille for longer assignments.

12 point: Visual impairment
14 point: Visual impairment
16 point: Visual impairment
20 point: Visual impairment
24 point: Visual impairment

Figure 14–1

Students who can use large print materials or regular materials with optical aids are taught reading in exactly the same way, and with the same scope and sequence, as sighted youngsters. Reading rate, however, is a universal problem among visually impaired students. Braille reading is slower than print reading and readers of large type read at about half the speed of sighted readers (Alonso, 1967), so teachers should allow them extra time.

Many factors should be taken into consideration when choosing large-print books and materials. It is important to check the space between words, between lines, and between the words and the lines. A crowded page is inappropriate. As well, the length of the lines, the width of the margins, the style of print, the width of the strokes of the letters, and the quality of paper will enhance or hinder the value of a book for a visually impaired student. Judging the quality of materials, however, is a subjective process based on what the student has seemed comfortable with in the past.

The reading environment is as important as the reading materials and aids. Teachers must check the brightness of the lighting and the contrast it produces between text and background in reading materials (Kirk, 1981). The amount of illumination depends upon the student's disability: the student with optic atrophy, for example, requires extra bright illumination, while the albino student needs less illumination than normal. Visually impaired students in general need maximum reflection without glare, an effect that can be facilitated by observing the following pointers:

- Avoid standing with your back to the window; it forces students to face the glare.
- Eliminate glare from desks and tables by moving them away from a direct source of light; place desks at a thirty-degree angle to the window.
- Cover glass cabinet doors with construction paper.
- Avoid visual aids that have surfaces with a high gloss.
- Adjust the lighting to suit the daily weather conditions.
- Keep the chalkboard clean; use a wide chalk stroke.
- Keep lighting behind the student's left shoulder.
- Adjust blinds to eliminate glare.

Large type helps the partially sighted student.

Braille

Most people immediately think of braille when they think of reading for severely visually impaired individuals, but only about 10 percent of visually impaired students will become braille readers. Braille is a complete medium for reading and writing. It is taught and learned in much the same way as ordinary reading and writing. In a unifying process, the braille reader learns to apprehend larger and larger units of material at a time, in a similar manner to sighted individuals who are developing reading ability. Some braille readers subvocalize or use silent lip movements, as sighted readers sometimes do. Reading efficiency takes longer to develop in braille, however, and attention must be paid to tactile tracking skills, posture, and smooth co-ordination of the two hands.

Braille uses an entirely different alphabet, formed by a series of raised dots, and has an elaborate shorthand system. The proficient braille reader must be familiar with the 26 letters of the alphabet, the 189 contractions and abbreviated words, and the 31 punctuation and composition marks (Brothers, 1974). There are also three braille codes: one for literary materials, one for mathematics and science, and one for music. Braille materials are cumbersome and are only available in a restricted range. Books are four times larger and cost ten times as much as regular materials.

The paperless brailler is a useful innovation.

The greatest limitation of braille materials, however, is that they are very slow to read. Most fluent adult sighted readers can read popular novels at roughly three to five hundred words a minute, perhaps faster when interest is high (Gillett & Temple, 1986). They achieve oral reading speeds of about two to three hundred words a minute. Even the most rapid braille readers only reach one-third of the speed of sighted readers (Alonso, 1967). Braille-reading students in the upper elementary grades average about ninety words a minute (Harley, Henderson, & Traun, 1979), and a really good braille reader may attain a speed of 150 to 200 words a minute (Lowenfeld, 1973).

Braille writing is also tedious and slow. It can be written either by using a mechanical brailler or with a slate and stylus. Children usually begin with the brailler and then learn the slate and stylus method. The manual, Perkins brailler is used to emboss braille. It has six keys, one for each dot of the cells, and the user depresses the key to leave a raised dot on the paper. The paperless brailler is a recent innovation that records information on a magnetic tape cassette. A cassette recorder is attached to the line of braille cells, and as the tape is played, reeds within the braille cells pop up to produce a line of "print" at a time. The message can then be read with the fingers.

Reading devices and optical aids

The *Optacon*, which converts print to tactile images, has proved a boon for many seriously visually impaired individuals. It is not intended to supplant braille but to supplement it. The Optacon is used to read printed material but not handwriting or fine print. It gives slow reading rates — thirty to sixty words a minute (Goldfish & Taylor, 1974) — and requires lengthy training.

The *Kurzweil Reading Machine* is about the size of a standard video cassette recorder and employs microprocessors programmed to apply over a thousand linguistic rules and fifteen hundred exceptions to convert printed materials in different type sizes and styles into synthetic English speech. The machine can read books, magazines, periodicals, typewritten letters, reports, and other printed documents (Bennett, 1982; Weinberg, 1980).

Compressed speech devices automatically discard small segments of speech from tape-recorded readings so that the speech is more rapid but still understandable. Compressed speech conveys information faster than normal listening does, and normal listening is faster than reading braille.

The most common types of optical aids are glasses, magnifiers, and telescopic devices, and many varieties are available to assist visually impaired readers. Of course, the simplest way to obtain magnification of print is to bring the book closer to the eyes. Certainly, many visually impaired children do this and should be allowed to hold materials in the position most comfortable for them.

Mobility and orientation

For visually impaired people, not only is the environment less appealing, less controllable, and less meaningful, but it can also present many hazards. Unknown obstacles, unpredictable noises, and the unexplained disappearance of objects and people are frequent experiences. Blind individuals must plan their every movement within a changing environment by using memory, concentration, and sensory information.

Mobility is always a concern for those involved with visually impaired students. It is not effective to use guide dogs with children; the dogs are too large and children tend to treat them as pets rather than mobility aids. Human guides are the safest and most flexible aids. The person being guided should grasp the upper arm of the guide, just below the elbow, with the thumb on the outside and fingers on the inside of the arm. This puts the visually handicapped person a half step behind the guide, so that the guide can alert him or her to obstacles and move directly ahead to go through narrow doorways.

Although humans make the best guides, in another sense they are impractical since they cannot be constantly available. The most common mobility device is therefore the *Hoover cane*, sometimes called the long cane or the prescription cane. Children may be introduced to this as early as the preschool years. *Sonic glasses* are an alternative. They consist of glasses frames equipped with an ultrasonic transmitter that scans objects. The beam bounces off objects and is then converted into audible sounds. The user can determine the distance of objects by the pitch of the echo sent back. The

There are various kinds of mobility devices available.

Hoover cane and sonic glasses are used by both partially sighted and blind people. The *laser cane* is another electronic device, and is designed to assist totally blind persons. It has the appearance of, and is used like, a long cane, but has a sensing device that emits beams of light. These are converted into sounds to detect objects in the environment. It gives off both high and low pitched tones as well as actuating an index finger stimulator that acts as an extra warning signal.

Although students must learn to use their own mobility devices, and will receive special mobility and orientation training, the classroom teacher can help. The following tips help visually impaired students' orientation, their sense of location, and their mobility:

- Make sure that the student is properly oriented about regular routes. Initially, allow her or him to travel with a companion to common places such as the washroom and the cafeteria.
- Allow the student to move about freely to learn the landmarks. Alert him or her to obstructions.
- Once the student has achieved independent mobility in the school, discourage the use of guides.
- If necessary, make special provisions during fire drills, field trips, and assemblies. Provide opportunities for the student to practise navigating the routes.
- Eliminate unnecessary obstacles in the classroom. If furniture must be moved, bring the changes to the attention of the student, in order to avoid painful accidents.
- Keep doors fully open or closed, passageways clear, and chairs pushed in.

As has been seen in this chapter, visually impaired students require greater emphasis and structure in certain curricular areas than other students do. They need daily living skills, orientation and mobility training, communication skills, vocational and career guidance, and instruction in the use of special aids that provide alternative means of reading, writing, and moving about. Visually impaired students are, however, prime candidates for integration as the curricular modifications are not extensive. The next chapter discusses another group of special learners for whom technical equipment is the main consideration in educational integration.

15 *Physically disabled and health-impaired students*

Dear Reader,

Children with physical disabilities and debilitating health conditions have been a source of great joy in my life as I have assumed the role of a teacher. I have also experienced the frustrations of a parent whose child has a physical disability. If you will excuse the personal reference, let me share with you some of my joys and frustrations in the hope that you may learn from my experience.

First, a little background information. My daughter's name is Aleta ReNae. She is eight years old and in grade two. She has a beautiful smile. One of her favorite pastimes is playing Barbies and house with her sister. Her mother has coined a pet name for all the kids in the family, and Aleta's special name is "Ponamena." At the moment, she is vehemently opposed to us calling her by that name. If you lend her an ear, she would love to bend it. A child with more spunk you couldn't find. Aleta has cerebral palsy. As a result, she must wear braces on both legs. If you ask her if she is handicapped she will probably reply with, "No, my arms and legs just don't work as good as yours." Aleta is an avid reader and for the most part enjoys school. Aleta has been a joy in my life.

The message that I am attempting to get across is that Aleta, and all other disabled people, are valuable members of our community. All disabled persons must be regarded in this manner. I emphasize the point because, in my experience as a parent and an educator, I often find a paternalistic attitude among those professionals whose services we have needed. There is no room in special education for paternalistic sentiments and behaviour. As Anderson (1988) states: "The person with two functioning arms and legs is not inherently better than the person with less dexterity or mobility. People should not need to feel economically, mentally or physically superior to another person in order to help them. In a truly human community, all are dependent upon one another to make life whole."

Much of the joy I have experienced comes from the "wholeness" that I have achieved in my own life as I have learned to depend on the physically disabled. I have learned to view Aleta as a child with cerebral palsy, rather than a child suffering from or afflicted with cerebral palsy, and I see other people with physical disabilities in the same way. As we learn to see people with physical disabilities and debilitating health conditions in this light, we will perceive them as they are: valuable and contributing members of our society, imbued with the same cognitive capacities and emotions that enrich our own lives.

We will then seek to help, not as a result of paternalistic sentiments, but because we understand that we all must depend on one another to make life whole.

L. Reed Mendenhall
Parent and teacher
University of Lethbridge

Physically disabled and health-impaired students form the most diverse population in all of special education. They have only one commonality: they each have a physical condition that can interfere with learning. Beyond that, it is futile to search for common psychological, social, intellectual, or emotional characteristics. Students may have conditions associated with mobility, stamina, time, environment, special equipment, or special medications. They may also have needs related to mental retardation or giftedness, learning disabilities, emotional or social problems, language or speech difficulties, or sensory impairments.

Chronic and disabling illnesses make it very difficult for physically and health-handicapped students to lead normal lives. Although their intellectual functioning is often not impaired, many factors militate against their school progress. Depending upon the specific type and severity of their impairment, these children may require extensive or frequent periods of hospitalization, special technical aids, and experiential, social, or psychological intervention. Physically disabled and health-impaired youngsters have special needs in academic and physical areas, and in mental health, that are different from those of other children, and they therefore often require special education services. They may have missed school for medical reasons or have begun school at a later age and therefore fallen behind academically. Physically disabled students may need assistance to meet personal needs such as toileting, going to the cafeteria, changing position, and moving between classes. Both physically and health-disabled youngsters may require extra work in self-help skills, ambulation training, leisure skills, and vocational training.

Teachers are responsible for informing themselves about the inhibiting circumstances that affect students, in order to individualize programs and adapt instruction. Students may also need strong emotional support in order to come to terms with certain conditions or diseases, and it is incumbent on teachers to respond to students' pain and emotional stress in positive and empathetic ways. Teachers may need skills in handling, health, movement, and medication. They should be aware of the side effects of medication, the procedures to follow in case of a seizure, a diabetic coma, or an asthma attack, and which activities to restrict for particular students. When a physically disabled student is in the classroom, the teacher will need to know about positioning, methods of communication, techniques for self-care, and technical equipment.

Armed with this information, and with sensitivity, teachers can lessen embarrassment and tension for the students and help them to become accepted and valued members of the regular classroom. The reactions of other class members to the disabled student are critical, from both a physical and a psychological standpoint, and teachers must do everything possible to ensure that those attitudes are positive. Everyone in the classroom should know something about the problem, appreciate the limitations of the disabled student, and be prepared to expect certain behaviours that are a part of the disability.

This chapter discusses some of the most common physical and health problems, including the special needs of abused and neglected children. It covers neither the whole range of conditions, nor etiologies and developmental consequences, but includes the conditions that a teacher is most likely to encounter in the regular classroom. The chapter focusses specifically on classroom needs, whether medical, physical, psychological, or academic. In contrast to other chapters, it deals with physical and technical modifications rather than teaching approaches. Physically and health-handicapped students do not need vastly different strategies in the curricular areas, and will benefit from the same sound teaching principles as all children do. They do, however, need certain modifications to function successfully in regular classrooms and teachers can help if they are familiar with various devices.

Teachers may not have had training in the care of braces, artificial limbs, and wheelchairs, for example. As a matter of fact, the management of orthopedically handicapped students is one of the least understood aspects of service delivery for exceptional students (Parette & Hourcade, 1986). Although occupational and physical therapists provide the most effective management strategies, they may not always be available and some responsibility, at least, falls to the classroom teacher.

The main objectives of this chapter are to

- make teachers aware of the role they play in helping physically disabled students to develop healthy habits and lifestyles
- describe the equipment used by physically disabled students
- discuss management techniques for orthopedically handicapped students and interventions for health-impaired youngsters
- discuss child abuse and the responsibilities of classroom teachers in Canada
- note possible curricular adaptations
- note the physical adaptations that schools can make to accommodate physically disabled students

The field of physical and health problems

Traditionally, the educational placement of physically disabled and health-impaired children has revolved around non-educational considerations. Although they present a wide range of abilities, potential, and educational needs, and there is little or no difference in their classroom performance as compared to that of non-disabled students, the majority of physically and health-disabled pupils in the past were restricted to special schools or special classes. Many school plants simply did not have the appropriate physical structures, technical equipment, and support personnel to accommodate disabled students. Given the difficulties that these children often have with mobility, it was considered more economical to construct one, barrier-free building than to alter all the plants in a school district. Students, teachers, therapists, and other interveners were then brought to a single, central location.

There also existed a traditional predisposition to stereotype both physically and health-handicapped children, to focus on their disabilities and ignore their strengths. Most terminology in the past was based on anatomy or medical evaluation and there was a strict adherence to a medical model. Additionally, teachers felt that these youngsters would be too difficult to handle in the classroom because they would take a disproportionate amount of time (Brulle, Barton, Wharton, & Brulle, 1983).

Such stereotypes are rapidly evaporating. Today, physically disabled students are provided with educational services in a variety of settings. Depending upon the severity of the condition, the related services available, and the prognosis, they may be served in the regular classroom, in a combination of the regular classroom and the resource room, in a special class, or in a more segregated setting. Physical accommodations are being made in the regular schools and numbers of physically and health-disabled students are appearing in regular classrooms. Because the conditions are not in themselves inherently intellectually handicapping, we should see almost all physically and health-disabled students who do not suffer additional conditions integrated into regular classrooms in the future.

Physically disabled and health-impaired students

Physically and health-disabled students differ markedly in behavioural, intellectual, and psychological functioning, and their conditions do not necessarily result in learning and behavioural problems. No two youngsters are affected in exactly the same way, since the impact of a physical disorder depends upon a number of variables: the age of onset of the condition, the degree of disability, the visibility of the condition, family and social support, attitudes toward the individual, and the individual's social status with peers (Lewandowski & Cruickshank, 1980). Definitions are far from orderly, and while a number of terms have been used to refer to these students, they generally indicate conditions grounded in objectively identifiable differences rather than needs (Reynolds & Birch, 1977).

While physical and health conditions are extremely varied, they also have a low incidence, only about 0.2 to 1.5 percent of the school-age population, although rates vary from locale to locale and from decade to decade. About half of physically and health-impaired children suffer from cerebral palsy or some other crippling condition and about half have chronic health problems or diseases (Kneedler, 1984). Further, almost half of the chronic health conditions are commonly met problems: hay fever, asthma and other allergies, sinusitis, and bronchitis and other respiratory diseases.

Identification and diagnosis

Before physically disabled students are placed in regular classrooms, they will need to be assessed. Their academic assessment will be the same as for other youngsters, but special areas of concern include gross and fine motor functioning, ability to communicate and to organize learning, personal care, and socio-emotional functioning. In addition, specialized methods of assessment must be employed for specific disabilities. Diagnosticians will attempt to assess the student's extent of mobility, the accommodations required for physical differences in the classroom, and the student's level, speed, and clarity of communication. At least part of the assessment will be concerned with the strategies and special devices necessary to facilitate learning. It must also determine the skills that the student needs to achieve maximum independence in physical functioning, including self-help skills such as feeding, dressing, and hygiene, which are crucial to the growing child. Although health-impaired students should also be assessed, they do not usually have school problems.

Students with mobility problems

A child's bony structure must be intact and function adequately if he or she is to attain normal development in physical skills. **Orthopedic conditions** in general refer to those deviations of the bones, muscles, or joints that cause abnormal functioning. In this sense, cerebral palsy, spina bifida, and muscular dystrophy are considered to be orthopedic handicaps even though their etiologies vary widely.

The mobility of children affected with cerebral palsy varies a great deal. Some pupils walk with no difficulty, others use braces or crutches, and some need either a manual or battery-powered wheelchair all of the time.

Spina bifida students often require assistance with locomotion, usually braces, crutches, or wheelchairs. Some children are fitted with modified skateboards that allow them to explore their surroundings. Because of the incontinence associated with more severe forms of the condition, good personal hygiene is important. The bladder can be emptied either by using a catheter or by exerting manual pressure on the abdomen. Children learn these procedures themselves although very young ones may need help. Currently, research is being conducted on electrical bladder-stimulating pacemakers to overcome the problems of incontinence (Brunner & Suddarth, 1982).

Physical handicaps do not necessarily have any bearing on cognitive development. (Sunny View #19, June 1965).

In the classroom, students with muscular dystrophy need special help. They have slow movements and generalized fatigue. They may be easily knocked down or be unable to perform simple tasks such as opening doors. Despite knowing the dire nature of this condition, it is important that teachers maintain a positive attitude and avoid overindulging or overprotecting the student. Short, attainable academic goals should be emphasized.

Students with spina bifida, muscular dystrophy, cerebral palsy, or other orthopedic conditions exhibit varying degrees of inability to handle their bodies. They have difficulty getting in and out of wheelchairs, in and out of cars or buses, or transferring from a wheelchair to a toilet. Such problems may hinder their educational progress because the decreased range and strength of motion or the addition of uncontrolled movement can dramatically affect the way that students perform, in terms of mobility, communication, and peer relationships.

Devices used to aid physically disabled students are classed under the general terms of orthotic, prosthetic, and adaptive. **Orthoses** prevent or correct deformity, provide support, or improve the movability of limbs. These devices duplicate normal body movements as nearly as possible while restraining normal functions as little as possible. **Prosthetic devices** replace an absent part of the body by an artificial one. **Adaptive devices** simply make living easier, and include items such as sporks (a combination of fork and spoon), toileting aids (portable urinals), Velcro openers on clothing, and TTDs (telephone devices) for deaf people.

Braces, crutches, and wheelchairs are the most common mobility devices. Orthopedic braces are designed for the lower extremities, and are available in three main types: short leg braces, long leg braces, and hip braces. A short brace is used on the ankle joint, a long brace on the knee to the ankle. Braces do not prevent contractures or develop walking skills but they do provide control and support. For cerebral palsied children, braces are used mainly for control. They help in ambulation, control involuntary movements, and prevent or correct deformities. Children with spina bifida and muscular dystrophy use braces chiefly for support. Support braces weigh less than control braces (Venn, Morgenstern, & Dykes, 1978). Teachers should be alert to circulation problems that may occur when children wear braces. These appear as swelling, coldness, change of colour, evidence of infection, or other skin problems.

Crutches are used for all children during periods of temporary disability. They assist balance and locomotion, and reduce weight on the lower extremities. The surface on which the crutches will operate is important. Rubber-tipped ends, spiked ends, or tripod legs should be provided for slippery surfaces.

Walkers also provide support and assist movement. There are various types of walkers, all of which can be adjusted to suit the individual. It is necessary to find a place in the classroom to store orthopedically handicapped students' crutches or walkers where they will not impede the other students yet are readily available to the disabled pupil. Placing the walker directly in front of, beside, or behind the desk is preferable because the student can readily locate the device. Hooks can be attached to the backs of chairs to keep crutches out of the way.

Individuals with spinal cord injuries, cerebral palsy, polio, multiple sclerosis, severe arthritis, amputations, spina bifida, muscular dystrophy, and so on for whom ambulation is unsafe, too strenuous, or impossible, will use wheelchairs. Wheelchairs come in a variety of shapes and sizes, may be manual or powered, and can include many attachments. Most have arms designed to fit under a desk or table, and others have trays that serve as desks.

When talking to a student in a wheelchair, ensure that you are at eye level, so that communication is effective and the student does not feel dominated or patronized. Teachers and students must remember too that the wheelchair is part of the person's body space and not lean or hang on it.

Sitting too long in a wheelchair can induce pressure sores (decubiti). The best way to deal with this problem is to avoid the conditions that cause it. Children with upper arm strength can lift their own body weight to reposition themselves. Some wheelchairs have special seat cushions to prevent pressure sores. The new stand-up wheelchair incorporates a powered lifting mechanism that enables students to stand erect and then return to a sitting position without leaving the chair and without assistance, allowing them to change positions frequently. Teachers should help students who are unable to reposition themselves. Repositioning should be performed every half hour or so for maximum protection against sores and muscle contractions. Generally, wheelchair-bound students will request assistance if they need it, and some very general tips for helping them appear in box 15–1.

Box 15–1 Tips for teachers of wheelchair-bound students

- Wear comfortable sturdy shoes with low rubber heels to prevent the possibility of slipping.
- Have the students wear sturdy belts.
- Students who can bear some weight on their feet should wear rubber-heeled shoes.
- Always lift with the legs, not the back. When lifting, keep the back as straight as possible.
- When positioning or transferring a student, maintain a wide base of support by placing one foot in front of the other. Move your feet in short steps.
- Always tell the student what you are going to do.
- Encourage the student to assist in positioning or transfer as much as possible.
- In a confined space, use the wall or furniture as a brace.
- Move the child slowly.
- Wait for the child to react.
- Be aware of the "feel" of the child.

Sources: King, 1987; Parette & Hourcade, 1986

If students must spend a large portion of the day in their wheelchairs, they must be helped to maintain sitting postures that promote good body alignment. Inappropriate positions can result in problems with respiration, digestion, circulation, and normal physical development, and sometimes promote other physical deformities (Parette & Hourcade, 1986). Teachers can position physically disabled students, but in order to prevent strained backs and pulled muscles they need some training in physical management. Steps to help in positioning are shown in box 15–2.

Box 15–2 Positioning physically disabled students

Moving the student forward
1. Lock the brakes and the forward casters on the wheelchair.
2. Stand in front of the student.
3. Grasp the student behind the knees, place one foot against the chair bumper, and pull the student forward.

Moving the student backward
1. Lock the brakes and forward casters on the wheelchair.
2. Stand behind the student.
3. Grasp the back of the student by the belt, pants, or dress and pull up and back.

Moving the student sideways
1. Lock the brakes and forward casters of the wheelchair.
2. Stand beside the chair.
3. Have the student place one arm over the pushing handle of the wheelchair on the side to be moved, and then grasp the student on that side by the belt, pants, or dress.
4. Pull the student up and toward you.

Sources: King, 1987; Parette & Hourcade, 1986

Teachers may also have to transfer students, particularly from the wheelchair to the toilet. To do so, position the student's wheelchair beside the toilet at about a thirty-five-degree angle. Lock the brakes and swing the footrests away if possible. If the arm rest can be removed, hook it onto the handgrip opposite the toilet. Stand in front of the student, who then leans forward and places his or her hands around your waist. Grasp the student securely by the belt, pants, or dress at the hips, lock the student's knees together by pushing against them with your own knees, and rock back on your heels, simultaneously lifting and pivoting the student toward the toilet (Parette & Hourcade, 1986). There are several other techniques for transferring, and the interested teacher is referred to Parette and Hourcade (1986).

Moving the wheelchair from place to place will also be necessary, but presents fewer problems than transferring students. To push a wheelchair down from a curb first place one foot on the long pole at the back of the chair. Grasp the handgrips firmly, tip the chair backwards, and gently lower it down from the curb. To go up a curb, follow the same procedure but lift the chair off its front wheels and onto the curb.

Students requiring medication

A number of students in any given classroom may be on medication for various mild medical conditions, but the students of concern here require controlled and consistent use of medication. Pupils suffering from epilepsy, allergies, asthma, and other chronic childhood conditions will be on a medication regime and teachers should be acutely aware of medication schedules, reasons for the medication, and possible side effects. There is some question whether or not the teacher should be responsible for administering medication. Teachers should check the procedures laid down by their particular school boards in this respect.

Epilepsy

Epilepsy is a chronic disorder and many children have to cope with the lifelong possibility of seizures. Although the majority of children with epilepsy are well controlled with medication and some may even outgrow the seizures, a cure is unlikely. Epilepsy is episodic and the occurrence of seizures unpredictable, which makes it particularly difficult to adjust to the disorder.

Seizures are most likely to occur, however, one to two hours after the person falls asleep or one to two hours before awakening. The likelihood of seizures during the waking hours is increased for some children by certain events such as flickering lights, loud sounds, too much heat, excitement, fatigue, or illness. Teachers should be aware of the precipitating factors and carefully observe epileptic students for signs of teeth gnashing, frequent stomachaches, and unexplained lapses of attention (Calhoun & Hawisher, 1979). They should be on the alert for more or less activity than normal, drowsiness, complaints of headaches, tremors in the fingers, loss of appetite, increased tension or talkativeness, or inarticulate speech. If a child has a grand mal seizure, it is important to remain calm, turn the child onto one side, and remove any obstructions.

Petit mal seizures are not nearly as dramatic. They may occur many times during the day, most often when the child is sedentary. Teachers should watch for fixed, blinking, or unfocussed eyes, short periods of rapid swallowing, repeated small nods of the head, and an apparent failure to hear when spoken to.

Epilepsy is primarily controlled with medication that either prevents seizures or reduces their frequency. When choosing a particular program of anticonvulsant medication, doctors take into account factors such as the patient's previous history of drug allergy, tolerance of side effects, age and weight, and the type and severity of the seizures being experienced.

Overmedication, an inappropriate dosage schedule, hypersensitivity, or long-term use can have side effects. Generally, side effects do not occur to such an extent that normal school activities are impaired, but school personnel must be watchful for them as the adjustment of drug levels is an ongoing process. Three widely used anticonvulsants—phenobarbital, phenytoin, and ethosuximide—can induce drowsiness, lethargy, hyperactivity, loss of muscular co-ordination, double vision, confusion, slurred speech, nausea, increase in body hair, tremor, anemia, sleep disturbances, loss of appetite, stomachaches, and groin swelling.

Teachers need to be very sensitive to the needs of epileptic children. They should record observations, especially of those children on medications (all those who have grand mal seizures), or in the process of changing medications. Data should include the time, length, and severity of seizures. Any abrupt changes in learning patterns or behaviour should be reported to the student's parents or physician.

Cystic fibrosis

Children with *cystic fibrosis* do not suffer any intellectual impairment and can function well in regular classrooms, on regular programs. They will, however, have frequent school absences and when in school may have a persistent cough. This cannot be controlled but is not contagious. The child may have an increased appetite and should be allowed second helpings. Although cystic fibrotic children may enter into school activities, teachers should observe them carefully, as their physical stamina can be impaired by the condition.

Arthritis

Arthritis is an episodic condition that can be crippling. Affected students may miss many days of school. Arthritis cannot be cured but some children do later experience remission. Treatment consists of aspirin and rest, and anti-inflammatory drugs now make it possible for individuals with rheumatoid arthritis to reduce some of the pain associated with the condition. Frequently, however, these medications cause side effects, usually drowsiness, that may substantially reduce the individual's academic, social, and behavioural performance.

Allergies and asthma

We are all familiar with the coughing, wheezing, and swollen and red-eyed allergy sufferer. An *allergy* is simply an unusual reaction to something in the environment. The most common allergies are reactions to pollen and dust but humans may be allergic to foods, fabrics, metals, inhalants, animals, and even other people. Allergies are very common among school children. The most common medication is antihistamines, which may cause the student to be sleepy in school.

Asthma is closely related to allergies (Kuzembo, 1980) but is far more serious. It is the most common disease of childhood, a chronic condition that occurs most frequently in young children. The symptoms include wheezing, laboured breathing, coughing, and increased respiration. The actual causes of asthma are not fully understood, although it is known that it tends to run in families. An attack may be brought on by a specific allergy or by stress. The creation of a non-threatening environment will reduce stress on the student and may prevent attacks. Drugs play a significant role in relieving the effects of asthma, and are frequently taken with inhalers. Other preventative techniques include avoidance of possible allergens, and exercise to improve postural drainage, strengthen muscles, and expand lung capacity (Butt, 1980).

During an asthma attack, the child's laboured breathing may frighten her or him and provoke crying, gasping, and much anxiety, which can complicate the effects of the attack (Best, 1975). If the student appears to be concentrating on breathing or if the lips are turning blue, seek medical attention immediately (Canadian Lung Association, 1985). In the classroom, the student should be allowed to rest until breathing takes on a regular and easy pattern. During this time, the student should receive no attention from the teacher or other class members.

Diabetes

Children with *diabetes* function no differently from other students in regular classes and can take part in all school activities unless a doctor has advised against it. There are, however, two potential problems to watch for when dealing with diabetic students.

Their school achievement may suffer because of emotional problems and increased absenteeism and tardiness, and they may sometimes have insulin reactions (hypoglycemia) while in school. Reactions can be caused by the failure to eat before taking vigorous exercise, by missed or delayed snacks, or by too much insulin. Teachers should not feel unduly alarmed by the onset of insulin reaction; virtually every well-controlled diabetic has mild reactions and these will pass off in fifteen or twenty minutes if sugar is taken. Diabetic reactions should not be frequent events, however.

Teachers should constantly be alert for warning signals. Abnormal behaviour may be the first sign and may consist simply of confusion, poor work, or poor handwriting deteriorating quickly over a few minutes. If these signs are recognized early, reactions may be promptly terminated by providing some form of sugar. If the reaction is not treated, unconsciousness and convulsions may result.

The teacher should keep a supply of sugar at hand. The student experiencing a reaction may need coaxing to eat or drink, and should receive either fruit juice (half a cup), non-diet carbonated drinks (four ounces), candy bars (in amounts specified by the parents), commercial glucose products, or two teaspoons of sugar. If improvement does not ensue in ten or fifteen minutes, the child should be given sugar again. The student should neither be left unsupervised nor sent home during a reaction. When he or she improves following the treatment with fast-acting sugar products, solid food should be taken and this will usually be in the form of the student's next regular snack or meal. After the student has completely recovered from a reaction, classwork may be resumed. If a decision is made to send the student home, he or she should be accompanied by a responsible adult.

Abused and neglected children

In the past, reporting child abuse was seen as the responsibility of physicians and social workers for the most part, but greater public awareness has led to substantial increases in the number of reported cases in recent decades. One might suspect that teachers have made great contributions because they are in the perfect situation for intervention, but of cases reported only a minority are from concerned teachers. Yet teachers hold both a moral and a legal responsibility for reporting suspected cases of child abuse. Since they are in daily contact with children and are trained observers of their behaviour, they are frequently the first adults to discover indications of abuse or neglect. In fact, the school may be the only place where an abused child feels safe and in contact with caring adults (B.C. Ministry of Human Resources, 1979).

Although teachers often believe themselves to be morally obligated to report cases of abuse, they may also feel that they know little about the symptoms, especially of sexual abuse (Hughes, 1985). All educators are responsible, however, for learning how to recognize the signs of abuse, how and where to report it, and what the school can do to offer support. Child abuse may have both physical and behavioural manifestations, as shown in table 15–1. When considering the significance of symptoms or behaviours, consultation with a public health nurse will prove very helpful. Not all of these signs will come to the attention of the regular classroom teacher, but it is important to be aware of them.

Table 15–1 Symptoms of child abuse

Physical abuse

- Extensive bruising, bald spots, burns, marks from blows, unexplained lacerations
- Refuses to discuss how an injury happened
- Gives doubtful reasons for injuries
- Sleep disturbances
- Often late or absent
- Comes to school early and does not want to leave
- Truancy, running away
- Inadequately dressed for the season
- Refuses to undress for gym class
- Intolerant of physical contact
- Overcompliance
- Speech disorders, hyperactivity, disruptive behaviour, extreme aggression, sucking, biting, rocking, or antisocial behaviour
- Sudden drop in school performance
- Memory or concentration disturbances
- Phobias, fear states, depression
- Fire setting

Neglect

- Always tired, listless; falls asleep in class
- Always hungry; appears to be undernourished
- Inadequate lunches, or no lunch
- Ill-clothed
- Obvious medical needs unattended
- Abnormal pain or headaches without a physiological basis
- Depression
- Destructive behaviour
- Truancy, running away
- Stealing
- Prostitution
- Pregnancy

Sexual abuse

- Difficulty walking or sitting
- Urinary tract infections, vaginal infections, anal fissures
- Complains of genital pain or itching
- Overly detailed knowledge of sexual behaviour, inappropriate to the child's age
- Excessively sexual and provocative behaviour
- More knowledge about drugs and alcohol than most children have
- Receives unexplained gifts of money
- Does not participate in school activities
- Sudden drop in school performance
- Infantile or withdrawn behaviour
- Afraid of change or new situations
- Sudden fears
- Poor self-image
- Extremely passive or aggressive
- Overly upset at mistakes
- Terrified or nervous if parents are contacted

Sources: B.C. Ministry of Human Resources, 1979; Harrison, 1985; McKittrick, 1981

Within the classroom setting, teachers should keep rigorous anecdotal records of any suspected abuse. If possible, they should talk to the student. Broussard (1973) suggests that the teacher confront the child in a private setting and explain that someone must be told. It is important to maintain an informal atmosphere and establish feelings of trust. It is also incumbent on the teacher to believe what the student says, to reassure the student that he or she has done nothing wrong, and to be ready with evident support.

Mainstreaming physically disabled and health-impaired students

Diagnostically, physical and health disabilities are primarily medical problems, but special education is often necessary because chronic illness affects academic achievement and children necessarily miss so much school. Nevertheless, many of these students can be educated in regular classrooms; a regular setting allows the special student to model peers and teaches other class members and teachers to be sensitive to individual differences.

Class members should be prepared for the integration of a physically disabled student by discussion sessions and simulation exercises, as outlined in chapter 6. They should be aware of, for example, the reasons for seizures and realize that such events are caused by non-catching conditions and certainly not equated with mental subnormality.

Physically handicapped students may require extra assistance in the regular classroom because their disabilities make it impossible for them to keep up in mobility, writing, and communication. They may have special equipment or communication systems and need intensive training to use them. As well, they may lack independence in some self-help skills and suffer a general inability to organize activities requiring physical skills. When considering the educational implications of a physical disability, it is important that educators be clear and open in their assumptions about placement, goals, objectives, and long-range perspectives. It is difficult to determine which students will function adequately in regular classroom settings, but table 15-2 presents some very general characteristics that students should possess, largely drawn from Gromek and Scandary (1977). The case study that follows introduces Shawna, a child with spina bifida who attends a regular grade one class, in order to illustrate one integration experience.

Table 15-2 Selected criteria for mainstreaming physically disabled students

Teacher
- Willing to accept the child
- Willing to adapt programs and learning environments
- Shows sensitivity to the specific problems

Student
- Sufficient mental ability to function within the range of intelligence existing in the classroom
- Sufficient mobility to move from place to place
- Sufficient indication of ability to interact with peers in the classroom and in recreational and social settings
- Sufficient emotional stability to cope with a normal educational environment without panicking at a change of setting, personnel, or schedule
- Sufficient ability to communicate his or her needs in some quick, understandable manner
- Wishes to be with non-handicapped peers in regular school
- Already has some exposure to integrated activities, whether in school, recreational, social, or church settings
- Able to function independently in most daily living activities
- Parents or guardians want the placement and feel confident of the child's success

Support services
- Resource-room personnel
- Physical therapist
- Occupational therapist
- Speech/language pathologist
- Instructor for adapted physical education
- School nurse
- Language specialist
- Counsellors

Case study 15–1, part 1

Shawna attends a regular grade one class in her neighbourhood school in a large Canadian city. At the outset, the school debated about accepting her because she has spina bifida and is confined to a wheelchair. The concerns centered less on Shawna's academic aptitude than they did on physical adaptations. When Shawna's parents came to enrol her for kindergarten, the local school had no ramps, special washrooms, widened doorways, or lowered drinking fountains. The physical barriers were relatively easy to overcome, however, and she began school when she was six.

Prior to Shawna's entry into the kindergarten class, the special education teacher had presented a unit that included books, pictures, and simulation activities involving the wheelchair. All the children had an opportunity to experience moving in the chair and learned how to push it safely. When Shawna finally arrived, the class was waiting for her and she was immediately accepted as an integral member. In fact, there was often a line-up waiting to push her chair outside for recess or to other activities.

Yet worries about mainstreaming Shawna did not end there. The next year, the grade one teacher expressed deep concerns about accepting her into a regular classroom. Although the teacher firmly advocated the principles of educational integration, she thought that a wheelchair-bound pupil would demand a disproportionate amount of her time and would cause disruptions in the classroom. She also believed, though not as strongly, that Shawna might be unable to compete academically and could be rejected by her peers.

The teacher asked the school team for techniques to maintain Shawna physically. In order to increase the teacher's confidence, the team planned an IEP that focussed only on physical modifications. They devised a checklist of management techniques and scheduled regular meetings between the teacher and Shawna's physiotherapist. The therapist visited the classroom and demonstrated to the teacher various aspects of handling and positioning. An aide was also found to take care of Shawna's toileting needs.

The mainstreaming team

No single profession or discipline has the full capability to plan intervention for physically and health-disabled youngsters. These children require a team of specialists to focus on their abilities and disabilities through therapy, training, and education. Parents, teachers, physicians, therapists, social workers, and many others play some role in helping physically and health-impaired children to become as independent as possible. From the teacher's point of view, therapists and homebound teachers are most important to the student's academic progress. Therapists will also serve as consultants for classroom teachers, as case study 15–1, part 2 indicates.

By working closely with physiotherapists, teachers can encourage orthopedically handicapped students' motor development. Physiotherapists specialize in improving physically handicapped children's physical strength, control, and mobility. The amount and quality of therapy that some children receive during the developmental period has a decisive effect on their potential for mobility and independence as adults. Physiotherapists provide children with opportunities for normal motor development; they use activities that inhibit unwanted reflexes and permit more useful movement patterns to occur. Occupational therapists are trained in many areas: they may develop physically handicapped youngsters' self-help skills and eye–hand co-ordination; or they may develop or adapt equipment to help youngsters to perform in a more efficient and effective manner.

Some children require long-term hospitalization—for orthopedic disabilities, kidney failure, or severe burns, for example—and others have to remain at home because of illness or recuperation. Students who are absent from school long enough to interrupt their educational programs may be provided with special instruction. The teaching is generally provided by an itinerant **homebound teacher** who serves students of various ages and levels.

Case study

15–1, part 2

Name: Shawna
D.O.B.: 7 May 1982

Diagnostic category: physically disabled, spina bifida

Need	**Technique**	**Responsibility**
Positioning	Change Shawna's position every twenty minutes. Stand behind the chair, grasp her firmly by the belt, and pull her up and toward you. Next time, stand in front of her, grasp her firmly under the knees, and pull her forward.	Classroom teacher
Toileting	Every hour	Aide
Seating	Seat Shawna as close to the other students as possible and near to where her group will work. She can use the tray of her wheelchair when doing small work, and can be moved to a table for art and other larger work.	Classroom teacher
Sitting	Consistently remind Shawna to maintain good posture and reposition her if necessary.	Classroom teacher
Communication	When speaking with Shawna on a one-to-one basis or in a small group, squat down to be at her eye level.	Classroom teacher

General educational approaches

For physically and health-impaired students, their conditions alone often imply special educational considerations. These may be slight, such as taping writing paper to the student's desk, or substantial, such as using sticks attached to a band around the student's head to enable him or her to operate an electric typewriter.

Setting realistic goals is one of the main problems in the educational management of these children. Educators tend to expect either too little or too much. Physically and health-disabled students need objectives similar to those of other youngsters, although teachers may need to drop some objectives, change others, and even add some. Physically disabled students who have limited stamina will not be able to fulfil as many objectives, and some other students simply cannot achieve certain skills. The athetoid child, for example, cannot play music or paint. Many pupils will progress more slowly through objectives, and teachers much accommodate their pace. Teachers should be guided by behavioural and functional evidence of abilities and disabilities, rather than by medical diagnoses or prognoses. They should view the physical impairment as only one of the student's many important attributes.

Physically disabled students should be treated as normally as possible and given as much independence as is reasonable. Behaviourally, they can adhere to class routines and expectations. Teachers should encourage students to meet reasonable standards of performance and to develop a realistic view of themselves and their conditions (Heward & Orlansky, 1980). Orthopedically handicapped students should be expected to participate in the same activities as other students do even though they may walk awkwardly and fall often. Teachers must guard against overprotecting disabled students or allowing them to develop a dependency on a non-disabled peer, or on the teachers themselves.

In the classroom, there are three types of adaptations that may be necessary: changes to classroom space, different types of communication, and adaptations to aid academic functioning. Teachers should ensure that students have access to materials and that students who use bulky equipment are included in small instructional groups. Teachers will also need to accept alternative forms of communication, such as augmentative devices of typewriters. Wherever possible, children should try to manage common classroom materials such as pencils and paper. They may also use a range of equipment designed to compensate for physical problems.

Reading, writing, and mathematics

Teachers must take care to incorporate the necessary supportive devices for physically disabled students into educational settings. Bookstands and page turners (either manual or electronic) help when students are reading and allow them to work alone or to take part in group lessons. A pencil eraser serves as an efficient page turner for some children. Talking books, cassette recordings, or compressed speech of textbooks, periodicals, and novels are also quite helpful if a student has difficulty turning pages or balancing a book.

Paper can be secured by taping it to the desk, by using writing frames, or by mounting the paper on a clipboard with a non-slip backing. Some students will find embossed, lined paper a useful writing aid because of its tactile quality. Students who find writing especially difficult can use special typewriters with covers that prevent the user from hitting more than one key at a time. As well, teachers should encourage students to use a tape recorder to prepare homework, creative writing, or projects.

For students who can handle writing implements, felt-tipped pens require less pressure than ball points and pencils, while giant pens and pencils are easier for cerebral palsied children to grasp. Any pen or pencil can be made easier to hold by increasing its diameter. A piece of rubber or plastic secured with tape around the pencil shaft will increase the diameter of an ordinary pencil if splint frame built-up pencils are unavailable. A larger handgrip can be made by inserting the pen or pencil through a foam rubber ball or a block of plastic foam. Taping a small pencil sharpener securely to a shelf allows disabled students to sharpen their own pencils. A student who has a writing table attached to his or her wheelchair can use magnetic rulers, triangles, and mathematical instruments, which stick to the table and remain within reach.

Students should be encouraged to use a backpack attached to the back of the wheelchair to carry books, homework, and school supplies. Some packs are designed to attach to the side of the wheelchair so that students can reach them more easily.

Language

Physically disabled students' receptive language may be far ahead of their expressive language. Some children are so physically involved that they cannot speak and must make use of communication boards or other methods of augmentative communication, as discussed in chapter 11. Physical problems often affect speech; cerebral palsy, for example, can affect the speech and mouth muscles, causing drooling when the individual tries to speak. About 70 percent of cerebral palsied children have speech defects. They have slow, laboured speech, and tend to slur sounds or omit them completely. They may expel air too quickly or not be able to exhale enough air to speak smoothly, causing a distortion of rhythmic patterns. Teachers should not hesitate, however, to ask a student to repeat a statement. Students may also have problems chewing and swallowing and teachers should be aware of the danger of students choking on hard candy, popcorn, and gum.

Vocational education

Career choices for physically disabled students are limited by their individual preferences, motivation, abilities, and performance in training programs. Some disabilities clearly rule out certain occupational choices, but others do not preclude exceptional professional status if the disabled person has high motivation and the full use of residual functions. Vocational education provides physically disabled students with employment opportunities, and includes job evaluation (to help students make realistic career choices), job placement, and follow-up.

Physical adaptations in the school plant

In many instances, physically disabled and health-impaired students are separated from their non-handicapped peers by physical barriers alone. Physical obstacles can prevent a student from entering a building, travelling easily from room to room or floor to floor, using the toilet, or getting along a crowded hallway. In order to accommodate physically disabled students, ramps into buildings and elevators to upper floors must be available. Other physical modifications include:

- support bars in bathrooms
- alterations to doors, which may be too heavy for the student to push open
- reinforcing straps to hold the physically disabled student in a comfortable position at a desk
- widened doorways
- lowered coat hooks, lockers, drinking fountains, and sinks
- specialized writing surfaces and seating
- footrests if the student's feet do not reach the ground
- grab bars near the chalkboard, the door, and the stairs

Although these physical adaptations are necessary, physically disabled and health-impaired students need few curricular modifications. Of course, teachers do need to be aware of students' special needs and medication, but the major adaptations for these students are technical. The students encountered in the next chapter, those considered to be gifted and talented, are the opposite. They require a wide range of curricular and administrative adaptations.

16 *Gifted, talented, and creative students*

Dear Reader,

As you learn about exceptional students, please do not forget gifted students. They are also exceptional students, and right now they desperately need help. If this assertion seems inconsistent with your understanding, remember the term "exceptional" as it is used in the context of this book. It simply means different, or more precisely, different from the norm. The most frequently used norm value is the arithmetic mean of a distribution of measured abilities, and given that the measured abilities of gifted students are significantly above the norm, it follows logically that they are exceptional students. Since their differences are as great as those of other exceptional students, they too require special assistance to reach their potential. Unfortunately, gifted students' exceptionalities are so difficult to define and often so difficult to detect that the students are frequently not identified. Worse, when their exceptionalities are detected, their need for special education is too often still not recognized or far too frequently challenged and denied (Hartman, 1987).

Perhaps the best way to alert you to the difficulties encountered by gifted students is to give you an example. Of the many gifted students with whom I have worked over the past ten years, none exemplifies the nature of the problems faced by gifted students more than one I'll call by the pseudonym "Katie." This four year old was asked to read the letters on a Snellen Vision Rating chart as part of her medical examination for entrance to kindergarten. After she correctly read all the separate letters, Katie then read aloud, with only a small bit of difficulty, the note printed at the bottom of the chart: "The above characters subtend the visual angle of 5 minutes at the designated distance in feet in accordance with the Snellen notation of visual acuity." Noting that such reading was exceptional for a preschooler, the school nurse recommended that Katie's intellectual ability be assessed by an educational psychologist prior to placing her in school. The school's principal contacted me and requested an assessment of Katie's intellectual and reading abilities. The assessment indicated that Katie was intellectually gifted and reading at a grade six level.

The evidence of Katie's exceptional ability prompted me to recommend that she be placed in a special educational program for gifted students. Unfortunately, no such program was available at her school. Furthermore, with genuine concern for the child's welfare, school authorities advised Katie's parents that it was best to keep her with children her own age, in order to avoid doing anything that might make her feel different. For the same reason, the school principal noted that he had dealt before with situations like this and found that when he put all the children together it usually, "didn't take very long before the other students caught up." Not surprisingly, Katie's parents were confused by the contradictory nature of the recommendations. In the sincere belief that they were doing their best for Katie and in the absence of an available educational program for gifted students, they approved her placement in a regular kindergarten program. Consequently, Katie spent most of her first academic year "learning" the letters, numbers, and basic sight words that beginning readers need to learn. Next, she spent three years "learning" the beginning reading series used in primary grades in her school. I last spoke to one of her teachers when Katie was in grade four. I was told that she was a good student who was doing well in school. Furthermore, this teacher also clearly indicated that Katie's performance was not exceptional. Apparently, the principal was right; the other students had caught up. In one sense, the "problem" caused by Katie's exceptionality was "solved." In another sense, the solution created a situation that was worse than the original problem. Sadly, almost everyone has forgotten that Katie still has to wait two more years before she receives instruction commensurate with the exceptional ability she demonstrated in kindergarten. By that time will the "catching up" have continued to the extent that her good performance becomes average performance?

The problem with the solution to Katie's exceptionality is that the "levelling off" was probably accomplished, at least in part, by retarding Katie's development in the area of her exceptionality. The practice of not providing curricular learning opportunities appropriate for one's level of ability constitutes a type of deprivation. More than one psychological investigation has suggested that withholding appropriate environmental stimulation can significantly retard human development (Bloom, 1964, 1982; Dennis, 1960; Skeels & Dye, 1959; Tarjan, 1970). Clearly, this "solution" is simply not a solution, and Katie's problem is not that *she* cannot cope with her exceptionality but that *her school* cannot cope with it.

Why should any child's exceptional ability to learn be a problem in an institution dedicated to the task of facilitating human learning? This question is—pardon the pun—not academic. Katie is required by law to attend school to be educated. Her parents are also required by law to pay their fair share of the cost of operating the educational system of which her school is a part. Given these obligations, Katie has a legal right to a proper education; that is, one that does accommodate her abilities, no matter how advanced or delayed they may be. A more significant problem is that Katie's story is not at all uncommon. She is just one of far too many gifted students who pass through our schools underserved. Clearly, these students also need help to cope with their exceptionality, and who better to understand and help them with their difficulty than one who is studying exceptionality; namely you.

On behalf of gifted students, I invite you to assist them. Yet as Katie's case demonstrates, concern, no matter how genuine, is not sufficient. Concerned people who are also well informed about the development of all exceptional students are needed. For this reason, I invite you to start by reading the following chapter very carefully, and then taking time to consider what you will do when a Katie comes your way.

Bryan D. Hartman, Ph.D.
Associate Professor
Department of Educational Psychology
Memorial University of Newfoundland

In the past, Canadian educators have directed only fleeting attention to the special needs of gifted, talented, and creative children and youth. Special education has traditionally been viewed as an effort to help children who do not perform well in school, and students possessing unique abilities and talents have rarely aroused the same level of concern as have handicapped pupils. Today, that situation is changing rapidly. The potential of Canada's gifted and talented youth is one of our greatest resources. Educators, researchers, legislators, and parents now agree that gifts must be fostered. Denied educational opportunity and challenges, gifted students may hide their abilities, underachieve, or even drop out of school (Winzer, Rogow, & David, 1987). As it becomes increasingly apparent that gifted pupils have special educational needs, schools across the country are developing programs to meet those needs.

Providing special education for gifted children helps them to master research strategies and systems of knowledge that enable them to become creative, productive, and enthusiastic in school and later life. Nevertheless, devising appropriate and challenging programs for gifted students is not easy. Three elements are crucial in programming for these youngsters: the teacher, the curriculum, and student selection procedures.

Some teachers feel that gifted pupils constitute almost an embarrassment of riches and parents also express concern about their ability to handle and nurture gifted children. Educating these students requires a great deal of professional skill and sensitivity. Providing appropriate programs taxes teachers' skills, knowledge, and resourcefulness. Teachers need to be aware of the multidimensional nature of giftedness, the uses of various test procedures and non-psychometric approaches, and the methods of designing innovative, flexible programs.

No matter how sophisticated the curriculum for gifted and talented students, it will be filtered through the teacher. The quality of the filtering device will affect the understanding of even the brightest student, and teachers who have gifted children in their classes must become perpetual learners. The students demonstrate wide diversity in ability and achievement and, by high school, may surpass their teachers in some areas.

Gallagher (1985) points out that the school program does not have to be dramatically different for gifted students. They need stimulation in the processes of creativity, originality, and solving problems. Their curriculum should contain greater stress on advanced conceptualization and increased depth and sophistication of content. Adaptations are not necessarily qualitative; programs for gifted youngsters involve elements in different proportions from those in other students' programs, rather than elements of an entirely different nature.

Although quite a number of administrative options have been attempted with gifted students, enrichment is the most common. Teachers sometimes wonder how to provide enrichment activities within the context of the regular classroom in a way that challenges gifted students. Yet not only can an enrichment program be implemented successfully but it will benefit all class members, as gifted students' enthusiasm for learning and social interactions influence the class.

The main objectives of this chapter are to

- outline the major issues and problems in the education of gifted students
- discuss methods for identifying and evaluating gifted students

- detail the various administrative arrangements used in the education of gifted students
- describe curricular modifications and instructional techniques suitable for gifted youngsters

Readers should note that while the chapter discusses issues and teaching approaches relevant to gifted, talented, and creative students, for the most part it uses the generic term *gifted* for the sake of simplicity.

The education of gifted students

Canada has been described as "a developing nation in terms of its recognition of the special educational needs of gifted children" (Newfoundland & Labrador Association, 1982, p. 13). Provisions for these students too often tend to be more dependent on chance than on commitment and good management. While good teachers have always attempted to enrich the learning experiences of all special children, real concern must be bolstered by legal mandates, school policy, administrative commitment, and adequate funding.

Education for gifted and talented students has lacked specific direction at the provincial level in the past. Teacher training programs have been limited both financially and in variety, and support for innovative school programming has wavered. The inadequacy of programming for these youngsters has rested partly on the misconceptions that have traditionally surrounded gifted students and their education. It has been believed, for example, that genius borders on insanity, that gifted students are all bookworms, that the term gifted is synonymous with upper middle class, and that gifted students are unpopular. Giftedness has often been equated with male students who excel at school performance, who are the "best" students. Compounding these myths is the concern that the principle of democratic education may be threatened by special education for gifted students. Critics bandy charges of elitism and discrimination, and predict the creation of a meritocracy within the school population.

The primary concern of educators in the area today is to come to grips with arguments concerning democratic education and the erroneous notion that gifted children will achieve under any circumstances. Another thorny problem centres on precisely how a school curriculum should be made different for gifted and talented students.

Identification of gifted students

Outstanding ability comes in a number of different forms and requires a variety of ongoing identification, assessment, and evaluative procedures as well as a variety of special education programs. The diverse characteristics of the gifted population, combined with intervening factors such as motivation and interests, make identification a complex and involved process, much more than just selecting individuals with high IQs.

The most effective identification procedures include a combination of standardized achievement and ability tests, assessments of general performance, and rating scales that explicitly identify commonly observed performance characteristics of gifted students (Gallagher, 1985). School grades, interviews, family histories, observations, case studies, tests of creativity, and auditions in the performing arts are also used.

While group intelligence tests are often used to screen for gifted pupils, individual intelligence tests appear to be the best predictors of giftedness (Gallagher, 1975). They can identify gifted children and pinpoint gifted underachievers. Moreover, these tests can show not only what a child can do at the present time but can also predict future functioning (Roedall, Jackson, & Robinson, 1980). Achievement tests are also used to identify gifted children. The tests have limitations, however, because they cannot select children who possess high potential but are nevertheless underachieving.

Creativity, a predominant characteristic of the gifted population, is particularly difficult to assess. Tests of divergent thinking are problematic because the performance of both children and adults on the tests is affected by the conditions of testing, the way that the instructions are phrased, and the frame of mind of the testers (Vernon, 1971). Additionally, the tests sometimes have little to do with a person's performance on everyday tasks.

Various nomination procedures — teacher, parent, peer, and self — are also extensively employed to identify gifted youngsters. Teachers have not shown themselves to be extremely successful at nominations (they may, for example, favour one sex in the procedures), but specific training can help them to become twice as effective at identification (Haywood Gear, 1976). Using rating scales also improves teacher perceptions in identification procedures. Parent nominations can provide information on a child's current hobbies and interests, books read, special problems or needs, leisure activities, extraordinary accomplishments or talents, and special opportunities available to the child, (Martinson, 1975). Finally, peer nomination is also used as an informal measure (see box 16–1). Peers are particularly good at choosing students with leadership abilities.

Identification procedures are sadly lacking in many respects. It is not only that teachers select students with high IQs rather than those who are highly creative, but they consistently overlook or ignore certain groups of children. Because teachers tend to focus on students' deficits, gifted handicapped children are easily passed over in identification procedures. In addition, culturally different gifted children may fare poorly in the procedures because they demonstrate different strengths from those of middle-class children. Boys are elected as gifted in overwhelming numbers, a bias that is then reflected in later achievements. Gifted underachieving students, who constitute a hefty proportion of the gifted population, are also overlooked in many identification and screening procedures (Winzer, Rogow, & David, 1987).

Mainstreaming gifted students

In any one classroom a teacher may actually have three different groups of students: one remedial, one average, and one above average. Education must address the needs of all three groups and all the diverse intra- and interindividual differences within each group. Gifted students can master the curriculum content of a grade two or three times faster than the average student and the higher a student's level of giftedness, the less likely she or he is to profit by the regular educational program. A program for gifted

Box 16–1 Informal peer nomination measures

1. The teacher tells the class that the school principal has asked the students to draw a special picture to place in the school lobby. Students complete the following statements:
   a) The three people in the class who would draw the best pictures are: ____________________
   b) The three people in the class who would draw the most unusual pictures are: ____________________
   c) The three people in the class who would think of the most good ideas for pictures are: ____________________

2. The teacher tells the class that a new game for physical education is needed. Students complete the following statements:
   a) The three people in the class who could think of the best new games are: ____________________
   b) The three people in the class who could think of the most unusual new games are: ____________________
   c) The three people in the class who would make good captains in a new game are: ____________________

3. The teacher tells the students that they are going to write stories and asks them to complete the following statements beforehand:
   a) The three people in the class who would write the best stories are: ____________________
   b) The three people in the class who would write the funniest stories are: ____________________
   c) The three people in the class who would write the most unusual stories are: ____________________

Source: After Gallagher, 1975.

students that is not intensive enough tends to sacrifice a student's academic performance in favour of socialization; but a program that is too intense tends to restrict the student's social needs for the sake of academic productivity. To create a perfect balance and to nurture the positive differences seen in gifted children, educators may have to consider seriously programs of denormalization rather than normalization.

Exceptional achievement is related to the amount of time that gifted students spend in special seminars or classes, increasing with special programming. Students may be removed from heterogeneous settings, or from groups in which they intimidate and overpower the other students, and placed in special groups or tracks according to their particular abilities and skills (Malone, 1979). They can receive instruction in special classrooms or special schools, or in small groups within regular classrooms, using carefully planned alternative activities.

Case study 16–1 details the story of Brian, a gifted but increasingly bored and frustrated eleven year old. An extract from Brian's IEP appears later in this chapter.

Case study 16–1, part 1

Brian's grade six teacher is becoming more and more frustrated and annoyed by Brian's behaviour in the classroom while Brian himself presents the appearance of a student attending school under great duress. Little in the classroom seems to grab his interest and he is becoming known as the class clown.

Early in his school career he was identified as having high ability and has always worked with the higher groups in reading and language arts. In previous years he has achieved well and passed through the curriculum at a good rate. Now, however, he seems bored with school and the standard of his work is falling. It may be that Brian did not learn organization and study skills in the earlier grades because he could get by without them, and now feels the lack as academic demands increase. It is more likely, however, that Brian is bored with the entire educational process and finds the teacher's style of presenting the same material and seatwork to the whole class stultifying. Brian challenges the teacher often and seems to enjoy posing strange ideas and answers. Although he helps out in the classroom by tutoring, this does not seem enough to keep him stimulated. The classroom does not contain learning centres or computer terminals.

The classroom teacher referred Brian to the school-based team because of the perceived increase in behavioural problems. The teacher was more concerned about Brian's behaviour than about his academic progress and asked for assistance in devising programs that would keep Brian "busy and out of his hair."

A complete psycho-educational assessment was conducted and the team reconvened to discuss Brian's levels of functioning, an appropriate placement, and a program that would stimulate him but could still be presented within the regular classroom.

The mainstreaming team

Classroom teachers will not be alone in their efforts to provide appropriate programming for gifted students. Although the school team may have a less complex structure than those for more problematic students, it will consist of at least the school principal, special education and resource-room personnel, an educational consultant, classroom teachers, and the school psychologist. To create effective programs for gifted students in regular classrooms, regular, resource-room, and special education teachers must coordinate their efforts. Their respective levels of involvement will, however, largely depend upon the organizational model favoured by the individual school — whether classroom enrichment, an enrichment model, acceleration, ability grouping, or some other construct.

Essentially, the team will endeavour to accommodate the basic intellectual, social, and psychological needs of gifted students within the context of the school and its existing programs. Areas that come under careful scrutiny when the team recommends placement and devises a program are presented in table 16–1. These are considered to be the minimal conditions for meeting the basic needs of gifted students.

Table 16–1 Minimal conditions to meet gifted students' basic needs

Intellectual	Social	Psychological
Interaction with true peers (intellectual and chronological)	Social and emotional support of true peers	Sense of success in a challenging intellectual environment
Contact with gifted individuals in a diverse range of ages, occupations, cultures, and so on	Climate of genuine respect and affirmation of self-worth	Flexibility
Encouragement to be creative	Honest and constructive feedback from teachers and peers on social expectations	Opportunities to develop capacity for self-direction
Exposure to bodies of knowledge in the arts and sciences	Development of social skills and leadership potential	Adequate balance of competition and co-operation
Integrated, interdisciplinary curriculum	Open communication with teachers and peers	Student-centered classrooms to allow students input into their own instruction
Differentiated curricular experiences		
Opportunities to pursue and share interests and abilities		

Source: Adapted from Whitmore, 1985.

General educational approaches

There is no magic in giftedness that will allow children to overcome all the obstacles to development without special assistance. The general tenor of research on gifted children indicates that they require social and emotional support from a group of true peers in order to maintain a positive self-concept; and intellectual interaction with those peers in order to transform abilities into productive reality. True peers are simultaneously the student's intellectual and chronological equal. Gifted students also need differentiated curricular experiences, which take into account the many different learning styles found among the gifted population (Goldberg, 1965; Gowan & Bruch, 1971; Malone, 1979; Meeker, 1969; Terman & Oden, 1959).

More specifically, gifted students need to be challenged in order to cultivate advanced cognitive abilities, to acquire competence at an accelerated rate, to integrate large amounts of information, and to explore specific areas of interest independently. They should always be told the objectives of learning since they are strongly motivated to pursue learning goals. Gifted students also need encouragement to become creative, rather than passive, learners. They should be placed in instructional environments that both prompt them to satisfy their curiosity and develop their abilities to analyse, hypothesize, synthesize, and evaluate. Stimulating learning settings must be accompanied by materials clearly built on concepts requiring higher reasoning skills.

Even though they can proceed at accelerated rates and with greater depth and intensity, gifted students still need to learn basic skills. Once they acquire them they will need a higher level of instruction in terms of both content and process. By employing more abstract and varied curricula, and greater economy of organization, *content* can be used to convey more complex ideas (Passow, 1979). Changes in the *process* of instruction lead to more advanced knowledge, greater open-endedness and freedom of choice, more rapid pacing, and opportunities for students to use more sophisticated reasoning. Changing the content and process of instruction alters the breadth and tempo of the program, and the kind of courses offered within it. The objectives for a class in mathematics, for example, might involve learning long division, and gifted students can be taught to conduct the operations using a base other than ten once they have mastered the basic process. Such a change increases the breadth of the program.

Some very general tips for teaching gifted students are given in box 16–2. These follow from Whitmore's minimal conditions for accommodating gifted students, presented above in table 16–1.

Adaptations for gifted students

Nobody is certain of the best methods to educate gifted students and numerous programs have been attempted, all of which are intended to come to grips with three major problems: the wide range of abilities among the gifted population, teachers' limited knowledge in content areas, and teachers' lack of special instructional methods (Gallagher, 1985). Such programs have been more impressive in their diversity, perhaps, than in their efficacy.

Gallagher (1985) points out that the individual school can make changes in the learning environment, in the content of lessons, or in the skills taught. There is as yet no evidence, however, that proves any method or curriculum to be better than another. Most gifted students are placed in enrichment programs simply because that is often all that is available. At the secondary level, the educational needs of gifted students are most effectively met by mentoring programs, directed study programs, and accelerated placement for specific academic subjects.

Changes in the learning environment

Changing the environment brings gifted students into contact with one another, so that they can profit from each other's ideas, and with an instructor who possesses the specific skills to help them reach their appropriate abilities more effectively. While enrichment in the regular classroom is the most common organizational model used to change the learning environment for gifted students, research does not yield clear support of such programs (Marland, 1972). Instead, the evidence of the literature advocates acceleration. (Tannenbaum, 1983). The academic achievement of accelerated students is generally superior to that of non-accelerated students of similar ability (Daurio, 1979), yet very few schools practise acceleration.

Acceleration

Acceleration for gifted students is an administrative construct that encompasses any method to move students through the educational system rapidly, although it is not synonymous with skipping grades. Acceleration programs emphasize reducing the time needed to complete the curriculum. The programs can maximize students' intellectual

Box 16–2 Tips for teaching gifted students

- Make the classroom flexible rather than authoritarian.
- Encourage students to risk failure.
- Expect the same behaviour as is required of other students.
- Carefully observe students for signs of emotional or learning problems.
- Provide opportunities for critical thinking, and encourage divergent thinking.
- Provide many opportunities for independent study.
- Provide opportunities for students to identify and clarify their standards of comparison; by cross-disciplinary work, for example.
- Provide opportunities for students to learn how to make decisions based on available information, individual needs and goals, and perceived consequences. Encourage students to apply their ideas to real situations.
- Expose students to aesthetic, economic, political, educational, and social aspects of the environment and culture.
- Allow students to work with adults and peers with expertise in special areas, and give them the chance to exchange ideas in a variety of ways.
- Create programs in which students can apply knowledge in inventive ways; encourage them to hypothesize and to test their hypotheses.
- Accelerate academic content.
- Concentrate on abstract concepts, thought processes, and advanced comprehension of principles and theories.
- Help students to generate new information and products.
- Transfer learning to other disciplines.

Sources: Clark, 1983; Gallagher, 1985

potential, permit early entrance to high school or post-secondary studies, and an earlier start on a career. Students, as well as their parents and teachers, however, prefer organizational structures that are flexible and not totally segregated (Marland, 1972). Partly because acceleration results in a different placement for all or part of the actual content of instruction, it has not been a popular option.

Nevertheless, if they are to be educated in the least restrictive environment, gifted students may need special programs that stress enrichment and acceleration. This is true only when the norms of the regular classroom impose a level of content, structure, or pacing that hampers gifted students' capacity to learn, or when the students' needs are so diverse that they obstruct rather than enhance learning opportunities for others in the classroom.

Ability grouping

Ability grouping can take the form of a special class of students from a single school or from several schools. A class will meet either during regular school hours or on an extracurricular basis, and can be full or part time. Ability grouping permits both acceleration and horizontal expansion of the curriculum. For students, it brings greater self-esteem, peer interactions, the exchange of ideas, and intensive involvement in studies. Critics believe, however, that it may foster elitism and limit gifted students' contact with their normally performing peers.

Group work is helpful to gifted students and their peers.

Enrichment Certainly, the most popular educational option for gifted students is **enrichment**, which involves adding to the instruction being provided at a particular content level (Newland, 1976). In other words, enrichment provides special activities in an otherwise regular class. Enrichment programs attempt to develop students' creative abilities and skills, and to motivate them to undertake creative projects. Activities within the programs are broader and deeper than those in the general curriculum, designed to challenge gifted students while accommodating their individual strengths and weaknesses. Enrichment thus involves some adaptation but gifted students remain in the regular classroom with their chronological peers.

Enrichment depends in great measure on how the classroom teacher can adapt the program and implies more than entertainment or a grab bag of activities. The teacher cannot simply patch a few experiences onto the program. Field trips, creativity exercises, and educational games loosely grouped together are not defensible as an enrichment program. Enrichment must be educationally relevant, and requires planned flexibility and evaluative methods. To ensure both relevance and flexibility a number of enrichment models are widely used, of which the most popular are probably the Enrichment Triad Model (Renzulli, 1977) and the Revolving Door Model (Renzulli, 1979).

Independent study Gifted students prefer loosely structured, open-ended learning experiences and need to pursue their own ideas. Such pupils must not always be confined to the classroom; they should be allowed to study independently in libraries, laboratories, museums, and other parts of the community. Museums are learning centres of unlimited resources, and libraries have workshops as well as book collections, documents, and the expertise of a professional staff.

Independent study is an approach that permits students to develop their own goals and therefore teaches them to become self-directed learners. It can be carried out in a variety of settings but is most often used as an adjunct to enrichment programs. Unfortunately, there seems to be a misconception about the proper role of the teacher in providing gifted students with intellectual freedom. Teachers must remember that while gifted students may learn easily, they are not necessarily wise; if children could learn completely alone there would be no need for teachers. When dealing with students on independent study programs, teachers only change their role somewhat, to become facilitators, rather than dispensers, of knowledge.

Teachers present the core of a discipline, the background information, the interrelated disciplines, the skills for independent study, and a sequence for the topics to be studied independently. The general guidelines for independent study also apply to other aspects of enrichment programs and mentoring sessions, and are given below:

1. Work with the student to select a topic. Webbing (see figure 7–12 in chapter 7) is an effective way to begin research.
2. Establish a schedule with the student.
3. Help the student to develop questions that will direct his or her research.
4. Assist the student in securing references and sources of data.
5. Oversee the student's research and note taking.
6. Help the student to develop further topics and objectives.
7. Oversee the student's creation of some product demonstrating the ideas that he or she has formed.

8. Provide opportunities for the student to display the product to an audience.
9. Evaluate the product.

Students must be provided with direction and encouragement before embarking on independent studies; the younger the child, the more direction necessary. Learning contracts are a useful method of providing guidance. The contract should contain a statement of need or intent, a description of how to accomplish the goal, and an agreed-upon evaluative procedure.

Mentoring programs

Because gifted students welcome change and diversity and are stimulated by new opportunities to observe, experiment, and discuss what they see happening, they profit from learning experiences outside the immediate classroom. **Mentoring programs** are an aspect of independent study that satisfies students' curiosity and provides learning experiences with some structure. The gifted student leaves the school for a period of time and comes under the supervision of a specialist in the community. A mentor, then, is a person of large experience in a particular area: a professional, a university student, or another person of interest to the gifted student and willing to work on a project. Using mentors is not only educationally sound but also economically feasible since they are volunteers. Mentors are particularly valuable when they possess some skill that the teacher cannot be expected to have.

At the outset, the mentor meets the classroom teacher, the principal, and the resource-room teacher. They identify various students' special needs and then match a particular student to the mentor's expertise. Together, the teacher, mentor, and student then select a topic broad enough to generate the student's interest and enthusiasm. Once the student and mentor are matched and have a topic, they write a proposed sequence of activities together. They discuss the project fully, in order to agree on responsibilities and scheduling. The completed proposal thus becomes a commitment or contract between the mentor and the student. As they delve into the topic, they gather, sort, examine, and analyse information, and then organize their findings so that the student can present them to the class.

Some people may assume that, compared to intellectually delayed youngsters, it is easy to teach gifted students and to prepare programs for them. Nothing could be further from the truth. The range of administrative options just outlined reflects by its diversity the difficulties of implementing appropriate programs.

Changes in instructional content

Programs for gifted students must be flexible enough to account for their range of abilities and must extend the breadth and depth of learning; students need content enrichment in a program as well as changes in tempo and kind. Teachers need to organize the curriculum in order to teach concepts primarily, rather than facts, and must allow more time for individual projects under supervision. Yet although gifted students can function at higher cognitive levels and move rapidly from information to concept, and then to generalizations, they initially require a thorough grasp of the core of the curriculum. The progression of instruction for gifted students is presented in figure 16–1.

The example of a grade three classroom teacher who wishes to present a new reading story to the class will illustrate instructional modifications. The teacher first teaches everyone the new vocabulary, discusses the title and the opening picture, and then breaks the class into groups. While she works with the slower children on extra drill for vocabulary and language structures, the average children read the story to answer specific comprehension questions, and the faster moving group completes an assignment designed to enhance their critical reading skills. They can, for example, answer such questions as "What might have happened after the book ended?" or "How would you change the story if you were to rewrite it?"

After students have acquired basic skills, their programs may be altered to provide either horizontal or vertical enrichment. It is actually very difficult to differentiate the two types of enrichment clearly. Essentially, horizontal enrichment activities provide more experience at the same level of difficulty. They concentrate on the application of acquired knowledge and involve practising learned skills, concepts, and generalizations. Content enrichment and content sophistication are part of horizontal enrichment. According to Gallagher (1985), *content enrichment* provides an extensive range of additional experiences and examples to strengthen students' mastery of important ideas embedded in the standard curriculum. *Content sophistication* takes advantage of gifted students' already superior knowledge and skills by prompting them to make use of more complex ideational systems.

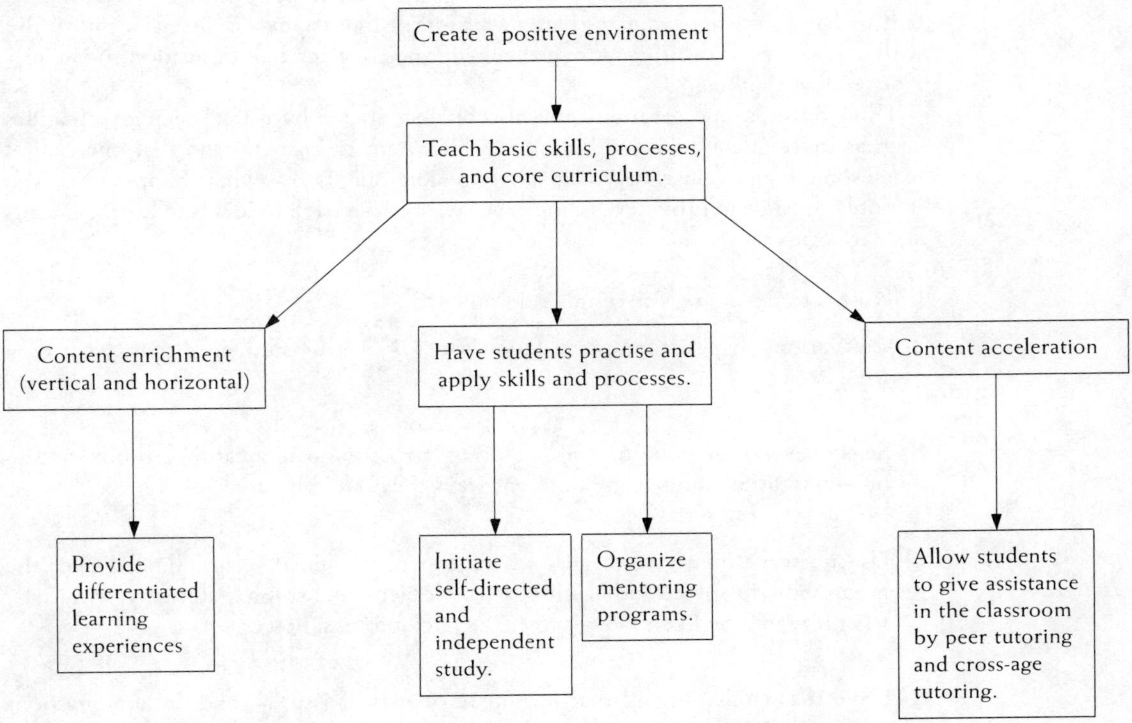

Figure 16–1 Accommodating gifted students

Vertical enrichment activities involve *content novelty*. They allow gifted students to learn through experiences beyond the core curriculum. Vertical enrichment therefore involves a higher level of activities, for the most part. It also includes *curriculum compacting*, which refers to substituting challenging work for learned material (Renzulli, Smith, & Reis, 1982), thereby eliminating some of the repetition found in drill and routine exercises and thus reducing boredom.

Changes in skills

The changes in learning environment and in content for gifted students discussed above can be complemented by instruction in special skills. The students have the capacity to develop their general thinking skills to a sophisticated level and to learn advanced skills appropriate to specific areas of the curriculum such as language arts, mathematics and science, social studies, and career education.

Developing thinking skills

The ability to discover new information by applying already acquired skills is one of the most impressive and valuable skills that human beings have, and one of the most highly prized in education. Gifted students excel at solving problems but require many activities that use these skills, in order to prevent them from becoming complacent about absorbing facts and uncomfortable when asked to apply reasoning. Teachers should gear their expectations to the students' levels, however. Too much pressure will only result in anxiety, frustration, resentment, and overcompetitiveness. It is also important to have students evaluate their own progress, either by discussing it informally with the teacher or by using more formal recording devices. Self-evaluation encourages independent thinking.

Thinking skills and creativity can also be encouraged by using specific techniques such as those given below, although it is important to bear in mind that one cannot teach something as elusive as imaginative thinking simply by giving children exercises. It is only possible to provide learning experiences that enable students to learn concepts and strategies rather than isolated facts.

Objective: to develop creative thinking skills

a) Cut various shapes from construction paper. Have the students discuss what they see.

K to grade 3

b) Select several common objects — a brick, a roasting pan, a cardboard box, and so on — and discuss how many different ways they could be used.

K to grade 6

c) Use nursery rhymes to discuss what happened when the cow jumped over the moon, how to solve Mother Hubbard's problem, and so on. Alternatively, discuss what it would be like to be a snowflake, a cloud, or a flower.

K to grade 6

d) Have the pupils pretend that inanimate objects can speak, and discuss questions such as "What does my math book say after I've gone home?"

K to grade 6

e) Tell the pupils to imagine that they are going on a trip to Mars. Now present some materials: clay, paper, glue, rocks, and crayons. From these they must create something that they would need on Mars and be able to explain its use.

K to grade 6

f) Have pupils list the attributes of a common object, such as a banana or a flowerpot.

K to grade 6

g) Have students give as many reasons as possible why people wear clothes, why we live in houses, why we go to school, and so on.

K to grade 6

h) Supply an answer and ask the students to come up with as many appropriate questions as they can.

K to grade 6

i) Discuss with the class how one could improve, for example, a bicycle.

Grades 3 to 9

j) Begin a story and have the students continue it by acting it out spontaneously. They take on roles, discuss observers' reactions, and draw conclusions about the story.

Grades 3 to 9

k) Have students discuss speculations; they might ask, for example, "What if I were an only child?"

All levels

l) Present students with an objective and ask them to invent ways to teach it to the whole class. Let them create a board game for the learning centre, for example.

All levels

Language arts

There is no dimension of the curriculum through which gifted children can operate more effectively than the language arts (Gallagher, 1985). As they learn language skills, students also learn to express themselves purposefully and with imagination, and develop new, unusual, and original ideas. Language teaches them to determine the worth of an idea and to see the subtle presence of values in society.

Once gifted students have a sound foundation in the mechanics of language, they can be given the opportunity to take upper level classes for additional credit and to become familiar with linguistic tradition through etymology, mythology, foreign languages, and literature. Students will need additional time to practise communicative and expressive skills and to study great intellects from the past.

Teachers should be involved with language and literature themselves in order to nurture pupils' creative writing and provide stimulating literature programs built on gifted students' voracious appetite for books. The activities given below are designed with the general intent to stimulate students in language arts:

a) Have the students construct the timetable of a typical day as if it were in a TV guide.

Grade 3 and up

b) Have the students invent myths, such as why Santa Claus wears a red suit or why witches fly on broomsticks.

Grade 3 and up

c) Ask the students to write an essay on how "isms" such as nationalism, Marxism, or social Darwinism have affected some event.

Grades 7 to 12

Book reports are particularly valuable to teach students the skills to interpret what they read. Reports should extend beyond mere summary of the story and characters to include criticism of the piece. After students read their chosen books, they answer questions and complete exercises such as the following:

1. Who was the hero(ine) of your book?
2. How would you describe the hero(ine) to someone else?
3. Why is the title of the book suitable?
4. Write a letter to the author to find out more about him or her.
5. Why do you think the book was written?
6. Design a new chapter to include a new incident or a new character.
7. Write a play using the book's characters in different situations.
8. Select music that creates the mood or shows changes in the mood of your book.
9. Suggest some changes you might make if you were to rewrite the story.
10. Choose a character from the story and one from another story. Plan a meeting between them and write their conversation as a play.
11. Compare one character in the story to a real person whom you know. How are they alike? How do they differ?
12. Pretend you are a news editor in the city where the characters lived. Write two articles, with headlines, that could have appeared in the paper at the time the story took place.
13. Invent a symbol alphabet. Write a message in your code to a friend about an exciting part of the book.
14. Write a letter to the main character in the story. Suggest what might have happened if he or she had acted in a different way.
15. Write an epilogue to your book. What happened after the book ended?
16. Choose a place mentioned in the story and write a legend about that place.

Mathematics

Students do not show as great a range of skill levels in mathematics as in other subjects at the elementary levels because they depend more heavily on the materials presented by the teacher. Nevertheless, students' mathematical skills in a regular elementary classroom may span grades one to eight. Gifted students may be able to complete exercises that extend beyond simple problem solving. They may, for example, not only find the area of a rectangle but also describe how they solved the problem and make up a further problem of their own to demonstrate the process.

As well, gifted students need interdisciplinary studies that incorporate science and mathematics. (See chapter 10 for instructional adaptations to the science curriculum.)

Units should make use of arithmetic, social competencies, communication skills, health, and vocational education. Students could, for example, investigate how adults use mathematics in their jobs or how they use the information on social insurance numbers, licence numbers, and the like. They could try their hands at weather prediction by keeping weather records, consulting past records of climatic conditions, and then applying the laws of probability.

Social studies

Gifted students are often fascinated by the distant past and future (Gallagher, 1985). Their ability to use concepts enables them to project themselves into imaginary lands, and their curiosity drives them to think about where the human race has come from and where it is going. These children also develop a system of ethics earlier than do other students, and are able to understand concepts such as democracy at a younger age.

In social studies, gifted students therefore require both horizontal and vertical enrichment and an emphasis on ethical issues. Teachers might present information by constructing an historical time line and thereby bringing events and issues into conjunction with one another. A time line can either connect kinds of issues — social, political, economic, and philosophical, for example — within a single period, or draw parallels between issues or events in different historical periods. For certain topics, teachers can ask students to devise a list of intentional and unintentional consequences of an invention; for example, of the automobile, of television, of nuclear weapons, or of computers. Similarly, teachers can set the task of assessing both sides of a story, such as British and American accounts of the Boston Tea Party or the War of 1812.

To explore values, students can create photographic essays or films to share information and opinions. Value sheets are also useful: they contain a provocative statement and a series of questions to which students respond, either individually or in a class discussion (Raths, Harmer, & Simon, 1966). The purpose is to take each student through the process of clarifying values.

Some commercial social studies programs are available for gifted students. The Trade OFF series (Sigler, 1984), for example, contains fifteen videotaped programs, each twenty minutes long, and a teacher's guide. The series uses a five-step decision-making model and is suitable for elementary gifted students. The selections deal with economics in the daily lives of the students and pose stimulating problems. Each segment presents key points and then dramatizes an economic problem. It then introduces another problem for students to resolve later. The series builds skills because it asks many questions, employs analysis, and demands complex intellectual processes.

Adaptations to the social studies program and other areas will make a great difference to students such as Brian, the grade six pupil introduced earlier in the chapter. The case study below presents an IEP extract for Brian. After making a psycho-educational assessment, the school-based team devised an enriched program to hold his interest and meet his educational needs. He was present at the second meeting of the team and talked about some things that he would enjoy doing in the classroom.

Case study
16–1, part 2

Name: Brian
D.O.B.: 14 October 1978

School: Rocky Mountain Elementary
Diagnostic category: Gifted

In many ways Brian's psycho-educational assessment bolstered the findings of earlier measures administered when he was in grade two. It was found that he was in the very bright to superior range and had the potential to function above most of his peers. In the areas of reading and the language arts, he demonstrated excellent aptitude, interest and, on achievement tests, performance, but was not as far ahead in mathematics, working a little above grade level. Brian confided to the psychologist that he enjoyed school and liked his friends but sometimes found the work boring. The best part of school was recess and the games during physical education classes. He especially disliked the readers and felt that they were "for kids." He responded to a comment about his declining grades with a nonchalant "Doesn't really matter much." To a question on his behavioural antics, he replied, "The other guys think it's funny!"

The school has no facilities for special class programming and so it was decided that Brian should remain in the regular classroom, with a more stimulating program in the language arts, specifically reading. He would pursue an independent study in an area of interest and work with a mentor in another area.

Long-range goals:

1. Brian will pursue an individual reading program that allows him to progress at his own rate.
2. Brian will receive guidance in an independent study of his own choosing.
3. Brian will study an area of special interest through an after-school mentoring program.
4. Brian will continue to take part in a structured peer tutoring program, which will help him to view himself as a valuable member of the class.

General techniques:

1. The teacher asked Brian to take six books and rate them for the class library as interesting, moderately interesting, or not interesting, and to comment about their levels of readability. Following this, the teacher asked him to choose a book and write a report on it, answering the type of questions just seen on p. 504.
2. In social studies, the class was studying the exploration of Canada. Brian worked with the group but then made a web of the topic to identify areas that he wished to follow. The teacher drew up a learning contract with him and assisted him with planning, research, and presentation for a three-week independent study.
3. As Brian expressed interest in the way that banks work, he was matched to a willing mentor at the local bank in an after-school mentoring program. With the mentor and the teacher, Brian drew up a learning contract. Once a week after school he would meet with the mentor at the bank to gather information to fulfil the contract.
4. In the classroom, Brian was asked to tutor a student encountering difficulties in mathematics and reading. The teacher drew up flow charts to structure the tutorial sessions, and Brian and the student worked together for short scheduled periods daily.

Computers

Gifted students especially must be allowed to take advantage of the new advances in information management and communication through computer technology, and computer activities should be placed high on the list of their educational priorities. Computers are capable of transmitting academic and thinking skills to gifted and talented students more rapidly and effectively than other instructional methods are. The classroom teacher can use computer instruction to accelerate students through subject areas in which they demonstrate high verbal or mathematical ability.

Gifted youngsters should begin to use computers as early as possible. They should learn programming and other computer skills, in order to use the computer as a tool to solve problems. It is important to remember, however, that computer instruction is only useful if it addresses curricular content that is significant and worthy of the student's time. It is particularly difficult to design complex programs to challenge gifted students.

Gifted youngsters are most effectively served by computer instruction in the tutorial mode, in which the computer instructs the student in some area of knowledge rather as a teacher would in a one-to-one situation. Tutorials attempt to teach the learner new skills by providing a fixed instructional sequence representing various stages of learning. The program presents a concept, prompts the student to answer, and then offers feedback on the response (Kolich, 1985).

Equally appropriate for gifted students are simulation activities, in which a computer model imitates a real or imaginary system. Common simulations include flying an airplane, piloting a lunar landing, managing a small business, and controlling the ecology of a small pond. Simulations build on drill and practice by adding a decision-making component. Students are encouraged to respond to complex situations with many solutions and are given feedback that helps them to choose an acceptable answer (Kolich, 1985).

As well, instructional games are an excellent use of the computer, although they should be provided sparingly. They offer a new dimension to the game formats that teachers often use and allow students to work independently. New interactive games are constantly appearing on the market.

Teaching gifted students programming, using Logo or Pilot, will improve their computer literacy and competence. They could, for example, start with Pilot (Programmed Instruction Learning Or Teaching), a programming language with eight basic commands that are mnemonic and easy to learn (Maddux & Cummings, 1987).

Many of the ideas applicable to gifted students can stimulate and enhance the learning of all children, including those with mild handicapping conditions. With adaptations, not only can gifted students receive greater benefit from instruction, but all students can profit from the contributions that gifted students themselves make to the class. Certainly, not all the approaches that can be used to stimulate gifted students have been discussed here. It is hoped, however, that this chapter and the earlier ones present a wide enough range of interventions and techniques to allow teachers to adapt to the specific needs of each individual student.

Glossary

Ability grouping. An administrative arrangement to serve gifted students, usually in a "pull-out" mode.

Acceleration. An administrative arrangement that encompasses any method to move students through the educational system in a rapid fashion, although acceleration is not synonymous with skipping grades.

Adaptive behaviour. The behaviour that is appropriate in specific situations and settings for a particular individual's age and culture.

Adaptive devices. Devices to make living easier, such as a modified fork and spoon (a spork), toileting aids (portable urinals), velcro openers on clothing, or TTDs for deaf people.

Assessment. The process that takes place as we form judgments about people, things, events, or performances.

Atypical youngsters. Individuals who do not reach the norm in some functional area or areas.

Augmentative communication. A term currently used to describe all communication that supplements or augments speech.

Axioms. The intuitive rules that arise from a study of numbers and underlie the discipline of mathematics.

Boundary conditions. Conditions, other than diagnostic data on the student, that are important to consider when constructing an IEP because they ensure that a certain teacher, working in an existing classroom situation, is in fact able to conduct the planned implementation for that exceptional student.

Chaining. Technique of breaking down a target objective into a number of component behaviours, which can be performed separately and which have a fixed order of performance. In language development, the term refers to a method of building up utterances slowly and systematically.

Classroom management. The manipulation of the classroom environment to facilitate the active engagement of students toward achieving academic and social goals.

Cognitive behaviour modification. The effect that self-talk or inner speech has on an individual's behaviour.

Cognitive competence. What an individual could do, in contrast to what she or he characteristically does.

Communicative competence. An individual's ability to understand and use communication commensurate with developmental levels.

Compensatory instruction. Counterbalancing or substituting one skill with or for another.

Computer-assisted instruction (CAI). Any method of instruction that uses the computer as the primary delivery system. Usually the student has direct interactive instruction and is on-line with the computer.

Computer-managed instruction. The systematic control of instruction by the computer, characterized by testing and diagnosis, learning prescriptions, and thorough record keeping.

Condition. The situation in which an individual is to perform the desired task. Conditions frequently include the materials used, the amount of verbal direction given, and the setting in which the behaviour is to be performed.

Construct validity. An assessment instrument's ability to measure a variable such as creativity, risk-taking, or intelligence.

Content validity. The appropriateness of the items on a test, and the level of mastery at which the content is assessed.

Criterion. How well an individual must perform a behaviour before the performance is considered sufficient to proceed to the next objective.

Criterion-referenced tests. Measures to assess a student's progress against criteria set for instructional objectives for that student, rather than against group norms.

Criterion-related validity. The extent to which a student's success on a criterion-related measure can be predicted from that student's score on a norm-referenced test or subtest.

Curriculum. A document written for a grade level and designed to benefit the greatest number of students.

Curriculum-based assessment procedures. Procedures to determine the instructional needs of students based on their ongoing performance in existing course content.

Delayed language. Language that demonstrates significant lags but still progresses according to the stages of normal language development.

Developmental disability. A severe, chronic disability, attributable to mental and/or physical impairment, which results in substantial limitations on behaviour in certain designated areas of human activities.

Deviant language (also **disordered language**). The language of children who may have the rudiments of a language code and may comprehend more easily than they produce language.

Diagnosis. The aspect of assessment that involves an intensive examination of various functional areas considered to be problematic.

Diagnostic tests. Tests designed to identify specific problems in perceiving or responding and used to identify the precise nature of the difficulties.

Diagnostic-prescriptive teaching. The practice of formulating instructional prescriptions on the basis of differential diagnostic results.

Differential diagnosis. The precise specification that a given set of symptoms is indicative of one disorder rather than another.

Direct instruction. The direct measurement of a student's performance on a learning task and the accompanying arrangement of instructional programs and procedures for each student.

Direct observation. Observation designed to permit assessment of a student's behaviour and achievement within the normal daily routine.

Disordered language. See *deviant language*.

Downtime. Classroom time when little or no instruction occurs and the students have little or no knowledge of what to do or what comes next.

Duration recording. Method of recording the intensity of a behaviour, rather than the frequency with which it occurs.

Dyslexia. A disorder of children who, despite conventional classroom experiences and instruction, fail to attain the language skills of reading, writing, and spelling at a level commensurate with their intellectual ability.

Dysnomia. Difficulty in remembering and expressing words.

Emotional overlay. An adverse reaction to learning problems and academic failure.

Enrichment. The provision of special activities in an otherwise regular class.

Error analysis. The process of analysing students' work samples in order to discover patterns of errors.

Event recording. Method of recording the number of occurrences of a behaviour over a given period, at least five days.

Exceptional children (or **special learners**). Those whose intellectual, emotional, physical, or social performance falls below or rises above that of other children.

Expansion. Acknowledgment and reinforcement of a child's utterances.

Expressive language. Language output.

Face validity. The general acceptance of a measuring instrument.

FM system. A miniature broadcasting system consisting of a microphone worn by the teacher and a receiver worn by the student.

Game. A pleasure-invoking rule-based

interaction between at least two people, with successful movement toward an agreed-upon terminal goal dependent on the mastery of academic skills.

Generalization. The development of strategies with which to discriminate the relevant dimensions of similar stimuli rather than the same stimuli.

Goal. A long-range general aim or direction that represents an estimate of accomplishment; the intent of a goal is based on identified student needs and defined in terms of the student's growth and development.

Grammatical approach. The traditional way of teaching language; the approach depends on teaching language structures with intense practice so that students can generalize.

Group contingency. A reinforcement that depends on the co-operation of every member of the group. If any member fails to exhibit the agreed-upon behaviour, then none receives the reinforcement.

Homebound teacher. A teacher who provides instruction for students who are confined because of illness, physical injury, or other problems.

Homophones. Words that look the same on the lips.

Hyperactivity. Behaviour characterized by abnormal patterns of inattentiveness, impulsivity, overactivity, extreme agitation, and over-responsiveness to stimuli.

Imitation. The technique of presenting the correct verbal structure for the student to repeat.

Individual education plan (IEP). A plan written, usually by a team, for an exceptional student and designed to facilitate individual instruction and learning.

Individualization. A way of organizing learning experiences so that the rate, content, schedule, experiences, and depth of the activities arise from the assessed achievements and needs of individual students.

Informal assessment. Activities for gathering data on which to base instructional plans for individual students. Informal assessment is designed to identify strengths and weaknesses within individuals.

Infusion method. Arrangement in which the basic curriculum is maintained but supplemented by activities and units related to career education.

Initial acquisition. The first or initial exposure that students are given to a skill or material.

Integration. See *mainstreaming*.

Interindividual differences. The differences that exist among members of an age group or grade level.

Interval recording. Method of recording behaviour that allows the observer to assess and chart both its frequency and its duration.

Intra-individual differences. The variations of performance that are observed as an individual performs several different sorts of tasks.

Language disorders. Impairments in the adequate use of the linguistic symbol system that humans use for communication.

Language experience. A student-centered program that capitalizes on the students' own language patterns and experiences.

Language hierarchy. Inter-related components in the development of language; listening, speaking, reading, and writing.

Language maturity. An individual's ability with the phonological, morphological, syntactical, and semantic elements of language.

Language samples. Examples of children's natural and spontaneous language collected during periods of social interaction.

Learning centre. An area in the classroom that contains a collection of activities and materials to teach, reinforce, and/or enrich a skill or concept.

Locational skills. The ability to scan or read over material rapidly in order to locate a fact or event, a specific piece of evidence for an argument, or a phrase that defines vocabulary.

Mainstreaming (also **integration**). Both a philosophy and a process. It is the physical, intellectual, social, and emotional integration of exceptional children and youth into the regular educational milieu. Mainstreaming demands individual programming, co-operative planning, and a range of educational options and support services.

Maintenance. The skill learned in an instructional situation is performed even after instruction ceases.

Mentoring program. A program in which the gifted student leaves the school for a period of time and comes under the supervision of a specialist in the community.

Metacognition. Strategies that command learning.

Miscue. An unexpected response to print.

Modelling. Adding more to a message in the hope that conversational interaction will continue, or presenting a stimulus behaviour for a student to imitate.

Natural approach. Language instruction that teaches language in the same way that children naturally acquire it.

Non-categorical approach. A way of placing and educating mildly handicapped youngsters that focusses on their behaviours and learning patterns rather than on diagnostic categories.

Normalization. The philosophical belief that every exceptional person, regardless of the type and degree of handicap, should be provided with a living environment as close as possible to normal.

Norm-referenced tests. Tests that have been administered to a large group of people so that any individual score can be compared to the average, or norm.

Objective. A very specific statement derived from the general goal. Short-term objectives are statements of intent or expectation, to be achieved within a specified period of time.

Observation. The process of systematically looking at and recording behaviour for the purpose of making instructional decisions.

Orthopedic conditions. Deviations of the bones, muscles, or joints which cause abnormal functioning.

Orthoses. Devices to prevent or correct deformity, provide support, or improve the movability of limbs.

Outward loci of control. Tendency to attribute all events, whether good or bad, to outside forces or luck.

Perception. The process by which an organism is aware of objects, qualities, and events stimulating the sense organs.

Precision teaching. The modification of instructional and other school variables based upon individual diagnosis in order to assist the student's learning.

Primary stuttering. Stuttering characterized by breaks in speech caused by repetitions of syllables and sounds and less frequently by prolongations.

Probe sheets. Work sheets containing problems that focus on a specific skill, tentatively identified as one in which an individual is experiencing difficulties. The work sheets are designed to provide data.

Process-oriented tests. Tests that attempt to assess how an individual integrates and uses stimuli.

Proficiency. The process of building on the original task by repeating it over and over again.

Prompting. Providing a student with a clue or clues, such as pointing or touching an object, in order to elicit a correct response.

Prosthetic devices. Devices that replace an absent part of the body with an artificial one, and therefore replace a lost function.

Readiness. A state of development necessary before a skill can be learned. It involves processing those skills and abilities learned at a preceding stage of development and is concerned with prerequisite skills rather than an assessed maturational level.

Receptive language. The comprehension of language.

Related services (also **support**

services). Services that augment and enhance special education.

Remedial instruction. The process of improving or correcting a skill in a particular area to normal or near-normal standards.

Resource room. A placement between the regular classroom and the special self-contained class; a setting that students enter for specific periods of time on a regularly scheduled basis.

Retention. What students remember over a given period of time after they have been taught a skill.

School-based team. A committee of people responsible for ensuring that appropriate procedures are used to refer, evaluate, and provide educational programs for exceptional learners.

Screening. Testing whole age groups of children in order to identify those achieving below the norm in certain areas of behaviour or attainment, or both.

Secondary handicapping conditions. Adverse physical or emotional conditions that arise as a result of the primary handicap.

Secondary stuttering. Stuttering characterized by terse, non-fluent speech along with facial grimaces, tics, or other forms of spasmodic movements.

Selective attention. The ability to focus on the relevant features of stimuli.

Shaping. A technique for task analysing targets, in which the same action is used in all the objectives but the materials change. It is generally more relevant for non-academic skills.

Slicing. A task analysis technique in which tasks are "sliced" into smaller, more manageable teaching units. The slicing technique is particularly useful in academic skill areas such as reading, spelling, and arithmetic.

Special learners. See *exceptional children.*

Specific reading disability. An inability to learn to read with the rapidity and skill required of an individual's mental age.

Speech disorders. Disorders present when a person's speech differs from the speech of others to the extent that it calls attention to itself, interferes with the intended message, or causes the speaker or listener to be distressed.

Speech reading. Interpreting visual clues about speech from lip movements and facial expressions.

Standardized tests. Instruments commercially prepared by measurement experts that provide methods of obtaining samples of behaviour under uniform procedures. Standardized tests have a fixed set of questions and of directions, timing constraints, delineated and precise scoring procedures, and are usually norm referenced.

Support services. See *related services.*

Sustained attention. The ability to scan the stimulus field, locate the relevant stimuli, and attend to the input over a period of time.

Task analysis. Breaking a skill into its smallest component parts.

Terminal behaviour. The eventual performance it is intended that the student produce.

Time sampling. Method of monitoring behaviour by checking it at prespecified intervals.

Voice therapy. Therapy to return an individual's voice to normal or near normal.

Whole language. An approach to teaching language that sees all learning as part of language; a natural approach.

Reference list

Abbey, R. (1979). Steps to good spelling. *Special Education in Canada, 53*, 15.

Abelson, M.A., & Woodman, R.W. (1983). Review of research on team effectiveness: Implications for teams in schools. *School Psychological Review, 12*, 125–136.

Abeson, A., & Weintraub, F. (1977). Understanding the Individualized Education Program. In B. Torres (Ed.), *A primer on individual education programs for handicapped children.* Reston, VA: Council for Exceptional Children.

Abrams, J. (1975). Minimal brain dysfunction and dyslexia. *Reading World, 14*, 219–227.

Abramson, R.M. (1973). *Rhythm games for perception and cognition.* New York: Music and Movement Press.

Adams, R.C. (1981). Adapted physical education. In J.M. Kauffman & D.P. Hallahan (Eds.), *Handbook of special education.* Englewood Cliffs, NJ: Prentice-Hall.

Adamson, D.R. (1983). Linking two worlds: Serving resource students at the secondary level. *Teaching Exceptional Children, 15*, 70–76.

Albert, W. (1980). Special education in the Yukon Territory. In M. Csapo & L. Goguen (Eds.), *Special education across Canada: Issues and concerns for the '80s.* Vancouver: Centre for Human Development and Research.

Allan, R. (1983). More Bionic Beaver. *Computing Now, 1*, 63–65.

Allan, R. (1984, June). Canadian computers and coursewear. *Computers in Education*, pp. 8–12, 14.

Allen, K.E. (1980). *Mainstreaming in early childhood education.* New York: Delmar.

Alley, G. (1977). Grouping secondary learning-disabled students. *Academic Therapy, 13*, 37–45.

Alley, G. & Deshler, D. (1979). *Teaching the learning disabled adolescent: Strategies and methods.* Denver, CO: Love Publishing.

Allingham, R. (1980). Word frequency and contextual meanings' effects on word identification of EMR children. *Education and Training of the Mentally Retarded, 15*, 118–120.

Allison, D.E. (1982). Some of the things you always wanted to know about measurement and evaluation but were afraid to ask. *B.C. Journal of Special Education, 6*, 111–120.

Allred, R. (1977). *Spelling: The application of research findings.* Washington, DC: National Education Association.

Alonso, L. (1967, November). The child with impaired vision. *NEA Journal*, pp. 42–43.

Alter, M.M. & Goldstein, M.T. (1985). The "G.S." paradigm: A tool for IEP preparation. *Teaching Exceptional Children, 18*, 135–138.

Anderson, A.S. (1979). *Public Law 94-142 and suggested areas of competencies for regular educators.* College Park, MD: University of Maryland.

Anderson, L.M., Evertson, C.M., & Brophy, J.W. (1979). An experimental study of effective teaching in first-grade elementary reading groups. *The Elementary School Journal, 79*, 193–222.

Anderson, R.J., & Sisco, F.H. (1977). *Standardization of the WISC-R Performance Scale for deaf children.* Washington, DC: Gallaudet College, Office of Demographic Studies.

Anderson, R.N. (1988). *Using language inclusively.* Unpublished paper, University of Lethbridge, Lethbridge.

Antia, S. (1982). Social interaction of partially mainstreamed hearing impaired children. *American Annals of the Deaf, 127*, 18–25.

Antia, S. (1985). Social interaction of hearing-impaired children: Fact or fiction? *Volta Review, 87*, 279–298.

Appell, L.S. (1979). Enhancing learning and enriching lives: Arts in the education of handicapped children. *Teaching Exceptional Children, 12*, 74–76.

Apter, S.J., & Conoley, J.C. (1984). *Childhood behavior disorders and emotional disturbance.* Englewood Cliffs, NJ: Prentice-Hall.

Armitage, D. (1978a). A multi-sensory approach to remediating spelling problems. *Special Education in Canada, 53*, 26.

Armitage, D. (1978b). Neurological impress method of reading instruction. *Special Education in Canada, 52*, 23.

Armitage, D. (1982). *Write on* (2nd ed.). British Columbia: Armitage Teaching Resources.

Aronson, E., Blaney, N., Sikes, J., Stephen, C., & Snapp, M. (1975). Busing and racial tension: The jigsaw route to learning and liking. *Psychology Today, 8*, 45–50.

Arter, J.A., & Jenkins, J.R. (1979). Differential diagnosis — prescriptive teaching: A critical appraisal. *Perceptual and Motor Skills, 49*, 517–554.

Ashcroft, S.C. (1963). Blind and partially-seeing children. In L.M. Dunn (Ed.), *Exceptional children in the schools.* New York: Holt, Rinehart & Winston.

Asher, S.R., & Hymel, S. (1981). Children's social

competence in peer relations: Sociometric and behavioral assessment. In J.D. Wine & M.D. Syme (Eds.), *Social competence*. New York: Guilford Press.

Asher, S.R., & Taylor, A.R. (1981). The social outcomes of mainstreaming: Sociometric assessment and beyond. *Exceptional Education Quarterly, 1*, 13–30.

Ashlock, R.B. (1986). *Error patterns in computation: A semi-programmed approach*. Columbus, OH: Charles E. Merrill.

Aukerman, R.C. (1972). *Reading in the secondary school classroom*. New York: McGraw Hill.

Axline, V.M. (1977). *Play therapy* (rev. ed.). New York: Ballantine Books.

Bachor, D.G. (1979). Using work samples as diagnostic information. *Learning Disability Quarterly, 2*, 45–52.

Bachor, D.G. (1983). Personnel preparation for learning assistance teachers: School based instruction. *Special Education in Canada, 58*, 16–20.

Bachor, D.G., & Crealock, C. (1986). *Instructional strategies for students with special needs*. Toronto: Prentice-Hall.

Ballard, M., Corman, L., Gottlieb, J., & Kaufman, M. (1977). Improving the social status of mainstreamed retarded children. *Journal of Educational Psychology, 69*, 605–611.

Balow, B., & Balow, E. (1982). Education of autistic children: Philosophy and program options. In C.R. Smith, J.P. Grimes, & J.J. Frielinger (Eds.), *Autism: Programmatic considerations*. Des Moines, IO: Department of Public Instruction.

Balow, B., Fulton, H., & Peploe, E. (1971). Reading comprehension skills among hearing impaired adolescents. *Volta Review, 73*, 113–119.

Bamberger, R. (1976). Literature and development in reading. In J.E. Merritt (Ed.), *New horizons in reading*. Newark, DE: International Reading Association.

Bangs, T.E. (1982). *Language and learning disorders of the pre-academic child* (2nd ed.). Englewood Cliffs, NJ: Prentice-Hall.

Bank-Mikkelson, N.E. (1969). A metropolitan area in Denmark, Copenhagen. In R. Kugel & W. Wolfsenberger (Eds.), *Changing patterns in residential services for the mentally retarded*. Washington, DC: President's Committee on Mental Retardation.

Bannatyne, A. (1971). *Language, reading, and learning disabilities*. Springfield, IL: Charles C. Thomas.

Barngrover, E.A. (1971). A study of educators' preferences in special education programs. *Exceptional Children, 37*, 754–755.

Barraga, N.C. (1976). *Visual handicaps and learning*. Belmont, CA: Wadsworth Publishing.

Bateman, B. (1967). Three approaches to diagnosis and educational planning for children with learning disabilities. *Academic Therapy Quarterly, 3*, 11–16.

Bateman, B. (1976, April, May, and June). *Teaching reading to learning disabled children*. Paper presented at the Reading Conference, National Institute on Education, University of Pittsburgh, PA.

Bates, E., Beningi, L., Bretherton, L., Camaioni, L., & Volterra, V. (1977). From gesture to the first word: On cognitive and social prerequisites. In L.M. Rosenblum (Ed.), *Interaction conversation and the development of language*. New York: John Wiley.

Beale, A., & Beers, C.S. (1982). What do you say to parents after you say hello? *Teaching Exceptional Children, 15*, 34–38.

Beare, P.L. (1985). Difficulties and alternatives in emotional/behavioral disorders. *B.C. Journal of Special Education, 9*, 1–10.

Beck, I.L. (1978). *Instructional ingredients for the development of beginning reading competence*. Pittsburgh, PA: Learning Research and Development Center, University of Pittsburgh.

Becker, L.D. (1978). Learning characteristics of educationally handicapped and retarded students. *Exceptional Children, 44*, 502–511.

Becker, W.C. (1975). *AAMD Becker Reading Tree Vocational Interest Inventory*. Washington, DC: American Association on Mental Deficiency.

Behr, M., Snyder, A., & Clopton, A. (1978). *Drama integrates basic skills*. Springfield, IL: Charles C. Thomas.

Behrmann, M.M. (1984). A brighter future for early learning through high tech. *The Pointer, 28*, 23–26.

Belch, P. (1975). The question of teachers' questions. *Teaching Exceptional Children, 7*, 46–47.

Bennett, R.E. (1982). Application of microcomputer technology to special education. *Exceptional Children, 49*, 106–113.

Bereiter, C., & Scardamalia, M. (1982). From conversation to composition: The role of instruction in a developmental process. In R. Glaser (Ed.), *Advances in instructional psychology* (Vol.2). Hillsdale, NJ: Laurence Erlbaum.

Beselt, H., & Patomares, V. (1970). *Magic Circle/Human Development Program*. San Diego, CA: Human Development Training Center.

Best, G.A. (1975). *Individuals with physical disabilities: An introduction for educators*. St. Louis, MO: Mosby.

Binkard, B. (1985). A successful handicap awareness program — Run by special parents. *Teaching Exceptional Children, 18*, 12–16.

Birch, J.W. (1976). Definitions, development, and characteristics. In J.B. Jordan (Ed.), *Teachers, please don't close the door*. Reston, VA.: Council for Exceptional Children.

Blacher-Dixon, J., & Turnbull, A.P. (1979). Preschool mainstreaming: Definitions, rationale and implementation. *Education Unlimited, 1*, 16–22.

Blackhurst, A.E., & Berdine, W.H. (1981). Basic concepts in special education. In A.E. Blackhurst & W.H. Berdine (Eds.), *An introduction to special education*. Boston: Little, Brown.

Blackman, J.A., Levine, M.D., Markowitz, M.T., & Aufsaeser, C.L. (1983). The pediatric extended examination at three: A system for diagnostic clarification of problematic three-year-olds. *Developmental and Behavioral Pediatrics, 4*, 143–150.

Blackman, L., Burger, A., Tan, N., & Weiner, S. (1982). Strategy training and the acquisition of decoding skills in EMR children. *Education and Training of the Mentally Retarded, 17*, 83–87.

Blackwell, P. (1978). *Sentences and other patterns*. Rhode Island: Rhode Island School for the Deaf.

Blair, T.R., & Rupley, W.H. (1980). New trends in spelling instruction. *Reading Teacher, 33*, 760–763.

Blake, K.A. (1976). *The mentally retarded: An educational psychology*. Englewood Cliffs, NJ: Prentice-Hall.

Blank, S.S., & White, B.R. (1984). Teachers and technological innovation. *B.C. Journal of Special Education, 8*, 71–80.

Blankenship, C.S. (1985). Using curriculum-based assessment data to make instructional decisions. *Exceptional Children, 52*, 233–238.

Blankenship, C.S., & Lovitt, T.C. (1976). Story problems: Merely confusing or downright befuddling? *Journal for Research in Mathematics Education, 7*, 290–298.

Blau, A.F., Lahey, M., & Oleksiuk-Velez, A. (1984). Planning goals for intervention: Language testing or language sampling? *Exceptional Children, 51*, 78–79.

Blau, H., & Blau, H. (1968). A theory of learning to read. *The Reading Teacher, 22*, 126–130.

Bley, N.S., & Thornton, C.A. (1981). *Teaching mathematics to the learning disabled*. Rockville, MD: Aspen Systems.

Bloom, B. (1964). *Stability and change in human characteristics*. New York: Wiley.

Bloom, B. (1982). The role of gifts and markers in the development of talent. *Exceptional Children, 48*, 510–522.

Bloom, L., & Lahey, M. (1978). *Language development and language disorders*. New York: Wiley.

Boder, E. (1970). Developmental dyslexia. *Journal of School Health, 40*, 289–290.

Boder, E. (1971). Developmental dyslexia: Pervading diagnostic concepts and a new diagnostic approach. In H.R. Myklebust (Ed.), *Progress in learning disabilities* (Vol. 2). New York: Grune & Stratton.

Bond, D. (1981). Aspects of behaviour and management of adolescents who are hearing impaired. *British Teacher of the Deaf, 2*, 41–48.

Bormuth, J. (1968). The cloze readability procedures. *Elementary English, 45*, 429–436.

Bornstein, M.R., Bellack, A.S., & Hersen, M. (1977). Social-skills training for nonassertive children: A multiple baseline analysis. *Journal of Applied Behavior Analysis, 13*, 113–117.

Bosno, R. (1981). Who's afraid of Individualized Education Plans (IEPs)? Or why individualization is the basic precept of enduring equal educational opportunity. *Special Education in Canada, 56*, 15–20.

Bower, E.M. (1961). *The education of emotionally disturbed children*. Sacramento, CA: California State Department of Education.

Brady, M.E. (1977). *A comparison of CATTS and audio feedback in developing teacher prompting skills in reading*. Paper presented to the American Educational Research Association, New York, NY.

Bragstad, B.J., & Stumpf, S.M. (1982). *A guidebook for teaching study skills and motivation*. Boston: Allyn & Bacon.

Brannon, J.B. (1966). The spoken syntax of normal, hard-of-hearing, and deaf children. *Journal of Speech and Hearing Research, 9*, 604–610.

Brannon, J.B. (1968). Linguistic word-classes in the spoken language of normal, hard-of-hearing, and deaf children. *Journal of Speech and Hearing Research, 11*, 279–287.

Bregman, S. (1984). Assertiveness training for mentally retarded adults. *Mental Retardation, 22*, 12–16.

British Columbia, Ministry of Human Resources. (1979). *Inter-ministry child abuse handbook*. Victoria, B.C.: Ministry of Human Resources.

Brito, T., & Reynolds, K. (1979). An epilogue. *Teacher Education and Special Education, 2*, 10–11.

Brolin, D. (Ed.). (1978). *Life-centered career education: A competency-based approach*. Reston, VA: Council for Exceptional Children.

Bromley, K., & Jalongo, M.R. (1983). Song picture books and the language disabled child. *Teaching Exceptional Children, 16*, 115–119.

Brophy, J.E. (1982a). How teachers influence what is taught and learned in classrooms. *Elementary School Journal, 83*, 1–13.

Brophy, J.E. (1982b). Successful teaching strategies for the inner-city child. *Phi Delta Kappan, 63*, 527–530.

Brophy, J.E., & Evertson, C. (1976). *Learning from teaching: A developmental perspective*. Boston: Allyn & Bacon.

Brothers, R.J. (1974). Classroom use of the braille code recognition materials. *Education of the Visually Handicapped, 6*, 6–13.

Brown, F. (1976). *Principles of educational and psychological testing* (2nd ed.). New York: Holt, Rinehart & Winston.

Brown, J.B. (1981). *Examination of the syntactic abilities of hard-of-hearing compared with normal hearing children.* Doctoral dissertation, Memphis State University.

Brown, J.B. (1984). Examination of grammatical morphemes in the language of hard-of-hearing children. *Volta Review, 86*, 229–238.

Brown, V.L., & McEntire, E. (1984). *Test of Mathematical Abilities.* Austin, TX: Pro-Ed.

Brozo, W.G., Schmelzer, R.B., & Spires, H.A. (1983). The beneficial effects of chunking in good readers' comprehension of expository prose. *Journal of Reading, 26*, 442–445.

Brueckner, L., & Bond, G. (1967). Diagnosis and treatment of spelling difficulties. In E. Frierson & W. Barbe (Eds.), *Educating children with learning disabilities: Selected readings.* New York: Appleton.

Bruininks, V.L. (1978). Peer status and personality characteristics of learning disabled and non-disabled students. *Journal of Learning Disabilities, 11*, 29–34.

Brulle, A.R., Barton, L.E., Barton, C.L., & Wharten, D.L. (1983). A comparison of teacher time spent with physically handicapped and able-bodied students. *Exceptional Children, 49*, 543–547.

Brunner, L.S., & Suddarth, D.S. (1982). *The Lippincott manual of nursing practice* (2nd ed.). Philadelphia: Lippincott.

Bryan, T.S. (1978). Social relationships and verbal interactions of learning disabled children. *Journal of Learning Disabilities, 11*, 107–115.

Bryan, T., & Bryan, J.H. (1978). *Understanding learning disabilities* (2nd ed.). Sherman Oaks, CA: Alfred Publishing.

Bryan, T.H., Donohue, M., & Pearl, R. (1981). Learning disabled children's peer interactions during a small-group problem-solving task. *Learning Disability Quarterly, 4*, 13–22.

Bryan, T.H., & Pflaum, S. (1978). Social interactions of learning disabled children: A linguistic, social, and cognitive analysis. *Learning Disability Quarterly, 1*, 70–79.

Bryant, D.N., Fayne, H.R., & Gellinger, M. (1980). *Designing spelling instruction for learning disabled youngsters: An emphasis on unit size, distributed practice, and training for transfer* (Technical Report No. 3). New York: Columbia University, Teachers College.

Bullock, L.M., & Mintz, J.A. (1979). A smorgasbord of ideas for classroom use with LD children. *Academic Therapy, 14*, 581–587.

Burke, C., & Goodman, K. (1970). What a child reads: A psycholinguistic analysis. *Elementary English, 47*, 121–130.

Burke, R.L. (1982). *CAI resourcebook.* Englewood Cliffs, NJ: Prentice-Hall.

Burmeister, L.E. (1974). *Reading strategies for secondary school teachers.* Massachusetts: Addison-Wesley.

Burns, P.C. (1968). *Improving handwriting instruction in elementary schools.* Minneapolis, MN: Burgess.

Burns, P.K., & Bozeman, W.C. (1981). Computer assisted instruction and mathematics achievement: Is there a relationship? *Educational Technology, 21*, 32–39.

Burt, M.A., & Myrick, R.D. (1980). Developmental play: What's it all about? *Elementary School Guidance and Counseling, 15*, 14–21.

Burton, G.M., & Meyers, M.J. (1987). Teaching mathematics to learning disabled students in the secondary classroom. *Mathematics Teacher, 80*. 702–709, 747.

Butt, K.R. (1980). *Breathing exercises for asthma.* Springfield, IL: Charles C. Thomas.

Caccamise, F. (1974). Musts for hearing people. *American Annals of the Deaf, 119*, 296–297.

Cacha, F.B. (1981). Managing questions for student participation. *The Clearing House, 54*, 263–264.

Calhoun, M.L., & Hawisher, M. (1979). *Teaching and learning strategies for physically handicapped students.* Baltimore, MD: University Park Press.

Calman, G., & Freeman, E. (1976). Pinpointing cursive writing. *Special Education in Canada, 50*, 31–33.

Campbell, D.P. (1974). *Strong-Campbell Interest Inventory.* Stanford, CA: Stanford University Press.

Canada, Health and Welfare. (1984). *Childhood hearing impairment: Report of a task force convened by the Health Service Directorate, Health Services and Prevention Branch.* Ottawa: Department of Health and Welfare.

Canadian Lung Association. (1985). *Willy and the wheeze.* Toronto: Canadian Lung Association.

Caparulo, B., & Zigler, E. (1983). The effects of mainstreaming on success expectancy and imitation in mentally retarded students. *Peabody Journal of Education, 60*, 85–98.

Carlsen, J.M. (1985). Between the deaf child and reading: The language connection. *The Reading Teacher, 39*, 421–426.

Carlson, G.P. (1982). Physical education is basic. *American Association of Health, Physical Recreation and Dance, 52*, 62–69.

Carpenter, D. (1983). Spelling error profiles of able and disabled readers. *Journal of Learning Disabilities, 16*, 102–104.

Carpenter, D., & Miller, L.J. (1982). Spelling ability and reading disabled LD students and able readers. *Learning Disability Quarterly, 5*, 65–70.

Carter, P.H. (1979). Teacher stress: Discipline,

paperwork top list of causes a M.T.A. survey has found. *Massachusetts Teacher, 59*, 7–11.

Cartledge, G., & Milburn, J.F. (1980). *Teaching social skills to children.* New York: Pergamon Press.

Cartwright, C.A., & Cartwright, G.P. (1974). *Developing observational skills.* New York: McGraw Hill.

Cartwright, G.P., Cartwright, C.A., & Ward, M.E. (1982). *Educating special learners.* California: Wadsworth Publishing.

Cartwright, G.P., Cartwright, C.A., & Ward, M.E. (1984). *Educating special learners* (2nd ed.). California: Wadsworth Publishing.

Case, R. (1982). *Reading critically.* Toronto: OISE Press.

Cawley, J.F. (1985). *Practical mathematical appraisal of the learning disabled.* Rockville, MD: Aspen Systems.

Chall, J. (1967). *Learning to read: The great debate.* New York: McGraw Hill.

Charlesworth, E.A. (1982). Music, psychology, and psychotherapy. *The Arts in Psychology, 9*, 191–202.

Chennault, M. (1967). Improving the social acceptance of unpopular educable mentally retarded pupils in special classes. *American Journal on Mental Deficiency, 72*, 455–458.

Chisanbop finger calculation. *California Mathematics, 3*, 2–10.

Clarizio, H.F. (1976). *Toward positive classroom discipline* (2nd ed.). New York: John Wiley.

Clark, B. (1983). *Growing up gifted* (2nd ed.). Columbus, OH: Merrill.

Clark, C.M., & Yinger, R.J. (1979). Teachers' thinking. In *Research on thinking: Concepts, findings, and implications.* Berkeley, CA: McCutchan.

Clark, M.M. (1957). *Left-handedness: Laterality characteristics and their educational implications.* London: University of London Press.

Clarke, B.R., Rogers, T., & Booth, J. (1982). How hearing impaired children learn to read: Theoretical and practical issues. *Volta Review, 82*, 57–69.

Clarke, K., Clarke, B.R., & Winzer, M.A. (1988). *A validation of competencies required by teachers of the hearing impaired.* Unpublished paper, Memorial University of Newfoundland, St. John's.

Clinchy, B., & Rosenthal, K. (1971). Analysis of children's errors. In G.B. Lesser (Ed.), *Psychology and educational practices.* Glenview, IL: Scott Foresman.

Cohen, S., & Plaskon, S. (1980). *Language arts for the mentally handicapped.* Columbus, OH: Merrill.

Coker, H., Medley, D.M., & Soar, R.S. (1980). How valued are expert opinions about effective teaching? *Phi Delta Kappan, 62*, 131–134.

Coleman, M.C. (1986). *Behavior disorders: Theory and practice.* Englewood Cliffs, NJ: Prentice-Hall.

Condon, D., & Maggs, A. (1986). Direct instruction research: An international focus. *International Journal of Special Education, 1*, 35–47.

Connolly, A.J., Nachtman, W., & Pritchett, E.M. (1979). *Keymath Diagnostic Arithmetic Test* (Canadian ed.). Circle Pines, MN: American Guidance Services.

Connolly, A.J., Nachtman, W., & Pritchett, E.M. (1982). *Keymath Diagnostic Arithmetic Test.* Circle Pines, MN: American Guidance Services.

Connor, F.P. (1983). Improving school instruction for learning disabled children: The Teachers College Institute. *Exceptional Education Quarterly, 4*, 23–44.

Copeland, A.P., & Weissrod, C.S. (1976). Differences in attitudes toward sex-typed behavior of non-retarded and retarded children. *American Journal of Mental Deficiency, 81*, 280–288.

Council of Ministers of Education. (1983). *Survey of special education in Canada, 1982–83.* Winnipeg: Candid Research and Council of Ministers of Education, Canada.

Council of Ministers of Education, Canada. (1982). *Social studies provincial curricula: A survey compiled for the curriculum committee of the Council of Ministers of Education, Canada.* Ottawa: Council of Ministers of Education, Canada.

Council of Ministers of Education, Canada. (1983). *Arts: A survey of provincial curricula at the elementary and secondary levels.* Ottawa: Council of Ministers of Education, Canada.

Cox, L.S. (1975). Diagnosis and remediating systematic errors in addition and subtraction computation. *The Arithmetic Teacher, 22*, 151–157.

Cramer, R.L. (1978). *Children's writing and language growth.* Columbus, OH: Merrill.

Crealock, C. (1983). Teacher and student behaviors in regular and special education settings. *B.C. Journal of Special Education, 7*, 321–330.

Criscoe, B.L., & Gee, T.C. (1984). *Content reading: A diagnostic prescriptive approach.* Englewood Cliffs, NJ: Prentice-Hall.

Crookall, P., & Land, J. (1983, September). Teaching exceptional children in the regular classroom. *FWTAO Newsletter*, pp. 20–23.

Crow, F., Johnston, D., Meeks, M., & Wilson, P. (1975). Punch me, I earned it. *Teaching Exceptional Children, 8*, 13–17.

Crum, M., & Matkin, N. (1976). Room acoustics: The forgotten variable. *Language, Speech, and Hearing Services in the Schools, 7*, 106–110.

CTC, McGraw Hill Ryerson. (1981). *Canadian Achievement Test.* Toronto: McGraw Hill.

Culatta, B., Page, J., & Culatta, R. (1981). *Improving language functioning: A manual for language clinicians and teachers working in regular educational settings.* Lexington, KY: University of Kentucky.

Cummings, S.T., & Finger, D.C. (1980). Emotional disorders. In H.E. Rie & E.D. Rie (Eds.), *Handbook of minimal brain dysfunction.* New York: John Wiley.

Curriculum Committee of the Council of Ministers. (1979). *Mathematics: A survey of provincial curricula at the elementary and secondary levels.* Nova Scotia: Curriculum Development Branch.

Currie, A.B. (1981). *Instruction in handwriting in Ontario schools.* Toronto: Ontario Ministry of Education.

Cypher, R., Hinves, D., Baine, D., & Sobsey, D. (1984). Contemporary considerations in educating students with severe and multiple handicaps. *B.C. Journal of Special Education, 8,* 137–148.

Dale, D.M. (1972). Towards individual integration programs. *Scandinavian Audiology, 2,* 28–29.

Dale, M. (1979). Peer tutoring: Children helping children. *The Exceptional Parent, 9,* 26–27.

D'Alonzo, B.J. (1974). Puppets fill the classroom with imagination. *Teaching Exceptional Children, 6,* 141–144.

D'Alonzo, B.J., & Miller, S.R. (1977). A management model for learning disabled adolescents. *Teaching Exceptional Children, 9,* 58–60.

Dangel, H.L. (1987). The coach's spelling approach. *Teaching Exceptional Children, 19,* 20–22.

Daurio, S. (1979). Educational enrichment versus acceleration: A review of the literature. In W. George, S. Cohn, & J. Stanley (Eds.), *Educating the gifted: Acceleration and enrichment.* Baltimore: Johns Hopkins University Press.

Davies, D.G. (1984). Utilization of creative drama with hearing impaired youth. *Volta Review, 86,* 106–113.

Davis, J.M. (1977). Reliability of hearing-impaired children's response to oral and total presentations of the Test of Auditory Comprehension of Language. *Journal of Speech and Hearing Disorders, 42,* 520–527.

Day, C., with S. Kirk & J.J. Gallagher. (1985). *Educating exceptional children* (Canadian ed.). Toronto: Nelson.

Deiner, P.L. (1983). *Resources for teaching young children with special needs.* New York: Harcourt Brace Jovanovich.

Dell, H.D. (1972). *Individualizing instruction.* Chicago: Science Research Associates.

De Magistris, R.J., & Imber, S.C. (1980). The effects of life space interviewing on academic and social performance of behaviorally disordered children. *Behavior Disorders, 6,* 12–25.

Denckla, M.B., & Rudel, R.G. (1976). Naming of object drawing by dyslexic and other learning disabled children. *Brain and Language, 3,* 1–16.

Dennis, W. (1960). Causes of retardation among institutional children: Iran. *Journal of Genetic Psychology, 96,* 47–59.

Deno, S.L. (1985). Curriculum-based assessment: The emerging alternative. *Exceptional Children, 52,* 219–232.

Deshler, D.D. (1974). *Learning disability in the high school student in monitoring of self-generated and externally-generated errors.* Doctoral dissertation, University of Arizona.

Deshler, D.D. (1978). Psychoeducational aspects of learning-disabled adolescents. In L. Mann, L. Goodman, & J.L. Wiederholt (Eds.), *Teaching the learning disabled adolescent.* Boston: Houghton Mifflin.

Deshler, D.D., & Graham, S. (1980). Tape recording educational materials for secondary handicapped students. *Teaching Exceptional Children, 12,* 52–54.

Dever, R.B. (1978). Language assessment through specification of goals and objectives. *Exceptional Children, 45,* 124–129.

Dewar, R.L. (1982). Peer acceptance of handicapped students. *Teaching Exceptional Children, 14,* 188–193.

Dietrich, D. (1973). Diserroneous spelling or the fine (language) art of spelling. *Elementary English, 49,* 245–253.

Dinkmeyer, D. & Dinkmeyer, D., Jr. (1982). *Developing Understanding of Self and Others — Revised.* Circle Pines, MN: American Guidance Service.

Ditchburn, S.J. (1987). Guest editorial. In *Teaching mathematics in early childhood classrooms.* Edmonton: Alberta Teachers Association.

Dolch, E.W. (1936). A basic sight vocabulary. *Elementary School Journal, 36,* 456–460.

Donaldson, J. (1980). Changing attitudes toward handicapped persons: A review and analysis of research. *Exceptional Children, 46,* 504–514.

Donlan, D. (1975). Teaching words through sense impressions. *Language Arts, 52,* 1090–1093.

Dover, A. (1983). Computers and the gifted: Past, present and future. *Gifted Child Quarterly, 27,* 81–85.

Drabman, R.S. & Patterson, J. (1981). Disruptive behavior and the social standing of exceptional children. *Exceptional Education Quarterly, 1,* 45–55.

Dreikurs, R. (1968). *Psychology in the classroom.* New York: Harper & Row.

Dry, E. (1978). Spanning the math-language bridge in the early grades. *Volta Review, 80,* 478–481.

Dubrov, E. (1968). *Learning to write, book 2.* Cambridge, MA: Education Publishing Service.

Dugues, S.L. (1986). An oral language bridge to writing. *Teaching Exceptional Children, 18,* 214–219.

Dunkin, M.J., & Biddle, B.J. (1974). *The study of teaching.* New York: Holt, Rinehart & Winston.

Dunlap, G. (1984). The influence of task variation and maintenance tasks on the learning and affect of autistic children. *Journal of Exceptional Child Psychology, 37,* 41–64.

Dunlap, G., & Egel, A.L. (1982). Motivational

techniques. In R.L. Koegel, A. Rincover, & A.L. Egel (Eds.), *Educating and understanding autistic children*. San Diego College, CA: Hill Press.

Dunlap, W.P. (1976). An attitudinal device for primary children. *Arithmetic Teacher, 23*, 29–31.

Dunn, L.M. (1968). Special education for the mildly retarded — Is much of it justifiable? *Exceptional Children, 35*, 5–22.

Dunn, L.M. (1973). Children with mild general learning disabilities. In L.M. Dunn (Ed.), *Exceptional children in the schools* (2nd ed.). New York: Holt, Rinehart & Winston.

Dunn, R., & Dunn, K. (1975). *Educator's self teaching guide to individualizing instructional programs*. West Nyack, NY: Parker.

Dunn-Rankin, P. (1968). The similarity of lower case letters in the English alphabet. *Journal of Verbal Learning and Verbal Behavior, 7*, 990.

Dupont, H., Gardner, O.S., & Brody, D.S. (1974). *Toward affective development*. Circle Pines, MN: American Guidance Service.

Early childhood. (1979). *Science and Children, 16*, 63–65.

Earp, N.W. (1970). Procedures for teaching reading in mathematics. *Arithmetic Teacher, 17*, 575–579.

Edge, D. (1984). Lecture presented to Ed. 441 class, University of British Columbia.

Ehly, S., & Larsen, S. (1980). *Peer tutoring for individualized instruction*. Boston: Allyn & Bacon.

Eisenson, J.J. (1971). Speech defects: Nature, causes, and psychological concomitants. In W.M. Cruickshank (Ed.), *Psychology of exceptional children and youth*. Englewood Cliffs, NJ: Prentice-Hall.

Elkins, J. (1983). The concept of learning disabilities: An Australian perspective. In J.D. McKinney & L. Feagans (Eds.), *Current topics in learning disabilities* (Vol. 1). Norwood, NJ: Ablex Publishers.

Ellis, E.S. (1983). *The effects of teaching learning disabled adolescents an executive strategy to facilitate self-generation of task-specific strategies*. Doctoral disseration, University of Kansas, Lawrence, KA.

Ellis, E.S. (1986). The role of motivation and pedagogy on the generalization of cognitive strategy training. *Journal of Learning Disabilities, 19*, 66–70.

Ellis, J.L. (1987a). *Handbook of creative problem-solving techniques*. New York: Trillium Press.

Ellis, J.L. (1987b). Mathematics and creativity for primary grades. In *Teaching mathematics in the early childhood classroom* (pp. 12–14). Edmonton: Alberta Teachers Association.

Ellis, N.R. (1970). Memory processes in retardates and normals. In N.R. Ellis (Ed.), *International review of research in mental retardation* (Vol. 4). New York: Academic Press.

Elman, N.M., & Ginsberg, J. (1981). *The resource room primer*. Englewood Cliffs, NJ: Prentice-Hall.

Emmer, E.T., Evertson, C., Sanford, J., & Clements, B.S. (1982). *Improving classroom management: An experimental study in junior high classrooms*. Austin, TX: Research and Development Center for Teacher Education, University of Texas, Austin.

Englert, C.S., & Thomas, C.C. (1982). Management of task involvement in special education classrooms. *Teacher Education and Special Education, 5*, 3–10.

Enster, G.I., & Winschel, J.F. (1976, January). Yes, no, it doesn't matter. *Exceptional Parent*, pp. 9–11.

Enstrom, E.A., & Enstrom, D. (1970). Right writing. *Grade Teacher, 87*, 105–106.

Epstein, L., & Lynch, W. (1974). *An experimental test of an attentional cuing technique in aiding mildly retarded children's recall of reading vocabulary.* Final Report, 29–32, Bloomington, IN: Indiana University Center for Innovation in Teaching the Handicapped.

Erber, N.P., & Cramer, D. (1974). Vibrotactile recognition of sentences. *American Annals of the Deaf, 119*, 716–720.

Evans, R. (1977). The prediction of educational handicap: A longitudinal study. *Educational Research, 19*, 57–67.

Ewoldt, C. (1982). Diagnostic approaches and procedures and the reading process. *Volta Review, 84*, 83–94.

Faas, L.A. (1976). *Learning disabilities: A competency based approach*. Boston, MA: Houghton Mifflin.

Faas, L.A. (1980). *Children with learning problems: A handbook for teachers*. Boston, MA: Houghton Mifflin.

Feagans, L., & McKinney, J.D. (1981). The pattern of exceptionality across domains in learning disabled children. *Journal of Applied Developmental Psychology, 1*, 313–328.

Fennel, F.M. (1981). *Elementary Mathematics Diagnosis and Correction Kit*. West Nyack: The Center for Applied Research in Education.

Fiester, A.R., & Giambra, L.M. (1972). Language indices of vocational success in mentally retarded adults. *American Journal of Mental Deficiency, 77*, 332–337.

Fiscus, E.D., & Mandell, C.J. (1983). *Developing individualized education programs*. St. Paul, MN: West Publishing.

Fisher, B. (1971). Hearing impaired children in ordinary schools. *The Teacher of the Deaf, 69*, 161–174.

Fisher, C.W., Berliner, D.C., Filby, N.N., Marliave, R., Cohen, L.S., & Dishaiv, M.M. (1980). Teaching behaviors, academic learning time, and student achievement: An overview. In C. Denham & A. Lieberman (Eds.), *Time to learn*. Washington, DC: U.S.

Government Printing Office.
Fitzgerald, E. (1934). *Straight language for the deaf.* Washington, DC: Volta Bureau.
Fitzgerald, F. (1979). Prizewinning author charges history textbooks present distorted picture. *ASCD News Exchange, 21*, pp. 1, 7.
Fitzsimmons, R., & Loomer, B. (1977). *Spelling research and practice.* Des Moines, IO: Iowa State Department of Public Instruction and University of Iowa.
Flesch, R. (1955). *Why Johnny can't read and what you can do about it.* New York: Harper & Row.
Flower, L.S., & Hayes, J.R. (1980). The dynamics of composing: Making plans and juggling constraints. In L.W. Gregg & E.R. Steinberg (Eds.), *Cognitive processes in writing.* Hillsdale, NJ: Erlbaum.
Fokes, J. (1976). *Fokes Sentence Builder.* Boston, MA: Teaching Resources Corporation.
Folio, M.R., & Norman, A. (1981). Toward more success in mainstreaming: A peer teacher approach to physical education. *Teaching Exceptional Children, 13*, 110–114.
Forness, S.R. (1981). Concepts of learning and behavior disorders: Implications for research and practice. *Exceptional Children, 48*, 56–64.
Foster, S.L., & Ritchey, W.L. (1979). Issues in the assessment of social competence in children. *Journal of Applied Behavior Analysis, 12*, 625–638.
Foulds, R. (1982). Applications of microcomputers in the education of the physically disabled child. *Exceptional Children, 49*, 155–162.
Fox, R.A. (1985). How to control and evaluate an essay examination: A practical approach. *Performance and Instructional Journal, 24*, 7–8, 15.
Freeman, F.N. (1954). *Teaching handwriting: What research says to the teacher* (Bulletin No. 4). Washington, DC: National Education Association.
Fry, E. (1977). Fry's reliability graph: Classification, validity, and extension to level 17. *Journal of Reading, 21*, 242–252.
Fuson, K.C., & Hall, J.W. (1983). The acquisition of early number word meanings: A conceptual analysis and review. In H.P. Ginsberg (Ed.), *The development of mathematical thinking* (pp. 50–102). New York: Academic Press.
Gagne, R.M. (1970). *The conditions of learning* (2nd ed.). New York: Holt, Rinehart & Winston.
Gajraj, I. (1982). Remediation of handwriting difficulties. *Special Education in Canada, 56*, 16–18.
Gajraj, I. (1983). Effective spelling instruction in special education. *Special Education in Canada, 57*, 25–27.
Gallagher, J.J. (1975). *The gifted child in the elementary school.* Washington, DC: American Educational Research Foundation.
Gallagher, J.J. (1985). *Teaching the gifted child* (3rd ed.). Boston: Allyn & Bacon.
Gallagher, P.A. (1979). *Teaching students with behavior disorders: Techniques for classroom instruction.* Denver, CO: Love Publishing.
Gambrell, L.M. (1980). Extending think-time for better reading instruction. *The Reading Teacher, 34*, 143–146.
Gardner, W.I. (1974). *Children with learning and behavior problems: A behavior management approach.* Boston: Allyn & Bacon.
Garrett, H.E. (1965). *Testing for teachers* (2nd ed.). New York: American Book Company.
Gast, D.L., & Nelson, C.M. (1977). Time out in the classroom: Implications for special education. *Exceptional Children, 43*, 461–464.
Geisser, P.J. (1985, August). *Art history: More than a cut and paste lesson for deaf education.* Paper presented at the Seventeenth International Congress on the Education of the Deaf, Manchester.
Gelman, R., & Gallistel, C.R. (1978). *The child's understanding of number.* Cambridge: Harvard University Press.
Gibson, E.J. (1969). *Principles of perceptual learning and development.* Englewood Cliffs, NJ: Prentice-Hall.
Gickling, E.E., & Thompson, V.P. (1985). A personal view of curriculum-based assessment. *Exceptional Children, 52*, 205–218.
Gilbert, R. (1987). Problem solving and graphing in the primary grades. In *Teaching mathematics in early childhood classrooms* (pp. 38–42). Edmonton: Alberta Teachers Association.
Gillespie, P.H., & Johnson, L. (1974). *Teaching reading to the mildly retarded child.* Columbus, OH: Merrill.
Gillet, J.W., & Temple, C. (1986). *Understanding reading problems: Assessment and instruction* (2nd ed.). Boston: Little Brown.
Gillingham, A., & Stillman, B. (1965). *Remedial training for children with specific disability in reading, spelling and penmanship* (7th ed.). Cambridge, MA: Educational Publishing Service.
Gillung, T.B., & Rucker, C.N. (1977). Labels and teacher expectations. *Exceptional Children, 43*, 454–465.
Ginsberg, H. (1977). *Children's arithmetic: The learning process.* New York: Van Nostrand.
Ginsberg, H.P., & Baroody, A.J. (1983). *The Test of Early Mathematics Ability.* Austin, TX: Pro-Ed.
Glazzard, M. (1977). The effectiveness of three kindergarten predictors for first grade achievement. *Journal of Learning Disabilities, 10*, 95–100.
Goldberg, M.L. (1965). *Research on the talented.* New York: Bureau of Publications, Teachers College, Columbia University.
Goldfish, L., & Taylor, H. (1974). The Optacon: A

valuable device for blind persons. *New Outlook for the Blind, 68*, 49–56.

Goldman, S., & Mosla, J. (1976). *Mainstreaming preparation for regular classroom personnel.* Athens, OH: Ohio University.

Goldstein, A.P. (1981). *Psychological skill training.* New York: Pergamon Press.

Goldstein, A.P., Sprafkin, R.P., Gershaw, N.J., & Klein, P. (1980). *Skillstreaming the adolescent: A structured training approach to teaching prosocial skills.* Champaign, IL: Research Press.

Goldstein, H. (1975). Schools. In N. Hobbs (Ed.), *Issues in the classification of children* (Vol. 2). San Francisco: Jossey Bass.

Goldstein, H., Moss, J., & Jordan, L. (1965). *The efficacy of special class training on the development of the mentally retarded child* (United States, Office of Education, Co-operative Project No. 619). Urbana, IL: University of Illinois.

Goldstein, M., Baker, J., Bruce, L., & Jamison, K.R. (1980). *Abnormal psychology.* Boston: Little Brown.

Goldstein, P. (1985). Art project prepared for special education students, University of British Columbia.

Goodman, K. (1972). Reading: The key is in children's language. *Reading Teacher, 25*, 505–508.

Goodman, K. (1976). Reading: A psycholinguistic guessing game. In H. Singer & R. Ruddell (Eds.), *Theoretical models and processes in reading.* Newark, DE: International Reading Association.

Goodman, K.S. (1982). Revaluing readers and reading. *Topics in Learning and Learning Disabilities, 1*, 87–93

Goodspeed, M.T., & Celotta, B.K. (1982). Professors' and teachers' views of competencies necessary for mainstreaming. *Psychology in the Schools, 19*, 402–407.

Gordon, E.W. (1973). Broadening the concept of career education. In L.M. Mcclure & C. Baun (Eds.), *Essays on career education.* Portland, OR: Northwest Regional Educational Laboratory.

Gottlieb, J. (1981). Mainstreaming: Fulfilling the promise? *American Journal of Mental Deficiency, 86*, 115–126.

Gottlieb, J., & Budoff, A. (1973). Social acceptability of retarded children in nongraded schools differing in architecture. *American Journal of Mental Deficiency, 78*, 15–19.

Gottlieb, J., Campbell, D.H., & Budoff, M. (1975). Classroom behavior of retarded children before and after integration into regular classes. *Journal of Special Education, 9*, 307–315.

Gottlieb, J., & Leyser, J. (1981). Friendship between mentally retarded and nonretarded children. In S. Asher & J. Gottman (Eds.), *The development of children's friendships.* Cambridge, MA: Cambridge University Press.

Goupil, G., & Brunet, L. (1984). Attitudes and behaviors toward the mainstreaming of exceptional children. *Canadian Journal of Exceptional Children, 1*, 28–31.

Gowan, J.C., & Bruch, C.B. (1971). *The academically talented student and guidance.* Boston: Houghton Mifflin.

Graham, S. (1982). Composition research and practice: A unified approach. *Focus on Exceptional Children, 14*, 1–16.

Graham, S., & Miller, L. (1979). Spelling research and practice: A unified approach. *Focus on Exceptional Children, 12*, 1–16.

Graubard, P.S. (1971). The relationship between academic achievement and behavior dimensions. *Exceptional Children, 37*, 755–756.

Gredler, G.R. (1978). Learning disabilities and reading disorders: A current assessment. *Psychology in the Schools, 15*, 226–238.

Green, J. (1975). *Teacher-made tests* (2nd ed.). New York: Harper & Row.

Greenberg, S.F., & Valletutti, P.J. (1980). *Stress and the helping professions.* Baltimore, MD: Paul H. Brooks.

Greenwood, C.R., Walker, H.M., & Hops, H. (1977). Issues in social interaction/withdrawal assessment. *Exceptional Children, 43*, 490–499.

Greenwood, J., & Anderson, R. (1983). Some thoughts on teaching and learning mathematics. *Arithmetic Teacher, 31*, 42–49.

Gresham, F.M. (1982). Misguided mainstreaming: The case for social skills training with handicapped children. *Exceptional Children, 48*, 422–433.

Gromek, I., & Scandary, J. (1977). Considerations in the educational placement of the physically or otherwise health impaired child. *Division of the Physically Handicapped, Hospitalized and Homebound Journal, 3*, 8–11.

Gropper, G., Kress, G., Hughes, R., & Pekich, J. (1968). Training teachers to recognize and manage social and emotional problems in the classroom. *Journal of Teacher Education, 19*, 477–485.

Grunwell, P. (1980). Procedures for child speech assessment: A review. *British Journal of Disorders of Communication, 15*, 189–203.

Guerin G.R., & Maier, A.S. (1983). *Informal assessment in education.* Palo Alto, CA: Mayfield.

Guthrie, F., & Cunningham, P. (1982). Teaching decoding skills to educable mentally handicapped children. *The Reading Teacher, 35*, 554–560.

Guthrie, J.T., Seifert, M., Burnham, N.A., & Caplan, R.I. (1974). The maze technique to assess, monitor reading comprehension. *The Reading Teacher, 28*, 161–168.

Hagen, D. (1984). *Microcomputer resource book for special education.* Reston, VA: Council for Exceptional Children.

Haisley, F.G., & Gilberts, R.O. (1978). Individualized competencies needed to implement PL 94-142. *Journal of Teacher Education, 29,* 30–33.

Hall, J.K. (1981). *Evaluating and improving written expression: A practical guide for teachers.* Boston: Allyn & Bacon.

Hallahan, D.P., & Kauffman, J.M. (1986). *Exceptional children: Introduction to special education* (3rd ed.). Englewood Cliffs, NJ: Prentice-Hall.

Hallahan, D.P., Kauffman, J.M., & Lloyd, J.W. (1985). *Introduction to learning disabilities* (2nd ed.). Englewood Cliffs, NJ: Prentice-Hall.

Hallahan, D.P., Kneedler, R.D., & Lloyd, J.W. (1983). Cognitive behavior modification for learning disabled children: Self-instruction and self-monitoring. In J.D. McKinney & L. Feagans (Eds.), *Current topics in learning disabilities* (Vol. 1). New York: Ablex Publishing.

Hallahan, D.P., Lloyd, J.W., Kauffman, J.M., & Loper, A.B. (1983). Academic problems. In R.J. Morris & T.R. Kratochwill (Eds.), *Practice of child therapy: A textbook of methods.* New York: Pergamon Press.

Hallahan, D.P., & Sapona, R.H. (1983). Self-monitoring of attention with learning-disabled children: Past research and current issues. *Journal of Learning Disabilities, 16,* 616–620.

Halpern, A., Raffeld, P., Irvin, L.K., & Link, R. (1975). *Social and Prevocational Information Battery.* Monterey, CA: CTB/McGraw Hill.

Hammill, D.D., & Bartel, N. (1975). *Teaching children with learning and behavior problems.* Boston: Allyn & Bacon.

Hanna, P.R. (1963). Revising the social studies: What is needed? *Social Education, 27,* 190–196.

Hannaford, A., & Sloane, E. (1981). Microcomputers: Powerful learning tools with proper programming. *Teaching Exceptional Children, 14,* 54–58.

Hannaford, A., & Taber, F. (1982). Microcomputer software for the handicapped: Development and evaluation. *Exceptional Children, 49,* 137–142.

Hardman, M.L. (1981). Learner characteristics of students with mild learning and behavior differences. In M.L. Hardman, M.E. Egan, & E.D. Lasau (Eds.), *The exceptional child in the regular classroom.* Iowa: William C. Brown.

Hargis, C.H. (1982). Word recognition development. *Focus on Exceptional Children, 14,* 1–8.

Haring, N.G., & Gentry, N.D. (1976). Direct and individualized instructional procedures. In N.G. Haring & R.L. Schiefelbusch (Eds.), *Teaching special children.* New York: McGraw-Hill.

Harley, R.K., Henderson, F.M., & Traun, M.B. (1979). *The teaching of braille reading.* Springfield, IL: Charles C. Thomas.

Harris, A., & Sipay, E. (1975). *How to increase reading ability: A guide to developmental and remedial methods* (4th ed.). New York: David McKay.

Harris, D. (1978). *Descriptive analysis of communication interaction processes involving non-vocal severely physically handicapped children.* Doctoral dissertation, University of Wisconsin, Madison.

Harris, J. (1978). Parents and teachers, inc. *Teacher, 96,* 85.

Harrison, R. (1985). How you can help the abused child. *Learning, 4,* 74–78.

Harrison, S. (1981). Open letter from a left handed teacher: Some sinistral ideas on the teaching of handwriting. *Teaching Exceptional Children, 13,* 116–120.

Hart, V. (1981). *Mainstreaming children with special needs.* New York: Longman.

Harter, S. (1978). Effective motivation reconsidered: Toward a developmental model. *Human Development, 21,* 34–64.

Hartman, B. (1987). *Reported educational provisions for Newfoundland's gifted students.* St. John's: Memorial University of Newfoundland.

Hasselbring, T., & Crossland, C. (1981). Using microcomputers for diagnosing spelling problems in learning disabled children. *Educational Technology, 21,* 37–39.

Haubrich, P.A., & Shores, R. (1976). Attending behavior and academic performance of emotionally disturbed children. *Exceptional Children, 42,* 337–338.

Hawisher, M.F., & Calhoun, M.L. (1978). *The resource room: An educational asset for children with special needs.* Columbus, OH: Merrill.

Hayden, A.H. (1974). Perspectives on early childhood education in special education. In N.G. Haring (Ed.), *Behavior of exceptional children: An introduction to special education.* Columbus, OH: Merrill.

Haywood Gear, G. (1976). Accuracy of teacher judgment in identifying intellectually gifted children: A review of the literature. *Gifted Child Quarterly, 20,* 478–487.

Hazel, J.S., Schumaker, J.B., Sherman, J.A., & Sheldon-Wildgen, J. (1981). *Asset.* Champaign, IL: Research Press.

Heckelman, R.G. (1969). The neurological impress method of remedial reading instruction. *Academic Therapy, 4,* 277–282.

Heinisch, B.S. (1981). Research implications on choosing a program to teach about disabilities. *Rehabilitation Literature, 42,* 344–346.

Heller, H.W., McCoy, K., & McIntyre, B. (1979). Group summary. *Teacher Education and Special*

Education, 2, 8–10.

Heller, J. (1983). A concrete mainstreaming experience: Cementing relations through art. *Teaching Exceptional Children, 15*, 90–93.

Henk, W.A., Helfeldt, J.P., & Platt, J.M. (1986). Developing reading fluency in learning disabled students. *Teaching Exceptional Children, 18*, 202–206.

Heward, W., & Orlansky, M. (1980). *Exceptional children*. Columbus, OH: Bell & Howell.

Hewett, F.M., & Taylor, F.D. (1980). *The emotionally disturbed child in the classroom: The orchestration of success* (2nd ed.). Boston: Allyn & Bacon.

Heyman, E. (1977). Cursive writing skills begin with chalk. *Teaching Exceptional Children, 9*, 106–109.

Hiebert, B., & Farber, I. (1984). Teacher stress: A literature survey with few surprises. *Canadian Journal of Education/Canadienne revue de l'education, 9*, 14–27.

Hill, W.F. (1977). *Learning through discussion*. Beverly Hills, CA: Sage Publications.

Hillerich, R.L. (1974). Word lists—getting it all together. *The Reading Teacher, 27*, 353–360.

Hirshoren, A., & McGuigan, C. (1984). Something isn't always better than nothing: On the use of educational and psychological tests. *B.C. Journal of Special Education, 8*, 99–106.

Honzig, M.K. (1976). Value and limitations of infant tests: An overview. In M. Lewis (Ed.), *Origins of intelligence: Infancy and early childhood*. New York: Plenum Press.

Hoover, R.C. (1972). Language for the deaf according to Henry. *American Annals of the Deaf, 117*, 590–594.

Hoskinson, K. (1979). A response to "A critique of teaching reading as a whole task venture." *The Reading Teacher, 32*, 652–659.

Howell, K.W., Caplan, J.S., & O'Donnell, C.Y. (1979). *Evaluating exceptional students*. Columbus, OH: Merrill.

Hresko, W.P., & Brown, L. (1984). *Test of Early Socioemotional Development*. Austin, TX: Pro-Ed.

Hughes, R.D. (1985). Sexual victimization of children: Implications for educators. *Behavioral Disorders, 10*, 175–182.

Hundert, J. (1982). Some considerations for planning the integration of handicapped children into the mainstream. *Journal of Learning Disabilities, 15*, 73–80.

Hunt, J. (1961). *Intelligence and experience*. New York: Ronald Press.

Hutt, M.L., & Gibby, R.G. (1976). *The mentally retarded child: Development, education, and treatment*. Boston: Allyn & Bacon.

Hutt, R.B. (1923). The school psychologist. *Psychological Clinic, 15*, 48–51.

Hymel, S., & Asher, S.R. (1977). *Assessment and training of isolated children's social skills*. (ERIC Document Reproduction Service No. ED 136–930.

Hymes, D. (1974). *Foundations in psycholinguistics*. Philadelphia, PA: University of Pennsylvania Press.

Iano, R.P., Ayers, D., Heller, H.B., McGettigan, J.F., & Walker, V.S. (1974). Sociometric status of retarded children in an integrative program. *Exceptional Children, 40*, 267–271.

Ibbitson, K. (1987). Money: A hands on approach. In *Teaching mathematics in early childhood classrooms* (pp. 78–79). Edmonton: Alberta Teachers Association.

Ife, B. (1982). *An introduction to the use of microcomputers in the classroom*. Unpublished paper, Jericho Hill School for the Deaf, Vancouver.

Illerbrun, D., & Greenough, D. (1983). Classroom/clinical diagnoses of young language learning disabled children: An integrated approach. *Special Education in Canada, 57*, 23–27.

Jamison, P.J., & Shevitz, L.A. (1985). RATE: A reason to read. *Teaching Exceptional Children, 18*, 46–50.

Jastak, J.F., Bijou, S.W., & Jastak, S.R. (1965). *Wide Range Achievement Test*. Wilmington, DE: Guidance Associates.

Jeffers, T., & Barley, M. (1971). *Speechreading (lipreading)*. Springfield, IL: Charles C. Thomas.

Jencks, S., Peck, D., & Chatterley, L. (1980). Why blame the kids? We teach mistakes. *Arithmetic Teacher, 28*, 38–41.

Jenkins, J.R., & Pany, D. (1978). Standardized achievement tests: How useful for special education? *Exceptional Children, 44*, 448–453.

Jenkins, J.R., Stein, M.L., & Osborn, J. (1981). What next after decoding? Instruction and research in reading comprehension. *Exceptional Education Quarterly, 2*, 27–39.

Jens, K.G., Johnson, N.M., & Attermeir, S.A. (1979). *Carolina Curriculum for Handicapped Infants*. Chapel Hill, NC: University of North Carolina.

Jesser, D. (1984). Career education: Challenges and issues. *Journal of Career Education, 11*, 20–24.

Johnson, A.B., Gold, V., & Vickers, L.L. (1982). Stress and teachers of the learning disabled, behaviorally disordered, and educable mentally retarded. *Psychology in the Schools, 19*, 552–557.

Johnson, D. (1982). Microcomputers and dyslexic students. *Educational Computer, 2*, 36–37.

Johnson, D.G. (1967). Educational principles for children with learning disabilities. *Remediation Literature, 28*, 317–322.

Johnson, D.G., & Myklebust, H.R. (1967). *Learning disabilities: Educational principles and practices*. New York: Grune & Stratton.

Johnson, D.W., & Johnson, R.T. (1978). Cooperative, competitive, and individualistic learning. *Journal of*

Research and Development in Education, 12, 3–15.
Johnson, D.W., & Johnson, R.T. (1980). Integrating handicapped students into the mainstream. *Exceptional Children, 47*, 90–98.
Johnson, D.W., & Johnson, R.T. (1981). Organizing the school's social structure for mainstreaming. In P. Bates (Ed.), *Mainstreaming: Our current knowledge base*. Minneapolis, MN: University of Minnesota.
Johnson, E. (1977). *The Weatherbee model: A full service learning disabilities/remedial teaching resource program for grades 4 to 8*. Paper presented at the annual Council for Exceptional Children convention, Atlanta, Georgia.
Johnson, K.A. (1977). A survey of mathematics programs, materials and methods in schools for the deaf. *American Annals of the Deaf, 122*, 19–25.
Jones, R., Gottfried, N., & Owens, A. (1966). The social distance of the exceptional: A study at the high school level. *Exceptional Children, 32*, 551–556.
Jones, T., Sowell, V., Jones, J., & Butler, L. (1981). Changing children's perceptions of handicapped people. *Exceptional Children, 47*, 365–368.
Jongsma, E. (1971). *The cloze procedure as a reading technique*. Newark, DE: International Reading Association.
Junkala, J. (1972). Task analysis and instructional alternatives. *Academic Therapy, 8*, 33–40.
Justman, J., & Maskowitz, L. (1957). *The integration of deaf children in a hearing class* (Publication no. 4). New York: Bureau of Educational Research, Board of Education.
Kaluger, G., & Kolson, C.J. (1978). *Reading and learning disabilities* (2nd ed.). Columbus, OH: Merrill.
Kamil, M.L. (1984). Computer literacy and teaching reading. In J. Baumann & D.D. Johnson (Eds.), *Reading instruction and the beginning teacher*. Minneapolis, MN: Burgess.
Kaminsky, S., & Powers, R. (1981). Remediation of handwriting difficulties: A practical approach. *Academic Therapy, 17*, 19–25.
Kates, B., & McNaughton, S. (1975). *The first application of Blissymbolics as a communication medium for non-speaking children: History and development, 1971–1974*. Toronto: Blissymbolics Communication Institute.
Katzen, K. (1980). An open letter to CEC. *Exceptional Children, 48*, 582.
Kauffman, J.M. (1981). *Characteristics of children's behavior disorders* (2nd ed.). Columbus, OH: Merrill.
Kauffman, J.M. (1985). *Characteristics of children's behavior disorders* (3rd ed.). Columbus, OH: Merrill.
Kauffman, J.M., McCullough, L.L., & Sabornie, E.J. (1984). Integrating exceptional students: Special problems involving the emotionally disturbed/behaviorally disordered. *B.C. Journal of Special Education, 8*, 201–210.
Kaufman, M.J., Gottlieb, J., Agard, J.A., & Kukic, A. (1975). Mainstreaming: Toward an explication of the construct. *Focus on Exceptional Children, 7*, 1–13.
Kehle, T.J., & Barclay, J.R. (1979). Social and behavioral characteristics of mentally handicapped children. *Journal of Research and Development in Education, 12*, 46–56.
Kelly, J.A., Furman, W., Phillips, J., Hawthorn, S., & Wilson, T. (1979). Teaching conversational skills to retarded adolescents. *Child Behavior Therapy, 1*, 85–97.
Kelly, T.K., Bullock, L.M., & Dykes, M.K. (1977). Behavior disorders: Teachers' perceptions. *Exceptional Children, 43*, 316–318.
Kennedy, L. (1984). *Guiding children's learning of mathematics*. Belmont, CA: Wadsworth Publishing.
Keogh, B., Becker, L.D., Kukic, S., & Kukic, M. (1972). *Programs for EH and EMR pupils: Review and recommendations — technical report*. Los Angeles: University of California.
Keogh, B.K. (1983). Early identification: One component of comprehensive services for at-risk children. *Topics in Early Childhood Special Education, 3*, 7–16.
Keogh, B.K., & Levitt, M.C. (1976). Special education in the mainstream: A confrontation of limitations. *Focus on Exceptional Children, 8*, 1–11.
Keogh, B.K., & Margolis, J. (1976). Learn to labor and to wait: Attentional problems of children with learning disabilities. *Journal of Learning Disabilities, 9*, 276–286.
King, C. (1987). *Movement of wheelchair bound students*. Unpublished paper.
Kinnison, L.R., Hayes, C., & Acord, J. (1981). Evaluating student progress in mainstream classes. *Teaching Exceptional Children, 13*, 97–99.
Kirk, E.C. (1981). *Vision pathology in education*. Springfield, IL; Charles C. Thomas.
Kirk, S.A., & Elkins, J. (1975). Characteristics of children enrolled in the child service demonstration centers. *Journal of Learning Disabilities, 8*, 630–637.
Kirk, S.A., Kliebhan, J.M., & Lerner, J.W. (1978). *Teaching reading to slow and disabled learners*. Boston: Houghton Mifflin.
Klas, L., Kennedy, L., & Kendall-Woodward, S. (1984). Factors which stress the special education teacher: A comparison to other educational specialists and regular classroom teachers. *Canadian Journal for Exceptional Children, 1*, 66–71.
Klausmieir, H., Rossmiller, R., & Saily, M. (1977). *Individually guided elementary education: Concepts and practices*. New York: Academic Press.
Klesius, S.E. (1981). Measurement and evaluation: The

neglected element in physical education for the handicapped. *The Physical Educator, 38*, 15–19.

Klockors, D.N. (1982). Counseling ideas for special education and learning assistance teachers. *B.C. Journal of Special Education, 6*, 189–193.

Kneedler, R.D., with D.P. Hallahan & J.M. Kauffman. (1984). *Special education for today.* Englewood Cliffs, NJ: Prentice-Hall.

Kniep, W.M. (1986). Social studies within a global education. *Social Education, 50*, 536–542.

Kolich, E. (1985). Microcomputer technology with the learning disabled: A review of the literature. *Journal of Learning Disabilities, 18*, 428–431.

Kolstoe, O.P. (1976). *Teaching educable mentally retarded children* (2nd ed.). New York: Holt, Rinehart & Winston.

Kottmeyer, W. (1970). *Diagnostic Spelling Test.* New York: McGraw-Hill.

Kounin, J.S. (1970). *Discipline and group management in classrooms.* New York: Holt, Rinehart & Winston.

Kraetch, G.A. (1981). The effects of oral instructions and training on the expansion of written language. *Learning Disability Quarterly, 4*, 82–90.

Kranes, J.E. (1980). *The hidden handicap.* New York: Simon & Schuster.

Kuzembo, J.A. (1980). *Asthma in children.* Tunbridge Wells, Kent: Pitman Medical.

L'Abate, L., & Curtis, L.T. (1975). *Teaching the exceptional child.* Philadelphia: W.B. Saunders.

Labour Canada. (1986). *When I grow up: Career expectations and aspirations of Canadian school children.* Ottawa: Labour Canada.

Ladd, G.W., Munson, H.L., & Miller, J.K. (1984). Social interaction of deaf adolescents in secondary-level mainstreamed programs. *Exceptional Children, 50*, 420–428.

La Greca, A.M., & Mesibov, G.B. (1979). Social skills intervention with learning disabled children: Selecting skills and implementing training. *Journal of Clinical Child Psychology, 8*, 234–241.

Lahey, B.B., Hammer, D., Crumrine, P.L., & Forehand, R.L. (1980). Birth order × sex interactions in child behavior problems. *Developmental Psychology, 16*, 608–615.

Lane, D., Pollock, C., & Sher, N. (1972). Remotivation of disruptive adolescents. *Journal of Reading, 15*, 351–354.

Langer, E.J., Fiske, S., Taylor, S.E., & Chanowitz, B.A. (1976). A novel-stimulus hypothesis. *Journal of Experimental and Social Psychology, 12*, 451–463.

Langford, K., Slade, K., & Barnett, A. (1974). An explanation of impress techniques in remedial reading. *Academic Therapy, 9*, 309–319.

Langone, J. (1986). *Teaching retarded learners: Curriculum and methods for improving instruction.* Boston: Allyn & Bacon.

Larrivée, B., & Cook, L. (1979). Mainstreaming: A study of the variables affecting teacher attitude. *The Journal of Special Education, 13*, 316–323.

Laycock, M., & Watson, G. (1975). *The fabric of mathematics.* Hayward, CA: Activity resources.

Laycock, V. (1980a). Environmental alternatives for the mildly and moderately handicapped. In J.W. Schifani, R.M. Anderson, & S.J. Odle (Eds.), *Implementing learning in the least restrictive environment.* Baltimore, MD: University Park Press.

Laycock, V. (1980b). Prescriptive programming in the mainstream. In J.W. Schifani, R.M. Anderson, & S.J. Odle (Eds.), *Implementing learning in the least restrictive environment.* Baltimore, MD: University Park Press.

LeBlanc, J.F. (1977). You can teach problem solving. *Arithmetic Teacher, 25*, 16–20.

Lee, M.L. (1981). Including the handicapped in junior high general music classes. *Music Educators Journal, 67*, 56–57.

Lerner, J. (1981). *Learning disabilities: Theories, diagnosis and teaching strategies* (3rd ed.). Boston: Houghton Mifflin.

Lerner, J., Mardell-Czudnowski, C., & Goldenberg, D. (1981). *Special education for the early childhood years.* Englewood Cliffs, NJ: Prentice-Hall.

Levine, E. (1981). *The ecology of early deafness: Guides to fashioning environments and psychological assessments.* New York: Columbia University Press.

Levy B., & Graf, P. (1984). Reading and remembering: Conceptual and perceptual processing involved in reading rotated passages. *Journal of Verbal Learning and Verbal Behavior, 28*, 405–424.

Lewandowski, L.J., & Cruickshank, W.H. (1980). Psychological development of crippled children and youth. In W.M. Cruickshank (Ed.), *Psychology of exceptional children and youth.* Englewood Cliffs, NJ: Prentice-Hall.

Lewis, A. (1980). The early identification of children with learning difficulties. *Journal of Learning Disabilities, 13*, 102–108.

Leyser, L., & Gottlieb, J. (1980). Improving the social status of rejected pupils. *Exceptional Children, 46*, 459–461.

Liebermann, L.M. (1981). Special education's perilous path. *Academic Therapy, 17*, 13–17.

Liedtke, W. (1982). Learning difficulties: Helping young children with mathematics — subtraction. *Arithmetic Teacher, 29*, 21–23.

Liedtke, W. (1983). Talking with young children about mathematics. *Special Education in Canada, 57*, 33–35

Lilly, M.S. (1971). A training based model for special education. *Exceptional Children, 37*, 745–749.

Lindfors, J. (1987). *Children's language and learning* (2nd ed.). Englewood Cliffs, NJ: Prentice-Hall.
Lindsey, J.D., & Kerlin, M.A. (1979). Learning disabilities and reading disorders: A brief review of the secondary level literature. *Journal of Learning Disabilities, 12*, 412–414.
Ling, D. (1986). Acquired hearing impairment. *Newsounds, 11*, 3.
Ling, D., & Ling, A.H. (1978). *Aural rehabilitation: Foundations of verbal learning in hearing impaired children.* Washington, DC: Alexander Graham Bell Association for the Deaf.
Linn, S.H. (1967). Spelling problems: Diagnosis and remediation. *Academic Therapy Quarterly, 3*, 62–63.
Lorenz, L., & Vockell, E. (1979). Using the neurological impress method with learning disabled readers. *Journal of Learning Disabilities, 12*, 420–422.
Lovitt, T.C. (1973). *Applied behavior analysis techniques and curriculum research* (Report). Washington, DC: National Institute of Education.
Lowenfeld, B. (1973). *History of the education of visually handicapped children: The visually handicapped child in school.* New York: John Day.
Lucas, E.V. (1980). *Semantic and pragmatic disorders: Assessment and remediation.* Rockville, MD: Aspen Systems Corporation.
Lund, K.A., Schnaps, L., & Bijou, S.W. (1983). Let's take another look at record keeping. *Teaching Exceptional Children, 15*, 155–159.
Lyman, R.D. (1984). The effect of private and public goal setting on classroom on-task behavior of emotionally disturbed children. *Behavior Therapy, 15*, 395–402.
McCall, R.B., Appelbaum, M.L., & Hogarty, P.S. (1973). Developmental changes in mental performance. *Monographs of the Society for Research in Child Development, 38* (Serial No. 150).
McClinaghan, B.A. (1981). Normalization in physical education, a reflective review. *The Physical Educator, 38*, 3–7.
McDermott, P., & Walkins, M. (1983). Computerized versus conventional remedial instruction for learning disabled pupils. *The Journal of Special Education, 17*, 81–87.
McDonald, D. (1975). Music and reading readiness. *Language Arts, 52*, 872–876.
McDonald, E.T., & Schultz, A.R. (1973). Communication boards for cerebral palsied children. *Journal of Speech and Hearing Disorders, 38*, 73–88.
McGinnis, E., Sauerbry, L., & Nichols, P. (1985). Skill-streaming: Teaching social skills to children with behavioral disorders. *Teaching Exceptional Children, 17*, 160–167.
McGinnis, P.J. (1977). *The McGinnis Hammandsport Plan.* New York: Walker Publications.
McGuigan, C.A. (1985). Increasing compliance and on-task behaviors of disruptive children: Procedure and sequence of instruction. *B.C. Journal of Special Education, 9*, 19–27.
MacIntyre, R. (1984). Special education. In H. Oliver, M. Holmes, & I. Winchester, *The house that Ryerson built.* Toronto: OISE Press.
MacKenzie, D.E. (1983). School effectiveness research: A synthesis and assessment. In P.C. Dettweiler (Ed.), *Educational productivity and school effectiveness.* Austin, TX: Southwest Educational Development Laboratory.
McKittrick, C. (1981). Child abuse: Recognition and reporting by health professionals. *Nursing Clinics of North America, 16*, 103–115.
McLeod, T.M., & Armstrong, S.W. (1982). Learning disabilities in mathematics: Skill deficits and remedial approaches at the intermediate and secondary level. *Learning Disability Quarterly, 5*, 305–311.
McLoughlin, J.A., & Lewis, R.B. (1981). *Assessing special students.* Columbus, OH: Merrill.
McMurray, J.G. (1980). Special education (mainstreaming): Teacher preparation for change. *Teacher Education, 17*, 67–71.
McNaughton, S. (1982). Augmentative communication system: Blissymbolics. In E. Bleck & D. Nagel (Eds.), *The physically handicapped child: A medical atlas for teachers.* New York: Grune & Stratton.
McNaughton, S., & Warrick, A. (1986, December). The special needs of nonspeaking children and their families. *Horizons.* In *Easter Seal Communication Institute 1986 Annual Report* (pp. 59–60). Don Mills, Ontario.
McNeil, J.D. (1981). *Curriculum: A comprehensive introduction* (2nd ed.). Boston: Little, Brown.
Macy, C.M. (1984). Art-as-education: A process for the development of confidence and communication. *Volta Review, 86*, 131–135.
Macy, D.J., & Carter, J.L. (1978). Comparison of a mainstreamed and self-contained special education program. *Journal of Special Education, 12*, 303–313.
Madden, N., & Slavin, R. (1983). Mainstreaming students with mild handicaps: Academic and social outcomes. *Review of Educational Research, 53*, 519–659.
Maddux, C. (1987). Issues and concerns in special education microcomputing. *Computers in the Schools, 3/4*, 1–19.
Maddux, C., & Cummings, R. (1987). Equity for the mildly handicapped. *The Computing Teacher, 14*, 16–17.
Maddux, C., & Johnson, D. (1983). Microcomputers in LD: Boon or boondoggle? *Academic Therapy, 19*, 113–119.
Malone, C. (1979). Gifted children in early childhood

education. *Viewpoints in Teaching and Learning, 55,* 25–28.

Mandell, C.J., & Fiscus, E. (1981). *Understanding exceptional people.* St. Paul, MI: West Publishing.

Mandell, C.J., & Gold, V. (1984). *Teaching handicapped students.* St. Paul, MI: West Publishing.

Mangieri, J., & Baldwin, R. (1979). Meaning as a factor in predicting spelling difficulty. *Journal of Educational Research, 72,* 285–287.

Mann, L. (1971). Psychometric phrenology and the new faculty psychology: The case against ability assessment and training. *Journal of Special Education, 5,* 3–65.

Mann, P., & Suiter, P. (1975). *Handbook in diagnostic teaching.* Boston: Allyn & Bacon.

Manson, M.L. (1985, May). Publishing students' stories. *Perspectives,* p.p. 5–8.

Manzo, A.V., & Sherk, J.R. (1971). Some generalizations and strategies for guiding vocabulary training. *Journal of Reading Behavior, 6,* 19–21.

Marfo, K. (Ed.). (1988). *Parent-child interaction and developmental disabilities.* New York: Praeger Publisher.

Marge, M. (1972). The general problem of language disabilities in children. In J.V. Irwin & M. Marge (Eds.), *Principles of childhood language disabilities.* Englewood Cliffs, NJ: Prentice-Hall.

Marland, S.P., Jr. (1972). *Education of the gifted and talented: Report to the Congress of the United States by the Commission of Education.* Washington, DC: U.S. Government Printing Office.

Marston, D. (1987). Does categorical teacher certification benefit the mildly handicapped child? *Exceptional Children, 53,* 423–431.

Martin, R.C., & McLaughlin, T.F. (1981). A comparison between the effect of free time and daily report cards on the academic behavior of junior high school students. *B.C. Journal of Special Education, 5,* 303–313.

Martino, L., & Johnson, D.W. (1979). Effects of cooperative versus individualistic instruction on interaction between normal progress and learning-disabled students. *Journal of School Psychology, 107,* 177–183.

Martinson, R.A. (1975). *The identification of the gifted and talented.* Reston, VA: Council for Exceptional Children.

Mason, G.E., Blanchard, J.S., & Daniel, D.B. (1983). *Computer applications in reading.* Newark, DE: International Reading Association.

Mathis, J.A., Fairchild, L., & Cannon, T.M. (1980). Psychodrama and sociodrama in primary and secondary education. *Psychology in the Schools, 17,* 96–101.

Maxwell, M. (1974). Teaching reading as a problem solving activity. *American Annals of the Deaf, 119,* 721–723.

Medley, D.M. (1977). *Teacher competence and teacher effectiveness.* Washington, DC: American Association of Colleges for Teacher Education.

Meeker, M. (1969). *The structure of the intellect: Its use and interpretation.* Columbus, OH: Merrill.

Meichenbaum, D. (1981, April). *Teaching thinking: A cognitive behavior approach.* Paper presented at the meeting of the Society for Learning Disabilities and Remedial Education, New York.

Mellor, M.C. (1981). *Aids for the 80s: What they are and what they do.* New York: American Foundation for the Blind.

Mendoza, M.A., Holt, W.J., & Jackson, D.A. (1978). Circles and tape: An easy teacher implemented way to teach fundamental writing skills. *Teaching Exceptional Children, 10,* 48–50.

Menyuk, P. (1971). *The acquisition and development of language.* Englewood Cliffs, NJ: Prentice-Hall.

Mercer, C.D., & Mercer, A.R. (1985). *Teaching students with learning problems* (2nd ed.). Columbus, OH: Merrill.

Mercer, C.D., & Payne, J.S. (1975). Learning theories and their implications. In J.M. Kauffman & J.S. Payne (Eds.), *Mental retardation: Introduction and personal perspectives.* Columbus, OH: Merrill.

Mesibov, G.B., & LaGreca, M.B. (1974). *Social adjustment of young children: A cognitive approach to solving real-life problems.* San Francisco: Jossey Bass.

Messerly, C. (1986). The use of computer-assisted instruction in facilitating the acquisition of math skills with hearing-impaired high school students. *Volta Review, 88,* 67–77.

Meyen, E.L., & Lehar, D.H. (1980). Least restrictive environments: Instructional implications. *Focus on Exceptional Children, 12,* 1–8.

Meyer, B.J. (1979). *Research on prose comprehension: Applications for composition teachers.* (ERIC Document Reproduction Service No. ED 174–999).

Meyerowitz, J. (1962). Self-derogation in young retardates and special class placement. *Child Development, 33,* 443–451.

Miederhoff, J.W., & Wood, J.W. (1988). Adapting test construction for mainstreamed mathematics students. *Mathematics Teacher, 81,* 388–392.

Milisen, R. (1971). The incidence of speech disorders. In L. Travis (Ed.), *Handbook of speech pathology and audiology.* New York: Appleton-Century-Crofts.

Miller, G.A., & Gildea, P.M. (1987, September 12). How children learn words. *Globe and Mail,* p. D5.

Miller, G.R., & Coleman, E.G. (1967). A set of thirty-six prose passages celebrated for complexity. *Journal of Verbal Learning and Verbal Behavior, 6*, 851–854.

Miller, J. (1978). Assessing children's language behavior. In R. Schiefelbusch (Ed.), *Bases of language intervention*. Baltimore, MD: University Park Press.

Miller, J.F., & Yoder, D.E. (1972). On developing the content for a language teaching program. *Mental Retardation, 10*, 9–11.

Miller, S.R. (1975). Secondary programming. In D.A. Sabatino (Ed.), *Learning disabilities handbook: A technical guide to program development*. De Kalb, IL: Northern Illinois University Press.

Milone, M.N., & Wasylyk, T.M. (1981). Handwriting in special education. *Teaching Exceptional Children, 14*, 58–62.

Mitchell, J. (1985). *Mental measurement yearbook*. New Jersey: Gryphon Press.

Mizen, D.W., & Lineton, N. (1983). Guess who's coming to PE? *Journal of Physical Education, Recreation and Dance, 54*, 63–65.

Moffet, J. (1978). *Teaching the universe of discourse*. Boston, MA: Houghton Mifflin.

Moog, J.S., & Kozak, V.J. (1983). *Teacher assessment of grammatical structures*. St. Louis, MO: Central Institute for the Deaf.

Moores, D. (1974). Nonvocal systems of verbal behavior. In R.L. Shiefelbusch & L.L. Lloyd (Eds.), *Language perspective acquisition, retardation and intervention*. Baltimore, MD: University Park Press.

Moores, D.F. (1986). *Educating the deaf: Psychology, principles and practices* (3rd ed.). Boston, MA: Houghton Mifflin.

Moran, M.R. (1979). Nine steps to the diagnostic prescriptive process in the classroom. In E.L. Meyen, G.A. Vergason, & R.L. Whelan (Eds.), *Instructional planning for exceptional children*. Denver, CO: Love Publishing.

Morgan, D.P., & Rhode, G. (1983). Teachers' attitudes toward IEPs: A two-year follow-up. *Exceptional Children, 50*, 64–67.

Mori, A. (1979). Vocational education and special education: A new partnership in career education. *Journal of Career Education, 6*, 55–69.

Morse, W.C., Cutler, R.L., & Fink, A. (1964). *Public school classes for the emotionally handicapped: A research analysis*. Washington, DC: Council for Exceptional Children.

Morsink, C.V. (1984). *Teaching special needs children in regular classrooms*. Boston, MA: Little Brown.

Mortimer, G., Jr., & Hammill, D.D. (1971). Who are the retarded? *Exceptional Children, 38*, 13–20.

Mulcahy, R., Marfo, K., Peat, D., Andrews, J., & Clifford, L. (1986). Applying cognitive psychology in the classroom: A learning/thinking strategies instructional program. *Alberta Psychology, 15*, 9–12.

Murray, M.E. (1981). Diagnostic psychological testing for reading/learning disorders in preschool children. *Reading Psychology, 2*, 146–157.

Musselwhite, C.R., & St. Louis, K.W. (1982). *Communication programming for the severely handicapped*. San Diego, CA: College Hill Press.

Naremore, R.C. (1980). Language disorders in children. In T.J. Hixon (Ed.), *Introduction to communication disorders*. Englewood Cliffs, NJ: Prentice-Hall.

Natheson, D.E., Cynamon, A., & Lehman, K. (1976). Miami snow poets: Creative writing for exceptional children. *Teaching Exceptional Children, 8*, 87–91.

National Council of Teachers of Mathematics. (1980). *An agenda for action: Recommendations for school mathematics of the 1980's*. Palo Alto, CA: Dale Seymour Publications.

Necco, E., Wilson, C., & Schiedemantel, J. (1982). Affective learning through drama. *Teaching Exceptional Children, 14*, 22–25.

Neill, K. (1980). Turn kids on with repeated reading. *Teaching Exceptional Children, 12*, 63–64.

Nelson, C.M., & Greenough Jansen. (1984). The case for non-categorical education programming for behaviorally disordered children and youth. *B.C. Journal of Special Education, 8*, 107–123.

Nesbit, W.C., & Karagianis, L.D. (1981). The teacher as facilitator: A crucial facet of integration. *Canada's Mental Health, 29*, 34–35.

Newcomer, P.L. (1980). *Understanding and teaching emotionally disturbed children*. Boston: Allyn & Bacon.

Newfoundland and Labrador Association for Gifted Children. (1982). *Educating gifted children: Brief presented to the Minister of Education, Newfoundland and Labrador*. St. John's: Newfoundland and Labrador Association for the Gifted.

Newman, R., & Simpson, R. (1983). Modifying the least restrictive environment to facilitate the integration of severely emotionally disturbed children and youth. *Behavioral Disorders, 8*, 103–112.

Noel, M. (1980). Referential communication abilities of learning disabled children. *Learning Disability Quarterly, 3*, 70–87.

Norman, C.A., & Malicky, G. (1986). Software: How to choose it and use it. *Canadian Journal for Exceptional Children, 3*, 61–62.

Northcott, W.H. (Ed.). [1984]. *Oral interpreting: Principles and practices*. Washington, DC: Alexander Graham Bell Association for the Deaf.

Ochoa, A., & Schuster, S.K. (1980). *Social studies in the mainstreamed classroom, K–6*. Boulder, CO: Social Sciences Education Consortium, ERIC.

Oden, S., & Asher, S.R. (1977). Coaching children in social skills for friendship making. *Child Development, 48*, 495–506.

O'Leary, K., & O'Leary, S. (1977). *Classroom management: The successful use of behavior modification* (2nd ed.). New York: Pergamon Press.

Oliver, L.I. (1974). *Behavior patterns of youths 12–17 years.* Washington, DC: Department of Health, Education and Welfare.

Otto, W., McMenemy, R.A., & Smith, R.J. (1973). *Corrective and remedial teaching.* Boston: Houghton Mifflin.

Page, W. (1978). *Teachers' decisions and basal readers' teachers' manuals.* Paper presented at the AERA Conference, Toronto.

Palincsar, A.S. (1986). Metacognitive strategy instruction. *Exceptional Children, 53*, 118–124.

Papert, S. (1980). *Mindstorms: Children, computers, and powerful ideas.* New York: Basic Books.

Parette, H.P., & Hourcade, J.J. (1986). Management strategies for orthopedically handicapped students. *Teaching Exceptional Children, 18*, 282–286.

Parke, B. (1978). Quick tricks for "cold" spellers. *Teacher, 26*, 74–76.

Passow, A.H. (Ed.). (1979). *The gifted and the talented.* Chicago: National Society for the Study of Education Yearbook.

Paul, J., Turnbull, A.P., & Cruickshank, W. (1977). *Mainstreaming: A practical guide.* Syracuse, NY: Syracuse University Press.

Paul, J.L., & Warnock, N.J. (1980). Special education: A changing field. *The Exceptional Child, 27*, 3–28.

Payne, R., & Murray, C. (1974). Principals' attitudes toward integration of the handicapped. *Exceptional Children, 40*, 123–125.

Peck, C., & Semmel, M. (1982). Identifying the least restrictive environment (LRE) for children with severe handicaps: Toward an empirical basis. *TASH Journal, 7*, 56–63.

Peckham, C.S., Sheridan, M., & Butler, N.R. (1972). School attainments of seven-year-old children with hearing difficulties. *Developmental Medicine and Child Neurology, 14*, 592–602.

Percevault, J. (1985). *The development of problem solving skills: Some suggested activities.* Unpublished paper, University of Lethbridge.

Perkins, W. (1977). *Speech pathology: An applied behavioral science* (2nd ed.). St. Louis: C.F. Mosby.

Peter, L.J. (1956). *Prescriptive teaching.* New York: McGraw Hill.

Peterson, P.L., & Clark, C.M. (1978). *Teacher planning, teacher behavior and student achievement.* Wisconsin.

Piers, E., & Harris, D. (1969). *The Piers–Harris Children's Self-concept Scale.* Nashville, TN: Counselor Recordings and Tests.

Pijl, S.J. (1986, April). *Two premises for IEPs.* Paper presented at the annual American Educational Research Association meeting, San Francisco.

Pointkowski, D., & Calfee, R. (1979). Attention in the classroom. In G.A. Herle & M. Davis (Eds.), *Attention and cognitive development.* New York: Plenum Press.

Polloway, E.A. (1984). The integration of mildly handicapped students into the schools: A historical review. *Remedial and Special Education, 5*, 18–28.

Polloway, E.A., & Polloway, C. (1981). Survival words for disabled readers. *Academic Therapy, 16*, 443–448.

Polloway, E.A., & Smith, J.E. (1982). *Teaching language skills to exceptional children.* Denver, CO: Love Publishing.

Polsgrove, L., & Reith, A.J. (1983). Procedures for reducing children's inappropriate behavior in special education settings. *Exceptional Education Quarterly, 3*, 20–33.

Ponder, G. (1979). The status of social studies. *Educational Leadership, 36*, 515–518.

Popp, R.A. (1983). Learning about disabilities. *Teaching Exceptional Children, 15*, 78–81.

Porter, R., Ramsey, B., Tremblay, A., Iaccobo, M., & Crawley, S. (1978). Social interactions in heterogeneous groups of retarded and normally developing children: An observational study. In B. Sackett (Ed.), *Observing behavior: Therapy and applications in mental retardation.* Baltimore, MD: University Park Press.

Pratt, D. (1983, June). *History in schools: Reflections on curriculum priorities.* Paper presented at the Canadian History Association annual meeting, Vancouver.

Prescott, G.A., Balow, I.H., Hogan, T.P., & Fan, R.C. (1978). *Metropolitan Achievement Tests.* New York: Harcourt Brace Jovanovich.

Price, M., & Goodman, L. (1980). Individual education programs: A case study. *Exceptional Children, 46*, 446–454.

Propp, G. (1973). Summary statements: Concluding remarks made at the Symposium on Research and Utilization of Educational Media for Teaching the Deaf. *American Annals of the Deaf, 118*, 617–624.

Quay, H.C. (1979). Classification. In H.C. Quay & J.S. Werry (Eds.), *Psychopathological disorders of childhood.* New York: John Wiley.

Quigley, S.P. (n.d.). *Some effects of hearing impairment upon school performance.* Springfield, IL: Division of special education services, Department of Title VI, E.S.E.A.

Quigley, S.P., Power, D.J., & Steinkamp, M.W. (1977). The language structure of deaf children. *Volta Review, 79*, 73–84.

Radatz, H. (1979). Error analysis in mathematics education. *Journal for Research in Mathematics Education, 10*, 163–172.

Rader, B.T. (1978). Competencies of mainstream teachers: An analysis. In J.K. Grasnich & M.C. Reynolds (Eds.), *Teacher education: Renegotiating roles for mainstreaming*. Minneapolis: University of Minnesota.

Ragsdale, D. (1982). *Computers in the schools: A guide for planning*. Informal Series 45. Toronto: OISE Press.

Rasche, D., & Dedrick, C. (1986). An experience in frustration: Simulations approximating learning difficulties. *Teaching Exceptional Children, 18*, 266–271.

Ratekin, N. (1979). Reading achievement of disabled learners. *Exceptional Children, 45*, 454–458.

Raths, L., Harmen, N., & Simon, S. (1966). *Values and teaching: Working with values in the classroom*. Columbus, OH: Merrill.

Redl, F. (1966). *When we deal with children*. New York: Free Press.

Reeve, R., & Kauffman, J.M. (1978). The behavior disordered. In N.G. Haring (Ed.), *Behavior of exceptional children* (2nd ed.). Columbus, OH: Merrill.

Reich, C., Hambleton, D., & Houldin, B.K. (1977). The integration of hearing impaired children into regular classrooms. *American Annals of the Deaf, 122*, 534–543.

Reich, P.A. (1986). *Language development*. Englewood Cliffs, NJ: Prentice-Hall.

Reid, D.K., & Hresko, W.P. (1980). Thinking and thinking about it that way: Test data and instruction. *Exceptional Education Quarterly, 1*, 47–57.

Reiter, S., & Levi. A.M. (1980). Factors affecting social integration of noninstitutionalized mentally retarded adults. *American Journal of Mental Deficiency, 85*, 25–30.

Renzulli, J.S. (1977). *The enrichment triad model: A guide for developing defensible programs for the gifted and talented*. Wethersfield, CT: Creative Learning Press.

Renzulli, J.S. (1979). *What makes giftedness*. Brief No. 6. Los Angeles: National/State Leadership Training Institute on the Gifted and Talented.

Renzulli, J.S., Smith, L.H., & Reis, S.M. (1982). Curriculum compacting: An essential strategy for working with gifted students. *Elementary School Journal, 82*, 185–194.

Reschley, D.J., & Gresham, F.M. (1981). *Use of social competence measures to facilitate parent and teacher involvement and unbiased assessment*. Iowa: Iowa State University.

Reynolds, M.C. (1979). Categorical vs. noncategorical teacher training. *Teacher Education and Special Education, 2*, 5–8.

Reynolds, M.C., & Birch, J.W. (1977). *Teaching exceptional children in all America's schools*. Reston, VA: Council for Exceptional Children.

Rider, R.A. (1980). Mainstreaming moderately retarded children in the elementary physical education program. *Teaching Exceptional Children, 12*, 150–152.

Ritter, D.R. (1978). Surviving in the regular classroom: A follow-up of mainstreamed children with learning disabilities. *Journal of School Psychology, 16*, 253–256.

Roberts, C.A., & Lazure, M.D. (Eds.). (1970). *One million children: A national study of Canadian children with emotional and learning disorders*. Toronto: Crainford.

Rockefeller, D., Jr. (1977). *Coming to our senses: The significance of the arts for American education*. New York: McGraw Hill.

Roedell, W.C., Jackson, N.E., & Robinson, H.B. (1980). *Gifted young children*. New York: Teachers College Press.

Ross, A.O. (1976). *Psychological aspects of learning disabilities and reading disorders*. New York: McGraw Hill.

Ross, M. (1978). Mainstreaming: Some social considerations. *Volta Review, 80*, 21–30.

Rourke, B.P., Young, G.C., & Flewelling, R.W. (1981). The relationship between WISC-R Verbal–Performance discrepancies and selected verbal, auditory-perceptual, visual-perceptual, and problem solving abilities in children with learning disabilities. *Journal of Clinical Psychology, 27*, 475–479.

Rowe, M.B. (1978). *Teaching science as continuous enquiry*. New York: McGraw Hill.

Rubin, D. (1980). *Teaching elementary language arts* (2nd ed). New York: Holt, Rinehart & Winston.

Rudel, R. (1977, February). *Psychology and reading: Teaching the learning disabled* [Televised discussion]. Columbia Broadcasting System.

Rupley, W.H., & Blair, T. (1983). *Reading diagnosis and remediation: Classroom and clinic* (2nd ed.) Boston: Houghton Mifflin.

Sabatino, D., & Mauser, A. (1977). *Intervention strategies for specialized secondary education*. Boston: Allyn & Bacon.

Salend, S.J. (1979). Active academic games: The aim of the game is mainstreaming. *Teaching Exceptional Children, 12*, 3–6.

Salend, S.J. (1984). Factors contributing to the development of successful mainstreaming programs. *Exceptional Children, 50*, 409–416.

Salmon-Cox, L. (1981). Teachers and standardized achievement tests: What's really happening? *Phi Delta Kappan, 63*, 87–89.

Salvia, J., & Ysseldyke, J.E. (1978). *Assessment in special and remedial education* (2nd ed.). Boston: Houghton Mifflin.

Salvia, J., & Ysseldyke, J.E. (1985). *Assessment in special and remedial education* (4th ed.). Boston: Houghton Mifflin.

Samuels, S.J. (1979). The method of repeated reading. *The Reading Teacher*, 32, 403–408.

Samuels, S.J. (1981). Some essentials of decoding. *Exceptional Education Quarterly*, 2, 11–25.

Scannel, D., Haugh, O., Schild, A., Ulmer, G., & King, E. (1988). *Canadian Test of Basic Skills—Revised.* Toronto: Nelson.

Scardamalia, M.C., Bereiter, H., & Goelman, H. (1982). The role of production factors in writing ability. In M. Nystrad (Ed.), *What writers know: The language process and structure of writing discourse*. New York: Academic Press.

Schaefer, C. (1979). *The therapeutic use of child's play.* New York: Jason Aronson.

Schiefelbusch, R.L., & Hollis, J.H. (1980). A general system for nonspeech language. In R.L. Schiefelbusch (Ed.), *Nonspeech language and communication: Analysis and intervention*. Baltimore, MD: University Park Press.

Schmidt, J. (1983). *The effects of four generalization conditions on learning disabled adolescents' written language performance in the regular classroom.* Doctoral dissertation, University of Kansas, Lawrence, Kansas.

Schubert, M.A., & Glick, H.M. (1981). Least restrictive environment programs: Why are some so successful? *Education Unlimited*, 3, 11–14.

Schultz, J.B., & Turnbull, A.P. (1984). *Mainstreaming handicapped students: A guide for classroom teachers* (2nd ed.). Boston: Allyn & Bacon.

Schwartz, C. (1977). Normalization and idealism. *Mental Retardation*, 15, 38–39.

Scott, E.P. (1982). *Your visually impaired child: A guide for teachers.* Baltimore, MD: University Park Press.

Searfoss, L.W. (1975). Radio reading. *The Reading Teacher*, 29, 295–296.

Seifert, E.P. (1960). Personal styles of handwriting in grades 6, 7, 8, and 9. *Dissertation Abstracts International*, 20, 3581–3582.

Semel, E.M., & Wiig, E. (1975). Comprehension of syntactic structures and critical verbal elements by children with learning disabilities. *Journal of Learning Disabilities*, 8, 46–51.

Shattuck, M. (1946). Segregation versus non-segregation of exceptional children. *Journal of Exceptional Children*, 12, 235–240.

Sherrill, C. (1982). Adapted physical education: Its role, meaning, and future. *Exceptional Education Quarterly*, 3, 1–9.

Shores, R.E., Hester, P., & Strain, P.S. (1976). Effects of amount and type of teacher–child interaction on child–child interaction during free play. *Psychology in the Schools*, 13, 171–175.

Siegler, R.S., & Robinson, M. (1982). The development of numerical understanding. In H.W. Reese (Ed.), *Advances in child development and behavior* (pp. 241–312). New York: Academic Press.

Sigler, J.M. (1984). An evaluation of Trade Offs as a program for the gifted. *Special Education in Canada*, 58, 59–62.

Silva, P.A. (1980). The prevalence, stability and significance of developmental language delays in preschool children. *Developmental Medicine and Child Neurology*, 22, 768–777.

Sitko, M.A., Bachor, D., & Slemon, A. (1980). *Teacher questioning techniques: The state of the art.* Paper presented at the annual meeting of the Canadian Society for Studies in Education, Montreal.

Sitlington, P.L. (1981). Vocational and special education in career programming for the mildly handicapped adolescent. *Exceptional Children*, 47, 592–598.

Skeels, H., & Dye, H. (1959). The study of the effects of differential stimulation on mentally retarded children. *Proceedings of the American Association on Mental Deficiency*, 44, 114–136.

Slingerland, B. (1971). *A multi-sensory approach to language arts for specific language disability: A guide for primary teachers.* Cambridge, MA: Educators Publishing Service.

Slobin, D.I., & Welch, C.A. (1971). Elicited imitation as a research tool in developmental psycholinguistics. In C.J. Lavatill (Ed.), *Language training in early childhood education*. Urbana, IL: University of Illinois Press.

Smith, F. (1978). *Reading without nonsense.* New York: Teachers College Press.

Smith, R.M. (1974). *Clinical teaching: Methods of teaching the retarded* (2nd ed.). New York: McGraw Hill.

Smoot, S.L. (1985). Exercise programs for mainstreamed handicapped students. *Teaching Exceptional Children*, 17, 262–266.

Speece, D.L., & Mandell, C.J. (1980). An analysis of resource room support services for regular teachers. *Learning Disability Quarterly*, 3, 49–53.

Splittgerber, F.F. (1979). Computer-based instruction: A revolution in the making. *Educational Technology*, 19, 20–26.

Spoder, B. (1985). *Teaching in the early years.* Englewood Cliffs, NJ: Prentice-Hall.

Squires, D. (1987). *Goals and objectives for a reading retarded child.* Unpublished material. Memorial University of Newfoundland.

Staab, W.J. (1978). *Hearing aid handbook.* Blue Ridge Summit, PA: Tap Books.

Stainback, W., Stainback, S., Etsheidt, S., & Doud, J. (1986). A nonintrusive intervention for acting and behavior. *Teaching Exceptional Children*, 19, 38–41.

Stassen, R. (1973). I have one in my class who's wearing hearing aids. In W. Northcott (Ed.), *Hearing impaired children in the regular classroom.* Washington, DC: Alexander Graham Bell Association for the Deaf.

Staton, J. (1985). Using dialogue journals for developing thinking, reading, and writing with hearing-impaired students. *Volta Review,* 87, 127–154.

Stauffer, R. (1975). *Directing the reading thinking process.* New York: Harper & Row.

Stein, M.L., & Glenn, C.G. (1978). An analysis of comprehension in elementary school children. In R. Freddle (Ed.), *Discourse processing: Multi-disciplinary perspectives.* Hillsdale, NJ: Ablex.

Stephens, T.M. (1977). *Teaching skills to children with learning and behavior problems.* Columbus, OH: Merrill.

Stephens, T.M. (1978). *Social skills in the classroom.* Columbus, OH: Merrill.

Stephens, T.M., Hartman, A.C., & Lewis, V.H. (1978). *Teaching children basic skills: A curriculum handbook.* Columbus, OH: Merrill.

Stephenson, W. (1953). *The study of behavior: Q-technique and its methodology.* Chicago, IL: University of Chicago Press.

Stevens, R., & Rosenshine, B. (1980). Advances in research on teaching. *Exceptional Education Quarterly,* 2, 1–9.

Stewart, D.M. (1977). Survey of community employer attitudes toward hiring the handicapped. *Mental Retardation,* 15, 30–31.

Stile, S., Cole, J., & Garner, A. (1979). Maximizing parental involvement in programs for exceptional children. *Journal of the Division for Early Childhood,* 1, 68–82.

Summers, E.G. (1984). A paradigm for developing QUICK word tests for reading assessment in secondary grades. *B.C. Journal of Special Education,* 8, 11–33.

Suydam, M.N., & Trueblood, C.R. (1974). Attitudes toward Mathematics Scale. In M.N. Suydam (Ed.), *Evaluation in the mathematics classroom: From what and why to how and where.* Columbus, OH: ERIC Information Analysis Center for Science, Mathematics and Environmental Education. Ohio State University.

Swett, S.C. (1978). Math and LD: A new perspective. *Academic Therapy,* 14, 5–13.

Tannenbaum, A.J. (1983). *Gifted children.* New York: Macmillan.

Tarjan, G. (1970). Some thoughts on sociocultural retardation. In H.C. Haywood (Ed.), *Socio-cultural aspects of mental retardation.* New York: Appleton-Century-Crofts.

Tarver, S.G., & Ellsworth, P.S. (1981). Written and oral language for verbal children. In J.M. Kauffman & D.P. Hallahan (Eds.), *Handbook of special education.* Englewood Cliffs, NJ: Prentice-Hall.

Telford, C.W., & Sawrey, J.M. (1981). *The exceptional individual* (4th ed.). Englewood Cliffs, NJ: Prentice-Hall.

Terman, L.M., & Oden, M.H. (1951). The Stanford studies of the gifted. In P. Witty (Ed.), *The gifted child.* Lexington, MA: D.C. Heath.

Thompson, B. (Ed.). (1980). *Science for the handicapped: An annotated bibliography.* Columbus, OH: ERIC Clearinghouse.

Thorndike, R., & Hagen, E. (1978). *Measurement and evaluation in psychology and education.* New York: John Wiley.

Thorndyke, G.G., & Symmach, R.D. (1982). CAI and the microcomputer. *Education Canada,* 22, 4–7.

Thornton, C., Jones, A., Graham, A., & Toohey, M. (1983). A multidisciplinary approach to thinking strategies for remedial instruction in basic addition facts. *Journal for Research in Mathematics Education,* 14, 198–203.

Thornton, C., Tucker, F., Dossey, J.A., & Bazik, E.F. (1983). *Teaching mathematics to children with special needs.* Menlo Park, CA: Addison-Wesley.

Thursky, D.D. (1977). Everyone's a star. *Teaching Exceptional Children,* 10, 77–78.

Tomblin, J.B. (1978). *Processes and disorders of human communication.* New York: Harper & Row.

Tompkins, G.E., & Friend, M. (1985). On your mark, get set, write! *Teaching Exceptional Children,* 18, 82–89.

Torgesen, J., & Dice, C. (1980). Characteristics of research on learning disabilities. *Journal of Learning Disabilities,* 13, 531–535.

Torgesen, J.K., & Young, K. (1983). Priorities for the use of microcomputers with learning disabled children. *Journal of Learning Disabilities,* 16, 234–237.

Touchings, D. (1989). *Attitudes of teachers toward computers.* M.Ed thesis, Memorial University of Newfoundland.

Towle, A. (1982). Learning how to be a student when you have a learning disability. *Journal of Learning Disabilities,* 15, 90–93.

Trifiletti, J.J., Frith, G.H., & Armstrong, S. (1984). Microcomputers versus resource rooms for LD students: A preliminary investigation of the effects on math skills. *Learning Disability Quarterly,* 7, 69–76.

Truch, S. (1980). *Teacher burnout and what to do about it.* Novato, CA: Academic Therapy Publications.

Trybus, R.J., & Karchmer, M.A. (1977). School achievement scores of hearing impaired children: National data on achievement status and growth patterns. *American Annals of the Deaf,* 122, 62–69.

Turnbull, A.P., Strickland, P., & Hammer, S.E. (1978).

The individualized education program: Part 2. Translating law into practice. *Journal of Learning Disabilities, 11*, 18–23.

Turnbull, A.P., & Turnbull, H.R. (1986). *Families, professionals, and exceptionality: A special partnership.* Columbus, OH: Merrill.

Tyack, D., & Gottsleben, R. (1974). *Language sampling analysis and training: A handbook for teachers and clinicians.* Palo Alto, CA: Consulting Psychologists Press.

Underhill, R.G., Uprichard, E.A., & Heddens, J.W. (1980). *Diagnosing mathematical difficulties.* Columbus, OH: Merrill.

Urbani, T. (1978). Fun, funny, funnies. *Teacher, 96*, 60–62, 64, 66, 68.

Vanderheiden, G.C., & Yoder, D.E. (1986). In S.W. Blackstone (Ed.), *Augmentative communication: An introduction.* Rockville, IL: American Speech and Hearing Association.

Van Dyke, L. (1982). An inservice training model for using the classroom FM system. *Volta Review, 84*, 344–351.

Van Riper, C. (1978). *Speech correction: Principles and methods* (6th ed.). Englewood Cliffs, NJ: Prentice-Hall.

Vaughan, J., & Gaus, F. (1978). Secondary reading inventory: A modest proposal. *Journal of Reading, 21*, 716–720.

Venn, J., Morganstern, L., & Dykes, M.K. (1978). Checklists for evaluating the fit and function of orthoses, prostheses, and wheelchairs in the classroom. *Teaching Exceptional Children, 11*, 51–56.

Vernon, P.E. (1971). Effects of administration and scoring on divergent thinking tests. *British Journal of Educational Psychology, 41*, 245–257

Vicker, B., Shurman, J.A., & Kladde, A.G. (1974). *Non-oral communication systems project.* Iowa: University of Iowa.

Vogel, S. (1974). Syntactic abilities in normal and dyslexic children. *Journal of Learning Disabilities, 6*, 103–109.

Vogel, S. (1975). *Syntactic abilities in normal and dyslexic children.* Baltimore, MD: University Park Press.

Vogel, S. (1977). Morphological ability in normal and dyslexic children. *Journal of Learning Disabilities, 10*, 41–49.

Wahlstrom, M.W., & Donley, R.D. (1976). *Assessment of student achievement: A survey of the assessment of student achievement in Ontario.* Toronto: Ontario Ministry of Education.

Walker, H.M., McConnell, S., Holmes, D., Todis, B., Walker, J., & Golden, N. (1983). *The Walker Social Skills Curriculum: The ACCEPTS Program.* Austin, TX: Pro-Ed.

Wallace, G., & Larsen, S.C. (1978). *Educational assessment of learning problems: Testing for teaching.* Boston: Allyn & Bacon.

Wallace, G., & McLaughlin, J.A. (1979). *Learning disabilities: Concepts and characteristics* (2nd ed.). Columbus, OH: Merrill.

Wang, M.C. (1981). Mainstreaming exceptional children: Some instructional design and implementation considerations. *Elementary School Journal, 81*, 195–221.

Wang, M.C., Resnick, L.B., & Boozer, R.F. (1971). The sequence of development of some early mathematical behaviors. *Child Development, 42*, 1767–1778.

Warnock, H.M. (1978). *Special education needs: Report of the Committee of Enquiry into the education of handicapped children and youth.* London: Her Majesty's Printing Office.

Warren, D.M. (1977). *Blindness and early childhood development.* New York: American Foundation for the Blind.

Watkinson, E.J., & Bentz, L. (1985). *Final report on the Canada-wide survey on the integration of physically disabled students into physical education in elementary, junior and senior high programs.* Ottawa: Canadian Association for Health, Physical Education and Recreation.

Wechsler, D. (1974). *Wechsler Intelligence Scale for Children — Revised.* New York: Psychological Corporation.

Weinberg, B. (1980). The Kurzweil reading machine: Half a miracle. *American Libraries, 11*, 603–604.

Weiner, M. (1979). *Clinical pharmacology and therapeutics in nursing.* New York: McGraw Hill.

Weinthaller, J., & Rothberg, J.M. (1970). The systematic selection of instructional materials based on an inventory of learning abilities and skills. *Exceptional Children, 36*, 615–619.

Wepman, J.M., Cruickshank, W.M., Deutsch, C.P., Morency, A., & Strother, C.R. (1975). Learning disabilities. In N. Hobbs (Ed.), *Issues in the classification of children* (Vol. 1). San Francisco: Jossey Bass.

Wesenger, G. (1980). *The enactive method: An interactive method for teaching language to young hearing impaired children.* Unpublished paper, E.C. Drury School, Milton, Ontario.

Whitmore, J. (1985, November). *Creating appropriate conditions for gifted students in the regular school program.* Paper presented at the British Columbia Council for Exceptional Children conference.

Wiederholt, J.L. (1974). Resource rooms for the mildly handicapped. *Focus on Exceptional Children, 5*, 1–10.

Wiederholt, J.L., Hammill, D.D., & Brown, V.L. (1983). *The resource teacher: A guide to effective practice* (2nd ed.). Boston: Allyn & Bacon.

Wiederholt, J.L., & McNutt, G. (1979). Assessment and instructional planning: A conceptual framework. In

D. Cullinan & M.H. Epstein (Eds.), *Special education for adolescents: Issues and concerns*. Columbus, OH: Merrill.
Wiig, E.H., & Semel, E. (1974). Productive language abilities in learning disabled adolescents. *Journal of Learning Disabilities*, 8, 578–588.
Wiig, E.H., & Semel, E. (1976). *Language disabilities in children and adolescents*. Columbus, OH: Merrill.
Wilbur, R.B. (1976). The linguistics of manual language and manual systems. In L.L. Lloyd (Ed.), *Communication assessment and intervention strategies*. Baltimore, MD: University Park Press.
Wilkinson, L., & Dollaghan, C. (1979). Peer communication in first grade reading groups. *Theory into Practice*, 18, 267–274.
Willings, D. (1983). Issues in career choice for gifted students. *Teaching Exceptional Children*, 15, 266–233.
Wilson, J.J. (1981). Notetaking: A necessary support service for hearing-impaired students. *Teaching Exceptional Children*, 14, 38–40.
Wilson, J.W., & McLaughlin, T.F. (1986). A review of management practices in three secondary resource room models: Teacher consultant, pull-out, and study period. *B.C. Journal of Special Education*, 10, 367–385.
Wilson, S. (1979). Beyond the spelling book. *Instructor*, 89, 128, 130.
Winzer M.A. (1982a). An approach to history for the handicapped child. *History and Social Science Teacher*, 17, 118–120.
Winzer, M.A. (1982b). Bill 82: Ideal and reality. *B.C. Journal of Special Education*, 6, 159–169.
Winzer, M.A. (1984). The effect of information on the attitudes of teachers and non-educators toward mainstreaming. *B.C. Journal of Special Education*, 8, 273–282.
Winzer, M.A. (1985a, July). *The enactive approach*. Paper presented at the International Conference of Educators of the Deaf, Manchester, England.
Winzer, M.A. (1985b). Teacher attitudes toward mainstreaming: An appraisal of the research. *B.C. Journal of Special Education*, 9, 149–161.
Winzer, M.A., & Clarke, B.R. (1987). Competencies required by educators of the hearing impaired: What do Canadian teachers view as important? *Canadian Journal of Special Education*, 3, 167–180.
Winzer, M., Rogow, S., & David, C. (1987). *Exceptional children in Canada*. Toronto: Prentice-Hall.
Winzer, M.A., & Rose, C. (1987). Mainstreaming exceptional students: Use of the Attitude Survey with teachers in British Columbia. *B.C. Journal of Special Education*, 10, 309–320.
Wittrock, M.C. (1983, April). *Generative reading comprehension*. Paper presented at AERA Conference, Montreal.
Woolfolk, A.E., & Nicolich, L.M. (1984). *Educational psychology for teachers* (2nd ed.). Englewood Cliffs, NJ: Prentice-Hall.
Worth, J. (1987). Problem solving in primary grades: Teacher activities. In *Teaching mathematics in early childhood classrooms* (pp. 23–28). Edmonton: Alberta Teachers Association.
Wright, B. (1980). Developing constructive views of life with a disability. *Rehabilitation Literature*, 41, 274–279.
Yatvin, J. (1981). A functional writing program for the middle grades. In S.M. James (Ed.), *Perspectives in writing in grades 1–8*. Urbana, IL: National Council for Teachers of English.
Yinger, R.J. (1978). *A study of teacher planning: Description and a model of practical decision making*. Michigan: Michigan State University.
Yinger, R.J. (1985). Journal writing as a learning tool. *Volta Review*, 87, 21–33.
Yoshida, R.K. (1983). Are multidisciplinary teams worth the investment? *School Psychology Review*, 12, 137–143.
Ysseldyke, J.E., & Algozzine, B. (1982). *Critical issues in special and remedial education*. Boston: Houghton-Mifflin.
Zemanek, D.H., & Lehrer, B.E. (1977). The role of university departments of special education in mainstreaming. *Exceptional Children*, 43, 377–379.
Zukow, P., Zukow, A., & Bentler, P. (1978). Rating scales for the identification and treatment of hyperkenesis. *Journal of Consulting and Clinical Psychology*, 46, 213–222.

Picture credits

An honest attempt has been made to secure permission for all material used, and if there are errors or omissions, these are wholly unintentional and the Publisher will be grateful to learn of them.

p. 1 Copp Clark Pitman files, uncredited.
p. 29 Photograph courtesy of the Metropolitan Toronto School Board. Photograph by Lorne Henne.
p. 33 Sunny View #18, June 1965, photograph, 12 × 12 cm, Records, Archives and Museum, Toronto Board of Education
p. 47 Photograph courtesy of F. Barry Brown.
p. 63 Photograph courtesy of The Ernest C. Drury School. Photograph by Douglas Mohun.
p. 88 Photograph courtesy of the Hugh MacMillan Medical Centre.
p. 133 Photograph courtesy of Normunds Berzins Photography.
p. 137 Copp Clark Pitman files, uncredited.
p. 139 Photograph courtesy of R. Gough.
p. 154 Photograph courtesy of the Hugh MacMillan Medical Centre.
p. 160 Photograph courtesy of Peter Chow.
p. 200 Photograph courtesy of F. Barry Brown.
p. 203 Photograph courtesy of Norm Scudellari Photography.
p. 224 Photograph courtesy of VOICE for Hearing Impaired Children.
p. 242 Photograph courtesy of the Markham Economist & Sun.
p. 273 Copp Clark Pitman files, uncredited.
p. 280 Photograph courtesy of Normunds Berzins Photography.
p. 287 Photograph by M. Howell-Jones. Material written and drawn by D. Peters.
p. 313 Photograph courtesy of the Hugh MacMillan Medical Centre.
p. 321 Copp Clark Pitman files, uncredited.
p. 325 Curriculum—Math #1, 1964, photograph, 15 × 15 cm, Records, Archives and Museum, Toronto Board of Education.
p. 355 Graham Bezant, Morse St. P.S. #7, 1979, photograph, 12 × 15 cm, Records, Archives and Museum, Toronto Board of Education.
p. 357 Photograph courtesy of the Markham Economist & Sun.
p. 361 Photograph courtesy of the Markham Economist & Sun.
p. 365 Photograph courtesy of the Hugh MacMillan Medical Centre.
p. 368 Grant Gibson, Curriculum—Physical Education #51, photograph, 16 × 12 cm, Records, Archives and Museum, Toronto Board of Education.
p. 371 Photograph courtesy of the Society for Manitobans with Disabilities Inc.
p. 381 Photograph courtesy of The Ernest C. Drury School.
p. 384 Photograph courtesy of the Hugh MacMillan Medical Centre.
p. 411 Photograph courtesy of The Ernest C. Drury School. Photograph by Douglas Mohun.
p. 416 Photograph courtesy of Phonic Ear Ltd., 7475 Kimbel St., Unit 10, Mississauga, Ontario, L5S 1E7.
pp. 433–34 Illustration courtesy of Alton Planners. Planners available at: Alton Planners, 229 Queen St., Chatham, Ontario, N7M 2H2.
p. 437 Copp Clark Pitman files, uncredited.
p. 444 Copp Clark Pitman files, uncredited.
p. 457 Photograph courtesy of the staff and students of The W. Ross Macdonald School.
p. 460 Photograph courtesy of the staff and students of The W. Ross Macdonald School.
p. 463 Photograph courtesy of the staff and students of The W. Ross Macdonald School.
p. 464 Photograph courtesy of the staff and students of The W. Ross Macdonald School.
p. 466 Photograph courtesy of the staff and students of The W. Ross Macdonald School.
p. 473 Sunny View #19, June 1965, photograph, 10 × 12 cm, Records, Archives and Museum, Toronto Board of Education.
p. 498 Photograph courtesy of Normunds Berzins Photography.

Index